THE BEST PLAYS OF 1942-43

THE BEST PLAYS OF 1942-43

THE BEST PLAYS
OF 1942-43

AND THE
YEAR BOOK OF THE DRAMA
IN AMERICA

EDITED BY
BURNS MANTLE

DODD, MEAD AND COMPANY
NEW YORK   -   -   -   1962

INTRODUCTION

OUR second war year was, in the theatre, a happier adventure than was the first. The comedies were gayer and there were more of them. The serious dramas recovered dramatic and literary qualities that were generally missing the first war year. Both the New York Drama Critics' Circle and the Pulitzer Prize Committee were able to agree with some enthusiasm on plays by American authors which they considered worthy of their respective awards, whereas it will be recalled they both passed the 1941-42 season by as having produced nothing worth mentioning as a prize play.

In one notable particular, however, the two war seasons reflected similar reactions in the taste of play-goers. They did not care for, nor would they support, plays written on war themes and plays reproducing, however impressively, an active wartime realism. During the season of 1941-42 there were eleven war plays produced, and only two of them, and these the less noisy and the more soundly foundationed in a universal emotional appeal, were successful—Robert Sherwood's "There Shall Be No Night" and Lillian Hellman's "Watch on the Rhine."

Last season we had twelve war plays offered for approval and only one of them, Maxwell Anderson's "The Eve of St. Mark," was successful. There have been numerous explanations of this American play-goer attitude toward war plays. One of the best and most recent was written by W. A. Darlington, the *New York Times* London correspondent. ". . . New York is in exactly the same state of mind about war plays now as London was during the last war, and for the same reason—that it is sharing the activity but is unexposed to the actuality of war," wrote Mr. Darlington.

"It is true that in London last time we had a few bombs dropped from Zeppelins and that nobody has as yet dropped anything on New York, but that does not affect the issue. Those Zeppelin bombs sent a good many old ladies scuttling to shelter, but did not have the slightest effect on London's attitude to or zest for its amusements. And then London definitely did not regard as coming under the head of amusements any attempt to deal realistically with the war. A sentimental piece by Barrie, or a roaring melodrama at the Lyceum, could be tolerated. But not a single management was so foolhardy, if I remember rightly, to attempt staging anything more serious; 'The Journey's End' had to wait until 1929. This time London is up in the front line, and the attitude is utterly different. War is in the air we breathe; we cannot escape it if we try. Sham horrors on stage are not disturbing because they are outdone by actual happenings yesterday, perhaps tomorrow, in the street outside. In other words if we leave war out of our plays we cannot have any contemporary drama at all."

The first of the prize-winning plays of this season was Sidney Kingsley's "The Patriots," one of the better native historical and biographical dramas having to do with the cradle of liberty while it was being rocked by President George Washington and two members of his cabinet, Secretary of State Thomas Jefferson and Secretary of the Treasury Alexander Hamilton. The Kingsley play is concerned principally with the Jefferson-Hamilton rivalries and antagonisms, with Washington serving as a disturbed and unhappy referee. It was impressively revealing in reviving vivid sidelights upon the early struggle for that liberty which America is now fighting to preserve.

The second prize-winner was the highly amusing, and likewise highly controversial, "The Skin of Our Teeth." This Thornton Wilder satirical fling at both the nobility and indestructibility of the human race aroused certain eminent literary authorities to shouts of plagiarism, they claiming that similar ideas, and even certain quotable phrases, are to be found in James Joyce's eighteen-year-old novel, "Finnegans Wake," for the use of which Mr. Wilder gave Mr. Joyce neither credit nor public mention. As for the non-literary and less excitable play-goers, they were content to divide into two fairly positive groups—one group insisting that this extravagant, yet meaningful, lampoon was the best comedy the stage had brought them in years, and the other group loudly insisting that it was probably the silliest and most meaningless mess of entertainment with which our theatre had recently been afflicted. Commercially the supporters of Mr. Wilder and his comedy won the day. "The Skin of Our Teeth," as more fully appears in later pages, ran through the season.

Anderson's "The Eve of St. Mark" was written originally at the suggestion of, and for the use of, The National Theatre Conference, an association of civic and college theatre groups. It was given something over 100 productions by these groups before it was taken over professionally by the Playwrights' Company, of which Mr. Anderson was one of the founders. It is, by common consent, the one war play concerned with America's participation in the struggle that adequately and effectively serves the purpose of stage presentation.

"The Doughgirls" is a frankly brazen war cartoon which moves its audiences to shrieks of mirth by making sport of both the stuffed hotels and the stuffed tunics of wartime Washington. It was greeted with respectful reservations by the professional reviewers, but there never was a moment's doubt as to the playgoing public's hearty endorsement.

"Tomorrow the World," which arrived late in the season, also boasts a war problem background of significant proportions. It deals dramatically with possible postwar complications having to do with the social readjustment of enemy nationals. The chief protagonist is a 12-year-old Nazi whose moral and physical reclaiming is attempted in New York with threateningly disastrous results.

"Harriet," the Florence Ryerson-Colin Clements biographical drama telling of the life and times of Harriet Beecher Stowe, undoubtedly owes much of its popularity to the presence of Helen Hayes at the head of its cast. But it does dramatize interestingly the story of how Mrs. Stowe came to write the immortalized "Uncle Tom's Cabin," and reveals, also interestingly and with acceptable authenticity, the environment and home and family conditions under which the story was written.

F. Hugh Herbert's "Kiss and Tell" brightly represents the domestic comedy. Expanding an adolescent theme no more extravagantly than a reasonable sense of showmanship warrants, it brings American family life into happy relief. In "The Damask Cheek" John Van Druten and Lloyd Morris tell the story of social conventions in an older New York and achieve a play that, as Richard Lockridge wrote of it, "is literate and at ease."

The two chief departures from routine in this 1942-43 issue of "The Best Plays" are found in the selection of the Oscar Hammerstein 2d-Richard Rodgers "Oklahoma," definitely a musical comedy, as a "best play," and the inclusion of Dan James's "Winter Soldiers" as an important contribution to the theatre season, even though it was produced in an experimental theatre far removed from the Broadway scene.

These selections, I feel, are justified. "Oklahoma" comes as near to being a "folk opera" as any musical comedy has since Edna Ferber's "Show Boat" was made over as a play with music by this same Oscar Hammerstein 2d and Jerome Kern.

In both its added lyric and musical content it is a superior sample of its type and may well stand as a model for future generations of American composers and libretto writers to study. In this sense it is an important contribution to the native theatre, and should be included in any year book of record.

"Winter Soldiers" was first shown at the Studio Theatre of the New School for Social Research in West Twelfth Street, New York. Dan James, the author, is a graduate of the Yale School of Drama who in 1941 was awarded the Sidney Howard Fellowship given to the most promising native dramatist of each season. This selection is made by the Playwrights' Company, of which Mr. Howard was a co-founder.

"Winter Soldiers" tells of delaying actions organized by the "little" people of Russia and their fellows in the occupied countries which helped to keep the Germans out of Moscow on their first big drive for that capital. It embodies the will to win of freedom-loving peoples all over the world and is, I think, one of the truly significant dramas inspired by the global war.

Statistically the season had little new to offer. There were fewer new plays brought to production, but a higher percentage of successes among them, and a better average in literary quality. There were ten revivals of past successes, as opposed to fifteen the previous season, which would seem to indicate that despite the war handicap creative effort is gaining.

Adding the new 1899-1909 volume of "The Best Plays," which is to be published this winter, and the recently re-issued 1909-1919 volume, to the twenty-three volumes that have been published since the series was inaugurated in the season of 1919-20, there is now available a complete record of the Broadway stage from the turn of the century to the present year.

More than that, with the covering of the twenty years extending from 1900 to 1920, we will have made available a record of the native theatre from its earliest beginnings in the seventeen hundreds to the present time.

The compilations have been in a large sense labors of love to one whose fondness for the theatre and its people is very genuine. The response of those friends of the series and of the theatre who have taken occasion to record their appreciation is gratifying and also a little demanding. It inspires us with the hope that we can go on with the work for another decade or two, starting, it may be, with a grand victory edition for 1943-44.

B. M.

Forest Hills, L. I., 1943.

CONTENTS

THE BEST PLAYS OF 1942-43

THE BEST PLAYS OF 1942-43

THE BEST PLAYS OF 1942-43

THE SEASON IN NEW YORK

THAT plays are better-written these days than they were in the old days that were presumed to be good, might be hard to prove, but they certainly run longer. At least they run longer in one spot. "Way Down East," "In Old Kentucky," "The Drunkard," "The Old Homestead," and the like, continued intermittently year after year, but their records were achieved on tour, city by city and town by town. "Abie's Irish Rose" and "Tobacco Road" ran five years and seven and a half years, respectively, and continuously, in New York. They were exceptions to what was supposed to be an established rule, but we now have "Life with Father," "Arsenic and Old Lace" and "Angel Street" continuing steadily toward records that may yet top those that have gone before.

Even intermediate runs seem to be more frequent than they used to be. "Junior Miss," starting in November, 1941, is still going fairly strong in June, 1943. "Claudia" ran up a sizable list of 722 performances before it finally took to the road, and "My Sister Eileen" has 865 performances to its credit in my record.

There were sixteen plays showing on Broadway in mid-June, when we closed last season's book. Six of them are still running. Of the other ten, "Blithe Spirit" quit temporarily after playing for 657 performances, "By Jupiter" after 427, "Let's Face It" after 547, and "Uncle Harry" after 430.

The 1942-43 season came through a pretty lively summer, in the face of the early war depression. There was but one major disappointment—Ed Wynn's vaudeville roundup, "Laugh, Town, Laugh," for all its admitted cleverness, was withdrawn after 65 showings. Against this was the sensational 4th of July debut of Irving Berlin's "This Is the Army," which came in for four weeks and stayed twelve, made thousands and thousands of dollars for Army Relief and later swept across country to build these figures into millions.

"Star and Garter," with Gypsy Rose Lee and Bobby Clark

3

at the top of its cast, has just completed a year's stay without any sign of weakening, and "Stars on Ice" at the Center Theatre ran for 427 performances before suspending for the summer and making ready for a second, or 1943-44, edition.

A brave young orchestra conductor, Joseph Tushinsky by name, took over Carnegie Hall for a revival of popular operettas in late June. Sets of make-shift scenery were introduced on a stage dedicated to concert programs for many years and, surprisingly, a popular-price success was scored. "The Chocolate Soldier" ran for three weeks, "The Merry Widow" for five and "The New Moon" for three.

The irrepressible William Saroyan took over the Belasco Theatre in August to try his hand at staging and directing a repertory of his own plays. "Saroyan Showcase" he wanted to call it, but settled for "The Saroyan Theatre." First he did a mysterious item called "Across the Board on Tomorrow Morning" and a dramatic one-acter entitled "Talking to You." A goodly number of Saroyan admirers and well-wishers applauded, but there were not enough of them. The plays were taken off after a single week.

Censors come and go, and sometimes they get in the way of that lusty old indestructible, "Tobacco Road," but the Georgia dirt drama goes on. Just to give a bit of impetus to another road tour this seven-year record holder came back for five preliminary weeks in New York.

The new theatre season opened pleasantly in September with a comedy by Josephine Bentham and Herschel Williams called "Janie." This proved another of the "Junior Miss" series, being concerned with the adventures of a 16-year-old heroine who wanted to do something for the boys in camp near her town. She gave a party the night her folks were out and they came home and found the house practically bursting with selectees. Starting slow, "Janie" made friends and was still flourishing in June.

Two other September openings followed. "The Morning Star," a tense war drama from London, written by Emlyn Williams with a blitz-bombing background, lasted only three weeks. New York audiences still preferred to take their war news from newspaper reports and not from the stage. This was followed by an unusual vaudeville visitation.

Clifford Fischer, the Parisian entrepreneur, introduced a "New Priorities" bill with Harry Richman, Bert Wheeler, Carol Bruce, Harrison and Fisher, Henny Youngman and a stageful of others on the 15th and the night following Fred F. Finklehoffe brought in a troupe he had organized on the Pacific Coast, headed by George Jessel and Jack Haley, and including the De Marcos and Ella Logan. "Show Time," Finklehoffe called it, and so popular did the combination prove that it played for weeks and weeks, twelve performances a week, achieving finally an all-time vaudeville record of 342 performances before it closed in April.

An effort to revive the cheaper forms of burlesque, and thus trade on the success of "Star and Garter," proved disastrous. The company was headed by Jimmy Savo and Margie Hart and the assorted entertainment, which was pretty coarse, was called after the old burlesque title of "Wine, Women and Song." Soon the police interfered, but with the aid of injunctions and other court delays, a final closing was fought off for 112 performances. This, however, meant no more than seven weeks in elapsed time, as sixteen performances a week were given.

Eddie Dowling decided to revive Gilbert Chesterton's "Magic" and play a new Saroyan short drama, "Hello, Out There" with it. There were encouraging words for the venture but not enough encouraging audiences. Six weeks and Mr. Dowling retired for the season.

A lusty bit of fun written by Howard Lindsay and Russel Crouse and called "Strip for Action" brought a burlesque company to a village near an army camp to give a benefit for the soldiers. The straight comedy framework, concerned with the gaining of Government permission for the show, was smartly written and hugely enjoyed, but when the boys got into the repetition of some pretty corny burlesque interludes audience interest lagged. With a cast headed by Keenan Wynn and Eleanor Lynn, "Strip for Action" lasted until after the holidays and was then withdrawn.

The National Theatre Conference, an association of non-professional theatres sprung from what used to be known as the Little Theatre Group, with college dramatic groups added, asked Maxwell Anderson to write a drama for production by Conference units. Mr. Anderson, not too happy over the critical reception of his recent plays, "Journey to Jerusalem" and "Candle in the Wind," agreed. "The Eve of St. Mark" was the result. Written with a view to simplified staging and to simple and human characterization, "The Eve of St. Mark" proved greatly to the liking of Conference audiences. The Playwrights' Company, of which Mr. Anderson was a co-founder, thereupon decided to exercise its option and make a professional production of the drama. It was brought to the Cort Theatre, New York, in early October and scored an immediate success with both play reviewers and play patrons. Thus the work from which he doubtless expected the least return, written with little if any thought of critical Broadway endorsement, turned out to be Dramatist Anderson's most popular success. It had been played 291 times on Broadway before it was withdrawn.

Friends and admirers of Molly Picon leased what was first called the Jolson Theatre in upper Seventh Avenue, New York, and renamed it in honor of the popular Yiddish star. There Molly made her debut in a dramatized version of her stage life, written by her husband, Jacob Kalich, and including her most successful songs. "Oy, Is Dus a Leben" it was called and it continued for 130 showings. Then Miss Picon went back to vaudeville.

George Abbott, hoping to capitalize the jive craze, staged a George Marion, Jr., musical comedy called "Beat the Band." It was spotted with new faces, including those of Susan Miller, a youthful prima donna who had sung with Rudy Vallée, and Jerry Lester, a floor show comedian. The music was loud and persistent and Mr. Abbott was forced to acknowledge one of his few recent defeats as a producer at the conclusion of 42 performances.

After having scored a string of successes as a character actress, notably in "Ladies in Retirement," Flora Robson was drafted to play the lead in a new play about New York society of the early 1890s. "The Damask Cheek" was the title, and Miss Robson played an English girl in her thirties come to visit her snobbish New York aunt and look for an American husband, as more fully appears in a digest of the comedy contained herein. Miss Robson's experiment with romance was less successful than she and her admirers, including John Van Druten and Lloyd Morris, the authors, had hoped it might be. "The Damask Cheek" enthused many, but not enough, patrons to keep it playing after 93 performances.

There was a popular-priced revival of Paul Green's and Richard Wright's dramatization of Mr. Wright's sensational novel, "Native Son," one of the minor sensations of the 1940-41 season. Canada Lee, the gifted Negro actor, had now become star of the troupe, but the production had been noticeably cheapened in staging and direction. An additional 84 performances were added to previous runs.

Now Mrs. Lytle Hull and her associate sponsors of the New Opera Company, determined that their efforts to bring quality to the musical entertainment of the theatre should seek a popular as well as an artistic endorsement, staged a new version of Johann Strauss' long popular "Die Fledermaus." This one, translated by Max Reinhardt and adapted by his son, Gottfried and John Meehan, Jr., was called "Rosalinda." It was staged elaborately at the roomy Forty-fourth Street Theatre, with a cast sprinkled with refugee artists as well as recently developed and trained American artists. Dr. Erich Korngold, famed in Europe before the war as a Strauss authority, conducted the orchestra, and Oscar Karlweiss, a favorite Berlin and Vienna comedian in the old days, sang the role of Prince Orlofsky. The leading feminine parts were given to Dorothy Sarnoff and Virginia McWatters, a favorite society amateur of Philadelphia. "Rosalinda" started modestly enough, but within six weeks was the talk of the town. It continued the operetta success of the year. Also it probably had a lot to do with inspiring later revivals of "The Student Prince" and "The Vagabond King."

Having satisfied herself on a fairly extensive road tour that Philip Barry's "Without Love" would prove sufficiently attractive to her particular following to warrant bringing it to New York, Katharine Hepburn began a season at the St. James Theatre early in November. Her conclusion proved correct. Not all the reviewers were as pleased with the new play as they had been with the first Barry-Hepburn contribution, "The Philadelphia Story," but most of them were. After fourteen weeks, however, Miss Hepburn decided she had played long enough, brought her season to a close and dismissed her company, headed by Elliott Nugent. Katharine had what are known in the trade as "motion picture commitments."

Then came Thornton Wilder's "Skin of Our Teeth." Controversy raged. Some insisted this was the greatest comedy of the year. Others contended that it was perhaps the worst play ever written. Some sat through the whole colorful life story of Mr. and Mrs. Antrobus, who represented the indestructible human race from the Stone Age until they finally settled in New Jersey; others sat through the first act and left. But "The Skin of Our Teeth" was still playing to a tidy profit when this record was compiled.

It was in November that Paul Muni revived Elmer Rice's "Counsellor-at-Law," which he first played successfully the season of 1931-32. So scarce had good dramas been the last two or three seasons, the Muni following, considerably expanded meantime by his successful career in pictures, happily endorsed the revival. It continued for an additional 227 performances and was still running at press time.

Alfred Lunt and Lynn Fontanne, after experimenting with S. N. Behrman's rewritten Ludwig Fulda comedy, "The Pirate," through several road weeks, brought it to the Martin Beck Theatre. Their reception was less enthusiastic than usual, so far as the play was concerned, but quite up to par in the matter of their personal popularity. They played "The Pirate" until late in the Spring. Then Miss Fontanne became ill and they decided to close, that they might embrace the restfulness of their Wisconsin farm.

The production of Dan James' "Winter Soldiers" at the New School for Social Research was a late November item. It caused more stir than had any other production in the history of that experimental theatre. It proved to be one of the most impressive of the war dramas and has been included in this volume as one of the ten outstanding plays of the New York season.

A succession of failures marked the December contributions, but the two successes that did punctuate the holiday period were top-hole. Katharine Cornell revived Chekhov's "The Three Sisters" with a starry cast that included Ruth Gordon, Judith Anderson, Dennis King, Edmund Gwenn, Tom Powers, Gertrude Musgrove and Eric Dressler, and Joseph Fields' "The Doughgirls," having to do with sleeping and extra-marital problems in an overcrowded Washington, kept the town buzzing for weeks. Miss Cornell went touring in the Spring, but "The Doughgirls" threatens at this writing to go on, it may be for weeks, it may be forever.

War plays were making crash dives all about us in mid-season. "Lifeline," a tense tragedy about a convoy straggler that was torpedoed but remained afloat and was later recovered by a part of its crew; "Flare Path," a popular English drama written around the delayed romance of a heroic airman; "Cry Havoc," a tense story of volunteer nurses who were expendable at Bataan, and "The Russian People," a dramatic, but also static, report from the Russian front—all these went down before the reluctance of sensitive play-goers to be made emotionally uncomfortable at this time and at standard theatre tariffs.

Ethel Merman was ready with a new Cole Porter show, "Something for the Boys," the first week in January, and New York is always ready for Ethel. Surrounded by a better than average cast of supporting personalities, including Allen Jenkins and Paula Lawrence, Betty Bruce and Betty Garrett among them,

Ethel sang herself into an all-season stay at a nice profit.

January also produced "Dark Eyes," an amusing comedy written by Elena Miramova with an assist from Eugenie Leontovich. These two Russian actresses evolved a lively plot in which two Russian actresses set out to find an angel for a comedy about three Russian actresses. The co-authors played leading roles until Mme. Leontovich quit in the Spring and returned to Hollywood and Gregory Ratoff, her husband. Tamara Geva took her place.

Sgt. Sidney Kingsley found time in the Army to finish the historical-biographical drama about Thomas Jefferson that he had been working on for four years. It emerged as "The Patriots," which title took in President George Washington and Secretary of the Treasury Alexander Hamilton as well as Jefferson. The play's reception was dignified and sincere, and the last weeks of its stay at the National Theatre were made particularly satisfying when the New York Drama Critics' Circle awarded it the plaque given each year to the best play written by an American author and produced in New York.

Out of another group of failures a Russian war drama, "Counterattack," rewritten from a Russian original called "Probyeda" by Janet and Philip Stevenson, emerged with some promise of success. It proved the most exciting of the war dramas based on Russia, being especially well acted by a company headed by Morris Carnovsky. But once past the lure of its excitements, "Counterattack" suffered the fate of other war plays.

Eddie Dowling thought to save a comedy called "This Rock" by casting Billie Burke in its leading role, that of a Lady Bountiful of the English countryside who takes in a group of East End évacuées. The task proved too much for her. The play was the first effort of Walter Livingstone Faust, a prominent industrialist.

Gertrude Lawrence came back from a highly successful tour with "Lady in the Dark" and added 83 performances to the previous record of that fairly amazing combination of psychoanalysis, music and charm. Then she departed for the West Coast and repeated her triumphs out there.

Helen Hayes was not ready with Florence Ryerson's and Colin Clements' "Harriet" until March. When she did arrive her reception was typical. The rather simple story of Harriet Beecher Stowe and the writing of "Uncle Tom's Cabin" which she helped to tell was accepted, with reservations, as a worth-while biographical drama.

March produced two other of the season's outstanding hits,

F. Hugh Herbert's "Kiss and Tell" and the Oscar Hammerstein 2d-Richard Rodgers-Lynn Riggs-Agnes DeMille "Oklahoma." It really is the work of the Hammerstein-Rodgers duo, but Riggs wrote the "Green Grow the Lilacs" from which it was taken and Miss DeMille put in the ballet which is its greatest novelty. They should, I think, be credited with a share of the success. More of this in later pages.

George Coulouris, a sterling actor, hoped to stimulate a re-awakened interest in the classic drama with a revival of "Richard III," but was disappointed. Milton Berle achieved a long-held ambition by appearing as the star of a "Ziegfeld Follies" at the Winter Garden. Critical approval was not too strong, but play-goer endorsement was generous and Mr. Berle was still a popular attraction when summer tourists began arriving in July.

The closing week of the season registered two fairly sturdy hits and a couple of interesting failures. The hits were James Gow's and Arnaud d'Usseau's "Tomorrow the World," presenting a post-war problem of Nazi youth, and Phoebe and Henry Ephron's "Three's a Family," a mild little domestic comedy which crowds three pregnant wartime mothers into one small apartment.

The interesting failures included Irwin Shaw's "Sons and Soldiers," which was staged by Max Reinhardt and beautifully set by Norman Bel Geddes, both of whom were investing partners in the enterprise. The dramatist's story, in which a wife who had been told that if she had a child she would likely die on the operating table at its birth, suffers a fainting spell during which she visions the life of the child, proved too thoughtful and too fantastic for the crowd.

Another worthy trial was that of Victor Wolfson's "The Family," taken from Nina Federova's novel of that title.

This was the story of a family of White Russians living in the British concession of Tientsin in 1937. To provide a living they open a superior sort of boarding house to which is attracted a curious assortment of troubled humans. The lives of a couple of derelicts are straightened out in the adventures that follow. Well acted by a cast headed by Lucile Watson, the play proved too scattered in attack to hold attention and was withdrawn at the end of its first week.

A third dramatic experiment was a first play by Charles Schnee called "Apology." In this the life of an average citizen in search of his soul is analyzed by a lady lecturer and dramatized as she goes along. This, too, was too fanciful to interest the crowd or the critics and was gone in a week.

Statistically the season's record was unexciting. There were ten fewer productions than there were in 1941-42, but four more success runs of a hundred performances or better; seventy-seven in place of eighty-seven new plays, and twenty-one against seventeen hits. The average of success and failure continues consistently to be at the rate approximately of three to one, three failures to one success.

THE SEASON IN CHICAGO

By Cecil Smith
Drama Critic of the *Chicago Tribune*

THE Chicago season of 1942-43 may be described, in the main, as prosperous but uninteresting. The legitimate theatres accounted for a total of 235 playing weeks between June 1, 1942, and May 31, 1943. This represented, if my feeble arithmetic is not at fault, an increase in tenancy of 20 per cent over the 1941-42 aggregate of 195½ weeks. Runs were longer in average duration, and the populace seemed to possess inexhaustible reserves of folding money to push over the tills of those theatres which housed popular attractions.

These data are encouraging, in a sense, for they show that people had not forgotten the theatre or learned to dislike it during the years of financial stringency, but were merely waiting until they had enough money to start going to the theatre again. But this observation is gratifying only to those who hold that indiscriminate play-going is a desirable activity for people, no matter what plays they are permitted to see. Obviously this is a purely quantitative judgment—a judgment appropriate to commercially minded managers and producers, but not to those who have the best development and growth of the drama at heart.

The bitter truth is that Chicago has seldom, if ever, sat through a more sterile season than the one now under consideration. Revivals and return engagements beset the city like a plague of grasshoppers. The number of productions which demonstrated the theatre as a dynamic, creative institution could be counted on the fingers of one hand. From reprises of "Arsenic and Old Lace" and "Claudia" to shabby Shubert restorations of "The Merry Widow" and "The Student Prince," the city's theatre-goers were glutted with entertainments whose flavor had gone stale. Out of 30 professionally produced plays, no fewer than 13 fell into the classification of revivals and return engagements; and only 2 of these, "Porgy and Bess" and "The Three Sisters," were able to lay claim to particular distinction and freshness of treatment.

The year's most curious phenomenon was the persistent success of "Good Night, Ladies." This farce, based upon "Ladies

Night" (In a Turkish Bath) of hallowed memory, came out of the Far West to make a bid for Chicago's favor on April 12, 1942. The story of its initial weeks was related in this chapter of last year's "Best Plays." To its beginning phases another portion—not the last one—of the saga must now be recorded. With the help of an impromptu cooling system pieced together in spite of priorities, the ribald farce spanned the Summer of 1942 easily, with Buddy Ebsen as the girl-shy professor who inadvertently invaded a feminine Turkish bath, and with Skeets Gallagher as his mentor. The cooler weather of Autumn apparently served only to fan the flames of desire within the potential patrons of "Good Night, Ladies," for the play continued to experience a rushing trade all through the Fall and Winter. On April 12, 1943, its first birthday was celebrated, with several hundred guests attending a program of skits and humor and availing themselves of the food and libations prodigally supplied by the management.

Not even a solid year was enough to satisfy Chicago's appetite for this hokey and uninhibited amusement. When May 31, the expiration date of run-of-the-play contracts, arrived, Mr. Ebsen withdrew to join the Coast Guard. He was supplanted on June 1 by Stuart Erwin, who approached his part with ripe comic device and lost no time in making himself at home in it. On July 10, attaining its 600th performance, "Good Night, Ladies" surpassed the all-time performance high of "Lightnin'" in Chicago. On July 18, having passed its 66th week, it exceeded the temporal span achieved by "Life with Father" in its initial engagement. It is possible that "Good Night, Ladies" will still be running in Chicago when this book reaches your hands, for nothing ever seems to impede its prosperity.

Many observers have been somewhat ashamed that Chicago should elect a play of this type to the honor of an all-time long-run record. In its favor, however, must be advanced the arguments that it is frequently funny and sometimes hilariously so; that its girls, although subject to the inevitable replacements from time to time, have been uniformly well-shaped and well-groomed; and that its principals, at least, are capable actors and attractive people. The farce may be—in fact, is—raucous and trashy, but it is not sordid or distasteful to observe.

With no advance warning whatever, a rival to "Good Night, Ladies" appeared—once again from the West Coast—in mid-September. A hill-billy comedy with a title of prurient *double entendre,* "Maid in the Ozarks," relighted the darkened Great

Northern Theatre, hoping to repeat the modest success which had kept it in Los Angeles, making a small weekly profit, for some six months. No play was ever more universally given a critical trouncing, and I assure you that no play ever more fully deserved what it got from the critics. But for some reason it did not close at the end of the first week, or the second, or the third. Its proprietor stood by his possession during these early weeks, hoping against hope that it would prosper.

Finally, along toward Christmas, he gave up hope. He was on the verge of closing the sorry spectacle when two young Chicagoans offered to buy it from him. Presumably he thought them demented, but he was glad to be rid of his feeble property. Forthwith the new managers flooded the city with the largest deluge of cut-rate coupons ever circulated in Chicago. They bought newspaper space for sensational Barnumesque advertising which employed come-on photographs and verbal descriptions implying that "Tobacco Road" was virtually a Sunday School tract alongside of "Maid in the Ozarks." They instituted Sunday matinees, which attracted crowds of young war workers on their day off. In short, they made a go of it, and the play began to make money. It is still making money, appealing for the most part to an audience to whom the legitimate stage is an unfamiliar novelty. It has found a new and huge group of potential theatre-goers with new money in their pockets, and without enough experience to be discriminating in their choice of an afternoon's or evening's amusement.

At the opposite pole of values, one of the outstanding events of the season was the engagement of Gertrude Lawrence in the Moss Hart-Kurt Weill-Ira Gershwin play with music, "Lady in the Dark." Wiseacres had knitted their brows forbodingly when the big Civic Opera House, seating 3,500, was named as the locale for the play. Dire pictures were painted of the bleakness of a comparative handful of auditors sprinkled among thousands of vacant seats, with the production invisible and inaudible on a stage gauged for "Aïda" and "Turandot." Even Miss Lawrence's management had serious doubts, for the original commitment was restricted to two weeks. But there was no choice; the Grand Opera House was the only theatre in town with a stage big enough to accommodate the revolving stages, inasmuch as the Grand Opera House was turned over to the movies six months before "Lady in the Dark" reached Chicago.

The world's most optimistic management could not have dared to anticipate the incredible popularity of Miss Lawrence's psychoanalytic entertainment. Before the curtain rose on opening night, a staggering advance sale had occurred. The two-week engagement was hastily expanded to four. When capacity business became the rule, night after night, on Mondays as well as Saturdays, a fifth week was added. If Ballet Theatre had not signed a prior contract for the house at the end of the fifth week, there is no telling how long Chicago would have continued to flock in Miss Lawrence's mesmeric direction. The star herself, by virtue of a percentage arrangement, drew a fabulous income reported to be as high as $6,000 a week. The total takings for the five weeks were, in round figures, $250,000.

The Irving Berlin army show, "This Is the Army," attained an equally high gross, relatively speaking. Its booking was severely limited to two weeks, and with the help of an opening night at an $11 top, the Army Emergency Relief took in $100,000 in Chicago. The engagements of these two top-flight musicals served to lift the Civic Opera House, once something of a white elephant, triumphantly out of the red, and the healthy blackness of the ledger was enhanced later in the Spring by a booking which falls outside of our record here—the Metropolitan Opera Company's first visit to Chicago in more than thirty years.

The visit of Katharine Cornell's star-packed revival of Chekhov's "The Three Sisters," occurring in May, proved to be the greatest remaining popular triumph of the year. Naturally enough, there was much diversity of opinion as to the merits of the various performers. Such divergences of opinion, however, served only to make those who had not seen the play rush down to buy tickets. A three-week engagement was extended to four. Not a single seat went unsold in all the four weeks, and the run could have been much longer if Miss Cornell and her colleagues had not wished to turn to Summer activities—either vacations or lucrative pieces of work in Hollywood.

In addition to "Good Night, Ladies" and "Maid in the Ozarks," Chicago saw a number of productions which were not revealed to New York. In January ZaSu Pitts, the movie actress with the fluttery hands and the disconsolate voice, made her initial try on the legitimate stage with a mystery farce known as "Her First Murder." The script was a painful hack job, offering little opportunity for the exploitation of Miss Pitts' somewhat restricted comic talents, and leaving the audience without the slightest impetus to discover who committed a certain very uninteresting murder. The play came to Chicago after a few preliminary weeks in Detroit and elsewhere on the road. At the end of its unpatronized fortnight in Chicago it was allowed quietly to give up the ghost, although at this writing I read that a revised version is to be tried out in the East. The only way to revise that play satisfactorily, I am afraid, would be to throw away everything except the stage setting and start writing a brand-new play.

"Cry Havoc," Allan R. Kenward's play about war nurses on Bataan, which had failed earlier in New York under the title of "Proof Thro' the Night," reached Chicago with an almost entirely new cast. The company ran to extremes of talent, from the strikingly effective and genuine gifts of Flora Campbell to the sensational presence of the former burlesque star, Margie Hart, who made her first venture into serious drama under the name of Bridget Hart, Bridget being the second name that actually belongs to her. The changes in cast may or may not have been improvements—I did not see the New York performance— but the faulty contrivances of the play were sufficiently obvious to keep it from gaining an audience. After leaving Chicago, the play toured to Detroit and Boston, and wound up in the sub-way circuit with Miss Hart enjoying star billing in it for the first time.

"Priorities of 1942," a considerable hit during the Fall season, employed a good many different principals from those seen in the vaudeville show in its New York days, and achieved special distinction in the presence of the gifted Argentinita and her brilliant partner Federico Rey, who left for the Army before the end of the Chicago engagement. An earlier variety show, presented in the summer of 1942 by Alfred Bloomingdale as the last flesh-and-blood attraction in the Grand Opera House, failed because it was badly paced and crudely put together, the talents of Bert Lahr, Joe E. Lewis and Bert Wheeler notwithstanding.

J. J. Shubert's contributions to the higher life were about as usual. In the summer a dismal warehouse musical, "Cocktails at Five," spent a desolate week at the Erlanger before expiring. A Christmas revival of "The Merry Widow" had neither taste nor talent to recommend it; it sank to a new nadir when the famous waltz was employed as an accompaniment to routine tap-dancing and to an arty and poorly executed ballet of the "Sylphides" genre. "The Student Prince," which received refurbished costumes and settings when it was brought back to New York some months afterward, still reveled in its ancient trappings on tour.

Several New York hits were brought to Chicago with second companies, of varying degrees of merit. "Junior Miss," the first to appear, suffered from special ineptitude of casting. It was also inadequately rehearsed, and investigation revealed that Moss Hart, whose name was listed as stage director, had never so much as seen the company act, and very likely has not to this day. A similar carelessness on Mr. Hart's part was evident in the third company, which invaded Chicago in the Summer of 1943, a period which does not rightfully belong in this survey.

"The Doughgirls" was treated better, and George S. Kaufman was conspicuously present, with furrowed forehead, in a box on opening night at the Selwyn Theatre. Taylor Holmes handled the part of Brig. Gen. Slade with skill and bravado, and the various young women all filled the prescription neatly. Better still, however, was George Abbott's second company of "Kiss and Tell," which proved in every way to be the full equal of the excellent New York company, and which accordingly prospered at the box office from the first night forward. Of "The Eve of St. Mark" not so much could be said. The men's parts, generally speaking, were quite satisfactory, but the women were uniformly weak. Perhaps because of the second-grade performance, and perhaps because of the immediacy of the subject matter at a time when the first impressive casualty lists were beginning to be published in the newspapers, Chicago did not take to Maxwell Anderson's drama, and its run amounted only to nine weeks.

A number of attempts at popular-priced performances were made, but most of them were not successful. Ruth Chatterton and Ralph Forbes, however, played in a revival of Noel Coward's "Private Lives" at $2.20 top, and enjoyed some of the best business in town for 11 weeks. The Boston Comic Opera Company, purveyors of somewhat homespun Gilbert and Sullivan, likewise found a friendly audience in two engagements of a fortnight each. Frank McCoy, who had made a good thing of popular-priced stock in Detroit, met his Waterloo when he brought two of his productions to Chicago with inferior and unrehearsed casts. These were "Stage Door," in which the brightly attractive Glenda Farrell was starred, and "You Can't Take It with You," in which Fred Stone returned after a decade's absence, but was not able to make his protracted curtain speech an adequate substitute for a dishearteningly sub-standard performance of the play.

Just before Labor Day the entrepreneurs of "Maid in the

Ozarks" brought Billy Bryant, the Ohio showboat impresario, to town with his version of "Uncle Tom's Cabin." They had thought that Helen Hayes' appearance in "Harriet" would have aroused great interest in Mrs. Stowe's story, but they were grievously mistaken. The play was presented in none too palatable surroundings in the auditorium of a lodge hall on the near North Side, well off the theatrical beaten track. Mr. Bryant's liberal ad libbing, which was supposed to save the show, made use of dated and unfunny gags, many of which lost their meaning when we stopped talking about the depression, the WPA, and kindred matters. The acting of the drama was altogether execrable, discovering neither the tone of a burlesque nor of a quasi-serious period treatment. After two weeks Mr. Bryant was forced to return to his river-side, to bemoan the fact that the government had commandeered his showboat for wartime purposes.

In addition to these various items, none of which was beheld in New York, the Chicago season also included visits of a number of Broadway attractions with their original casts more or less intact. These were: "Café Crown," which was too esoteric in locale to strike a sympathetic chord in Chicago; Grace George and C. Aubrey Smith, who were welcomed generously in their fluffy trifle called "Spring Again"; "Best Foot Forward," which did well for three weeks at the Erlanger, and then slipped off when it had to move to the less centrally located Studebaker; "Porgy and Bess," successful for 11 weeks; and the above-mentioned "This Is the Army" and "Lady in the Dark."

Repeat engagements included "My Sister Eileen," "Arsenic and Old Lace" (with Boris Karloff), "Claudia" (with the original New York cast), "The Merry Widow" (with Muriel Angelus), "Watch on the Rhine" (with most of the original cast), "The Student Prince" (with Everett Marshall and Ann Pennington), "New 1943 Hellzapoppin," which was not new at all; "Life with Father" (with Percy Waram and June Walker); "Private Lives"; "Stage Door"; the new "Porgy and Bess" production, which involved many changes from the original Theatre Guild staging; and the Boston Comic Opera Company's repertory of seven Gilbert and Sullivan operas. (The Fred Stone performance of "You Can't Take It with You," which I included to round out the picture of Frank McCoy's activity, did not open until May 30, and therefore really belongs in next season's résumé.)

The 30 plays which constituted the 1942-43 season may be classified in the following categories: new comedies, farces and melodramas, 7; new serious dramas, 2; new musicals and vaudeville entertainments, 7; farce held over from previous season, 1; revivals and return engagements of all sorts, 13. Compared with 1941-42, this classification reveals a 50 per cent decline in the number of new serious plays, and virtually a 100 per cent increase in the number of revivals and return engagements.

The most significant alteration in the real estate picture was the removal from the scene of the Grand Opera House, Chicago's oldest playhouse with a continuous history of legitimate stage entertainment. After the theatre had passed from Shubert control back into the hands of its owners, the Hamlin estate, it did not receive as enthusiastic co-operation as formerly from the United Booking Office. The season of 1941-42 brought only three or four really profitable weeks, and in discouragement the management signed a long-term contract with movie interests.

The elimination of the Grand Opera House brought the Studebaker back into much greater prominence, with the result that that theatre enjoyed its busiest season in many years. The Blackstone, of course, was busiest of all, for "Good Night, Ladies" occupied the house for 52 weeks. The record of the other houses is as follows: Harris, 45; Great Northern, 37; Erlanger, 35; Selwyn, 32½; Studebaker, 23; Civic Opera House (exclusive of opera, ballet, concerts, Jewish plays, etc.), 7; Grand Opera House, 2½; Foresters Theatre (the home of "Uncle Tom's Cabin," which opened a week before the end of the season under consideration, and continued for one week into the new season), 1.

The augury for 1943-44 in Chicago looks somewhat more hopeful. Many of the good products of the past season in New York will find their way westward, and it is possible that the forthcoming season will recover a higher degree of intrinsic interest. The chief future problem is a potential theatre shortage, which is likely to be serious enough throughout the Autumn to force many plays to defer their Chicago engagements until mid-Winter.

THE SEASON IN SAN FRANCISCO

By Fred Johnson

Drama Editor, *The Call-Bulletin*

TOURING difficulties that were expected to deprive San Francisco of its usual share of road shows during the 1942-43 season were so well overcome that this distant port of army embarkation became instead a showman's bonanza town.

The wartime activities of shipbuilding and the growth of army and navy stations drew a prosperous new bay district population of amusement-seekers, creating a welcome drop-in trade at the theatre box offices.

"What's a good show?" became the stock query of brief visitors and new residents, with the result that all legitimate houses made sure they were not without an attraction. And their bookings became solid for the first time in many seasons.

On no previous year in the city's theatrical history had even the more outstanding Broadway successes risked return engagements at so frequent intervals. "Arsenic and Old Lace," for instance, made its third visit in less than nine months, playing its last to almost capacity business.

"Claudia," with its original cast almost intact, came again within ten months, and "Life with Father," which in 1942 had broken the town's long-run record of recent years, came back within almost a year for fat profits.

Of three Coast productions, two went on to Broadway with contrasting results. One was "Show Time," first of the Paul Small and Fred Finklehoffe "variety revues," starring George Jessel, Jack Haley and Kitty Carlisle. Its San Francisco launching was good for a run of six weeks. But Jess Smith's production of "The Barber Had Two Sons," a drama of the Norway invasion, starring Blanche Yurka, forced its stay of three lean weeks in the face of unfriendly notices before venturing on to New York for similar critical attention.

A third première was that of Eugene S. Bryden's "Adamant Eve," a costume comedy with music based by Francis Edwards on Sardou's "Divorcons." It was "adamant" in the stretching of even a brief sojourn, with the aid of Carol Stone's beauty and charm and the valiant acting of Rex O'Malley and Barry Norton.

"Junior Miss" was so well received in a Curran Theatre engagement of five weeks that it was moved next door to the Geary for three more stanzas. Of the Broadway hits, "Watch on the Rhine" alone failed of its expected acclaim and the answer is yet to be supplied. The geographical hint in its title was seen as one reason for its merely fair patronage of less than a month. And yet "The Student Prince," with its locale of old Heidelberg, fared well for as long a period and to excellent business.

Everett Marshall, after starring in "The Student Prince" at one theatre, took over the lead in "Blossom Time" on another stage for a fortnight longer.

Ethel Barrymore in "The Corn Is Green" found her San Francisco popularity undimmed and her engagement of one month was well supported.

A musical highlight of the year was the return of Gilbert and Sullivan after a long absence, with the Boston Comic Opera Company playing to capacity at the Geary for three weeks in a full repertoire that included the seldom-staged "Ruddigore."

Another Finklehoffe and Small variety show, which matched the success of "Show Time," was Ed Wynn's "Big Time," which did an excellent six weeks' business and might have stayed on to good profit. The producers' second venture decided them to lay plans for the later production, "Laugh Time," starring Frank Fay, Ethel Waters and Bert Wheeler.

Fourth season of the San Francisco and Los Angeles Light Opera season was rated as the association's best. It was unusual in its drawing of two Broadway hits as guest attractions—"Porgy and Bess" and Gertrude Lawrence in "Lady in the Dark." "The Gypsy Baron," starring Irra Petina, the Metropolitan Opera soprano, and "The Firefly," with Francia White and Rudolf Friml (at the piano) were hits in the shorter engagements allotted.

An event extraordinary was the Memorial Opera House run of Irving Berlin's "This Is the Army," prior to its settling down in Hollywood for the show's filmization.

The Alcazar Theatre, long the home of Henry Duffy stock and productions, was relighted for several months by Hollywood's Sid Grauman, first with his "Highlites of 1943" vaudeville and then for Bill Robinson's all-colored revue, "Born Happy," both rewarded by lengthy runs. Another and less successful venture was the Turkish Ali M. Ipar's production of "The Chocolate Soldier."

A loss to the city's rialto was the death of George Warren,

former drama critic of the *San Francisco Chronicle,* after an illness of several years. He had continued as a member of the plays committee of the nationally prominent Berkeley Playmakers, which has been busied this season in staging both comedies and dramas at the near-by army and navy bases, besides conducting its annual playwrighting competition which brought in a record grist of 424 manuscripts. The George Pierce Baker award went to Harold Bassage of Berkeley for his documentary of China's long struggle, "Gung-Ho." The play now is being broadcast to the Orient.

The Little Theatre (without a theatre) on the University of California campus made a red-letter production of Maxwell Anderson's "The Eve of St. Mark" and Stanford University's drama department had another active year.

THE SEASON IN SOUTHERN CALIFORNIA

By EDWIN SCHALLERT

Drama Editor of the *Los Angeles Times*

THE theatre, distinctly as a medium of "release" in wartime, renewed some of its lost popularity in Southern California during the 1942-43 season. Hardly anybody would be so sanguine as to regard this as a period of great accomplishment, as it has occasionally been known in the past, but at least the interest in the flesh-and-blood form of entertainment was increased, and certain events, mostly those of musical character, were greeted with great enthusiasm.

The real climax was arrived at during the light opera season, which began with the New York production of "Porgy and Bess" and culminated with the sold-out engagement of Gertrude Lawrence in "Lady in the Dark." It otherwise included a revised version of Johann Strauss' "Gypsy Baron," starring Irra Petina, and "The Firefly," with the composer Rudolf Friml himself present on the stage to provide a medley of his famous songs rendered with many arabesques and other technical decor.

Important in the impression he made on audiences was John Tyers, who had sung in light opera in the East, and who is under contract to Metro-Goldwyn-Mayer. He became an idol both because of his personality and voice. The studio immediately began to think of him as a discovery for the screen, where he had previously been given little or no attention, though it was also believed that he would face the familiar fate of younger men these days, namely, being called to the colors.

Each light opera had a good two weeks, instead of one, and the Gerrtude Lawrence stay was even longer. It was a personal triumph for her, because "Lady in the Dark" lost a little of its glow in the comparatively large expanse of Philharmonic Auditorium. The production would have carried greater appeal in a more intimate setting. It was liked by the majority, though with some reservation. But that reservation was not reflected in the box office.

The Los Angeles Civic Light Opera Association, which had assured the visit of the attraction to the Coast by virtue of its financial backing, profited luxuriously as the result of its enter-

23

prise, and the showmanship in arranging for the two New York offerings undoubtedly stimulated the attendance for those operettas which were Coast originated. It was by far the best series in general quality that had ever been given.

The "straight play" record had some noteworthy highlights. These comprised the advent on the road of "Watch on the Rhine," with practically all of its original cast, including Lucile Watson, Paul Lukas and Mady Christians, "Arsenic and Old Lace," with a full complement of Manhattan players like Boris Karloff, Jean Adair, Josephine Hull, etc., "Claudia," with Dorothy McGuire, Donald Cook and Frances Starr; "The Corn Is Green," starring Ethel Barrymore; "Junior Miss," with the touring company; a return engagement of "Life with Father," this time featuring Percy Waram and June Walker.

The potpourri soldier show "This Is the Army" enjoyed enormous business, climaxing its Coast engagement with its entry into the film. A rival presentation of much simpler fabric, created at Ft. MacArthur, near Los Angeles, thrived both before and after the visit of the Irving Berlin creation. This was called "Hey, Rookie!" and lasted from October to May at the Belasco Theatre. It was distinguished by its pleasant spontaneity, and cast the spotlight on Sterling Holloway as the primary comedian. It was sold out much of the time.

Very popular, too—and again we return to musical entertainment—were the performances of R. H. Burnside's Boston Comic Opera Company, which had in its personnel Florenz Ames, Robert Pitkin, Morton Bowe, Philip Tully, Bertram Peacock, Catherine Judah, June Winters, Marjorie Hayward and Margaret Roy, among others. The work of the troupe was distinguished by its spirit, and its repertoire was made up of "The Mikado," which was the opening bill; "Pirates of Penzance," "Gondoliers," "Iolanthe," "Trial by Jury" and "Pinafore" together, and "Patience." A proposed giving of "Ruddigore" had to be canceled because the service call took its toll of the cast. The audiences grew day by day for this Gilbert and Sullivan manifestation, proving that as always their devotees, even in a changing world, are numerous.

There were no great stirrings in the way of Coast productions, although several hovered in the 1943 summery middle distance, which is beyond the purview of this recapitulation. "Cry Havoc" caused the most excitement, but that was chiefly when it was produced at the Beachwood Studio Playhouse, a little theatre environment. Here it ran for several weeks, and an effort was then made to commercialize the play at the Music Box, but it languished. The film adaptation, which has a lustrous cinema cast, promises to reach the greater public.

Probably if it had been kept in its original setting "Cry Havoc" might have fared better on the Western stage. Show-goers in Southern California seem sometimes to lean toward novelty in theatres, as well as entertainment. Witness the 10-year run, still continuing, of "The Drunkard" and the perennial allure of the Turnabout, with its puppet shows and its slight vaudeville revue which retains Elsa Lanchester as the star, and was winding up its second year at the end of the 1942-43 season.

Rather conspicuous were the return engagements of "Arsenic and Old Lace," which came on the scene first in August of 1942, revisited toward the end of September, and then reappeared in May of 1943. It possessed some of the endurable attributes of a "Tobacco Road," despite their remoteness from each other in content.

Any show that spelt laughter was warmly greeted, and at the very end of the year, "The Doughgirls," with a specially organized company from the East, was attaining a marked vogue. This was practically the only one of the newer attractions from New York to reach the Coast in the professional sphere.

Joy Hodges gave the liveliest impetus to the comedy, and the cast was in other respects acceptable. The bright sophistication of the lines garnered plenty of response, notwithstanding the solid residential group in Los Angeles is inclined to be conservative about this smart stuff. The more worldly-wise are, however, constantly gathering new forces, and may someday confute the testimony that Los Angeles is not a good show town when it comes to ultra-modernity, and incidentally the price question.

The price question is, of course, a big factor. Ken Murray has been doing a tremendous business with a vaudeville revue for more than a year at $1.50 top. Ensconced in the new El Capitan Theatre on Vine Street this affair gives every indication of remaining there more or less indefinitely. The anniversary celebration drew a full complement of first-nighters, and Murray, who has Marie Wilson as his feminine aide-de-camp, wins victories again and again with his quick resourcefulness of wit and his versatility. His vaudeville started after George Jessel's during the 1941-42 season, opened much less brightly but has remained. The show plays two matinees on Sundays (drawing many war industry workers), as well as a night performance. The theatre is nearly always packed week-ends, and the crowds are never too light at other times.

Ed Wynn came to town with a higher-priced production called "Big Time." He played the Mayan Theatre, which has been dark so much since it was built. He had several very successful weeks, made money for himself and his backers, but though he was vastly clever and ingenious himself, and never in the "blue" zone with his humor, he did not seem to have the chance to become an institution in the same sense as Murray, who often resorts to very snappy innuendoes to enliven his presentation.

Wynn and his sponsors were naturally not looking for a protracted success. They did exceptionally well. But the sort of divertisement that really has the success "edge" is the source of some mystification. Murray's show, for instance, is one of the exhibits like "The Drunkard," the Turnabout Theatre, "Meet the People" and "Hey, Rookie!" which makes the theatrical pattern an odd one. The element that all these have in common is their informality. This seems to be liked above all else by the greater populace.

When it comes to dramatic or "legitimate" events, so-called, said populace will usually turn out and (above all) pay a price for seats if there is a famous star in the cast. But they want someone of the celebrity of a Barrymore, Alfred Lunt and Lynn Fontanne, Katharine Cornell, or Helen Hayes, and even these have to proffer just the right play.

For the basic drama one must continue to look toward the Pasadena Community Playhouse, where the annual program is always representative. Were it not for the fact that this organization brings to life a number of the more notable New York plays, these would probably never have been seen in the Southern California territory. The repertoire at the Playhouse is varied, and it never fails to include something either out of the current, or at least recent seasons on Broadway.

In that setting during the year was given the Coast "first" of "The Eve of St. Mark," which, by the way, was day and date with the Boston advance "break-in" of the Maxwell Anderson tragedy of war. This preceded the New York première.

Digressingly, it might also be noted that this same "Eve of St. Mark" was given a very good rendition in Hollywood by workers in an airplane plant, with some members of the cast boasting actual theatrical experience prior to their present occupation.

At Pasadena during 1943 were also offered the Coast "firsts" of "Jason," "Quiet Wedding," "Heaven Can Wait" and "Lights of Duxbury." The premières were "Very Unusual Weather" by Jack Robinson and Gene Stone, and "Return of Ulysses" by Emil Ludwig, the former faring much better than the latter.

"Arsenic and Old Lace," "Watch on the Rhine" and "Cry Havoc" found their way onto the Playhouse list, notwithstanding they were professionally performed during the year. "The Moment Is Now" by Hallie Flanagan, "Cuckoos on the Hearth," "Family Portrait," "Papa Is All," "The Women" and a revival of "Charley's Aunt" were among the novelties.

The Midsummer Drama Festival for 1942 scanned 50 years of American comedy by eight famous playwrights—started with "The Fortune Hunter" by Winchell Smith and wound up with "Abie's Irish Rose" by Anne Nichols. The festival for 1943, which began a little earlier than usual in June, was dedicated to Booth Tarkington.

One returns to the professional theatre to note that in June an effort was made to resurrect the dynamic lure of the Grand Guignol type of playlet, under the title of "Horror Tonight," with Howard Young sponsoring. Primary stars were the splendid Flora Robson and Henry Hull, who individually made "Thirsty Death," of French origin, and "Silver Nails," with its Irish background, convey an impact. "The Needle," of genuine Grand Guignol derivation, and "Behind the Mask" were the other constituents of the program.

Short plays were the mainstay of the Brentwood Service Players, a most interesting assembling of professional folk who, in a suburb, sought to divert service men gratis, while civilian support was depended on to keep the project going. This did very well and featured famous stars not only in the regularly scheduled part of the show, but also in an impromptu olio.

Motion picture people really like the excuse to get before audiences in reality, and are finding numerous reasons for managing this during the wartime. This is again a hopeful trend along lines laid out in the past by the glamorous staging of "Tonight at 8:30" in 1940, the David O. Selznick venture in Santa Barbara in 1941, and others.

Permanence prevails for the restaurant shows like Earl Carroll's and Nils Thor Grandlund's at Florentine Gardens. These partake almost as much of the theatre as they do of the cabaret. Sign of the times is that Carroll has not found it necessary to alter the character of his production at mid-year as has been his wont. His December (1942) revue was proceeding on into the 1943-44 season. Audiences have multiplied.

Bill Robinson followed the revue prescription with his show, "Born Happy," which opened at the Biltmore after an engagement in San Francisco, and moved to the Mayan, Sid Grauman being its original impresario. Paul Small, who was the Ed Wynn producer, was preparing to introduce still another revue toward the end of the year with Frank Fay. A late arrival was "Money Girls," presented by H. M. Horkheimer, formerly of the films.

There was light opera apart from the civic. Everett Marshall was especially well recognized in "The Student Prince" and "Blossom Time." Charles Purcell and Florence George headlined "The Chocolate Soldier." A revival of "Topsy and Eva" with the Duncan Sisters added to the lighter musicals.

"Out of the Frying Pan" had a brief trial with a film town cast. Maurice Schwartz and his Yiddish Art Theatre Players did a repertoire.

The miscellany further included "She Lost It in Campeche," which finally totaled up about 100 weeks, "The Nudist," which was produced for three months, "Keep Your Distance," which was in a much different vein but a very poor play, a mild revival of "Rain" and various other items over which there need be no particular tarrying.

The little theatres as usual went on their determined way, apart from the Pasadena Community, and accomplished some very interesting things, both in the discovering of talent, and in actual staging. A debut that proved arresting was that of Maria Manton, daughter of Marlene Dietrich, in "The Little Foxes" at the Geller (formerly the Reinhardt) Workshop. Consistently active were the Callboard, Bliss-Hayden and a few other establishments.

All in all, there is considerable new leaven in the theatre hereabouts, even though much of it may not be yielding more than casual, gaily distracting, wartime show history.

THE PATRIOTS

Historical Drama in Prologue and Three Acts

By Sidney Kingsley

SIDNEY KINGSLEY, whose "Men in White" won him a Pulitzer Prize, and whose "Dead End" brought him great praise and generous profits, had been working for two years on a play he had tentatively titled "Thomas Jefferson," when along came the war.

Soon Sidney Kingsley was Sgt. Kingsley and a part of the war, being stationed at the time on Governors Island, New York. The play had been put aside. Whatever the urge to finish it, there was little time in which to do it, and no place in which to write it. Finally the urge was too strong to be denied, and time and place were found. It is related by a fellow sergeant that among Sgt. Kingsley's other adventures was that of hiding himself away in the attic of the barracks building, where he thought he could work with some degree of quiet and without too frequent interruption. And he could have done so had it not turned out that the barracks' attic was also used as a rifle range.

A second two years slipped by before "Thomas Jefferson," now retitled "The Patriots," was ready for production. By this time the play had acquired an added backer in the person of Rowland Stebbins, who will be known to the end of the century at least as the noble soul who had enough faith in Marc Connelly's "The Green Pastures" to bring it to production after so-called wiser heads of Broadway had neglected to do so.

Mr. Stebbins, seeking the best in the way of contributing technical aids to production, suggested an association with the Playwrights' Company, which two seasons previously had had a happy adventure with another historical drama, Robert Sherwood's "Abe Lincoln in Illinois." The Playwrights' Company was sincerely interested and promptly set about casting and rehearsing "The Patriots," bringing it to production January 29, 1943.

The drama's reception was most favorable. The reviewers agreed upon its outstanding quality as a transcript of those historical years which immediately followed the founding of the republic, and disagreed only mildly over the author's evaluation

29

of the characters of Thomas Jefferson and Alexander Hamilton, his leading protagonists. That he favored Jefferson as the founder of our democracy and rather over-emphasized the opposition of Hamilton and his followers as a crew of doubtful loyalists who were really "itching for crowns, coronets and mitres," was their common contention, but they in no way intimated that by so doing he had unbalanced either the drama or its argument.

"Mr. Kingsley is, of course, a Jeffersonian," wrote Wilella Waldorf in the *New York Post*. "His play uses Jefferson as a symbol of Democratic government in its most enlightened form, and it is therefore at its best, not when he is exalting Jefferson at the expense of Hamilton in the final act, but earlier, during Washington's lifetime, when Jefferson and Hamilton were at each other's throats as Secretaries of State and the Treasury, and the riotous echoes of the French Revolution were stirring the minds and emotions of Americans who had so lately staged a Revolution of their own."

Our introduction to "The Patriots" is by way of a prologue. We are in a ship at sea. The year is 1790. It is a star-lit night. There is a sound of rushing water and the creak of tackle. Dimly outlined, standing at a bend in the rail, looking over the dark ocean, a middle-aged man and a girl are discovered. "The man is very tall and thin, his face fine, supersensitive, a gentleness almost womanish written on it. He has dispensed with the wig of the period. His hair, ruffled by the winds, is reddish, streaked with gray, right long. The girl is in her late teens, vibrant, lithe, handsome." They are Thomas Jefferson and his daughter, Patsy.

Presently the Captain appears. He would warn them that it may blow up a bit and advises their thinking of going below. But the Jeffersons are loath to leave the scene. The sea and their thoughts hold them fascinated. They are nearing the American shore. Like all voyages home, this one has seemed to Jefferson to last forever. But it is nearly over, and the plans for their immediate future interest them.

Patsy had thought they would be going to New York first, but her father has decided to go direct to Monticello. Then, after they have completed plans for Patsy's wedding, he will go on to New York for his conference with President Washington.

Patsy has been wondering about these plans—and about her wedding. Perhaps it would be better to put it off a little while. "If you accept the President's offer you will have to live in New York," Patsy reminds her father. "You'll be alone for the first

time in your life. You'll be utterly miserable. I know you too
well, Papa. Who'd take care of you?"

"But I have no intention of accepting the Secretary of State."

"You haven't?"

"The President gave me the option of refusal. And I certainly mean to take advantage of it."

"Why didn't you tell me?"

"It never occurred to me. You see, darling—I discovered a
long time ago that Nature didn't intend me for office. I accepted the French post, dearest, only because . . . at the time
. . . your mother's death had left me so blank . . . I . . ."

"I know, Father . . ."

For a long time they stand staring into the darkness. Then
Jefferson would talk of Monticello; of his wish that Patsy's
mother were still there to meet them; of his fond memory of her.

"She used to love to tell me about *your* wedding night," Patsy
tells him. "In the garden cottage, midst such a clutter of your
drawings and your books and your inventions, you could hardly
move about. . . . And how you lit a fire, and found half a bottle
of wine a workman had left behind some books. . . . And
Mother played the piano-forte and you your violin, and you sang
old songs." . . .

The wind has risen. Jefferson would go below to make sure
that Patsy's sister has not kicked her blanket off, but Patsy insists on doing that errand herself. After she has gone the darkness deepens, the moonlight fades. As Jefferson gazes upon the
sea out of the mists "the exterior of an enchanting house mate-
rializes. Monticello! Snow is falling and has piled deep around
it."

Now there are sounds of galloping horses, muffled by the snow;
sounds of laughter; sounds of a barn door opening. And soon
Martha Jefferson comes into the vision. She is laughing, shaking
the snow from her cloak, and talking to someone following—

"Phew! Was there ever such a wedding night?" Martha is
saying. "I declare, Tom Jefferson, those last few miles the
horses fairly flew through the snow."

"They smelled home," Jefferson answers, coming to stand beside her.

"Are they stabled now?"

"Yes, indeed."

"A true Virginian. First your horses, then your women."

"Shocking talk for a bride of one night, Mrs. Jefferson. . . ."

And now he is happy to turn Monticello over to his bride;

the most beautiful home, she says, that she ever dreamed of;
"an incredibly lovely house."

"It'll be ready for us to move into by April," he says. "Till
then we'll use the garden cottage. It's only one room."

"Like a couple of dormice. We won't stir till Spring," decrees Martha.

The picture fits Martha's vision of what Monticello was like in
Tom Jefferson's youth, and he fills in the scene with memories
of his happiness there. Suddenly her eyes begin to twinkle, and
when he presses for a reason she confesses—

"I was thinking I hardly recognize the man I married. I
declare, Tom Jefferson, you're a different person here. Sort
of . . ."

"Sort of what?"

"Tipsy!"

"It's the rarefied atmosphere."

"It's most becoming. I thought I'd married a sober, red-headed,
raffish young lawyer who was clever with the fiddle and who had
all the propertied squires a little worried because he wanted to
change the laws of Virginia from top to bottom."

"You know, Martha," he says, quite seriously, "I've been
thinking of giving up the law. I'd like to spend all my time
here—farming . . . some day. I don't like lawyers much."

"I fell in love with one. (*Seriously.*) Tom, dearest . . ."

"Yes, Martha."

"I can't tell you what you've done for me."

"What I've done for you?"

"Yes. Before I met you, circumstances and the intolerance of
little men had begun to make me lose faith. The world had
begun to shrink. Living had become something quite unimpor-
tant. Then . . . the night I met you . . . after the gay chatter,
when you began to talk gravely, I suddenly fell in love, not only
with you, but I fell in love with the possibilities of the whole
race of man. The earth expanded. I saw a future. Oh, Tom,
it's so exciting just to be alive and to be here with you. What
a wonderful adventure the world can be, can't it? If we . . .
(*She stops short. He is gazing at her adoringly.*) Now, what are
you looking at, Mr. Jefferson?"

"If I live to be a thousand and close my eyes—this is the
way I'll see you, my love. With snow on your face and your
eyes shining!"

"Oh, Tom, I'm only trying to say I'm happy."

He has taken her in his arms and kissed her and quoted a bit of verse and promised to love her forever and ever. And then he realizes that she must be getting cold, picks her up in his arms and carries her toward the house as the vision of Monticello fades. . . .

The wind that the Captain had predicted begins to sweep through the rigging of the ship. The deck light comes up enough to show Jefferson in silhouette still standing looking out at sea. The Captain's orders roar around him and the voices of the crew can be heard answering "Aye, sir," from many posts.

Again, as the darkness deepens and the winds howl, the voices of men raised in anger supplant those of the ship's crew. Out of the darkness there emerges a second picture; a picture of Jefferson seated at a desk with a manuscript before him.

"Georgia votes nay!" . . . "This document is a mass of glittering generalities." . . . "Carolina votes nay!" . . . The voices boom in Jefferson's ears, as he looks anxiously from one antagonist to another. "Motion to strike out clause condemning the slave traffic. Hands! For? Against? Motion is carried. You will please strike out that clause."

Jefferson bitterly scratches out the offending clause. "That second sentence. Don't like it!" booms another voice.

"But this is the heart of it, man," protests Jefferson. "Are we going to have to creep up on liberty, inch by inch?"

VOICE—Where does this lead? No wonder we're driving all our men of property into the arms of the loyalists.

JEFFERSON—I was asked to write the declaration and I wrote it. I haven't tried to be original. This is a simple expression of the American mind. Our people want this.

REID'S VOICE—From a legalistic viewpoint . . .

JEFFERSON—The men who migrated to America, who built it with their sweat and blood were laborers, not lawyers.

REID'S VOICE—Plague on't, boy! You want some precedent. Where can you show me anything like this in history?

JEFFERSON—Where in history do we see anything like this new world or the man of this new world? Where have we ever seen a land so marked by destiny to build a new free society based on the rights of man? Precedent? Let's make precedent! Better to set a good example than follow a bad one.

REID—I'll debate this point all day.

JEFFERSON (rising)—No member of this Congress is more eager than I to settle the business on hand and go home. My wife is ill and bearing me a child, and while I stay here she's doing all my work at home. I'm half mad with anxiety, but I'll stay on all summer if necessary to fight for this one sentence. There is not a man in the whole empire who wished conciliation more than I. But, by the God that made me, I would have sooner ceased to exist than yield my freedom. And in this I know I speak for America. I am sorry to find a bloody campaign is decided on. But since it is forced on us, we must drub the enemy and drub him soundly. We must teach the sceptered tyrant we are not brutes to kiss the hand that scourges us. But this is not enough. We are now deciding everlastingly our future and the future of our innocent posterity. Our people have already been fighting a year . . . For what? (*He taps the document.*) For this. Let us give it to them . . . in writing . . . now. Now is the time to buttress the liberty we're fighting for. By law, by the written word. I would go beyond this simple sentence. In my own state I would tear up all the laws we inherited from the old world, discard all the trappings of monarchy and tyranny, write a whole new legal code! Build a whole new structure. It can't be too strongly emphasized. Now is the time, while men are bleeding and dying. Tomorrow they may grow careless and a new despot may find in the old laws an instrument to rob their liberty again. Now is the time to build a free society. Now! Not later.

REID'S VOICE (*wavering*)—Well . . . er . . . Read that clause again. Let's examine it again!

JEFFERSON (*sitting, reading from document*)—We hold these truths to be self-evident; that all men are created equal; that they are endowed by their Creator with certain inalienable rights; that among these are the right to life, liberty and the pursuit of happiness; that a just government derives its power from the consent of the governed . . .

The Liberty Bell begins to peal. "Jefferson's face is transfigured by an almost sacred light which glows brighter and brighter."

Now there is a sudden crack of thunder and lightning streaks across the sky. In the flashes of light the outline of the ship is seen again; the winds howl and gradually fade away. The Captain's orders are heard hurtling from man to man. The lights go out again and when they are renewed the scene is that of a room in Monticello. "Martha is lying on a bed, waxen-white, struggling for breath Jefferson sits by her side, his face a mask of grief. A doctor stands in the half shadow nearby."

Martha has thought that she dreamed the war was over. It was not a dream, her husband assures her, taking her hand tenderly; the war is over, and their side has won. Now all she has to think of is getting well—

"Oh, Tom . . . My . . . good . . . husband . . . I love you," Martha says haltingly. "Ten years . . . the richest happiness . . . any woman . . . ever knew . . . you've given me. In spite . . . of war . . . in spite of . . . everything . . . They couldn't . . . take that . . . from us . . . could they?"

Jefferson's tears mingle with his pleading with her to get well. They have done their jobs. Now they can rest and take no part in the worries of the world. Martha's thoughts are with her children. He must promise to take good care of them—

"I don't want to die, Tom! I want to stay here with you . . . I don't want to die . . ." She has grown visibly feebler. "So tired . . . Forgive me, dearest . . ." Her eyes close and her labored breathing stops. The doctor comes from the shadow. It is over.

"No . . . No . . . Martha, darling . . . Martha, dearest . . . Martha . . . I can't go on living without you . . . In every picture I ever painted you were in the foreground . . . without you there's no picture. There's nothing . . ."

Faintly Patsy's voice is heard calling out of the darkness. The lights, slowly brightening, reveal Patsy standing by her father's side on the ship. She has come to tell him that Maria is all right. She had kicked the blanket off, as he feared, but now she is tucked in tight again.

"You were so deep in meditation," says Patsy, a little anxiously. "What were you thinking?"

"Oh . . . nothing, dear. Just . . . thinking."

Suddenly there is a cry of "Land, Ho!" from the watch. "Two points to the starboard! Land, Ho!"

"Father! There it is! Do you see?"

"No. Where, Patsy? Where?"

"That light . . . There. . . ."

"Yes. Yes. It's land! It's America, Patsy!" He has shaded his eyes, his face working with emotion.

"We're home again!" says Patsy. The curtain falls.

Later in the Spring of that year, in the MacComb mansion on lower Broadway, serving now as the residence of President Washington, James Madison and Alexander Hamilton are in conference with the President, "Washington, tight-lipped, grave; Madison, prematurely wizened, scholarly; Hamilton, a small, handsome man who carries himself with princely assurance." In the party, but not of it, is Col. Humphrey, "foppish and affected."

Washington is listening as Madison and Hamilton argue. "I tell you—if Col. Hamilton's treasury bill is re-introduced, Congress will kill it again," protests Madison, vehemently.

"Mr. Madison, I am tempted to seize your Congress by their separate heads and knock them together into a collective jelly," answers Hamilton, with spirit.

Now the charge of speculation flies back and forth. The South is afraid the North will profit a little more. It will, Hamilton admits. What of it? It's a damnable petty sectionalism that is the curse of the country—

"The crying need of this infant government now—at this moment—is confidence in its financial policy," thunders Hamilton.

"Exactly. And is this the way to achieve it?" demands Madison.

"Question! Can the wise and learned Congressman from Virginia propose any better plan?"

"Gentlemen! Gentlemen! . . . Thank you, Mister Madison, for your views. Of course it is not in this office to interfere with the people's legislature," interposes the President.

The decision satisfies Madison, but not Hamilton. "My congratulations! You've won a noble victory . . . over unity and honor," snaps Hamilton as Madison is leaving. And to the President he adds, when Madison has gone: "I can't build a treasury out of thin air."

"All right, my boy. All right," agrees Washington, paternally.

A sergeant has appeared to announce "His Excellency's Ambassador to the Court of France, Mr. Jefferson." The announcement gives the President pleasure, and Mr. Hamilton hope. "Providence is with us," declares Hamilton, excitedly. "Mr. Jefferson could easily persuade the South to vote for my treasury bill. I have never met him . . . so if you'd speak to him . . ."

"I can't do it," answers Washington, a little wearily.

"Why not?"

"Again?" groans Washington. "Must we go over the ground again, and again, and again?"

"It seems nothing but a catastrophe will make any impression.

But I am optimistic. I expect very shortly we will see a colossal catastrophe."

Hamilton and Col. Humphrey have left when Jefferson walks in. The greeting of the President is enthusiastic and friendly. Jefferson has brought a package of lily buds from the South of France, and one of rice seeds from Italy for the President. These are appreciatively received. Soon the two, farmers at heart, are talking of their respective estates; the prospects for a good harvest; the worries that ignorant and careless overseers bring upon them. "Mine complained the rabbits always ate the outside row of cabbages," Jefferson reports.

"Humph! What did you tell him?"

"Told him to remove the outside row," laughs Jefferson.

Conversation turns to reports of the Ambassador's six years abroad. ". . . So Lafayette is trying to establish a republic in France?" prompts Washington.

"Slowly, by constitutional reform," answers Jefferson. "In my room in Paris he drew up the first bill of rights for France. The people are all looking to our experiment. It is a heart-warming thought that in working out the pattern of our own happiness, we are inadvertently working for oppressed people everywhere. There's a great danger there, though. I toured France, incognito. Visited the peasants in their hovels. The poverty and ignorance. Appalling! —If they should ever lose Lafayette . . ."

"Anarchy?"

"Yes." The President sighs heavily.

"Mr. President, you look tired."

"I'm not accustomed to this indoor life. I need activity."

"Long walks. The best exercise."

"It is not permitted. The dignity of State forbids it . . . I'm told. When we lived on Cherry Street, I couldn't go down the street without a parade. But I can tell you since we moved here to Broadway . . . it's a Godsend. Now occasionally I can steal out that door to the back yard . . . across the meadow . . . and down to the river."

"What do you do down at the river?"

"Go fishing."

"Ah!"

"I've had two attacks of illness this year. I doubt if I'd survive a third. Oh, well, tomorrow or twenty years from now, we are all in the hands of a Good Providence . . ."

The President has gone to his desk and picked up a sheaf of papers. "I'm organizing the ministers of the various departments into a council—a cabinet to advise me," he says. "As our Secretary of State, you're—"

JEFFERSON—General Washington.

WASHINGTON—Mm?

JEFFERSON—In your letter you did give me the option of refusal.

WASHINGTON—You can't mean to refuse?

JEFFERSON—I must.

WASHINGTON—Why?

JEFFERSON—I've been away so long. I know none of the duties of this office. I may bungle it. I have . . . forebodings.

WASHINGTON—We're all groping . . . This will be a government of accommodation.

JEFFERSON (*shaking his head*)—I'm sorry. (*Pause.*) I want you to understand. Whatever spice of political ambition I may have had as a young man . . . has long since evaporated. (*Pause.*) I believe every man should serve his turn. I think I've done my share. Now I want to go home. I must complete my house. Twenty years it's waited. Patsy and her husband have come to stay with me at Monticello. The truth of the matter is, I've lived with my children so long, I've come to depend on their affection and comfort.

WASHINGTON—Tom . . . Have you ever thought of marrying again?

JEFFERSON—No.

WASHINGTON—She was a wonderful woman . . . your Martha.

JEFFERSON—Yes. (*Pause.*) When I came home . . . she was in every room.

HUMPHREY (*entering*)—Excuse me, sire.

WASHINGTON—Yes, Humphrey?

HUMPHREY—The theatre box and the guard of honor are arranged.

WASHINGTON (*drily*)—Good.

HUMPHREY—And I've discovered the Ambassador of the Sultan of Turkey *is* going to be present.

WASHINGTON (*with a notable lack of enthusiasm*)—Mm, Mm.

HUMPHREY—A suggestion, Excellency?

WASHINGTON—Yes?

HUMPHREY—Wouldn't it be advisable to return to six horses on the coach?

WASHINGTON—I thought we compromised on four.

HUMPHREY—When I was at the court of Louis . . .

WASHINGTON (*slowly making an effort to restrain his violent impatience*)—Colonel Humphrey, I recognize the importance of these forms to the dignity of a state, particularly one so young as ours. Understand, I know nothing of these matters. I've never been to the courts of Europe. I'm just an old soldier. I leave the ceremonies in your hands. (*The impatience erupts, and he growls.*) But it seems to me four horses and that canary coach with the pink and gilt angels will be enough to impress even the Ambassador of the Sultan of Turkey.

HUMPHREY—But, sire . . .

WASHINGTON—Four will do—that's final. (*He ruffles the papers, frowns.*) On second thought, I won't be free to go to the theatre tonight. Cancel it!

HUMPHREY—Sire, if I may . . .

WASHINGTON (*rising, thundering*)—Don't sire me! How many times must I tell you? By the Eternal . . . I am not a king. I am the elected head of our people. This is a republic. Can you get that through your skull? All right! Go!

HUMPHREY—Yes, Mr. President. (*He goes.* WASHINGTON *looks at* JEFFERSON.)

WASHINGTON—I was offered the crown, Tom.

JEFFERSON—The crown!

WASHINGTON—Twice. (*Pause.*) I don't want to be a king, Tom.

JEFFERSON—I know you don't, Mr. President.

WASHINGTON—You've no idea! Every eye is on this office. A number of our people suspect me. As God is my judge, I would rather live and die on my farm than be emperor of the world.

JEFFERSON—I know how you feel. Since I've been back—particularly here in New York—I find alarming yearnings. Our fashionable folk appear to be looking wishfully for a King and a court of our own.

WASHINGTON—Yes. I suppose so. (*Pause.*) On the other hand, there is the equal danger of anarchy. We came close to it, while you were away! We walk between these two pitfalls. (*He shakes his head.*) Our people do not take to discipline. But without it . . . we shall be lost. We've yet to see how large a dose of freedom men can be trusted with. Tom—you are the good genius of our common people. From the earliest days in Virginia—in all you said—in all you wrote—you were close to them—you seemed always to understand them. In this office I find myself far removed from direct contact with them

. . . I need your agency. I need their faith in you. This is the last great experiment for promoting human happiness. I need the hand that wrote, "All men are created free and equal." I can't let you go home yet, Tom. I need you here.

JEFFERSON (*after a long pause*)—It's for you to marshal us as you see fit.

WASHINGTON—Good!!

JEFFERSON—It's a great honor. I hope I can be worthy of it.

The Minister of the King of Spain has called; the appointment had been arranged; President Washington must, Col. Humphrey feels, extend the expected courtesies. . . .

Hamilton has come into the room and found Jefferson alone. The Secretary of the Treasury introduces himself. The response is friendly. Jefferson has read Hamilton's Federalist papers and found them brilliant. Hamilton has been looking forward to Jefferson's help in shaping the affairs of the new country—

"Mr. Jefferson, it's enough to make any man who loves America want to cry," says Hamilton. "Forgive me! I really shouldn't burden you with this. It's a matter of my own department."

"If I can be of any assistance . . . ?"

"It's often been remarked, that, it's given to this people here to prove once and for all whether men can govern themselves by reason or whether they must forever rely on the accident of tyranny. An interesting thought, Mr. Jefferson."

"God, yes. We live in an era . . . perhaps the most important in all history."

"An interesting thought. An . . . awful thought. For if it is true . . . then . . . we dare not fail."

"No."

"But we *are*. The machinery is already breaking down. *United* States? A prayer—not a fact, Mr. Jefferson. We're insolvent. We haven't that much foreign credit. The paper money issued by the States is worthless. We are in financial chaos. It's a pity. So young a country, with such promise. The galling part is . . . I have the remedy at hand. And the solution is so simple. A nation's credit, like a merchant's, depends on paying its promissory notes in full. I propose to pay a hundred cents on the dollar for all the paper money issued by the States. Our credit would be restored instantaneously."

Jefferson is worried. Mr. Madison had spoken to him of Mr. Hamilton's bill, and of his (Madison's) fear of the speculative feature. Jefferson feels that he will need time to study the facts—

But there is no time, Hamilton thunders. The North is about to secede. Unless his bill is passed there is every reason the Union will dissolve—

If the situation is that serious, protests Jefferson, it seems to him that reasonable men sitting around a table discussing the matter coolly could arrive at some compromise. Let Hamilton have dinner with him the next night. He will ask a few others. He may include Madison, for all the latter is bitterly opposed to the Hamilton plan—

"I have a way to sweeten the pill," promises Hamilton. "The cost of living in New York has become so unreasonable there's talk of moving the capital. It's already been promised temporarily to Philadelphia. Give me my bill and I can promise Madison the nation's capital will go to the South. Permanently. I was born in the West Indies—I have no local preference. However, for the sake of the Great Man, I'd like to see it go to Virginia."

"Well . . . I'll bring you together and sit at the table to see you don't shoot each other."

"Fair enough."

"You see, Colonel Hamilton, we must never permit ourselves to despair of the republic."

"My dear Jefferson, if I haven't despaired of this Republic till now, it's because of my nature, not my judgment."

The President has returned as Hamilton is leaving. "Remarkable young man," observes Washington, as his Secretary of the Treasury disappears. "They call him the Little Lion."

Jefferson can understand that. And now he is ready to submit his report on the French tariff situation. "Just before I left France, I had conversations with Monsieur Neckar on the matter of fishing rights," he begins.

The President, staring out the window, heaves a huge sigh. He plainly is not paying much attention to what Jefferson is saying. "Nice day out . . . isn't it?" observes Jefferson. As Washington answers, a little vaguely, he adds: "Have you a fishing pole for me?"

"How'd you know?" The President is obviously pleased. He turns to open a closet from which he removes an assortment of poles and fishing tackle. "You don't mind, now?"

"No, I can't think of a better way to discuss the affairs of the republic."

Washington has taken off his ruffles and his jacket and replaced them with old ones from the closet. He calls the sergeant. "Sergeant, I'm in conference with my Secretary of State," he says. "I'm not to be disturbed by anyone." The sergeant understands.

The President has set his wig on a stand and replaced it with a battered old hat. "If Humphrey caught me in these clothes, I'd never hear the end," he whispers to Jefferson as he picks up documents from the desk and takes a precautionary peek out the back door. Seeing one of the servants, he motions Jefferson to wait, pointing to his old coat—

"Don't they approve of democracy?" asks the Secretary, smiling.

"No!"

Another peek. Now the coast is clear. The President signals the Secretary. "Come!" he whispers.

Stealthily they go out the back door. The curtain falls.

At curtain rise we stand outside the smithy of an inn in New York. Through the wide gate of the courtyard a group of men can be seen around a table. Their chatter and laughter float in. At the forge Jacob is hammering out a horse-shoe on an anvil, while Mat, his apprentice, pumps the bellows. Shortly a pot-boy crosses the doorway with an armful of tankards. Col. Hamilton wants his horse saddled, reports the boy. He's leavin'.

The party is breaking up early, observes Jacob, the smith. "They ain't hardly started a-belchin' yet."

They've belched enough to displease the pot-boy and Mat, too, it appears. "Listenin' to that Tory talk out there gets me mad," says the boy. "Braggin' about the millions they made in paper money! I keep thinkin' about my sister."

"And me! Don't fergit me! Three hundred dollars—whish—right out-a me pocket!" adds Mat.

"Know what one was a-sayin'? President ain't a good title for the head of the United States. Ain't got enough distingay."

"French words!" sneers Mat.

"'At's what he said. There are presidents of cricket clubs and fire companies, he said."

"What the plague do they want? Royal Highness?"

"Yep. That's it."

"You mean that?"

"'At's what they said."

"Fer cripe's sake!"

Jefferson, Monroe and Madison have arrived with various jobs for the smith. They had not heard of the party in the courtyard. Some of Col. Hamilton's friends are celebrating the passage of his bill, they're told.

The idea does not sit well with Monroe. Nor with Madison, though he thinks that the bill stood for the lesser of two evils. Jefferson hopes Madison is right—but he doesn't know—

Jefferson has found a set of metal fittings Jacob has forged for him. They are for a "convenience" Jefferson has invented— "A sort of closet on pulleys," the inventor explains, "that will come up from the kitchen to the dining room—carry the food hot and the wine cold right in . . . without people running up and down stairs."

"Now. Say, that's a purty good invention," agrees Jacob, heartily. "Told my wife about the collapsible buggy top you invented. Kinda useful idea, she said. But this'll catch her fancy. What do you call this here invention?"

"A 'dumb-waiter.' "

"Dumb-waiter?" Jacob is puzzled, but soon he gets it. "Oh, yeah! A dumb-waiter. Purty good!"

Mr. Jefferson would sound out the Tavern boys on the Hamilton bill. It doesn't take him long to discover that they are bitter about it. "A blood-suckin' swindle, Mr. Jefferson," says the one named Ned. "Take my sister . . . her husband was killed at the battle of Saratoga. Left her two little ones and some paper money they paid him. She's been savin' that for years. Two months ago the speculators told her it would be years more before she got anything on it . . . if ever. Got her to sell it for forty dollars. Six hundred dollars' worth!"

They got Jacob's savings, too—nine hundred dollars; his pay from the Revolution. "This ain't what we fit the Revolution for," says Jacob. And Jefferson agrees.

Col. Hamilton has come from the courtyard. He is in high spirits and pleased to have good reports for Mr. Jefferson. Mr. Jefferson, however, is still disturbed by what he has heard from the tavern employees. "Apparently a handful of speculators, many of them in high places, have taken advantage of the bill to feather their own nests," says Jefferson.

Hamilton would make light of the report. The victims should have had more faith in their government. "The Treasury can't ask every man who submits a paper note how he came by it.

At least, this way they have received something," Hamilton protests.

JEFFERSON—There must have been a means to avert this speculation.

HAMILTON—Avert it? I did all I could to encourage it!

JEFFERSON—You did?

HAMILTON—Of course.

JEFFERSON—I wasn't aware of that. You said nothing of that to me.

HAMILTON—Look here . . . I don't quite understand your attitude toward the bill. If we want to develop this country we've got to create great personal fortunes. Those men out there are building manufactories and industry. They're building America.

JEFFERSON—Good. Encourage them! But not at the expense of the people!

HAMILTON—You and Madison! The people whisper . . . you tremble.

JEFFERSON—That's as it should be, isn't it?

HAMILTON—I am determined this country shall be sound. I think its only hope now lies in a moneyed aristocracy, to protect it from your people.

JEFFERSON—I see. And this bill is to lay the foundation for such an aristocracy?

HAMILTON—Yes.

JEFFERSON—I must be quite honest with you. I regret that I have been made a party to your bill.

HAMILTON—Made? You have been in politics twenty-four years. Don't play the innocent with me. Are you dissatisfied with your bargain?

JEFFERSON—Bargain?

HAMILTON—The capital of the nation is going to your state— not mine.

JEFFERSON—Oh, for God's sake. (MONROE and MADISON *have entered and stand silently watching.*)

HAMILTON—Yours, by agreement! . . . Frankly, your alarms smell abominably of hypocrisy. One minute you say you know nothing of Treasury matters; the next you set yourself up as an authority.

MONROE—What do you propose, Colonel? Shall we scrap the Constitution at once?

HAMILTON (*seeing* MONROE *and* MADISON)—The Constitution!!

JEFFERSON—You don't approve of it?

HAMILTON—A frail and worthless thing.

JEFFERSON—Then why did you support it?

HAMILTON (*flaring up*)—I had no choice. I couldn't stand by and see the country go down in convulsions and anarchy. I must confess that it's my opinion this government won't last five years. However, since we've undertaken this experiment, I'm for giving it a fair trial . . . But be certain of this: while it lasts it will be an aristocratic republic. If you want a democracy, proceed to the confines of some other country. Good day, gentlemen.

It seems reasonably clear to Madison now that Hamilton is prepared to pervert the Constitution into something it was never intended to be. And Monroe not only has a statement from a man who swears Hamilton gave him money out of the public treasury with which to speculate, but he also knows of letters in Hamilton's hand to the same effect.

These things Jefferson refuses to believe. Hamilton, he insists, is personally honest. He is willing to vouch for that. Nor will he promise to confront Hamilton with the letters in an effort to fight fire with fire, as Monroe suggests. "I'm no salamander. Fire's not my element," says the Secretary.

"His bill has made the fortunes of half the prominent men in the Federalist party," protests Monroe. "It's a ring he's put through their nose. Now he can lead them about. They'll follow him anywhere. And it's clear enough, God knows, where he intends to lead them. . . . We can't allow that. You've got to fight him. You've got to wrest the leadership of the Federalist party away from him!"

"If there's one thing makes me sick to death—it's the whole spirit of party politics," answers Jefferson. "James, if the only way I could enter heaven was on the back of a political party, I'd rather burn in purgatory." His voice has grown harsh and lifeless. "You're wrong about the letters, James," he goes on. "For the rest . . . this bill has values . . . but it's hurt our people. Through it, he's created a corrupt squadron. I've blundered. . . . Naturally, if he does try to pervert the Constitution, I shall oppose him. But I must do it in my own way. I'm not a brawler. . . . I'm not a politician."

Monroe and Madison are worried about the change that has come over Jefferson. He has been living in the past again. After nine years he has just ordered a new stone for Martha's grave. They will have to think of some way to rouse him.

The boy Ned has come from the courtyard, hoarse with rage as he tears off his apron. "I'll be damned if I'll wait on them any more," shouts Ned. "Know what they're saying now? Dukes and Lords we oughta have!"

"Dukes and Lords?" repeats Mat, pausing in his bellows-blowing.

"Aye! The bloodsuckin' swindlers."

"Pump her, Mat! Pump her!" prompts Jacob.

"What do they want to do? Make serfs outa us." Mat's anger rises.

"Is this what we fought Lexington and Bunker Hill for?" screams Ned. "Is this the freedom my brother and my sister's husband died for? . . . Where's your goddam Revolution now?"

"Pump her, Mat! Come on! Pump her!"

Mat pumps furiously. The forge is glowing red. Jacob's hammer clangs on the anvil. The curtain falls.

ACT II

A year later, at the Alexander Hamilton home in Philadelphia, coffee is being served by Mrs. Hamilton. Surrounding her are her husband, Col. Humphrey and Henry Knox. Their talk concerns the dreadful state of France in the midst of a revolution.

To Mrs. Hamilton the thought of Louis and Marie in jail is distressing. To Col. Humphrey it is almost beyond bearing. The Colonel has not slept a wink since the Palace fell. To Knox the situation appears to be growing steadily worse. How does Mr. Hamilton feel about it?

"Dangerous. Highly dangerous," answers Hamilton. "I'm particularly disturbed by the effect it may have on some of our inflammables."

"You certainly lashed Mr. Jefferson on that score!" Col. Humphrey recalls with satisfaction. "Ma foi! Ma foi! Gave it to him. But proper!"

"Mr. Jefferson isn't really one of these filthy democrats?" queries Mrs. Hamilton, passing Mr. Knox the sugar.

"I'm afraid so, my dear."

"Horrors!" exclaims the lady. And as they laugh heartily she adds: "Does he *really* believe every man is as good as every other man?"

"Even better," her husband assures her. The guests are quite convulsed. "Our people are so jealous of their rights," Hamilton goes on; "one has the feeling these people can't wait for the Union to fall apart so they'll be free to cut each other's throats at leisure."

At least the government has made some progress, they admit. "The Chief" has made an army out of a rabble. There's no doubt of that. But the Chief is getting old. "Sometimes I lay awake nights wondering how we can ever hold this country together when he's gone," admits Hamilton.

"Personally, I think it's his character alone that keeps us together now," says Knox. "I wouldn't give a penny for the Constitution without him."

"I agree with Alec. A monarchy would be our salvation," Humphrey chimes in.

"I think so," agrees Hamilton. "Well—I've always said the sole value of this Constitution is a stepping-stone."

The situation is quite frightful, Mrs. Hamilton repeats. All her lady friends are agreed that to go into the streets is quite frightening. What the country needs is a *real* king.

Senator Monroe is announced. A country bumpkin, Humphrey insists. A good soldier, General Knox admits. A good soldier, with the soul of a clerk, in Hamilton's estimation. He probably has come on some errand for Mr. Jefferson.

Monroe is quick to state his mission. He would like to see Mr. Hamilton alone. He has been trying unsuccessfully to make an appointment with him at his office for weeks.

Hamilton would explain that he has been extremely busy— what with the new taxes, the stock market expansion, and so forth. Let Mr. Monroe state his errand now. If not let him come to his office next day at 4:30.

That will not do. Mr. Monroe is seeing the President at four next day, on a matter that vitally concerns Mr. Hamilton. He will be submitting papers to the President—papers he thought Mr. Hamilton would like a chance to explain. There have been charges leveled at Mr. Hamilton—charges of his having appropriated treasury funds—

"What!!? You dare to come into my house and accuse me of . . ." Hamilton flushes with anger.

"*I'm* not accusing you—I'm inquiring into the facts."

"Gen. Knox, will you act as my second?" Hamilton's anger mounts.

"Your servant."

"Sir, you will name your friend to this gentleman. They can

arrange weapons, time, and place. Good night."

"I'll be very happy to oblige you. But I must first demand that you explain these letters to Mr. Reynolds."

The name of Reynolds and the sight of a letter in his own handwriting, quickly change Hamilton's attitude. Now he has no objection to a fair inquiry. If Senator Monroe will come to his office in the morning all necessary letters and documents will be supplied him—

"Mr. Reynolds charges that you gave him money from the public treasuries to speculate with in your behalf," says Monroe.

"Where is Mr. Reynolds now?"

"I've no idea."

"He's in jail. Subornation of perjury in a fraud case. You take the word of such a character?"

"Did you give him this money?"

"I did. But it was my own."

"And why did you give money to such a character?"

Hamilton hesitates. "He was blackmailing me," he says.

"What for?"

"A personal matter which has nothing to do with the treasury. I'll prove that to your full satisfaction."

"Under any circumstances, I shall ask for an accounting to Congress."

"As a senator that is your privilege. And I shall oblige you. I will invite all America to look into the window of my breast and judge the purity of my political motives. Not one penny of the public funds have I ever touched. I would sooner pluck out my eye by the roots."

Knox and Humphrey have left. Alone with his wife, and under her pointed questioning, Hamilton is forced to admit that the man Reynolds had been blackmailing him because he, Hamilton, had been philandering with Mrs. Reynolds—

"It was a game they were playing together," he insists. "She and her husband. He suddenly appeared one night, claimed I'd ruined his life, and threatened to inform you, unless I gave him a thousand dollars. I gave it to him. He's been bleeding me dry ever since. Now he's gotten himself in jail, and wants me to use my influence to release him. I refused. This is his revenge. . . . Forgive me, dearest. I would do anything—"

"Let's not discuss that, Alec. The question is: what shall we do . . . now . . . to clear you? . . ."

"My accounts will do that, Betsy. Congress will clear me."

Mrs. Hamilton is distressed. Why hadn't she been told of this before? Why should she ever be told?

"I'm forced to do it, Betsy," pleads Hamilton. "Jefferson obviously wants to destroy my position as leader of the party. As long as these letters in his hands go unexplained . . . by insinuation . . . he could undermine belief in my honesty. I must be prepared to publish the facts, if necessary."

He would take her in his arms, pleading for her forgiveness, but she will have none of him. She is convinced now that he had never loved her; that he married her only because she was the daughter of Governor Schuyler.

"And I the illegitimate son of a Scotch peddler!" exclaims Hamilton. "I married you for your wealth and your position! Is that what you *believe?*"

"Have you left me any other belief?"

The butler has appeared to announce a Mr. Fenno. Shown in, Fenno, in great excitement, tells them of late news that the King and Queen of France have been guillotined, and that the mobs in France are utterly out of hand— "Burning, looting, killing! A blood bath! Unbelievable, isn't it? Simply unbelievable!"

"No. I was afraid of that."

"Worse even. I've heard ugly rumors here. I passed a house yesterday, and I heard a group of men down in the cellar, singing 'Ça Ira'! Rufus King told me he heard open threats against us. Even against General Washington."

"I've no doubt of it."

"I fear this is going to spread like the smallpox."

"Yes, yes! And who've we to thank? Jefferson! Jefferson!"

"Oh, no, I don't think he would dare—"

"I tell you, yes. The man's a lunatic. He's been encouraging our people to all sorts of wild illusions. Bill of rights! Freedom! Liberty! License! Anarchy! This is the fruit of his disordered imagination. That man will stop at nothing to achieve chaos. But there'll be no more of him here! I promise you. I will see to it. There's no longer any room in this country . . . in this world . . . for both me and that . . . that . . . fanatic!"

The curtain falls.

In 1793 Jefferson is living in a rather depressing rented house in Philadelphia. The room in which he spends most of his time is a curious jumble of a few pieces of fine furniture, a center table piled high with books and papers at one end, a small vise, tools and a machine in course of construction at the other. When Jefferson comes in he strikes a flint and tinder and lights an oil lamp. By the dull light of this he tries to read a journal he has brought with him. Outside can be heard the wild, discordant chanting of a crowd, mixed with strains of "Ça Ira."

Jupiter, the Jefferson servant, pleased that Mist' Tom has got home at last, is a little insistent that his master should "tuck sumpin' " in himself right away, but can arouse no response in Mist' Tom, who is not the least interested in food. Jupiter knows what that means—Mist' Tom has just come from one o' dem cabinet meetin's. They compromise on a cup of mint tea.

A bandage on Jupiter's hand has attracted Jefferson. What does that mean? It means that Jupiter, buying supplies at Randolph market, had heard three men talking, calling Mr. Jefferson a devil, and saying that Col. Hamilton had told them that Mr. Jefferson was going to bring the French Revolution over here. And when Jupiter had told them that that wasn't true, they had set upon him. In trying to ward off a blow from a club, a nail in the club had gashed his hand—

"Then a crowd came down the street, yellin'," reports Jupiter. "De men see dat crowd. Dey get scared. Run away. Mister Tom . . . dem crowds in de street—dey're talkin' wild, Mister Tom. Yellin' 'Kill de aristocrats! Break dere windows! Burn dere houses!' Singin' French songs. . . . Dey talkin' bad about President Washington. Dat got me all mixed up. I know he fight for liberty. I remind me you tell me General Washington try to free my people."

"That's right. He did."

"I remind me, how you try, Mister Tom. I like to see my little Sarah free some day. An' I remind me how you say we gotta some day open all that land in the Northwest and ain't gonna be no slaves there. An' how we gotta git my people education, an' we gotta git 'em land, and tools."

"Some day, Jupiter. It's written in the book of fate. Your people will be free."

"Mister Tom. Dat crowd. Git me mixed up. Git me all mixed up. I don't like it. Dey jus' gonna make trouble."

"I'm afraid you're right, Jupiter. You see, the men who beat you—they're monarchists. They want a king here. The others . . . the crowd . . . they're mixed up. It's what's happening in France now. It's gone wild. The French Ambassador is getting all our people mixed up, too."

Jefferson, who has been bandaging Jupiter's hand, finishes that job just as the doorbell rings. A moment later a flushed and happy Patsy rushes into her father's arms on a surprise visit.

Hooray! Let Jupiter kill the fatted calf. "It's chicken," corrects Jupiter. Patsy's father is much pleased. His satisfaction grows with Patsy's report of his flourishing grandchildren.

But the talk shortly takes a serious turn. Patsy's coach had been stopped by the crowds in the streets. Her father is forced to admit that everything is not as it should be, in Philadelphia. The French Ambassador has been openly defying the President and there have been some disorders. "This epidemic of fever here seems to have a moral contagion, too," says Jefferson.

Patsy is worried. She has been reading some of the attacks upon her father in *Fenno's Journal*. They are positively horrible; much worse than anything she could have imagined. Jefferson would make light of them, if he could— "It's very flattering," he says. "Especially that bit about the harem! At my age! Pretty good . . ."

Patsy can see no humor in the situation. Surely her father will answer such charges? No, Jefferson doesn't think he will. If he answers one lie, his enemies will print twenty others. He thinks it would be wiser to ignore them.

Then, it is Patsy's conviction, the time has come for her father to quit being Secretary of State. He has sacrificed enough. When he would deny this, she reminds him of some things he may have forgotten.

"A few weeks ago I found a pamphlet Mother had written during the Revolution to the women of Virginia on the necessity for them to make sacrifices to help win the war," says Patsy, bitterly. "I remember Mother so ill she could hardly walk, doing ten men's work at home. I remember, after she died, sitting on the cold floor outside your door, listening to you sob . . . till I thought you, too, must die. I remember hearing you cry out, you'd sacrificed her to the Revolution."

"Patsy."

PATSY—The morning and afternoon of your life you sacrificed. Wasn't that enough?

JEFFERSON—Patsy, dear! Please!

PATSY—No. If you won't think of yourself, what of us? A child of twelve and a baby of four, torn from our home, from all we loved . . . taken to a foreign land . . . seeing you only on occasion, dreaming always of home again and security and . . . Why? For what? Is there no end to it!

JEFFERSON—Patsy, I beg of you!

PATSY—Don't you owe anything to yourself? Don't you owe

anything to us? I tell you, Father, everything at home is going to pieces. If you don't come back soon, there'll be nothing left. Nothing!

JEFFERSON (*rising*)—Patsy! Will you, for God's sake, stop!

PATSY (*going to him*)—Father! Oh, Father, I didn't mean to . . .

JEFFERSON (*taking her in his arms*)—I know. I know.

PATSY—Forgive me.

JEFFERSON—Of course.

PATSY—I've been so confused and unhappy. I had to come and talk it out with you.

JEFFERSON—Of course you did. I should have been very hurt if you hadn't.

PATSY—You see . . . it's the business of running Monticello and the farms. We try . . . Lord knows we try . . . But Mr. Randolph has no talent for it. And his failure makes him irritable. And I worry so. I'm afraid the way things are going you may lose everything you own.

JEFFERSON—I see, my dear. I see. (*Pause.*) I haven't been altogether insensible to this. It's weighed on me very heavily, the trouble I put your good husband to.

PATSY—I shouldn't have said anything. I know what your work here means to you.

JEFFERSON (*moving away; a sudden burst of bitterness*)—I have never loathed anything as much in my life. You've no idea, Patsy, of the rank and malignant hatreds. Politics and party hates destroy the happiness of every being in this city . . . I'm surrounded here by hates and lies. Lately I've seen men here who once called themselves my friends go so far as to cross the street to avoid tipping their hats to me.

PATSY—You of all people! Why?

JEFFERSON—There is a gang of king-jobbers here who are bent on changing our principle of government—by force, if necessary. Since Mr. Madison and Mr. Monroe have left, I'm alone against them. I can't contend with them, Patsy.

PATSY—What of the President?

JEFFERSON—Only his strength and his stubborn purity oppose them. But he's old, and he's sick.

PATSY—Oh, my poor father.

JEFFERSON (*sitting*)—I work from morning till night. They undo everything. This isn't spending one's life here. It's getting rid of it. Do you know, my dear, my only pleasure? For an hour or so every evening I sit and dream of Monticello. I find myself more and more turning to the past and to those I loved first. Your mother . . . (PATSY *moves over to him; kneels at his feet; he draws out the locket hanging around his neck.*) She was a beautiful person, Patsy. She loved you all so dearly. (*He puts the locket back.*) You're right, Patsy. If I hadn't neglected my duties at home, she might have been alive today. It's true. I sacrificed your mother to the Revolution. And now I'm doing the same to you. Darling, your happiness is more important to me than my life. And, like a fool, I've been jeopardizing it. For the privilege of being . . . (*Rising, he picks up the pamphlet.*) called in the public prints "lecher, liar, thief, hypocrite!" But no more . . . You mustn't worry, dearest. Everything's going to be all right. I promise you. I'm tending to my own from now on.

Grim-faced and serious he takes down his portable writing desk and begins to write furiously. A moment later he has called Jupiter, to send him to the President's home with a letter. They're going home. They're going home together and to stay. He is sending his resignation to the President.

The noise of the crowd outside grows in volume. They move to the window and are listening. At first they cannot make out what it is the crowd is chanting. "Down with who?" Patsy asks.

Now they can hear it. "Washington? Wash . . .!!" Jefferson stands for a moment in shocked surprised. "He is all that stands between them and their enemies," he says, turning to Patsy. "Patsy! When all our names are sponged from the records, his will burn brighter, wherever men fight for freedom."

Now he turns, a little irritably, to send Jupiter on his way. Then he comes again to Patsy. "No, darling," he says, "it isn't going to make any difference. If our people won't deserve their liberty, no one can save it for them. I'm going home."

The curtain falls.

A few days later Jefferson is sitting at his desk in the same room of his Philadelphia house, writing grimly. Patsy is with him, sitting stubbornly in a corner, watching. Most of the furniture has been moved from the room, which is heavy with the smoke sent up from scattered braziers.

The pestilence is spreading. From time to time the "ominous rumbling of a cart outside" can be heard. Jefferson has been trying to induce Patsy to let Jupiter take her to Germantown.

where he will join her in a few days and they will go to Monticello together. Patsy refuses to budge. So long as her father
is held in town she intends to stay with him.

Col. Hamilton is announced. He has an appointment to meet
President Washington at Jefferson's house. He would have
waited in his carriage, but there is a man dead of the plague
lying on the sidewalk. It is not a pleasant sight. He has sent
for the death cart. He is, Jefferson assures him, welcome to
wait there for the President.

Jefferson goes on with his writing. Hamilton casually picks
up *Fenno's Journal*. He "smiles mischievously" as he reads it.

"When I read this article, I said . . ." begins Hamilton.

"Read it? It's commonly supposed, Mr. Hamilton, that you
wrote it," interrupts Jefferson, with some spirit.

"It's written by some person called—Pa . . . ci . . . fi . . .
cus." Hamilton is peering at the *Journal* mockingly.

"Pacificus. Peaceful. A proper pen name." Jefferson's tone
savors of irony. He puts aside his writing. "Col. Hamilton,"
he says, "almost since our first cabinet meeting—you and I have
been thrown at each other like cocks in a pit. The cock fight is
over. Peaceful will soon have the cabinet to himself."

"How is that?"

"Hasn't the President informed you?"

"No."

"I've resigned."

Hamilton expresses some surprise at the announcement, and
likewise his regret. It is possible, he agrees, that they will not
be meeting again.

"I should like to ask you as man to man, without rancor or
warmth," Jefferson continues, picking up *Fenno's Journal*, "is
this fitting to the dignity of a Minister of State?"

Hamilton laughs bitterly. "Was it fitting the dignity of your
high office to send your henchmen prying into my private life?"
he demands.

"I never did that."

"You thought I would keep silent, did you? You thought
sooner than risk my personal happiness I'd let you call me thief?
Well! You see what you've done? Congress has cleared my
public name, and I'm all the stronger for it! I didn't run away!
However, in your case . . . I think it wise for you to go home
and sit on your mountain-top. The philosophic experiment is
over. Your Democracy is finished."

"You really think that?"

"I know it. I knew it six years ago. When I first saw Mr. Madison's Constitution, I knew it couldn't last. And it hasn't. What do you think of your people now? Your fellow dreamer in Paris, Lafayette, in irons forged by the ones he sought to free. And perhaps, even now, his head lying in the basket, and his blood flowing in the gutters . . . running into a river of the noblest blood of France . . . while your drunken swine, the people, swill in it. I tell you—it nauseates me to the very heart. And now—the same rioting mobs here—and next, perhaps, the same terror."

General Washington has arrived. "He is getting very old. His face is tired and bewildered, but a bulwark of grim, stubborn determination." His greetings are friendly but reserved. He is distressed by the sweep of the plague, as well as the citizen unrest. What does it mean? "Aren't men fit to be free?" he asks. "Is that the answer?" Turning to Jefferson he adds: "Have you spoken to the French Minister?"

"Yes. One can't reason with him. He's a lunatic. I've demanded his recall."

"They're all lunatics. Lafayette imprisoned. Lafayette! And here now . . . mobs rioting . . . what does this mean? We must do what we can to help Lafayette."

"I've already dispatched a letter to Ambassador Morris, urging him to make every solicitation in his power."

"I don't know if it'll help. I doubt it."

His eye has caught the copy of *Fenno's Journal*. He picks it up, glances at it and throws it down impatiently. Turning to Col. Hamilton he asks him if he would mind waiting below. As Hamilton bows his way out the President continues—

"I shall have to speak to him again. He's very difficult. He's always been that way, though. Once during the war, when he was my aide, he kept me waiting two hours. When I rebuked him, he resigned. Sulked like a little boy. (*Softens, with evident love of* HAMILTON.) Finally I gave him what he wanted—a command in the field. He was a very good soldier. Led his troops in the first assault on Yorktown. He's an invaluable man. Why can't you two work together?"

"Our principles are as separate as the poles."

"Coalesce them!"

"It can't be done."

Now the matter of Jefferson's resignation comes into the conversation. The President cannot accept it. Jefferson cannot withdraw it. He feels that he has failed and he is through—

JEFFERSON—I've spent twenty-four years in public life. I'm worn down with labors that I know are as fruitless to you as they are vexatious to me. My personal affairs have been abandoned too long. They are in utter chaos. I must turn to them and my family.

WASHINGTON—And the good esteem of your fellowmen?

JEFFERSON (*moving away*)—There was a time when that was of higher value to me than anything in the world. Now I prefer tranquillity. Here for everything I hate you ask me to give up everything I love. I'm sorry, no! I want a little peace in my lifetime.

WASHINGTON—I know. I know. I'm sick, Tom, and I'm getting old, and I catch myself dreaming of the Potomac and Mount Vernon— (*He almost shouts.*) Don't you think I hate this, too? Don't you think I yearn for the peace of my own farm? Don't you think all this . . . all this . . . (*Pauses. Controls himself. There is a long silence. He murmurs.*) Peace in our life. (*Smiles.*) Thomas Paine wrote . . . It's in the Crisis. (*His memories turn back. He quotes.*) "These are the times that try men's souls. The summer soldier and the sunshine patriot will in this crisis shrink. . . ." (JEFFERSON *wilts into a chair; unwittingly, the President has dealt him a stunning blow.*) How that brings back the picture. As if it were yesterday. My men starved, naked, bleeding. I read Paine's essay. You know, it lent me new strength. I had it read to my men through trumpets. Nailed it on trees for them to read. It helped them. Gave them sore-needed courage . . . Yes . . . yes. Do you remember the passage on the Tory innkeeper who was opposed to war because —that's it— "He wanted peace in his lifetime"? And Paine looked down at the innkeeper's children crawling on the floor and thought, "Were this Tory a man, he would say: If there must be conflict with tyranny, let it come in my time. Let there be peace and freedom in my children's time." Yes. That's the answer, I suppose. The only answer. (*Suddenly, desperately, he grabs* JEFFERSON's *arm.*) Tom! The fabric is crumbling. Our Republic is dying. We must bolster it, somehow . . . some way. (*Fiercely, a grim, stubborn, determined warrior fighting a ghost, he pounds the desk.*) It must have a chance. It will, it will, it will! I'll defend its right to a chance with the last drop of my blood. (*The fierceness goes. Again he becomes a tired man.*)

You'll stay on a few days more? Till I find someone else?

JEFFERSON—Yes.

WASHINGTON—Good! You see I'm like a man about to be hanged. Even a few days' reprieve makes me rejoice. (*Sighs heavily, starts to go, turns.*) I wouldn't stay here. Take your papers, go to the country. You can work there, Mr. Jefferson.

Patsy has come to rejoin her father. She has found a little music box which she thinks she will take home to her daughter Anne, but Jefferson, deep in thought, hears little of what she is saying. Her father's attitude worries her. She is worried, too, about General Washington. He looks so old—

"He's a dying man, Patsy," her father says. "He's dying. And when he's gone, they'll take the reins. And that will be the end, Patsy. That'll be the end of the Republic."

"Perhaps we weren't ready for it, Father."

"If not here and now, where then? Where will men ever have such a chance again? This was my dream, Patsy! From my earliest youth."

"You've done your best, Father."

"Not good enough, apparently. Summer soldier. (*Pause.*) It was seventeen years ago, here in Philadelphia, I wrote the Declaration of Independence. That's how I dreamed of America, Patsy. A beacon for all mankind. (*Pause.*) Patsy! It's not our people who've failed us. It's we who've failed them. I'm convinced of it. Yes. I see that now. (*Paces about the room.*) These fermentations are a healthy sign. Our people are groping. They're jealous of their rights? Good! They want a larger share in their government. Most of them today haven't even the privilege of voting. It would take so little education to make them understand these disorders are not to their advantage. That's where we've failed them, Patsy. It's not enough to create a form of a republic. We must *make* it work. We must see that our people get the right to vote. We must educate them to use it and be worthy of it. We must give them free schools and universities and a liberal press. Only an enlightened people can really be free. Till now, the genius of the common people has been buried in the rubbish heap. We must rescue that! I'm convinced of it! We must make war on ignorance and poverty. We must go into the streets and the squares and the smithys—"

Col. Hamilton has come back, at the President's suggestion, he explains, to see Jefferson. The President had hoped that they might try to coalesce their differences. Jefferson sees no hope of that. He and Hamilton are natural enemies.

"Well, I offered peace," Hamilton protests.

"The wolves offered the sheep peace . . ." snaps Jefferson.

HAMILTON—You don't flatter me!

JEFFERSON—It is not an American art.

HAMILTON—I am an American by choice . . . not by accident.

JEFFERSON—Yet you bring here a lie bred out of the vices and crimes of the old world.

HAMILTON—Lie?

JEFFERSON—The lie that the masses of men are born with saddles on their backs, and a chosen few booted and spurred to ride them legitimately by the grace of God.

HAMILTON—It's laughable! You, born to wealth and land and slaves, driveling about the common people!

JEFFERSON—Search your own birth, Mr. Hamilton, and you'll . . .

HAMILTON—Don't say it! (*Trembling, white with rage.*) I must warn you.

JEFFERSON—Say what? That you as a boy were poor? That you came to this country and it gave you honor and wealth? I believe every boy in this land must have that opportunity.

HAMILTON—Why do you think I want the country strong?

JEFFERSON—It can only be strong if its people govern it.

HAMILTON—You think the peasants on my farm can make it strong?

JEFFERSON—There are no peasants in America.

HAMILTON—Words! What do I care for them! Call them yeomen! Call them what you will! Men cannot rule themselves.

JEFFERSON—Can they then rule others? Have we found angels in the forms of kings and dictators to rule them?

HAMILTON—I've made my last gesture. Go. Run back to your hill! From here on, I promise you, you will never again dare raise your head in this party.

JEFFERSON—I hate party. But if that's the only way I can fight you—then I'll create another party. I'll create a people's party.

HAMILTON—Now it comes out. You want two parties! You want blood to flow! At heart you, too, are a Jacobin murderer.

JEFFERSON—That's another lie you believe because you wish to believe it. It gives you the excuse you need to draw your sword! I'm sick to death of your silencing every liberal tongue by calling "Jacobin murderer."

HAMILTON—Well, aren't you? Confess it!

JEFFERSON—Go on! Wave the raw head and bloody bones!
Invest your scares and plots! We were asleep after the first
labors, and you tangled us and tied us, but we have only to
awake and rise and snap off your Lilliputian cords.

HAMILTON—Very well. Let it be a fight then. But, make it a
good one. And, when you stir up the mobs, remember! We
who really own America are quite prepared to take it back for
ourselves, from your great beast "The People."

JEFFERSON—And I tell you, when once our people are free and
have the government securely in their own hands, they will be
strong as a giant. They will sooner allow the heart to be torn
out of their bodies than their freedom to be wrested from them
by *any* Caesar!

HAMILTON (*bowing*)—Good day, Mr. Jefferson.

JEFFERSON—Good day, Colonel Hamilton. (HAMILTON *exits.*
JEFFERSON *turns to* PATSY.) Patsy, this is a fight that may take
the rest of my life . . .

PATSY—Yes.

JEFFERSON—But I have to! I hate it but I have to, Patsy.
I want Anne and Jeff and their children to grow up in a free
republic. I have to, Patsy.

PATSY—Of course you do. (*Rises and moves toward* JEFFER-
SON.) Of course you do, Father.

The curtain falls.

ACT III

In the "new city of Washington," in 1801, in his rooms at
Conrad's boarding house, Mr. Jefferson is writing at a desk.
Near by Patsy sits crocheting. Her two children are playing
on the floor.

Outside the door there is an excited babble of voices. When
the door is opened by Patsy, in response to a knock, a group of
boarders gathered in the hall press forward. A messenger has
brought a message, which is relayed to Mr. Jefferson and read.
It is a report of the twenty-seventh ballot just taken in Congress.
The situation remains the same. The boarders are disappointed.
They had heard that Mr. Burr had lost a vote to Mr. Jefferson.
That is not true, so far as she knows, Patsy informs them. The
situation is unchanged.

Now Mrs. Conrad has pushed her way through the crowd in
the hall. She would send all the boarders down stairs to the

parlor. She cannot have them "a-pesting Mr. Jefferson."

Presently there is more excitement. Another messenger—a Frontiersman, this time, armed to the teeth—makes his way into the room. He has ridden hard all the way from Richmond with a message from Governor Monroe of Virginia, which he has been ordered to deliver to Mr. Jefferson personally, and await an answer.

Presently Mr. Madison arrives. He has just come from the House of Representatives, and reports the streets jammed with people. Congress is a sight. Representatives are falling asleep in their chairs, red-eyed and haggard. One of them, Mr. Nicholson, is ill in a committee room. He sleeps between ballots. They wake him up to vote, ply him with medicine and water. Nicholson should be removed to a hospital, but he will not budge. Swears he will go on voting for Jefferson until he dies.

Mrs. Conrad, getting Patsy's ear, would state the case for the people she knows. To her and her husband the whole way of voting just ain't right. "Take my husband," says Mrs. Conrad. "We wanted your father for President, Mr. Burr for Vice President. Well, he should be allowed to put that down on the ballot instead of just the two names and lettin' Congress decide. Stands to reason, don't it? See what happens? We beat the Federalists, and then the old Congress, most of 'em Feds themselves, don't know who to pick. Deadlocked six days now. They might like as not go on bein' deadlocked four years, and we'll have no president at all. Now, I say, it's deliberate. Everybody's sayin' that!"

Mr. Madison is worried. Not only does he feel that he has bungled the electoral system, but that the Constitution will have to be amended so that a man can put down who he wants for President.

"Well, it can be amended," Jefferson reminds Madison; "that's the great virtue of your Constitution. It can grow."

A handsome young man has appeared in the doorway. He is looking for Mr. Jefferson and he is, it soon appears, the son of Lafayette. George Washington Lafayette is his name, and he is pleased to meet them all, including Patsy's little son, Thomas Jefferson Randolph. Having come recently from France, young Lafayette is glad to report that his father has been released, after six years in prison, but that he still does not dare write his friends in America. "Bonaparte watches him. He is only out on . . . a string."

"I had hoped at first Bonaparte would value the real glory

of a Washington as compared to that of a Caesar," says Jefferson, glancing at a bust of Washington.

"When we heard he died, my father wept . . . like a child."

"A great man fell that day. America now must walk alone."

"Here . . . forgive me . . . this isn't the America I expected. This is like . . . like . . . when Bonaparte came to us."

"There is an ominous note in this dissension. You've sensed it correctly. Our own little Bonaparte may step in with his comrades at arms and force salvation on us in his way."

"That must not be." Lafayette has risen quickly. "This is the message my father asked me to deliver. Tell Jefferson, he says to me, tell him the eyes of all suffering humanity are looking to America. It is their last hope on earth."

A courier has brought a message to Jefferson. It warns him that there is to be a meeting of Federalists that night to set aside the election. "Like hell they will!" exclaims the Frontiersman. "Nobody's gonna take my Republic from me!"

Now it becomes imperative that Patsy and the children must leave. There may be trouble. The Frontiersman is ordered to ride like the wind back to Governor Monroe with a message from Jefferson. Apparently General Hamilton is again active. This puzzles Lafayette.

"Hamilton?" he queries. "But during the war, he was my father's friend, too. My father often speaks of him."

"People changed here after the war, Monsieur Lafayette," explains Patsy. "The real revolution was fought in the last six years."

"And our people have won, Monsieur Lafayette," adds Madison. "Through the ballot they've taken the government into their own hands. But now the Federalists intend to drag everything down with them rather than admit defeat."

"They've turned President Adams completely against my father,—one of his oldest friends. Do you know *why* he didn't write your father all these years? He couldn't! They opened his mail! They twisted phrases he used in his letters, and printed them against him."

"These are things, Patsy, that are best forgotten. This isn't like you . . . to . . ."

A knock at the door is followed by the entrance of General Hamilton. For a long moment those in the room stare at him. Now, Patsy, with expressed disgust, sweeps past the General into the hall. A moment later Madison and Lafayette have followed.

Jefferson and Hamilton face each other. There is no exchange of compliments. Hamilton is quick to assert that his feelings toward Jefferson remain unchanged. "I still despise you and everything you represent. Is that understood?"

"I think pretty widely," calmly answers Jefferson, motioning the General to a chair.

For a little they exchange pleasant inquiries as to the health of their respective families. Soon they come to the important matter. Who is to be President? Burr or Jefferson? Congress will decide, says Jefferson. With the friends he has, Hamilton thinks he can influence the decision either for or against Jefferson—

"In the matter of the public good, men must consult their reason, not their passions," says Hamilton. "I believe I can swing Congress over to you if you will accede to certain conditions."

First, Hamilton would have Jefferson's promise that all his (Hamilton's) friends shall be continued in office. Jefferson refuses to consider this or any other bargains. Hamilton is shouting mad—

HAMILTON—I came here to compromise. I hoped to avert the more drastic alternative. But the years have made you even more pig-headed, if possible. I might have spared myself this trouble.

JEFFERSON—I couldn't enter the presidency with my hands tied.

HAMILTON—Don't concern yourself. You won't enter it at all! (*Ominously.*) My friends are meeting tonight. You oblige them to act to set aside this election altogether and choose their own man.

JEFFERSON (*grimly*)—They would be smashing the Constitution.

HAMILTON—Stretching it!

JEFFERSON (*rising*)—Smashing it, I say. (HAMILTON *shrugs his shoulders and turns to go.*) Have you seen the crowds about the capitol building?

HAMILTON—One volley from my troops, and they disperse.

JEFFERSON—Don't deceive yourself! Our people will not be "*put aside.*" (*Hands him a letter.*) From Maryland. Fifteen hundred men met last night. Resolved: If anyone dares usurp the presidency, they will come here in a body and assassinate him. (*He picks up a communiqué.*) From Governor McKean of Pennsylvania . . . From Governor Monroe of Virginia. Their militias are ready to march at a moment's notice. If you put aside this election tonight, tomorrow morning there will be blood in the streets.

HAMILTON—I am an old soldier, Mr. Jefferson. If you give us no alternative . . .

JEFFERSON—But you have an alternative. End this deadlock at once! Use your influence with your friends. I shall use mine. Make Aaron Burr President.

HAMILTON—Aren't you being whimsical?

JEFFERSON—No. I should honestly prefer that.

HAMILTON—So you want Aaron Burr to be President?

JEFFERSON (*turning away*)—He's a superior man, energetic, sharp, believes in our people.

HAMILTON—God! You're gullible! I know the man. He despises your democracy more than I. Yet he has chimed in with all its absurdities. Why? Because he is cunning, and audacious, and absolutely without morality—possessed of only one principle, to get power by any means and keep it by all.

Burr, charges Hamilton, has been bankrupt for years, yet he has spent vast sums on his campaign. Where did the money come from? From Bonaparte, in Hamilton's opinion, for which he can offer proof.

"Burr is the Cataline of America," continues Hamilton. "He'll dare anything. You may as well think to bind a giant by cobwebs as his ambitions by promises. Once President, he'd destroy all our institutions. Usurp for himself complete and permanent power. Make himself dictator."

Jefferson would still put his faith in the American people. They would fight, Hamilton admits, although he has no real faith in them. That would bring down upon the country a bloody civil war, which would be all that Bonaparte would need. "Now you know my motive," Hamilton concludes. "I'm afraid, I'm profoundly afraid for the happiness of this country."

Jefferson is miserable. It may be he had been duped, when he suspected only Hamilton. It may be, too, that Hamilton is himself planning to be America's Bonaparte. The thought is not new to Hamilton. He could have been a Bonaparte when Washington died. And why didn't he?

"Burr asked me that question," he admits. "Contemptuously. This may be difficult for you but try to grasp it. I happen to love this country too. I have fought for it in field and in council.

Above every small, selfish, personal desire, I want to see it peaceful and prosperous and strong."

Now will Jefferson meet his terms? No. Then Hamilton knows how to proceed. His conscience at least is clear. And he is not afraid that there will be bloodshed, because he still is counting on Jefferson to prevent that extremity.

"You're wrong, my friend," cries Jefferson, with a sudden new fierceness. "I'd be part of it."

"You really mean it."

JEFFERSON—By the God that made me, I mean it. I'd open my veins and yours in a second.

HAMILTON—You amaze me.

JEFFERSON—Why? Isn't the blood of patriots and tyrants the natural manure for liberty?

HAMILTON—You've become a tough old man.

JEFFERSON—Who made me tough?

HAMILTON (*turning away; smiling*)—Then I haven't lived in vain.

JEFFERSON (*growling*)—That's right. (HAMILTON *is staring at* JEFFERSON.) Listen to me, Hamilton. . . .

HAMILTON—This is a strange . . .

JEFFERSON—Listen to me. I know you love this country. But you have never understood it. You're afraid of Bonaparte? Well, there's no need to be. Bonaparte will die and his tyrannies will die, and we will be living, and we will be free. You're afraid of Burr? If Burr tries any quixotic adventures he will smash himself against the rock of our people. You see, this is the mistake you have always made. You have never properly estimated the character of the American people. You still don't understand them. At this moment.

HAMILTON (*after pause*)—I confess it. I don't. (*Sits down.*)

JEFFERSON (*standing over him; gently*)—This is not the way, Hamilton. Believe me. If you really love this country, this isn't the way. Our people who fought the Revolution from a pure love of liberty, made every sacrifice and met every danger, did not expend their blood and substance to change this master for that. But to take their freedom in their own hands so that never again would the corrupt will of one man oppress them. You'll not make these people hold their breath at the caprice, or submit to the rods and the hatchet of a dictator. You cannot fix fear in their hearts, or make fear their principle of government. I know them. I place my faith in them. I have no fears for their ultimate victory.

HAMILTON—I wish I had such faith. (*Pause.*) I don't know. I frankly don't know. I find *myself lost here*. Day by day, I am becoming more foreign to this land.

JEFFERSON—Yet you helped build it.

HAMILTON—There is a tide here that sweeps men to the fashioning of some strange destiny . . . even against their will. I never believed in this . . . and yet as you say, I helped build it. Every inch of it. (*Pause. Rises.*) And still, I must admit it has worked better than I thought. If it could survive . . . if . . . ?

JEFFERSON (*very softly*)—It can. And it will. This tide is irresistible. You cannot hold it back. This is the rising flood of man's lost freedom. Try as you will, you cannot stop it. You may deflect it for a moment. But in the end you will lose. Try the old way of tyranny and usurpation and you *must* lose. Bonapartes may retard the epoch of man's deliverance, they may bathe the world in rivers of blood yet to flow, and still, still, in the end, they will fall back exhausted in their own blood, leaving mankind to liberty and self-government. No, General Hamilton, this way you lose. Believe me . . . (*Moves away.*) I shall not compromise, General Hamilton. You do whatever you choose. I cannot compromise on this.

HAMILTON (*holding out his hand after a long pause; it is shaky*)—Since the fever took me, I cannot hit the side of a barn with a pistol. Burr is cool as a snake, and one of the best shots in America. He will challenge me. I have no doubt of that. I am a dead man already. But at least you are honest. I shall urge my friends to end the deadlock. You will be President. Your victory is complete.

JEFFERSON—There is no personal victory in this for me. I didn't *want* this for myself. I still don't. If it will give you any satisfaction, my own affairs have been neglected so long . . . In another office, with time to mend them, I might have saved myself from bankruptcy. As President, I am certain to lose everything I possess, including Monticello, where my wife and four of my children lie. Where all the dreams of my youth lie. No matter. I thank you—for a glorious misery.

HAMILTON—I must go. Some of my . . . friends . . . are waiting.

Hamilton turns at the door and bows to Jefferson as he goes

out. Jefferson looks after him a second, then turns his gaze to the statue of Washington. The curtain falls.

Out of the darkness a hall in the Capitol at Washington is dimly seen. On a platform, Jefferson, his hand raised, is facing Chief Justice Marshall as the oath of office is administered. Monroe and Madison are standing at one side, and Patsy and her children can be seen in the shadow.

Justice Marshall completes the oath and waves the President to the assembled audience. Jefferson steps forward nervously, hesitantly. For a moment his gaze rests on Patsy, "standing proudly with Anne and Jeff." They smile at him, and he smiles faintly back as he turns to the audience and begins to speak.

For a little he speaks of the grave duties he is assuming; of his grateful thanks for the honor and for the stimulation and hope he finds in the presence of those before him. "To you, then," he continues, "I look for that guidance and support which may enable us to steer with safety the vessel in which we are all embarked amid the conflicting elements of a troubled world. This is the sum of good government: Equal and exact justice to all men, of whatever state or persuasion; a jealous care of the right of election; absolute acquiescence to the decisions of the majority, the vital principle of republics, from which is no appeal but to *force,* the vital principle and parent of despotism . . . Freedom of religion, freedom of press, freedom of person, and trial by juries impartially selected. These form the bright constellation which has gone before us and which has guided us in an age of revolution and reformation. The wisdom of our sages, and the blood of our heroes have attained them for us. They are the creed of our political faith, the touchstone of our public servants. Should we wander from them in moments of error or alarm, let us hasten to retrace our steps and to regain the road which alone leads to peace, liberty and safety."

For a brief moment the President pauses. Then with new force and prophetic vision he continues. "During the present throes and convulsions of the ancient world, during those agonizing spasms of blood and slaughter abroad, it was not strange that the agitation of the billows should reach even this distant and peaceful shore; that this should be more felt and feared by some than by others. I know, indeed, that some honest men fear that a republic cannot be strong, that this government is not strong enough. But would the honest patriot in the full tide of successful experiment, abandon a government which has so far kept us free and firm, on the theoretic fear that it may possibly want energy to preserve itself? I trust not. I believe this, on the contrary, the only government where every man would fly to the standard and meet invasion as his own personal concern. I believe this the strongest government on earth. I believe, indeed, I know, this government is the world's best hope . . ."

The President is still speaking as

THE CURTAIN FALLS

THE EVE OF ST. MARK

A Drama in Two Acts

BY MAXWELL ANDERSON

THE Broadway theatre had been offered a generous assortment of dramas concerned with the Second World War by the time Maxwell Anderson's contribution, "The Eve of St. Mark," was introduced in early October, 1942. Most of them had failed. Most of them, in fact, had been practically bombed out of the theatre. By applying his widely publicized blitzkrieg to London in his first desperate effort to knock Britain out of the war in 1940, Herr Hitler had set a new and vicious style in warfare which, naturally, the playwrights were quick to observe and to capitalize, insofar as stage limitations permitted.

It is still too early to determine whether or not the bombing itself, being hard on sensitive ears as well as sensitive imaginations, was the chief factor in establishing the reactions of audiences, but unquestionably it played a definite part. The fact that "The Eve of St. Mark," among the major war dramas in which the simulation of actual bombing is featured, is the only one to have been favored by audiences is in itself significant. "The Wookey," "The Heart of a City," "The Morning Star," "Flare Path," "Cry Havoc," "Counterattack" were all subjected to a vigorous off-stage pounding, and none of them lived, though "The Wookey" did hold on for upwards of a hundred performances in light competition.

However, war dramas without bombs, or with very little bombing, have also generally failed of audience popularity. Notable exceptions were Robert Sherwood's "There Shall Be No Night" and Lillian Hellman's "Watch on the Rhine." Anderson's "Candle in the Wind" was saved, in the opinion of many, by Helen Hayes' playing of the heroine. But there were quick exits for Steinbeck's "The Moon Is Down," the humanly appealing "Letters to Lucerne," Elmer Rice's dramatic "Flight to the West," and several lesser war-time exhibits.

"The function of the theatre in war time is not easy to define," wrote Howard Barnes in a *Herald Tribune* review of "The Eve of St. Mark." "To many of us it has seemed quite proper that it should avoid the ultimate, desperate issues which confront us.

So long as it has afforded a brief release, we have argued, it was doing fine. 'The Eve of St. Mark' makes it apparent that it can do far more than that. For this gallant tribute to high courage in the face of death has such clarity and understanding that it resolves the burden of current emotional tension, instead of merely sidestepping it."

In general the opinion must hold that play-goers do not favor war plays during a war. Vivid reminders of yesterday's horrors and today's fearful apprehensions, whatever the emotional overtones, are avoided rather than sought after in such hours of relaxation as the theatre normally offers. But it also is apparent that good drama is still good drama, whatever its subject, whatever its setting. And "The Eve of St. Mark" definitely belongs in that category.

The play was written originally for the National Theatre Conference, representing the organized "little theatres" and the college dramatic groups of the country. It had been produced at the Pasadena Playhouse in California, and in no less than seventy-five other minor theatre centers before it reached Broadway. The dedication is to Mr. Anderson's nephew, Sergeant Lee Chambers—"one of the first to go, one of the first to die that we may keep this earth for free men."

Because of the limited equipment at the command of the smaller Conference units the staging problems were simplified as much as possible. For the setting of the first scene, for example, the author's instructions read: "A background of curtains, against which is set the furniture of a farm kitchen." The furniture consists of a white enameled range, a kitchen cabinet, a leaf-table and seven or eight chairs.

This would be the kitchen of the Deckman Wests, somewhere in upstate New York. As we meet the Wests they are finishing breakfast on an early April day in 1941. There are Deck and Nell, his wife, both about forty-five; their two sons, Neil, eighteen, and Zip, sixteen, and Cy, a lean old neighbor of fifty or so. Cy explains his presence by reporting that his family has left him. The last he'd seen of Mother and the boys they were goin' off down the road in the county wagon. "Come to find out," says Cy, "she asked for it. She complained the windows was broke out in the upper story and the boys wasn't getting vitamins. Which was true."

Being a bachelor from now on, Cy is wondering if the Wests wouldn't be needin' a hired man—a hired man "with a good team of loggin' horses and a natural affinity for manure."

Deck is inclined to think that with his son Quizz in the army and his other two boys in school a lot, he could do with another hand on the farm. Nell is agreeable, too. Having another to cook for doesn't matter, but it is going to be pretty hard for her to be seeing Cy sitting in Quizz's place at the table.

The Wests are expecting Quizz today. "I don't know how much time I'll have," he had written in the letter Nell knows by heart; "but I'll see you, and that'll be good. And I'll have a chance to show you the most wonderful person in the world."

That last rather puzzles them. Quizz can't be married, so he must be bringing the girl along with him. "Can you understand it, Mother—our being grown up and having grown-up children, old enough to wear a uniform?" asks Deck.

"No, I just can't understand it," agrees Nell.

"And I can't. Doggone it, I go rushing around here, buying hay and selling hay and suddenly I'm an old man and my son's fighting a war."

"Yes."

"And I keep wondering about us when we were twenty. Did we look as young as that?"

"I wonder."

"And why did I have to have a funny little girl with glasses? There I was, a dashing young Lothario, come of a family of dashing young Lotharios, the pick of the town at my feet, writhing for mercy, and what do I do? I pick me a funny little girl with glasses that didn't care whether I came or stayed."

"I never understood that either."

"Well, it's too late to change now. All those beautiful girls are grandmothers now."

There's a car in the yard. It has brought Deck's older brother, Ralph, "a tall, dreamy farmer, with graying hair." Ralph is just back from the creamery. "If gasoline and milk cost the same I'd break even," he tells them; "but with prices being the way they are I lose money on the trip."

Ralph had seen Quizz down the road, sitting on the Fellers' porch. He was wearing a kind of khaki-colored suit of clothes, and had refused a hitch. He would be right along, Quizz had said.

When Pete Feller arrives with the mail, Janet, his daughter, is with him. So is Quizz, as it turns out. He comes in now with his bag. And he has no intention of letting Janet turn around and go right back.

"Look—Janet—there's only one of me—and I've got only one

day," he says. "I don't want to waste it traveling up and down a dirt road. You stay here."

Then the secret's out. "Doggone it, Mother, you can leave it to Quizz to keep things neat and handy," explodes Deck, heartily. "He's picked himself a neighbor girl. I was wondering when some bright boy would notice there was a pretty girl at the Fellers'."

"I thought you meant you were bringing someone—" Nell has begun, but Quizz stops her. "No, what I said was I wanted to show you the most wonderful person in the world. It was kind of a surprise when she turned out to be a next hill neighbor. But there it was—and there she is."

By now Janet is standing in the corner, blushing one of the prettiest blushes, Deck insists, he ever saw on a face.

"I've got a lot of things to explain all at once," Quizz says, "so maybe I'd better start right in. I just managed to wangle this one day. I'm supposed to be on my way to Fort Grace, you see, but I was able to prove to the old man I'd get there sooner by coming a little out of my way, so I can be here till five o'clock."

"Oh."

QUIZZ—Yes, just till five, Mother.

DECK—I must say your soldier clothes become you, son.

QUIZZ—That's how I managed to waylay Janet. It's the uniform does it.

NELL—But where in the world did you see Janet?

QUIZZ—Ah—trust Mother to put her finger on it. That's the funny thing. That's the thing you'll never believe, because I don't believe it myself. I was at Camp Upton, Mother, and when I got my first day off I went to New York, naturally. There was nothing much to do in New York, not for a jeep with no money, so I took in Rockefeller Center. —There was a guide showing a whole crowd of us around, and when we got to the tower—

JANET—Quizz—

QUIZZ—Yes?

JANET—Don't tell it. Please.

QUIZZ—Why not?

JANET—I don't know. I just don't want you to tell it.

QUIZZ—Well, that's the whole point of the story. It's the whole point of everything. Everything up to now.

JANET—No. No, please. You mustn't, Quizz. Nobody knows

about that. Nobody can ever know it.

QUIZZ—Listen, darling, I don't know what you mean. Dad and Mother—they naturally—they said where in the world did we meet. —Well, there's nothing wrong with it, only it was completely unbelievable—that's all—so why not tell them?

JANET—I never dreamed you'd tell anybody—I—to save my life I wouldn't tell anybody. And you can't—

QUIZZ—Well, look, Janet—you're making it seem as if we had something to hide. There's nothing wrong with the way we met. It was fun, and it was certainly unusual, but—you see, I was standing beside this girl in the tower. I'd been watching her all along, and then when I found myself standing beside her I said the first thing that came into my head. I said, "You're the most beautiful person I've ever seen in my life."

JANET—I'll never forgive you! Never! (*She rushes out.*)

NELL—What's the matter?

QUIZZ—I've no idea. I didn't want to hurt anybody's feelings.—Well, I'll finish it anyway.—I said, "You're the most beautiful person I've ever seen in my life," and I meant it. And she looked at me very pleasant and cool and said, "Thank you." And I said, "After this barker gets through barking maybe we could have a little lunch together." And she looked me all up and down and looked at my uniform and said, "Yes, that would be very nice, thank you." Well, I thought she looked a little familiar, but she was so blossomed out and beautiful it wasn't till we were half through lunch that I found out she was little Janet Feller that lived two miles away from here. And she didn't know who I was till I told her. Then we had the afternoon and evening together—and then we seemed to feel the same way—so—

DECK—How'd she get to Radio City?

QUIZZ—Won a contest. Maybe that's what she doesn't want me to tell. It was some silly business for high school girls in domestic economy classes. She baked the best cake with a certain kind of flour, and that was the prize, the trip to Radio City.

Deck has gone into the other room to see if he can find Janet. Quizz would know whether his mother is pleased and if she is disappointed because he can't be more with her this last visit. "You'd be a poor specimen if you hung around your mother much today, I guess."

"But—I love you. Just as much. And I've never forgotten what you said to me."

"I'm not very wise, Son."

"You're wise enough to tell me."

"Some things we think we've learned, just by living, Deck and I, and one of them is—that's the best part of life—loving somebody and being true. I think she'll always love you."

"So do I. And it makes me—" He has gone to his mother and kissed her. "Never mind. You know what it does to me."

"It's made me rich all my life," she says.

Deck has induced Janet to come back into the room. He has been telling her how much he and Nell have always wanted a daughter—and now they've got one. As for Quizz, he is sorry if he had hurt Janet. He had only wanted to tell it the way it happened.

Nell thinks, perhaps, Janet was afraid it would look like Quizz had picked her up, and she wouldn't like that. Quizz wouldn't care. "Personally, I like the way it happened," he says. "What's a pickup, anyway? It's love at first sight. So why not say it the way it was?"

"But you couldn't say it the way it was—because you had no idea what was happening."

A moment later Janet is telling her side of the story. "You see, I knew who you were. From the beginning."

Now the older folks have gone about their work and left Quizz and Janet to themselves. "If you're hungry or anything, come and see us, but it's your day, what there is left of it," Nell says. "And it's Spring."

They thought maybe they'd walk back to the Fellers'. All the country is new to them now, seeing it together for the first time. But before they can do that there are a couple of other Wests to take into account. The boys, Zip and Neil, have come rushing in to greet Quizz. "Boy, you look like Napoleon!" says Zip, proudly.

The boys have taken time out today to inspect their big brother. School? Not while Quizz is home on leave!

ZIP—You know what we thought? We thought maybe we ought to climb up and look at the maples. The sap's running like a brook and Ralph says his syrup's thick enough to fill a tooth.

NEIL—We thought we'd like to candy a little on a snow-drift, the way we used to.

QUIZZ—I certainly would like to—

NELL—You boys run along and let Quizz take a walk with

Janet. They're starting back toward her house together.
  ZIP—With—
NEIL—Hello, Janet.
JANET—Hello.
ZIP—What's going on here?
DECK—Good God, they can take a walk, can't they?
QUIZZ—Mind you, we'll be back. We'll see you later.
NEIL—Sure.
QUIZZ—So long.
ZIP—So long, General.
JANET—Good-by. (QUIZZ *and* JANET *go out.*)
ZIP—What the hell is going on here?
DECK—Looks a little to an old man like they was fixing to get engaged.
ZIP—Yeah. I see.
NEIL—I could run them down in Old Faithful.
NELL—They want to walk.
ZIP—In all that slush?
NELL—That's right.
ZIP—Looks like we lost the best brother we ever had.
NEIL—Looks that way.

The curtain falls.

The curtained background is the same when the curtain rises but the furniture has been changed. Now there are six army bunks in pyramids of two each stretching lengthwise across the stage. Quizz is sitting on one of them at the back, writing a letter on a pad which he holds on his knees. In front of another section Corporal Tate, Private Shevlin and Private Mulveroy are rolling dice against a cardboard placed beside a cot.

The game doesn't last long. Mulveroy soon has all the Corporal's money and they can't get Quizz in. "The way I work it out I've got just enough to buy cigarettes and stamps and get my pants pressed," explains Quizz.

"You mean you figured all that out?" Mulveroy is disgusted. "I had to."

"You got to get over that, soldier. That destroys ambition. That eliminates the element of chance. You're in the army for a whole year, remember! You gotta reorganize, gotta get on army time!"

Mulveroy's eloquence favoring life in the army as it should be, with every guy in rhythm and the crap game running free, is about to lure Quizz into the game when the appearance of Pvt. Francis Marion takes the gamblers' attention. Francis is a handsome Southerner and he has just been paid. He doesn't keep his wages long. Mulveroy, Tate and Shevlin are on him like a pack of not too polite loan sharks and strip him of all his cash, which they divide. "What is this, a gang?" Quizz wants to know.

"No, suh, this is my holding company, a perfectly legal arrangement," Marion explains. "To tide me over one crisis after another these gentlemen have lent me money. Finding that my total borrowings had grown to an enormous sum, they organized to administer my affairs—also to prevent any addition to the list of my creditors. They are now a closed corporation, dedicated to supplying my modest needs and collecting my monthly honorarium. You, for example, could not extend me credit. They wouldn't allow it."

It further appears that Pvt. Marion has so far borrowed the sum of $97, largely on the security of his ancestral estates in Marion County, the existence of which Mulveroy is already beginning to doubt. "Mulveroy is the cynic of the enterprise," says Marion. "He refuses to believe that I am descended on my father's side from Francis Marion and on my mother's side from Patrick Henry. He refuses to believe that only three aunts, two uncles, seven cousins and a grandfather stand between me and my inheritance."

Pvt. Marion's weakness, it appears, is Cuba Libras, which are expensive. And he drinks a lot of them, being by nature a sorrowful fellow. There is another complication. This would be Pvt. Buscemi, who has just arrived. He also is a member of the syndicate, and he wants his bit. There is wrangling over this, but the other three finally agree to disgorge three dollars each of what they have taken, and this satisfies Buscemi.

With money in hand, the urge is to go places. They can all go except Corp. Tate. Sergt. Ruby had said something about Tate being appointed Charge of Quarters and he will have to wait and see about that. Ruby was supposed to be there at 7. He is half an hour late now.

"He's down at the mess-hall," Buscemi reports. "All the tops are being lectured by a couple of staff officers down there."

"What are they getting lectured about?" Tate wants to know.

SHEVLIN—What do you care? We'll get it all from Ruby tomorrow.

BUSCEMI—You won't get what I heard. I was standing guard right outside the window. There's a sprout up in front with charts and figures and he's discussing sexual intercourse.

MULVEROY—Did he know about it?

BUSCEMI—He's got a theory about it. He says they made a study and he's got it all down in percentages. Twenty per cent of the men in an army camp will refuse all temptations to sexual intercourse because they've got wives or sweethearts and so they don't want to play. And then another twenty per cent will take anything they can get. You know, the way it is with you, Mulveroy.

MULVEROY—They got to have shoes. I draw the line there. They got to go home and get their shoes.

BUSCEMI—But then he goes on and says, there's sixty per cent in between that maybe will and maybe won't, depending on the temptation.

TATE—The loot said that?

BUSCEMI—That's what he said.

SHEVLIN—I don't know why he's talking to the non-coms. They all belong to that lower twenty per cent.

BUSCEMI—And he's got a project, the loot. He wants all the non-coms to help him. Look, he says, there's twenty per cent that don't need no help. And there's twenty per cent you can't do anything with. But the big sixty per cent in between, there we can exert an influence, he says. There we can save a lot of boys from contamination. And if you ask me how, he says, there's only one way—offer them something better.

MARION (*after a pause*)—For instance?

BUSCEMI—That's where the guard came to relieve me. I never did hear what they're going to offer.

It further appears that Sergt. Ruby has come out of that highly moral lecture and immediately laid his plans to get down to Amityville with Sergt. Kriven and keep a date with a couple of girls named Lill and Sal. Pvt. Shevlin had heard them making a rendezvous over the telephone. They are to meet the girls at the Moonbow at 8 o'clock.

This gives Mulveroy an idea. He knows Lill and Sal, too. He used to board at their house. And he doesn't propose to let Sergt. Ruby get any inside track. Those gals are much too good for a goon like Ruby.

"Sergt. Ruby appears to be unpopular around here," ventures Quizz.

"Sergt. Ruby?" shrieks Mulveroy. "You don't know him yet. Wait till he tears into you." He begins to imitate Ruby's enunciation, "which sounds like Brooklynese dragged through all the slums in the world."

" 'Tenshun! Fall in! Give ta boy a taste of what he's gonna get! Get ta hell on your feet and take ta position of a soldier! Don't you know ta position of a soldier, ya dumb bunny? (*They all line up except* TATE *and* QUIZZ.) Pull in at pod! (*He walks up and down in front of them, addressing remarks as he stops before each one.*) Inspection! Arms! Look, you! We're doing Inspection Arms!"

Sergt. Ruby, "an elderly, rather stolid-looking, old-line sergeant," has come into the room back of Mulveroy and stands quietly watching his imitator's performance. Mulveroy continues in complete ignorance of his added audience—

"At a Command Arms take a position a Port Arms! You hear? Port Arms! Is dat a way to hold a gun? Gimme da gun! (*He snatches an imaginary Springfield.*) See dat! At's a way to hold a gun! Take da gun! (*He slams it back at* SHEVLIN, *half knocking him down.*) Stand up! Stay on your feet when addressed by ya officer! You heard me! Inspection! Arms! At a Command Arms take ta position a Port Arms! Wit ta fingers of ta left hand closed place ta left thumb on ta operating rod handle and push ta handle to da rear— What ta hell you tink you're doing there?—to da rear! Da rear! till caught by operating rod catch, at ta same time lower da head an' eyes sufficient to glance in da receiver! Lower da God-damn head! Having found ta receiver empty— (*He stops, feeling a presence behind him, and turns around. The line melts away. There is a pause.*) I was just trying to give them an idea of Inspection Arms, Sergeant."

"Ya charge of Quarters tonight, Tate," barks Ruby.

"O.K., Sergeant." Sergt. Ruby has started to leave. Before he leaves he turns and faces them. "Tanks for ta ad. Yeah, tanks for ta ad," he says.

"I hope you won't take our games too seriously, Sergeant Ruby," says Pvt. Marion, pleasantly. "The psychologists say that a certain amount of irreverence and disrespect is healthy in the armed forces, and should be encouraged."

"Yeah? Well, I don't know what it says in da books, but when I see a smart, brainy squad like dis it gives me ideas, see? It makes me tink of tings. Tings like poimanent K.P., and duty wit da foitilizer wagon, and latrine detail. It makes me tink of yard duty special, and policing up, and twenty-four hour guard duty and runnin' the lengt of da company street carrying da God-damn rifle over ya ruttin head. Dis whole ruttin squad is goin' to have more ruttin fun dan you could write home about. I'm going ta take a poisonal interest in every ruttin one of you. Toin in and get ya ruttin sleep. Ya gonta need it."

Sergt. Ruby leaves, and the boys hop on Mulveroy. "Now we're in good and deep," growls Shevlin. "You're a genius, Mulveroy, just a blatting genius."

Buscemi has an idea. While Sergt. Ruby is taking a shower the rest of them should beat it down to the Moonbow and meet the guineas. Shevlin has his own plans. But Mulveroy can go. Lill's his gal. Buscemi can have Sal.

Quizz and Marion decline the invitation. Later they start out to mail Quizz's letter. "You haven't been talking much," Marion observes.

"I'm listening mostly, so far," answers Quizz.

MARION—When you make up your mind about anything, let me know. I'd be greatly obliged.

QUIZZ—I only know one thing. You can't run out on it. You have to go along and do your damnedest.

MARION—What's the chance of us all being let out after our year's up?

QUIZZ—Not a chance in the world.

MARION—That's what I think.

QUIZZ—Would you want to get out?

MARION—For myself, I have infinite natural gall and great presence of mind, but I'm in a hell of a fog. I walk around and around in it, but I can't think it through.

QUIZZ—What's the problem?

MARION—Well, there's going to be a hell of a war, some of us are going to die young, and others are going to benefit by it. Which are the lucky ones? Which would I rather be?

QUIZZ—You'd rather be one that almost got killed and didn't.

MARION—Yes, but then another question arises. How close do I have to come to being horizontal before I earn the right to remain perpendicular?

QUIZZ—I don't know that.

MARION—I guess nobody knows or we'd God damn well been told by this time.

QUIZZ—I know this much. I read the entire manual of arms coming down on the train, and it's not in there.

MARION—No. I looked for it there. I shall look for it to-night at the bottom of a coke with rum. That's the bus now.

The curtain falls.

The curtain rises. Briefly we catch a glimpse of Janet Feller's bedroom. The bed is set back against the curtains in a splash of light. There is a small table alongside, with an oil lamp on it. Janet is sitting on the edge of the bed writing a letter on a tablet. She is wearing a robe, from the pocket of which she takes a khaki handkerchief and smoothes it over her knee.

From outside the room her father calls. He has come to tell her that he is going to town. Does she want a letter mailed, or anything? She'll have a letter finished in a minute, Janet calls back.

Also, Charlie Lane's boy is downstairs. He wants to see Janet. But Janet doesn't want to see him. She had told him not to come.

"Shall I say you're going to town with me?" Feller asks.

"Will you, Daddy?"

"Sure. And you can mail the letter yourself."

"I'll just put on a dress," she says.

Janet slips into a dark dress. She smooths her hair before the mirror, kisses the end of her letter before she seals it and starts to go. The khaki handkerchief has fallen from her knee. She picks it up, puts it in the pocket of her dress and runs out. The curtain falls.

Again the scene changes. One fairly large restaurant table is now set before the curtains. Lill and Sal are seated at the table, drinks in front of them. "Mulveroy, Buscemi and Marion have just come up and negotiations are in progress. Lill and Sal are both wearing a little too much of everything, but they are attractive."

"Sure, you can sit down if you want to, Mr. Mulveroy," Lill is saying. "That is, as far as I'm concerned you can sit down, but as far as Sal's concerned I can't speak for her, because we make a point of being entirely separate and distinct personalities."

"Look, Lill—" He has taken the proffered seat.

"So as for her I can't decide, but I will say, Mr. Mulveroy,

when a soldier comes in and sits down at a table a girl's got the
privilege to say she was waiting for somebody else."

"You better let me sit beside you, girl, because you've been
taking that one extra drink and you're getting elaborate for this
early in the evening."

"I am not elaborate! I'll murder anyone that says I'm elaborate! Was I, Sal?"

"Just a little, Lill, just a little."

"Gee, was I? Maybe I was, at that."

Mulveroy's campaign for reinstatement in Lill's affections
doesn't make very much headway. She is a girl of changing
moods, especially with Cuba Libras. She also suddenly becomes
aware of the handsome Marion.

Mulveroy and Buscemi talk fast, trying to convince Lill and
Sal that they are about to be made game of by a couple of irre-
sponsible sergeants. They'd be much better off if they were to
eat their hamburgers and drink their Cuba Libras and go out
with Mulveroy and Buscemi before Ruby and Kriven arrive.
Sergeants aren't to be trusted. Look at the way they talk about
girls. Look at them, stopping in a drugstore to lay in medical
supplies before they go on a date!

Lill is stirred by the attack, but her emotional reactions are
general. "I hate sergeants, and I hate you, and I hate the whole
damn army," declares Lill. "What did you have to come to this
town for, anyway, with your whole army, spoiling everything!
We didn't ask for you! We didn't want you here! We had
everything nice, and we went to church on Sunday, and I could'a
got married, and then you come along with your army and it's all
spoiled! I want it to be the way it was before you came along!"

A moment later Lill and Sal are made conscious of their competition. Two other pretty girls have appeared. Mulveroy
recognizes them, too. They are Flash and Dimples, and they
would have a word with Mulveroy. Presently Mulveroy has
called Buscemi into the conference and the four of them go into
a huddle. "I guess they had a little something to talk over,"
guesses Lill.

"He's their spiritual advisor. They come to him for guidance
and religious instruction," explains Marion.

"You hear that, Sal? Religious instruction!"

"For the best instruction you got to get under a good teacher,"
says Sal.

"I wouldn't be surprised."

Mulveroy and Buscemi have completed their arrangements and

are on their way. Lill and Sal are not greatly concerned. They turn to Quizz and Marion with new interest. Sal is particularly impressed with Quizz. "You know, I like this silent job here," says Sal, as Quizz insists on paying the bill. "When he speaks he says something. That's the first word he spoke, but, boy, did he make it count?" She lifts her glass. "Silent job, I love you. Come on, drink to the silent job. He's paying."

"It's nice to be quiet for a change," says Lill.

Sal has moved over and put her arm around Quizz. He is not too enthusiastic about it. "You don't like my arm around you, do you?" she says.

"Certainly I like your arm around me. What do you think I'm made of?"

"You're blushing."

"I do that for a come-on, you know. I start blushing, and the girls say, look, he's bashful. And then they throw their arms around me."

"Look, the silent job can talk, and he's got a technique."

There is some danger, Quizz points out, that the expected Ruby and Kriven will walk in on this happy quartet and do things to it. Of course, as Sal suggests, they could say that while they waited these new friends had kindly bought them a drink. But, as Quizz says, non-coms aren't very good at taking explanations like that. It would be better if the girls were to go in one of the booths and draw the curtains. Then when the sergeants came they (Quizz and Marion) could explain that the girls waited for a while and then went home.

"Will you give me a kiss, darling?" asks Sal.

"Absolutely," answers Quizz, meeting the situation politely.

"Tell me you love me."

"You want me to tell you the truth?"

"Sure I do."

"There's somebody else I love better."

Sal is silent for a moment. "That's all right," she decides. "I don't mind. You'll—you'll forget about her when you know me. You'll forget her."

"Anything can happen."

"That's it. Anything can happen."

It isn't easy for Lill to leave Marion. He has been doing his duty by the drinks and has found, as usual, that alcohol stimulates his love of the beautiful and the good. That, Lill decides, would be her. "What was that poem you said?" she demands. And Marion repeats—

"The host with someone indistinct
Converses at the door, apart;
The nightingales are singing near
The Convent of the Sacred Heart.

"And sang within the bloody wood
When Agamemnon cried aloud,
And let their liquid droppings fall
To stain the stiff dishonored shroud."

Lill is moved. "It's the God damn poetry gets me!" she says.
"I don't know what it means!" She turns to Marion. "Any
time, baby, any time."

"Yours until the dust-cart calls," he answers.

The girls disappear into the booth. "Are you interested?"
Quizz would know.

"They begin to verge on the professional," Marion admits,
"but I'm inclined to believe the whole of Amityville verges."

Mutual confessions lead to their also admitting the importance of the girls at home. Quizz has just mailed a letter.
Marion has written letters, but does not mail them. Recently
they haven't been answered.

It is Quizz' idea that Marion gives up too easily. He should
keep on writing letters. And mail them. They will be answered
in time. No girl could forget a man who can quote poetry to
her. Marion is not sure his Iseult still cares for poetry. Anyway—

"Didn't we promise to love and cherish Lill and Sal?" demands Marion.

"We promised to save them from worse than death, that's all."

MARION—Don't you have any hankering after the flesh-pots?
QUIZZ—Some. It's the drinks mostly.
MARION—I have a hell of a hankering.
QUIZZ—It won't kill you.
MARION—What if there's never anybody else, not even Lill and
Sal? What if we never lie with anything warmer than the Pacific
Ocean?
QUIZZ—You're maudlin.
MARION—On three free Cubas? No, no. I'm philosophic,
delicately apprehensive. And I hanker. I definitely hanker.
QUIZZ—For those two flesh-pots? (SERGEANTS RUBY and
KRIVEN enter. QUIZZ rises.)

Marion—One of them. Will you make a fourth?

Quizz—Oh, Sergeant Ruby, there was somebody looking for you.

Ruby—Yeah?

Quizz—A couple of girls, in fact. Named Lill and Sal. They said to say they waited as long as they could, and then went home.

Ruby—Dey did? Who da hell dey tink dey are? (*To* Kriven.) Dat's what comes a missin' da bus, see?

Kriven—I guess we missed da bus, all right.

Ruby—So you hadda change da ruttin shirt— (Ruby *and* Kriven *go out.*)

Marion—Now what do we do?

Quizz—We take the bus back to camp and crawl into our own truckle beds.

Marion—I don't know as I like a man with that much character.

Quizz—It's not character. I just belong to the twenty per cent the loot was talking about.

Marion—Very well. You're the strong solid man, and you bear the purse. I bow to your judgment and follow. What am I, after all? The weakling scion of a decaying house. Do you mind if I put a sandwich in my pocket? (*He scoops one up.*)

Quizz—Finish the drinks if there's any left.

Marion—I will. (*He empties a glass.*) "So out went the candle and we were left darkling." Taps! Heel-taps. And thus the evening ends.

They go out as the curtain falls.

It is in September of 1941 that Quizz gets his first leave. We find him now at home, standing in the kitchen, regaling his mother and father, his brothers, and the Fellers, Janet and her father, about his experience getting home. The battery commander had given him three days and said: "You better make the most of it. I can't promise you any more."

"So I grabbed my extra shirt and started for Amityville," Quizz continues. "Well, before the bus came along, I got picked up by a fellow in a station wagon that wanted me to help him drive. Sure I could help him drive, and then, on the way into town, he told me he was driving to Buffalo, New York, to deliver some pedigreed sheep."

The sheep were in the back of the station wagon. Quiz and

the sheep man were going to drive all night, taking turns at the wheel. But after dinner the sheep man disappeared and it was hours before Quizz found him, drunk in a Harrisburg saloon. Quizz drove that night and the next day, and the next night the sheep man disappeared again in Wellesville. He had given Quizz all his money and the key to the car, but he had stolen two tires off his own car and got himself stinking on the proceeds of their sale. This time Quizz quit. He gave the sheep man back his money and the key to the car and trained the rest of the journey. Fooling around with those damned sheep cost him most of two days.

"No matter how much time you start out with it always whittles down to one afternoon," sighs Nell. "Can't you be here this evening, Quizz?"

"Just for dinner, Mother. I'll have to take the ten o'clock in Olean. I'm sorry."

"It's worse for you than for us."

It is Nell's idea that Quizz and Janet should go in her room to talk. They'll never get rid of that family gang if they don't. Quizz is of the same opinion, and Janet, too, except she thinks she should help with the dishes. Deck does his part by calling Zip and Neil. "Look, boys, you can't keep bankers' hours on a farm, not unless you want the bank to take it away from you."

The lights fade out on the kitchen, and when they come on again they reveal a corner of Nell's bedroom. Janet is sitting on the one chair. Quizz would have her come over and sit beside him on the bed. "You said things in your letters—about wanting to see me," he reminds her.

JANET—Of course I did. Only when I see you again, after a long time, it always seems as if I don't know you at all. As if we had—almost to begin all over again.

QUIZZ—I hope not. Oh, God, I hope not.

JANET—No, no, not really—but—I have to look at you and hear your voice. I can't believe it's—

QUIZZ—What?

JANET—You see, you've been with—so many people—and you've done so many things I don't know about. It can't be—quite the same for you as it was. Is it just the same?

QUIZZ—Oh, darling—just more so, that's all. I've lain awake at night, whenever I wasn't too tired, just thinking about you—and all day, whenever I didn't have to think about something else, you'd slip into my mind, and I'd think about you. And your letters—how I loved you and thanked you for those letters.

JANET—I was always afraid they'd sound—

QUIZZ—They came—oh, they came like rain in a dry year, darling—and you can't imagine how dry—and how much I needed them.

JANET (*her hand on her bosom*)—I carried yours here, all the time.

QUIZZ—You see? (*He kneels at her feet, taking her hand, looking up at her.*)

JANET (*with a long breath*)—I—I just couldn't believe it was true.

QUIZZ—Couldn't I kiss you now?

JANET—I kept thinking there must be somebody else. Wasn't there anybody else?

QUIZZ—No. Nobody.

JANET—You see—one hears so many things—about the camps. The girls have brothers there—and it isn't like being at home, being in camp.

QUIZZ—No, God knows it isn't. And, I'll tell you the truth, Janet, if it hadn't been for you I could have got mixed up in all sorts of things. Because the things are there to get mixed up in. But, darling, I just used you for a north star and I steered straight for you as fast as I could come.

JANET—Yes, it's true. (*She runs her hand over his hair.*) Yes, you are Quizz, and you're not changed.— You didn't mind what I said?

QUIZZ—No, sweet; you're right about it. It's—so different it's—well, I couldn't believe this farm was here—or you—or any of it. I'd feel your letter in my pocket some time when I was out on maneuvers or in a restaurant—or at chow—and I couldn't believe there was such a girl. You have to kind of hang on anyway.

JANET—Did you want to believe—?

QUIZZ—Did I want to believe—? A fellow hangs on to somebody the way he hangs on to life. God, I wish I could tell you.

JANET—You don't need to. I know now.

They hear Zip slam the door when he goes out. Quizz sees his mother pass the window on her way to the upper orchard to get some apples. The house is theirs now. They have moved over to the bed, and Quizz' arms have tightened around Janet. "If we only had our own house," Janet is saying. Quizz has thought about that, too. Another furlough? There probably won't be another. Quizz is most likely to be getting on a train pretty soon—a train for San Francisco.

"And this is the last time—before you go?" Janet has straightened up sharply at the thought.

"I think so. You know, if anybody ever wished he had a house I'm wishing it now," says Quizz. "A house for you and me."

JANET—There's no use being angry—and no use holding you back, because you just have to go.

QUIZZ—I just have to go. And I think I should. I only wish it came a few days later.

JANET—I won't see you—till after—it's all over.

QUIZZ—I guess not.

JANET—What can I do? How can I live?

QUIZZ—Will you wait for me, Janet?

JANET—I'll have to wait for you.

QUIZZ—Janet?

JANET—Yes?

QUIZZ—Couldn't we be together?

JANET—I—don't know. (*Her breath comes fast.*) I don't know anything about it.— We couldn't—be married?

QUIZZ—There wouldn't be time.

JANET—Suppose—there was a child. And we weren't married. And you never came back.

QUIZZ—I know.

JANET—You see, I don't know about it. What one does, so there won't be a child.

QUIZZ—I don't either.

JANET—Quizz, have you ever—?

QUIZZ—No, darling. You see, somebody told me—the way to be happy—was to wait till you were in love—and I waited.

JANET—Who told you?

QUIZZ—My mother.

JANET—I want to be good to you.

QUIZZ—Kiss me. (*They kiss.*)

JANET—But it couldn't be here.

QUIZZ—Why, darling?

JANET—I don't know this house. It's not ours. No, no—I couldn't.

QUIZZ—There isn't any house for us, darling. I haven't any house.

JANET—But let's go somewhere. Not here. (*The telephone rings in the kitchen—one long ring, two short.*)

Quizz—That's our ring. (*He goes out toward the kitchen. She sits waiting.* Quizz *is heard answering in the kitchen.*) Yes. Yes. Yes, Mrs. Boon. Yes, that's who it is. I see.— Will you say that again?— Before twelve?— Yes, I have it. Thanks. (Quizz *returns.*) There's been some mix-up. I have to be in camp before noon tomorrow. I can just catch the two o'clock train.

Janet—It's one now.

Quizz—Yes. You'll drive me. We'll have to hurry.

Janet—Oh, darling, darling— (*She runs to him.*)

Quizz (*kissing her quickly*)—Start the car, sweet. I'll get my things.

"They go into the kitchen, leaving the bedroom empty and lighted for a moment. The lights dim down quickly, then go out."

The curtain falls.

ACT II

It is October, 1941. We are standing on a pier, facing a gangplank that juts out in front of the curtains. Quizz' outfit is waiting at ease at the foot of the gangplank. Ruby, Marion, Quizz, Tate, Mulveroy, Shevlin and Buscemi are wearing their overseas packs. They can hear a faint roar. That would be "the Pacific Ocean beating at the Golden Gate," according to the poetic Marion. It's the first time Tate has ever been closer to an ocean than Lake Michigan.

Sergt. Ruby is regaling his mates with reminiscences of the last time he crossed this old Pacific. That's the time they were coming home from the Philippines. About a million men came home then, and they all got paid off at once. "Tree years' pay. Boy, was 'at a crap game? On ev'y ruttin' ship dey played till one guy got all da paychecks. All night, ev'y night, dey was playin', under da ruttin' blankets wit' da candles." The sergeant is deeply impressed by the memory.

And when all the ships put into Honolulu, according to Ruby, the winners got together and really "run it up." "Dey was about seven guys an' about seven million dollars in dat Honolulu game and da whole God-damn army was stony broke except dem seven."

"Was gambling allowed back in those days?" asks Tate.

"Soitenly not. It was strictly against da ruttin' regulations, same as now."

Sergt. Kriven is going back on the pier for a couple of minutes. Quizz asks him to mail a letter. "Sure. Gimme the heifer dust," jokes Kriven.

"You know, it sort of sounds like a big ocean," says Tate.

" 'Roll on, thou deep and dark blue ocean, roll!' " quotes Marion.

"Yeah, bo. Da ships rolled an' da ocean rolled, an' da dice rolled. Seven million bucks dem guys got," adds Ruby.

A whistle blows from the ship. "O.K., Sergeant," booms a voice.

"O.K., boys," answers Ruby, and the soldiers begin to climb the gangplank. The curtain falls.

On Deckman West's farm the men are in the fields putting in winter rye. A seeder stands at one side and there are several sacks of seed grain lying around. Nell has brought out the men's lunch. She is sitting with Deck and Cy while they finish their lunch.

Cy is telling them of the Welfare Society's interest in his children. The Society folk are probably going to make legislators out of a couple of the boys, but he won't hold that against them.

Presently Janet comes running across the fields with the mail. There's a letter for Janet from San Francisco. She hasn't had a chance to finish it yet. There are a couple of gun catalogues for Zip, but he's lost interest in guns since you can't buy anything but a twenty-two. That's a popgun.

Deck thinks perhaps Janet had better glance through her letter "and skim those kisses off" before she tries to read it to them, but Janet is willing to let them hear as far as she's got. That much is to all of them—

" 'Tell Mother and Dad and the boys I haven't had time for much writing,' " she reads. " 'We've been on the way from one place to another mostly, or trying to catch some shut-eye. And tell Mother and the others I was sorry not to say good-by or eat that dinner that was in the oven. Several times since I've wished I had a dinner like that handy. It's a good thing I caught the train, though. I'd have been A.W.O.L. otherwise.' "

She pauses now and then to "hurdle the love stuff," as Zip suggests, and then goes on—

JANET—"You remember I told you about Sergeant Ruby? Well, he's not so bad when you get to know him. He's served all over the world, Brooklyn, Haiti and San Diego and the

Philippines, and he talks like all of them. 'Sure ting I had a goil when I went out dere,' he says. 'But when I come back ta goil's married. So what? You're a soldier, so you go get you anoder goil.' Only you've got to wait for me, darling. I don't know how to say it the way I want you to hear it, but you've got to wait for me. (*She stops, reads a little, then goes on.*) Maybe you think it's funny I'd talk about you to the Sergeant, but I couldn't help it. Everybody knows all about everybody else here. Who your girl is and what she looks like and whether you've got more than one. You can't keep anything to yourself. And after a while you don't even try. So they know all about you—and now I'm rather glad they know, because I can talk about you sometimes—and that helps.— Oh, darling, if we'd only had—" (*She stops again, reading on to herself.*)

DECK—All right, sweetheart. I guess the rest's up to you, and we'll let you off now.— Come on, boys, we're wasting farm labor.

NEIL—He gets it on paper. It sounds like Quizz.

ZIP—It makes you realize he's a long way off, though. Doesn't it, Janet?

JANET (*folding her letter*)—Yes.

NEIL—We're going your way with the wagon, Janet, if you want to ride.

JANET—Yes, I'll go with you.

"The men go. Janet runs over to Nell, who takes her hands silently. Janet turns quickly and runs out. Nell puts the dishes in the lunch basket and goes to the house." The curtain falls.

The scene has changed. Before the same curtains empty cartridge cases are scattered about; there is a stack of guns; a few army blankets and miscellaneous equipment. This is a corner of an ammunition dump hollowed out of the rock on a Philippine island. "A cannon booms miles away. From outside come the commands for loading and firing an artillery piece." It is April, 1942.

The voice of Tate can be heard giving directions: "Base deflection, left one zero seven; on number one open seven; number one adjust; six three five zero; corrector five zero; charge V; time two two; number one, one round; three seven zero; fire. (*A howitzer fires near the mouth of the cave.*) Battery adjust; right five. Fire at will."

Under a blanket at one side of the cave Mulveroy is sleeping.

A Filipino girl sits watching him, a water gourd in her hand.
Shevlin and Marion cross the cave, pick up a full cartridge
case and start out with it. Shevlin speaks to the Filipino girl as
they pass her. "How's the big boy?" he asks. "Mabuti," says
she. "Attagirl!" Evidently it's good news. Buscemi and Quizz
come on for more ammunition. They are enthusiastic about the
hits the boys have been making. All three of the gun emplace-
ments they were shooting at have disappeared. But before they
were blasted they sent one shell that got Lieut. Siegel, the field
kitchen, the pharmacist's chest and the pharmacist.

"Ruby's crawling around down there trying to find the quinine
tablets," reports Quizz. "He tastes everything he picks up, and
if it's bitter he puts it in the bottle."

There is a rumbling report from the howitzer at the mouth
of the cave. It awakens Mulveroy. He sits up with a startled
"What's that?" "They fire the gun," the Filipino girl tells him.
Slowly he gathers his senses. How long has he been there?
Three days, she says. "I've been out so far I can't remember
your name. That's the truth," he says. "That's what malaria
does to you. What's your name?"

"You say Pepe."

"That's right. Peppy. What day is it?" She shakes her
head. "No, you wouldn't know." There is another report from
the gun. "Somebody must have been taking my place in the
section.—Listen, Peppy, you been away from your home three
nights now. Your maman will raise hell. You better go home
pronto. Will you go home now? (*She shakes her head.*) I'll
tell you how it is, Peppy. I'm no good for you. (*He sits up
to talk to her.*) You stick around me for a while and nobody'll
marry you—and I won't marry you and you'll be a Goddam
social outcast. So you better go home."

Peppy leans over and lays a hand on his forehead. "Not hot
now. You see?" she says.

"I see what?"

"You see. Not hot."

"We haven't got enough vocabulary in common, kid. No
exchange of ideas. Nothing gets across. (*He lies back.*) All
right, you stay and be my water boy. Everybody's got to give
up something in this war. Your maman is giving you up."

Outside Marion has keeled over with the fever. Ruby carries
him in and they fix blankets for him over near Mulveroy.

"He'll be O.K. Just da malaria," Ruby is saying, as the
others gather around him. "We lost da kitchen, see? Ya gotta

eat ya iron rations. And we lost the pharmacist and da pharmacist supplies, see? And we lost da lieutenant. And on top a dat we all got malaria."

"All but two of us. Quizz and me. We haven't shivered yet," Tate reminds him.

"We all got it, see?" Ruby isn't to be fooled. "Maybe you don't feel it yet, but you all got it, just like Patrick Henry here. And all de quinine's in dis bottle, see? As long as you got quinine you can fight it off, and you can keep going, but you run outa quinine and ya done, see? Now I got da quinine, and da pharmacist's gone, so I give da stuff out. And when I give it out you take it, see? Because if you don't take it ya won't be fit for duty, and if ya ain't fit for duty because ya don't take it dat's malingering."

They've got three days' iron rations, and maybe two days' quinine, Ruby reports. Sergt. Kriven has taken the outrigger to the north island. He may fetch more rations and a nurse back. Or maybe he won't even get there. So, they'd better go easy on the iron rations.

Pepe is trying to get Marion to take his quinine tablets, and a sip of water from the gourd, but it's a hard job. "Hold it for him, girl; he's shaking so much he'll knock his God-damn teeth out," advises Mulveroy.

"You mix your Cuba Libras very bitter, Vision of Delight," sighs the shaking Marion. A moment later his mind wanders back to the gun and he has trouble getting his firing directions right. He is partly delirious when Quizz comes to ask after him.

" 'How cold are thy baths, Apollo,' " murmurs Marion. "I was dreaming. Dull dreams. Classical. I was the young Alexander. Dying, I think. Dying of fever, I think, in the Temple of Serapis. I called for, you know, Roxana, and she came, and said I was to go home. 'Come home,' she said. 'It's not necessary to conquer the world. Besides, you have malaria.' " . . .

Marion is still rambling a little incoherently about his letters when Mulveroy decides that he, too, wants to write a letter. "I want to write to me dear old mither on Delancy Street," says Mul, reverting to his most Irish Irish. "Living there amongst the Polacks and the pushcarts. Sure, it'll gladden the bitter old heart of her to hear from her wandering son. She niver liked me. I was born to her old age, be accident, and me arrival was a shame and a calamity to her from the beginning. But I'll write to her anyway."

There is trouble finding the date for him, but Tate finally gets one from an old New England almanac he has in his kit. "April," reads Tate. "Fourth month. Reset fence-posts. Mulch strawberry beds. This is the twenty-fourth. High tide at eight five in the morning, at eight one at night. Yesterday was St. George's Day. Tomorrow is St. Mark's. This is the Eve of St. Mark. 'Weather, wind, women and fortune change like the moon.' "

"What pertains to the Eve of St. Mark?"

"It's a long story. (*He reads.*) "On St. Mark's Eve, if a virgin stand at the church door at dusk she will see entering the church all those of the parish who are to die that year. If her lover should enter among the others he will turn and look at her, may perhaps speak."

"Has to be a virgin or she won't see anything?" This from Mulveroy.

"That's right."

"The legend has naturally fallen into disrepute," observes Marion.

There's an argument now as to where they are. "There's a nest of small rocky islands east of Tawi," says Tate. "We're on one of them. I'm damned if I know which one, and I doubt if it makes much difference."

Wherever they are, writing letters, to Shevlin, is a waste of time. They'll never get anywhere. Who's going to take them? Neither Tate nor Quizz knows, but someone might. A boat got through yesterday. There might be another tomorrow. "I still don't think the postman is going to come around," persists Shevlin.

Marion is having another spell with his visions. His fever has shot up to a hundred and six, Quizz reports. Everybody better get ready to hold him down. "Quizz, will they laugh at me if I talk to her?" whispers Marion . . . "Because she's here. This is the ends of the earth and she followed me here." He has raised up and is staring dully at the others. "They're all ghostly, like shadows from a fire flickering on the ceiling," he says. "And you're a ghost—and Pepe. But the Wraith's as cool and clear as an April morning. Lady sweet, you've been la belle dame sans merci so long, I don't know how to welcome you. She's not really here, Quizz. She smiles at me, but she says nothing. It's just the fever that makes my eyes think they see her."

"She's as real as I am, boy. As real as any of us," says Quizz.

A moment later there is a thunder of airplanes overhead. They're the Japs looking for the howitzer, Quizz thinks. Now there is the explosion of a bomb some distance away. Quizz is up and out of the cave before they can stop him. He's quickly back. "They didn't get the gun, but they certainly got the path," he reports. "Laid one right in the middle of it. There's a hole thirty feet deep.—Kriven's in with the boat. They must have just missed him."

Kriven has brought more quinine, and that's good. "Also I got about a quarter cord of stinkin' dried fish, and that's all. . . . And the C.O. says we can get the hell out of here any time," he adds.

"What's that?" Shevlin and Mulveroy are all excitement. "You talked to the C.O.?" demands Buscemi.

"That's right. And he says we can get the hell out of this island any time."

They're all on their feet now, milling around, slapping each other on the back. "Well, by God!" shouts Mulveroy. "Lord love the C.O.! May he live forever!" adds a revived Marion.

"And the C.O. gives me a letter for Lieut. Siegel," Kriven is saying.

"He was killed this morning, Sergeant."

KRIVEN—Yeah? Jeez! Well, da letter's got instructions in it, so I better give it to Ruby. (*He fishes out a note, then pauses.*) Dere was two men coming down ta path when I came in wit ta outrigger. Dat Jap bomb got bot of dem. Is everybody here but Ruby and Tate?

SHEVLIN—That's right.

KRIVEN—Den dat bomb got dem. (QUIZZ *starts out.*) You won't find anyting. Just nuttin'. (MULVEROY *crosses himself.* QUIZZ *remains.* KRIVEN *gives him the note.*) You read it out loud. I ain't no ruttin' Harvard man.

QUIZZ (*reading*)—"Dear Siegel: Considering your reported scarcity of food, quinine and ammunition it appears necessary to evacuate H 23 moving all remaining personnel to H 25, the nearest base where hospitalization is available. The Japs are moving in, and it will not be possible to hold any of this group permanently while Tawi is in their hands. This is not an order, however. Your defense of H 23 and your destruction of batteries and shipping have slowed the enemy considerably. Every day you can hold your position is an incalculable gain. Just for the record let me say that your gunnery has set a high standard, and we're all proud of you. We've seen some of your shells land. If you have to fall back don't think for a moment you haven't done yourselves proud. G. Solway, C.O. H Sector."

KRIVEN—I don't know wot to hell 'at means, but you better get ya duffle ready so we can start before da sun comes up.

SHEVLIN—Yes, sir. (*They begin to pack up. Nobody speaks for a moment.*)

QUIZZ—You think we ought to go?

KRIVEN—What do you tink?

QUIZZ—I don't know.

KRIVEN—Look, when ya in a army ya don't have to make it tough for yaself. You can leave dat to da C.O. and da Japs.

SHEVLIN—We had it tough enough, buddy.

KRIVEN—You tink we ought ta stay here?

QUIZZ—I don't know.

KRIVEN—Listen. Dere was tirty-two men on dis island besides Gooks. Now we down to what's here. Some of us sick and da rest of us going to be sick. Maybe we get off a' here tonight, but if we don't go tonight maybe we never get off here. Da C.O. says dese islands can't be held. He says go ahead an' evacuate. And you want ta stay.

QUIZZ—No. I want to go home. More than I ever wanted anything in this world. More than I'll ever want anything again. But I don't want to—run out.

MULVEROY—He says, "If you have to fall back don't think you didn't do yourselves proud."

QUIZZ—I know.

BUSCEMI—Then for God's sake what's eating you?

MARION—How close does a man have to come to being horizontal before he's earned the right to remain perpendicular?

SHEVLIN—We've come close enough.

QUIZZ—It sounded to me as if he was pleading with us—to hold on. If we possibly could.

MARION—There are tens of millions back home who have hardly been touched at all, tens of millions who have risked almost nothing.

QUIZZ—I know. But they aren't here. And we are.

KRIVEN—Listen, if you guys want to stick on dis rock we stick, see?

MULVEROY—Mother of God! I thought we was out of here!

QUIZZ—I'm not deciding it.

MULVEROY—You started it, farmer! Nobody else started it! And now we got to think about it!

QUIZZ—I'll shut up. (*He gets his letter, and sits down.*)

MULVEROY—Maybe we ought to stay, at that. The C.O.'s staying on his ruttin' rock.

SHEVLIN—Damn it, now you're saying it!
MULVEROY—I'll shut up.

He picks up his letter. There is a general silence as the curtain falls.

At curtain rise the head of Nell West's bed is seen in a circle of light. Nell is asleep. From out the darkness Quizz' voice is heard calling her. "Mother!" . . . "Mother!" She stirs restlessly, then sits up in bed, muttering: "No, it couldn't be!"

"Mother—I haven't much time," Quizz is saying. "I want to ask you something." The light faintly outlines his face now. "Mother, I've come to a place—"

"Yes?"

"Mother, I've come to a place where we have to choose. It's a question whether we'll let ourselves be driven back—or hang on here. But if we do hang on—I doubt if we'll all live. I doubt if any of us will. And, Mother, in the night, one wonders what to do. So I've come to you."

"Isn't there some way—to do what you must—and still come home?"

"Yes. We're not ordered to stay here. It's only—that we're needed, and we know it. And this is what troubles me most. I'm in love, Mother. I'm so much in love it's a pain to be away. Every mile away from her was a hurt in my side. And we've never been together. I've never made her mine."

"I know."

"Oh, Mother, I've never taken any woman, because you said I should keep myself pure for my love. So I kept myself for her—and now—if I'm true to myself—it's too late.— Oh, Mother, sometimes it seems it's better to stay alive, no matter what guilt you feel—if only you can take your love in your arms again—and lie on her breast—and live. Live a little at least before you die."

"Oh, my son, does it matter about giving up one place to the enemy? It won't matter as much as your lives. It's better to live. If you live now you can fight them again. And we'll see you. We'll see you here again."

"Should I choose to come home, Mother? Oh, don't make it easy for me."

"Must you choose? Doesn't someone choose for you?"

"It seems they'll do as I say. They'll go as I go."

"Oh, Quizz! It doesn't matter about the other things! Only come home!"

"There's no one. Oh, God, I'm here alone!"

The light dims on his face and goes out. The curtain falls.

Again the scene is dark, save for a ring of light thrown upon Janet, asleep. Again from the darkness comes the voice of Quizz, calling her. Janet is still asleep when she answers, but soon she, too, awakes and sits upright, startled to see Quizz' face faintly in a shaded light.

"Then it's true," Janet is saying, tremulously. "You've come home! Oh, darling, please never leave me again!"

QUIZZ—I must ask you something.
        Sweet, we had no house. No place and no time,
        and it seems to me I'm only a ghost forever
        if I should die and you've never been mine in the
            night,
        as if I'd never lived, and left no record—
        no son and no name—and another must take my love,
        my lost uncompleted love.
JANET—Oh, darling, I'm yours
        or never never anyone's.
QUIZZ—The earth
        won't have it that way—the dark old plodding earth
        says if you're dead you're dead, and a living girl
        must mate among the living. So if I die now
        I give you to another, and I know that—
JANET—No, Quizz, never—and you mustn't die!
        What makes you speak of dying?
QUIZZ—It's noon on this rock
        and torrid hot, and six of us who are left
        sit in the cave to vote, do we go or stay,
        do we make a try for H 25 and home
        or man a gun while we can, fire a few shells,
        sink the invasion barges, never let them in
        till they've paid the last death. And when they come
            in be then
        the threshold, lie there with this foreign earth;
        never with those we love.
JANET—Who asks this of you?
        They shouldn't ask it!
QUIZZ—Nobody asks it, dear.

It's something in myself I don't understand
that seems to require it of me. It seems to be
the best of me—the same inner self that turned
to love you and love no one else, that says
give more than is asked of you, be such a man
as she you love could honor at a secret altar
knowing all you've thought and done. But as for orders
we have none now. We're free to go back or stay
save for what's in our minds. And so it seemed
I must talk with you—for you're at the heart of me—
either way it's for you what choice I make—
and I thought it might all come clear if I saw your face
and heard you speak.

JANET—But you say such terrible things—
that I'd love someone else if you were gone—

QUIZZ—Oh, darling,
because I must see what's true and then decide—
because I must look at our dark old plodding earth
the way she is, and then do what I must.
Please, help me see truly!

JANET—Oh, Quizz, come home!
And, oh, forgive me, please forgive me now
for knowing so little when you went away,
for letting you leave me, mine and yet not mine—
for I didn't know—but the empty days and nights
have taught me now how if you've missed your love
there's nothing to put in its place.
So you must come home.
Oh, come and find me. Don't leave me empty here.
What could you win worth losing what could be ours?—
What could you win?

QUIZZ—Seeing you there in your bed
where I've never lain, it seems that I'd give all heaven
and all the earth, and all men ever had,
to put my arms round you once. You're more beautiful even
than I remembered.

JANET—Only for you. Never for anyone else.
Please come home to me here. If you should die
I think I'd die too. And I don't know what to say.
I say the wrong things. But I love you more than
you know—
more than there's any word for.

QUIZZ—Darling, it doesn't matter,
    anything you say—it's there in your eyes—
    all I wanted to know—and it's here in mine—
    all I could tell you—
JANET—Yes—
QUIZZ—And now I must go—
JANET—Oh, please—
QUIZZ—Yes, I must.
    It's high noon here on the island,
    and things to do, and voices calling. And so
    God keep you.
JANET—Oh, my darling!—He was here.
    He was here, and he's gone.

The curtain falls.

We are back on the island. Mulveroy and Marion are sitting up, cleaning their guns. Buscemi has come running in looking for Quizz to report a line of barges being towed into the inlet on the west island. Quizz has been counting cartridges deeper in the cave. He comes out now and he and Buscemi go in search of Sergt. Kriven.

With an effort Mulveroy and Marion are able to pull themselves to their feet. "According to my draft board if a man can stand up and see lightning and hear thunder, he can fight," says Marion. . . .

Quizz is back with Sergt. Kriven. "If we wait until they begin to come out through the narrows we ought to be able to sink them one at a time," says Quizz. "It's a perfect shot for the howitzer."

"O.K., boy, you take over," answers Kriven, throwing off his helmet. "My eyes ain't good enough. I can't see 'em wit ta glasses, even."

He sees the wabbling Mulveroy and Marion, and orders them back to their blankets, but he takes back the order when they don't want to go.

Shevlin has come in. "What are we going to do?" he wants to know.

"We're going to make holes in the bottoms of those barges, as fast as they come out," says Quizz.

"We're going to try to hold the island?"

"Wasn't that what we decided last night?"

"We didn't decide anything last night. We just sat around.

Then it looked like it was too late to do anything. But we could still get out of here, you know. We could take the outrigger and cross to H 25 before those barges were anywhere near here."

"Dat's right. Dat's a trut'."

"What do you want to do?"

"Why don't we take a vote on it?"

"All right," agrees Quizz. "Let's do that. Let's vote on whether we stay on the island one more day. Tomorrow we can take another vote if we feel like it."

"If we're still here."

"Right. If we're still here. Then if there's ever any question what happened—it was a vote. Who's got a pencil?"

Marion makes a little speech of considered protest, beginning: "Gentlemen, I find that my natural cynicism is not decreased by tropical malaria and short rations," and ending with: "Who the hell picked us out to save the world, anyway? And are we perfectly sure it's worth the effort? And what's the good of saving the whole world if you happen to die in the process? But I vote to try it another day."

"What?" demands Buscemi.

MARION—I vote to try it another day, and probably another day after that.

BUSCEMI—Why in hell do you do that?

MARION—Because man is not a reasonable creature. Because I'm essentially a fool like those rutting ancestors of mine.— And, you know, I want to sink those God damn Jap boats. I want to sink all of them. I only hope you have more sense than I have. Here's my vote. (*He writes it, places it in a helmet. Quizz passes the helmet around. They all vote silently.*)

QUIZZ—Shall I count them?

KRIVEN—Go ahead.

QUIZZ (*looking at the six votes*)—There's something wrong here. Everybody votes aye. Everybody votes to stay.

SHEVLIN—What's the matter with that?

QUIZZ—You voted to stay?

SHEVLIN—Sure I voted to stay.

QUIZZ—Attaboy. (*A bomber is heard outside. Then a crash. Quizz looks out.*) They missed the gun. They just can't seem to locate that gun. And there's a string of barges coming toward the point. It's our move.

KRIVEN—Positions! (*They all run out. Kriven is heard outside giving commands.*) Aiming point—dat first boat. You take it, Quizz. I can't see ta damn ting!

Quizz (*outside*)—Target, that first boat, deflection one zero, fire as the boats come out! Fire!

The howitzer is heard. Once, twice, three times as the curtain falls.

In the kitchen of Deck West's farm there is a small radio on the table. Deck and Nell are listening:

"It is quite possible that the Philippines have not been entirely abandoned by American forces," a commentator is saying. "In those numberless islands there are many natural fastnesses, well equipped for defense, difficult to attack. Mopping-up operations may take many months—and may never be completed. How many American soldiers still hold out in that wilderness of atolls and volcanic peaks is, of course, a military secret, but even if it were not, there is nobody either in Washington or elsewhere who knows all the facts as of today."

Nell has switched it off. "I guess we can do without the rest," she says. "He doesn't know any more than we do, and he admits it."

There are two extra plates on the table. They look mighty good to Nell. Neil and Zip are coming on the afternoon train. Deck thinks perhaps he had better go over and try to meet the train, but Nell is afraid he might miss the boys if he did.

A moment later Deck is at the window. He sees Pete Feller dropping Janet at the gate. She has run into the house now, excitement in her greeting. There's a letter from Quizz. Good news? Janet doesn't know. "I've only just looked inside. I didn't dare read it alone. It came in an army envelope, and there's a note from his captain—but there's a letter from Quizz too."

She has taken out the letters and holds them a second before she begins to read: "Dear Miss Feller. You have of course been notified that Private West is listed as missing. H 23, the island on which he was stationed, was captured by the Japanese about two months ago. It is impossible to report definitely concerning our men who were on the island, but it is supposed that some are prisoners. They acted with extraordinary courage and effectiveness and we hope they all turn up later to receive the medals they have coming to them. I am writing you now to enclose some fragments of a letter delivered to me, along with other messages and letters, by a Filipino girl who escaped from H 23 in an outrigger canoe. I have only recently reached a point within our own lines where I could sort the papers and mail them. Unfortunately only a few pages of your letter reached me. Sincerely yours, Captain G. Solvay."

"Then here are the pieces of his letter," Janet goes on. " 'April 29th. Dear, I haven't written you for two days. It seems I had malaria pretty bad and didn't know what was going on. Today I'm a little shaky but I'm up. Sergeant Kriven died in the night, and I'm the only excuse for an officer there is around here. The Japs are certainly determined to blow us out of this place. This gun of ours covers the north and south channel through the islands and we're holding up a lot . . .' "

"That's all of that page—and then, there's one more little piece: 'Some nights I try to think myself clear out of this place, and round the world to you, and once or twice I seemed to be there in your room, but I'm never sure I found you. And now I can only say, all my love, Quizz.' "

That's all. They are silent for a moment. Then Deck declares himself. He's going to think that Quizz is alive and well, and will come through. And he knows what he is going to do—he's going to enlist.

"Maybe we're more good here on the farm, Deck, both of us," Nell suggests quietly. . . . It's better to keep on with the same things. You're doing better here than you could in any armed service."

Deck has gone back to his work. Janet stays on to help Nell. They talk of Quizz as they clean up the dishes. "Did you ever have a feeling he was near you in the night?" asks Janet.

"Yes, more than once."

JANET—I suppose one imagines.—But that's why I think I won't see him again. It's—as if he told me. They made a decision that meant they wouldn't come home.

NELL—A decision?

JANET—Yes.

NELL—Could it be that we have the same dreams?

JANET—Did you have it too?

NELL—Wait.—It's shadowy now, the way dreams are in the daytime. But for a moment.—No, it's gone.

JANET—I suppose it was dreams. But the last time it was so real I could have touched him—so real I can remember words he said.

NELL—What did he say?

JANET—He said, "Those who love you can't tell you what you must do. They can only say, Save yourself. If they love you they can't say anything else. But the soldier, there with his comrades, and with the enemy in front of him, he must decide for himself." That's why I think he won't come home.

NELL—Janet, darling, you've been carrying this with you, all these weeks!

JANET—But something happened between us that last night—that gave me a way to live. He said, "Don't think it's all loss. There's a kind of glory between us we couldn't have had. We eat our iron rations at a secret altar." It's as if it was our marriage.

NELL—He must have loved you terribly, for his words reach you clear round the earth.

JANET—I love him terribly. But—if they'd left the island they'd have been defeated—in their own hearts—and when they stayed there—that was a victory. I wouldn't want him to be defeated. We can't decide for them because we love them.

NELL—He's yours now forever, darling. He was mine for a little while, but you'll have him always, even if he doesn't come back.

Deck is back. His brother Ralph is with him. If they don't mind, he'd like to turn on the radio again.

"Have you noticed that our soldiers almost never talk about the war, almost never discuss our reasons for fighting," the commentator is saying. "I've noticed it. And have you wondered why? I think I know. This is the first war in history where there's no possible argument about who's right and who's wrong. We're fighting for our lives and fighting to keep men free. You can't argue about that. You don't need any oratory to convince people, nor songs to keep up their spirits in such a war. And so it's a war without oratory and without songs—because we know very well what we're doing."

Cy has appeared at the door. He seems a little flustered. He had just seen Zip get out of the car at the corners. There was a soldier with him. A soldier that looked a lot like Quizz—

Deck has jumped up from the radio and turned to the door, just as Neil comes in, wearing a uniform, followed by Zip.

"What's this mean?" demands Deck, huskily.

"It's mine, Dad," says Neil.

DECK—No wonder he said you looked like—

NELL—Oh, Neil, Neil!

NEIL—I know I should have said something first, but I was afraid you'd say no.

DECK—I guess we would have.

NELL—Oh, Neil! You could have waited till later. Till you were called.

NEIL—No, I couldn't, Mother.

ZIP—And I can't either.

NELL—You, Zip. What do you mean?

ZIP—They wouldn't take Neil in the air force because of his eyes. So he joined the artillery. But they'll take me.

DECK—You signed up for a pilot?

ZIP—I have to get your permission.

NELL—If it had come a little later. Today—Janet has a letter from Quizz. We don't know whether he'll come back. It's a sort of a last letter—

NEIL—That's why we had to go, Mother. That's why we couldn't wait. Because of Quizz. It's what Quizz would want us to do.

DECK—How do you know that?

NEIL—I don't know. But it's as if I could hear him saying it. We couldn't stay here on the farm, and know he'd left something unfinished out there. We had to take it up—and carry it on.

ZIP—I'm the age they want, Mother. For the air force. And if I'm old enough to fight, I'm old enough to make up my mind.

NEIL—As a matter of fact I haven't been at the U. for a couple of months. Zip's been kind of covering for me. I didn't write because it seemed better to talk about it, Mother.

NELL—Yes.

NEIL—And, Dad, it seemed wrong, when there was only one important thing to do in the world, to look the other way and let somebody else do it. I know you thought I was coming back to the farm, and I know they need farm workers, but—tell the truth I want to get out there where the fighting's going on. Suppose they make the world over, more the way it ought to be, and everybody has a better chance—well, I want to pay for my ticket.

DECK—I suppose it might turn out better.

NEIL—Anyway, if it isn't I don't want it to be my fault.

ZIP—That's right.

DECK—Mother, what can we do with these two? What can we do?

NELL—What can we do, Janet?

JANET—I guess Quizz would say—we had to let them go.

DECK—Maybe I'm just holding back from being old, but they look mighty young to me. I'd rather go myself.

RALPH—The army don't want us any more, Deck. I tried it.

DECK—You tried it?

RALPH—I went down and tried to enlist. But they want these young fellows. They're the men of the house now. They're the fighting men.

NELL (*going over to* DECK)—And it's true we can't hold them back because we love them. Every man has to follow his own vision. That's the way new worlds are made.

DECK—All right, boys. You go out and make things over your way. We old folks, we'll stay here, damn it, and milk the cows and run the baler. (NEIL *and* ZIP *cross to kiss* NELL.) Make a new world, boys. God knows we need it.

THE CURTAIN FALLS

THE SKIN OF OUR TEETH

A Fantastic Comedy in Three Acts

By Thornton Wilder

THE production of Thornton Wilder's "The Skin of Our Teeth" provided another of those fabulous stories of the theatre that will long be quoted by historians and statisticians. Written in 1940-41, the manuscript was first acquired by Jed Harris, who had produced Mr. Wilder's "Our Town." It was rejected by Mr. Harris after a struggle. Early in 1942 the play went to Michael Meyerberg, an operatic impresario, and Mr. Meyerberg started on a still hunt for fellow backers. During the next few months "The Skin of Our Teeth" was read and rejected for a vast variety of reasons, all of them sounding quite sane at the time, by no less than thirty-seven different prospects, ranging from novices to experts, from speculators to the wisest of investors.

By the date of its first production in New Haven in October, 1942, Mr. Meyerberg had disposed of 20 per cent of his investment, making up the balance himself. After "The Skin of Our Teeth" had both mystified and charmed audiences in New Haven, Baltimore, Philadelphia and Washington, another 10 per cent was disposed of. The morning following the New York opening Mr. Meyerberg could probably have sold the 70 per cent interest he had retained in the play for a great deal of money.

Incidentally, among those with a lasting faith in this most extravagant of fantasies was Fredric March, the actor, who not only acquired a 5 per cent interest, but, by the record, gave up $200,000 in motion picture contracts so that he and Mrs. March (Florence Eldridge) could play the leading roles.

So much for the financial romance. "The Skin of Our Teeth" was produced November 18, 1942, in New York and was something of an overnight sensation. There were modest reservations by the critics, and the sight of bewildered and discouraged, if not disgusted, patrons walking out at the first intermission and not returning to their seats was not uncommon. The public's endorsement, whetted by its curiosity, continued to create a generous attendance through the season.

"What he [Mr. Wilder] is trying to say is by no means new," wrote John Anderson in the *Journal-American*, "but it is eternally
105

pertinent, since it is forever remembered, and always forgotten. It is the fact that humanity is as indestructible as its hopes, that from the glacial age up to right now, from the invention of the wheel to the perfection of high altitude bombing, man is forever improving himself and eternally falling in ruins, forever building and tearing down, but that somehow, through hell, high water, and, as the playbill says 'double feature movies,' he manages to survive."

A projection screen appears in the center of the curtain as we, as spectators, start wondering about "The Skin of Our Teeth." On the screen the legend, "News Events of the World" is shown. Shortly the voice of an announcer is heard explaining the slides. The first is of a slightly lopsided sun appearing above an irregular horizon. "Freeport, Long Island," announces the announcer. "The sun rose this morning at 6.32 A.M. This gratifying event was reported by Mrs. Dorothy Stetson of Freeport, L. I., who promptly telephoned the Mayor. The Society for Affirming the End of the World at once went into a special session and postponed the arrival of that event for twenty-four hours. All honor to Mrs. Stetson for her public spirit."

The next slide is a view of the front door of the theatre and of three cleaning women—the Mesdames Simpson, Pateslewski and Moriarity—who, as the announcer explains, frequently find lost objects in the theatre. Recently one of them picked up a wedding ring, inscribed: "To Eva from Adam. Genesis 2-18." The ring will be restored to the owner or owners, promises the announcer, if their credentials are satisfactory.

There is a slide of a glacier resting lightly on Tippehatchee, Vt., and a report of the unprecedented cold weather in that neighborhood. According to rumor a solid wall of ice is moving across the northern countries, but the report that it has already pushed the Cathedral of Montreal as far as St. Albans, Vt., is given little credence. However, the disruption of communications has rendered exact information difficult.

In an Excelsior, N. J., view our attention is drawn to the modest suburban home of Mr. George Antrobus, the inventor of the wheel. The wheel has followed closely upon Mr. Antrobus' discovery of the lever and thus has focused the attention of the country upon him. "This is his home," the announcer is saying; "a commodious seven-room house, conveniently situated near a public school, a Methodist Church, and a firehouse; it is right handy to an A & P."

There is a slide of Mr. Antrobus himself standing on his front steps, smiling and lifting his straw hat. "He comes of very old stock and has made his way up from next to nothing. It is reported that he was once a gardener, but left that situation under circumstances that have been variously reported. Mr. Antrobus is a veteran of foreign wars, and bears a number of scars, front and back."

Now we have a slide of Mrs. Antrobus, "the charming and gracious president of the Excelsior Mothers' Club. Mrs. Antrobus is an excellent needlewoman; it is she who invented the apron on which so many interesting changes have been wrung since that time. Here we see the Antrobuses with their two children, Henry and Gladys, and friend. The friend in the rear is Lily Sabina, the maid. I know we all want to congratulate this typical American family on its enterprise. We all wish Mr. Antrobus a successful future. Now the management takes you to the interior of this home for a brief visit."

The curtain rises and the somewhat disordered living room of a commuter's home is revealed. Sabina, "straw-blonde, over-rouged," is standing by a back window, a feather duster under her elbow. The room is ceilingless and the walls seem none too secure.

"Oh, oh, oh!" wails Sabina. "Six o'clock and the master not home yet. Pray God nothing serious has happened to him crossing the Hudson River. If anything happened to him, we would certainly be inconsolable and have to move into a less desirable residence district. The fact is I don't know what'll become of us. Here it is the middle of August and the coldest day of the year. It's simply freezing; the dogs are sticking to the sidewalks; can anybody explain that? No. But I'm not surprised. The whole world's at sixes and sevens, and why the house hasn't fallen down about our ears long ago is a miracle to me."

At that moment a fragment of the left wall does lean precariously over the stage, but gradually rights itself as Sabina regards it nervously. "Every night this same anxiety as to whether the master will get home safely," Sabina goes on; "whether he'll bring home anything to eat. In the midst of life we are in the midst of death, a truer word was never said."

This time the doubtful fragment of scenery does fly up into the loft. Sabina is "struck dumb with surprise," but only for an instant. With a shrug of her shoulders she goes on with her story—

"Of course, Mr. Antrobus is a very fine man, an excellent husband and father, a pillar of the church, and has all the best interests of the community at heart. Every muscle goes tight every time he passes a policeman; but what I think is that there are certain charges that ought not to be made, and I think I may add, ought not to be allowed to be made; we're all human; who isn't? Mrs. Antrobus is as fine a woman as you could hope to see. She lives only for her children; and if it would be any benefit to her children she'd see the rest of us stretched out dead at her feet without turning a hair—that's the truth. If you want to know anything more about Mrs. Antrobus, just go and look at a tigress, and look hard. As to the children— Well, Henry Antrobus is a real, clean-cut American boy. He'll graduate from High School one of these days, if they make the alphabet any easier—Henry, when he has a stone in his hand, has a perfect aim; he can hit anything from a bird to an older brother— Oh! I didn't mean to say that!—but it certainly was an unfortunate accident, and it was very hard getting the Police out of the house. Mr. and Mrs. Antrobus' daughter is named Gladys. She'll make some good man a good wife some day, if he'll just come down off the movie screen and ask her. So here we are! We've managed to survive for some time now, catch as catch can, the fat and the lean, and if the dinosaurs don't trample us to death, and if the grasshoppers don't eat up our garden, we'll all live to see better days, knock on wood."

Sabina is not too pessimistic. After all they have rattled along, hot and cold, for some time now. "Enjoy your ice cream while it is on your plate, that's my philosophy," says Sabina. "Don't forget that a few years ago we came through the depression by the skin of our teeth! One more tight squeeze like that and where will we be?"

She is looking angrily at the kitchen door now. ". . . where will we be" is the cue line, but there is no response. Sabina goes back and repeats the speech. Still no one appears to carry on. Flustered and a little mad, Sabina goes back to the window and starts the act all over—"Oh, oh, oh! Six o'clock and the master not home yet. . . ."

She skips to the cue line and repeats that. This time the hoarse whisper of a prompter is heard from the wings. "Make up something! Invent something!" Sabina tries. "Well . . . uh . . . this certainly is a fine American home . . . and . . . uh . . . everybody's very happy . . . and—uh . . ."

But she cannot go on. Now she has flung pretense to the winds and come defiantly to the footlights.

"I can't invent any words for this play, and I'm glad I can't," she announces, leaning toward the audience. "I hate this play and every word in it. As for me, I don't understand a single word of it, anyway,—all about the troubles the human race has gone through, there's a subject for you. Besides the author hasn't made up his silly mind as to whether we're all living back in caves or in New Jersey, and that's the way it is all the way through. Oh—why can't we have plays like we used to have— *Rain—Peg o' My Heart,* and *Smilin' Thru,* and *The Bat,* good entertainment with a message you can take home with you?"

"I took this hateful job because I had to. For two years I've sat up in my room living on a sandwich and a cup of tea a day, waiting for better times in the theatre. And look at me now: I—I who've played "Rain" and "The Barretts of Wimpole Street" and "First Lady"—

The stage manager has stuck his head through a hole in the scenery. "Miss Somerset!" he calls. Sabina doesn't appear to hear, but presently she has picked up her cue line again—

"We came through the depression by the skin of our teeth,— that's true!—one more tight squeeze like that and where will we be?"

This time Mrs. Antrobus gets the cue. Striding in from the kitchen Mrs. A—"a majestic matron"—faces her angry servant—

"Sabina, you've let the fire go out," she says sternly. Sabina continues to mumble. "You've let the fire go out. Here it is the coldest day of the year right in the middle of August, and you've let the fire go out."

SABINA—Mrs. Antrobus, I'd like to give my two weeks' notice, Mrs. Antrobus. A girl like I can get a situation in a home where they're rich enough to have a fire in every room, Mrs. Antrobus, and a girl don't have to carry the responsibility of the whole house on her two shoulders. And a home without children, Mrs. Antrobus, because children are a thing only a parent can stand, and a truer word was never said; and a home, Mrs. Antrobus, where the master of the house doesn't pinch decent, self-respecting girls when he meets them in a dark corridor. I mention no names and make no charges. So you have my notice, Mrs. Antrobus. I hope that's perfectly clear.

MRS. ANTROBUS—You've let the fire go out!—Have you milked the mammoth?

SABINA—I don't understand a word of this play.—Yes, I've milked the mammoth.

MRS. ANTROBUS—Until Mr. Antrobus comes home we have

no food and we have no fire. You'd better go over to the neighbors and borrow some fire.

SABINA—Mrs. Antrobus! I can't! I'd die on the way, you know I would. It's worse than January. The dogs are sticking to the sidewalks. I'd die.

MRS. ANTROBUS—Very well, I'll go.

SABINA (*barring the front door, then sinking on her knees*)— You'll never come back alive; we'd all perish; if you weren't here we'd just perish. How do we know Mr. Antrobus'll be back? We don't know. If you go out, I'll just kill myself.

MRS. ANTROBUS—Get up, Sabina.

SABINA—Every night it's the same thing. Will he come back safe, or won't he? Will we starve to death, or freeze to death, or boil to death or will we be killed by burglars? I don't know why we go on living. I don't know why we go on living at all. It's easier being dead.

Sabina has flung her arms on the table and buried her head in them. Mrs. Antrobus is not to be fooled by such actions. She knows Sabina—always throwing up the sponge. But give her a new hat, or a plate of ice cream, or a ticket to the movies and she wants to live forever.

Sabina thinks she knows Mrs. Antrobus, too. What does she (Mrs. A) care about the rest of them? Nothing. Only her children. They are all she's interested in. Does she understand Mr. Antrobus? She does not! All that work he does, trying to discover the alphabet and the multiplication table— "Whenever he tries to learn anything you fight against it," charges Sabina. But Mrs. Antrobus has an answer for that, too—

MRS. ANTROBUS—Oh, Sabina, I know you. When Mr. Antrobus raped you home from your Sabina hills, he did it to insult me. He did it for your pretty face, and to insult me. You were his new wife, weren't you? For a year or two you lay on your bed all day and polished the nails on your hands and feet: You made puff-balls of the combings of your hair and you blew them up to the ceiling. And I washed your underclothes and I made you chicken broths. I bore children and between my very groans I stirred the cream that you'd put on your face. But I knew you wouldn't last. You didn't last.

SABINA—But it was I who encouraged Mr. Antrobus to make the alphabet. I'm sorry to say it, Mrs. Antrobus, but you're not a beautiful woman, and you can never know what a man could do if he tried. It's girls like I who inspired the multiplication table. I'm sorry to say it, but you're not a beautiful woman, Mrs. Antrobus, and that's the God's truth.

MRS. ANTROBUS—And you didn't last—you sank to the kitchen. And what do you do there? *You let the fire go out!* No wonder to you it seems easier being dead. Reading and writing and counting on your fingers is all very well in their way— but I keep the home going.

With this last shot Mrs. Antrobus goes to the window to shoo a baby dinosaur off the front lawn. If the animals insist on hanging around the house, let them go around back, where they belong.

When Mrs. Antrobus calmly leaves the room, Sabina raises her head and again confides in the audience. "Now that you audience are listening to this, too, I understand it a little better," she says. And adds with a sigh: "I wish eleven o'clock were here; I don't want to be dragged through this whole play again."

Now there is great excitement. Out the window Sabina spies a strange man coming down the road. With a wild shriek for help she gets Mrs. Antrobus back and the two of them begin hurriedly to barricade the front door with furniture. Presently Mrs. Antrobus recognizes the voice. It is the Telegraph Boy. He has brought a message from Mr. Antrobus in the city. When they let him in, a Dinosaur and a small Mammoth sneak in with him and make themselves comfortable.

The Telegraph Boy is full of news; at least he has heard that there's a wall of ice moving down from the North. "We can't get Boston by telegraph, and they're burning pianos in Hartford. It . . . it moves everything in front of it, churches and post offices and city halls. I live in Brooklyn myself."

Finally he gets around to the telegram, which he has some little difficulty remembering. "This telegram was flashed from Murray Hill to University Heights! And then by puffs of smoke from University Heights to Staten Island. And then from Staten Island to Plainfield, New Jersey. What hath God wrought," he marvels.

TELEGRAPH BOY (*clearing his throat*)—"To Mrs. Antrobus, Excelsior, New Jersey: My dear wife, will be an hour late. Busy day at office. Don't worry the children about the cold just keep them warm burn everything except Shakespeare."

MRS. ANTROBUS—Men! Men! He knows I'd burn ten Shakespeares to prevent a child of mine from having one cold in the head. What does it say next?

TELEGRAPH BOY—"Have made great discoveries today have separated em from en."

SABINA—I know what that is, that's the alphabet, yes, it is. Mr. Antrobus is just the cleverest man. Why, when the alphabet's finished, we'll be able to tell the future and everything.

TELEGRAPH BOY—Then listen to this: "Ten tens make a hundred semicolon consequences far-reaching." (*Watches for effect.*)

MRS. ANTROBUS—The earth's turning to ice, and all he can do is to make up new numbers.

TELEGRAPH BOY—Well, Mrs. Antrobus, like the head man at our office said: a few more discoveries like that and we'll be worth freezing.

There is more of the telegram, but the Telegraph Boy finds it a little difficult to deliver it. He clears his throat again and begins to sing: "Happy w'dding anniversary to you, Happy w'dding anniversary to you—"

The animals begin to howl and Sabina screams with pleasure. It is too much for Mrs. Antrobus. If they've taken to singing telegrams she thinks the world is getting so silly it is no wonder the sun turns cold.

There is nothing in the house with which Mrs. Antrobus can tip the Telegraph Boy, but she generously gives him one of her two needles. That is the one thing his wife wants most.

At the door Mrs. Antrobus calls to her children, Henry and Gladys. They are to come in and get warm. But, first, Henry is to put down the stone he is threatening to throw at something or someone. Henry should remember what happened last time. And Gladys—Gladys should put down her dress and try to be a lady. The children rush in and begin throwing their things in a heap on the floor. "Mama, I'm hungry. Mama, why is it so cold?" "Mama, why doesn't it snow?"

"Settle down, both of you. I want to talk to you." The children pile up at her feet, leaning against her lap. "It's just a cold spell of some kind. Now, listen to what I'm saying: When your father comes home I want you to be extra quiet. He's had a hard day at the office and I don't know but what he may have one of his moods. I just got a telegram from him very happy and excited, and you know what that means. Your father's temper's uneven; I guess you know that. (*Shriek.*) Henry! Henry! Why—why can't you remember to keep your hair down over your forehead? You must keep that scar covered up. Don't you know that when your father sees it he loses all control over himself? He goes crazy? He wants to die? (*After a moment's despair she collects herself decisively, wets the hem of her apron in her mouth and starts polishing his forehead vigorously.*) Lift your head up. Stop squirming. Blessed me, sometimes I think that it's going away—and then there it is: just as red as ever."

"Mama, today at school two teachers forgot and called me by my old name. They forgot, Mama. You'd better write another letter to the principal, so that he'll tell them I've changed my name. Right out in class they called me: Cain."

"Don't say it! Don't say it!" cries Mrs. Antrobus, hoarsely, putting her hand over Henry's mouth. "If you're good they'll forget it. You didn't . . . throw any stones today, did you, Henry?"

"Oh . . . no-o-o!"

"And, Gladys, I want you to be especially nice to your father tonight. You know what he calls you when you're good—his little angel, his little star. Keep your dress down like a little lady. And keep your voice nice and low. Gladys Antrobus!!! What's that red stuff you have on your face? (*Slaps her.*) You're a filthy, detestable child! (*Rises.*) Get away from me, both of you! I wish I'd never seen sight or sound of you. Let the cold come! I can't stand it. I don't want to go on."

Gladys is sent to the kitchen to have her face scrubbed. Mr. Antrobus can be heard roaring in song up the road. "I've been working on the railroad, all the livelong day—" Sounds like a drunken tramp, Sabina is convinced, and again the furniture must be piled against the door. But not for long. Mrs. Antrobus soon recognizes her husband's familiarities. "Broken-down camel of a pig's snoot! Open this door! . . . She-bitch of a goat's gizzard! I'll break every bone in your body. Let me in or I'll tear the whole house down!"

The door is flung open and Mr. Antrobus has a wild welcome, the whole family piling into his arms, the animals dancing wildly about the group. His arms are full of parcels, including a large stone wheel with a center in it.

Mr. Antrobus is very proud of the wheel, which Henry is soon rolling about the floor. Suddenly he gives Henry a slap. That's to make him remember this day. The day the alphabet's finished; the day that they have first seen "the hundred—the hundred—the hundred—there's no end to 'em." He has turned exultantly to Mrs. Antrobus—

"Take a look at that wheel, Maggie—when I've got that to rights you'll see a sight," he says. "There's a reward there for all the walking you've done."

"How do you mean?"

"Maggie—we've reached the top of the wave. There's not much left to be done. We're there!"

Wherever they are Mrs. Antrobus thinks something should be done about the cold. What are they going to do? Freeze to death! Mr. Antrobus wouldn't be at all surprised if they did. That's what people are doing up north.

Outside a number of people have gathered. Mr. Antrobus suddenly sees them and remembers that they came with him. He goes to the door to explain that they will have to be patient a little longer, until he can explain them to his wife. While they are waiting they might keep busy pulling up the stakes of the fence. There will be a need of firewood presently. They will have coffee and sandwiches in a moment—

Mrs. Antrobus comes back as he is talking. She is definitely opposed to the idea of having company right now. Mr. Antrobus is not going to let another soul in that house. Mrs. Antrobus is carrying on a conversation with her invisible ancestors when Sabina decides to step out of character again and set the audience straight—

"Ladies and gentlemen: Don't take this play serious," she advises, across the footlights. "The world's not coming to an end. You know it's not. People exaggerate! Most people really have enough to eat and a roof over their heads. Nobody actually starves—you can always eat grass or something. That ice-business—why, it was a long, long time ago. Besides, they were only savages. Savages don't love their families—not like we do."

Again the voice of the Stage Manager is heard calling Sabina to attention. She is to get back into the play. Finally Sabina agrees on a compromise. "All right. I'll say the lines, but I won't *think* about the play."

The question of the company comes up again. Mr. Antrobus would have Sabina make a lot of sandwiches and a pail of coffee, but Mrs. Antrobus is still firm. Not another soul is going to get in that house over her dead body.

"Maggie, there's a doctor there," pleads Mr. Antrobus. "Never hurts to have a good doctor in the house. We've lost a peck of children one way and another. You can never tell when a child's throat will get stopped up. What you and I have seen!!!"

He has put his fingers on his throat to imitate diphtheria. Mrs. Antrobus weakens a little. "Well, just one person then, the Doctor. The others can go right along the road."

ANTROBUS—Maggie, there's an old man, particular friend of mine—

MRS. ANTROBUS—I won't listen to you—

ANTROBUS—It was he that really started off the A.B.C.'s.

MRS. ANTROBUS—I don't care if he perishes. We can do without reading or writing. We can't do without food.

ANTROBUS—Then let the ice come!! Drink your coffee!! I don't want any coffee if I can't drink it with some good people.

MRS. ANTROBUS—Stop shouting. Who else is there trying to push us off the cliff?

ANTROBUS—Well, there's the man . . . who makes all the laws. Judge Mohzes!

MRS. ANTROBUS—Judges can't help us now.

ANTROBUS—And if the ice melts? . . . and if we pull through? Have you and I been able to bring up Henry? What have we done?

MRS. ANTROBUS—Who are those old women?

ANTROBUS (*coughing*)—Up in town there are nine sisters. There are three or four of them here. They're sort of music teachers . . . and one of them recites and one of them—

MRS. ANTROBUS—That's the end. A singing troupe! Well, take your choice, live or die. Starve your own children before your face.

ANTROBUS (*gently*)—These people don't take much. They're used to starving. They'll sleep on the floor. Besides, Maggie, listen: no, listen: Who've we got in the house, but Sabina? Sabina's always afraid the worst will happen. Whose spirits can she keep up? Maggie, these people never give up. They think they'll live and work forever.

MRS. ANTROBUS (*walking slowly to the middle of the room*)— All right, let them in. Let them in. You're master here. (*Softly.*) But these animals must go. Enough's enough. They'll soon be big enough to push the walls down, anyway. Take them away.

ANTROBUS (*sadly*)—All right. The dinosaur and mammoth—! Come on, baby, come on, Frederick. Come for a walk. That's a good little lady.

DINOSAUR—It's cold.
ANTROBUS—Yes, nice cold fresh air. Bracing.

He holds the door open and the animals go out. He beckons then to his friends to come in. Each of them brings two fence stakes and lays them on the fire. Antrobus introduces them— the Doctor, the Professor, the Judge, and the three Misses Muse. The last of the crowd is a young man wheeling a wheelbarrow filled with food. That is a stirring sight to Mr. Antrobus. "Archimedes and I have been putting that together all week," he tells Maggie, proudly.

"How do you do?" Mrs. Antrobus is curtly formal. "Just . . . make yourself comfortable. Supper'll be ready in a minute." She goes to the kitchen and is shortly followed by Mr. Antrobus, who wants to help.

Archimedes has found several benches in the yard. After a cursory examination of the room the crowd settles itself variously. Homer is sounding his guitar. There is a whispered call for him to do something. Presently he strikes a chord and recites in Greek the opening lines of the Iliad. The guests sigh and nod reminiscently.

The next call is for Moses. "In the back row an old man rises, parts his beard, and says, in Hebrew, the first three verses of Genesis." Again there is a murmur of appreciation, mingled with pleased responses.

Now the Antrobuses and Sabina, with plates of sandwiches and a pail of coffee, come from the kitchen. One look at the group of refugees is enough to start Sabina off again. She is giving the Antrobuses notice. Two weeks. That's the law.

Mrs. Antrobus is trying to make polite conversation. "The roads are crowded, I hear," she begins. The guests assure her they certainly are. It may be sun spots, Mrs. Antrobus suggests. It may indeed, they agree. Mr. Antrobus ventures the opinion that things just can't go on getting worse. "I can't believe it. Professor! Have we worked for nothing? Judge! Have we just failed in the whole thing?" Before anyone can answer Mrs. Antrobus is talking about the children. She wants the Doctor to meet them. How many has she? Two. A boy and a girl.

But the Judge thought there were three! This is enough to throw Mrs. Antrobus into a spell of "blind suffering." Presently she is muttering, "Abel, Abel, my son, my son, Abel, Abel!" The refugees move toward her, comfortingly. Suddenly there is a shriek from the kitchen. The next moment Sabina has burst into the room. It is that awful boy, Henry! He isn't fit to live with respectable people, insists Sabina, emotionally. Henry has just thrown another stone, and if he hasn't killed the boy next door it's a miracle. Stark murder, Sabina calls it.

Now Mrs. Antrobus has brought Henry into the room. There is a scarlet scar in the shape of a C on the boy's forehead. He has his own explanation. The boy next door had tried to take the wheel away from him. Also he had thrown the first stone. Mrs. Antrobus understands. It was just a boyish impulse. Henry's so young. Let his father remember Henry is only 4,000 years old.

Mr. Antrobus is disgusted. There is no use trying to go on. Let them put out all the fires. What's the use of trying to live.

Sabina and Mrs. Antrobus have seized Mr. Antrobus and are trying to force him into a chair. Gladys is sent for her father's slippers. Perhaps if the guests were to sing a little something it would help, Mrs. A suggests. The guests are agreeable and as they swing into "Jingle Bells" a little hesitantly Mrs. Antrobus appeals earnestly to the discouraged Mr. A:

"George, remember all the other times," she pleads. "When the volcanoes came right up in the front yard. And the time the grasshoppers ate every single leaf and blade of grass, and all the grain and spinach you'd grown with your own hands. And the summer there were earthquakes every night."

"Henry! Henry!" wails Mr. Antrobus, putting his hands to his forehead. "Myself! All of us, we're covered with blood!"

"Then remember all the times you were pleased with him and when you were proud of yourself. Henry! Henry! Come here and recite to your father the multiplication table that you do so nicely."

Henry begins his "two times two is four"; little Gladys, back with the slippers, tries to do her part by reporting that she really was good in school that day; the teachers said so. The singers have got to "Tenting Tonight." Mrs. Antrobus thinks that if Gladys were to recite the piece she did in Assembly it might help. Gladys responds with " 'The Star,' by Henry Wadsworth Longfellow." Still Mr. Antrobus is not cheered. The fire continues going out. Quickly Mrs. Antrobus sends Henry upstairs to fetch the chairs and to begin breaking up the beds. Everybody will have to do something. Gladys is at her father's feet trying to convince him of what a good girl she is and remind him of all the happy times they can have again when Spring comes.

Suddenly Mr. Antrobus responds to the treatment. Getting to his feet he strides to the window and back again. The singing stops.

"Build up the fire!" shouts Mr. Antrobus. "It's cold. Build up the fire! We'll do what we can. At least the young ones may pull through. Henry, eat something. Gladys, have you had some supper?"

"We ate in the kitchen, Papa."

ANTROBUS—If you do come through this—what'll you be able to do? What do you know? Henry, did you take a good look at that wheel?

HENRY—Yes, Papa.

ANTROBUS—Six times two are—

HENRY—Twelve; six times three are eighteen; six times four are— Papa, it's hot and cold. It makes my head all funny. It makes me sleepy.

ANTROBUS (giving him a cuff)—Wake up. I don't care if your head is sleepy. Six times four are twenty-four. Six times five are—

HENRY—Thirty, Papa!

ANTROBUS—Maggie, put something into Gladys' head on the chance she can use it.

MRS. ANTROBUS—What do you mean, George?

ANTROBUS—Six times six are thirty-six. Gladys, you sit by your mother and learn the beginning of the Bible.

GLADYS—But, Papa, it's so cold and close. (HENRY has all but drowsed off. His father slaps him sharply and the lesson goes on.)

MRS. ANTROBUS—"In the beginning God created the heavens and the earth; and the earth was waste and void; and the darkness was upon the face of the deep— (The singing starts up again louder.)

SABINA (coming down to the footlights)—Will you please start handing up your chairs? We'll need everything for this fire. Save the human race. Ushers, will you please pass the chairs up here? Thank you.

HENRY—Six times nine are fifty-four; six times ten are sixty. (In the back of the auditorium the sound of chairs being ripped up can be heard. Ushers rush down the aisles with chairs and hand them over.)

GLADYS—And God called the light Day and the darkness he called Night.

SABINA—Pass up your chairs, everybody.   Save the human race.

The curtain falls.

ACT II

Again the highlights of the day's news.   The screen is showing scenes at the Pennsylvania Station; "timetables for trains leaving for Atlantic City; advertisements of Atlantic City hotels, drugstores, churches, rug merchants, fortune tellers, Bingo parlors." The voice of the Announcer is clear and enthused as he explains the advantages of the great resort:

"This great convention city is playing host this week to the anniversary convocation of that great fraternal order—the Ancient and Honorable Order of Mammals, Subdivision Humans," he is saying.   "This great fraternal, militant and burial society is celebrating on the Boardwalk, ladies and gentlemen, its six hundred thousandth Annual Convention."

There is a brief projection of Atlantic City scenes, one showing Mr. and Mrs. Antrobus seated on a bench along the Boardwalk.

"It has just elected its president for the ensuing term—Mr. George Antrobus of Excelsior, New Jersey.   We show you President Antrobus and his gracious and charming wife, every inch a mammal.   Mr. Antrobus has had a long and chequered career. Credit has been paid to him for many useful enterprises including the introduction of the lever, of the wheel and the brewing of beer.   Credit has also been extended to President Antrobus's gracious and charming wife for many practical suggestions, including the hem, the gore, and the gusset; and the novelty of the year,—frying in oil."

There are, it appears, many conventions of rival orders also being held at this time—the Wings, the Fins, the Shells among them.   They have all sent delegates to the Convention of the Mammals, sent them in pairs, two of a kind.   Later in the day President Antrobus is to broadcast.

But here are President Antrobus and Mrs. Antrobus in Atlantic City posed as they were shown upon the screen a moment ago. "Mrs. Antrobus is wearing a corsage of orchids.   Mr. Antrobus wears an untidy Prince Albert; spats; from a red rosette in his buttonhole hangs a fine long purple ribbon of honor.   He wears a gay lodge hat,—something between a fez and a legionnaire's cap." Now President Antrobus has risen to speak—

ANTROBUS—Fellow-mammals, fellow-vertebrates, fellow-humans, I thank you. Little did my dear parents think,—when they told me to stand on my two feet,—that I'd arrive at this place. My friends, we have come a long way. During this week of happy celebration it is perhaps not fitting that we dwell on some of the difficult times we have been through. The dinosaur is extinct—(*Applause.*) the ice has retreated; and the common cold is being pursued by every means within our power. (MRS. ANTROBUS *sneezes, laughs prettily, and murmurs: "I beg your pardon."*) In our memorial service yesterday we did honor to all our friends and relatives who are no longer with us, by reason of cold, earthquakes, plagues and . . . and . . . (*Coughs.*) differences of opinion. As our Bishop so ably said . . . uh . . . so ably said . . .

MRS. ANTROBUS (*closed lips*)—Gone, but not forgotten.

ANTROBUS—They are gone but not forgotten. I think I can say, I think I can prophesy with complete . . . uh . . . with complete . . .

MRS. ANTROBUS—Confidence.

ANTROBUS—Thank you, my dear.—With complete lack of confidence, that a new day of security is about to dawn. The watchword of the closing year was: work. I give you the watchword for the future: Enjoy yourselves.

MRS. ANTROBUS—George, sit down!

ANTROBUS—Before I close, however, I wish to answer one of those unjust and malicious accusations that were brought against me during this last electoral campaign. Ladies and gentlemen, the charge was made that at various points in my career I leaned toward joining some of the rival orders—that's a lie. As I told reporters of the Atlantic City *Herald*, I do not deny that a few months before my birth I hesitated between . . . uh . . . between pinfeathers and gill-breathing,—and so did many of us here,—but for the last million years I have been viviparous, hairy and diaphragmatic.

Mrs. Antrobus follows. She doubts that she should say anything, seeing that it is Mr. Antrobus who has been elected, and yet, as President of the Women's Auxiliary Bed and Board Society, she has collected a few notes that may prove of interest. For one thing, it has just been decided that the tomato is edible.

For another, she has with her a sample of cloth made from the thread woven by a silkworm. Very nice, but rather shiny on the surface.

The debate as to whether the windows of a sleeping apartment should or should not be left open at night is still going on, Mrs. A reports, without a decision having so far been made. As for her own opinion it does seem to her that night air must be unhealthy for children. Reminded of the imminence of her wedding anniversary Mrs. Antrobus adds a few words on that happy subject—

"Yes, my friends, this Spring Mr. Antrobus and I will be celebrating our five thousandth wedding anniversary," she admits proudly. "I don't know if I speak for my husband, but I can say that, as for me, I regret every moment of it. (*Sneeze. Laughter of confusion.*) I beg your pardon. What I *mean* to say is that I do not regret one moment of it. I hope none of you catch my cold. We have two children. We've always had two children, though it hasn't always been the same two. But as I say, we have two fine children, and we're very grateful for that. Yes, we've been married five thousand years. Each wedding anniversary reminds me of the times when there were no weddings. We had to crusade for marriage. Perhaps there are some women within the sound of my voice who remember that crusade and those struggles; we fought for it, didn't we? We chained ourselves to lampposts and we made disturbances in the Senate,—anyway, at last we women got the ring. A few men helped us, but I must say that most men blocked our way at every step: they said we were unfeminine. I only bring up these unpleasant memories, because I see some signs of backsliding from that great victory. Oh, my fellow mammals, keep hold of that. My husband says that the watchword for the year is Enjoy Yourselves. I think that's very open to misunderstanding. My watchword for the year is: Save the Family. It's held together for over five thousand years: Save it! Thank you."

It was the announcer's hope that he could show upon the screen some views of the Beauty Contest held that day, but there is time only for the announcement that President Antrobus, "an experienced judge of pretty girls," had given the title of "Miss Atlantic City 1942" to Miss Lily-Sabina Fairweather, the charming hostess of the Bingo Parlor.

Now, with the raising of the curtain, a section of the Boardwalk is revealed, backed by a Salt Water Taffy stand, a Bingo Parlor, a Fortune Teller's tent, a Turkish Bath, etc. The audience view is from the ocean. A hand rail of scarlet cord is looped across the stage at the footlight line, and a ramp leads to the orchestra pit below. In the right-hand corner of the pit a great scarlet beach umbrella stands. From the opposite corner a weather signal rises, like the mast of a ship, with cross bars. From time to time "three roller chairs, pushed by melancholy Negroes, file by empty."

Gradually the scene is taken over by groups of conveeners, several of the men dressed much like Mr. Antrobus. They are trying a little desperately to have a gay time, cutting up monkey-shines. From the Bingo Parlor the voice of the caller is heard: "A—Nine; A—Nine; C—Twenty-six; C—Twenty-six," and so on. Suddenly there is a great shout of "Bingo!!" and this literally lifts the Bingo Parlor off its foundations.

The Fortune Teller, an aging gypsy, smoking a corn-cob pipe, is pointing mechanically to the backs of passers-by and shouting their fortunes after them: "Bright's disease! Your partner's deceiving you in that Kansas City deal. You'll have six grand-children. Avoid high places!"

Sabina has come from the Bingo Parlor. "She hugs about her a blue raincoat that almost conceals her red bathing suit." Sabina is eager to talk with the Fortune Teller. Particularly eager to know where President Antrobus is. "President Antrobus!!!" she thrills. "And I'll be his wife! If it's the last thing I'll do, I'll be Mrs. George Antrobus! Esmeralda, tell me my fortune."

Esmeralda is too busy shouting at the passersby. "All right, I'll tell *you* my future," Sabina continues, laughing dreamily and tracing the lines of her hand. "I've won the Beauty Contest in Atlantic City,—well, I'll win the Beauty Contest of the whole world. I'll take President Antrobus away from that wife of his. Then I'll take every man away from his wife. I'll turn the whole world upside down."

It is the Fortune Teller's advice to Sabina that she shut her foolish mouth and wait until President Antrobus comes along. Then she can see what she can do. Presently several playful conveeners have rushed the queen of the Bingo Parlor back into her booth.

And now the Fortune Teller would have a word with the audience. She rises from her stool, "unfurls her voluminous skirts, gives a sharp wrench to her bodice and strolls to the footlights, swinging her hips like a young woman." She can tell the future, she assures her listeners. Because everybody's future is in their face. But who can tell the past? Nobody!

"Your youth—where did it go?" she demands. "It slipped away while you weren't looking. While you were asleep. While you were drunk? Puh! You're like our friends, Mr. and Mrs. Antrobus; you lie awake nights trying to know your past. What did it mean? What was it trying to say to you? Think! Think! Split your heads. I can't tell the past and neither can you. If anybody tries to tell you the past, take my word for it, they're charlatans. But I can tell the future." . . . "And what's the immediate future of our friends, the Antrobuses? Oh, you've seen it as well as I have, keck,—that dizziness of the head; that Great Man dizziness? The inventor of beer and gunpowder. The sudden fits of temper and then the long stretches of inertia. 'I'm a sultan; let my slave-girls fan me.' (*Distant thunder. She puts out her hand for raindrops and looks up at the ceiling.*) You know as well as I what's coming. Rain. Rain. Rain in floods. The deluge. But first you'll see shameful things—shameful things."

Again there'll be the narrow escape, she prophesies, and the survival of a handful, including the animals; "two of a kind, male and female." Conveeners have been edging in and listening to the direful prophecies. Now they have surrounded the Fortune Teller and are jeering at her. "Charlatan! Madam Kill-joy! Mrs. Jeremiah! The croaking raven. Old dust and ashes. Rags, bottles, sacks!"

"Yes, stick out your tongues!" she shouts back. "You can't stick your tongues out far enough to lick the death-sweat from your foreheads. It's too late to work now—bail out the flood with your soup spoons. You've had your chance and you've lost."

"Enjoy yourselves!!!" shout the conveeners, as they quit the scene. "They're coming," warns the Fortune Teller. "Your hope. Your despair. Yourselves."

Mr. and Mrs. Antrobus and Gladys stroll in. They've lost Henry, but he soon appears. He is dancing around a roller-chair and the Negro pushing it. Henry has a slingshot in his hand and is threatening the Negro, who is doing a little threatening on his own account. "Nobody can't touch my chair, nobody, without I allow them to," warns the Negro. "You get clean away from me and you get away fast!"

The Antrobuses take a hand and finally get Henry quieted. Mrs. Antrobus again is ready to forget everything. But again

Mr. Antrobus is all through with Henry. Mr. Antrobus, in fact, is about through with the whole family. There has been too much nagging to suit him. Aren't they on a vacation? Why shouldn't they have a good time? But Mrs. Antrobus is still inclined to protest. There's a rainy day coming. They'd better prepare for it. Besides, Mr. Antrobus still has his broadcast to make.

From the Bingo Parlor Sabina appears. "She wears a flounced red silk bathing suit, 1905. Red stockings, shoes, parasol. She bows demurely to Antrobus and starts down the ramp."

Mr. Antrobus smiles appreciatively and speaks pleasantly to Sabina as she heads for her beach umbrella. Mrs. Antrobus, suddenly aware of what's going on, demands an explanation. Who was that woman? Mr. Antrobus would evade the question if he could, but Mrs. A persists.

ANTROBUS—Maggie, that's the girl I gave the prize to in the beauty contest—that Miss Atlantic City 1942.

MRS. ANTROBUS—Hm! She looked like Sabina to me.

HENRY (*at the railing*)—Mama, the life-guard knows her, too. Mama, he knows her well.

ANTROBUS—Henry, come here.—She's a very nice girl in every way and the sole support of her aged mother.

MRS. ANTROBUS—So was Sabina, so was Sabina; and it took a wall of ice to open your eyes about Sabina.—Children, come over and sit down on this beach.

ANTROBUS—She's a very different matter from Sabina. Miss Fairweather is a college graduate, Phi Beta Kappa.

MRS. ANTROBUS—Henry, you sit here by Mama. Gladys—

ANTROBUS (*sitting*)—Reduced circumstances have required her taking a position as hostess in a Bingo Parlor; but there isn't a girl with higher principles in the country.

MRS. ANTROBUS—Well, let's not talk about it.—Henry, I haven't seen a whale yet.

ANTROBUS—She speaks seven languages and has more culture in her little finger than you've acquired in a lifetime.

MRS. ANTROBUS (*with assumed amiability*)—All right, all right, George. I'm glad to know there are such superior girls in the Bingo Parlors.—Henry, what's that? (*Pointing at the storm signal, which has one black disk.*)

HENRY—What is it, Papa?

ANTROBUS—What? Oh, that's the storm signal. One of those

black disks means bad weather; two means storm; three means hurricane; and four means the end of the world.

Mrs. Antrobus has gone to buy the children raincoats. The storm is going to get worse and worse, she's sure of that. And it will be as bad on land as it will be at sea. A person would be as safe in a boat. Fortunately there is a boat at the end of the pier. Henry discovers it. It will be well for Henry to keep his eye on it while his mother's gone and it would be well for Mr. Antrobus to shut his eyes and get a little rest before his broadcast.

"Thundering Judas, do I have to be told when to open and shut my eyes?" explodes Mr. Antrobus. "Go and buy your raincoats."

Several conveeners stick their heads out of the Bingo Parlor and would mock their president. "Geo-r-r-rge! Leave the old hen-coop at home. Enjoy yourself. Do-mes-ticated Georgie!"

"Low common oafs!" retorts Mrs. Antrobus, shaking out her umbrella and continuing on her way. "Guess a man has a right to bring his wife to a convention, if he wants to. What's the matter with a family, I'd like to know. Hm'p—what else have they got to offer?"

The children have gone to have a look around. Mr. Antrobus closes his eyes and would rest. The Fortune Teller comes from her booth and stations herself at the side of the stage near the entrance to the ramp. Sabina has come halfway up the ramp. "What's he doing?" she calls in a hoarse whisper.

"Oh, he's ready for you," answers the Fortune Teller. "Bite your lips, dear, take a long breath and come on up."

"I'm nervous. My whole future depends on this. I'm nervous."

"Don't be a fool. What more could you want? He's forty-five. His head's a little dizzy. He's just been elected president. He's never known any other woman than his wife. Whenever he looks at her he realizes that she knows every foolish thing he's ever done."

"I don't know why it is, but every time I start one of these I'm nervous"

"You make me tired," sniffs the Fortune Teller.

Sabina finally decides to come on up the ramp. She receives a smart slap on the behind as she passes the Fortune Teller, and stands hesitantly before Mr. Antrobus. She coughs a little to attract his attention—

"Oh, Mr. Antrobus—do I dare speak to you for a moment?"

"What? Oh, certainly, certainly, Miss Fairweather." Mr. Antrobus is quite awake now.

SABINA—Mr. Antrobus . . . I've been so unhappy. I've wanted . . . I've wanted to make sure that you don't think that I'm the kind of girl who goes out for beauty contests.

FORTUNE TELLER—That's the way!

ANTROBUS—Oh, I understand. I understand perfectly.

FORTUNE TELLER—Give it a little more. Lean on it.

SABINA—I knew you would. My mother said to me this morning: Lily, she said, that fine Mr. Antrobus gave you the prize because he saw at once that you weren't the kind of girl who'd go in for a thing like that. But, honestly, Mr. Antrobus, in this world, honestly, a good girl doesn't know where to turn.

FORTUNE TELLER—Now you've gone too far.

ANTROBUS—My dear Miss Fairweather!

SABINA—You wouldn't know how hard it is. With that lovely wife and daughter you have. Oh, I think Mrs. Antrobus is the finest woman I ever saw. I wish I were like her.

ANTROBUS—There, there. There's . . . uh . . . room for all kinds of people in the world, Miss Fairweather.

SABINA—How wonderful of you to say that. How generous. Mr. Antrobus, have you a moment free? . . . I'm afraid I may be a little conspicuous here . . . Could you come down, for just a moment, to my beach umbrella?

ANTROBUS—Why-uh . . . yes, certainly . . . for a moment . . . just for a moment.

SABINA—There's a deck chair there. Because: you know you do look tired. Just this morning my mother said to me: Lily, she said, I hope Mr. Antrobus is getting a good rest. His fine strong face has deep deep lines in it. Now isn't it true, Mr. Antrobus: you work too hard?

FORTUNE TELLER—Bingo!

Sabina has got Mr. Antrobus to the beach umbrella and seen him stretched out and relaxed before she steps out of character again to speak to the audience. She has decided, she says, not to play the next scene. She will tell the audience what takes place and then she and Mr. Antrobus will go on from there.

"I'm sorry, but I have to skip it," she repeats, when Mr. Antrobus indicates his displeasure. "In this scene I talk to Mr. Antrobus, and at the end of it he decides to leave his wife, get a divorce at Reno and marry me. That's all. So that now

I've told you we can jump to the end of it."

The stage manager, Mr. Fitzpatrick, is furious, but Sabina remains firm. She can't, and she won't, play the scene. There are lines in it that might hurt certain people and the theatre is not a place in which feelings should be hurt. Nor can her understudy play it, because she has sent the understudy to the corner for a cup of coffee. If Mr. Fitzpatrick reports Sabina to Equity, as he threatens to do, she will carry the case right up to the Supreme Court.

"Why can't you play it . . . what's the matter with it?" demands Mr. Fitzpatrick, testily.

"Well, if you must know, I have a personal guest in the audience tonight. Her life hasn't been exactly a happy one. I wouldn't have my friend hear some of these lines for the whole world. I don't suppose it occurred to the author that some other women might have gone through the experience of losing their husbands like this. Wild horses wouldn't drag from me the details of my friend's life, but . . . well, they'd been married twenty years, and before he got rich, why, she'd done the washing and everything."

"Miss Somerset, your friend will forgive you. We must play this scene."

"Nothing, nothing will make me say some of those lines . . . about 'a man outgrows a wife every seven years' and . . . and that one about how 'the Mohammedans being the only people who looked the subject square in the face.' Nothing."

Mr. Fitzpatrick would send Sabina to her dressing room, while he reads her lines, but the other actors insist that the play should go on. In the end Sabina wins. She and Mr. Antrobus pick up the scene at his line: "Lily, it won't be easy to lay all this before my wife. It'll hurt her feelings a little."

"Listen, dear: *Other* people haven't got feelings," replies Sabina, getting quickly back into her part. "Not in the same way that we have,—we who are presidents like you and prize-winners like me. Listen, other people haven't got feelings; they just imagine they have. Within two weeks they go back to playing bridge and going to the movies. Listen, dear: everybody in the world except a few people like you and me are just people of straw. Most people have no insides at all. Now that you're president you'll see that. Listen, darling, there's a kind of secret society at the top of the world—like you and me—that know this. The world was made for us. What's life anyway? Except for two things, pleasure and power, what is life? Boredom!

Foolishness! You know it is. Except for those two things, life's nau-se-at-ing. So,—come here! (*She kisses him.*) So. (*He kisses her.*) Now when your wife comes, it's really very simple; just tell her."

"Lily, Lily: you're a wonderful woman."

"Of course I am."

Sabina has tipped the red umbrella forward so that she and Mr. Antrobus are hidden from view. Above on the Boardwalk Mrs. Antrobus has returned from her shopping with her arms full of bundles. Shortly she is joined by Gladys, also wearing red stockings and carrying a red parasol. Mrs. Antrobus is horrified, and a little disgusted. The fact that Gladys' father admires red is no excuse. Gladys should go back to the hotel at once. However—if she wants to risk it, let her stay. Let her see what her father will say. Mrs. Antrobus is ready to give up. What if the biggest storm in the whole world comes, she doesn't care. Let Henry get into trouble if he wants to. Let—

Where is Mr. Antrobus? He is talking to the lady in the red dress, Gladys reports. Well, they will sit there until he is through, decides Mrs. Antrobus, covering Gladys' red stockings with a raincoat.

Now there is more excitement. Three conveeners have rushed in with a microphone on a standard and the paraphernalia for the broadcast. The spokesman for the three is greatly excited. They have been hunting everywhere for Mr. Antrobus. It is almost time. Where is he?

One of the other conveeners, peeking over the rail, is able to answer that. There is Mr. Antrobus with a lady in red. The Chief rushes to see. Seeing, he calls wildly:

"In the name of God, Mr. Antrobus, you're on the air in five minutes. Will you kindly please come and test the instrument. That's all we ask. If you just please begin the alphabet slowly."

Mr. Antrobus comes ponderously up the ramp. He'll be ready when the time comes, he assures the broadcast official. Meantime he has something to say to his wife. He moves over to stand beside Mrs. Antrobus, and Sabina follows. "Don't let her argue," whispers Sabina. "Remember arguments have nothing to do with it."

"Maggie, I'm moving out of the hotel," begins Mr. Antrobus. "In fact, I'm moving out of everything. For good. I'm going to marry Miss Fairweather. I shall provide generously for you and the children. In a few years you'll be able to see that it's all for the best. That's all I have to say."

He moves back to take up the broadcast, somewhat to the relief of a very excited official, who has gone on feverishly setting up and testing his paraphernalia.

"George," calls Mrs. Antrobus, lowering her eyes, "I can't talk to you until you wipe those silly red marks off your face."

"I think there's nothing to talk about. I've said what I have to say."

"Splendid!" approves Sabina.

"You're a fine woman, Maggie, but . . . but a man has his own life to lead in the world."

"Well, after living with you for five thousand years I guess I have a right to a word or two, haven't I?"

Mr. A turns a worried expression on Sabina. "What can I answer to that?" he asks.

"Tell her that conversation would only hurt her feelings. It's kinder-in-the-long-run-to-do-it-short-and-quick."

Besides the excitement of the imminent broadcast the storm signals are rapidly changing. The hurricane signal already has gone up. "I want to spare your feelings in every way I can, Maggie," Mr. Antrobus is saying. To this Mrs. Antrobus replies calmly, even a little dreamily:

"I didn't marry you because you were perfect. I didn't even marry you because I loved you. I married you because you gave me a promise." She has taken off her ring and is looking at it. "That promise made up for your faults. And the promise I gave you made up for mine. Two imperfect people got married and it was the promise that made the marriage."

"Maggie, I don't deny . . . but . . . I was only nineteen."

"And when our children were growing up, it wasn't a house that protected them; and it wasn't our love that protected them —it was that promise. And when that promise is broken—"

With a sweep of her hand she has pulled the raincoat away from Gladys' legs. The sight of his daughter's red stockings is enough to threaten Mr. Antrobus with apoplexy. Has everybody gone crazy? Did Sabina give Gladys those stockings? Let Gladys go straight back to the hotel and take them off!

Again Mrs. Antrobus takes command. "Stop your noise!" she shouts at George, clapping her hands peremptorily. "I'm taking her back to the hotel, George. Before I go I have a let-ter . . . I have a message to throw into the ocean. (*Fumbling in her handbag.*) Where is the plagued thing. Here it is. There! (*She flings something—invisible to us—far over the heads of the audience to the back of the auditorium.*) It's a bottle. And in the bottle's a letter. And in the letter is written all the things that a woman knows. It's never been told to any man and it's never been told to any woman, and if it finds its destination, a new time will come. We're not what books and plays say we are. We're not what advertisements say we are. We're not in the movies and we're not on the radio. We're not what you're all told and what you think we are: We're ourselves. And if any man can find one of us he'll learn why the whole universe was set in motion. And if any man harm any one of us, his soul—the only soul he's got—had better be at the bottom of that ocean,—and that's the only way to put it."

Mrs. Antrobus would drag Gladys after her, but the girl breaks away long enough to tell her father about Henry. Henry has hit one of the colored men and the police are looking for him. And as for herself, Gladys doesn't care whether her father likes her or not, so there!

Mr. Antrobus would follow after his family, but Sabina stops him. Let him remember he's on the air. Let him say anything —it doesn't matter. He's only talking to a lot of birds and fishes and things.

He looks up from the microphone and sees the animals gathering, two of a kind. In the water the fishes are having a great time, jumping and leaping about. There are even two of Maggie's whales. Maggie should see those. It is getting dark when Mr. Antrobus starts his broadcast—

"Friends. Cousins. Four score and ten billion years ago our forefather brought forth upon this planet the spark of life."

There is a roar of thunder and a crash of lightning. When it is over the Fortune Teller is there, standing by Mr. Antrobus—

"There's not a minute to be lost," she is saying. "Don't you see the four disks on the weather signal? Take your family into that boat at the end of the pier."

Some of her excitement is passed on to Antrobus. He is calling a little wildly for Maggie, now. The Fortune Teller insists that the family will come, all right. Let him start getting the animals into the boat, two of each kind. Sabina, too, would calm Mr. Antrobus' excitement. This is just another storm. But Antrobus is still calling for his Maggie.

Presently Mrs. Antrobus arrives with Gladys. She knows what is happening. She knows they are going aboard the boat, but she won't stir a step until she finds Henry.

Suddenly Antrobus decides to get busy. He begins to herd the animals toward the boat. "Elephants first!" he calls.

"Gently—gently—look where you're going! Is the kangaroo there? There you are. Take those turtles in your pouch, will you?"

The rollicking conveeners have appeared again. They find it great fun watching Mr. Antrobus herd the animals toward the boat. "George! What, are you scared, George? Fellas, it looks like rain— 'Maggie, where's my umbrella?' George, setting up for Barnum and Bailey!"

The pier is about to break up. Mr. Antrobus would hurry, hurry. But Mrs. Antrobus will not stir without Henry. "Henry! Cain! Cain!" she shouts in desperation.

That brings him. Henry is with them now. He was afraid they didn't want him. Sabina, too. Sabina is begging to be taken along. She'll help. She'll work. "Don't leave me here," she begs. And Mrs. Antrobus sweeps her in with the family. "Yes, go back to the kitchen with you," sneers the Fortune Teller.

"I don't know why my life's always being interrupted—just when everything's going fine!" wails Sabina.

The conveeners are doing a serpentine dance on the Boardwalk. "Get a canoe!" they shout at the Fortune Teller. "There's not a minute to be lost! Tell me my future, Mrs. Croaker."

"Paddle in the water, boys—enjoy yourselves."

"Rags, bottles, and sacks."

"Go back and climb on your roofs. Put rags in the cracks under your doors— Nothing will keep out the flood. You've had your chance. You've had your day. You've failed. You've lost."

"B—Fifteen. B—Fifteen."

"They're safe. George Antrobus! Think it over! A new world to make—think it over!"

"Bingo!"

The curtain falls.

ACT III

From the stage back of the curtain two sounds are heard. First, the wail of a baby; then a cracked bugle call. Out of the darkness there emerges the Antrobus house as it was when the play began, but rather completely devastated. Parts of the walls lean crazily forward; some sections appear to be missing. In the distance a red fire is burning.

Sabina is the first to appear. "She is dressed as a Napoleonic camp follower in begrimed reds and blues." She comes in calling lustily and a little excitedly for Mrs. Antrobus and Gladys. The war's over! *Mrs. Annnntrobus! Glaaaadus! The war's over!* Mr. Antrobus is coming home! "He says that now the war's over we'll all have to settle down and be perfect!" calls Sabina.

There is an interruption. Mr. Fitzpatrick, the stage manager, appears, followed by the entire acting company. There is an explanation that has to be made to the audience. He turns to the actor playing Mr. Antrobus. (Fredric March, in this instance.) "Mr. March, will you explain the matter to the audience?"

The lights are turned up, revealing an elevated runway crossing the stage back of the rear wall of the Antrobus house. Mr. March steps to the footlights. "The management feels, in fact we all feel, that you are due an apology," he says. "And now we have to ask your indulgence for the most serious mishap of all. Seven of our actors have . . . have been taken ill. Apparently, it was something they ate. I'm not exactly clear what happened."

He seeks confirmation from the other members of the company. Mrs. Antrobus (Florence Eldridge) agrees that the actors had eaten something that disagreed with them. Sabina (Tallulah Bankhead) is more emphatic. "Disagreed with them!!!" she sniffs. "They have ptomaine poisoning. They're in Bellevue Hospital this very minute in agony. They're having their stomachs pumped out this very minute, in perfect agony."

Fortunately, Mr. March continues, word has come from the hospital that they will all recover. Right now, however, something has to be done to fill their places. There are, as it happens, a number of splendid volunteers available. They have watched the rehearsals and are quite certain they know the lines. There is Mr. March's dresser, Mr. Tremayne, himself an old Shakespearian actor; the wardrobe mistress, Hester; Miss Bankhead's maid Ivy and Fred Bailey, the captain of the ushers of the theatre. The volunteers step forward and bow politely.

"Now, this scene takes place near the end of the act," Mr. March is explaining. "And I'm sorry to say we'll need a short rehearsal, just a short run-through. And as some of it takes place in the auditorium, we'll have to keep the curtain up. Those of you who wish can go out in the lobby and smoke some more. The rest of you can listen to us, or . . . or just talk quietly among yourselves, as you choose. Thank you. Now will you take it over, Mr. Fitzpatrick?"

"Thank you.— Now for those of you who are listening perhaps I should explain that at the end of this act, the men have come back from the war and the family's settled down in the house. And the author wants to show the hours of the night passing by over their heads, and the planets crossing the sky . . . uh . . . over their heads. And he says—this is hard to explain—that each of the hours of the night is a philosopher, or a great thinker. Eleven o'clock, for instance, is Aristotle. And ten o'clock is Spinoza. Like that. I don't suppose it means anything. It's just a kind of poetic effect."

Miss Bankhead is inclined to take issue with Mr. Fitzpatrick. "Not mean anything! Why, it certainly does. Twelve o'clock goes by saying those wonderful things. I think it means that when people are asleep, they have all those lovely thoughts, much better than when they're awake."

Ivy, too, has an idea. At least Ivy's father, who is a Baptist minister, had come to one rehearsal and he said that the author meant that "just like the hours and stars go by over our heads at night, in the same way the ideas and thoughts of the great men are in the air around us all the time and they're working on us, even when we don't know it."

The rehearsal proceeds satisfactorily until suddenly Mr. Fitzpatrick discovers that they have forgotten the planets! The planets, the stage manager explains, are singers. Of course there are no substitutes handy for them, so the audience will just have to imagine the singing.

When the run-through is finished the curtain is lowered again. Now the baby's wail and the cracked bugle call are repeated and the act begins all over with Sabina entering as the camp follower, calling Gladys and Mrs. Antrobus.

Sabina has gone into the backyard to continue her search when a trap door near the fireplace opens and Mrs. Antrobus emerges. "She is disheveled and worn; she wears a tattered dress and a shawl half covers her head." She reports what she can see through the trap door to Gladys, who shortly comes half way up the stairs holding a baby.

Soon Sabina is back to give them her report of the end of the war and to advise them to get themselves fixed up against the return of the men. Mr. Antrobus will be home in the afternoon and probably Henry, too. Let them be dressed and clean. Peacetime's coming awful fast.

"Sabina, how soon after peacetime begins does the milkman start coming to the door?" asks Gladys.

"As soon as he catches a cow," answers Sabina. "Give him time to catch a cow, dear." She has turned to Mrs. Antrobus: "Mrs. Antrobus, guess what I saw Mr. Antrobus doing this morning at dawn. He was tacking up a piece of paper on the door of the Town Hall. You'll die when you hear: it was a recipe for grass soup that doesn't give you the diarrhea. Mr. Antrobus is still thinking up new things. He told me to give you his love. He's got all sorts of ideas for peacetime, he says. No more laziness and idiocy, he says. And, oh, yes! Where are his books? What? Well, pass them up. The first thing he wants to see are his books. He says if you've burnt those books, or if the rats have eaten them, he says it isn't worth while starting over again. Everybody's going to be beautiful, he says, and diligent and very intelligent. . . . Yes, peace will be here before we know it. In a week or two we'll be asking the Perkinses in for a quiet game of bridge. We'll turn on the radio and hear how to be big successes with a new tooth paste. We'll trot down to the movies and see how girls with wax faces live—all *that* will begin again. Oh, Mrs. Antrobus, God forgive me, but I enjoyed the war. Everybody's at their best in wartime. I'm sorry it's over. And, oh, I forgot! Mr. Antrobus sent you another message—can you hear me?"

A blackened and sullen Henry comes through the door. "He is wearing torn overalls, but has one gawdy admiral's epaulette hanging by a thread from his right shoulder, and there are vestiges of gold and scarlet braid running down his left trouser leg." The others are in the cellar. Sabina is calling to them. Henry listens for a moment and then goes over and sits on a broken couch.

"Listen!" Sabina continues. "Henry's never to put foot in this house again, he says. He'll kill him on sight, if he sees him. You don't know about Henry??? Well, where have you been? What? Well, Henry rose right to the top. Top of *what?* Listen, I'm telling you. Henry rose from corporal to captain, to major, to general. I don't know how to say it, but the enemy is *Henry;* Henry *is* the enemy. Everybody knows that."

HENRY—He'll kill me, will he?

SABINA—Who are *you?* I'm not afraid of you. The war's over.

HENRY—I'll kill him so fast. I've spent seven years trying to find him; the others I killed were just substitutes.

SABINA—Goodness! It's Henry!— (*He makes an angry gesture.*) Oh, I'm not afraid of you. The war's over, Henry Antrobus, and you're not any more important than any other unemployed. You go away and hide yourself, until we calm your father down.

HENRY—The first thing to do is to burn up those old books; it's the ideas he gets out of those old books that . . . that makes the whole world so you can't live in it. (*He reels forward and starts kicking the books about, but suddenly falls down in a sitting position.*)

SABINA—You leave those books alone!! Mr. Antrobus is looking forward to them a-special. Gracious sakes, Henry, you're so tired you can't stand up. Your mother and sister'll be here in a minute and we'll think what to do about you.

HENRY—What did they ever care about me?

SABINA—There's that old whine again. All you people think you're not loved enough, nobody loves you. Well, you start being lovable and we'll love you.

HENRY (*outraged*)—I don't want anybody to love me.

SABINA—Then stop talking about it all the time.

HENRY—I never talk about it. The last thing I want is anybody to pay any attention to me.

SABINA—Oh, I can hear it behind every word you say.

HENRY—I want everybody to hate me.

SABINA—Yes, you've decided that's the second best, but it's still the same thing.— Mrs. Antrobus! Henry's here. He's so tired he can't stand up.

Mrs. Antrobus and Gladys are excited when they find Henry, but he will have none of them. He has not come back to live there. They might as well know that. Before they can convince him that he is foolish, Henry has practically fallen asleep. They take his gun away from him and make him comfortable on the couch.

With the aid of ropes they find hanging from the ceiling Mrs. Antrobus and Sabina are able to pull parts of the house into line. "That's all we do—always beginning again," mutters Sabina, as they straighten up the furniture. "Over and over again. Always beginning again. How do we know that it'll be any better than before? Why do we go on pretending? Some day the whole Earth's going to have to turn cold anyway, and until that time all these other things'll be happening again: it will be more wars and more walls of ice and floods and earth-quakes."

But Mrs. Antrobus has no sympathy with this kind of talk. "I don't want to hear any more of it," she exclaims, taking the rope from Sabina, and, with one mighty pull, setting the whole house to rights. "Do I have to explain to you what everybody knows,—everybody who keeps a home going? Do I have to say to you what nobody should ever *have* to say, because they can read it in each other's eyes? Now listen to me: I could live for seventy years in a cellar and make soup out of grass and bark, without ever doubting that this world has a work to do and will do it."

Henry is stirring restlessly in his sleep. Mumbling, too. What he is saying sounds very much like the harangue of a street-corner agitator: "All right, you tell me. What have you got to lose? What have they done for us? That's right—nothing. Tear everything down. I don't care what you smash. We'll begin again and we'll show 'em."

Mr. Antrobus has arrived, his arms full of bundles. He has a slight limp and is wearing an overcoat much too long for him. Hearing Henry he lets his bundles fall and takes out a revolver. He is backing away from Henry, the revolver pointing at the floor, when Henry awakes and sitting up defiantly, stares at his father. "All right! Do something!" he shouts. "Don't think I'm afraid of you, either. . . . Shoot me, I tell you. You don't have to think I'm any relation of yours. I haven't got any father or mother, or brothers or sisters. And I don't want any. And what's more I haven't got anybody over me: and I never will have. I'm above, and that's all I want to be: alone. So you can shoot me."

Slowly Antrobus walks back to the window and tosses the revolver into the yard. "You're the last person I wanted to see," he says. "The sight of you dries up all my plans and hopes. I wish I were back at war still, because it's easier to fight you than to live with you. War's a pleasure—do you hear me?— War's a pleasure compared to what faces us now: trying to build up a peacetime with you in the middle of it."

"I'm not going to be a part of any peacetime of yours. I'm going a long way from here and make my own world that's fit for a man to live in. Where a man can be free, and have a chance, and do what he wants to do in his own way."

"You do?" Antrobus has become suddenly thoughtful. "Henry, let's try again," he suggests, pleadingly.

"Try what? Living here? Oh, no.— Speaking polite downtown to all the old men like you? Standing like a sheep at the
street corner until the red light turns to green? Being a good
boy and a good sheep, like all the stinking ideas you get out of
those books there? Oh, no. I'll make a world, and I'll show
you."

"How can you make a world for people to live in, unless
you've first put order in yourself." The hard tone has come
again into the Antrobus voice. "Mark my words: I shall continue fighting you until my last breath as long as you mix up
your idea of liberty with your idea of hogging everything for
yourself. I shall have no pity on you. I shall pursue you to
the far corners of the earth. You and I want the same thing;
but until you think of it as something that everyone has a right
to, you are my deadly enemy and I will destroy you."

From the kitchen comes the voice of Mrs. Antrobus. That
reminds Mr. Antrobus to warn Henry that when his mother comes
in he must behave himself. Henry must have some feeling for
his old home and his family, else he would not have come back
there. But the injunction sets Henry off again. There are to be
no more "musts" for him. "All my life everybody's been crossing me," he shouts: "everybody, everything, all of you. I'm
going to be free, even if I have to kill half the world for it.
Right now, too. Let me get my hands on his throat. I'll show
him."

Henry has started furiously for his father when Sabina jumps
between them and calls out excitedly: "Stop! Stop! Don't
play this scene! You know what happened last night! Stop the
play!" The men have fallen back, panting, and Henry has
covered his face with his hands. Sabina turns again to the
audience. "Ladies and Gentleman, I forbid these men to play
this scene. Last night Henry here almost strangled Mr. March.
He becomes a regular savage."

HENRY (*also out of character*)—It's true. I don't know what
comes over me in this scene. I have nothing against Mr. Antrobus personally. I respect him very much. . . . I . . . I admire
him. But in this scene something comes over me. It's like I
become fifteen years old again. I . . . I . . . listen: my father
used to whip me and lock me up every Saturday night. I never
had enough to eat. He never let me have enough money to buy
decent clothes. I was ashamed to go downtown. I never could
go to the dances. My father and my uncle put rules in the way

of everything I wanted to do. They tried to prevent my living at all.— I'm sorry. I'm sorry.

MRS. ANTROBUS (*quickly*)—No, go on. Finish what you were saying. Say it all.

HENRY—In this scene it's as though I were back in High School again. It's like I had some big emptiness inside me— the emptiness of being hated and blocked at every turn. And the emptiness fills up with the one thought that you have to strike and fight and kill. Listen, it's as though you have to kill somebody else so as not to end up killing yourself.

SABINA (*calling him by his real name*)—Henry, that's not true. I knew your father and your uncle and your mother. You imagined all that. Why, they did everything they could for you. How can you say things like that? They didn't lock you up.

HENRY—They did. They did. They wished I hadn't been born.

ANTROBUS (*in his own person, with self-condemnation, but cold and proud*)—Wait a minute. I have something to say, too. It's not wholly his fault that he wants to strangle me in this scene. It's my fault, too. He wouldn't feel that way unless there was something in me that reminded him of all that. He talks about an emptiness. Well, there's an emptiness in me, too. Yes,— work, work, work,—that's all I do. I've ceased to *live*. No wonder he feels that anger coming over him.

MRS. ANTROBUS—There! At least you've said it.

SABINA—We're all just as wicked as we can be, and that's the God's truth.

Mrs. Antrobus would take Henry out and put his head under cold water, but Sabina takes that job off her hands and Henry is led away, protesting that he will be all right, he'll not lose control again. This leaves Mr. and Mrs. Antrobus to skip to the end of the scene and go on with the play. She moves up to the door and the window, preparing to fasten them for the night. "George, did I see you limping?" she asks.

"Yes, a little. My old wound from the other war started smarting again. I can manage."

From the window Mrs. Antrobus can see that the lights are coming on—the first in seven years. People are walking up and down and looking at them. And over in Hawkins' open lot they have built a bonfire to celebrate the peace. People are dancing around it like scarecrows.

"George should sit down and rest," insists Mrs. Antrobus. He's tired. He is, George admits, but he's restless, too. He is pacing the room when suddenly he stops before her with a cry of despair. "Maggie! I've lost it! I've lost it!"

"What, George? What have you lost?"

"The most important thing of all. The desire to begin again, to start building."

"Well, it will come back."

"I've lost it," repeats Antrobus, walking to the window. "This minute I feel like all those people dancing around the bonfire— just relief. Just the desire to settle down; to slip into the old grooves and keep the neighbors from walking over my lawn.— Hm. But during the war,—in the middle of all that blood and dirt and hot and cold—every day and night, I'd have moments, Maggie, when I *saw* the things that we could do when it was all over. When you're at war you think about a better life; when you're at peace you think about a more comfortable one. I've lost it. I feel sick and tired."

"Listen! The baby's crying." She is at the door, listening. "I hear Gladys talking. Probably she's quieting Henry again. While Gladys and I were living here—like moles, like rats, and when we were at our wit's end to save the baby's life—the only thought we clung to was that you were going to bring something good out of all this suffering. In the night, in the dark, we'd whisper about it, starving and sick.—Oh, George, you'll have to get it back again. Think! What else kept us alive all these years? Oh, George, even now, it's not comfort we want. We can suffer whatever's necessary; only give us back that promise."

Sabina has brought in a lighted lamp. She is dressed again as she was at the play's beginning. If it is all right with Mr. and Mrs. Antrobus Sabina would like to go to the bonfire and celebrate the war's being over. Besides, at the Gem Movie Theatre they are giving a hand-painted soup tureen to every lady. Seems as though one of them ought to go.

He hasn't any money, Mr. Antrobus reminds them. That doesn't worry Sabina. They are taking anything they can get at the theatre, and she has a little something she has picked up— beef cubes. She should turn them in to the Center downtown, as Mrs. Antrobus says, but—

"Mrs. Antrobus, I didn't make this war," protests Sabina. "I didn't ask for it. And in my opinion, after anybody's gone through what we've gone through, they have a right to grab what they can find. You're a very nice man, Mr. Antrobus, but you'd have got on better in the world if you'd realized that dog-eat-dog was the rule in the beginning and always will be. And most of all, now. (*In tears.*) Oh, the world's an awful place, and you know it is. I used to think something could be done about it; but I know better now. I hate it. I hate it."

A little reluctantly Sabina turns over her beef cubes to Mr. Antrobus and then begs one back for the movies. She is grateful to him for that. Although she is only an ordinary girl, she knows how bright he is, and what he has done. If he has any other plans she wouldn't want to upset them. She does have to go to the movies every now and then, or her nerves couldn't stand it. But she is ready to help with any improvements Mr. Antrobus has for the world, she really is.

Mr. Antrobus is laughing softly and with a certain exhilaration as Sabina leaves them. "Now I remember what three things always went together when I was able to see things most clearly," he says to Maggie. "Three things: The voice of the people in their confusion and their need. And I thought of you and the children and this house . . . And . . . Maggie! I didn't dare ask you: my books! They haven't been lost, have they?"

"No. There are some of them right beside you. Kind of tattered."

"Yes. Remember, Maggie, we almost lost them once before? And when we finally did collect a few torn copies out of old cellars they ran in everyone's head like a fever. They as good as rebuilt the world." He is standing, a book in his hand, looking a little dreamily upward. "Oh, I've never forgotten for long at a time that living is struggle. I know that every good and excellent thing in the world stands moment by moment on the razor-edge of danger and must be fought for—whether it's a field, or a home, or a country. All I ask is the chance to build new worlds and God has always given us that. And has given us (*Opening the book.*) voices to guide us; and the memory of our mistakes to warn us. Maggie, you and I will remember in peacetime all the resolves that were so clear in the days of the war. We've come a long way. We've learned. We're learning. And the steps of our journey are marked for us here. (*He stands by the table turning the leaves of a book.*) Sometimes out there in the war—standing all night on a hill—I'd try and remember some of the words in these books. Parts of them and phrases would come back to me. And after a while I used to give names to the hours of the night. (*He sits, hunting for a passage in the book.*) Nine o'clock I used to call Spinoza.

Where is it? "After experience had taught me—"

The back wall of the Antrobus house has disappeared. On the elevated runway Fred Bailey is standing, carrying the numeral IX. As he starts across he begins to quote Spinoza—

"After experience had taught me that the common occurrences of daily life are vain and futile; and I saw that all the objects of my desire and fear were in themselves nothing good nor bad save insofar as the mind was affected by them; I at length determined to search out whether there was something truly good and communicable to man."

Mrs. Antrobus was sitting by the table sewing. Mr. Antrobus has risen from his chair and is standing in moved thought. Gladys comes from the kitchen and sits by her father's empty chair, leaning her head against it. Hester, carrying a numeral X, starts across the runway, reading from Plato—

"Then tell me, O Critias, how will a man choose the ruler that shall rule over him? Will he not choose a man who has first established order in himself, knowing that any decision that has its spring from anger or pride or vanity can be multiplied a thousand fold in its effects upon the citizens?"

Hester disappears and Ivy takes her place as Numeral XI. Mr. Antrobus has gone back to his chair. Henry appears in the shadow of the door and stands watching. From the distance the music of the planets can be faintly heard. Ivy represents Aristotle—

"This good estate of the mind possessing its object in energy we call divine. This we mortals have occasionally, and it is this energy which is pleasantest and best. But God has it always. It is wonderful in us; but in Him how much more wonderful."

The music rises as Mr. Tremayne starts across the runway, reading from the first chapter of Genesis—

"In the beginning, God created the heaven and the earth; and the earth was waste and void; and darkness was upon the face of the deep. And the Lord said, Let there be light and there was light."

Out of the darkness the strokes of a midnight bell can be heard. At the stroke of XII there is light. The scene is as it was at the beginning of the play. Sabina is standing at the window. "Oh, oh, oh! Six o'clock and the master not home yet," she repeats. "Pray God nothing serious has happened to him crossing the Hudson River. But I wouldn't be surprised. The whole world's at sixes and sevens, and why the house hasn't fallen down about our ears long ago is a miracle to me. (*She comes to footlights.*) This is where you came in. We have to go on for ages and ages yet. You go home. The end of the play isn't written yet. Mr. and Mrs. Antrobus! Their heads are full of plans and they're as confident as the first day they began—and they told me to tell you: Good night."

THE CURTAIN FALLS

WINTER SOLDIERS

A Drama in Two Acts

By Dan James

THE directors of the Playwrights Company—they being Maxwell Anderson, S. N. Behrman, Elmer Rice and Robert E. Sherwood—wanting to do something to honor the memory of their late co-founder, Sidney Howard, decided upon the creation of a Sidney Howard Memorial Award. This, they agreed, should be given annually to the young American playwright showing the most promise, and should consist of $1,500 in cash. In 1940 the prize went to Robert Ardrey, whose "Thunder Rock" was a production of that season. There was no award in 1941, and in 1942 it was given to Dan James, who had submitted the script of "Winter Soldiers" for the Playwrights' consideration.

As producers they decided that this drama would be too expensive an experiment for them to undertake, but as drama it was entitled to their fullest support. Shepard Traube, who had served as Mr. James' representative, thereupon arranged for the production of "Winter Soldiers" in the Studio Theatre of the New School for Social Research in West Twelfth Street, New York, where production expenses could be reduced to the minimum.

Most of New York's first string play reviewers saw "Winter Soldiers" and their reports were highly favorable. There was considerable talk at the time of a later Broadway production, but still the item of expense could not be easily met and the project was finally abandoned. Feeling that Mr. James' play would surely have found its way into these pages if it had been produced professionally on Broadway, the editor could see no reason why it should be barred because of its failure to make that particular grade.

"Winter Soldiers" is a story of the part the "little people" of the occupied countries of Europe played in the defeat of Hitler and his persistently advertised juggernaut the time the Nazis organized their first drive on Moscow. It was the little delays, the frequently broken Nazi schedules, the mysterious acts of sabotage that threw the German army machine frequently out of gear. These so harassed and delayed the drive on Moscow as to result

143

in Hitler's second major defeat, counting the Battle of Britain the first. Mr. James' multiple-scene visualization of that campaign furnishes an episodic but steadily interesting drama of the war.

It is near dawn of a late November morning in 1941 when "Winter Soldiers" opens. At a German staff headquarters somewhere in Russia Marshal von Seldte and General Kessel, Chief of Staff, are awaiting rather anxiously the arrival of Marshal von Falken. It is "a large barren room, classic and cold, with tall French windows at the rear" in which they wait. There is a huge detail map of the Moscow front on a side wall; a long table in the center of the room covered with detail maps, phones, etc. The lamps are still lit and "the cold light filtering through the windows and the yellow electric glare of the lamps give a nightmare tinge to the room."

Marshal von Seldte is packing books into an open dispatch case on the table. "He is a Prussian in his early sixties—a heavy set, Hindenburg of a man." Gen. Kessel, "chubby, efficient within his own narrow range, unimaginative but a confirmed sentimentalist," is standing at the window, listening for the first faint roar of Von Falken's plane. From the conversation it is quite evident that Gen. Kessel is bitter. The approaching Von Falken, he is willing to admit, is brilliant—

"Brilliant at Berchtesgaden! Brilliant at playing politics behind the lines while you win the victories at the front! Poland, France, Greece, Russia to the gates of Moscow! And now—recalled! . . . I shall resign myself—in protest!"

"Don't be sentimental! You're needed here," answers Von Seldte, continuing with his packing.

"Would you care to participate in this offensive on Moscow?"

"Von Falken is no fool. Perhaps he'll listen. After all, he was an old protégé of mine."

"Do you think friendship means anything to him? The man's inhuman, I tell you. You'll only humiliate yourself by pleading with him."

"That I can risk."

"And if he doesn't listen?"

"I shall take the matter to the Fuehrer himself."

Herr Tieck of the Gestapo has interrupted them. "He is smartly dressed in civilian clothes; a very small man with an unbelievably villainous face and a most engaging insolence. For some reason he enjoys playing the part of a buffoon." He is spirited with his "Heil, Hitler!" and its accompanying salute. And he comes bearing gifts—tulip bulbs from Holland which, he hopes, will serve to cheer Von Seldte's declining years on his ancestral acres. Von Seldte is not impressed.

Von Falken's plane has roared to a stop, practically outside the door, "as graceful as one of Mr. Wagner's Valkyrie," according to Herr Tieck. A moment later, following a flurry of "Heil, Hitlers!" Marshal von Falken is with them, followed by two of his staff generals, Gerhardt and Kranz. "Von Falken is a tall, unmilitary man, thin to emaciation, with head thrust forward like a bird of prey as he peers nearsightedly through thick-lensed glasses."

The greetings are general and perfunctory, followed by a smattering of compliments. Von Seldte is glad that he is to be succeeded by his one-time brilliant protégé, but Von Falken is suspicious. Aren't these compliments leading up to a warning about the Moscow offensive?

Without blinking an eye, Von Seldte is free to admit that they are. "You read my report?" he asks.

"Yes. I disagree. So does the Fuehrer," snaps Von Falken, and would hear no more of it.

Von Seldte persists. "First, there is the matter of the army," he reports, walking up to Von Falken. "The men are tired, Von Falken. They've been attacking now for weeks without relief. They must have rest to bring them up to battle pitch. This is a factor not fully appreciated in Berlin."

Von Falken—And your second point?

Von Seldte—The question of communications. The entire rear must be reorganized. Pockets of resistance cleared out, railroads rebuilt, bridges repaired and so forth. This is absolutely necessary for an offensive on such a scale . . . If action could only be postponed a few short weeks—

Von Falken—Yes. A few short weeks. Of course. With you, Marshal, it's always "postpone—delay!" If the Fuehrer and I hadn't forced you to attack we'd still be facing your "impregnable" Maginot Line.

Von Seldte—We're not prepared, I tell you. (*His emotions breaking through.*) Listen, Von Falken, I love this army. Twenty years of my life I've given to make it perfect. I won't stand by and see it smashed!

Von Falken—Who made that army grow from ten divisions to three hundred, may I ask? Was it you, Marshal, in the shameful years, coming hat in hand to the giants of Weimar, the Jew commission merchants, the retired plumbers and brewery barons

—coming to beg a few revolvers for your glorified police force? Or was it our party, planning and fighting, hated and despised, yes, even by you, Marshal, till our revolution came. And only then, your army got room to grow in—air to breathe.

VON SELDTE—I believe in leaving politics to the politicians.

VON FALKEN—So? You have such a short memory, Marshal. Perhaps you don't recall that politics lost the last war? Perhaps you've forgotten 1918 with the mobs howling through the streets of Berlin? Sweaty peasants—common soldiers playing the master everywhere—ripping the straps and medals from our uniforms? . . . No, Marshal, not again! This time we keep driving, and let me warn you, anyone opposing us will be eliminated.

VON SELDTE—I shall lay my objections before the Fuehrer.

VON FALKEN—The Fuehrer's mind is made up.

VON SELDTE (*grimly*)—That I shall determine for myself.

VON FALKEN (*shrugging*)—As you wish, Marshal von Seldte.

At the door Marshal von Seldte turns for an exchange of salutes. A moment later Tieck has run after him. Von Seldte has forgotten his tulip bulbs. . . .

Von Falken settles quickly to business. Kranz will see that all departments receive their orders for the following day. Gen. Kessel will remain on as Chief of Staff. Kessel salutes the honor, but would respectfully suggest that in one respect the Von Falken plan of campaign has not been thoughtfully worked out. It is the question of time. That is the stumbling block. Three times they have taken a great deal of territory, but three times they have had to revise their time schedules—

"It affects not only our rate of advance—but also the paramount question of bringing up the reserves," Kessel points out. "From the first there have been unavoidable delays in getting our troops to the front. This applies not only to the Russian end of the line—but all across Europe. The Red Army has secret allies everywhere. They must not be underestimated."

It is Gen. Kessel's suggestion that the drive be put off until fresh divisions can be brought in from the West. Von Falken feels strongly that such a decision would only give the Russians a chance to bring in *their* reserves and fortify the city. "No, thank you, Kessel. The drive begins tomorrow as scheduled. . . . The matter is settled."

Von Falken and his aide, Gen. Gerhardt, are poring over their plan for the attack on Moscow, quite pointedly ignoring Gen.

Kessel. They have put in a call for Gen. Holz in Zagreb and decided that they will bring their troops up by the quickest route —north through Czechoslovakia and east through Poland. Again Gen. Kessel would make a suggestion—

"With the Czechs it is always risky," he says. "And in West Poland—guerrillas. The troops may be delayed. Now, if I might make a suggestion—"

"Kessel, do you seriously think I'll allow a few packs of starving peasants to alter my entire plan of campaign? The 18th army will go to the front as planned. Today is Monday. They will entrain tomorrow night. They will go into action Saturday morning."

"Saturday morning! Impossible! Marshal von Seldte always allowed at least ten days—"

"Kessel, may I ask you to forget the Marshal. Things are going to move somewhat differently from now on."

"But if those troops should arrive late it would be disastrous!"

"They will not arrive late!"

"If you gave us just three more days—"

"Not another minute! Already there is snow on the ground. The Reds are rushing troops forward from the Urals. Time, Kessel, time!"

Herr Tieck interrupts them to report, with restrained excitement, that Marshal von Seldte's plane has crashed in the take-off. The Marshal and all aboard were killed, the plane completely destroyed by fire. Gen. Kessel stands speechless. The others receive the news calmly.

"Such things don't just happen! Good God—" Kessel stares about him at the cool faces of the others.

"A tragedy for the entire nation," says Von Falken. "Tieck, see that the flag is flown at half mast, will you? Attend to all the details."

"Of course." Tieck moves toward the door. "The first casualty of your offensive, eh, Marshal?" He is gone.

Kessel is still stunned when Gen. Holz is reported on the wire. Gradually his voice strengthens as he passes along Von Falken's orders. "Holz, you are to assemble your troops at once. Pack all equipment! Prepare to evacuate Zagreb. You are rolling to the Russian front!"

The lights fade.

In the darkness a pin spot of light picks out Gen. Holz at the phone. He has difficulty hearing Gen. Kessel. When he does hear he has trouble understanding. His troops have just moved into winter quarters. Their supplies have been ordered.

"All plans are changed. You roll east tomorrow night," booms the voice of Kessel.

"Tomorrow night! Impossible!"

"In the German language that Jewish word no longer exists!" Gen. Kessel has hung up.

Gen. Holz would get Col. Shreiber of the Death's Head Regiment in Kotor Varos on the wire. The wires are down, reports his operator. They have been down nearly every night in the Kotor Varos district. Gen. Holz decides to drive over and investigate.

The lights come up on the interior of a Yugoslav peasant hut, now serving as regimental headquarters for Col. Shreiber. The Colonel is stripped to the waist. His neck and back are being massaged by Janez, a hulking Croat peasant, "a mountain of a man with a shock of hair falling over his eyes." The Colonel is a little man "with a petulant, spoiled baby face."

When Gen. Holz is announced Janez continues stupidly massaging the Shreiber neck until he is shaken off. Shreiber grabs excitedly for his tunic as he tries to explain to the General that it is the climate that plays the devil with his rheumatic back. Gen. Holz should have let him know— The General would have done so, if the wires had not been cut. Funny why they are always being cut in Shreiber's district—

The General is pointing significantly to the kneeling Janez, now polishing the Shreiber boots. There is nothing to fear from that quarter, Shreiber is quick to indicate. As proof he walks back of Janez and claps his hands loudly. The peasant pays no attention. "Deaf mute," explains Shreiber.

To emphasize his point Col. Shreiber takes a bit of chocolate and, facing the grinning Janez, who is now on all fours, calls to him. "Speak for it, Janez! Speak, sir!" And Janez, grinning, growls like a dog. When the Colonel tosses him the chocolate he catches it deftly and wolfs it down.

There is nothing to fear from Janez, insists the Colonel. He is devotion itself. Once he had saved his master's life, and would again if called on. Interesting, admits the General, but that doesn't explain the mystery of the cut wires. As to that, Col. Shreiber is at pains to explain that his is a particularly difficult district. When they had first taken over they rounded up the trouble makers and strung 'em up. Next morning not only were the bodies cut down, but two of Shreiber's own men had been strung up in their places.

Since then a train has been derailed, a warehouse burned and a dozen men have disappeared. Shreiber has taken five lives for one in reprisal, but the system doesn't work. He can't kill everybody.

"There is an underground broadcasting unit in this district," Gen. Holz reminds him. "Why hasn't it been silenced?"

"We can't locate it," admits Shreiber. "I defy anyone to do better. You don't know this district. They're peasants by day, but by night they're devils. Holz, you have no idea how they hate me. I find threats tacked up on trees. A bomb exploded during inspection. I've been shot at through windows. Now they're trying to poison me. I can't eat. I don't dare sleep. My nerves are all shot. I tell you, Holz, I need a leave—a chance to rest up—to see a specialist."

Holz is firm. There is no chance for a leave. But if it is a change that Shreiber needs—he is going to get that. He is leaving for the Russian front next day. The Death's Head Regiment has been chosen to lead the attack on Moscow. They will entrain at Zagreb. All further instructions will be found in the dispatches which the General tosses on the table as he leaves the hut.

For a moment Shreiber stares angrily after him, picking up the dispatches only to toss them disgustedly back. With an angry shout he summons a sentry and passes on Gen. Holz' instructions to Major Bauer. He returns the departing sentry's salute grumblingly.

"Heil Hitler, indeed!" he mutters. "Ordered all over Europe on a moment's notice. A sick man, but it makes no difference to them, sitting in their cushy general staff. A man half dead with frayed nerves. . . . Stop grinning, you idiot." He kicks viciously at Janez. He has gone back to his chair and opened his tunic. "Well, what are you waiting for? Come here, dumbhead!"

Janez resumes the massage. Gradually the Colonel is soothed. He reaches over and turns on the radio. An orchestra is playing a Wagner overture. "Ah, that's good," he exclaims. "Yes. What a devil of a nuisance this war is. Slavs, kikes, Polacks, Greeks, why weren't they wiped off the map long ago?" His eyes close sleepily.

A change has come over the peasant's face. "The stupidity seems to drain from it, to be replaced with hatred and determination." Janez looks over toward the dispatches. His great hands move over the Colonel's throat. Suddenly Shreiber wakes up. "What do you think you're doing?" he demands.

The Colonel would cry out for help, but the great hands have closed over his windpipe. In agony he struggles, but gradually his struggles grow weaker till, with a final spasm "he slumps to the floor like an empty sack of manure."

"Janez reaches down and takes his revolver, then picks up the dispatches from the table, stuffs them under his shirt, turns off the radio and hurries out. Gradually the lights fade into darkness. . . ."

Out of the darkness comes a sentry's voice calling to Col. Shreiber. Soon a note of worry creeps into the voice. There is no answer. Now a pin spot of light picks out Gen. Holz at the telephone. From Maj. Bauer he hears the report of Col. Shreiber's murder. No dispatches had been found in his room. "This is vital!" declares Gen. Holz, in alarm. "Take command of the regiment at once. Organize searching parties! Call out the entire regiment. Capture the murderer and recover those dispatches!"

The lights have gone out. From the darkness an insistent bugle call, followed by shouts and orders from the distance. "Then the sound of tanks and trucks starting up and driving off . . ."

A German officer's voice is heard. A pin spot picks him out at a microphone: "Assigned area thoroughly covered," he is saying. "No trace of murderer. Awaiting orders. . . . Attention, motor attachments three, six and ten. Attention, infantry detachment seven. Attention all search parties in area C 3. . . ."

The lights have faded.

The lights come up on a mountain cave. A beam from the setting sun lights up one wall. Through the mouth of the cave blue sky can be seen. "A shortwave radio has been set up on a ledge of rock. Franke, the technician, squats at the dials. Janez, the peasant, sits near him on the floor of the cave. Prof. Hoffman, "a man of sixty, with white hair and delicate features, sits on a rock listening. He seems terribly out of place, with his tattered classroom clothes augmented here and there with cast-off peasant garments."

A little to one side sits Maxo, "a man of indeterminate age, for years an organizer of the European underground, short on speech but long on nerves."

The German officer's voice is still coming over the radio. "Proceed at once to Sector C 4. . . . Search the ridge thoroughly. Every bush, every ravine, every possible hiding place. Scour every inch of this area. The murderer must be found. Message ends. Heil, Hitler!"

Maxo and Prof. Hoffman have found the ridge on their maps. It is quite close. The Professor is worried, but Maxo's order is that they stay where they are. The cave is not easy to find and, anyway, it will soon be dark.

"So we wait!" mutters the Professor. "What a catch for them. Their murderer—the Colonel's dispatches there—their old enemy the shortwave—all in one glorious afternoon!" Maxo is not moved.

Franke has gone to watch at another entrance of the cave. He'll be back for the Professor's broadcast. Maxo has been going over the Colonel's papers. "Look here at the map! They're routed through Vienna northwards," he shows the Professor. "They join the main line at Prerau, Czechoslovakia, then roll east across Poland. Twelve hundred miles they've got to travel and we have centers all along the line."

"What is your plan?"

"West Poland. That's where we'll strike. We have guerrillas there who will operate from the marshes. They'll attack at night—tear up the rails for miles. It could slow the Nazis down a day at least."

"A day is very little."

"A day can make the difference between victory and defeat."

The Professor has been studying the dispatches. "This says the trains pass through West Poland in the afternoon. You said a night attack."

"We'll delay them down the line," answers Maxo.

"But, Maxo—how?"

"Strikes—slowdowns—sabotage. Our centers must use every weapon that they have. Everything to give the Poles their chance. . . . When the sun goes down you speak on the shortwave to Austria, the Czechoslovakians, Poland. We follow each speech with directions in code to all our centers. Details to be worked out on the spot. . . ."

There is the distant roar of motors from the valley. Janez senses that the enemy is approaching and turns to Maxo for instructions. The Professor can see the enemy now—armored cars, trucks—

"A company at least," Maxo decides. "They'll be in full view coming up, except along the east slope. . . ."

Quickly he assigns them to their posts. Janez is to keep behind a rock and warn them if the Nazis should start up the slope. The Professor and Maxo will guard the cave. Janez has started out when suddenly he stops. He turns quickly, rips a small wooden cross from about his neck, shoves it at the Professor, tries desperately to speak and hurries out. The Professor doesn't understand.

"This is a funny country, Yugoslavia," Maxo offers as his explanation. "They worship men of learning here—for some reason."

Maxo thrusts a rifle into the Professor's hands and indicates his post. "What a glorious finish for a pacifist," mutters the Professor.

"Aim for the knees. That'll catch them in the belly. I'll tell you when to fire," instructs Maxo. He plainly doesn't understand this man of learning and peace. Suddenly he turns on the Professor—

"Hoffman, what the devil made you join us?" he demands.

PROFESSOR—A photograph in a newspaper. A picture of the Parthenon—with the Swastika flying over it. The issues then looked sharp as a knife's edge. But a man gets tired you know.

MAXO—That happens to us all. Even to me and I was born into it. . . . Miner's son. We've always had our Hitlers, one sort or another.

PROFESSOR—Tell me, Maxo, are we really doing any good, I talk and talk over the shortwave. What happens—more Nazi victories. Does anybody really listen?

MAXO—They listen. I've seen your words scrawled in pencil—passed from hand to hand.

PROFESSOR (looking off toward the Nazis)—How methodical those soldiers are—a bayonet in every bush.

MAXO—Yes, they're good soldiers. Good soldiers in the summertime when the sun is hot and the wind's just right—and the odds are in their favor. . . . But let them be icebound, with their tanks stuck in the snow—then it takes soldiers of a different sort—the sort we have—the winter soldiers. In Spain we had no tanks. Winter all the year around. No tanks—just a stick of dynamite and a lit cigar.

PROFESSOR—Yet in the end the Fascists won— Now it's Moscow. Again we'll fight like heroes. And again we'll lose.

MAXO—We won't lose this time. This time we've got an army on our side with tanks and planes and guns. The Red Army, my friend.

Two pistol shots ring out in the valley. Maxo moves out to the mouth of the cave. Soon he is back with the report that Janez has charged the advancing armored cars. Now the Professor has looked out and seen Janez die. "Do they have to keep shooting him?" he pleads, his face lined with horror. "He died for us, Maxo, do you know that?"

"They are dumping his body in a truck," answers Maxo, tonelessly. "They're driving off. . . . Come on! Let's get to work. Get ready, Professor."

"You ask me to speak—after that? Haven't you any heart?"

"What do you think he wanted—marble tombstones? Saintly silence? Tears trickling down somebody's nose?" shouts Maxo, in fury. "He died for the radio, you hear me? For words he couldn't speak! You're going to speak 'em, by God! German, Czech, Polish, every language! You're going to be his voice!"

Maxo has called again for Franke, the radio operator, and ordered him to heat up the shortwave. The Professor, still in a fog, paces the cave. "It's getting dark. . . . Tell me—we've been staring at defeat so long—what will it be like if we win, I wonder. What shape future will it be after all this is over?"

MAXO—It will be the shape of the people who build it. You with your speeches, Professor, the dead peasant Janez down there, Franke, myself. All the people your voice carries to tonight.

FRANKE—Ready with the radio.

MAXO—Austria first. Nothing now about the trains, Professor. That goes later—coded. (*Glancing at watch.*) Six o'clock. We're right on time. What do you think of that?

FRANKE—Ready, Professor.

PROFESSOR (*taking the microphone . . . the light fades slowly, till finally he's just a silhouette against the sky*)—This is Freedom Station—Yugoslavia—I am speaking now to you, my fellow countrymen of Austria. Tonight—as on many other nights, the news is black. But days and nights have been black before. This monster Hitler's nothing new. We've known him by a hundred names: Persian King and Greek tyrant; Feudal Lord and Emperor of the French; Russian Czar and Oriental despot. They all made edicts: "It is forbidden." "Verboten." "Defendu." "History ends with me." And where are they now?

Buried in the trash of history for all their swords and guns and lies. (*The lights fade out. Then in darknss over the loud-speaker.*) The Nazis tell us it is hopeless to resist. They tell you: "We have the railroads and the highways, the communica-tion lines. We have the factories and the armies and police. We have a state machine that will last forever. We're steel. You're human. You bleed and die. But we go on forever!" They lie! I tell you they lie! Machines rust and rot, but Man is inde-structible! It is the people who go on—not the machines!

There is a moment of dead silence. From out the darkness comes a voice announcing the loading of trains. Sounds of trains moving, of locomotives getting up speed, the clanging of a bell, the rumbling of wheels on the tracks come through the darkness.

Then a spot of light picks up a German officer making a re-port over a telephone. "Capt. Bruckner reporting. Fifty troop trains are now leaving the Zagreb Yards at five-minute intervals! General warning! Beware of sabotage! Extra police detach-ments at all bridges and strategic points. Message ends. Heil Hitler!"

The distant rumble of the trains comes through. A low whis-tle is heard in the distance. Presently the discords of a tiny orchestra playing a Viennese waltz are heard.

The lights come up on a tiny bedroom and an unmade bed. A chair, a washstand, a screen over which hangs a woman's robe. "An Austrian soldier is sitting on the bed lacing up his boots. His hair is mussed. His tunic is open. He has a certain veneer of soldierly hardness, but very close to the surface is the naive peasant boy who joined up a few years ago. From behind the screen a woman's bare arm is seen taking down the robe."

As he dresses the soldier is talking to the girl back of the screen. "You're a funny one," he is saying. "I'm damned if I ever ran into your sort before. And I have been out with the best of them here in Vienna, let me tell you."

He waits but she does not answer.

"Anyone ever tell you you talk like a school teacher?" he asks. "So very polite: 'Would it please you to visit my apartment?' Calling this crib over the tracks an apartment!" Still no answer. "I can't understand why you picked me up in the first place—with the whole park crawling with Prussian officers. Nothing is too good for the noble Prussian. You know that."

The girl has come from behind the screen, fastening her robe.

Her hair streams loosely down her back. She is tiny and delicate.

"It happens I don't like Prussians," she says, quietly.

"Like—like—whose talking about 'like.' Their pockets are stuffed with marks. That's what pays the room rent."

He watches her fasten her robe. Suddenly he grabs her and kisses her on the neck. "You're so lovely, chick. So dainty and delicate." He finishes buttoning his tunic. "Well, as they say, the finest things in life have to end sometime. And business is business. You'll be throwing me out now."

"You don't have to hurry," she says. "It wouldn't hurt to get acquainted, would it?"

"Very well. We shall get acquainted," he says, sitting himself importantly on the bed. "I know. You want to tell me the story of your life. They all do when business is slack."

It would be, he thinks, the story of the governess and Prince Shineyboots, the Prussian, but it doesn't turn out to be very funny. Then it is his turn to tell his story. Nothing fancy or fictional about that. He had joined up before the Anschluss. There seemed nothing else to do. It made a sort of hero of him in his village. At least the first time home. But after that there was no food. The Nazis took everything in the neighborhood to feed the Prussians. He had been pretty lucky at that. He hadn't been shipped off to the front yet.

"Tell me," the girl says, "is it true what they say, that in the attack our Austrian regiments go over first?"

"Sometimes."

"And the Prussians move up behind?"

"Perhaps."

"Some even say more Austrian soldiers are shot by Prussians than by the Reds."

"They'd better not try that on us, by God! We'll give 'em cold steel. Right in their guts!"

"It'll be a little late then, won't it?"

"I'm waiting my time, chick. When the day comes they'll hear from me and don't forget it."

She thinks perhaps the day is there. Tonight, for example, the 18th Prussian Army is rolling up from Zagreb. He goes on duty at midnight. Never mind how she knows. He will be in command of a detachment guarding the tracks just north of Baden. The track is single there, and one of the rails has been pried loose. Suppose his detachment should fail to notice that! The locomotive would pile up and the train would hang there for hours—

The Soldier is stunned. "Who are you anyway?" he demands. "What do you want? Do you think I'll stick my head in the noose for you? Do you think for a half hour's fun—"

"I didn't ask you to do it for me! You said yourself—" She breaks off. "But you were only bragging," she adds.

He has grabbed her by the arm. His voice is tense and excited. What is she up to? Why aren't there men to do men's work? They have been jailed, she tells him, by another man who bragged he hated Nazis. If he is afraid why doesn't he run along?

He knows her now. She's one of those crazy university students. She, a girl with an education, ought to be ashamed of herself. "Dirtying yourself like this!" he sneers. "You should get down on your knees and ask God to forgive you!"

"With this war on, don't you think he'll be a little too busy to bother about details?"

SOLDIER—Wait a minute. . . . You did this for our country. . . . You took me to your room and now you ask me to— (*He breaks off.*) It's not that I'm afraid. I fear nothing—nobody! And when the day comes I'll show you. . . . But this business doesn't make sense—a few trains delayed—how does that make our country free?

GIRL—Do you think freedom will come by itself while we sit here and talk about the day? Do you think it will come flying down from the skies? . . . No, soldier, freedom only comes because men fight for it. (*Outside the whistle of a train.*)

SOLDIER—Trains in the night—an unholy sound.

GIRL—You go on duty in ten minutes.

SOLDIER—It's dark outside?

GIRL—There is no moon.

SOLDIER (*relaxing*)—What the devil then, is a man a cat to see in the dark? If a rail or so were loose—more or less, how could a man be blamed for missing it. (*She kisses him.*) Mama, your boy's a crazy fool. . . . One thing more—in case we should not meet again—I'd like to know your name.

GIRL—Lisl.

SOLDIER—Mine's Adolph. Isn't that a riot!

The Girl has crossed to the door and is looking after him as the light fades.

Through the darkness comes the whistle of a train, followed by the roar of an engine and the rumbling and grating of cars.

A light picks up a German officer reporting from Observation Post 113, twenty miles south of Baden, that the last train is now passing that post. Another light and another officer at post 112. The schedule is working perfectly.

But suddenly a third voice, that of a Gestapo officer, breaks in excitedly. "Stop all trains bound north to Vienna! . . . At once! Repeat: Stop all trains bound north to Vienna!" There is the sound of steam brakes going on and the screech of wheels coming to a stop. "Trouble north of Baden! . . . Sabotage discovered north of Baden! . . . Section of track damaged by enemy agents. Tracks will be repaired in fifteen minutes. Traffic will then be resumed. . . . I am shipping you Sergt. Adolph Muller for questioning."

Again the darkness. The sound of moving trains is resumed. Through the darkness comes the voice of Prof. Hoffman: "Brothers of Czechoslovakia! Marshal von Falken's headquarters report that the Germans have driven ten miles closer to Moscow in the past twelve hours. What are you doing to help your Russian comrades in their hour of need? . . ."

The lights come up on a narrow tenement room lit by a feeble lamp. A radio on a center table is turned very low. A man past middle age, "a small man but powerful, with a fine head and a magnificent flowing lion's mane of white hair," Antonin by name, is listening with his wife, Marya. Over the radio the Professor is saying: "Brothers of Czechoslovakia! Take your place in the battle line! Your own lives and the lives of your children are at stake! I call on you to strike with every weapon that you have—"

There is a knock at the door. Marya would not have Antonin open. Through a crack of the door Antonin recognizes Jan Bordevyk, a friend. They let Jan in. He is just out of a concentration camp. The prison doctor had discharged him as harmless, with six weeks to live. In his late twenties, tall and emaciated, Jan is a sick man. He is sure that he has not been followed. The bad weather is keeping the Gestapo off the streets. After a racking coughing spell, Jan is able to tell them of his need of help.

There has been a code message. A German Army Corps is coming through Prerau bound for the Russian front. It must be stopped. That means the railway workers must call a strike. Antonin is president of the union—

But Antonin will have nothing to do with such a plan. That

would be suicide. Jan must know that. Marya, too, would keep Antonin out of any plotting. Even to relieve the pressure on Moscow.

"You've always been too friendly with the Reds," Antonin charges. "In God's name haven't we enough troubles of our own without throwing away our lives for other people?"

"It's not for other people. It's for ourselves, Antonin. For God's sake, man, if Russia falls where are our hopes for freedom?" Jan can't understand the change in Antonin. "Remember Munich?" Jan demands. "The day news came the Nazis were marching on the city? The people jammed the square before the City Hall. Remember? I saw one woman with a pair of scissors begging to go fight the German tanks. The crowd called for you, Antonin, and you walked up the steps of the monument. 'Our heroes will be killed,' you said. 'We must save our heroes until we're ready. When the day comes I will give the word.' "

Antonin does not speak. "The people are still waiting for that word," says Jan.

And then the truth comes out. Antonin and Marya's son, Sasha, is not safe in England, as they had pretended. He is in prison, held as a hostage by the Nazis, to keep Antonin in line. They will kill him now that Antonin has told, wails Marya. Antonin had no right to tell. But Jan will keep their secret. If he had known he would not have come to them. Now he must go back to the delegates. He waits to hear Antonin's final answer—

"Damn you! What do you want? Is it a crime for a father to love his son and want to see him live?" cries Antonin, in a torment of indecision. "I won't let him be killed, do you hear? I won't!"

"I told you, Antonin, I didn't know."

"It only means waiting a little, Jan," pleads Marya. "We're working now for an escape. Karel Kubaryk has gotten a job in the prison. He's coming to see us later on tonight to let us know about our boy. We have a little money saved, you see. The Nazis will do anything for money. Then once Sasha's safe— then we can give the word. Wait till then, Jan."

They have given Jan a coat against the weather. He is leaving when Karel Kubaryk appears. "Kubaryk is a stooped old man in working clothes." They are eager for his message. Jan is their friend. Karel can speak before Jan. What about their boy?

"I didn't see your son," says Karel Kubaryk calmly, sadly. "Your son is dead!"

"He isn't dead! They promised—" Marya is screaming her grief.

"He fought them bare handed. He made them kill him. He knew then you'd be free to fight, Antonin."

"We'll make them pay," says Jan, quietly.

"Antonin! Antonin! What will we do now?" Marya is clinging blindly to her husband.

"It all happened two months ago," Karel whispers to Jan. Antonin stands speechless, his body stiff with agony. The lights fade.

In the darkness the trains are heard. Then the figure of a German soldier comes into the light. He is at a telephone. "But I tell you the night shift left ten minutes ago. The day shift is not here yet! Not a man! Yes, this is the north gate. Let me speak to the Railroad Commissioner right away."

The Railroad Commissioner, "a bald-headed man in civilian clothes," is sound asleep at his desk when the light finds him. On his desk there are two phones. He jumps up when one phone rings. He would inform the world that he is not to be disturbed. Whatever is wrong, let them take it up with the proper authorities. The other phone rings and is given the same answer. Finally the Commissioner can think of nothing to say except that the yard men are probably late, but when a strike is suggested he comes actively to life—

"WHAT? A strike? My God!" There is a train whistle in the distance. "The train's coming into the yard!" screams the Commissioner. "Change your signals right away! What? No switchmen? Then flag it down yourself! If you haven't a red flag, wave your handkerchief! Wave anything! But stop that train! For God's sake!"

In continued panic he calls the Gestapo and makes an excited report. They demand particulars. "Particulars be damned!" shouts the Commissioner. "All I know is fifty troop trains are coming into the yards right now and there's not a soul here! No engineers! No mechanics! No coal loaders! No switchmen! Nobody! For God's sake do something!"

The lights have faded. Now they pick out a Berlin Announcer assuring his listeners that Germany is destined to rule the world because of the superior blood of the master race.

"This shows itself in the efficiency of our people's state," the announcer is saying; "the most perfectly organized, the most perfectly functioning machine in the history of the world. For every problem there is an answer. For every task a competent authority—"

We go back to the Railroad Commissioner. "No," he is shouting into his phone. "The trains are NOT running yet. No. They are still standing in the yards. . . . All right, can soldiers repair electric switches? . . . Can soldiers drive locomotives? . . . Yes, I'll keep you informed. . . ."

Now Herr Tieck is on the phone. He would like very much to know what is going on. He is in Warsaw. If the Commissioner has rounded up all the strikers, as reported, they can be made to talk, guarantees Herr Tieck. Spontaneous? Strikes are never spontaneous.

There's a ring on the other phone. The Commissioner excuses Herr Tieck to answer. This is good news. The strike is all settled. Settled in just four hours to the dot. What time will that bring the trains through West Poland? The Commissioner isn't sure, but he thinks about nine o'clock. Yes, nine o'clock at the earliest. The news seems to excite Herr Tieck. He hangs up immediately.

Trains in the yards can be heard getting up steam and pulling away. The Commissioner is mopping his brow and shouting: "Hey! You in there! Telegrapher! Take a message: To all section and division points. To all stations on the Poland main-line . . ."

A train whistle blows. There is the tap of a telegraph key, and then another growing more pronounced as the lights fade.

The lights reveal the small Polish railway station of Midzyrzek. There is a telegrapher's bench under the window that looks out upon the tracks. Under the bench there is an assortment of electrical wires and appliances. Midzyrzek is 617 miles from Berlin, according to a sign on the wall.

At the bench a young Pole is taking down a message as it comes over the wire. He is small, pale and sickly looking, in his early twenties and very nervous. His name is Stefan.

Outside the angry barking of soldiers giving orders can be heard. Stefan has finished his message, has noted by the wall clock that it is now 8.45. He is peering through the window into the darkness when the door is burst open and a German soldier roughly throws a bearded peasant into the room, aiming a kick at him as he does so.

The peasant is Nikolai, in his fifties, short and stocky. As the door bangs Nikolai turns to shake his fist in the direction of the soldier. The soldiers have just finished searching his house, Nikolai reports. They found nothing, much to the delight of his old woman and his daughter Masha, too. Masha is Stefan's bride of a month. Love is a silly thing at a time like this, Nikolai gruffly insists, but he is willing to admit to the nervous Stefan that Masha is safe.

The trains, Stefan reports, are due in fifteen minutes. They are most beautifully late, Nikolai is happy to note. And the dynamite is ready. Stefan has attached the wires. He has only to set the switch and everything will be as planned. The guerrillas in the marsh will attack when they hear the dynamite, and Nikolai and his fellows will tear up the tracks. But Stefan is worried. The telegram he has received tells him that the Nazis have been warned. Also a new garrison has taken over the old. That's bad.

"The plan goes through," announces Nikolai, brusquely. "You hear me, son-in-law?"

"With the old garrison it would have been so easy," wails Stefan. "In the name of God why did this new one have to come tonight?"

"Keep your head, son-in-law! No good howling after the soup's in the ashes." . . .

The door has been kicked in by a Nazi Captain. "He is a big fellow; a hard-boiled professional who glories in his sense of power and his personal strength."

The Captain had sent Nikolai for bread and salt, and when the peasant offers what he has brought, which looks a bit mistreated, the Captain promptly throws it on the floor. "What sort of garbage do you call that?" he shouts.

"It seems the bread and salt met with an accident," ventures Nikolai, mildly.

"An accident. Yes. Too many accidents around here. Too much laxity. There must be order, understand? Discipline! Going to be some changes made around here." Nikolai tries to speak. "Quiet! "You know where I was born? Danzig, that's where. So you see I know you Polacks. And so long as you Polacks do as you're told, and keep to your place you got nothing to be afraid of. Is that clear? But if you forget you're Polacks—if you step out of line so much as a single inch—" The Captain taps his revolver. "Do we understand each other?"

"Yes, your excellency."

"You're the telegrapher." The Captain has turned to Stefan. "Yes. I've got a card on you. From my predecessor." He finds the card in his pocket and reads: " 'Stefan Bershowski—Polack —German mother. Valuable agent. Came over to us early in the war. . . . Devoted, trustworthy. Gives information.' Very pretty."

The Captain snatches the telegram Stefan is holding, reads it and turns to grab Stefan roughly by the arm. "Guerrillas, eh?" he sneers. "What about the attack on the garrison to-night?"

"Attack?" gasps Stefan. "Your excellency, I know of no attack."

That Stefan is lying the Captain is convinced, but decides a warning will do for the present. Dragging the frightened boy to the window he shows him the soldiers, each with an automatic rifle. If anything should happen, whether he is implicated or not, it will go hard with Stefan, promises the Captain. "You'll find yourself lashed to two tanks going in opposite directions. Is that clear?"

Before Stefan can answer the door opens and Masha comes in. "She is a peasant girl of seventeen, very lovely in her traditional costume of the district." Masha, frightened, would back away, but the Captain is interested. He would know how long she and Stefan have been married. "A month, eh? Not tired of it yet, eh? Keep it locked up nights where the soldiers can't get at it?" The Captain is leering at Stefan. "And yet—if a man weren't so close with his information he might be permitted to be a little more selfish about other things." He has turned again to Masha when the door is thrown open and a soldier enters.

The Captain has been summoned by the Lieutenant. He gives Masha an appraising glance and a pat on the hip as he passes. "Plump, too, eh?"

A moment later the Captain has gone, Masha is trembling in Stefan's arms and Nikolai is railing at them. Masha has been much too docile. Stefan, however, has fooled them neatly. "He took you for a lad who wouldn't blow his nose with Germans present," chuckles Nikolai. "And you in charge of fifty sticks of dynamite! Now get busy with your switch!"

Nikolai is wild with enthusiasm for what is going to happen this night. First he will capture a machine gun. Then he will let the Germans have it—in the belly, in the head, anywhere—in memory of all the dastardly things they have done. They are setting up a machine gun at the end of the platform, are they? Well, a stick of dynamite from the Widow Kashowitz's roof could take care of that neatly.

"Ai, it always falls on us old dogs to do the dirty work," chortles Nikolai. "Don't worry, son-in-law— The devils will never know where their train was blasted from. And when we take over the village we'll come and get you out. Understood?" Stefan nods. "About the dynamite—careful not to blow it off too soon. Let the train pass the station. Then count five—"

Nikolai has gone, leaving a panicky Stefan and a frightened Masha in the station. Nervously Stefan sets the switch on the table. Masha can hardly believe that such a little toy can blow a steel train to pieces; Stefan must keep warning her not to touch it. . . . There is nothing to do now but to wait.

Stefan paces the room nervously. From the window he can see nothing but soldiers, soldiers and more soldiers everywhere. That makes it bad. "A hundred other towns like this in Poland. A million others to do this work." Stefan has pulled himself away from the clinging Masha. "Why did it have to be here? Why us two?"

"The good God willed it, Stefan."

STEFAN—All my life I've wanted just one thing—to be left alone—to live in peace. Was it my fault I wasn't born strong like others? Must every man fight and claw like a wild beast? Masha, when I was a boy the others beat me. I hid my head. I covered my eyes. . . . Later, when the Nazis came, the others fought. I couldn't! Do you understand? I couldn't! I had no shame. I served them—like a dog I served them. And then you. Masha, you're the first good thing that's come to me. I don't want to lose you. Masha!

MASHA—Husband! Husband!

STEFAN—Masha, do you know how a bayonet would feel— ripping up through your bowels, tearing flesh and muscle till you felt its chill against your heart?

MASHA—Stefan! Stefan! Don't!

STEFAN—Nothing's worth that, Masha, do you hear? Moscow's a place I've never seen! Those fine words—Freedom, Victory, Liberation—they're only words. But Death is a Thing— a horrible, devouring Thing! Death and killing pain!

MASHA—Stop it, Stefan!

STEFAN—Masha, I haven't the strength to do this! I can't go through with it! I can't! I can't! I can't! (*His fists pound like hammers on the bench. Again the whistle sounds.* STEFAN *breaks off.*) Masha, it's not too late. We could let the train go through. Before dawn I could rip up the wires. No one will find out. We'll say the fuse was damp. Masha—tell me—shall I let the trains pass by?

MASHA—You are my husband, Stefan. It is for you to decide.

STEFAN—If I decide not to do this thing—?

MASHA—I only wonder—if this thing we failed to do might not stay with us all our days. Those people down the tracks—those dead people who gave their lives to give us this chance. Some day men won't have to do such things. Some day . . . (*Now the drumming of the engine comes through the night. Suddenly* MASHA *sees something.*) Stefan! The Captain! He's coming back! He's running! (*She rips off her shawl and throws it over the switch. The* CAPTAIN *bursts into the room.*)

CAPTAIN—Pig! Swine! Want to stop the train, do you? (STEFAN *is too stunned to answer.*) The light, blockhead! The green light!

STEFAN—The light! (*He stumbles to the switch. Turns it on. A green glare comes through the window, giving a ghastly look to the faces of the three.*)

CAPTAIN—Thought you'd slow us down, did you? By God, a man's got to keep his eyes open round here. Lucky for you they didn't have to stop or, by God, I'd of put a bullet through your head.

The Captain's eyes light on Masha's shawl. Perhaps she is cold. He would hand the shawl to her, but she touches his arm gently. Cold? Masha isn't cold. Not with his excellency there! The train is roaring into the station. Perhaps the Captain will show Masha the tanks and guns as the train passes by? The Captain will be glad to, if Masha will come over by the door.

They are standing in the door as the Captain points out the tanks—three to a flat car. And the big gun—big enough to blow their whole town to bits. Masha has turned a little to look over her shoulder at Stefan. Tremblingly Stefan reaches for the switch and disentangles the shawl that hides it.

"See there? Those cars are for the soldiers! A great sight, eh?"

"Yes, Excellency."

"And forty-nine more like that to come! In three days their guns will pound Moscow to a heap of rubble! Let them try to stop us now! Today Europe is ours! Tomorrow all the world!"

Stefan's hand presses on the switch. There is a terrible crash.
A sudden glare lights up the station. The Captain wheels and
sees Stefan, who stands as in a trance. The Captain whips out
his revolver. "Damn you!" he yells, facing Stefan. Masha tries
to snatch the gun from him. He flings her off as Herr Tieck
of the Gestapo bursts through the door, followed by two soldiers.

"Put up your revolver, Captain," commands Tieck. "Gestapo
taking charge."

Masha is clinging to the frightened Stefan. Should they be
held for questioning? the Sergeant asks. "Not this scum," Tieck
answers. Not this "small fry," as they say in America. "Stand
them over there where the slugs won't harm the telegraph!"

Masha and Stefan are shoved over against the wall. Stefan
staggers like a drunken man.

"Thought you'd stop us, didn't you?" sneers Tieck. "A very
pretty plan. Very pretty. But you bungled it. Like amateurs.
You're waiting for your guerrillas, eh? Your guerrillas have
been destroyed."

"We stopped your train! We stopped it!" Stefan's voice is
dull and hollow.

"What's one train to us?" demands Tieck, as a final torture
before the kill. "We've got them by the thousands. For that
one train we'll wipe out this entire town, you hear? We'll wipe
it clean until it is just a blackened patch of ground, where nothing
grows. And then we'll see how many more Poles wish to make
heroes of themselves. . . . Sergeant!"

The two German soldiers take up their positions. "It's too
bad to die so young, isn't it? And your wife's so pretty. What
do you think she'll look like after she's been lying in the street
a week?"

This is too much for Stefan. "She had nothing to do with it!
I swear to you . . ." he screams. He has fallen to his knees,
with Masha begging him not to beg favors.

"I thought you'd crawl. They always do," sneers Tieck.

"Stefan, get off your knees!" pleads Masha, and when he cannot move she kneels beside him. Her lips are repeating a formal
prayer: "Praised be Jesus Christus and Mary His Mother, for she
is worthy of it. Praised be—"

Outside there is a tremendous explosion. The Captain rushes
out to investigate. With a glad cry of "Nikolai!" Masha is trying to help Stefan to his feet. The second train is grinding
toward the station.

"Hear that? That's our second train." Tieck has whipped

around to Stefan, his eyes gleaming. "It carries engineers. In two hours' time they'll have the track repaired. Did you really think you could stop us?"

"We slowed you down two hours," announces Stefan, struggling to get to his feet.

"Two hours!"

"One day you'll pray to God for those two hours." Stefan is standing straight and defiant now. "And we've taken them away from you! We! Something will stop you! Something will!"

"Sergeant!" The soldiers raise their guns.

"Ready!"

"Stefan, I love you. Stefan, hold me close!"

"Aim!"

"Something will stop you!" shouts Stefan.

Tieck's hand is raised. Suddenly it falls. The lights black out. The guns flash.

ACT II

At German General Staff Headquarters Marshal von Falken and Generals Kranz and Kessel are in conference. On the wall a large detail map of the Moscow front. Von Falken stands by the map, checking troop movements. The Reds have massed their troops in the center, as expected, Kranz confirms. Von Falken is pleased. The attack will start at 6 A.M. Sector K and the armies of Gen. von Block are properly set—

"These divisions will drive forward to point K 1 as planned," announces Von Falken. "They then pivot and drive south to cut communications between Moscow and the front. The Russians become demoralized and we drive into the city from all sectors. . . . We drive in for the kill and no force in the world can stop us. . . . Like a theorem in Euclid, Q.E.D."

Gen. Kessel would raise a point. The fresh troops for Sector K have not yet reached the front. Herr Tieck confirms Kessel's statement. "Marshal, your trains are just coming into the junction at Rzhev now," reports Tieck.

"Six hours late!" explodes Von Falken.

"Sabotage."

"Damned incompetence!"

"I'm sorry, Marshal," says Tieck. "It's a little difficult maintaining the railroad schedules these days, you know."

"The entire plan was perfectly worked out, down to the last mathematical detail."

"So you still believe in mathematics, Marshal?"

"By God, the Fuehrer's going to hear about this. . . . Kranz, I want a complete report on all highways and communication lines between the railroad junction at Rzhev and the front. Distances, condition of roads, etc."

Again Kessel would object to moving the troops up that night, but Kessel is always objecting and that doesn't worry Von Falken. The Marshal goes with Gen. Kranz to check the roads from Rzhev. Tieck and Kessel fall into a general discussion. They talk of the tricks mathematics can play; of the virtues of psychology. Kessel would contend that psychology is rubbish, but Tieck is not so sure. "There must be something makes us tick the way we do," says he. "Take myself, for example. I used to work in a laboratory torturing rats for science. Now I've graduated to the Gestapo. I'm a clear case. But what about Von Falken? What's his secret, I wonder?"

"Secret? I know of no secret," explodes Kessel. "The man's a monomaniac, that's all. Still there was 1918."

"Quite an interesting year for us all," admits Herr Tieck.

"The Von Falken family owned one of the great estates in East Prussia," Kessel continues. "After the armistice agitators came to the peasants and started dividing up the land. The authorities were powerless. So Von Falken rounded up a group of officers . . . They had machine guns. . . . They ambushed the peasants and slaughtered them. In the melee young Von Falken was almost killed. A hand grenade exploded under his feet. God knows how he pulled through at all. He's all plates and wires below here." He taps his stomach. "No friends, no affections, no human ties of any kind. And yet to this man is entrusted the most crucial offensive of the entire war."

"These are desperate days, General," observes Tieck. "Perhaps they call for desperate men. Still . . . one hates to put all one's eggs in a single basket. . . ."

Von Falken and Kranz are back. Von Falken has put in a call for Gen. Holz. The Marshal has checked on the highways and found them well guarded. The troops from Yugoslavia will be moving up to the front tonight.

Again Kessel would protest. How can Von Falken send troops through the forest at night when he knows guerrillas are operating in that sector? "What if they don't reach the front? What if you have to attack with exhausted troops?"

"Perhaps you would like to fly back to Berlin and lay your objections before the Fuehrer?" suggests Von Falken. "By God, we've driven to within twenty miles of Moscow! We can take the city by tomorrow night. And for fear of a few guerrillas you would call the whole thing off!"

Kessel—I warned you about those trains. You're making the same mistake again.

Von Falken—I made no mistake. Am I to be held accountable for blundering subordinates? . . . You'd stop the whole offensive now—now when we've built up an overwhelming superiority. Five tanks to their one! Enough planes to blast a path clear to the center of Moscow. And you'd call the whole thing off, by God!

Kranz—Your call, Marshal von Falken.

Von Falken (into phone)—Hello, Holz? We're moving up your troops at once. They start rolling at five o'clock this afternoon. They will reach the front at 4 a.m. They will lead the attack at dawn!

A spot of light picks Gen. Holz out of the darkness. He is at the phone protesting to Von Falken that there are guerrillas all along the road. Gen. Holz refuses to take the responsibility. He holds the phone away from his ear as Von Falken answers and then quietly says: "Yes, Marshal, I'll give the order at once! Operator, get me Col. Bauer, Death's Head Regiment. This is important. . . . Hello, Bauer. . . . Cancel all previous orders. Death's Head Regiment up to the front immediately!"

"But, General, my troops aren't unloaded yet!"

"Not my idea. Headquarters'."

Col. Bauer should take every precaution against guerrillas, Holz advises, but he must start his regiment rolling at once. "You must reach the front before dawn." The lights fade.

Out of the darkness a bugle call and the rumble of orders and troop movements. "Motorcycle scouts, forward!" "Tank columns, forward!"

There is the clatter of great tanks as they gain momentum. Then a voice on the loudspeaker in the darkness: "Radio Moscow! Word has just come that fresh Nazi divisions are now unloading at the railroad junction of Rzhev. They will move up to the front tonight to take part in the attack tomorrow. . . ."

The radio voice can still be heard as the lights come up on the corner of the common room of a Russian Collective Farm.

"There are large poster portraits of Lenin and Stalin and a large graph labeled 'Kalinin Collective Farm' in Russian. . . . A large peasant girl stands by the table listening to the radio. She is Katya. At the window stands an old peasant with a rifle. He wears a great flowing mustache and has a habit of stroking a non-existent beard—his sacrifice to progress."

The radio voice continues quietly, earnestly: "Order of the day. To all partisan and guerrilla units! To all men and women behind the German lines! Redouble your efforts! Strike at the enemy wherever you find him! Cut his roads! Destroy his bridges! Everything to delay these troops. No sacrifice is too great. Moscow is in danger!"

Katya and Grigori are waiting for a Red Army man. Katya is confident. Grigori is doubtful. To bolster his confidence Grigori has retrieved an ikon he has had for twenty years. Now, while Katya stands guard, he sets it up on a barrel head and gets down on his knees before it.

"I shall pray with one eye only," he assures Katya, when she begs him to be on his guard. . . . "Little Father, I humbly beg you to look down and help us out here in Russia. It is I— Grigori Stepanitch Shilov—though I don't know as you'll recognize me without my beard. It's true I haven't paid so much attention to you these last twenty years. But we've been terribly busy, Little Father. First it was the White Guards—those agents of the devil—we made short work of them, I can tell you. Then —the electricity situation and the five-year plans—"

"Grigori—you're an old fool!" declares Katya. But Grigori is not to be turned from his devotions. He goes on with his prayer —praying that the Nazis may go by without killing them, but asking particularly that the Little Father take good care of Comrade Stalin, whatever happens. "Because, if you don't," concludes Grigori, "I'll never believe in you again—even if I AM dead."

The door is flung open and a tall Red Army Soldier darts in and closes the door quickly after him. They have been waiting, Katya tells him. Yes, this is the Kalinin Collective Farm; yes, they have taken their ton of dynamite into the forest.

"I'm the mechanic here," Katya tells the Soldier. "I drive the tractor."

It is a thorough job Katya is doing, the Soldier admits, but there is no time for that now. There are a hundred and fifty guerrillas waiting in the woods, with the dynamite. That's good!

"Listen, Citizens, there's a German column coming to the front tonight on this same highway. It's a crack column of motorized troops and tanks, to be used as spearhead for the offensive to-morrow against Moscow. These troops have been delayed six hours. As a result they are moving up after dark. Our guerrillas are to wipe them out!"

Everything else has been attended to. The cattle have been driven into the forest. The grain has been buried. The tractor? —No, the tractor has not been destroyed. Katya has hidden some of the parts— That isn't enough. The Germans carry replacements. But Katya wouldn't see anything happen to that tractor—

"Listen, I was a Stakhanovite last year," she pleads. "We fin-ished the harvest two weeks early. They sent me to Moscow. I saw Comrade Stalin. The tractor did all that for me."

"Now you listen to me, Katya," interrupts the Soldier. "Last month we blew up Dneiprostov. You heard that?" Katya nods. "It wasn't easy. No one would blow the dynamite. Finally our Commissar had to push the switch himself. You know what he said? 'This is our greatest victory. It proves that we will build again,' he said. 'Only in despair a people gives its treasures to the enemy.' . . . Well, Katya?"

"Burning is quickest, I suppose," says Katya.

"I'll do it, if you wish."

"No, I'll do it." She turns and hurries out.

The house will have to go, too. Grigori will attend to that. The thatch is dry, and there is a pile of rags soaked in gasoline. He starts to light the rags and notices the portraits on the wall. They must not be left behind—nor the ikon, which he puts under his shirt. Grigori has turned in the doorway, taking one last look around the room. "You've been a good friend to us these last years, Kalinin Collective," he says. "You've sheltered us from the cold and damp. You've helped us feed a hundred thousand mouths in your day. . . . Standing here, I, Grigori Stepanitch Shilov, swear for every stick of you we'll take a life. Yes, for every twisted nail. Today we run away. But our time will come. Believe me, it will come!"

The lights black out.

In a spot of light the Soldier who had come to the Kalinin farm is speaking over a shortwave transmitter. His head is bandaged. He is calling Guerrilla Headquarters to report that the guerrilla group with which he had made contact had success-fully blown up a German motorized column and shot down its

men. "The German regiment was completely destroyed," he reports. "Forty-seven tanks—thirty armored cars—seventy-one
trucks." It was the Death's Head Regiment.

"Special mention should be made of tractor driver Katerina
Michaelovna Pogodin, who attacked the Nazi staff car with hand
grenades," the soldier goes on. "She was killed in action. . . .
Any further instructions?"

"Continue to operate in the German rear. Disrupt communications wherever possible. Cut all lines of supply to the front.
Let us know all developments. That is all. . . . A good night's
work, eh, Markov?"

"Yes, Commander, a good night's work."

There is darkness and then another light picks out a German
officer at a field phone. He is calling the Death's Head Regiment
for General Holz and has been calling for some time. There is
no answer. There is no more time. Let him call the 89th Regiment instead, orders Gen. Holz. The 89th will have to lead the
attack now, even though they have been attacking for over a
week and have been promised their leaves.

"How can they get their leaves when the Death's Head Regiment hasn't come up to relieve them?" demands Holz. "Is it
my fault those damned trains were delayed six hours? Was it
my idea to send up the Death's Head troops after dark? The
regiment must go into action! Support will follow. The men
will get their leaves in Moscow! Tomorrow!"

"Yes, General. . . ." The German officer has turned back to
the phone. ". . . calling the 89th Regiment. Gen. Holz calling the 89th Regiment. . . ."

The lights are out.

As the lights come up a German armored regiment is discovered camped in a clearing in the forest. Soldiers can be seen
huddled under blankets; thick brush hides the outline of a tank.
A sentry is dozing on his gun when there is a stir in the brush
that brings him into action. A moment later a young Sergeant
comes into the clearing. His uniform is torn and he has lost
his equipment. A stocky soldier with an unpleasant voice grabs
the Sergeant. Others pinion his arms and throw him to his knees.
He is, they shout, a lying bastard of a spy. They twist his arms
back of him amidst his howls of protest. One, Weiskopf, the
roughest of them, rips open the soldier's tunic, examines his

papers and pulls out a shawl. It is the shawl Masha wore in the telegraph office.

They demand further explanations. The Sergeant tells them of the ambush that wiped out the Death's Head Regiment. That proves he's a liar. The Death's Head is to relieve these men tonight. "There's less than a company of us left alive," insists the Sergeant. . . .

From the direction of the Russian lines a booming voice is heard over a loudspeaker: "German soldiers of the 89th Armored Regiment. . . . You are listening to the voice of the Red Army—"

"I command you not to listen," orders a Lieutenant.

"You are waiting for your leave," the voice continues. "The Death's Head Regiment was to take your place in the line. Last night the Death's Head Regiment was ambushed by guerrillas and wiped out. . . ."

"Propaganda!" shouts the Lieutenant as the men demand to know if their leaves have been canceled. He sends two men to search out and silence the broadcast.

"German soldiers, ask yourselves this question," booms the voice. "What are you getting from our Russian soil? The Goerings and the Krupps are coining millions, but what of yourselves? What do you get but blood and wounds and suffering?" . . .

"I promised you leaves and leaves you'll get," shouts the Lieutenant in an effort to drown out the loudspeaker. "Not in chilly barracks in a muddy village! No! You'll get your leaves in Moscow! Not just two weeks, but the whole winter! Get the picture, Tigers! Steam-heated apartments! Clean, warm beds! Plenty to eat! Plenty to drink! Women!" He is talking fast to overcome the voice booming in the background. "You'll get the run of the city! The stores! The apartments! The warehouses! What about it, Tigers? Vodka, caviar, fur coats, silk stockings!"

The German soldiers are excited by the promise. Their questions swamp the Lieutenant. They are ready now to smash on through to Moscow—

"Think it over, German soldiers," booms the voice. "This is your last chance! In a few minutes we'll meet again!"

There is the boom of artillery in the distance. "That's M Sector. It's starting!"

"Pack your equipment!" orders the Lieutenant. "Tank drivers, to your tanks! Get those actors rolling! . . . We're driving forward, men! Forward to Moscow!"

The tank motors are starting. In the distance the artillery fire increases. The men are rushing out to their machines. The roar of battle is on as the lights fade.

The lights have come up on a section of the Russian front lines, a hilltop screened by sandbags and camouflaged for an anti-tank gun. There are a stack of shells and a row of bottles nearby. There is still a rumble of big guns in the distance, a rumble which keeps coming nearer.

The Gunner, "a squat, powerfully built man with an Oriental cast," is testing the breech of his gun. Presently he is joined by the Company Commissar, carrying a sub-machine gun under his arm.

Nothing has been heard from Sergei and his loudspeaker yet, which worries the Commissar, because it is beginning to get light. The Gunner had also heard a couple of rifle shots a minute ago, and that is not too good. But even as they worry the hearty voice of Sergei greets them. Sergei "is a huge fellow, good-natured and grinning. In one hand he carries the loudspeaker and in the other a rifle. Across his back are slung two more rifles."

Sergei has been having his experiences. He had heard the Commissar talking over a loudspeaker and holding forth eloquently in a plea for "International solidarity." For himself Sergei doesn't think much of international solidarity. It's a one-way affair. "Look! There I sit in a snowdrift listening to your pretty voice over the loudspeaker. Up creep two Nazis with their guns ready for business. 'Brothers,' I say, 'Tovarischi, don't forget your international solidarity.' Do they answer, the brutes? No. They want to play rough. Both of them!" He reaches under his coat and pulls out Masha's shawl. "And look! The thieving devils! Midwinter, and some poor peasant girl is freezing for want of this." . . .

The machine gun the Commissar has brought is a present from the Colonel. It is American made, very pretty, very light and certain to be of great help if they are rushed. Sergei can't make out the name stamped on it, however. "They have such a damned difficult alphabet, those Americans!" he insists.

As to the order of the day, Moscow is in danger. They are calling out volunteers from the factories and there is going to be a big push right through where they are. "The Nazis have massed fresh troops from Yugoslavia down there," reports the Commissar. "Our orders are not to yield a single inch."

There can be no hope of reserves being brought up for another two hours. Two hours! Sergei knows what that means. There is a long whistle, followed by a long silence. Then Sergei begins to talk again. But not about the present war. He talks about his father who lived past 72, through two wars and three revolutions. "Yet in all those years he never learned to read or write," muses Sergei. "He never left our little village."

He pauses as though he were puzzling something out. "On the other hand, you take me now. I've lived in Moscow a whole year. I was in Vladivostok once. I've seen cotton growing in the Uzbek desert—and the North Sea all frozen over. Would you believe it? I've even gone fishing with an ax and chopped fine salmon right out of the ice."

"Is that the truth?" Gunner wants to know.

"Strictly. But that's nothing to my little Sergei. What a life he'll have, eh, when he grows up! Fly to the moon, perhaps, and cruise around the sky inspecting stars. What a place our Russia will be then! Tell me, did the Fascists think we'd really let them snatch it from us?"

France had a fine country, too, the Gunner would remind him, but Sergei is not impressed. "They chop no fish out of the ice in France," says he.

There are signs of movement in the forest. Sergei is itching to fire a few rounds into the woods to stir up the enemy, but the Commissar won't let him.

"So you think you'll take Moscow!" mutters Sergei, defiantly, throwing a vicious glance in the direction of the Germans. "When you can see your ears! That's when!"

But that two hours before the reserves can be brought up is still worrying Sergei, which prompts the Commissar to tell him the story of the Persian Xerxes and the Greeks at Thermopylae. "There were six hundred against a million then, yet when King Xerxes shouted: 'Surrender, Greeks!' they, too, answered: 'When you can see your ears.' "

And when Xerxes called over: "I have ten thousand archers. Their arrows will come so thick that they'll shut off the sunlight," the Greek general, Leonidov, called back: "Then we'll fight in the shade!" Leonidov, Sergei is proud to note, is a Russian name.

The Persians attacked and the Greeks cut them down by dozens and hundreds. For a week the Greeks held. Then Xerxes sent an army around by another road to pinch them off. Leonidov ordered his men to retreat, but they built a barricade behind them and faced both ways instead.

"Then, you know what?" the Commissar concludes; "they "combed their hair and bathed and dressed up in their finest uniforms—and every man died fighting!"

For a moment there is silence. "Unconsciously Sergei's hand reaches for his throat. He buttons up his tunic and runs his hand through his hair to comb it."

"I'm a mess, to tell the truth," mutters Sergei. "Look at this beard! Torn pants—a mess. About those Greeks—what happened in the end?"

"In the end King Xerxes' army fled and Greece was free. After that no Persian army ever dared cross the sea to Europe."

The sound of battle draws closer. Machine guns start banging close at hand. "Come—Tovarischi . . . A fine shooting gallery we'll have here!" shouts Sergei.

The Commissar has taken several of the bottles. "I'll dodge down the ravine. If they try to climb up here I'll cook one or two of them . . ." he says. "You can fire when ready. So long."

The battle increases to a roar. A ray of sunlight strikes the two soldiers as they aim their guns. "The sun! We'll have a lovely day," shouts Sergei over the battle.

"What?"

"I said we'll have a lovely day," answers Sergei, going back to his shooting. The lights fade.

Out of the darkness come the sound of shelling and dive bombers. Cutting through it radio voices are heard:

"This is the British Broadcasting Corporation in a program beamed to Free Frenchmen everywhere!" says an English announcer.

"The eyes of the world are turned East today as the German war machine batters at the very gates of Moscow . . ." booms a voice speaking French. "The liberty, not only of the Russian people, but of all Europe—and not only the liberty but also the very existence of free people hangs in the balance. Moscow is in danger. . . ."

"Radio Berlin!" speaks up a German voice. "The valiant National Socialist Army of the Fuehrer is still grinding forward. . . . The end of the war is in sight as Field Marshal von Falken predicts that Moscow will fall tomorrow!"

"Radio Moscow!" cuts in a voice in Russian. "The Fascist barbarians have driven ten miles closer to our Moscow but they

are paying for it with their life's blood for every inch of the
way. Red Armymen! Citizen volunteers! Partisans! Men
and women! Everything to smash the Nazi war machine. Moscow is in danger! . . ."

"On the bloody battlefield outside Moscow is being fought the
most gigantic battle of the entire war." The English speaker
has returned to the microphone. "Our hearts go out to our gallant allies, the courageous Russian people in their hour of need.
Their battle is our battle, for if Moscow falls that last free capital of the continent of Europe is gone!"

The lights come up on German General Staff Headquarters. It
is noon of the day of the big push. Marshal von Falken and
Gen. Kessel are seated at the table, studying stacks of reports
in front of them. Gen. Gerhardt brings in more dispatches.

In the reports received Sector K has not been heard from.
Other sectors are advancing according to plan. Herr Tieck slides
in and is pleased to hear that everything is progressing satisfactorily, despite Sector K. It was Sector K, he recalls, that
Von Falken considered the key to the entire offensive. Tieck
also brings news. Gen. Lechner has just joined their little band.
And Lechner, he understands, is hoping for a promotion.

Von Falken stares hard at Kessel. Kessel is visibly uncomfortable and quick to deny that he knew anything about Lechner's
coming, a statement Von Falken obviously doubts. Breaking
under the Marshal's accusing glance Kessel leaps to his feet—

"I at least think more of my country than of my personal
feelings," he shouts. "If this offensive is smashed the responsibility is yours! We all advised you from the first—"

"Don't worry, Kessel. I have not failed."

How could he fail? "With three tanks to their one. With
numerical superiority and mastery of the air? . . . It's quite
obvious. After today the enemy is through—everywhere," insists Von Falken.

"Aren't you forgetting about America, Marshal?" inquires
Tieck.

"America? You know, Herr Tieck, there's one pleasure I've
permitted myself—sports. . . . Have you ever seen an ex-world
champion prizefighter? A soft-headed hulk with flabby, sagging
muscles? He hasn't seen a fight in years. One morning suddenly he decides to enter the ring again. He trains. He says
good-by to his whores and his liquor and his great swilling gluts
of food. He goes to a gymnasium where he wheezes and sweats

and gives off a nauseous smell. Finally, the day comes. He
steps into the ring in a gorgeous dressing gown. In the other
corner is a lean killer, with his belly stretched tight across his
spinal cord. Which one has your money, Herr Tieck?"

"A striking metaphor," admits Tieck.

Gen. Kranz is in with reports from Sectors H and I. Still
nothing from K. Ominous reports of "pressure on their left,"
which the Marshal cannot understand. Sector K should be to
their left. It could be a by-passed unit trying to break out. . . .

Finally Kessel gets through to Gen. von Bloch. A moment
later Von Falken has snatched the phone out of Kessel's hand.
"Hello," he calls, excitedly. "Von Falken speaking. What's
going on out there?"

As he listens his foot starts tapping nervously. Tieck and
Kessel exchange glances. Suddenly the Marshal bursts out:

"What do you mean 'bogged down'? I don't give a damn
for their anti-tank batteries and their fortified hills and their
gasoline bottles! You have enough tanks to smash through
anything. Throw in your reserves. . . . WHAT? Your reserves
are gone? . . . No! No, it isn't all over, I tell you. . . . Let
me think, will you? Give me a chance to think? . . . Yes,
yes . . . Stay by the phone. I'll call you back." He has hung
up and is fumbling through his papers.

KESSEL—You couldn't be wrong, could you? (VON FALKEN
seems not to hear him.) You wouldn't listen to us, would you?
Not when we told you this offensive was insane—suicide!

VON FALKEN (*pitifully*)—Be quiet, won't you? I'm trying
to think.

KESSEL—The whole staff told you it was impossible! Von
Seldte told you it was impossible! So you had him murdered because he stood in your way! You knew better! Yes, you went
ahead and killed a hundred thousand men—the flower of our
beautiful army!

VON FALKEN—By God, you've been waiting for this—you and
your third-rate military hacks! Waiting and hoping with the
juice drooling out at your mouths like a pack of hungry jackals!

TIECK—Gentlemen, really this is undignified.

VON FALKEN—You've been against me from the first—betray-
ing me at every step! Calling in Lechner behind my back!

TIECK—You give the General too much credit, Marshal.

VON FALKEN—You! . . .

TIECK—The smart boys don't put all their eggs in one basket,

MARSHAL. Surely you've learned that by this time!
VON FALKEN—I'll take it to the Fuehrer!
TIECK—You've had your chance, Marshal.

A sentry's voice is heard announcing: "Marshal Lechner!" A moment later Gen. Lechner storms in. "He is short and stocky. A powerful man in the best Prussian tradition." He drops his dispatch case on the table and turns to Von Falken: "I'm to take command. The Fuehrer's instructions. By God, you've distinguished yourself, Von Falken. The finest army we've ever mustered—the greatest opportunity of the entire war, and you've thrown it all away!"

"I made no mistake. There was nothing wrong with my plan! Not a single flaw."

"Nothing wrong! The greatest defeat in our history! Nothing wrong!"

"We're not defeated."

"We've had enough of invalids—cripples! Kessel, the map!"

The Fuehrer, reports Lechner, wants to see Von Falken in Berlin. "There's a plane waiting for you outside," says Tieck.

"The Fuehrer is too kind," mutters Von Falken, as he goes into an inner room.

Lechner is busy with the maps, pointing out the errors in this "hastily conceived offensive." Kessel explains the positions. From the inner room a pistol shot is heard. The Generals go on with their conference.

Tieck goes to the room, from which he returns a moment later. "He was evidently quite a student of anatomy," he says, coldly. "Tell me, Marshal Lechner, why did Von Falken fail?"

LECHNER—He miscalculated—criminally.

TIECK—So? It's difficult to put one's finger on the exact spot, I suppose. There were so many unpredictable factors—an incompetent Colonel murdered in a tiny Croatian village—a few sticks of dynamite in Poland—an hour lost there, another there—trains delayed—snowdrifts—cold—Russian fanaticism—and intangible factors of morale. Each cause in itself insignificant—yet add them up and it's defeat. . . . Yes, when it comes to people, mathematics has a strange way of breaking down. . . . Which straw broke the camel's back? A real question for the philosophers, eh?

KRANZ (hurrying in)—Sector E is calling for reserves! The Reds are counter-attacking!

LECHNER—Counter-attacking!

KESSEL—That's impossible!

KRANZ—We've been pushed back almost a mile. Other sectors report counter-attacks too. All down the line they're calling for more troops.

LECHNER—All down the line! (*The phone rings.*) Yes? Marshal Lechner speaking. . . . You must prevent a break-through, do you hear? You've got to hold your lines or, by God, I'll have you broken for it! Yes, I'll send up all available reserves.

TIECK (*as the siren sounds*)—What's that?

KESSEL—Air raid!

LECHNER—Counter-offensive by God, in dead earnest!

TIECK—Excuse me, gentlemen. Air raids are not in my de-partment. (*He hurries out.*)

LECHNER—Counter-offensive! Kessel, front line reports! Try the shortwave! (KESSEL *switches on the radio.*)

GERHARDT (*coming in*)—The Reds have broken through in two more sectors. Von Bloch is calling for instructions. What shall I tell him?

LECHNER—Tell him— (*He clenches his fist, and breaks off.*) Tell him— Tell him to burn his tanks and retreat southeast! (KESSEL *turns, horrified.* GERHARDT *hurries out.* KESSEL *turns back to the radio. A voice booms out.*)

RADIO VOICE—Radio Moscow. Today our troops in the Mos-cow sector counter-attacked in force all along the front! The enemy is being pushed relentlessly back. Let the Fascist butcher remember Moscow as they run like rats! Let them remember Moscow when they fall freezing in the snow! (*Dive bombers zoom over the building.*) Brothers behind the enemy lines! We are coming to liberate your homes and cities. The Red Army is driving to the West! *Victory will be ours!*

"Outside bombs rain down. Planes scream. The lights black out. And through the darkness comes the sound of Red Army soldiers singing."

THE CURTAIN FALLS

TOMORROW THE WORLD

A Drama in Three Acts

BY JAMES GOW AND ARNAUD D'USSEAU

IT was mid-April before "Tomorrow the World" reached Broadway. The drama had been discovered by Theron Bamberger, the producer, some months before that, but it had taken time, first, to raise sufficient funds to cover the cost of production and, second, to assemble a proper cast after the funds were available. There are twenty-eight stockholders in the "Tomorrow the World" company, which, I think, is seven more than subscribed to the production of "Arsenic and Old Lace" the season before. This was also quite a season for co-operative play producing.

"Tomorrow the World" was written by two young men who have for some years been devoting their talents to the preparation of picture scripts in Hollywood, James Gow and Arnaud d'Usseau. They had sent the script of this play East, to a play agent, and he had decided that it was not only salable, but also promising. It happened, purely by accident, that the agent was in a bank prepared to cash a check, or deposit one, when he met Mr. Bamberger, similarly engaged.

The two exchanged greetings, and, as often happens, the agent suggested that he had a play which he thought might interest Mr. Bamberger. True, it had been read and refused by several better known producers, but so had other scripts that had later made a good deal of money for those who had invested in them.

Mr. Bamberger thought he might be interested and promised to read the play if the agent would send it to his office. He read it. He got others to read it. And finally, as noted, successfully assembled the funds for its production. The drama caused no particular excitement during its preliminary tour, and was received with mixed enthusiasm in New York.

The play-going public, however, was quick to respond to its dramatic appeal and to the compelling performances given by its youthful protagonists, the "Skippy" Homeier, who played the 12-year-old Nazi who is smuggled out of Germany after his liberal father had been murdered in a concentration camp, and Joyce Van Patten, a 10-year-old actress of exceptional gifts, who played his American cousin. Both children had had considerable experience in radio drama, which gave them confidence and poise, and they were quickly acclaimed.

After its late start "Tomorrow the World" ran through the summer. It must have stimulated literally hundreds of dinner-table discussions. These would concern the winning of a world peace by the United Nations after they have succeeded in winning a global war.

It is a morning of early Autumn, 1942, when we walk into the living room of Prof. Michael Frame in a large university town in Middle West America. It is a pleasant room. A hall at back is the real hub of the entire house, running through to the front door at one end and a door into the kitchen at the other.

There is a stairway leading to the second floor, and under the stairway a door to the cellar. There is a fireplace, and over the fireplace an oil portrait of Karl Bruckner. "The style of the painting is academic. Its only claim to merit is its faithful reproduction of Bruckner's features—his small nose and mouth, his mild blue eyes, his hair, which had begun to thin at the time he posed for it." In front of the fireplace is a couch and back of the couch a long table.

Across the room a large bay window looks out on a deep lawn. There is a large desk in front of the window, littered with papers, and with a row of books between heavy brass book-ends. "Although Prof. Frame has an office in the University, this is his living room, and to him living requires his desk, his many books, the daily clutter of magazines, journals, etc. This does not make for order, but it suggests a certain exuberant vitality."

The front door bell is ringing. Commotion on the stairs is followed by the appearance of Patricia (Pat) Frame, 10, lively as a cricket and cute as a button, who comes running down the steps, stops deliberately on the third step from the bottom and jumps from there. "This apparently is one of her latest accomplishments."

Pat is shouting lustily for Frieda. The taxi-man has arrived and they are going to be late. She continues shouting until her Aunt Jessie Frame, "forty-five, pleasant in appearance but rather sharp in manner," takes a hand in quieting her.

Pat and Frieda, it presently appears, are on their way to the train to meet a young man who is coming by train; a young man who is at least two years older than Pat (which really isn't anything that Pat is going to worry about), whose name is Emil.

The prospect of having a new playmate attached to the family is exciting to Pat. "If he can't talk English, do you know what we can do?" she demands excitedly. "We'll talk in deaf and dumb language. I already know two letters. Look, Aunt Jessie!" And Pat proceeds to demonstrate her learning.

Presently, Frieda, the maid, appears. "Frieda is thirty-five, a blonde-haired rather homely woman, who speaks with a German accent." She is wearing her hat and coat and is carrying a small vase of flowers. These she would put in the expected Emil's room—

"I wanted to make his room nice for him—I remember how frightened I was when I came to this country—I felt real homesick—"

"I'll take the flowers up. (JESSIE *takes the vase from* FRIEDA.) And don't think we're going to let you spoil the boy just because he comes from your country. He'll take things as he finds them —and he's a very lucky boy to come to a home like this. Now go on."

In place of taking the flowers to Emil's room when Pat and Frieda go, Jessie adds them to another bouquet on the table. She is just assuring an Associated Press man who has called up from Chicago that it will be impossible for him to talk with Prof. Frame because the Professor is working at the Bronson Foundation Laboratory, which hasn't any phone, when the Professor walks in. He "is forty, not handsome, not too careful in his dress; but blessed with enormous vitality and charm."

Now Michael has taken the phone from Jessie. "Hello . . . this is Michael Frame," he is saying. ". . . That's right, I couldn't be reached—and now I *can* be reached. What would you like to know? . . . Yes . . . Yes, that's right . . . No, no. He's the only son of my sister and Karl Bruckner . . . Karl Bruckner, my ignorant young friend, happened to win a Nobel Prize—in 1933—you might consult the Almanac on your desk there . . . Well, for one thing, he wrote a score of books. May I suggest that you read one of them in particular. It's called 'Superstition, Religion and Reality.' "

"H'mmm. He won't get any further in that book than I did."

"Yes, on the exchange ship—the *Drottningholm*," Michael continues, ignoring Jessie. "Well, it was part of a complicated deal between the German government and our State Department. . . . Well, if he arrives with a couple of dead Nazis slung over his shoulder, I'll call you back . . . Right. (*He hangs up.*) My God. The temporary mortality of the world's great."

"Now what does *that* mean?"

"Today Karl is dead and already forgotten. But fifty years from now every school child will know the story of his life."

Jessie sees no good reason why she should get excited about Emil's coming. It wasn't she who invited him. In fact she hadn't even been consulted. Michael doesn't seem to realize the work involved in bringing another person into the house—

"I wonder if he'll look at all like Karl," Michael muses, as he looks across the room at the Bruckner picture. "We've got to take good care of him, Jessie. He's undoubtedly been through hell. He'll need everything we can give him."

JESSIE—That's what I want to talk about. I can see that you're going to spoil the boy.

MICHAEL—Now wouldn't that be tragic!

JESSIE—The way you spoil Pat. And you do spoil her. I know you're brilliant and very advanced in your ideas, but as a father you leave much to be desired. You treat Pat exactly as if she were a grown-up person.

MICHAEL—Is that bad?

JESSIE—All right. But when you suddenly adopt a twelve-year-old boy, it seems to me you should determine what attitude to take.

MICHAEL—Of course we'll take an attitude. He's our nephew and Karl Bruckner's son. We'll love him.

JESSIE (*after a moment*)—I may learn to love him, but not because he's Karl's son. Yes, I know he was a great man, but I haven't forgotten what Mary went through.

MICHAEL—Mary loved Karl.

JESSIE—Oh, yes—he was a fine romantic figure when he came over here and married her. The great German professor. But after he took her back to that horrible country—always in some fight, some political squabble, until they had to fire him from his University. Those books he wrote may be very impressive, but they didn't furnish any bread and butter. How many times did you and I have to send them money, or they would have starved to death, literally.

MICHAEL—Yes, indeed. And every time you delivered the same oration.

JESSIE—And I was right. If it hadn't been for him, Mary would have been alive today. Well, maybe it's a good thing that she didn't live. Look what happened to him. Practically a criminal, and then he died in prison.

MICHAEL—For God's sake, Jessie! He died in a concentration camp!

JESSIE (*shrugging*)—Well, he must have done *something*.

MICHAEL—He did plenty. Can't you understand! Karl was fighting then the very thing we're fighting now! He was on our side!

JESSIE—He was a German, wasn't he?

MICHAEL (*after an astonished moment*)—Jessie, I adore you, you're the most wonderful mass of contradictions I've ever known. Have you ever given five minutes' thought to what this war is about? Just because you didn't like Karl personally—

JESSIE (*mildly*)—Don't worry, Michael. I'll love the boy for a different reason. He's Mary's son, too.

Leona Richards has let herself in the front door. Leona is thirty and attractive. She has hurried over to help with the welcoming of Emil. She, like Jessie, has found it pretty difficult to get in touch with Michael. And should, according to Michael. There is every reason why the work he is doing in the laboratory should continue to be a military secret. But, if they must know, it isn't munitions.

As soon as Jessie leaves them Michael rises deliberately, walks over to Leona, kisses her, and demands to know what is troubling her.

"Good Lord, is it that obvious?" Leona would know.

"No. But last night you told me you'd be busy all day. And then you walk in at eleven-thirty announcing you've come to see Emil. And then—the way you kissed me."

LEONA—Well, you're right.

MICHAEL—Let's have it.

LEONA—Sally Praskins, who is a horrible person, was at my door at nine o'clock this morning. She said she had to tell me something for my own good.

MICHAEL—Dear Sally.

LEONA—It seems it all happened at the faculty tea. Margaret Bates had it from somebody else that you were seen leaving my apartment at a quarter of twelve last Thursday night.

MICHAEL—It's a damn lie. It was a quarter *after* twelve and it was Wednesday.

LEONA—Of course, this tasty morsel reached the ears of Dean McGrath's wife. She was elaborately horrified.

MICHAEL—Well, in her position, it's her Christian duty to be horrified. Besides, she disapproves of my politics.

LEONA—"Disapproves" is a weak word, darling. She told Sally that knowing your radical ideas, she's not surprised to learn that you're also a *libertine.*

MICHAEL (*bursting into laughter*)—That's great! And what did she call *you?*

LEONA—Oh, she knew better than to call me names. But it gave her a chance to deplore the fact that I'm principal of the Experimental School.

MICHAEL (*after a pause*)—Nine-tenths of our colleagues and their wives are intelligent, decent people. But that woman's a hideous old harridan. What are you worried about?

LEONA—I'm not, really. Because it's so ridiculous. But I was afraid you'd be upset.

MICHAEL—What?

LEONA—Because of Jessie and Pat.

MICHAEL—Nonsense. Jessie and Pat both know how I feel about you. So let's forget it.

LEONA—All right, Professor. It's forgotten.

The next minute a new idea strikes the Professor. Why shouldn't he and Leona get married. And he means it. Leona is not so sure. There are several things and a few people to be considered. Jessie and Pat especially.

"Jessie has her own income. She's a free agent," counters Michael.

"That's just like you, Mike. You've accepted her adoration all your life—she's bound herself to you hand and foot. And then you casually say, 'She's a free agent.' "

"She's always known I might get married again. Besides, Jessie's tough."

"And Pat? I suppose she's 'tough' too."

"You're not worried about Pat?"

"Worried? I'd be scared stiff."

"Pat worships you. She comes home from school every day telling me you're the only teacher who has any sense. What's more, she's asked me to get married. To almost anybody! She wants me to have more children. Three of them, to quote her precisely."

"Mike."

"As soon as we're married. I'm sure she'll take it up with you."

"Oh, my God!"

"You'll find she has a startling knowledge of the facts of life. It seems we no longer believe in the stork."

"You know where she got that startling knowledge? Me. Right from me. It was I who revealed the mysteries of sex according to the newest methods of progressive education. Pat was very bright about it, and awfully matter-of-fact—seemed to regard it chiefly as a problem in plumbing."

Still Leona is not convinced. She refuses to be rushed. For one thing she is not at all certain she would be a good mother. And if she weren't, she couldn't resign after three months, as she could a teaching job. Then there is Emil. He might not even like her. He might not even like his new father, Michael reminds her.

"How could I, or anyone else, take the place of Karl Bruckner?" he asks seriously. "But should I hesitate because of that to adopt the boy? The world we live in today doesn't allow for hesitations. We're at war. We can't afford the luxury of a 'maybe' or a 'perhaps'—(*With a swift look.*)—or a long engagement."

He has put his hand on her shoulder and kissed her. There is no resisting his last plea, and Leona agrees. They will be married in two weeks.

Pat and Frieda are back. There was no Emil on the train and the conductor is sure he had not seen him. Pat is plaintive in her disappointment. Frieda is excited with fear that the boy has been lost. Aunt Jessie is not surprised. She knew there would be trouble. "Letting a child of twelve travel alone halfway across the country—"

But Michael refuses to be dismayed. Emil may have missed the train in New York. If he got on the wrong train he probably had his address pinned on his coat. Anyway, he will put in a long distance call for New York.

"After all, if the kid survived the Nazis and got out of Germany, he should be able to change trains in Chicago. He'll probably arrive this evening."

Meantime Michael has an important announcement to make to the family. Leona would stop him if she could, but she can't. He has sat down and drawn Pat to him. "Lee and I are going to be married in two weeks," he tells her, adding quickly: "That is if it's all right with you."

"Are you really asking my permission?"

"We certainly are, Pat," says Leona, seriously.

"Naturally," adds Michael, "we can't get married unless we

have your permission. And Jessie's."

Jessie has turned her head away. Leona was right. Mike should not have been in such a hurry with his announcement. He should have first talked with Jessie—

"Why should he?" Jessie demands, a little sharply. "It's none of my business if he wants to get married." With a brave attempt at a smile she turns to Leona. "I'm sorry, my dear— it's just that Michael has such a way of springing surprises. I hope you'll be very happy."

Aunt Jessie has gone to her room. They shouldn't worry, Pat thinks. Aunt Jessie always gets a headache whenever things turn out the way she doesn't expect. As for her own permission, Pat is enthusiastic about giving them that, running into Leona's arms and accepting a big hug with enthusiasm—"I think it's wonderful," she squeals delightedly. "Now we can walk to school together every morning."

Suddenly Frieda appears in the hallway all excitement. "Professor! He's here! Das Kind. Ganz allein!" She is gesturing wildly for Emil to enter. Now the boy appears in the hall, slowly, carrying a small suitcase. "Emil Bruckner is twelve, blond, tall for his age. He is a startlingly handsome boy. He wears a threadbare black suit; knickerbockers. In his manner there is an inner uncertainty, a critical reserve."

For a moment Emil stands, holding his suitcase and looking at the people in the room. When Michael steps forward to welcome him he clicks his heels smartly and bows from the waist.

"Herzlich willkommen, mein Kind! Du bist willkommen!" says Michael, taking his suitcase and handing it to Frieda. He embraces Emil and kisses him. "Wir hoffen dass du sehr glücklich in deinen neuen Heim fühlen wirst."

Emil draws himself up stiffly, including them all in his explanation. "Thank you. You are very hospitable. You see, I speak acceptable American, although grammar I have not quite mastered."

"Splendid! Splendid! Take his bag, Frieda. Take it up to his room."

"Er ist hübsch, nicht wahr?" Frieda has hardly taken her eyes off the boy, and speaks in hushed tones. "Ein liebes Kind!"

Emil turns on her sharply. "Please do not call me a child, and I am not beautiful. I am brave but I am not beautiful."

With proper apology Frieda has gone to the kitchen. "Frieda will adore you; you will have to tolerate it," Michael explains, smilingly. "This is my daughter, Patricia. She has fallen in love with you, sight unseen." Ignoring Pat's disgusted "Aw—!" Michael, standing with his arm around Emil's shoulder, calls her over. "Come here, Pat—you've at last got your Emil."

Pat comes hesitantly forward and tentatively holds out her hand. Emil ignores the hand, bows stiffly and clicks his heels. "Miss Patricia . . . I am happy to be acquainted with you."

Pat is all friendliness. She is even willing to bow and click her heels, too, if that is what is expected of her. Leona, too, when it comes her turn, would be friendly and informal, which is the way people are in America. She would, Leona explains, like to meet Emil more than half-way. "That means that I want for us to become very good friends," she explains.

"But of course," agrees Emil. "I shall try to make myself as delightful as possible."

"Relax, Emil, relax." Michael is laughing. "Sit down. Are you hungry? We're going to have lunch in a few minutes. And incidentally, how the devil did you get here?"

Emil's story is interesting. He was not on the train because he had preferred to be "transported by airplane." And how did he talk Miss Lewis, who was to meet him in New York, into that?

"If I may have pardon, Miss Lewis is a blockhead," explains Emil. "She made difficulty. It was necessary that I insist."

A moment later Emil has observed that they seem to be possessed of a "very extreme house," and when he is surprised that they should think him funny, Michael explains that to be strictly American he should have said: "Quite a dump you've got here!" This, Emil assumed, is an idiom. He will remember it.

"Don't let them tease you, Emil," warns Leona. "I think your English is wonderful. And you'll pick up our American slang fast enough."

"I shall apply myself."

"You shall apply yourself to having a good time," says Michael. "You'll play games, and eat lots of food, and sleep like a log. No more unhappiness, no more fear. This is your family; and we hope you'll love us."

Also, Michael adds, Emil is to call him Mike. It may not be exactly American, but it is the custom in that house. "No barriers here between youth and age. We're all equal. We're all friends."

Discovering that Emil will not be twelve until the nineteenth

of that month, and that he never has had a birthday party, Pat
has gone shouting into the kitchen to warn Frieda of the party
he is going to have.

"Emil, can we talk about your father?" Michael asks. Emil
doesn't answer. "He was a wonderful friend and a great teacher,"
Michael goes on. "I studied under him at Leipzig. I hope you
will like this portrait of him. (EMIL *turns and looks up at the
portrait.*) He was my teacher in philosophy, and not only in the
lecture room. We drank a lot of beer together, and once we
went skiing in the Bavarian Alps. It was Karl, the philosopher,
who persuaded me to become a chemist. He believed that the
philosophers of the future must be men of science—men of action.
That's why it was inevitable that he became a great fighter when
it was necessary to fight. (*After a slight pause, gently.*) You
must be very proud to be his son."

"Please do not speak of my father." Emil's voice is trembling
with emotion.

Leona has crossed quickly to him. "Of course not, Emil," she
says sympathetically. "Of course not. We know how it is. Being the son of a great man can be a heavy burden."

Pat has come rushing in. She would like to take up the matter
of showing Emil her clubroom. And her electric train. She has
dolls, of course, but she likes trains better. Emil is surprised.
Was Emil afraid when he went up in the plane? Naturally not.
He is going to be an aviator, Emil explains. When Pat thinks
that she will be an aviator, too, Emil is not so sure. Girls get
sick. One got sick in the plane he was on. Was he sitting near
her? He was not. "I was forced to sit beside a big, fat Jew!"
sneers Emil.

The silence is momentary but intense. "Miss Richards is
Jewish," Michael says, quietly.

"You are joking?" Emil is incredulous.

"No."

"That is regrettable."

"It's not regrettable," says Leona, evenly. "You'd better remember that."

Pat is urging Emil to follow her upstairs. "Come on before
you make any more bum cracks!" she says.

The children have disappeared around the landing. Michael,
looking after Emil, is plainly worried. "Karl's son . . . Good
Lord!" he mutters.

"Children say those things," says Leona, with a shrug. "Children who should know better. The Thorndyke kid pulled a honey the other day, right in the classroom."

MICHAEL—That's no excuse for this boy.

LEONA—Michael, who took care of Emil—I mean, after his father was arrested?

MICHAEL—For a while, a younger brother of Karl's had him; after that, I don't know who. For a long time we thought he was dead. I tried to get him out in 1938, and our consul in Berlin couldn't even find him. Then he finally turned up in the custody of an old woman who claimed to be a distant aunt. Apparently she was happy enough to get rid of him. (*He looks at* LEONA *perceptively.*) You're wondering if the kid's a Nazi?

LEONA (*mildly*)—Only wondering.

MICHAEL—I thought of that, too, but it's ridiculous. He was undoubtedly ostracized, starved, life made miserable for him, because he was Karl Bruckner's son.

LEONA—I'm wondering, anyway. How much of the filth rubbed off on him . . . You'll send him to the Experimental School, won't you?

MICHAEL—Do you want him?

LEONA—Certainly.

MICHAEL—You've got him. And let's remember, no matter what the kid says, he'll turn out all right. He's Karl's son.

LEONA (*laughing*)—Mike, you're wonderful. Every now and then you go back to the lovely, old-fashioned belief in inherited characteristics. Blood's-thicker-than-water. Good stock there, Major. I knew his great grandfather.

JESSIE (*coming downstairs; has regained her composure*)— Well, I've met him. He's the perfect image of Mary.

LEONA (*pleasantly*)—Your sister must have been a beautiful woman. The boy is striking.

JESSIE—Yes. And I must admit, he seems to have nice manners.

MICHAEL (*smiling*)—I hope that means you've decided to like him.

JESSIE—Well, I'm not sure. I don't think I'll be here long enough to find out. (*She crosses to* LEONA.) You understand, don't you, dear? It's better for all of us if I leave.

LEONA—I hoped you wouldn't. I honestly hoped you'd stay with us. This is your home as much as Michael's. Surely we can work things out. I have my own work—and you're much better at running a house than I am—I'd never dream of interfering.

MICHAEL—I'm asking you to stay, too, Jessie. But I also know you'll do exactly as you please.

JESSIE—Thank you, Michael. (*To* LEONA.) I know, dear. It would be convenient for you to have me as housekeeper. It's been very convenient for Michael. But by now I deserve a vacation. Don't you think?

It is Jessie's idea that she will go to Mexico. An old friend has long been insisting that she should come. But, with Leona's pleading, she agrees to stay on for a week or two.

Frieda has announced lunch. The children are called from upstairs. Pat comes complaining that Emil is changing his clothes and wouldn't let her stay and watch him, a suggestion that horrifies Aunt Jessie.

They have all gone into lunch and the room is empty when Emil appears on the stairs. "He is wearing the uniform of the Nazi Jungvolk—the tan shirt with red arm-band, the black shorts which leave the knees bare, the tan stockings and the black shoes. A sheathed dagger is thrust through his belt. He comes down the stairs, stops in the hall, glances toward the dining room, then deliberately comes into the living room. He surveys the living room professionally, as if establishing the precise strength of the enemy. The tremendous number of books is, of course, highly suspicious. He walks over to the shelves, and starts to examine them. But there are too many, and he doesn't know much about books anyway. So, after leafing through one or two, he gives it up. Then his eye is caught by the desk. Obviously it is the desk that holds all the secrets. He approaches it and cautiously sits down in Michael's chair. He picks up a letter, reads it, but it doesn't appear to be of military importance. He then very carefully opens the top drawer of the desk. The contents are disappointing. As he is closing the drawer, his eye is caught by the heavy brass book-ends on top of the desk. He picks one of them up, and is in the process of examining it when the front door-bell rings. Quickly he puts down the book-end, and glances toward the hall. Frieda, passing through the hall to the front door, doesn't see him. We hear her opening the front door."

When Frieda comes into the room carrying a telegram, she stands rooted at the sight of the Nazi uniform.

"Frieda. Komm hier!" commands Emil.

Surely he must be joking, thinks Frieda. Just trying to scare people. "Heil Hitler!" shouts Emil, extending his arm in salute. When she fails to respond he repeats: "Heil Hitler!"

"You are insane!" mutters Frieda, and turns to go.

"Halt! Ich will mit dir sprechen. Ich habe sofort gemortt dass du für Das Vaterland arbeitest."

"No. I am an American. And I speak only English."

"Very wise. We will speak English. Also, I am glad to see you are correctly suspicious of me, because you think I am a child. But you can trust me. We will work together to defeat the enemy."

"You are insane."

"Please—don't try to deceive me. I have been informed. There are eight million of you in America—all good Germans— all working for Der Fuehrer. Don't you understand? I know all about it. I am prepared."

"What are you prepared for? In your Nazi uniform?" Frieda is sarcastic.

"You and I will have collaboration. We must find out *every-thing*. The Herr Professor is engaged in important work; I discovered that before I even left New York. We must examine all the letters; we must open all the telegraphs. Give me that telegraph!"

"You're also a fool."

As Frieda turns to go, Emil jumps in front of her and would take the telegram from her. She shouts lustily for Professor Frame. Michael and the others come from the dining room. Emil stands arrogantly defiant under the family's stares.

"Well, you Nordic superman. What the hell do you think you're doing?" demands Michael.

FRIEDA—He's a devil, Professor! A devil, like they make them in Germany these days! He thinks he's a spy for Hitler. He wanted to open your telegram!

MICHAEL (*taking telegram*)—Thank you.

FRIEDA (*turning on* EMIL *bitterly*)—You! It is you fellows who make everyone hate Germans! You wear your swastikas. You march! You kill! And all the Germans get blamed— people like me get blamed!

MICHAEL (*summarily*)—All right, Frieda. We can take care of him. He'll do no marching or killing. You can go.

FRIEDA—And I wanted to put flowers in his room. (*She goes out through the dining room.* MICHAEL *tears open the telegram and glances at it.*)

MICHAEL (*to* EMIL)—You were interested in this telegram, Herr Bruckner. I will read it to you and you can convey its contents immediately to Herr Goebbels. (*He reads.*) "Emil Bruckner arrives plane 11.13 A.M. You have my deepest sympathy. Ruth Lewis." (*Holds out the telegram to* EMIL.) You'll want this for your file? You'll doubtless find many interesting finger-prints.

LEONA—Michael. You'll never get anywhere that way.

JESSIE (*sharply*)—Of course not! There's only one thing to do! Tear that uniform off! What are we waiting for?

LEONA—To hear from Emil.

JESSIE (*turning on* LEONA)—We're at war, aren't we? He's the enemy. He's a German, just as I knew he would be. They're all the same. Lying, arrogant, deceitful, goose-stepping—if it was up to me, I'd exterminate the entire German race!

LEONA (*mildly*)—Including Frieda?

JESSIE—Oh, I know you and your progressive education! Letting people do as they please, that's what it is! That's what you do with Pat. That's what you'll do with Michael—

MICHAEL—That's enough, Jessie—

JESSIE—And that's what you'll do with this little beast! You'll keep him here in this house, and let him grow up to be a lying, thieving little monster. Well, I'm glad I won't be here to see it! (*Takes* PAT'S *hand.*) Come on, Pat. This is no place for you.

Michael would talk with Emil. He would find out what has happened to the boy. "Tell me this. What did you hope to accomplish by wearing that uniform? Is that being a clever spy?"

"I'm not afraid . . . If there is the necessity I will die for Der Fuehrer!" announces Emil, stoutly.

As Michael walks toward him Emil draws himself up, waiting for Michael's fist. Michael puts a kindly hand on his shoulder and pushes him toward a chair.

"Emil, you're in a new country now," he begins. "There are many things you'll have to learn. I think you'll *want* to learn them. You'll be making new friends; you'll be living in the same house with Pat. You can be very happy here, if you will accept what we can give you. And if you will accept *us*. Do you understand what I'm saying, Emil?"

"I am a German, and I shall always be a German," announces Emil, stiffly. "America is a cesspool. To be an American is to be a member of a mongrel race. The American blood stream is a mixture of the scum of the earth. The only pure-blooded American is the Sioux Indian. . . ."

Leona would like to ask Emil a few questions. In a few weeks, she tells him, she is going to marry his uncle. Also she is going to be his (Emil's) teacher. She thinks she knows why he is wearing the Nazi uniform. It is because it is the only good suit he has. Naturally he is proud of it. It was clever of Emil, admits Leona, to fool the authorities who examined his baggage by putting on his uniform under the threadbare suit he had arrived in. But she can't quite understand, if the Fuehrer is so generous, why he doesn't give his boys more than one suit and one uniform. That, according to Emil, is because of the Versailles Treaty.

Emil should have more clothes, Leona tells Michael. At least two or three suits, and with long trousers, like the other boys in the school he will be going to.

"You know, Emil, I've just been thinking about something," continues Leona. "I don't know if I should say this, because I don't wish to make you unhappy—but after all, I'm sure other people will notice it, too—. From that picture, I'd say you look somewhat like your father. Your eyes—"

"That's a lie!" shouts Emil, rising abruptly from his chair. "I have no resemblance to my father. I've been told otherwise many times."

LEONA (*patiently*)—Maybe I'm wrong. But why are you ashamed to look like him?

EMIL—My father was a traitor to the Third Reich.

LEONA—I suppose a great many people have told you that? Your teachers . . . Your military instructors . . .

EMIL (*forensically*)—In 1918 Karl Bruckner betrayed Germany on the home front. He fomented revolution. If it had not been for him and the Jewish Bolsheviks, Germany would have won the war. He was one of those who made Germany weak. He was responsible for the inflation and the Communists.

MICHAEL (*who has been watching* EMIL *intently*)—Is that the end of the phonograph record?

EMIL (*turning to* MICHAEL)—You drank beer and read philosophy with my father. It was that which gave Germany trouble. Too many people drank beer and read philosophy. We Germans were soft. We forgot our great destiny. Then Der Fuehrer came. He gave us back our courage. With Der Fuehrer

to show us the way, it is our position to conquer the world. You
will find out that I speak the truth.

MICHAEL—Yes? You're not doing so well at Stalingrad.

EMIL—That is a lie! Your Jewish Capitalist newspapers
feed you lies! We captured Stalingrad weeks ago.

LEONA—And those are the only reasons why you are ashamed
of your father?

EMIL—Because of my father, they would never permit me to
be trusted. I excelled in all endeavor, yet they would not make
me captain of my troop, because my name was Bruckner. I did
everything I could. I informed the Gestapo about the mother
of my best friend, though it pained me greatly, and I lost my
friend.

LEONA—Did the Gestapo reward you?

EMIL (*bitterly*)—Yes. But they still laughed at me. Because
my name was Bruckner. No matter what I did, I could never
be like the others. They always spoke of my father.

MICHAEL—Thank God, Karl can't hear you say these things.

EMIL—My father was a coward. He committed suicide.

MICHAEL—Damn their rotten souls! Those lying—

LEONA (*quickly*)—No, Mike. (*To* EMIL.) You'll learn the
true story of your father. There's no use our telling you now.
You wouldn't understand it.

EMIL (*calmly*)—I am prepared that you should tell me lies.

MICHAEL (*bringing his fist down on the desk*)—Lies! How
the hell would *you* know what's a lie and what's the truth?
You've been drugged; you've been poisoned! But we've got the
antidote—we know what to do— We'll get it out of you!

EMIL—You can beat me. You can torture me. I am prepared
for the most horrible experiences.

MICHAEL (*relaxing*)—Now listen to me. In America, we don't
beat little boys. Nor do we torture them. We *persuade* them.
That is our secret weapon. (*He hesitates a moment.*) Can you
understand that? (EMIL *does not answer.* MICHAEL *puts a
friendly hand on his shoulder.*) Go upstairs and take off the
uniform. Put on your other suit, and this afternoon we'll buy
you those long trousers. Now go on. (EMIL *stands motionless.*
MICHAEL *regards him quietly.*) All right. Stay here, if you like.
But you can't sit down to lunch with us until you take off that
uniform. (*Turns to* LEONA.) Come on, Lee.

"Emil, with hostility, watches them go. He turns, looks up at
the picture of his father. Then, deliberately, he pushes a chair

under the picture. He carefully takes his dagger from its sheath, steps up on the chair, and slashes the picture from top to bottom —not once, but several times, furiously."

The curtain falls.

ACT II

Ten days later, the day of Emil's party, the telephone has been ringing constantly. Most of the invited guests have found that they will be unable to attend. Frieda, who is fixing up the playroom in the cellar for the festivities, remarks slyly that it should be a fine party because "Mr. Fine Manners" will have to eat all the cake himself. There's a boycott on.

"You didn't put poison in that cake, did you?" asks Jessie.

"It came into my mind," Frieda admits.

Emil, it appears, has been making himself about the best-hated boy in the neighborhood. The crimes charged against him are many. He had knocked one little boy down and taken his bicycle. He had killed the dog next door. And now, as he comes into the room, it is plainly evident that he has been in more trouble. "His forehead is cut, his face is black with dirt, the collar of his shirt is half torn off, and one knee is exposed through a rip in his trousers."

"There were four of them," Emil explains, proudly. "It was four against one. Robert Amery called me a liar. No one can tell me I've never shot a machine gun."

"You hit Robert Amery?"

"Such a little boy! Much smaller than you!" Frieda is disgusted.

"But I did shoot a machine gun," insists Emil. "It was my reward. Because I was the best spy in my troop."

It was after that that the four attacked him—just like American gangsters. "It was their desire to make me cry," boasts Emil. "But they could not accomplish it. I did not cry once. I have never cried. They cannot understand that a man of my education will never cry."

"A man of your education should blow his nose," suggests Frieda, handing him a handkerchief.

Aunt Jessie plans to leave next day and Emil would now convince her that he is quite sorry she is going. He has been sent home from school by Leona, the Jewess, he reports, and when Aunt Jessie reproves him for talking that way, he frankly tells her that he knows her "accurate feelings" are much the same as his about Miss Richards.

"You have the same lack of fondness for her that I do," ventures Emil, keeping a close watch upon the effect of his words. He knows, he tells Jessie, that she does not like him and he is sorry. But it is not for that she is leaving. It is because of Leona. One night he had heard her crying in her room, and that had made him sad. He will not tell anyone, but he knows. Now they can be friends.

Jessie would stop Emil talking that way, but her inner curiosity is great. Besides she does not feel as Emil suspects. If Michael wants Leona for his wife, she insists, that is his right.

"But you and I know what is best for Uncle Michael," slyly suggests Emil. When Jessie demands to know what it is he is trying to get out of her, Emil pretends that his feelings are hurt by her suspicions. Nothing he does is understood properly. It was for Jessie that he had killed the big dog next door—because he had heard her say that the dog barked and kept her awake, and she wished someone would wring its neck.

"Anyway, it was only a mongrel, and it tried to bite me," says Emil, and adds plaintively: "It is difficult for me to know what is expected."

"Mercy. When I think of your mother—poor Mary. If she were here now—" Jessie shakes her head sadly.

"Aunt Jessie, maybe sometime you will tell me about my mother. I was only a little baby when she died. . . . Won't you tell me about her?"

"Of course I will. She would have wanted you to be a good boy. Please be a good boy."

"Was she beautiful?"

"Yes, dear. She was very beautiful."

"Yes. It is difficult to be without a mother. Uncle Michael speaks always of my father. He never speaks of my mother."

"You poor child. There's been no one to understand you." Jessie's voice is tremulous.

"No . . . Please don't go away, Aunt Jessie. Please don't go away and leave me with her."

Pat has rushed in, carrying her school books. Her words come tumbling over each other in her excitement: "Hello, Aunt Jessie! Hello, Emil! I heard all about your fight. Did you get hurt? You don't look hurt—much. Where's Frieda? Is everything ready for the party? I have to see the cake—Emil can't see it because it's a surprise—I have to put the candles on—"

"Calm down, Pat," Aunt Jessie advises. "Just calm down.

The cake will be a surprise for both of you. I'll go and put the candles on myself. Right now. (*She takes* PAT's *school books from her.*) You'd better go up and change your clothes, Emil. You can put on your Sunday suit if you want to. Of course, there's great danger nobody will come to your party, but we'll hope for the best."

Pat is optimistic. She is sure the boys will come to the party. Just now she is more interested in finding out what Aunt Jessie had said about Emil's fighting, and is greatly surprised when he explains that he and Aunt Jessie now understand each other; that they have been having a discussion. "I can make anybody like me if I want to," says Emil.

"Then why don't you? And then you wouldn't have to fight so much," suggests the practical Pat.

"If people will not believe what is true, I have to fight them."

"Why?"

"Well, you know how it is." Emil is a little vague.

"Can't you just argue with them? I argue with people all the time. And if you have to, you call them names. But you don't fight. (*Very grown-up.*) Really, Emil, you make it very difficult for me socially."

Pat thinks Emil should make a special effort to be nice at his party. He can be nice if he tries. Of course everybody will bring presents. That's what birthday parties are for. Did she buy him a present? Of course she did. What? Pat only smiles knowingly in answer to that question.

"I told you what I wanted. I made it most clear." Emil is quite annoyed.

"I guess I forgot," says Pat, still smiling. "What's the only thing you wanted, Emil?" she asks roguishly.

"A watch! A good watch with seventeen jewels and an illuminated face. One useful for night marches. So, you forgot. If you wanted something, *I* would not forget."

"But that would be a very *expensive* present! I couldn't afford ever to buy a *watch!* Anyway, no one around here goes marching at night."

Emil would bribe Pat to tell him what his present is to be by promising to show her his credentials as a member of the Universal Spy System, Inc. The idea is exciting. Perhaps, suggests Pat, at the party they could initiate all the fellows as spies, and then take turns being G-men. Emil doesn't think much of that game. Pat is the only one he trusts. He could train her.

"I was trained to follow people—and watch everything they

do. I have been educated," boasts Emil.

"But not as a *real* spy."

"Yes, as a real spy."

"Aw—! When you left Germany, I bet they didn't tell a little boy like you to be a real spy in America. Did they?"

"No. But some day I will show them . . . Do you want to see what I have in my pocket?"

"All right. What is it?"

"It is the oath which you must take as a spy."

"But I *told* you, Emil. I don't want to take the oath. I don't want to die."

"You do not show the proper bravery. Unless you die for something, your life is worthless."

"Why?"

"Death is the highest honor."

"But I wouldn't like it. When you're dead, they close your eyes and you can't see your friends."

"But a brave man must die for his country."

"But, Emil, don't you understand? I don't want to die."

"Not even for America?"

"Well—not if I could get out of it."

"I don't think you will make a very good spy. You would be afraid—"

Michael has come in from the hall and been greeted with squeals of delight by Pat. Michael is too tired for much playing. He has soon quieted Pat and, with a glance at Emil, suggested that she run out and play. As he sinks into his chair at the desk he takes a key from his jacket pocket, unlocks a drawer, drops in a key-ring with other keys attached, locks the drawer again and returns the desk key to his pocket. As he looks up he discovers both Pat and Emil watching him intently—

"We're just spying," announces Pat, with a giggle, running into the hall. Michael turns to Emil. Now he is ready for his nephew's explanation, and his alibis. Michael has had the story from Miss Richards. It is Leona's opinion that what Emil needs is a good licking. Michael can't understand Emil. Doesn't he ever get tired of being disciplined?

All Emil's defiance has disappeared. Now he is contrite. He would like to make amends. He would like to make Michael a promise that he will make his conduct satisfactory. He would even like to pay Michael for having his father's picture mended. He could, if Michael would let him, mow the lawn until he had earned enough to pay Michael—

"Mowing that lawn out there is hard work," warns Michael. "It's a good half acre. If you're doing this just to impress me, you're making a bad deal."

EMIL—No—no! . . . Yes, it is so. I *am* trying to impress you, because I *am* sorry. When I arrived here in America, I was a savage.

MICHAEL—What do you think you are now?

EMIL (*thoughtfully*)—I am still a problem, but not a savage.

MICHAEL—All right, problem child. You can mow the lawn. We'll make it a dollar and a half. It's a big lawn, and you're a big problem.

EMIL (*as they shake hands*)—Thank you.

MICHAEL (*reflectively*)—If Karl were here, I wonder what he would do? Would he regard you as hopeless? (*He crosses to the table behind the couch; he fills his pipe.*) You see, Emil, you're more than just my exasperating nephew. To me, you're also a test case. I'm an optimist. I've always been an optimist about the German people. Your father was an optimist, too. He believed that human nature *can* be changed. . . . Many's the time we sat together dreaming up a brave new world—

EMIL—Uncle Michael, I tried to read my father's book, but I could not understand it.

MICHAEL—Which book?

EMIL—I will show you. (*He goes to the book-shelves, and takes down a book.*) You like this book. You have marked it in many places. (MICHAEL *takes the book, idly leafs through it.*) It is a very large book. It must possess a great deal of information. What does it say that is so shocking? Why did they burn it in the bonfire of the books?

MICHAEL (*reading from the book*)—"Original sin does not reside within the individual soul of the human being, but within the structure of society. A person is born neither good nor bad; he is born only with incalculable capacity for both virtue and evil. The flowering of these capacities depends upon the social incentives with which the individual finds himself confronted. If he finds the rewards for evil-doing are great, the individual will quite logically and sensibly become an evil man."

EMIL—What does it mean?

MICHAEL—It means your father doesn't think your case is hopeless. It means the capacities you were born with are still there—somewhere.

EMIL (*disappointed*)—Is that all? Why did they burn the book?

MICHAEL—Because it contains *ideas*. Your Nazi teachers are cowards. They're afraid of ideas. That's why they had to burn the book; and that's why they had to kill your father. They were afraid of him.

EMIL—But I told you before. He committed suicide.

MICHAEL—Stop repeating that damn lie! Your father couldn't take his own life—not in a million years. A man doesn't spend his life in struggle, just to end up hanging himself.

EMIL—But he left a note. It was in all the newspapers.

MICHAEL—It couldn't occur to you that it might not have been Karl who wrote that note?

EMIL (*thoughtfully*)—Perhaps. But how do you know?

MICHAEL—Have you ever heard of Conrad Reiss?

EMIL (*frowning*)—No.

MICHAEL—No, of course not. They wouldn't have told you about *him*. Because *he* escaped. Reiss and your father were in the same concentration camp.

EMIL—Dachau?

MICHAEL—Yes. . . . The Nazis knew there was a plan to escape. But they did not know who the plan involved . . . So the Nazis took Karl, they took Reiss, and they took six other men—all of them suspects. They chose Karl as their first victim. He was older than the other men; they thought he would break more easily. . . . First they used whips and rubber truncheons. They wanted Karl to betray which men were his comrades. They forced the others to stand there and watch Karl being tortured. If Karl would not betray his comrades, perhaps his comrades would betray themselves to save Karl.

EMIL—Did they?

MICHAEL—No. No one spoke. Nor did Karl.

EMIL—What did they do?

MICHAEL—They told the seven men that unless the plan was confessed they would put out Karl's eyes. And they told Karl that if he named his comrades, they would let him go free. . . . Still no one spoke. They put out Karl's eyes. . . . Then, in a fury, they killed him. They put four bullets into him. (*There is a pause.*) My friend Conrad Reiss is working in Washington now.

EMIL (*puzzled*)—But if what you say is true, they could not call my father a coward.

MICHAEL—Couldn't they? Figure it out for yourself—why

they called him a coward. Think about it.

EMIL—This Conrad Reiss—did he tell you the story himself?

MICHAEL—He told me, and he told thousands of other people. He wrote it in a book.

EMIL—If this man is an author, is it not possible that it is a made-up story—like the American cinema?

MICHAEL (*disappointed*)—So you don't want to think about it. You prefer to believe it's a lie. You'd rather remain convinced that your father was a coward.

EMIL—Perhaps I should read Herr Reiss' book.

MICHAEL (*briefly*)—Perhaps you should.

Michael takes the Reiss book from a shelf and hands it to Emil just as Jessie brings in Fred Miller. "Miller is a man of fifty. His manner is quiet and respectable." Michael introduces Miller to Emil. Miller is quite pleased with the young man's appearance and interested that he should have come all the way from Germany alone.

Miller's errand is concerned with his getting into the laboratory to clean it up. He has apparently asked for the key, and Michael has tried to get one for him. But the college authorities have refused. If Miller wants to clean, let him work while the others are there. But as Superintendent of Buildings and Maintenance the Miller pride is stirred.

". . . Looks like after nineteen years folks around here don't trust me," wails Miller.

"Now, Fred. Not even President Gilbert could have a key to that laboratory."

"It ain't President Gilbert that's got to keep things clean . . . I wish you could see your way clear to— Naturally I'd hold on to the key personally."

"No, Fred. Government orders." Pat is calling for help from upstairs and Michael is growing impatient. "Sorry I can't do anything about it, Fred. Now you'll have to excuse me. It seems I have an appointment with my daughter. (*As he goes.*) See you later."

Miller watches Michael go up the stairs and turns to pick up his hat. The sight of Emil on the sofa reading arrests his attention. It looks like a good book the boy's reading. Emil thinks perhaps Mr. Miller has heard of the author—Conrad Reiss. Nope. Miller hasn't. "He is a friend of my uncle," Emil explains, reading an inscription from the book: " 'To Michael Frame. Good friend of Karl Bruckner. Good friend of Ger-

many.' I do not think I will read it. I think that it is propaganda. Don't you?"

"Well, now, that's frequently the trouble with books. Too
many opinions."

Miller has put on his hat and started to leave. Emil watches
him a long moment and then speaks:

EMIL—If you have the custody of all the University buildings,
your job is very important.

MILLER—Oh, they keep me plenty busy. Well, young fellow,
I'm certainly glad to have met you.

EMIL—Wait a minute, Mr. Miller. (MILLER *stops, a little
surprised.*) Why do you want the key?

MILLER—Now,˚ that's a strange question to ask. You were
sitting right here. You heard me.

EMIL—Isn't Miller a German name? War dein Name einmals,
Müller?

MILLER—Sure, my father's name was Mueller. What of it?

EMIL—You must want the key greatly. I'm surprised the
Herr Professor was not suspicious. You were awfully crude.

MILLER (*laughing*)—That's rich. I've heard of you. Little
Emil Bruckner. They say you're a devil, and I guess they're
right.

EMIL—It is useless to deceive me, Mr. Miller. I know what
you are trying to do. I am working on it also. I have examined
the contents in my uncle's desk. But there is nothing about the
laboratory. (*Grudgingly.*) I'm afraid the Herr Professor is a
very intelligent man.

MILLER (*smiling*)—Well, that's the general opinion around
here . . . Kid, you're better than a movie. You've certainly
got a lively imagination.

EMIL—All right. You distrust me because I am a child. But
remember what Der Fuehrer says: "We must put our faith in
the youth. They belong to Germany completely. They are more
reliable than the old people." You do want the key, don't you?

Frieda has come from the cellar. Miller greets her with an
informal "Hello, there," which apparently surprises her somewhat. She goes on into the dining room.

EMIL—You know this woman who works here? Her name is
Frieda.

MILLER—Of course. She's been here for years.

EMIL—She is a bad German. When the times comes, we will have to report her to the Gestapo.

MILLER (*amused*)—That's a hot one, too. Keep going.

EMIL—She is not one of the eight million who are loyal to the Fatherland. I tried to work with her.

MILLER—And what happened? Did she spank your bottom?

EMIL (*drawing himself up stiffly*)—All right. You may treat me like a child if you wish. But if you do, you are the one who is being stupid. (*He moves closer to* MILLER.) I will take the key and have a duplicate made.

MILLER (*sharply*)—Wait a minute, youngster. A joke's a joke, but—

EMIL—I will return the key, and the Professor will never guess. I will bring *you* the duplicate key.

MILLER—You just do that, my young friend. And when you arrive, I'll turn you over to the police.

EMIL (*confidently*)—You cannot deceive me, *Herr Mueller*. You may tell your *superior* that I will bring you the key. I will prove that *I* am working faithfully for Der Fuehrer! (*He clicks his heels sharply.*)

MILLER (*angry and frightened*)—Will you shut up! You don't know what you're talking about! You'll get me into trouble!

There is a ring at the door bell. With a warning "Shhh!" Emil goes to the window and peeks out. The caller is Leona Richards, he announces. Miller is not interested. With a hearty good-by he meets Aunt Jessie at the foot of the stairs and goes with her to the front door. While they are in the hall Emil makes a quick survey of the room and then goes quickly to hide back of the draperies in the bay window.

A moment later Jessie and Leona have come in. Jessie welcomes Leona's visit because of the chance it will give them to talk a few things over before she (Jessie) leaves the next day, and before Leona and Michael's wedding the day following. Leona, however, is in no mood for such a talk just now. She is anxious to see Emil, but she will not tell Jessie why. She had rather talk with Michael about that.

"If you want my opinion," ventures Jessie, to Leona's astonishment, "you are entirely too hard on the child." With that she goes into the hall and up the stairs.

Emil has left his place of hiding and is tiptoeing toward the hall. He reaches the first step of the stairs before Leona turns

and sees him. She calls to him sharply. He would continue on
up the stairs. She orders him to come to her. Hesitantly he
obeys.

"When did you write those obscene things about me on the
sidewalk?" Leona demands.

Emil ignores the query. "Uncle Michael has accepted the fact
that my conduct will become satisfactory," he says, calmly.

"It was after I sent you home for fighting, wasn't it?"

"I think you are confused. I do not write on sidewalks."

"Come here." Emil does not move. "I said come here!"
Leona is firm. He moves toward her. She reaches in his coat
pocket and takes out a piece of chalk. "Why are you carrying
this chalk?" she demands.

"I can carry chalk. This is a free country."

"Then you did write it?"

"It's a lie! A Jewish lie! . . . A Jewish lie from a Jewish
whore!"

Leona slaps him hard across the face. For a moment they
stare at each other with burning hatred. Then Emil turns and,
shoulders back, walks toward the stairs. At the stairs he meets
and passes Michael without a word.

"That's the first time I ever struck a child," says Leona, her
voice trembling.

Michael would know what has happened, but Leona is re-
luctant to tell him. Emil has just been up to another of his nasty
little deeds. He had set out to make her angry, and he had
succeeded. "It never does any good to lose your temper," admits
Leona.

Michael wouldn't have Emil get on Leona's nerves. The boy,
he thinks, is improving. At least he is becoming curious as to
facts. "For the first time he has begun to wonder," reports
Michael, and cites Emil's asking about his father as an example.

Leona is not convinced. Emil is growing more clever, that's
all. "We've got to see this thing clearly, Mike," she says.
"We've considered him a child, more or less like other children.
Being rational people, we've treated him as if he were a normal
human being. And he isn't. (*She shrugs.*) Oh, I grant you
he's changing, outwardly. He's given up clicking the heels and
heiling Hitler. But inwardly, he hasn't changed at all. He's just
become more cunning, more shrewd. As far as he's concerned,
we're still the enemy. So, he's got to split us up. He's got to
turn us against each other. Divide and conquer!"

Michael would laugh Leona's worries away. Let them at least

wait until they are married before they get divided and conquered. But Leona is not to be laughed out of this mood. She
knows what she is talking about. Emil, to her, is not a monster—
he's just a Nazi.

"Darling, he's a child. You've handled problem children before," persists Michael.

"Plenty of them," agrees Leona. "But I could always get at
the root of the problem. Malnutrition—a drunken father—a
neurotic mother. We understand those things. We know how
to remove the cause, or to help the child overcome his ob-
stacles. . . . But Emil isn't just a case of maladjustment. He's
perfectly adjusted—but to a Nazi society! He's been taught
contempt for people who don't use force. He's been taught that
Americans are soft. And sure enough, we've been soft with him.
He's found that he can push us around. And he'll go on pushing us around until we give him the one answer he understands—
a licking."

"That's what you said on the telephone."

"And I'm still saying it. . . . Oh, yes, I know. We don't beat
children. It's passé, outmoded. A great way to relieve the feelings of the parent, but no good for the child. I can quote you
three dozen child psychologists. (*Insistently.*) But it's long
overdue, Mike. A licking. Not in anger, not in haste. But a
deliberate, carefully planned licking."

"Sure, revert to that good old American custom. Irate papa
takes recalcitrant offspring to the wood-shed. Do you favor the
harness strap or the peach whip, Mrs. Gilhooley? (LEONA *turns
away impatiently.*) All right—so we give him a beating. And
what does that do? It's merely a confession of failure. And I
don't think we've failed yet."

"Well, we're pretty close to it . . . May I quote a Michael
Frame proverb of five years ago—'The Democracies must stand
together and take action.' "

"I'll give you one more ancient than that. 'Beat your child
at least once a day. If you don't know the reason, the child
does.' Old Chinese Saying."

Again Michael would make light of Leona's excitement, but
she does not respond very freely. It is all very well for him to
exert his charm on his students. It is nice that he is the most
popular teacher on the campus. But Emil Bruckner is not a
student. The only way to handle him is to get tough.

"Great!" snorts Michael. "Instead of using my head, I'm

going to get out the rubber truncheon and start playing Storm Trooper!"

"Don't be stupid! Are the Nazis the *only* ones who can use force? Do you think our soldiers in Europe will be Storm Troopers?"

"Our soldiers won't go around beating up children!"

There is an angry silence between them, broken by Leona's insisting that if it is a matter of principle with Michael, it is also a matter of principle with her. She is coming to live in that house, as Michael's wife, but she cannot live in the same house with Emil, and that's final. Before he can change her determination Leona has hurried out of the room.

Jessie has come downstairs. Seeing that Michael is disturbed she would comfort him if she could. She would even cancel her reservations and stay on, if Michael needs her. That he does need her she decides for herself, when she can drag no definite statement from him.

Michael is about to go upstairs for a nap when Emil appears. He has washed, combed his hair and changed his clothes. Aunt Jessie is quite pleased, and thinks Michael should be, too. It certainly shows that Emil is trying. "You remember what you said—we must love Emil?" Jessie reminds Michael. "First thing you know, I'll be loving him, not for Karl's sake, nor Mary's, but for himself."

"Apparently you're willing enough to exercise your winning ways on Jessie," says Michael. "Why couldn't you try it with Miss Richards?"

"I try to please Aunt Jessie because she is reasonable. She would never slap me in the face."

When Michael has gone Jessie is curious to know what had happened between Emil and Leona. Leona had slapped him, Emil reports, but he is glad of that. Now he does not have to apologize for hating her.

Jessie would not have Emil feel that way. It makes his Uncle Michael very unhappy. She puts her arms around Emil and tells him that she has decided to stay, because Michael needs her.

"You must not show me too much affection," warns Emil, as he draws away from Jessie. "Uncle Michael will think that you encourage me to be rude to Miss Richards. (*With an ominous look.*) It would be unfortunate if he were to think that."

Jessie would be shocked if Emil did not smile and assure her that he loves her very much. "Now we are compatible, you

must do me a favor," he says. "Tell Frieda I am to be shown
more respect."

"Well, really!" Jessie is frowning, but soon her mood changes.
"If you're a good boy she'll treat you all right," she promises.

Aunt Jessie has no sooner left the room than Emil "exultantly
throws out his chest and does an exaggerated goose step half
across the room. Then, laughing, he runs and dives on to the
couch. Lying on his back, still laughing, he kicks his legs into
the air."

But there is work to be done. Suddenly Emil remembers.
Making sure, with hasty glances, that he is alone, he takes the
key from the pocket of Michael's coat, unlocks the desk, gets
the key-ring and is working to get the laboratory key off it when
Pat comes quietly down the stairs and stands watching him
working with the key-ring. She is dressed in her white party
dress, with ribbon knots on it to match the ribbon in her hair.

Now Emil looks up and sees Pat. Angrily he demands to
know what she means by sneaking in like that and she, good-
naturedly, is as curious to know what he is doing with Mike's
keys. Emil would explain that he was just looking at them, but
Pat saw him put the new key in his pocket and he'd better put
it right back on the key-ring.

Pat is holding something behind her back. Emil wants to
know what it is. Is it his present? At first Pat refuses to tell.
It is to be a surprise. Finally she admits that it is the present.
She will give it to him if he puts the key back.

"Don't alter the subject," says Emil, with conscious dignity.
"You're just trying to get out of giving me a present."

"Oh, Emil, you're terrible," Pat protests. "You know perfectly well I *have* to give you a present, because it's your birthday. So *there!*"

She has taken her hand from behind her back and handed him
a small white package wrapped in white tissue paper. "It's not
a watch," she warns. "Really, Emil, you must think I'm a millionaire. Anyway, I gave you your present. Now you've got
to put back Mike's key."

"I haven't got any key."

"All right, then. I'll go tell Mike! I'll tell him you stole his
key!"

"Don't you dare! Why do you want to be a little tattle-tale?"

"I don't want to! But you stole his key! I'll go upstairs
right now and tell him."

"Oh, no, you won't."

"Get out of my way, Emil Bruckner!"

"If I put the key back on the ring, you will promise not to tell him?"

"Oh, all right. I won't tell him."

"It is a promise. We will keep each other's secrets, no?"

Emil has taken the key from his pocket and has started to put it back when Aunt Jessie comes down the stairs. To cover the situation Pat starts singing "Frère Jacques" very innocently. Jessie, "throwing Emil a cozy smile," joins in the song with Pat and turns to go into the dining room. Pat continues the song after Jessie disappears. Emil works feverishly to get the key back on the ring, the ring back in the drawer of the desk and the desk key in the pocket of Michael's coat. When he has done this he turns to Pat, and holds out his hand. "There," he says. "Now it is all forgotten. We can shake hands on it. You have promised not to tell Uncle Michael."

"Unless he asks me."

"But you promised."

"But I didn't cross my heart! You didn't even ask me to!" Playfully Pat gives Emil a shove that sets him down on the couch.

"Why should one cross one's heart?"

"Well, unless you cross your heart, a promise doesn't count. Gee, you ought to know by this time."

Emil gets up quickly from the couch. "You promised! To make a promise is to make a contract!" He has grabbed Pat's arm.

"Let go of me, Emil, or I'll kick you in the shins! I'm not afraid of you!"

"All right, then," hisses Emil, through clenched teeth. "Cross your heart! Cross your heart, or I'll kill you!"

"Aw, nuts! Stop talking like that, Emil! You know you can't scare me!"

"If you will not make a contract, it will be very bad for you. You promised not to tell Uncle Michael."

"Well, maybe I will and maybe I won't. Maybe I ought to tell Mike anyway. I don't like the way you're acting. You seem awfully funny."

Jessie has heard the scuffling and calls from the dining room to know what they are doing. Pat assures her that nothing is happening and turns again to Emil. "Aw, you get so serious about everything," she protests, good naturedly. "Don't be such a jerk! . . . Come on, let's go down to the clubhouse, and see if Frieda fixed everything like I told her. When those guys get here, Aunt Jessie can let them in."

She has gone down the cellar stairs. Emil is still apprehensive. He goes to the foot of the stairs and looks up nervously. Then back to the cellar door. "Are you going to tell him?" he calls after Pat.

Pat's voice comes back in a taunting sing-song. "Maybe I will and maybe I won't!"

Emil is worried. He comes into the room, looking about him desperately. His eyes light on the heavy brass book-ends as he approaches Michael's desk. Quickly he picks one up and goes back to the cellar door, closing it quietly after him as he disappears. . . .

The front doorbell is ringing. For several minutes no one appears. The ringing continues. Finally Frieda comes, glances into the living room and goes to answer the bell. The moment she is out of sight Emil looks out cautiously from the cellar door. Seeing no one, he comes hurriedly into the room, brushing his forehead with the sleeve of his coat. Frieda can be heard welcoming guests to the party. Emil, hearing her, tries hard to appear casual, standing rigidly erect and waiting.

Presently three small boys, of Emil's age, though not as tall, come through the hall with Frieda. They are Dennis, Butler and Tommy. Each carries a package awkwardly in his hand. Seeing Emil they stand reluctantly in the hallway.

"Go on in, boys. Make yourselves at home." Frieda turns to Emil. "Well, you're lucky," she says, in a half aside; "three of them, anyway." She goes on into the dining room. For a moment the boys stands as they were and then move hesitantly toward Emil.

"Hello, dope," says Dennis, gloomily.

"Welcome. I am pleased to see you." Emil's politeness is excessive.

"It ain't mutual. Here." Butler thrusts his package into Emil's hand. The other boys silently do the same.

"Thank you. You are most kind."

"Skip it! It wasn't our idea," says Tommy.

"Shut your trap, Tommy." This from Dennis.

"Where's Pat?" demands Butler. "She said there would be cake and ice cream," adds Tommy, looking around. "Where is it?"

"Let's get Pat. Where is she? Downstairs?" Dennis has started for the cellar door.

"No—no—! She is upstairs! She will be down. Please be seated." Emil would motion them to seats.

"Aw, go squat yourself!" commands Butler, pugnaciously.

Emil is still holding the three packages in his hands. Why doesn't he open them? Perhaps he has to wait for Pat.

"What's the matter, jerk? You look sick," says Butler.

"It's something he ate, we hope," says Tommy.

Jessie has come from the dining room with affable greetings for the guests. It is so good of them to come to help Emil celebrate. Now Frieda appears from the dining room, carrying a birthday cake adorned with twelve unlighted candles. She starts for the cellar door. Emil watches her, horror-stricken. He is gesturing helplessly as Dennis holds the door open for her. Now he is standing transfixed in the hallway, Dennis on one side of him, Tommy on the other, and both staring at him curiously.

"And what do I see here?" Jessie chirps, as she discovers the presents. "Did the boys bring all those lovely presents? My goodness, where's Pat? Where is she, Emil?" Her eyes search the room and come back to Emil, standing rooted in the hallway. "Emil, I asked you a question. Where's Pat?" There is no answer. Struck by Emil's strange appearance, Jessie crosses quickly to him. "Emil, what's the matter with you?"

Suddenly there is a shrill scream from the cellar. No one moves. All eyes are turned toward the cellar. Then Jessie starts for the door. Before she can reach it Frieda appears breathless at the top of the stairs.

"Professor Frame! . . . Professor Frame!" . . . she is shouting. "Come here!" She runs up the stairs.

"What is it, Frieda?"

"It's Pat! *Professor Frame!*"

Jessie has hurried through the cellar door. Butler and Tommy would follow her, but Dennis holds them back. "What happened?" He has turned to Emil, who is again nervously brushing his forehead with his sleeve. "What happened? Did she get hurt?" demands Dennis.

"She—she must have fallen down! That's it! She must have fallen down."

Michael comes hurtling down the stairs in his dressing gown, followed by Frieda. He disappears quickly through the cellar door.

The boys are still puzzled. They do not know what to do. Dennis is again at Emil, demanding an answer. Emil can only repeat that Pat must have fallen down. Did he see her? No.

Then how does he know?

"She must have. She must have, that's all! She tripped and fell down the stairs. She—"

He gets no further. Frieda has come through the cellar door. She is carrying the heavy book-end, which she thrusts toward Emil. For an instant his eyes are held by the sight of it. Then Jessie's sobs can be heard from the cellar, and a weeping cry: "Oh, Michael!"

From the cellar comes Michael. In his arms is the limp body of Pat. For a second he stops, his eyes meeting Emil's with accusative hatred.

"She must have fallen down," repeats Emil, in choking tones. Michael continues on upstairs with Pat. Jessie follows. Frieda and the three boys are standing gazing after them.

"She must have fallen down! She hurt herself! She fell down! SHE FELL DOWN!" shouts Emil, hysterically. He turns and sees the open window into the yard. He runs wildly out.

The curtain falls.

ACT III

As early as six o'clock the following morning the family is stirring. Frieda has brought into the living room the picture of Karl Bruckner that had been out being repaired and is taking it from its wrappings. When she has finished she stands it face outward, in front of the fireplace.

Michael comes slowly down the stairs. He is in his dressing gown and he is pretty haggard. Pat, he reports, is apparently all right. She has gone back to sleep.

"Poor darling. So many stitches on that dear little head," mutters Frieda. "When I found her there I thought he'd killed her."

"Well, he tried," says Michael, looking grimly at the key-ring he is holding in his hand.

The police have called, Frieda reports. They haven't been able to find Emil, but she hopes they will. Michael is convinced the boy can't get far.

Frieda goes for the coffee and Michael calls Leona on the phone. "I'm not going to apologize for waking you up," he says, shortly. "Yes, Jessie told me last night that you called; we hope she'll be all right. It may be no more than a laceration of the scalp. . . . Lee, will you come over? . . . I'll expect you."

Michael wanders restlessly about the room. He finds the

book he had given Emil to read and puts it back where he found it. He sees the Bruckner picture and walks slowly over and turns the face toward the wall.

From Frieda, when she brings his coffee, he would know what she knows about Fred Miller. Frieda doesn't know much. Once, in Chicago, where she had gone to visit a cousin, she had met Miller at what they called a German picnic. It wasn't a picnic. It was a German Bund meeting, and Frieda didn't like it. Miller was sitting on the platform. Frieda didn't like that, and she doesn't like Miller.

"Until the war began he was for Hitler," says Frieda. "Now he doesn't say anything. He's afraid, of course. But I tell you, Professor, there's something about him—"

"Yes?"

"Well—I think he hates himself because people look upon him as a janitor. He would like to make himself important."

Aunt Jessie appears wearily on the stairs. She is wearing a bathrobe and her face is pale and drawn. She hopes the police will catch Emil, the loathesome little beast, and lock him up for life. "I knew you should never have brought that boy from Germany. I warned you."

"Yes, Jessie, you warned me," admits Michael.

"I hated that child the moment I laid eyes on him. And now, the way things have turned out— Well, I was right."

Now Jessie believes that every last German should be exterminated. But, Michael reminds her, she did not feel that way yesterday. Yesterday she was talking about loving Emil for himself. And today— What has happened?

"Really, Michael. I don't know what you're talking about."

"Yes, you do. You *must* have some reason," persists Michael. "He was sent home from school yesterday for fighting, and lo and behold, you were treating him like a new-found friend. Why was it? Tell me, Jessie. Was it because he hated Lee? And you resented her, too."

Jessie has found her handkerchief and is weeping miserably. Michael walks over and puts a hand on her arm, gently. "Suppose you tell me, Jessie. Let's get this out in the open."

"It's true, Michael. It's all true. That's why I couldn't sleep last night. I let that child deceive me."

"He found the weak spot in all of us," admits Michael, sympathetically.

"It was worse than that. I let him talk against Leona. I let him brag that he would make it impossible for you to get married. Then when he almost killed Pat, it was as if I had been in league with a murderer. . . . Michael, I wasn't really opposed to your marriage. You know that. Of course, it shocked me, it hurt me. I'm a selfish woman, I suppose. But I was prepared to go away. I wanted you to be happy—all my life, that's all I've ever wanted."

"Yes, I know. And I've been pretty rough with you sometimes."

"No; just thoughtless! You see, Leona is so different from me. That's what shocked me, somehow. It is hard for me to like people who are different. She can't possibly take care of you the way I have. It's water under the bridge now, but she never even asked me where we keep the linen. (*Apologetically.*) That's silly, isn't it? (*After a moment.*) As soon as Pat is better, I'm going to leave for Mexico as I planned."

The doorbell has rung. Jessie has dashed upstairs. A moment later Frieda has let in Fred Miller who is dragging a frightened Emil after him. All the boy's self-assurance, all his bravado, are gone. "He is a thoroughly terrified little boy."

"Here he is, Professor," Miller is shouting. "This is a terrible thing. I'm more shocked than I can possibly say. . . . If I just knew how to express my sympathy, sir. Such a tragedy! Such a great tragedy!"

MICHAEL—Thank you.

EMIL—Uncle Michael—

MICHAEL (*harshly*)—Keep away from me, Emil.

MILLER—The little murderer. Yes, he confesses it. We'll have to turn him over to the police.

MICHAEL—He told you he—killed her?

MILLER—Yes.

MICHAEL—I see . . . Have you seen the morning paper, Fred?

MILLER—I didn't stop for nothing, sir—after he told me what he had done. I know how you're feeling, Professor. It's tragic enough without the newspapers—I don't wonder— (*To* EMIL.) Here—get over there and sit down where we can keep an eye on you.

MICHAEL—How'd you happen to catch him?

MILLER—Do you know what he did? He came to my house! Can you imagine that? At five-thirty this morning.

MICHAEL—Where was he last night?

MILLER—Wandering in the woods, he says. (*Smoothly.*) I

guess you'd like to know why he came to me.

MICHAEL—I expect he was hungry.

MILLER—I expect he was. But why should he come to *me?*

MICHAEL—Well?

MILLER—I tell you, the only way I can figure it, yesterday I spent a few minutes chatting with him—just to be friendly, you know how it is.

MICHAEL—That's natural enough.

MILLER—Thank you, Professor. I wanted to clear that up before we took him to the police.

MICHAEL—Why?

MILLER—Well, if a person'll commit murder, he'll lie about anything. He'll implicate anybody he can—and I've got my reputation to think of. Nineteen years with this University.

MICHAEL—You reminded me of those nineteen years yesterday.

MILLER (*a trifle nervous*)—Well, I'm very proud of my record. (*He looks at* EMIL.) God knows why he did it, Professor. I think he's insane. He'll give the police a dozen cock and bull stories, I know. He's tried them on me already, and they don't make sense, believe me.

MICHAEL—You have no idea why he did it?

MILLER—It's beyond me, sir.

MICHAEL (*insistently*)—Are you sure?

MILLER—I really can't figure it.

MICHAEL—You should have read the morning paper, Fred.

MILLER (*uneasily*)—Yes?

MICHAEL—You see, he didn't kill her.

EMIL—Then she is all right. It was just an accident—and it was not my fault—

MILLER (*turning on* EMIL)—You little fool, you told me—

MICHAEL—You seem upset, Fred.

MILLER (*hastily*)—No—I'm so happy, Professor. I am so happy. Your little girl is going to be all right. That's wonderful. You realize I am very happy?

EMIL (*turning on* MILLER *venomously*)—You traitor! You're just trying to save yourself! You're a coward!

MICHAEL—Shut up, Emil!

MILLER—You see, Professor? He's likely to say anything. We'll probably never find out why he did it. Even your little girl may be confused. The blow on the head—

MICHAEL—No. She knows why Emil hit her. She told me exactly what Emil was trying to do. She's not confused.

MILLER—No, you are right; she is a smart girl. (*Indicates*
EMIL *accusingly.*) But don't let *this* one fool you. Well, I have
to be going now. I'm late. I'll leave him here for you to deal
with as you think best. And if you want me for any testimony,
just remember you can count on me, Professor. I'll be in my
office most of the day. . . . Well, I'm certainly glad the little
girl is going to be all right. Good-by.

Before Miller can leave, Michael sharply calls him back for
further questioning. What did he expect to find in the laboratory? Did he hope to stumble on something that would make
him a big, important spy? "You've been a Nazi sympathizer,"
says Michael, "and you might be a Nazi agent. But whatever
you are, you're a stupid fool."

"Professor Frame, I've never done anything," whines Miller.
"I've been here nineteen years. I'm a good American citizen."
He points accusingly at Emil. "It was all *his* idea—I didn't—"

"All right, all right. I'm going to notify the Federal Bureau
of Investigation. They'll look up your record."

Miller would repeat his protests, but suddenly his manner
changes and he turns on Michael with angry bravado. "All
right," he snarls; "all right, but let me tell you something! Sure
I wanted that key. But what if I did? And suppose I did
want to get into that laboratory—and not to clean it up. There's
nothing you can prove, because I haven't done anything! You
professors, with your many books and your great thoughts!
Educated fools, that's what you are!"

"Get the hell out of here!"

"Just because I'm a janitor you think you can wipe your
feet on me! Always being polite to you! Always cleaning up
your messes! Well, some day we'll see who are the janitors
around here! This war isn't over yet!"

Miller hurries out and Michael turns on Emil, who is trembling with excitement. "He is guilty, Uncle Michael. He made
me do everything! He said he would report me—the Gestapo—
he frightened me—" Emil is stuttering nervously.

"You'd better be frightened, Emil—you have good cause to
be frightened—"

Emil is moving toward the stairs. His voice takes a higher,
more hysterical tone. "Ask Aunt Jessie! She loves me! She
knows I tried to be good! She's my friend—that's why I was
rude to Miss Richards! It was all for Aunt Jessie!"

Emil has sprung toward the stairs. Michael follows him,

warning him to come away before he disturbs the sleeping Pat. Emil is screaming hysterically. "I won't! You can't make me! I'll scream! I'll wake her up! Then she will die! I'll tell everybody you beat me—and you killed her—"

Michael leaps for Emil and grabs him by the throat. "Uncle Michael—don't hurt me— You're a kind man—you knew my father—"

Michael does not stop. He has forced the boy across the table. Suddenly Emil's body goes limp. Michael is still choking him when Leona comes into the hallway. Horrified at what she sees she rushes over and grabs Michael's arm. "Mike! For God's sake, Mike! You're killing him!"

Michael does not hear. She grabs his other arm and succeeds in loosening his grip. Emil lies limp across the table. Leona picks him up and carries him to the couch. Michael stares at her, dazed, as she loosens Emil's collar.

Michael has sunk into a chair. "I wanted to kill him!" he mutters, tonelessly. Leona would send him upstairs to finish dressing. Mechanically he obeys her, reaching the stairs slowly.

Leona has come back to Emil. He used to do a lot of talking about the honor of dying, she reminds him. Now that he almost died, did he find it much fun? Emil's reply is weak but positive. She makes him sit up. She would have him tell her why he did what he has done. Probably he thought he was being brave? Maybe he thought he was being a hero—

"You know, it's a funny thing," Leona is saying. "Pat could be brave, too. She could be a hero. She could sneak up behind you and hit you over the head. But I don't think it would ever occur to her. Of course, she's not a member of the Master Race."

"Please leave me alone, Miss Richards," pleads Emil, wiping a corner of his mouth with the back of his hand.

Leona has moved over to the desk and is noting the birthday presents that are still there, unopened. She calls Emil's attention to them. He is not interested. She doesn't blame him for that, but it does seem a pity—

"Pat went to a lot of trouble for that party," Leona tells him. "The boys didn't want to come, you know. Pat bought the presents; all of them. And then she paid each boy twenty-five cents to come and bring the presents." Emil is looking at her bewilderedly. "She had to borrow the money from me," Leona goes on. "That's how I know. It seems she spent everything her father gave her for the present she wanted to give you herself." She has picked up the smallest of the packages and is examining it thoughtfully. "Pat's so affectionate. It was rather silly of her, wasn't it?" Emil averts his eyes. Leona goes over to him and holds out the package. "You may as well open it."

Emil shakes his head, but when she repeats the suggestion as a command he slowly obeys her. Inside the first tissue paper wrapping he finds a card and stops to read it. "What does it say? Read it to me," commands Leona.

" 'For Emil—who will now know the time, but has yet to learn the score,' " reads Emil.

"Oh, that's very good, isn't it? I wouldn't be surprised if Mike helped her write that."

"It must be a watch," says Emil, tremulously.

"I suppose it is. Why don't you look?"

He takes off the last wrapping and opens the little case. He stares at it and begins to cry. "With an illuminated—face!" he mutters. He is sobbing now, his face contorted with childish misery. The next moment he has pressed his face into the pillows. His body is shaking convulsively. Leona is watching him with satisfaction.

Presently Michael comes down the stairs. He is fully dressed. Without paying any attention to anyone he walks over to the telephone and calls Police Headquarters. As Frieda appears in the hall he calls to her to take Emil upstairs and pack his clothes, and not let him out of her sight. Getting Sergeant Thompson on the phone, Michael tells him that Emil is there and the sooner they come for him the better.

Leona is not happy. She cannot feel that the police are the final answer in Emil's case. What would she do? She would keep him right there in the house. "He's been crying, Mike," she says. "He was crying like any other child."

Michael does not find that even touching. "Alexander the Great bawled like a baby because there were no more worlds to conquer," he says.

LEONA (*earnestly*)—Don't you see, Mike? He shed tears. He's actually by way of becoming a human being.

MICHAEL—He's too late.

LEONA—I thought so, too, but I was wrong. There's a flaw in his Nazi armor.

MICHAEL—You're being sentimental. The kid finally breaks down and it touches your heart. So you become a great humanitarian. Don't be so gullible, Lee. Of course the kid cried.

It was the only device he had left.

LEONA—No. I watched him. He tried not to cry. They did a good job on him, all right—those beasts. But there's one thing they didn't count on.

MICHAEL—What?

LEONA—They couldn't quite kill his wanting to love.

MICHAEL (*impatiently*)—What the devil are you talking about?

LEONA—Pat.

MICHAEL (*incredulously*)—You're crazy. He crowns her on the head with a brass book-end, then you say he loves her . . . Do you think I'd consider for a moment having him in the same house with Pat? He can't stay here. It isn't safe. He's dangerous.

LEONA—How does Pat feel about it?

MICHAEL (*a trifle shocked*)—You don't think I asked her!

LEONA (*gently*)—So you assume that she feels as you do. Maybe what you are really saying is, How dare we have him in the same house with Michael?

MICHAEL (*stopped cold*)—All right. Dare we? I tried to kill him. (*He looks at* LEONA *unhappily*.) Yesterday I didn't even want to give him a spanking. And today— Yes, it's true. I'm also thinking of myself.

LEONA (*sympathetically*)—That's important. Maybe it's the *most* important.

MICHAEL—You and I are going to be married. We *are*, aren't we?

LEONA—We are indeed.

MICHAEL—You and I have got our own lives, and we've got Pat. We haven't got room for Emil Bruckner, too.

LEONA—So we just ship him off to the reformatory.

MICHAEL—Yes.

LEONA—No . . . Oh, no, Mike. Yesterday I made a bad mistake. I walked out on something we should have faced together. That was stupid. Today you're trying to do the same thing. You don't want to face it . . . Right now, Mike, I don't know any more than you how to handle this boy. But I know we've got to try. We can't turn our backs. We can't put him behind bars, nor simply wipe him out. You can call it pride, if you want, but I won't admit failure like that, and I won't let you. . . . And it's not just our problem. There are twelve million other children just like him in Germany. They can't all be put behind bars They can't all be exterminated.

MICHAEL (*shaking his head*)—Of course not. But what we decide for Emil Bruckner has nothing to do with post-war Germany. You're talking way up in the clouds.

LEONA—But don't you see, Mike. If you and I can't turn one little boy into a human being—then God help the world when this war is won, and we have to deal with twelve million of them!

MICHAEL—All right, then. God help the world!

Frieda has brought Emil back. He is carrying his suitcase. She could take him to wait in the kitchen, but Michael will keep him there. For a moment there is an impressive silence. Emil sits stiffly and miserably in his chair.

Leona has walked over to the fireplace and stands looking at the back of the Karl Bruckner picture. "Are you going to banish the father along with the son?" she demands, turning to Michael. "You'll have to, you know. You can't forget about Emil, unless you get rid of Karl, too. Take his picture off the wall. Take his books off the shelves. After all, it was really his fault, wasn't it? His and the Germans' that came before him. The sins of the children shall be visited upon the fathers unto the third and fourth generation."

"Damn it, Lee, will you keep quiet?"

"Yes, Michael. And if the police would only come and take him away we could all have breakfast, couldn't we?"

Pat has appeared on the stair landing. She is in her bathrobe and there is a bandage on her head. Emil gets quickly to his feet and backs out of her line of vision.

"Pat! What are you doing out of bed?" shouts Michael.

"Well, darn it, I'm hungry. And Frieda didn't bring me anything yet."

"You're a sick girl. Now get back up there."

"Oh, I feel fine. *Please*, Mike."

She is on her way down before he can answer. "On the fourth step from the bottom she stops to make her jump, then thinks better of it and walks down sedately."

Leona goes to Pat and brings her tenderly down to the couch. On the way Pat sees Emil and faces him.

"Emil Bruckner, *you stink!!*" she says. "Really, you're the sneakingest coward I ever saw."

Emil takes the watch from his pocket and humbly hands it back to Pat.

She considers the matter judiciously. "Well, I certainly ought to take it back," she decides. "But—no, you can keep it. But, remember, I'm plenty sore!"

"I'll remember."

"You'd better, or you'll *really* be out of luck. You won't have *anybody* to play with."

There is a ring at the bell. That will probably be the police, says Emil. They are coming to take him to jail. Pat doesn't understand. "Because you bopped me on the bean?" she asks incredulously. "Oh, Mike won't actually let them put you in jail. Will you, Mike?"

Mike doesn't answer. Let Frieda tell them Emil will be right out. Emil, with ceremony, bids them all good-by. He has walked to the hall and picked up his suitcase when Michael stops him.

"Emil, do you know why we are sending you away?" he asks. Emil doesn't answer and Michael continues. "It's because I don't think there's any hope for you. You're lost. They did their job too well, the Nazis. They lied to you, day after day, year after year. They told the same things over and over. Repetition! Repetition! They grooved your brain. They turned you into a sly, clever puppet. I doubt that even now you realize the kind of creature you are. . . . Am I wrong? Have you anything to say for yourself? Do you still feel that you're a superior martyr? Do you still believe that your Fascist cause is invincible?"

"I do not understand."

"I mean don't you know you're losing? . . . There are no questions you'd like to ask as a member of the Master Race? . . . You're quite satisfied with yourself?"

Emil is puzzled. He admits it. He had seen his Uncle Michael trick Miller and make a fool of him. Yet Michael is not a German. "Your uncle is Irish, French, Swedish," puts in Leona.

"A mongrel. An American," adds Michael.

"That is the only thing I have not been able to understand. There are times when the Americans do not have entirely the appearance of an inferior race."

Leona and Michael exchange glances. Then Michael calls Emil over to him. "Are you admitting that your Nazi teachers might have lied to you?" he demands.

Emil's "No . . ." is slow and irresolute.

"Give us that record about your father again," prods Michael. "Is it still clear? Is it still sharp? Go on. Tell us about your father. 'In 1918 Karl Bruckner—' "

Slowly, laboriously, Emil tries to pick up the familiar Nazi statement. "In 1918 Karl Bruckner betrayed Germany—" Falteringly he proceeds, prodded by Michael, or Leona, until he reaches the statement that his father was a coward—

"Go on!" commands Michael. "Tell us the rest! You're absolutely right! Your father was a coward! He committed suicide!"

EMIL (*tortured*)—*Is that true?*

MICHAEL—You know it's true! Your father was a stupid man! He was weak! You're right to be ashamed of him!

EMIL (*tortured*)—Uncle Michael, why are *you* saying this?

MICHAEL (*harshly*)—Because it's true! Isn't it? Karl Bruckner was a degenerate coward!

EMIL (*protesting loudly*)—No! No! My father was a brave man. He *must* have been a brave man. Why else were they afraid of him? Why did they burn his books if they weren't afraid of him? (*His voice rises hysterically.*) Why did they hit me? Why did they lock me up in the dark? (EMIL *breaks off in bewilderment.*)

MICHAEL (*after a look at* LEONA)—Who hit you, Emil?

EMIL (*helplessly*)—I—I don't know. . . .

MICHAEL—When did they lock you in the dark?

EMIL (*shaking his head in hopeless confusion*)—I can't remember . . . A long time ago. . . . (*On the verge of tears.*) Please, Uncle Michael. I'm all mixed up.

MICHAEL (*gently; firmly; again meeting* LEONA's *eyes*)—Why were the Nazis afraid of Karl Bruckner? *Why,* Emil? Why? That's what you've got to ask. Every time anybody tells you anything, you've got to ask why! In our country we're not afraid of questions. We want people to ask questions. . . . Lee says you can be turned into a human being. Pat seems to think so, too. Perhaps they're right. (*Very quietly.*) But get this straight, Emil. What happens is really up to you. You can be a decent member of society, if you want to. But if you insist on being a Nazi, we're just as tough as you are, and a lot tougher. We'll destroy you—along with your Nazi soldiers . . . You have your choice. (*To* LEONA.) We're going to keep Emil here. (LEONA *nods.*) I'll tell the police we don't need them—and then we'll have breakfast.

PAT—Breakfast! Hot dog! Can I eat down here, too? I don't want to go back to bed.

MICHAEL—All right. You don't have to. (*To* EMIL.) Are you hungry?

EMIL—Yes, sir.

MICHAEL—Very well. Go out in the kitchen and tell Frieda politely that you're staying. We'll fill your stomach before we attempt your re-education. . . . Come on, Lee. Come on, Pat. (*He goes out.*)

LEONA (*to* EMIL)—We all have things to learn, Emil. (*She takes his hand.*) If we all try, some day we can all be good friends.

PAT (*turning back to* EMIL)—Say, Emil, after breakfast, do you want me to show you my stitches? (*She points to her bandaged head.*) Seven of them!

"She goes out. Emil is left alone on the stage. His eyes go to the portrait of his father. He walks over and stands looking at it irresolutely. Then he pulls the chair in front of the fireplace. Michael reappears in the hallway and stops to watch Emil. The boy takes the heavy picture and with difficulty lifts it to the chair, and then climbs on the chair himself. He is lifting the picture to the mantelpiece, and Michael is watching him with satisfaction—"

THE CURTAIN FALLS

HARRIET

A Drama in Three Acts

BY FLORENCE RYERSON AND COLIN CLEMENTS

IT was not until March 3, 1943, that Helen Hayes and "Harriet" arrived in New York. They had done a bit of touring before then, Miss Hayes being abnormally anxious about a Broadway opening, however sure she may rightfully feel about her place in the public's affections. The road's reception of Florence Ryerson and Colin Clements' biographical drama had been cordial and frequently enthusiastic, but still the popular star was not sure. She had seen such verdicts set aside too many times to be sure. But a little after eleven o'clock that night she was convinced. A dozen curtain calls and an uproarious stage reception, in response to which she had to make one of those nervous little speeches of thanks, convinced her. Next day the press reviews confirmed her conviction.

"Life is so funny," Miss Hayes told Catherine Maher, a newspaper caller from the *Times*, a few days later. "I had my summer all planned. I was going to be a very serious farmer. Now here I am with a success on my hands. I really don't know what to do. It upsets me."

What she did was to play "Harriet" through till June and then take a five-week vacation to work on the farm.

That "Harriet" was helped greatly by Miss Hayes' suggestions and by her performance is true, but it also commands definite character and dramatic values stemming from the wisdom and skill of its authors.

"They contrast her amusingly with the other Beechers—the stern, Old Testament, God-walloping preachers of hellfire and damnation," John Anderson wrote in the *New York Journal-American*, "and they suggest that in her political ideas Harriet began as an escapist, turned into an appeaser, and finally found that there can be no compromise over liberty. If she shaped the events, she was also shaped by them. She thought that slavery was ugly but none of her business; she believed that for every Southern slave-holder there were 10 Northern mill owners opposing abolition because it would hurt their profits, and she wrote 'Uncle Tom's Cabin,' so the playwrights say, in the hope that it would bring peace—not the sword. It was only when she talked to Lincoln that she learned the true proportions of the struggle, and saw it as part of a fight for freedom to release —someday, somehow—all men, white and black, from bondage of all sorts, political and economic."

It was in January, 1836, that the newly married Harriet Beecher Stowe and her husband, Calvin Stowe, moved from Columbus to Cincinnati, Ohio. Just before their arrival in their new home we find Catherine and Henry Beecher, Harriet's brother and sister, doing what they can to make the Stowe cottage a little more homey before the bride and groom arrive.

The sitting-dining room is comfortably but sparsely furnished. There is a small Franklin stove in front of the fireplace, a large padded chair by a pillar table, a sideboard set with inexpensive china.

Auntie Zeb, "an ample, pleasant-faced Negro woman in her middle forties," lugs in a wash boiler filled with iron cooking utensils. Henry, "in his twenties, pink-cheeked, square-shoul-dered, full of vitality," is burdened with a large basket filled with crockery. Catherine, "thirteen years older than her brother; a spinster who hides her warm affections under a cloak of severity," is doing most of the directing as to the disposition of the things.

Henry has an idea that perhaps Harriet would like to arrange her own things when she comes, but Catherine has no patience with that idea. "Harriet is as incapable of managing a house as a chipmunk, and you know it," she sputters. "I have no patience with this wild idea of hers—rushing into matrimony, and with a *widower!* I can't see what a husband can give Harriet she couldn't find in her own family."

It appears further that Harriet had also chosen an unhappy time for her wedding, in that it happened right in the midst of a Beecher family reunion. This has already added to the confusion and is certain to add more as soon as the Beecher clan arrives.

Harriet herself appears in the doorway in time to catch the drift of Catherine's criticism, and to agree heartily with her. "Harriet is twenty-six. To many people she is plain; others say she is beautiful. Undoubtedly it depends upon whether her face is seen in repose—when the strong Beecher modeling of her nose and chin are most in evidence—or when, as now, her eyes are merry and her mouth is curved in laughter. Her hair is crisp and so curly that it is perpetually escaping from its decorous confinement. Her figure is slender, her voice low, but distinct. She wears a full-skirted coat, a very large, very becoming bonnet which frames her face like a halo, and carries a small, round muff."

The brother and sister greetings are affectionate. It was good of Henry and Catherine to have arranged this cheery homecoming for the bride and groom, Harriet agrees. She and Calvin have had a long, hard drive from Columbus, and were bogged in the mud more than once. "It was Calvin's books sank us," says Harriet. "He has brought home at least two hundred weight. Where *is* Calvin?"

"He probably has forgotten he lives here," suggests Henry.

"I shouldn't be surprised. In Columbus, he kept forgetting my existence and starting off without me."

But Calvin hasn't forgotten. He is standing in the doorway now, gently chiding his wife for her exaggeration. "Calvin Stowe is ten years older than his wife; a scholarly man, with a large head and a shock of curly hair, which is already receding from his brow. To make up for this desertion, he is cultivating sideburns, which have, as yet, crept down only to the level of his ears. Not a romantic figure, yet he has a child-like sweetness and charm."

Calvin is burdened with an enormous carpetbag and several parcels. He still is mistily excited about his purchases at a recent book auction, at which much of the household money has disappeared, according to Harriet. But Calvin is happy. He had gathered in several prodigious bargains. He has them in his bag. The "De Agesilae Rege Oratio," Xenophon, 1748; Whaley's answer to the John Cotton tract on "The Keyes of the Kingdome of Heaven" and two volumes of Hagiz' commentaries.

When Harriet searches his pocket she finds one small, fat volume and another smaller one. "I always carry my Greek Testament and the 'Divina Commedia,'" protests Calvin.

"Not any more!" Harriet announces. "And hang up your other suit, or it won't be fit to wear to class tomorrow."

"You're right, my love. Yes, yes. Indubitably you're right."

Calvin takes his bag upstairs with him, but leaves behind his other parcels. One is discovered to be a painting in oils of Eliza Stowe, Calvin's first wife. He had given it to Harriet as a wedding present. The gesture shocks Catherine, though Harriet accepts it gracefully. Eliza had been a good friend of Harriet's.

The settling goes on. As Henry suspected, Harriet likes the easy chair near the table rather than by the fire, where Catherine thinks it should be—

"Kate, this is my house—*my* house," declares Harriet, with

some firmness. "At last I have a house of my own with a hearth—and lovely fire tongs—and a beautiful, beautiful coal scuttle."

Auntie Zeb is in to report that the kitchen range is not working, and to bring pieces of wedding cake Harriet had saved for the family. There is quite a lot of the cake—a neatly tied small package for each of them—fifteen in all. Spread out in a row Harriet finds them a vivid reminder of the home she is leaving—

"Henry, do you see this beautiful little table?" Harriet is saying.

"I see it is little."

HARRIET—That's why it is beautiful. A table for *two*. When I think of that spread at home—yards and yards of Beechers, and where the Beechers leave off, the boarders begin. Then the grandchildren—shoals of grandchildren. (*Angrily, she sweeps the packages back into her basket.*) Guinea pigs!

HENRY—You always hated it at home.

HARRIET—Yes. I hated the noise. The arguments and confusion. Squalling babies—children and animals under foot! Pa and Catherine always crusading for some cause! And brooding over it all. Pa's horrible, gloomy God.

HENRY—Harriet!

HARRIET—Oh, come, Henry. You don't believe in Father's God—a cruel monster who condemns His people to eternal torment. I am through with all that! I am turning my back on the Old Testament and putting my faith in the New.

HENRY (*slowly*)—So that is why you married—to escape from home.

HARRIET (*turning to him*)—No. No. I really love Calvin. He may not be the Prince Charming of my girlhood dreams, but a Prince Charming would want me to worship him, and wait on him. *I* mean to be the one who is waited on, and worshiped. Oh, dear. Am I very selfish?

HENRY—I hope so.

HARRIET—So do I. It's a quality I mean to cultivate. I've planned my new life down to the last detail. Take this table and chair—they are going to be mine. Mine, and nobody else's. I shall sit here every day and write—two hours after breakfast, and three hours after dinner.

HENRY—Aren't you afraid the dishes will give out, with nobody to wash them?

HARRIET—Calvin will pay for that. (*Quickly.*) I know he is only a professor in a small seminary, now, but he has a brilliant mind. Brilliant and profound. He can write . . .

HENRY—In Latin, Greek, Sanskrit, Hebrew—

HARRIET—*And* Arabic. Did you know he is taking it up for mental relaxation?

HENRY—Very useful.

HARRIET—It will be. Henry—for years he has been doing research for a book on the sources of the Bible. I've interested Catherine's publishers and now—

HENRY—Now all you have to do is to interest Calvin.

HARRIET—Laugh if you like.

HENRY—I hope— Oh, I *do* hope—that you find happiness in your ivory tower.

HARRIET—I shall. You'll see!

Henry and Catherine have left on a personal mission. They are going to try to head off the Beechers, and they carry Harriet's prayers for their success. Now, for the first time, Harriet and Calvin are in their new home alone. It is a moving moment for Harriet. She circles the sitting room with satisfaction and pride. She dismisses Auntie Zeb for the night. She is muttering the new name softly to herself—

"Mrs. Stowe!" "Mrs. Calvin Ellis Stowe . . ." when Calvin comes into the room. "Do you want me, Hatty?" he asks, gently.

"Always. Oh, Calvin—I *do* love you."

"Of course, my dear. Is anything wrong?"

"Why?"

"You said that so— (*Pause.*) combatively."

"Perhaps I hoped you would put up an argument," she says, taking his arm and marching him to the center of the room.

"Do you know, dear, at times you are lovely."

"Oh, no . . . I've always been quite plain. Homely little Hatty Beecher."

"Not now. There is something about your face—your eyes, I think—" He has tilted her face up, and is quoting softly: " 'Sad and laughing eyes, whose lids make such sweet shadows when they close.' "

"Why, Calvin—you quite take my breath away! Is that from the Greek?"

A pleased ejaculation escapes Calvin, but his tone is rebuking as he answers. "No, Hatty—Sanskrit." He has taken a chair at the table and she follows him and sits on the hassock at his feet.

"I wonder if any woman before was ever courted in *all* the dead languages," she says, looking up at him. "Shall we be able to hold on to it? Will we always be happy?"

"Perhaps not in the same way."

"We mustn't let it slip away from us. I have seen so many wretched marriages, where people have made compromises with life. I refuse to compromise!"

"My dear—"

"I warn you, Calvin—I intend to teach you to be gay. You've no idea how gay you can be if you try."

"I will make the attempt, Hatty. I will certainly make the attempt."

"And above all—I mean this, Calvin, for it is most important —we must respect each other as individuals."

It is Harriet's plan to arrange the parlor as a library for Calvin, where he can work with all his books close to his hand. And then she is sure that he will have his new book finished in no time. . . .

Catherine and Henry are back—with evil tidings. The Beechers are coming! At least all the true Beechers are coming. The non- or in-law Beechers are in the throes of a disagreement.

It is the feeling of Father Beecher, Catherine reports, that the family should tender Harriet a visit of welcome, for which she is to make no formal preparations. "Just tea and coffee for the adults; milk for the young—" suggests Henry, in imitation of his father; "with a few sandwiches, cookies, cakes . . . soda biscuits with honey—"

Calvin would get away, if he could, but Catherine pulls him back. Harriet will need his help. Harriet herself has gone to find or to borrow such refreshments as she can. Then the Beechers begin to "spill in"—

"William, Edward, and Mary are the first to enter. They are in their thirties. Like all of the family, they are full of vigor and bounce; often pompous and opinionated, but seldom intentionally disagreeable. William and Edward are ministers; they both wear whiskers."

Now there is a rattling crossfire of conversation. The chief topic of interest would appear to be Father Beecher's most recent sermon. A powerful utterance, his sons are agreed, and a credit to all of them, collectively and individually. Henry is the only one inclined to scoff gently. "Did Papa do his usual 'My six stalwart sons consecrated to God through the ministry'?" asks Henry, and is immediately sat upon.

"If you do not abandon your scoffing attitude, Henry, you will never climb to the ministry," warns William.

"You will have to content yourself with being a lawyer, or a senator," adds Edward.

They are all pleased to welcome Calvin in his new home, and a little anxious to know what has become of Harriet. Sister Isabella and Brother James have now arrived and reported that Father Lyman has been delayed by a newspaper man, a Mr. Tuttle, who writes weekly letters for the press and hopes to write something about the Beecher reunion—

"He says we're the most notable family in America," reports James; "with more brains, and more influence, and more ministers."

"James!" Edward is sharp.

"Beechers do not boast!" adds Mary.

"That is for *others* to say," cautions Catherine.

"Mr. Tuttle did say it," insists James. "He said the public would rather read about us, than about a balloon ascension—"

"*Much* rather," corrects Isabella.

Harriet is back. She comes from the kitchen with a tray of cookies, cocoa and milk, and is loyally welcomed. William, if they would listen, would make a little speech about the pleasure it gives the family to welcome their sister as the Queen of her domain.

But now Father Lyman is trumpeting his arrival in the hall and for the next few minutes everything revolves about that event. A chair must be drawn up for Father, and not too near a window, either. That's where the drafts come from. And there should be a pillow for Father, although Catherine happens to know that he scorns them.

When Father comes into the room he has retained his muffler to offset the chill he had felt in the church, however warm William may think his sermon was. "I always preach straight to the conscience, like a bullet to the bull's-eye," declares Lyman, pleased at their praise. "Life is on the wing! No time for shilly-shallying. Immortal souls are sleeping on the brink of hell . . . Eternity is at stake!"

"Welcome to our home, Pa!" Harriet is trying to get in a word, even edgewise.

"God has chosen me his humble instrument to awaken the sinners—to cry to those who slumber with a great and terrible voice. (*Turning to her. Suddenly smiling.*) Well, well, daughter, so you are with us again—and looking very hearty, Praise to Providence, very hearty indeed."

Now Calvin is brought forward to be greeted. That over, Lyman has time to notice that Harriet is wearing a new garment —a dress, she reports, that she had bought with money she had earned by writing. "I mean to earn others. I mean to earn a *silk* dress," declares Harriet.

"And you will be charming in it, Hatty." Calvin beams approvingly.

LYMAN—Do I gather from that you approve of her writing, Professor?

CALVIN—The Lord has obviously intended Harriet for a literary woman. Who am I to oppose the Lord?

LYMAN—I am disappointed. Gravely disappointed!

CALVIN—S—Sir?

LYMAN—I had hoped that marriage with a man like yourself —not only a minister of the gospel but also connected with an educational institution—would serve to steady Harriet.

CALVIN—But we have only been married a week.

HARRIET (*demurely*)—In what way do you consider me unsteady, Pa?

LYMAN—In many ways, Harriet—but most specifically in the matter of your literary fabrications.

HARRIET (*kneeling beside him*)—Surely you do not take my poor little stories seriously!

LYMAN—It is *that* I deprecate, their lack of seriousness.

EDWARD—You are constantly embarrassing us, Hatty.

WILLIAM—People are beginning to ask if you can possibly be my sister.

HARRIET (*delighted*)—And do you admit it, William—or do you cast me off?

WILLIAM—Really, Harriet!

LYMAN—I warn you, Daughter, levity is an insidious vice. If you are not constantly on guard the habit of Fiction will grow on you. We Beechers have always been writers, yes. We have prided ourselves on our power with the pen, but always we have employed that power worthily—never without high purpose.

HARRIET (*much too meekly*)—Do you suggest I should write sermons, Papa?

LYMAN (*sharply*)—Decidedly *not*.

CHARLES—Unthinkable!

WILLIAM—A female in the pulpit!

CATHERINE—And what would be wrong with a female in the pulpit?

WILLIAM (*to* CATHERINE)—If it is necessary for me to tell you—

CATHERINE (*not waiting*)—A female in the pulpit might not waste so much time in pompous platitudes but—

LYMAN—Catherine!

CATHERINE—I am sorry, Father, but it is a subject upon which I feel deeply!

MARY—So do I!

EDWARD—Quiet!

CATHERINE—A female in the pulpit *might* have the courage to air a few questions which stand in need of airing.

WILLIAM—Such as?

EDWARD—For instance?

CATHERINE—Such as Abolition, for instance!

Now the fat is in the fire. "Like a pack falling on a bone the Beechers seize upon the word." Edward is constantly bringing up abolition in his pulpit, which William considers a grave mistake, but Henry doesn't. Neither does Charles.

"Where do you stand?" Edward would know of Harriet.

"I stand opposed to anything which may cause conflict, either in my house or in the nation."

They are mostly shocked at Harriet's stand, though Lyman would agree, if he could make himself heard above the racket his sons are making. Presently Harriet escapes into the kitchen, but the argument goes on right merrily without her. Now Lyman has agreed with Mary that there is far too much talk about abolition, which is appalling to Catherine and to Henry, but not to William.

"I contend the whole question of slavery can be left to the Southern states," contends William. "The planters are already learning that slave labor is economically unsound."

Edward is excited about the border outrages, and so is Henry. It is quite terrible when the Kentucks cross the river and invade the Negro district, and these are not merely local riots, as William would imply.

"They are not local," shouts Edward. "They are beginning to occur wherever slave territory touches free."

"And your friends, the Abolitionists, are feeding the flames," says Charles.

"I agree with Charles," booms Lyman. "The Abolitionists

are fanatics, madmen, willing to burn down the house in order to destroy the rats."

"By 'the house' I presume you mean the nation?" demands Edward.

"I do, Sir!"

"Then you prefer to have the rats destroy the *nation.*"

Now the pack is off in full cry again, snapping at each other with sharp and caustic, but mostly unfinished, sentences. Even the entrance of Harriet, followed by her efforts to attract and hold the attention of her father long enough to tell him that Mr. Tuttle is turning in at the gate, at first have little effect. But the family realizes that a gentleman from the press is approaching and there is complete silence.

Mr. Tuttle is, of course, to be admitted. And when he is admitted it is Lyman's wish that the whole family shall be discovered singing one of their favorite hymns. Harriet should stay with the family. Calvin can receive the guest. Charles will accompany the family at the melodeon, Isabella may turn the pages of the music and the rest will be grouped in the order of their ages—Catherine, William, Edward, Mary and Harriet. The hymn will be "Old Hundred," Lyman decrees, though Harriet would have preferred "There Is a Happy Land, Far, Far Away."

The Beechers have burst into song just a split second before Calvin appears with Mr. Tuttle, "Who is very oily and effusive." For a moment Mr. Tuttle stands surveying "the exaggeratedly unconscious Beechers" and then mutters his entire approval. "Charming! Charming! Too delightful!" insists Mr. Tuttle. And as Lyman, with a brave start of surprise, calls his children's attention to the arrival, Mr. Tuttle adds: "I beg of you, do not let me interrupt such a joyful occasion."

"Ah, yes," Lyman agrees. "What a sensation for a father to behold his offspring—without exception—gathered together— Where are you going, Harriet?"

Harriet has thought she would go to the kitchen, but Lyman, and Mr. Tuttle, too, insist that she shall stay. Mr. Tuttle has brought a Mr. Wycherly with him. Mr. Wycherly, "a smallish man in a long frock coat," is "the Gainsborough of Lightning Delineators," Mr. Tuttle explains. They are both very anxious to have a picture of the inspiring Beechers. Lyman would protest, but is finally persuaded, without too much difficulty, to pose. "You owe it to your public. A heart-warming picture of family devotion," points out Mr. Tuttle, and the others add their endorsements of the idea in a babble of enthusiasm.

The wordless Mr. Wycherly, however, is a little worried. He whispers to Mr. Tuttle, and Mr. Tuttle explains to Lyman, that there may be too many Beechers for a really good picture. Perhaps it would be better to take in just a few—

"Suppose we say—just the members of the family of most— How shall I put it? Of greatest interest to the public—"

With that he proceeds to arrange the group, calling them one by one and posing them as they step forward— "Dr. Beecher. Miss Catherine. Mr. Edward. Mr. Charles. And Mrs. Stowe. Would you mind holding the lamp?"

Harriet picks up the lamp and is a little in doubt as to what she is expected to do with it.

"For the delineator, Mrs. Stowe," instructs Mr. Tuttle.

"For the artist, Hatty—the artist," booms Lyman.

"Yes, Pa."

Mr. Wycherly has started to sketch as the curtain falls.

When the curtain rises several years have passed. It is a July morning. The living-dining room appears much the same, although the slip cover on the padded chair is worn and faded and the center table is piled high with Calvin's heavy tomes and littered with manuscripts. There are eight chairs at the dining table now, including a high-chair. There are children's toys scattered about, and a curtained baby carriage stands in the center of the room.

Auntie Zeb can be heard singing in the next room. Presently she appears with a blanket for the baby carriage, and is closely followed by Celestine, "a small black limb of Satan who wears a single garment, belted at the waist." Celestine's kinky hair is in curl papers, and she is plainly a problem to Auntie Zeb. She grabs up the children's toys and unties Auntie Zeb's apron as she dashes out of the way when she is about to be "whammed."

Brother William has come to suggest to Auntie Zeb that the children be kept in the upper part of town if they go out. Kentucks have been crossing the river all morning searching for two runaway slaves.

Auntie Zeb knows. She has been trying to keep the Kentuck reports from Miz Stowe all morning. "Every time trouble starts wid de Kentucks, she goes mos' crazy worryin' about de chillun."

Harriet comes from the kitchen with the baby and is surprised to find William, who explains that he has come to tell her the steamboat is in and that he will be back to take Calvin and his bags to the landing. Calvin is upstairs packing for the journey, but it is Auntie Zeb's idea that he already has forgotten that he is going.

Now Harriet, anxious about the children, would round them up. Standing in the doorway she rings a small bell and calls: "Children! . . . Hatty . . . Eliza . . . Freddie . . . Georgie . . . Harry . . ." Freddie is the only one to appear, but he can report on the others. The twins are down at Grandpa's playing hopscotch, Georgiana and Brother are fishing in the big puddle. . . .

Auntie Zeb has found Calvin sitting at the edge of his bed reading. When he comes he has one shoe on, and one slipper; his hair is rumpled and his vest unbuttoned; his carpetbag is half packed.

"Do not be perturbed, Harriet . . . do not be perturbed . . . I am quite ready to start," Calvin assures his distressed wife. She sits him in a chair and proceeds to comb his hair, while Freddie hunts for his father's other boot. The boy would like to go with his father on the steamboat, but being told that he must stay home to take care of his mother, he would like to have a gun. You can't take care of anybody without a gun. "You got to have a gun fo' shootin' dem Kentucks," the playful Celestine advises. "Lot's of 'em in town today," she adds, before Auntie Zeb can stop her.

"What's that?" Harriet quickly demands.

"Jest Celestine givin' out fool talk." Auntie Zeb is preparing to do a little more whamming. "What makes you such a bad girl?"

"Nobody made me—Ah jest growed!" answers Celestine, whom the children call Topsy.

Calvin is a little apprehensive, too. He doesn't think he should be going East at this time, leaving Harriet alone with the children. But Harriet is determined he shall go. She will not be alone. Catherine is canceling a lecture tour to be with Harriet. Besides, this is a business trip. Calvin must go East to sell his book, and to find a new position.

"I am no good at business without you, Hatty," sighs Calvin.

HARRIET—Then you must force yourself! We can't go on like this any longer . . . the Board not paying you . . . all of us without money . . . without clothes, almost without food.

CALVIN—The Board isn't to blame.

HARRIET—I'm not blaming anyone—but I am sick of being

always tired, always worried, always wondering how soon we will be forced to surrender and ask for charity.

CALVIN (*in the depths*)—I should never have married you, Harriet, and brought the children into the world.

HARRIET—Now, Calvin, you are *not* going into one of your indigo moods! (*Forcing herself into gaiety.*) Don't look so woe-begone, dear. Before you know it you will be back with your book sold, and a fine professorship in a big college. (*With an affectionate pat.*) Where *is* your manuscript? I don't see it.

CALVIN—As a matter of fact—it isn't there.

HARRIET—That is half the reason for your going!

CALVIN—I know, but—

HARRIET—We are counting on the advance money to pay for our move East.

CALVIN—I—I feel it is not quite ready to show the publishers. Not quite. I need just a few more weeks . . .

HARRIET—You said that last year—and the year before.

CALVIN—Harriet! You seem to care nothing for my reputation as a scholar.

HARRIET—But, Calvin—

CALVIN—No, no—I cannot and *will* not permit any interference with my literary affairs. Before I submit the book for publication there are a number of references I desire to verify. I shall do so on this trip.

HARRIET—I know. Instead of looking for a position you will go and bury yourself in a library. I shall have to send a rescue party to excavate you. Why didn't I marry a man who merely *drank?*

CALVIN—Perhaps none of them asked you, my love.

HARRIET (*laughing*)—You are right.

CALVIN (*once more in high good humor*)—Oh, Hatty—I am going to miss you.

HARRIET (*turning and smiling*)—Are you sure?

CALVIN—Positive. You are quite the most intelligent and agreeable woman in the whole circle of my acquaintance.

HARRIET—It is good to hear you say that . . . it is such a long time since you've made love to me, even in Greek.

CALVIN (*ever literal*)—Why, Hatty, we have six children. (*As* HARRIET *begins to laugh again.*) I was not intending to be humorous.

HARRIET—I'm not laughing, really. I am crying. (*Burying her face in his bosom.*)

CALVIN—You are my very dear wife, and I love you.

HARRIET—If you were not already my very dear husband, I should certainly fall in love with *you*. (*After a moment.*) You know if you had that manuscript in your bag you could give the publishers a glimpse— (*Quickly, at his withdrawing movement.*) Just a tantalizing glimpse, Calvin. They would surely be impressed by that magnificent first chapter.

CALVIN—I had thought of that . . .

HARRIET—You shouldn't deny them the pleasure.

CALVIN—Perhaps you are right, Hatty. (*She is already halfway to the table.*) Yes, indubitably, you are right. If they appreciate the chapter I may even be able to negotiate a small advance.

With some additional confusion they get Calvin off to the boat. Harriet has dropped wearily into the padded chair. She is tired, she admits, "tired clear into the future." She is discouraged, too—discouraged remembering the fine things she was going to accomplish in that chair.

"I've *scribbled*—in between washing, and baking, and babies," Harriet admits. "But I haven't achieved anything. Not even a silk dress. (*She looks around the room.*) I am glad Henry isn't here to see me in my ivory tower."

Catherine had visited Henry in Brooklyn on her last lecture tour. Found him well and very successful. "His congregation adores him. He has a magnificent salary . . . his own horse and carriage . . ."

"Is he happy?"

"You think too much of happiness, Harriet. Henry is doing the Lord's work. He is conceded to be the country's foremost crusader in the Temperance cause."

"I know. And you're crusading for Female Education. Edward for Abolition. Belle for Women's Rights, James and Charles for—what are James and Charles crusading for now? They must be galloping at the head of some cause."

"At least we are doing our duty by our fellow men. That is more than you can say!"

"I? What can I do?"

"You can declare yourself publicly for Abolition. You are not deceiving me, Harriet. All this talk about Calvin's obtaining a professorship in an Eastern University, I can see what is back of it."

"It's no secret. Everyone knows Father's Seminary is failing. Every day we are sinking deeper into poverty."

"When were you ever afraid of poverty?" demands Catherine, scornfully. "You have been poor all your life. All the Beechers have been poor, and never given it a thought."

Outside there is the noise of a crowd passing. It is only people going down to the boat, Catherine reports from the window. She is still impatient of Harriet's fear. It isn't fear of poverty, she insists, but of the Kentucks—

"Certainly, I'm afraid. Why shouldn't I be?" Harriet is quick to answer her. "You've been away on your lecture tours. You don't realize how outrageous they've become. We never know when a mob will cross the river and burn and loot the colored district. They pretend they are coming after runaways, but it is only an excuse for kidnaping free Negroes and dragging them back into slavery."

"You let this abomination go on! You do nothing to stop it!"

"I have no money, so little strength. I have my children to think about."

"You are hiding behind your poverty, your children, anything and everything, to keep from taking a stand on the slavery question."

"That is not true!"

"No? Then prove it by joining the Abolitionists. Stand up and be counted!"

"I am against violence! I refuse to join any group which advocates meeting force with force."

"Force is the only language the crowd understands."

Suddenly Brothers Edward and Thomas have burst into the room. Thomas, "an excited young chap in his twenties," carries a gun, and Edward has a pistol strapped on. The Kentucks are running amuck, they report, and they want to use Harriet's stove to melt lead for bullets. The Citizen's Committee is calling for arms.

But Harriet is firm. They are not going to mold bullets in her kitchen. Bullets never settled any argument. "How about the Revolution?" Catherine would know.

Now Lyman Beecher has come storming in. He sides with the boys. "The time for reasoning is past," booms Lyman. "The devil is loose—riding the land with his cohorts! The wrath of Jehovah will descend upon them! God will destroy the destroyers!"

Outside there are screams, and shots are fired. Harriet's anxiety about the safety of the children—about the baby and Freddie —starts her toward the door. Nor will she listen to her father's command to come back.

Catherine would follow Harriet, but she, too, is ordered back. Catherine has work to do, Lyman reminds her. Let her build up the fire for the melting of the lead. There will be need of bullets before the day is done.

Auntie Zeb, distraught and all but speechless, appears with the baby, muttering over and over: " 'Twern't mah fault!" She had tried to hold Freddie, it appears, but he got away from her. Freddie was "boun' to see de Kentucks." "Ol' nigger runnin' . . . Kentucks catch him . . . Catch him right by Freddie."

From the hall come Freddie's screams and Harriet's comforting words. The boy is clinging to her skirts as they come into the room, and sobbing hysterically.

"Yes—yes, dear. Stop trembling. Try to stop. Mama won't leave you. Mama's right here—holding you. Nothing can hurt you." She has turned to her father. "I knew this would happen. I've always known!"

LYMAN—The boy has not been injured. He will forget.

HARRIET—After what he has seen? Never—never! So long as there are Kentucks to remind him—

FREDDIE (*hysterical again*)—Kentucks! Kentucks!

HARRIET—No, Freddie, they can't hurt you! I won't let them— (*There is a boat whistle in the distance. She goes on her knees.*) Listen, darling, we are going away—hundreds and hundreds of miles away—where there aren't any Kentucks. You are going to live where you'll never see any of those wicked men again! . . .

CALVIN (*offstage*)—Harriet— (*He enters, followed by* WILLIAM.) We've just heard . . .

WILLIAM—We got word at the boat.

CALVIN—Is the boy safe?

LYMAN—Quite unharmed!

HARRIET—Calvin!

CALVIN—Yes, dear. I won't leave you. I won't go—

HARRIET—You *must*—go—

LYMAN—Surely, daughter, he should stay with you.

CALVIN—At least—until the emergency is over.

HARRIET (*beginning to get hysterical*)—Oh, my God—don't you realize we can't stay here? You must get us away from this horrible place. Some place where our children can go out and play without a mob of murderers trampling them under foot. You do that, do you hear me—

LYMAN—Daughter—control yourself! You will leave in God's good time.

HARRIET (*bringing herself up short*)—Yes, Father. (*With quiet intensity, to* CALVIN.) Calvin, I am counting on you. You catch that boat—go East, find a position— I don't care how poor, how small. But you try, keep on trying, because if you fail, I warn you, I'll forget I am a woman, I'll go East myself— I'll go to the colleges, beg on my knees, I'll do everything, anything, to find safety and peace. (*She pauses.*) Now you go catch that boat.

She has turned again to Freddie and drawn him against her with a fierce, protective gesture.
The curtain falls.

ACT II

It is a Spring morning in the early 1850s. The Calvin Stowes have just arrived in Brunswick, Me. The back parlor of their new home is a pleasant, livable room, but still unsettled. At the moment Harriet is sitting on the floor upholstering a chair made from a barrel. "She is taking the last stitches in the seat cushions. This is the third appearance of the material from her trousseau dress."

Candice Hobbs, "a thin, uncompromising New Englander of the lady-helper type," is tacking gimp on the back of a sofa which she is upholstering, and getting as much news of the Stowes as she can between her attacks upon her job.

Thus she learns that the trip from Cincinnati had been a hard one. It was made on steamboats, trains and stage coaches, with all the young 'uns and Mrs. Stowe "in a condition." Prof. Stowe is still in Cincinnati, finishing a book. He had had to wait years before the college could make a place for him. "It isn't always easy to find a Professorship in Revealed Religion, you know," Harriet points out. But Mrs. Hobbs doesn't know.

"Oh, it is so beautifully peaceful here." Harriet has gone to the window and is looking out, dreamily. "This is what I've been looking for these seven years—peace."

A moment later Freddie has bounded in. He is now "a good-looking boy at the gawky age. He wears pantaloons, a short jacket and a peaked cap." Freddie carries a picture of Eliza Stowe. He thought perhaps his mother would like to hang it over the mantel again, but Harriet thinks it would look better now in the spare room.

A moment later Georgie Stowe bounces in. "She has reached her full height, but is still a tomboy in short skirts, white ruffled apron and pantalettes."

Georgie comes to report that the four-poster bed has fallen on the man who couldn't find the screws for it. "Oh, Mama, moving's so exciting! I wish we moved and moved all the time, don't you?" adds Georgie.

"Well, not all the time," her mother answers.

Now Hatty and Eliza come in through the dining room. They are "very young girls; pretty and well-mannered; identical twins. Since it is a warm day, they wear gowns of India print, drop-shouldered and full-skirted."

Between them Hatty and Eliza are carrying a small horsehair trunk in which are the clothes that their mother had kept after the baby died. And there is some question about the baby carriage. "Is it worth while taking it up to the attic?" Hatty would know. No, her mother doesn't think so.

Hatty thinks perhaps she had better walk down to the store and get more soap for the window washing. Eliza is in favor of getting more soap, but she insists it is her turn to go. Hatty has already been four times, and she only three.

"Aren't they ridic'lous?" sneers Georgie. "All they want is a chance to swish at the Denton boy."

"A chance to what?" Harriet is a little startled.

"Swish at Lowell Denton—that boy two houses down. He's been clipping the front hedge ever since we moved in. Every time they go to the store they swish past him."

And what has she (Georgie) been doing, the twins would remind their sister. "Tom-boying all over the place, with your pantalettes all crooked!"

Eliza gets the chance to go for the soap, but Hatty finds a job hanging curtains at the window from which she can watch the hedge clipper. A moment later she has heard Mrs. Hobbs ask for more gimp and is off like a shot to fetch it. "Just a-swishin'," mutters Mrs. Hobbs.

Jerusha Pantry has arrived with a hogshead from the cotton factory. That is going to be Harriet's cistern. There's a pump down the street, but she prefers water in the house, even though, as Jerusha points out, there is a school of thought that holds the 'pinion water in the house is unhealthy.

Harriet has gone to see about getting the hogshead through the cellar door, which Jerusha assures her can't be done, and Jerusha has gone down to the station to throw the switch for the steam train that is standing waiting for him, when Eliza comes back, leaning a little heavily on the arm of Lowell Denton, "a handsome youngster of about her own age." Eliza is also limping in exaggerated fashion.

It is with some difficulty and a good many "Ouches!" that young Mr. Denton gets Eliza to the couch and finds the vial of smelling salts she tells him is in the work basket. He is fearfully afraid that she may swoon, and would go at once in search of her mother, but Eliza recovers sufficiently to make that unnecessary.

She considers herself quite lucky that her twisting her ankle on the cobblestones should have happened so close to where Mr. Denton was clipping the hedge, and he, too, considers it a fortunate coincidence. He had been conscious of Eliza's many trips to the store—fourteen in all, he had counted. Eliza would tell him that only seven of those trips were hers, but thinks better of that—

"After you have seen a young lady walk past fourteen times," Lowell is saying, "you kind of feel you are acquainted with her."

"Do you?"

"Yes—let me get you a cushion."

"Please don't discommode yourself. There's one over there."

It is while Lowell is getting the cushion that he turns and comes face to face with Hatty. "In her flowered dress she is an exact duplicate of Eliza. The shock almost bowls the young man over. He turns, looks at Eliza, discovers she is still there and looks back at Hatty."

Eliza is "inarticulate with embarrassment," but she manages an introduction. "Mr. Denton this is Hatty. Hatty, this is Mr. Denton . . . my twin sister, Hatty. We are twins. . . . Mr. Denton just happened to be clipping the hedge when I just happened to turn my ankle on a cobblestone."

"—Right where I was clipping the hedge. That's what makes it such a coincidence."

"Does it not!" Eliza adds, brightly.

But Hatty is not impressed. It sounds too much like a story that Mother had in *The New Era* the week before. That's the real coincidence. Lowell manages a nervous laugh, as he sits uncomfortably between the two sisters. Then he suddenly remembers that Mrs. Stowe's writing for *The New Era* would indicate that the Stowes are Abolition, and he is pleased.

"Oh, yes. We are Abolition—and Presbyterian," says Eliza.

"So are we Presbyterian," admits Lowell, with new enthusiasm.

"I have an uncle who is a minister."

"We have a grandpa, and a papa, and six uncles who are ministers," says Hatty, proudly.

"Cracky!" Lowell is certainly impressed. "Old School Presbyterian, or New School?"

"New School, of *course*."

"Then that's all right." The girls sigh in momentary relief; then a new cloud forms on the horizon. "Are you Freedom-by-decree Abolition, or Freedom-by-purchase?"

"We are Freedom-by-purchase."

"*We* are Freedom-by-decree."

For a moment the situation is a little tragic, but they soon find a new common ground for friendship and understanding. For one thing, Uncle Edward is a station on the underground railway for smuggling escaped slaves. So are the Dentons. And that's lovely.

Harriet and Georgie appear, looking pretty messy. Harriet has a towel around her head. She has been working with the hogshead in the cellar. Georgie's hair is disheveled and she carries a torn apron in her hand. She had been fighting with an Irisher who had pushed her off the fence when she was watching the train. Eliza and Hatty are quite embarrassed, and Harriet quickly apologetic.

Harriet is pleased that Mr. Denton has dropped in. He can help her move the furniture. Again the girls are fussed, but there is nothing they can do about it. They are greatly pleased a moment later when Harriet asks Lowell to stay to supper. Eliza's ankle is suddenly quite strong again.

In some excitement Henry Beecher appears. He had been lecturing in Boston and could not resist the temptation to run up. Henry "has grown heavier and attained a dignity which is beginning to verge on pomposity. He is still clean-shaven, but he now wears his hair long, brushed back from his brow and behind his ears in a rather theatrical fashion. He has already adopted the familiar cape and broad-brimmed black hat."

Harriet is delighted to feast her eyes on Henry and all the evidences of his new prosperity. She has heard of his expanding fame, of his great church that seats three thousand and has people standing in the aisles every Sunday. "My pulpit is in the middle—on a raised platform," Henry proudly relates. "I can see everyone."

"And everyone can see you," adds Harriet, knowingly.

As for herself, Harriet has little to report. Calvin is still in

Cincinnati finishing his book. Of all the books she was going to write none has been written. There are many reasons for that, but Henry refuses to accept any of them.

"I shut myself in my study every day—and allow no one to disturb me," announces Henry, and when Harriet chuckles he demands to know what she is laughing at.

HARRIET—I'm afraid it is at you. Don't be too successful, Henry. Don't grow sleek and smug. (*Quickly, at his gesture of annoyance.*) I'm sorry, dear. Sometimes I grow afraid for you. I keep hearing about your popularity, your success.

HENRY—You need have no fears for me, Harriet. Of the Almighty's servants, your brother is the humblest, the most self-effacing, the most— (*Suddenly eager.*) Did you hear about my auction?

HARRIET—Your *slave* auction? Yes, they—

HENRY (*excited by the memory*)—An auction in a church! Picture the scene! It was—indescribable!

HARRIET (*a trifle drily*)—I thought the newspapers did very well.

HENRY—Think of it. An exquisite young slave girl—beautiful hair, beautiful eyes, beautiful figure—(*Recollecting himself.*)—a professing Christian, standing, suppliant, before the congregation.

HARRIET—Didn't she distract the congregation's attention?

HENRY—From what?

HARRIET—From the pulpit, Henry.

HENRY—Only for a moment . . . (*His eyes widen.*) Harriet!

HARRIET—I'm sorry. That was really wicked of me. And you did marvelously. Raised a thousand dollars, wasn't it?

HENRY—Eleven hundred. More than enough to buy her freedom. (*Again ecstatic.*) Strong men wept, women became hysterical. Tore off their rings and bracelets. Threw them on the platform. The following Sunday the church was packed. Packed! Since then I have redeemed four more slaves.

HARRIET—All of them beautiful?

HENRY—*All*. Especially the last. She— (*Suddenly suspicious.*) What does your editor want?

HARRIET—My—?

HENRY—Your editor. You say he nags you.

HARRIET—Oh, yes, yes. He wants a three-part serial—an abolitionist story illustrating the evils of slavery.

HENRY—A capital idea! Have you started writing?

HARRIET—No! I mean to put the whole slavery question out

of my mind. In Ohio, I could never forget. The dreadful thing was there—under my eyes every minute. Now—that is past. I have escaped.

HENRY—So you hope to solve the problem by closing your eyes?

HARRIET—It is not my duty to solve it. We have statesmen in Washington—

HENRY—Not any more! They've turned into vote-grabbing, pandering politicians!

HARRIET (*smiling*)—Henry—do you remember Father's prayer? "Oh, Lord—grant that we may not despise our leaders, and grant that they may not act so that we cannot help it!"

HENRY (*grimly*)—This is no time for humor, Harriet. While you, and thousands like you, evade your responsibilities, Congress meddles and muddles and makes matters worse—selling out states and territories, passing laws like this last filthy enactment . . .

HARRIET—The Fugitive Slave Act?

HENRY—The Act that makes fugitives of American decency and honor! Think what it means, Harriet! Think what it does to the rights of the human being; not just to the slave—but to you, and me, and the man down the street! If I permit a freezing Negro to sleep in my barn—if I so much as give him a crust of bread, I am a criminal!

HARRIET—The Act will never be upheld. The authorities will flout it.

HENRY—Read your newspaper! Slave hunters are already kidnaping victims in Boston and Philadelphia.

HARRIET—And crowds are rescuing them as fast as they are kidnaped.

HENRY—So the Governor threatens to call out the militia to aid the kidnapers. Americans will be ordered to shoot down other Americans because the wise and reverend judges have decreed that slavery is guaranteed by the Constitution.

HARRIET—They believe they can frighten us into obeying such a law? What kind of people do they think we are?

Jerusha Pantry pops in just in time to hear Henry insist that the thing for them to do is to come out squarely for emancipation. Jerusha doesn't agree, and boldly says so. "Slaves is proppity" to Jerusha. True, he never has seen a slave, at least "not when he was slavin'," but he has a brother who owns a mill over Lynn way.

"If the slaves was freed, who'd raise the cotton for his mill?'

Jerusha wants to know. "They'd have to pay white men t' do it. Cotton'd go sky high, an' you'd be ruinin' the value of his *prop-pity*."

Mrs. Hobbs has come to remind Jerusha that he'd better be about his lamp-lightin' job. That stops the argument. "And they blame the South," Henry continues, after Jerusha has gone. "For every slaveowner, you can count ten Northerners like that. Selfish, greedy—"

"Only blind. They don't know what slavery is. Because it is so far away, they can't picture the evil they are defending."

"Then you must picture it for them, Harriet."

"I dare not. I am afraid of what it might do to me. There is something insidious about that subject, Henry. It's so dark and terrible, it seems to drive everyone who touches it into a sort of insanity. I did try to write, Henry. An idea came to me in church. I call it an idea, but it was really more of a picture—a scene unrolling before my eyes. An old, gray-haired slave— very gentle, very religious—was being beaten to death by order of an overseer. I even seemed to know the overseer's name— Simon Legree. A horrible man. When I reached home it was still so vivid I was literally compelled to put it down. (*She opens her writing case, hands him several squares of brown paper.*) There was no paper in the house. I used the wrappings from the groceries."

"The Death of Uncle Tom."

"Don't try to read it. It is only a rough sketch, and the whole thing is too painful . . . too harrowing. After finishing it, I could not sleep all night. (*Picks up envelope from table.*) I have written a letter to my editor, giving him my reasons, and refusing to undertake the commission."

Now there are excited cries from Georgie, rushing through the hall, followed by Eliza and Hatty. The cause of the excitement shortly appears. Lowell and Freddie half lead, half push a frightened colored woman in a rusty black cape and bonnet with a widow's veil of bedraggled black crepe into the room. When her bonnet is pushed back her face is disclosed, "a brown face, strained and livid with terror." Her name is Sukey and she is trembling in fear. When Harriet puts out a friendly hand Sukey draws back. "No—no! You ain't Mr. Denton . . . dey tell me ask fo' Mr. Denton," she says.

"Mr. Denton isn't here," Harriet gently explains. "But we are your friends, Sukey. We are Abolitionists. You are safe here—safe. We shall take care of you. We will not let any harm come to you."

With some difficulty they get Sukey on the couch. Harriet sits beside her on the hassock and tries to calm her, as she would calm a frightened animal. Henry would help, too, if Sukey will accept him as a friend.

Gradually they piece the story together. Sukey had been smuggled out of Savannah by the captain of a coast-wise vessel. She was trying to get from the Denton underground station to the next station, which is Randall's farm, up near Lewiston. Henry thinks he might drive Sukey there, if Lowell could go along and point out the way. But Lowell wonders if Henry should take that risk. "They caught Dr. Willard and his son and put them in jail," he warns.

The word "jail" is enough to throw the frightened Sukey into another panic of fear. She tries to struggle to her feet. Georgie brings her a glass of milk, which she gulps ravenously. This revives her a little. As Sukey's eyes brighten and her nerves relax she notices the shawl that Freddie has tucked around her. "My ol' missus . . . she had a shawl like dat!" she says. "Jus' like. When she die . . . dey bury her in dat shawl. Dey bury her . . . den dey sell all de niggers. Sell ma husban' . . . sell me . . . sell ma chillun . . . sell ma baby . . ."

"Oh!"

"Ma baby . . . wasn't even weaned yet . . ." Freddie, "in complete frustration," turns away, pounding one palm with the other hand.

"When you get to Canada you can find work," Harriet comforts her. "You can earn money to buy your children."

Sukey shakes her head, slowly and sadly. "No, mam, dey's all scattered. Scattered an' sold . . . Scattered an' sold . . ."

There is a commotion in the hall. Jerusha, followed by a man named Haley, pushes his way roughly past Eliza, who is trying to hold him back while she calls a warning to her mother. The men have come for "Mrs. Stowe's nigger friend," as Haley puts it. They have had a warning from Savannah and have been watching the Denton house for two days for this runaway slave.

Sukey has sunk to the floor and is crying out her fear of being beaten. Freddie is all but hysterical. Harriet would calm them all if she could. She would also reason with Haley and Jerusha. She appeals to Henry and Henry suggests that perhaps if the reward money were matched, or even increased. the law would be satisfied. That would be bribery, Haley warns Henry. If he (Henry) were not a reverend, Haley would knock him down for trying it.

"The law says she is common proppity." Jerusha has turned to Harriet. "You're lucky if you don't end up in court yourself. They could throw you both in jail for what you done already. You could be fined every cent you own, get three or four years in prison."

"I'm afraid we're helpless," Henry admits.

Harriet stands firm. There must be some way. And then a happy idea occurs to her: Henry's church will buy Sukey's freedom!

Henry cannot promise that. He can't ask too much of his congregation. "Why don't you say it?" demands Harriet, wrathfully. "She isn't young. She isn't *beautiful*."

"That is unfair!" shouts Henry. "We have already bought five slaves—"

HARRIET (*slowly*)—Five slaves—out of three million.

JERUSHA—Sorry, Mrs. Stowe, we gotta be getting started. Come on, gal!

HARRIET—No— No—

SUKEY (*to* HARRIET)—You ain't goin' to let me go—

JERUSHA—Please, Mrs. Stowe, it's the law. Don't make any trouble. (*Takes* HARRIET *by shoulders—moving her up out of the way.*) Come on, gal. (*Takes* SUKEY *by the arm—starts dragging her across the room.*)

SUKEY—The missus she promised, the missus she promised. Let go my arm— (*Turning to* HARRIET.) You promised! You won't let me go—you promised you gonna buy me. You say I'm safe here with you. And I believed you!

HARRIET—I won't give up. I'll find some way.

JERUSHA—Come on.

HALEY—If you come along quiet I won't put the chains on you.

SUKEY—Oh, Lord— Lord—gotta help me, Lord— Nobody can do nothin' for me now, but you! (*Her voice dies away.*)

HENRY—Harriet— (HARRIET *turns her head, looks at him; he is unable to sustain her gaze.*) I'll go with them . . . see that she is well treated. (*He hurries out.*)

FREDDIE (*coming to her*)—It's not your fault.

ELIZA—You did all you could.

HARRIET—No.

ELIZA—Ma, shall I tell Mrs. Hobbs just the family for dinner? (HARRIET *does not answer.*) Mama, shall I tell Mrs. Hobbs?

HARRIET (*absently*)—Yes, dear— Yes. (*She makes a little motion dismissing the children.* ELIZA *leaves through the dining room.* FREDDIE *takes several steps then lingers, troubled.* HARRIET *picks up the letter to her publisher, which she left on the table after showing it to* HENRY. *Slowly, she tears it to shreds. She makes a strange sound.*)

FREDDIE—Are you crying, Mama?

HARRIET (*her breath catches—turning to him*)—Oh, Freddie— I am frightened. I am being forced into an undertaking which is beyond my powers. I haven't the wisdom. I haven't the strength. I haven't the courage.

ELIZA (*calling*)—Freddie . . .

HARRIET—Run along, dear.

FREDDIE—But, Mama—

HARRIET (*patting his cheek and smiling*)—Don't worry. I'll manage . . . (*To herself.*)—God helping me.

"Harriet moves slowly around the table and picks up the brown paper notes on 'Uncle Tom.' As she looks at them, she sinks into her writing chair. For a moment she does not move, then, very simply, she clasps her hands, leans her head upon them. We see that she is praying."

The curtain falls.

It is late afternoon the following December. The Stowe parlor has assumed "the natural clutter of a room which is used by a large and busy family. . . . In the corner stands a Christmas tree partly decorated with strings of cranberries, pop-corn and homemade ornaments."

Calvin, sitting in the barrel-chair close to the fire, "is busily annotating a volume of manuscript. . . . Calvin is plumper. His sideburns have crept down and met under his chin, framing his face in a fringe of whiskers."

Catherine Beecher is sitting bolt upright on the sofa intently reading a copy of *The New Era*. A group singing Christmas carols has been heard approaching the house. They stop outside now and Calvin, searching for a coin to toss out the window, borrows one from Catherine, almost without her knowing it, so intent is she on her reading. Suddenly Catherine gives a little crow of laughter.

"Harriet's story seems to amuse you, Catherine," suggests Calvin.

"I find a certain element of humor in the delineation of Topsy," admits Catherine. "Of course it is quite out of place in a work of this character."

"I thought so too at first, but it is astonishing the number of readers who relish a little humor. . . ."

"That is scarcely the class to which Harriet should appeal. Levity has always been her principal weakness— Calvin, you should try to repress it."

"I do, but it won't stay repressed—"

It appears further that since Harriet has been so wrapped up in her writing of "Uncle Tom" she has not had much time either for her family or her housework. But Calvin wouldn't have Catherine refer to that.

And now Harriet, followed by Freddie and Georgie, their arms filled with Christmas greens, come barging through the hall lustily singing "We Three Kings of Orient Are." "The relief from indecision combined with the birth of her baby has changed Harriet. She is full of vitality and sparkle. She wears a jacket, fur hat and mittens."

The three report a glorious afternoon. Mama, reports Freddie, has been bobsledding down Turnpike Hill. She beat Deacon Thompson by three lengths. Mama also landed in a snowbank.

Harriet is pleased to see that Catherine has been reading "Uncle Tom" and hopes she enjoyed it. Catherine did. She feels it a duty to enjoy everything the family writes. But she still questions what Calvin describes as the lighter passages.

"I was afraid of that," admits Harriet. "I never made a little joke without thinking 'Kate won't approve.'"

"I contrived to write my 'Remedy for the Wrongs of Women' without descending to humor."

"You certainly did, dear. You most certainly did."

Harriet has a chapter to finish before Christmas overwhelms her, and would get at it now. Freddie and Georgie are back to finish the tree and go about that job with a good deal of argument and not a little clatter. Calvin also takes a hand in the tree trimming, but Harriet goes bravely on with her writing.

Now Catherine has finished the last installment of "Uncle Tom" and would like another. Harriet finds it hard to believe that the story has been running so long. "I thought it would be completed in three issues," she says. "I sold it for three hundred dollars."

"Mercy!" ejaculates Catherine. "That's less than I demanded in *advance* for my treatise on household management."

"Well, after all, *you* have a reputation," Harriet reminds her.

Nor has Harriet much hope of royalties from the book. She will be perfectly satisfied with enough to buy a silk dress, and for that she has already selected a design from *Godey's Lady's Book*. She thinks Catherine will approve of the next chapter of "Uncle Tom." She will at least find it "unsullied by humor." "It is the death of Little Eva," warns Harriet. "Be sure you have a pocket handkerchief."

The hubbub over the trimming of the tree continues, but Harriet writes on. Then Catherine becomes excited because Harriet is sitting in a draft and insists on moving her, her writing case, papers, pen and inkwell, all to the couch near the fire.

Now Calvin has taken a tin star and is mounting a stepladder to put it at the top of the tree. Would he be needing help? Oh, no. All he asks is to be let alone. Harriet lets him alone. But presently she hears a plaintive call for help. Calvin has dropped the star. The children are at the moment out of the room, and Catherine is lost in "Uncle Tom."

"My dear, would you mind— I said, would you mind—just— Hatty! The star, my love. The star. I dropped it."

"Yes, dear . . . certainly." Harriet puts aside her writing case and recovers the star. Then she finds the wire to fasten it with. Then she steadies the ladder.

Harriet finally gets back to her writing, just as Mrs. Hobbs comes to announce that Jerusha Pantry has come to fix the front door bell. Again Harriet's writing is interrupted, but she is glad to stop long enough to tell Mr. Pantry that subscribers to *The New Era* raised enough money to free the girl, Sukey, he had helped send back into slavery. "It wasn't me sent her, Mrs. Stowe. It was the law," pleads Jerusha, who had read about Sukey, and has also been reading "Uncle Tom."

"I ain't sayin' it's convinced me, but it's shook me up considerable," admits Jerusha. "I got t' admit, it's shook me up." Harriet is delighted to hear that.

"They's one thing, if you don't mind my askin'," continues Jerusha. "I haven't been able t' lay my hands on the last issue. Are y' planning to— Does little Miss Eva—"

"Y-yes. She dies," Catherine answers, in a voice choked with emotion.

Mr. Pantry is greatly saddened. "I didn't think you'd hev the heart . . ."

"To tell you the truth, I didn't either," Harriet confesses frankly.

Once more Harriet returns to her writing, only to be interrupted time and again. Eliza and Hatty are dressing for a party and they can't decide whether they should wear blue over pink or pink over pink. Harriet hears their excited queries only vaguely.

Presently Lowell Denton has arrived and the twins have swarmed upon him and forgotten their dresses. Lowell has sent a note inviting one of them to be his supper partner at the party, but which one? Lowell himself is in a quandary. So, if they don't mind, he will take them both.

That exciting and noisy controversy having been settled, practically over Harriet's head, word is brought from the kitchen by an outraged Catherine, who has only been trying to bring some little order out of the huddle-muddle she found in there, that Mrs. Hobbs is leaving. Mrs. Hobbs is prepared to confirm the news when she stalks in and faces a still oblivious Harriet, who calmly goes on writing—

"Mrs. Stowe, I've been a saint for patience," declares Mrs. Hobbs. "I've put up with boys, and babies, and cuttlefish in the sink—but Miss Beecher is the camel's straw!—With her book-writin' and her recipes and her burnt-black puddin's— (*She takes off her apron.*) It's past all bearing. I beg to give notice."

"Yes. Yes, indeed," mutters Harriet, without taking her eyes from her work.

"Mama! You're not listening!" yell the twins.

"Do you hear? I'm giving *notice*," repeats Mrs. Hobbs. "I'm through workin' for a family of shatter-pates!"

"There! The chapter is finished!" Harriet pushes her hair back from her eyes and gazes at those around her as though she were coming out of a daze. "Oh, Mrs. Hobbs! Was there anything you wanted to ask me?"

"Ask you? I'm tellin' you! Good-by!" And she hurls down her apron and bangs out.

The children try to make their writing mother understand that Mrs. Hobbs is leaving, but Harriet still doesn't quite get it. "Oh! Tell her to bring some ink when she comes back."

Now the children are convulsed with laughter. With many

terms of endearment for their funny mama they gather around her.

"Will you read us your chapter?" Freddie cries, as he gathers up the pages.

"Just try to stop me!" says Harriet.

LOWELL—May I listen too, Mrs. Stowe?

HARRIET—Of course. I'm particularly anxious to reach young people.

LOWELL—I'm not so young any more.

ELIZA—In two years he'll be in West Point.

LOWELL—Father says the North and the South will be fighting before I graduate.

HARRIET—No, no—never believe that.

GEORGIE (*sitting on floor at her feet*)—Mama's story is going to keep 'em from fighting.

ELIZA (*sitting on hassock*)—She's making all the *bad* people from the North, and all the *good* people from the South, so's the South will like the story and give up their slaves—aren't you, Ma?

HARRIET—It isn't quite as simple as that—but it's the general idea. (*As* FREDDIE *hands her the manuscript.*) Thank you, Freddie. Remember where we left off?

HATTY—Oh, yes! George and Eliza were just getting on the boat—

FREDDIE— —to escape to Canada.

GEORGIE—They *do* reach it, don't they, Mama?

HATTY (*on arm of sofa*)—I can't bear it if they don't.

HARRIET—Wait and see. (*She reads.*)

"Their night was now far spent, and the morning star of liberty rose fair before them. Liberty!—electric word! What is it? Is there anything more in it than a name,—a rhetorical flourish?

(*By now the family is grouped around her.*)

"Why, men and women of America, does your heart's blood thrill at that word, for which your fathers bled, and your braver mothers were willing that their noblest and best should die? Is there anything in it glorious and dear for a nation—that is not also glorious and dear for a man? What is freedom to a nation, but freedom to the individuals in it?

(JERUSHA *and* MRS. HOBBS *are standing in the door.*)

"It is the right of a man to be a man, and not a brute; the right to protect and educate his children. . . .

(GEORGIE *drops her head on her mother's knee;* HARRIET

smiles, puts her hand over her curls.)

"The right to have a home of his own, a religion of his own, a character of his own, unsubject to the will of another . . ."

The curtain falls.

Five months later, on a sunny afternoon in Spring, Harriet's long-dreamed-of silk dress has arrived. She is standing on a hassock as Catherine and Georgie are helping to lower it over a series of full-ruffled petticoats. It is a handsome dress. Harriet is so excited about it that she finds it difficult to close her eyes, hold her breath and stop wriggling, as Catherine demands.

The new dress is finally adjusted and, according to Georgie, Harriet looks "too absolutely sumptuous in it," which she does. Even Catherine must admit that she does look "fetching" and Freddie is called to confirm the verdict.

"Mrs. Stowe, may I have the honor of the next waltz?" asks Freddie, bowing very low.

"With pleasure, sir."

With that Harriet and Freddie whirl into a dance, humming a waltz, which Georgie is singing. Even Catherine has forgotten her dignity for the moment. And then the door is thrown open and who should stride in but Henry Ward Beecher. "He is wearing an Inverness and carrying a broad-brimmed hat and cane. There is no longer any doubt of his pomposity."

Henry is amazed, and says so. Surely they must know his sentiments on dancing. "Dancing in one's own home leads to dancing in other homes," thunders Henry, "and dancing in other homes leads to dancing in low dives."

The family is not greatly impressed. When Harriet finds that Calvin was at the station to meet Henry, but stopped off at the library on the way home, she must send Georgie after her father at once. They are due at the Freeman's League in half an hour. The Freemen are to present Harriet with a plaque.

Now Hatty and Eliza are back with the mail—two baskets of it. They are so excited by their mother's grand dress they hardly see Uncle Henry.

"Here's a letter from Senator Horace Greeley," exclaims Eliza, as the twins report that their mother's mail continues to grow and grow. "He says he tried to read 'Uncle Tom' on the train, but he cried so hard he had to get off and finish it in a hotel."

"Mr. Longfellow sent her a letter, too," beams Catherine.

"The ladies of the Dorcas society of North Pinkham are fashioning you a bed quilt," reports Eliza, handing Harriet a letter.

" 'Tastefully worked with their names and addresses,' " Harriet reads.

"And a lovely poem was written for her by Mr. Whittier," says Hatty, reading—

> " 'Dry the tears for holy Eva,
> With the blessed angels leave her;
> Of the form so sweet and fair
> Give to earth the tender care . . .' "

One group of admirers has sent Harriet a live pig, which Jerusha has delivered to the kitchen, and she flies out to see that. The week before a goose and two turkeys were among the contributions, and hundreds and hundreds of letters—

"Such touching letters, Henry," Catherine is saying. "So full of love and admiration."

"And what about the others? The letters which vilify her . . . the threats and accusations—"

"We hide them," admits Hatty.

That there are wicked letters, too, the girls confess. But neither they nor Catherine can see any reason why they should be permitted to distress Harriet.

"Their malice is unbelievable," says Catherine. "Full of blasphemy and abuse. Last week, there was a small box containing a human ear—a black ear."

"We burned it! We burn all the very bad reviews, too. Before Mama can see them . . ."

"And how long do you think you can keep her in this state of blissful ignorance?"

"Not long, perhaps. But at least she will have had a little happiness."

Harriet has come back from her inspection of the porker. Catherine would have her rest and compose her mind for the Freeman's meeting, but Harriet had rather visit with Henry. In any event, Catherine is hopeful that Harriet will not excite herself—

"I am not to excite myself!" repeats Harriet, when, save Henry, they have all gone. "In the midst of all this! Great men writing me letters, and poetry, showers of presents—flowers, shawls, bedspreads—"

HENRY—Pigs!

HARRIET—Pigs. And the money, Henry. It's rolling in in a flood. Twelve thousand dollars already and they say it is only the beginning. This can't be happening to me—a little house-wife—mother of six children. I'm bewildered, I'm living in a dream.

HENRY—I hope, Harriet, you will not permit all this public attention to induce vanity and pride. Remember, the applause of the multitude is a terrible danger. It puffeth up the heart. It generates sinful self-glorification. It undermines the Christian character.

HARRIET—I never did like that sermon, Henry, and it doesn't grow better with age.

HENRY—Harriet!

HARRIET—I know, dear. Yes, dear, it's your turn. Now. Don't let me grow smug and pompous.

HENRY—You have become insufferably light-minded!

HARRIET—Perhaps it's an improvement, like the sparkle in wine.

HENRY—Harriet!

HARRIET—No, I haven't taken to drink. I thought you would be so happy in my success. What's the matter, Henry? Don't you like the book? I see you don't. It was you who first urged me to write—

HENRY—A reasoned and temperate novel, not a rabble-rousing melodrama.

HARRIET—A temperate novel would never have sold twenty thousand copies in the first three weeks. It would never have been read and discussed in every city, every cross-roads, hamlet—

HENRY—By the butcher, the baker, the candle-stick maker—

HARRIET—And farmers, and merchants, and ministers of the gospel. Yes, Henry, by men who never before read fiction! (*Sits beside him.*) Do you realize that eight presses are running night and day to supply the demand? Already it is being published in England—translated into French and German. There is even talk of adapting it for the theatre.

HENRY—With your permission?

HARRIET—No permission is necessary. Anyone has the right to dramatize a book. But were they to ask, I should give it.

HENRY—Harriet!

HARRIET—What difference does it make how the message reaches the public?

HENRY—I cannot, I will not, believe it! You—my sister—a Beecher—deliberately encouraging the moral assassins upon the stage to debauch the purity of your fellow Christians!

HARRIET—Oh, come, Henry—

HENRY—Reared in a home where the very word "theatre" is anathema! That wellspring of wickedness! (*Slipping unconsciously into his favorite sermon.*) If you would pervert the taste —go to the theatre! If you would imbibe false views—go to the theatre! If you would become infected with each particular vice in the catalogue of human depravity—go to the theatre—

HARRIET—Henry, have you ever gone to the theatre?

HENRY—Never! I have never set foot in— Have you?

HARRIET—No. But I mean to see "Uncle Tom"!

HENRY (*almost unable to speak*)—You are planning to attend a theatrical performance?

HARRIET—I am too far away from your church to attend your slave auctions, Henry.

HENRY—I was right! Success has ruined you. It has corrupted your character, made you frivolous and worldly. You sit there, smug and complacent in your new silk dress, confident that your book has become the Bible of Abolition. That your writing has united the country against slavery!

HARRIET—Darling—I have seen my letters—read all the newspapers.

HENRY—Not all, not nearly all, or you would know the South is beginning to rage, the North as well. Catherine and the girls are deceiving you, Harriet—they have made you believe the press and public have accepted "Uncle Tom" with open arms. The *Observer* says your writing is anti-Christian. The *Journal* calls it a mass of exaggeration where it isn't downright lies.

Catherine is the one who takes Henry down. She walks in as he is assuring Harriet that it is entirely probable that she "has started a conflagration which may destroy the union . . . fired hatreds which can only lead to war."

Harriet shouldn't listen to Henry, insists Catherine, with spirit. "What he really can't forgive is the fact that your success has really eclipsed his own," she says. And when he protests she adds: "Don't deny it, Henry. The women in your congregation have flattered your vanity until you are eaten up, rotten with jealousy."

"If you can believe that—"

"I can and do believe it. Furthermore, I believe you are well on your way to becoming a flatulent old windbag with nothing to offer but a booming voice and a head of hair!"

"And what have *you* to offer! A cross-grained, grasping virago!"

Harriet will have no more of that; her house is no place for
Beecher squabbles. What they have been keeping from her she
should have known. "It was all too beautiful to last."

Calvin has arrived. There are crowds of desperate characters
in the street, he reports. It would be a foolhardy risk for Harriet
to think of going to the meeting.

Harriet is firm. She sends Georgie for her bonnet and shawl.
None of their arguments will stay her—not even the threat that
the roughs will throw mud on her pretty silk dress.

The crowd has gathered around the house now. "Where's old
Hatty?" they shout. "Where's the old nigger-lover?" And
then they chant: "Go, go, go, old Harriet Beecher Stowe—
You're nothing but a dirty crow—so go, go, go—"

The racket, punctuated with insults, continues outside. Now
Calvin begs off. He cannot go with Harriet. He knows he
would run away and disgrace them both. Harriet understands.
Nor will she let Freddie go with her. Catherine is the first to
volunteer. And then Henry.

Harriet's knees don't seem to be holding her up very well, she
admits. But a moment later, when the mob throws a burning
copy of "Uncle Tom" through the window—the knees strengthen
miraculously.

The crowd is singing again: "Go, go, go, old Harriet Beecher
Stowe——"

"Hatty! I forbid it! You'll be injured! You'll be killed!"
protests Calvin.

"Don't worry, my love!" answers Harriet, turning to kiss him.
"You can't beat the Beechers!"

Almost gaily she takes the arms of her brother and sister.
They start for the door. The curtain falls.

ACT III

It is Spring, 1861, in Andover, Mass. "Again it is a beautiful
Spring day, and again the Stowes are moving into a new house.
This time a 'gentleman's domicile, replete with elegance' as
Godey's Lady's Book would have it." The settling has been
pretty well taken care of. Practically everything is in place.
The twins are clearing up the final clutter, helped by Jane, an
Irish maid. "Eliza and Hatty are as pretty as ever, in a prim,
Victorian way. That they are still unmarried is a surprise to
everyone, including themselves."

Georgie, "now a vivid girl in her early twenties," dashes into the room from the garden. She has been out on the Common, playing croquet with the boys, and has lost a petticoat, which she carries over her arm until she can toss it to Jane. The twins are still given to being mildly shocked by Georgie. All three girls are excited by the thought that Lieutenant Lowell Denton is expected this afternoon. Lowell, it appears, has been in the West fighting Indians. Now Harriet also sweeps in from the garden—"a different, much handsomer Harriet. She is fifty, well dressed, plainly a personage."

Harriet has been to a reception. On the way home she has been thinking about and declaiming a new chapter opening for one of the two novels she has been writing, "Pearl of Orr's Island" and "Agnes of Sorrento." She thinks what she has in mind will fit Agnes best. Harriet does not know whatever possessed her to involve herself in two books at the same time, and she is quite perturbed when Hatty tells her of a letter that has come from *The Atlantic*.

"The editor will advance five hundred, but not another penny until he has the manuscript in hand," reports Hatty.

"Now, I do think that's unfriendly," declares Harriet.

"After all, Mama, you're had nine thousand already," Eliza reminds her. . . .

Lieut. Denton has arrived. He wears the uniform of the cavalry. Harriet is enthusiastic in her greeting. The twins prettily fussed. Of course Lowell mistakes Eliza for Hatty, but the girls don't mind, Harriet assures him.

Lowell has come from Boston, and has seen Freddie in Cambridge. Freddie is studying medicine. Dr. Oliver Holmes has taken him under his wing, and in two years, they say, he will be a doctor. Lowell had also heard of Harriet's triumphs in London —of the Lord Mayor's banquet, and all. The girls can add to that. Their mother had met Mr. Dickens, and Mr. Ruskin, and Mr. Thackeray. She had even met the Queen—

"How did you find Her Majesty?" Lowell would know.

"A trifle snooty—but awe-inspiring," answers Harriet. "But that's enough about me. Do tell us—oh, dear, you have been gone so long and there is so much we want to know. Tell us about the West. What are they doing out there? What are they saying?"

"Much the same as here. Talking politics, and grumbling about the government."

"No wonder . . . with an utterly incompetent President!"

"Oh, they're not objecting to Mr. Lincoln, Ma'am. The West

is quite satisfied with him."

"You astound me. I didn't suppose he satisfied anyone—not even the men who elected him."

"He is such an unshapely person."

"Mr. Stanton says it is like having a baboon in the White House." This from Eliza.

"When I first heard of his nomination I was unable to credit my senses," admits Harriet. "At a time like this—when we are desperately in need of strength in the White House—we have foisted upon us a political huckster from the backwoods . . . 'Honest Abe!' In his speeches the man is as slippery as an eel! Mark my words, he would be perfectly willing to cast the whole anti-slavery cause overboard if he thought it would pacify the secessionists!"

"You may be right, Ma'am. Out West they say—first, last, and always,—come hell or high—(*To the twins.*) beg pardon, ladies—come *heaven* or high water, Mr. Lincoln stands for the Union."

"But the Union is in no danger. This uproar in the South— it is all sound and fury, signifying nothing."

"But, Mama," Hatty reminds her mother, "six states have already seceded."

"Seven," adds Lowell. "And there's that business of Sumter. When they demand the surrender of one of our forts, and we refuse to surrender it, then war can't be far off."

"My dear boy. The South does not want war. We do not want war. War is impossible when nobody wants it."

"I hope you are right, Ma'am."

"I am right. You shall see."

Calvin has come, a little excited because a brute of a horse is eating the elm tree at the front gate The horse, it turns out, is Lowell's, but before either Lowell or Harriet can go to the rescue of the elm tree, Georgie has hung her hoops on the tree and gone for a ride on the horse. . . .

Harriet has a surprise for Calvin. She has sent half the manuscript of his book to the printer and told him to put it in type. This, sputters Calvin, is an unpardonable intrusion in his literary career, but he has not read more than a few paragraphs of one proof before he is intensely interested and quite pleased. "Upon my word, this isn't bad. Not bad at all," admits Calvin.

A moment later a wild "Hallo!" in the hall is followed by the appearance of Freddie. He had driven up from Cambridge with some of the boys. No, he is quick to assure his mother, he is not sick. Neither is he bankrupt, nor has he been expelled. He has come home, Freddie confesses, to tell her that he is leaving college to enlist. He wants to go to war.

War? There is no war, Harriet insists. But there will be shortly, Freddie assures her. "Haven't you heard? They've fired on the flag! At Sumter! Any minute the President will be calling for volunteers."

HARRIET—It is monstrous, unthinkable!

FREDDIE—The Rebs have been preparing for months . . . They've been raising troops . . .

HARRIET—But they have no guns . . . no ammunition.

FREDDIE—That's what we've believed, but the truth is coming out. Colt, Sharpe, and half the armament factories in Connecticut have been running night and day . . .

HARRIET—Those arms went to Europe.

FREDDIE—Via the Southern harbors.

HARRIET—If that's true, why hasn't our government stopped it?

FREDDIE—Stopped our manufacturers from making a profit?

CALVIN—Frederick!

FREDDIE—I'm sorry, Sir, but I may see those shells tear some of my friends to pieces.

HARRIET—It is madness! Freddie, I do want to be reasonable. I want to understand your point of view. I know that in the midst of the hysteria you are bound to be carried away by your emotions. But, Freddie dear, you must keep your head. All your life you have planned to be a doctor . . . a healer. You're in the middle of your training. Now you want to throw everything away and rush wildly into the terrible business of killing.

CALVIN—Your mother is right. You should wait—

FREDDIE—I can't wait! After the President calls I can't wait an hour.

HARRIET—Freddie, for my sake, I beg you—

FREDDIE—Mother, it *is* for your sake. (*Desperately.*) Don't you understand?

HARRIET—What? What is it, Freddie? What are you trying to tell me?

FREDDIE—Mother, I can't put off enlisting and let the others do the fighting . . . because I am your son. They are saying this is your war . . . that's what some people are saying.

HARRIET—Oh, no—no—

FREDDIE—I'm not blaming you, Mother. I *want* to go—

HARRIET (*not hearing*)—How could they misunderstand? I only tried to make them see!

FREDDIE—You wrote what you believed. But writing just isn't enough. The truth must be fought for too. You yourself taught me that.

HARRIET—Yes— (*The twins run in excitedly.*)

ELIZA—Freddie . . . there is a carriage full of boys outside . . . they're calling for you—

HARRIET—They're waiting to drive you back to Cambridge.

FREDDIE (*going up to the window and calling*)—Just a minute . . . I'll be there . . .

ELIZA—Oh, Mama . . . Is Freddie really going to war?

FREDDIE (*going back to* HARRIET)—Mother—I want to enlist with my friends—but I told them I would never go without your consent—

HARRIET—What can I say?

FREDDIE—I know what you will say.

HARRIET (*after a moment she takes his hand*)—Fight well, my son.

CALVIN—God keep you.

HARRIET—Amen.

The boys are waiting. Freddie is ready to go. Harriet and Calvin decide to go to the carriage with him. The twins are following, assuring their brother that they will be sending him cookies every week. Outside the boys are calling to Freddie to hurry up.

"Mother . . . I promised the boys they could meet you . . ." Freddie is saying.

"Did you, dear? Of course, Freddie, my son!"

Harriet "straightens her shoulders . . . raises her chin bravely" —as they both start out. The curtain falls.

We have come to a Summer evening in 1861. It is dark and the lamps in the Stowe living room are lit. A large table has been brought in and at this Catherine Beecher is separating lint. There is a pile of rolled bandages before her. The twins are rolling gauze into bandages, and Georgie is sewing on a nightshirt. Somewhere in the house several women's voices can be heard singing softly "Let My People Go."

The conversation is desultory and concerned mostly with war work and such gossip of the fighting as the gossips bring. Reports of the wounded lying in the broiling sun, and the need of thousands of more bandages, has made Georgie jittery. When she can stand it no longer she runs for the stairs and goes up.

Upstairs Lowell Denton is recovering from an attack of typhoid-pneumonia. He is still weak, but determined to rejoin his regiment. To test his strength, Catherine reports, Lowell is to try coming down stairs today and the twins agree that they should see if they can't help him.

Before they go both Hatty and Eliza have confessions to make to each other. The night before, when Hatty had taken up his gruel, Lowell had held her hand—she thinks. "He dropped his napkin and we both picked it up . . . then he just—didn't let go."

"Did he make you an offer?" Eliza would know.

"He couldn't. Georgie came in. You don't feel I was shameless to permit such a liberty?"

"No." Eliza has put her cap and apron on the table. "Hatty—he held my hand, too. We must make up our minds, sister. Whichever one of us Lowell chooses—we won't let it part us."

"It couldn't. We're twins. (*Wistfully.*) I wish he'd been twins, too."

At that moment Lowell appears at the head of the stairs followed by Georgie. He is pale and evidently not yet recovered from his illness, and the twins are solicitous.

"I'm still a trifle shaky," the lieutenant confesses, "but I wanted you two to be the first to know—"

"Know what?"

"I tried to tell you last night."

"But I wanted to tell you myself," puts in Georgie, as Lowell puts his arm around her. "Oh, sisters, I'm so happy!"

The twins exchange a hurried glance. "So are we, dear," says Eliza. "Aren't we, Hatty?"

"Yes . . . oh, yes!"

". . . I've always wanted you two for my sisters," says Lowell.

"We've always wanted you for our—brother. Haven't we, Hatty?"

"Yes—yes."

Georgie has taken Lowell's arm and they have gone in search of Calvin and Harriet to get their consent. The twins fall consolingly into each other's arms. . . .

Harriet is back from the postoffice with the new casualty list. She tries bravely to read it, but it is not easy. "The oldest Jackson boy—missing—Tom and Will Morris—" There is a catch in her throat. "Your cousin—George—and—and—Freddie—"

The twins and Catherine would come to her, but Harriet puts them off. Let them find Calvin. Freddie will be all right. He is only wounded. The women have started singing "When Johnny Comes Marching Home." Harriet can't stand that. Catherine sees that the singing is stopped abruptly.

"Do not try to control yourself," Catherine suggests. "Tears will relieve you."

"I have no tears, Kate. I am like a cold, dead, leafless tree."

"Harriet . . ."

"I speak as though there is no sorrow like mine, yet I know this heart-break is everywhere. There is scarcely a house in the land without its dead. And what are they fighting and dying for?"

"If *you* do not know—"

"I knew once—I was very sure once—I promised so much, so glibly. Abolition would cure all evil. Free the slave—and a brave new world would dawn for black and white!"

"Slavery has been abolished, Harriet. The President has issued a proclamation—"

"Are you still innocent enough to believe that will end slavery?"

"When we have won the war."

"You should read my mail! Letters from men, white men rotting in coal mines. Women coughing out their lungs in cotton mills. Mothers forced to watch their children work at machines, ten, twelve, fourteen hours a day. They ask why we are only interested in *black* slaves. They want to know what this war will do for *them*. Kate, for two dreadful years we have battled, strained every nerve, given ourselves, our money, our flesh and blood to a fight for freedom. Now I am beginning to see the bitter truth. It has all been for nothing. Nothing—when it is over we will find the world as far from freedom as ever."

"God would not permit such a futile waste!"

"Who are we to say what God will permit?"

"Oh, Harriet—"

"I'm sorry, Kate— Years ago I turned away from Father's Old Testament God of wrath. I created a God for my own worship— A God of compassion— This war has killed that illusion too."

Calvin has hurried in. He is searching for Harriet and is too intent to see the casualty list she holds out to him. He has come from the Recruiting Committee. They want Harriet to speak on the program of their rally—

"They feel—everyone feels—that you are the proper person to bring comfort and courage to the families of the volunteers."

"I? Do you hear that, Kate?"

"What is it? What is the matter?" Calvin doesn't understand.

"I am the one to bring comfort and courage!" Harriet has broken suddenly. "I am— Calvin . . . Freddie—Freddie—"

"My dear, my love . . ."

The curtain falls.

Two weeks later, just before sundown, the Stowe living room is full of Beechers "come to Andover to attend the recruiting rally, and to greet their famous sister upon her return from Washington." They are putting up decorations about the room and running frequently to the window to see if the parade has started.

Mary is ready to serve coffee and interested to find she will need only six cups this time. That's a small number for the Beechers, but Father Lyman has died, James is in the army, and Henry is in London—"putting the British Empire in its place," according to Isabella.

Hatty and Eliza are back from seeing Lowell off at the station. They had a time getting through the crowd on the Common. Everybody kept stopping them to ask about Freddie, and when their Father and Mother would be back, and what the President had said—

"We told them Freddie was better, but about Mama and the President we only knew what we read in the paper," reports Hatty.

Georgie is a little bitter about Lowell's having gone back to his regiment. He didn't have to go—even as an officer who could help train the recruits—

There is a call from the hall. Harriet is home. She goes gaily among her girls, kissing them and chattering her news. Freddie is much better. The last day they were with him he talked to them a little—about getting back to his regiment. Lowell has gone back, they tell her and she would sympathize with Georgie—

"Yes, he's gone, and I may never see him again," says Georgie. "If he had only waited we might have been married . . . had a little time together . . ."

"Oh, my dear . . ."

"Why should we care because some men somewhere want to keep slaves? What possible difference does it make to us? I say let them keep their slaves so long as it ends this ghastly war. Let them do what they like, and give us a chance for happiness!"

"If it were only as simple as that! There was a time when *I* tried to turn my back on life. Tried to build a small, secure world for myself and my family. I said, 'These, alone, are my responsibility. What happens to others is not my affair.' But I found life was too strong for me. You would find it too strong for you."

"If I believed that, I should want to die."

"Yes, and I have often wanted to die. When I have seen all my hopes swept away, all my faith. But somehow, we find the strength to keep on. (*She smiles sadly.*) There are times when that is all we can muster—just the strength to keep on keeping on."

"Then what is there to live for?"

"There is love, and the dear beauty of the human family. . . ."

"Mother—"

Now the Beechers come trooping back from the parade and there are more demands for a report of the trip. How's Freddie? Where's Calvin?

Calvin answers in person, though he is practically unconscious of the Beechers. The parade is over and the crowd is coming across the Common. "They want to see you, Harriet," Calvin reports a little excitedly. "The crowd wants to see you."

"Oh, no, no—I have had too long a trip," protests Harriet, a little wearily. "I cannot see anyone tonight."

"But they want to hear about the President!"

"You owe it to them, Harriet," William and Edward are agreed.

And now the crowd itself is heard outside the window. "Mrs. Stowe, Mrs. Stowe. Are you there?" . . . "Come to the window, Mrs. Stowe." . . . "Tell us about the President." . . . "Tell us about Mr. Lincoln." . . . "Tell us about Old Abe—"

Harriet is worried. There are so many—she can't go out. She isn't tall enough to speak to them from the window. She can only see half their faces.

Catherine brings the hassock to the window and Harriet stands on that. The crowd calls to her. "I'm sorry," she calls back. "I'm afraid I'm not like Topsy—I never 'just growed.' (*The crowd chuckles.*) I never realized that so strongly as in the White House when I met our President. When I stepped forward and put my hand into his great prairie of a palm I became as a grasshopper in my own eyes. You know he is a tall man, very tall, and a plain man at first sight, but when he smiles—then he becomes Father Abraham."

"What did he say to you? What did Mr. Lincoln tell you, Mrs. Stowe?" the crowd yells.

"What did he say? Well, first he led me over by the window and then he said, 'So you are the little woman who made this great war.' Two weeks ago, when I went from among you to the bedside of my son, that would have seemed an unbearable accusation, for I took with me a heart full of bitterness and doubt. One hour with our President has lifted my spirits and endowed me with new strength. He has made me see that this war, which seems so final to us now, is but one small pattern in a vast tapestry of struggle. Since the dawn of history there have always been tyrants, great and small, who have seized upon and enslaved their fellow men. But equally always there have been noble souls who have bravely and gladly given their lives for the eternal right of man to liberty. The hope of today lies in this: that we, as a people, are no longer willing to accept these tyrants and the world they make, without question. (*She pauses.*) Yes, that is our hope. Our danger is this, that when the conflict is finished, and the war-weariness has set in, we may be tempted to forget, to slip back into the old ways. Then, and then only, will our sons have died in vain. Then will the battle have to be fought again, and perhaps yet again. A day will come when all of us here engaged in this struggle will be gone. When this our little life will be ended—all will be gone, but eternity will never efface from our souls whether we did well or ill—fought bravely or failed like cowards—it is for us to decide, whether, in the end, we may say with truth—'I have fought the good fight, I have kept the faith.' " (*She pauses, then adds softly.*) " 'For Mine Eyes Have Seen the Glory' "— (*A soprano voice sings.*) "Of the coming of the Lord"— (*The crowd outside joins in.*)

"He hath trampled out the vintage
  Where the grapes of wrath are stored—" (*People on the stage join in.*)
"He hath loosed the fateful lightning of his terrible swift sword,
  His truth is marching on—
Glory, glory, Hallelujah—
Glory, glory, Hallelujah—
Glory, glory—"

THE CURTAIN FALLS

THE DOUGHGIRLS

A Comedy in Three Acts

By Joseph Fields

JUST before "The Doughgirls" arrived on Broadway in late December there had been a run of fairly serious plays with a wartime background. A romantic story of the R.A.F. called "Flare Path" was counted a little too trivial to be deserving of critical endorsement. A turgid little tragedy of the Bataan defeat, with a cast of nurses' aids, titled "Cry Havoc" when it first was played in the West, and retitled "Proof Through the Night" when it was brought East, was dismissed as being too obviously on the fiction side to command respect. And an authentic but depressing drama from the Russian of Konstantin Simonov, called "The Russian People," had been given a dignified and respectful reception, but had aroused no enthusiasm.

The time was ripe for a comedy that would reflect wartime conditions but also keep the audience mind free of wartime miseries. Joseph Fields' "The Doughgirls" was made to order for the time. A bold satire of life among the overstuffed civilian war-workers, with and without service commissions, in the overcrowded capital of wartime Washington, "The Doughgirls" is frankly and boastfully written and staged to appeal to the broader and lustier American sense of humor. Sophistication is its aim, and whenever a question of taste obtrudes it is promptly set aside in the cause of a general merriment. There were protests from the guardians of a play-going public's morals, naturally, but the larger public flocked to the theatre and the comedy ran triumphantly and prosperously through the season.

Report has it that Mr. Fields found his inspiration for the comedy on a business trip to Washington, when he found himself without hotel accommodations and was compelled finally to go over to Baltimore to find a place to sleep. Adding his own experiences to those of friends, it was easy to collect such a series of extravagant adventures and reminiscences as gave the gifted George Kaufman, who staged the comedy, a wealth of amusing material with which to work.

It is a hot August afternoon in Washington when "The Doughgirls" gets under way. The scene is a rather attractive living room in a fashionable hotel. "It is one of the pseudo-Louis XV affairs, but it still has a forcibly functional look." There are double doors letting in from the hall at back, and side doors leading to bedrooms. "Over the mantelpiece a decorative copy of Washington having tea at Mount Vernon. A note of Americanism in case of a chauvinistic transient." The usual divan, French secretaire and telephone. "The general effect reflects the personality, the delicate sensitiveness and the innate refinement of the Capital Hotel Holding Corporation."

Edna is packing. So is Julian Cadman. Edna "is a striking girl of 28, dressed in a smart negligee." Julian "is a tall, pleasant-looking man in his late thirties. He wears a linen suit and a black bow tie, a typical product of the Middle West." There is a good deal of hurrying, and, as it appears, pressing need for it. The people who have rented this suite are on their way upstairs to get into it. This worries Julian, but not Edna. "If they are going to live in Washington they've got to wait outside of closed doors like everybody else," says she. And she goes on with her plan to take a bath.

"Now, look, they told us we could have this suite for only forty-eight hours," pleads Julian.

"But that doesn't apply to us. You're trying to help the Government, aren't you?"

"Yes, darling. But the Government doesn't know that yet. Now why don't you be a good little soldier and . . ."

"How the hell can I be a good little soldier when they're throwing us out on that blistering street?"

"Now, Edna. You know our situation, and you know I can't afford any notoriety. Any day I might be in the public eye."

"I'm so mad I could spit in the public eye!"

There is a knock at the door, which is immediately opened. Mr. Jordan, the manager, "a correct little man in morning coat," walks in, followed by Harry Halsted and a bellboy carrying several pieces of baggage. "Halsted is about thirty-five. He is good looking and has a jovial manner. He carries a cardboard carton under his arm and a shining new sword."

The situation is plain to Halsted and he is a little embarrassed. He could wait outside— But Manager Jordan will have none of that. The Cadmans are already in their forty-ninth hour. Julian, too, is understanding. But not Edna. The newcomers, snaps Edna, might at least have waited until the beds were cold.

Nor is she moved by Col. Halsted's report that Mrs. Halsted suffers from the heat: that she is just off the train, after having stood all the way from New York, and that she is now waiting downstairs in the lobby.

"That's a damn shame," agrees Julian. "Colonel, why don't you ask her up?"

"Yes, do, Colonel, I'd love to have her. She can scrub my back," explodes Edna, barging into the bedroom and slamming the door.

A moment later Vivian Marsden arrives, leading a boxer on a leash, and followed by a bellboy with her bags. "Vivian is a very pretty red-head, very feminine, and chuck full of sex. She appears a little vague at times, but back of it is a supernatural knowledge of men."

The bellboy has no sooner disappeared with the dog and the bags in the second bedroom than Vivian is in Harry's arms and being generously kissed. When she has time to notice the room Vivian is happily pleased. "I was hoping it would be just like this when we got together," she says. "Two months—Harry, don't ever do that to me again." Harry won't. "Promise me you won't let the Army send you any place you can't come home to sleep," pleads Vivian. Harry promises.

And now Harry would order a drink and Vivian would get into something light. She heads for the bedroom that is still occupied by Edna. Harry stops her just in time. Vivian is pretty indignant at the gall of some people, but the only response she gets to her knocking on the door is the muffled advice from Edna that there is another bathroom if she wants one.

Now Harry must change into his uniform and report to the General. That's a big disappointment to Vivian. Why can't he telephone?

"Now, now," chides Harry, taking her in his arms. "I'll be back in a couple of hours—then we'll have the whole evening to ourselves. We'll have a beautiful dinner up here, just the two of us—I'll get some of those lousy Cherries Jubilee that you're so crazy about, and, I know! Remember that magnum of champagne the boys gave me at the office?"

"You didn't bring that down here?"

"I brought it down for the General, but right at this moment you outrank him a mile. Remember what Mark Twain said— he would rather go to bed with Cleopatra without a stitch on than General Grant in full uniform."

"I thought Mark Twain just wrote about boys."

Harry is dressing in the other room when a porter arrives with the Halsted wardrobe trunks. Vivian is about to have them put in with Harry when she gets a better idea. Let the porter take them into the room where that woman is. And he does. A second later there is a loud scream, and out comes the porter on the run, without his truck. He doesn't stop until he is well down the hall.

"What the hell is this, the Aquarium?" Edna is shouting from the other room.

"I'm sorry," Vivian calls back, pointedly. "You've been in there so long I forgot all about you."

"I'd like a little privacy!"

"So would we!"

"You'll get it when I'm damned good and ready," declares Edna. And she means it.

The telephone is ringing. Vivian hurries to answer. "Hello— yes, this is Colonel Halsted's suite . . . Oh, the War Department . . . Who? General Slade . . . Well, put him on . . . (*She pauses.*) Hello, General . . . This is Mrs. Halsted . . . You're lucky . . . We just got in . . . He's dressing at the moment . . . Can I take a message? Oh, that's all right, the Colonel tells me everything . . . I see . . . I'm looking forward to meeting you, General . . . as soon as we get settled here, you must come up. You and Mrs. General . . . There isn't . . . Oh, that's too bad. We must do something about that . . . Yes, I'll tell him."

Harry is not at all pleased when he hears that Vivian has been helping him with the General. He would prefer to run his own life. But Vivian isn't worried. Harry's really just like a little boy who'll never grow up. She wants the General to respect him.

Soon Harry is dressed and ready to keep his appointment. He looks very nice in his uniform, and even better when he gets his insignia fixed on his collars. He didn't know exactly how they went, but Vivian fixed that, too. She asked the waiter. The waiter knew, because he had fixed so many for other military gentlemen—and ladies, too.

"Harry, when you get a chance will you tell the General that I'd like to get into something to help win the war?" Vivian asks, as she warns him not to forget his "knife."

"If you want to help win the war you'd better stay out of it."

"I could brush up on my shorthand—and . . ."

"Vi, you were a lousy secretary."

"You thought enough of me to have me transferred from the receptionist desk to your office."

"I had to get you out of there. We got tired waiting for our callers."

"But you brought me into your office. And then people got tired waiting for *you*."

Vivian has sent her Harry off to war. Now she is ready to give her full attention to that woman in the bathroom. She knocks vigorously on the door. "If you're not out of there in two minutes, I'm going to call the manager," she shouts, angrily.

"I'll be out of here in one minute, and I'm coming out swinging," answers Edna.

"Why, you . . ." Vivian can't find a word.

"Get out of my way, here I come!"

The door opens. Edna barges in. "Now, you crummy little—"

She sees Vivian. With an excited scream she spreads her arms wide. "Darling!" she calls, excitedly.

"Edna!"

"Darling, I haven't seen you in months. . . . What did you do to your hair?"

"Harry likes it red— You look marvelous."

Edna is pleased, but she still feels that she has put on a few pounds—and right where they will do her the least good. Spying a bottle of Scotch on the table she is quick to call room service and order club soda. Then she is ready to relax. It is so wonderful to know where she and Julian are going to sleep tonight. She thought they might have to go to Baltimore. Married? No, they're not married. "It's just sort of a lend-lease arrangement."

Of course, Edna explains, she and Julian are engaged—over-engaged, in fact. Julian's wife, from whom he has been separated for ten years, refuses to divorce him. What is Julian's business? He and a chemist from the Soviet Embassy have invented a formula for making artificial rubber from corn—

"Corn?" exclaims a wide-eyed Vivian. "No wonder I could never digest it."

"It seems you can make rubber out of practically anything— radishes, huckleberries—"

"If they can make it out of all those things, what's the trouble?"

"Darling, in the Government just because you can do a thing doesn't mean that you do it. Julian's been trying for weeks to meet Warren Buckley."

"Who's he?"

"He's a millionaire wet-wash king. He's just been made head of the rubber administration."

"He has? But what's wet-wash got to do with rubber?"

"It hasn't anything to do with rubber. It's just that he's a business man and a multi-millionaire. He invented the system of having people call for their own laundry."

It is when they are disputing each other's right to sign the check for the soda that Vivian is forced to confess that she and Harry Halsted aren't married, either. Why? Harry's peculiar. "He feels that everything is so uncertain these days—"

"Hmm—he doesn't want to bring another wife into the world, the way it is today," Edna adds.

Vivian and Harry expect to get married just as soon as Harry is sure his Army job is permanent. Meantime he is, of course, terribly nervous about their living together. That, Edna assures her, is another worry Vivian can dismiss. Now they will both be chaperoned. Vivian can't see that—

"You've got to go, Edna . . . I can't do that to Harry— —tonight is our big reunion. We haven't seen each other for two months—we want to be alone."

Edna is completely deaf to any such pleading. A moment later she is phoning her goods news to Julian, who has been waiting exasperatedly in the lobby for her. ". . . But we don't have to find a place," Edna shouts joyfully into the phone. "We're going to stay right here in the suite we have—with Vi . . ."

"Edna—you can't . . ." Vivian protests, weakly.

"What do you care, 'Vi who'? Vi anybody. She's my oldest and dearest friend."

"Please, Edna, now . . ."

"Yes . . . they know all about us . . . *They're* not either. It's the same set-up as ours, only they have a place to sleep."

A moment later the door opens and in walks Nan Curtis. She is leading Vivian's dog, Duke, and is followed by the bellboy who had taken Duke for a walk. Nan, too, is a pretty girl, blessed with "a devastating sense of humor which pierces all sham and pretense." With a glad cry of "Nan!" Vivian flies to embrace her. The next instant Nan has discovered Edna, and there is a second explosive reunion.

"I had no idea you gals were in town till the Duke picked me up in the lobby. He barked at me and I barked at him. The first friendly face I've seen in Washington."

The reunion settles cozily to a series of further confessions, or would if Vivian were not so anxious. Nan, it appears, is now Mrs. Thomas Dillon—though not strictly in the Biblical sense of the word. "I didn't know you even got a divorce," declares Vivian.

"Listen—my decree is due in another two weeks," says Nan, "and the minute it comes we're getting married. Only until it gets here it looks like a hot couple of weeks."

Edna and Vivian would hear the story and Nan tells it, with amusing flourishes, as it might be told to John J. Anthony, the radio consultant. It seems that Nan had met a fella. He was an aviator and they fell in love. Not having her divorce, Nan had agreed to follow her aviator to Bolling Field and live with him as man and wife.

This temporary arrangement might have worked out perfectly if Dillon had not signed certain papers naming Nan as his wife, which she wasn't, nor had been nor is. This, too, might have been adjusted if the sister of the Commander of Bolling Field had not turned up. Sister was a lady Judge from Montana and she was feverishly organizing a War Wives' Relief Corps. Also she was insisting that Nan should join. If Nan joined she would have to be investigated, finger-printed, and so on. Therefore it was absolutely necessary that she and Tom should keep in hiding for the present.

"I've got to keep away from camp and that lady judge for the next couple of weeks," concludes Nan, "because if I sign that application as Mrs. Tom Dillon and it's investigated, Tom could be court-martialed."

Edna is sure that can be arranged. Nan and Tom can stay right here in the suite, if they don't mind sleeping on a couple of cots. The porter, come for his truck, assures her the hotel can furnish the cots. The suggestion is, however, received by Vivian with vigorous protests—

"You can't do that. Edna, you'll have to go. Nan, you'll have to go, too! Harry's paying for this suite, and he's entitled to his money's worth, and we want to be alone."

Nan is of a mind to agree with Vivian, but Edna will not have it. She is prepared to murder Vivian if she has to. She—

The buzzer sounds. On their invitation to come in, the door opens and General Slade appears. He is carrying a large box of candy with a big red bow. "He is a well-preserved man in his early fifties. He wears a neatly trimmed mustache and his hair is gray at the temples."

Confused by the sight that greets him, Gen. Slade fears that he is in the wrong room, but, learning he is looking for Col. Halsted, Vivian is quick to assure him that he isn't. She is also pleased to introduce him to the girls as "Harry's new employer." On his part, the General is charmed to meet them, is pleased to accept the invitation to sit down and, after a split second's deliberation, will be pleased to join them in a drink.

"Is the candy for—Col. Halsted?" Nan inquires, casually.

"No, no. I—uh—took the liberty . . ." The General, a little flustered, turns quickly to Vivian. "You were so charming over the phone. I was coming this way on business . . . uh—Army business . . . and I just happened to pass a little candy kitchen —Aunt Delilah's—they call it—and as long as I'd talked to you —over the phone . . . (*Hands her the box.*)—well!"

"General, you didn't have to do this."

"Oh, yes, he did," drily insists Edna.

"Oh, that's all right," fidgets the General. "That's all right. It's a pleasure."

Soon General Slade is comfortably relaxed, practically for the first time since he left Wall Street. Ah, those were peaceful days! No, he cannot remember ever having met Edna in Wall Street. Still Wall Street was not his only activity. He also had a show at the World's Fair. "South Sea Beauties" it was called—

"Very talented girls," the General recalls. "We had a big tank and they'd go down in it. Then this man—he was got up as an octopus—(*He shows the movements of an octopus.*)—he'd swim after them and try to get his claws around them, and they'd fight him off with a knife. Wonderful girls. Practically lived under water."

"Just came up for their salary, I suppose."

"Uh—yes, yes. Well, this has been very pleasant—sort of brought me back to Wall Street."

The General has finished his drink and thinks he must be going. He wouldn't like to keep Col. Halsted waiting. Vivian would know, before he goes, if he doesn't think there is something she can do to end the war.

"I can type, and I take shorthand, if it isn't too fast," Vivian tells him; "and I can file things and generally I can find them."

"Well, now," admits the General, appraising Vivian with pleasure, "it seems to me that a young lady of your—uh—talents ought to be squeezed in somewhere. It so happens that I could use a secretary—"

"You could?"

"Just social, you know . . . I mean just take a little dictation

—speeches, you know—perhaps attend some function or other—
might take up some of your evenings—would you mind that?"

"Not if it's for the war."

"Oh, certainly, certainly. Suppose I call you—make an appointment?"

"I'd be thrilled, General."

"Fine—fine! Well—good day, ladies."

The General leaves them. He will be expecting Vivian next
day about one. And, if she hadn't had any lunch by that time,
that, too, can be arranged.

Now Tom Dillon has telephoned from the lobby. Judge
Honoria Blake is with him, and before Nan can warn him not
to bring the Judge upstairs he has hung up. This is where Nan
disappears. She has recovered her things and is about to fly
down the hall when the door opens and the Judge is there.

There is nothing for it now but the usual introductions. Mrs.
—er—Halsted, and Mrs.—er—Cadman are pleased to meet Judge
Blake. Tom is charmed to see Nan's friends again. Remember
them? Surely he remembers them. They were the girls who
were thrown out of the Stork Club. Edna has a quick explanation for that one. "You've got to drink a certain amount or they
don't like it," she explains to the somewhat startled Judge.

Judge Honoria is right in her element, and this is her lucky
day. Not only is she glad to have found Nan, naughty girl, but
with her these other perfect recruits. Fortunately they are all
eligible, seeing that eligibility demands no more than that they
shall be married.

"But we don't even know what the War Wives' Relief Corps
relieves," objects Edna. And Tom thinks the girls really should
be given a little time to think the matter over. The Judge, however, is not to be put off. She is willing, even eager, to tell them
the whole story of the War Wives right then—

". . . I tried to think of something in war work for which
there was a crying need," the Judge is saying; "and the crying
need brought me to the thought of—babies."

"Babies?" Vivian is puzzled.

"I suppose babies are the last thing you young women think
of."

"I wouldn't say that," ventures Edna, with a quick glance at
Nan.

"Having children is nothing to me," boasts the Judge, who is
the mother of four girls and two boys. "Why, I can have a baby
at the drop of a hat."

"You can?" Vivian is impressed.

"Yes, and I'd be having one now if my husband hadn't left for Australia."

"He did?"

"Yes, and he took the hat with him," concludes Edna.

Judge Blake has returned to her subject. Day nurseries for war workers' babies—that's the idea. And who has the greatest love for children? Married women, of course. So, now—

But Vivian simply has to get dressed. Her husband's coming home. That's all right. The Judge will go with Vivian, and take Mrs. Cadman along, so she can continue her story while Vivian dresses.

They're gone but a minute. Nan just has time to explain the situation to Tom, and Tom to reassure Nan of his love for her and to repeat the promise that they will surely be happily married in another two weeks, when back comes the Judge with the application papers all ready to be signed and her fountain pen poised.

On a call from the desk Nan tells the clerk he can send up the magnum of champagne that has arrived, addressed to that room. Now, if the Judge will excuse her, she really must wash her hands. Edna, too, really should take a bath. And Harry, reports Vivian, will never let her sign anything any more—not since they got the whole Modern Library.

The Judge will just have to leave the applications with the girls, Tom thinks. Again there is a timely interruption. This time it is Julian Cadman who has come from the Soviet Embassy and brought with him Natalia Chodorov. Natalia "is a beautiful Russian girl of twenty-five. She has short-cropped hair and bright sharp eyes. She has a mannish stride and is dressed from cap to boots in the masculine uniform of a guerrilla fighter. She wears several campaign ribbons and decorations. A rifle, with a telescopic sight, slung over her shoulder, hangs diagonally across her back."

The visitor, Julian's introductions disclose, is none other than the famous Sergeant Natalia Chodorov, the great guerrilla fighter. This revelation greatly impresses Judge Blake. The Sergeant takes the introductions in stride.

"Wouldn't you like to take your gun off and sit down?" asks Edna, the perfect hostess.

"No, I keep her with me," sharply answers Natalia.

JULIAN (*enthusiastically*)—Natalia has shot three hundred and ninety-six Nazis!

NATALIA (*correcting him*)—Three hundred ninety-*seven!*

NAN—That's terrific, Sergeant.

NATALIA—My mother shoot more as four hundred twenty-five. My mother best sniper in Russia!

VIVIAN—Four hundred and twenty-five. That's marvelous!

NATALIA—She would do better as that, but any day now she gone for to have baby.

JUDGE—Baby!

NATALIA—In small village where I am coming from, we have it custom. When woman is going for to have baby, she tell her husband—then he is running quick to window with gun for to fire salute three times—*one* for *mother, one* for *baby,* and *one* for *Joe*—

VIVIAN (*puzzled*)—Joe?

NATALIA (*proudly*)—Joe *Stalin!*

EDNA—Nothing for the father?

NATALIA (*staring wide-eyed at* EDNA's *large piece of costume jewelry, and pointing to it*)—What for is this decoration?

EDNA (*wisely*)—I sniped *one* man.

NATALIA—You kill him?

EDNA (*with a look at* JULIAN)—Boy, do I kill him.

NATALIA (*looking around at the girls*)—Why all you women paint your fingers? This is stupid!

VIVIAN—Sorry!

NATALIA—I'm hungry—I like to eat a fish.

VIVIAN—A live one?

NATALIA—Dead one.

VIVIAN—Nan!

NAN—Huh!

EDNA—A fish!

NAN (*picking up phone*)—Room service, please. What kind of fish do you like?

NATALIA—Big one! (*Makes large gesture.*)

NAN—Will you call me?

NATALIA (*surveying room*)—Nice place.

EDNA—Where are you living, Sergeant?

NATALIA—I am living on Soviet Embassy.

EDNA—Do you like it there?

NATALIA—Yes, is nice but too much people. Is big delegation . . . Is not so many people here.

VIVIAN (*fearfully*)—Oh, yes, there are.

NATALIA—I like better here . . . I sleep here.

VIVIAN (*protestingly*)—But you can't stay here!

NATALIA (*with firm decision*)—This is free country . . . I stay here!

VIVIAN (*tearfully*)—Harry'll kill me!

EDNA—She'll kill Harry!

NAN—It'll be a Round-Robin.

There is a timid knock at the door, followed by the entrance of a sad, tired little man carrying a valise. Without paying much attention to anyone he sidles over by the couch and runs his hand caressingly along its back. Would anybody be sleeping on the couch tonight? He really wouldn't disturb anybody. He would get up early— But they cannot help him. All the space in that room has been taken. Sadly the tired little man takes a list from his pocket and begins checking it— "Carleton. Mayflower. Smithsonian Institution—" He is still muttering as he disappears.

There is another knock at the door, followed by the entrance of a waiter, carrying a magnum of champagne in a silver bucket filled with ice. Judge Blake is greatly pleased—

"Now, isn't this nice," she cries, gleefully. "Tom, you did this! To celebrate Nan's signing up!"

Before Tom can stop her she has taken the champagne from the waiter. "This is just the nicest gesture," the Judge continues, enthusiastically. "Why, there's a card."

Now Vivian would protest, but it isn't any use.

"What a patriotic sentiment!" the Judge is saying as Harry Halsted appears in the doorway, a single long-stemmed rose in his hand. To Harry's evident amazement the Judge reads the card: " 'We've done it before and we're going to do it again!' "

The curtain falls.

ACT II

Two weeks later the prized hotel suite has been pretty thoroughly taken over by the four girls. "The Royalist Louis XV décor has lost some of its old-world elegance." A large photograph of Natalia's guerrilla mother stands over the mantel, and there are rifles and cartridge belts leaning against the fireplace.

A typewriter has been placed on a long table back of the divan. At the typewriter, Vivian, smartly dressed and wearing a celluloid identification button on her bosom, is picking out a military order. A patient Army orderly waits near by. He is greatly relieved when the order is finished and he can take it to General Slade.

Edna has been trying to borrow a dress from Vivian to wear to a reception for the whole Rubber Administration, where, as Mrs. Julian Cadman, she will be expected to look important. Of course, she would pick the dress Vivian has bought to wear to the Peace Conference. No, she can't have that one. Edna will have to be content with Vivian's black lace.

Nan appears in a highly nervous state because a special delivery air mail letter has not arrived with her decree of divorce. She tries to get long distance on the phone. All wires are busy. Can it be that Donald Nelson is on all of them? Nan's situation is desperate because she is expecting Tom Dillon any minute now, and Tom is bringing an army chaplain who is going to marry them.

This news increases the complications. How can Nan and Tom be married when General Slade is coming up to make out his income tax? And Julian has invited Warren Buckley, the Rubber Chief, for cocktails. That, to Edna, is very important.

"Why do you have to be turned into a good woman just today, when we're all so busy?" demands Edna of Nan. "Why can't you get married Sunday, when there's nothing else to do?"

"I'll tell you why. Because Tom got his flying orders this morning. He's leaving this afternoon."

No, nobody knows where Tom is going, because Tom can't tell. Vivian knows, but she can't tell, either. Vivian has learned a lot being a General's secretary. She knows where the Navy is, and, Edna suspects, she knows who lives in the White House. But she can't tell. Anyway, Tom is leaving and he and Nan have to be married before he goes, or Tom might be court-martialed.

A moment later Harry Halsted has burst into the room, as mad as mad. He wants to speak to Vivian alone. It's the publicity they're getting and the hotel bill that have made Harry furious. Vivian doesn't see what she can do about either, but, she says, Harry wouldn't have to worry about publicity if they were married—

"Let's get in a taxi and sneak off to Gretna Green," suggests Vivian.

"In Washington you can't get any taxis," storms Harry. "Anyway, how can we have our marriage announced in the papers when we've been registered at this hotel for the past two weeks as man and wife—and that reminds me. Four hundred and sixty-three dollars, and I haven't even slept in the joint!"

VIVIAN—You could have slept here, but you preferred to sleep at the Officers' Club with a lot of strange men.

HARRY—I certainly did. I preferred that to curling up at the foot of the guerrilla's bed like Shazlik on a hot bayonet!

VIVIAN—Now you're exaggerating.

HARRY (*reading items from the bill*)—Valet service—pressing and cleaning, $46. How do you dames get your clothes so dirty? What are you, Commandos?

VIVIAN—But, Harry . . .

HARRY (*glaring at the bill*)—Beauty parlor, $102!

VIVIAN—It can't be that much, Harry!

HARRY—Here it is, written in blood! Shampoos, manicure with wax, rinses, facials, mud packs, pedicures—four permanent waves! Taxis! C.O.D.'s. Cash at the desk. Room service. Sturgeon flown from Barney Greengrass' in New York, $36. Who has to have sturgeon?

VIVIAN—Natalia. She likes fish.

HARRY (*peeling off the attached restaurant checks as if he were counting a deck of cards*)—What's the matter with sardines! Add tip! *Add tip! Add tip!! I'm not going to pay it!*

VIVIAN—We're all working for the war . . . There's a war going on, Harry.

HARRY (*enraged*)—You don't say! What the hell do you think I'm dressed up for, Lieutenant Pinkerton in *Madame Butterfly?*

VIVIAN—Well, if you can't see it, I can't explain it to you.

HARRY (*flatly*)—I *can't* see it!

VIVIAN—Then I can't explain it.

HARRY—Well, I *can*. I'm not going to pay this bill! And another thing. I'm damned if I'm going to eat my dinners alone, spend my evenings alone, and sleep alone!

VIVIAN (*fearfully*)—But, Harry—the General does his best work at night.

HARRY—So do I! And furthermore I want this arsenal evacuated. This is our home, God damn it, and I don't want it overrun with a lot of hysterical hags. (*Indicates portrait of Natalia's mother, over the mantel.*) And take that old tramp's picture down before I lose my appetite for you. (*Glares at it.*) Who is it, anyhow?

VIVIAN (*weakly*)—It's—Natalia's mother.

HARRY—Looks like her father. Now I want this whole place aired and fumigated!

VIVIAN (*rising*)—I'll try to get them all out, Harry, but how can I do it?

HARRY—I don't care how, but you'd better, if you want any part of me.

VIVIAN (*coyly*)—Harry, aren't you going to kiss me good-by? Aren't I a cute little—punk—any more?

HARRY (*firmly*)—I can't handle it—you can't sell me a thing —and to conclude, I will be back here at 5 o'clock—5 o'clock sharp—by which time I expect to see these barracks stripped of everything but you.

VIVIAN (*kittenishly*)—All right, Harry, but are you sure you won't marry me?

HARRY (*disgustedly*)—Right now I'd just as soon marry *him*.

With a sweeping gesture toward the portrait of Natalia's mother, Harry leaves her. Vivian is on the verge of tears, but her returning roommates soon get her mind off her troubles. It is silly, they think, for Harry to think he can get out of paying the bill. What's $463? It's easy to raise money. Why not try lease lend, Natalia suggests. A moment later Natalia is called to the phone. The Soviet Embassy is relaying exciting news. Natalia has a new little sister.

"Mamushka! She have her baby!" announces Natalia, gleefully grabbing her rifle. "I must salute her!"

With that announcement she goes to the window and fires three shots into the court. A moment later Jordan, the hotel manager, closely pressed by an assortment of frightened maids and bellboys, crowds into the room.

"Who fired those shots?" Jordan demands.

"Me! One for Mother, one for baby and one for Roosevelt!" cheerfully answers Natalia.

"One of the oldest rules of this hotel is that people who have not paid their bills must not fire guns out of the window," sputters the manager. Then, with the further announcement that he will allow them just one hour in which to raise the $463, Mr. Jordan retires.

"Your mother has a baby in Russia and we get thrown out of a hotel in Washington, notes Edna.

But Natalia is not impressed. A moment later she is busy directing a small stream of the hotel help into one of the bedrooms. A meeting of the workers from the third floor has been called. Natalia must go join them. If others come let them be sent in.

And now the hall door opens, and with something of a flourish Julian Cadman ushers in Warren Buckley, head of the Rubber Administration. Buckley "is tall and dignified, dressed in the height of fashion and carries a ten-gallon hat. His hair is a white mane."

Mr. Buckley is quite pleased to meet them all, and especially pleased that they should be interested in his war work. He has fifteen hundred men in his department, and three thousand stenographers, which, Vivian can see, would naturally keep the men pretty busy. It is Vivian, too, who remembers that Mr. Buckley, before the war, was the wet wash man. "Wet Wash Will Win the War!" That's the slogan. "We had a contest in the laundry—just among the employees—little fellow on the mangler won it. First prize was two weeks on a dude ranch— never been on a horse before and broke his leg."

"He was a lucky little fellow, wasn't he?" observes Edna.

The waiter has appeared, prepared to take orders for a dinner for four. But, as it turns out, that order had been put in the night before and nothing ever came of it.

Julian, having brought Mr. Buckley to the suite, thinking it would be more quiet than the office, is worried because it is not working out that way. Presently the little man who is looking for a place to sleep reappears. He hasn't slept for two weeks. The night before he had spent walking around Bernie Baruch's park. He found a committee meeting on every bench.

Now Judge Blake has arrived. And she is glad to meet Mr. Buckley! Her Nursery Home is short of rubber teething rings. "The babies have been cutting their teeth on cigarette holders, but they're not as good," the Judge explains. The Rubber Chief will do what he can.

When things get too complicated Edna takes a hand. Calling Natalia from the new Soviet Headquarters in the bedroom, Edna insists that the Third Floor Workers be disbanded for the moment. Julian and Mr. Buckley will be needing the room. Reluctantly Natalia calls off the meeting, but with a promise: "Next time you come I will have all these Republicans out of here," she assures the help, as they file solemnly into the hall.

"Shall we say—thirty minutes?" calls a smiling Mr. Jordan from the doorway.

Which reminds Vivian that something will have to be done about the hotel bill. The only thing to do, Edna concludes, is to pawn Vivian's diamond and ruby clips. They've been "in" before.

They have, Vivian admits, but Harry had just taken them out for her birthday. She can't put them in again unless the girls swear on everything they hold sacred that they'll never tell. They swear and Natalia knows a reliable pawnbroker in I Street.

"How much you like to got?" asks Natalia.

"I got five hundred last time, but I had to cry a little," says Vivian.

"I get six hundred—he cries a little," promises Natalia, patting her gun.

General Slade has arrived. He is happy to see Vivian, but a little distressed to learn that she had sent the speech she had typed for him to the War Department. It happens to have been something the General was preparing for a stag dinner. He is on the phone trying to trace that speech when Col. Halsted arrives. The Colonel is not at all pleased at sight of the General, and a good deal less pleased when his superior officer immediately suggests that he (Col. Halsted) return at once to the War Department, get the General's speech and take it to the Officers' Club.

"But, General, I wanted to speak to Vivian," protests the Colonel.

"Don't worry about Vivian. Just leave Vivian to me."

"Yes, sir." The Colonel swallows hard, but goes, slamming the door after him.

Word comes that Tom Dillon is on his way over with a chaplain. The General and Vivian are shooed into the other bedroom for their work, and Nan and Edna begin to straighten up the room for Nan's wedding. For one thing, they get the shotguns out of the way. Edna is afraid the guns might give someone the wrong idea.

Nan is still worrying about the non-arrival of her divorce decree when there is a buzz at the door. That might be the decree, but it isn't. It is Sylvia, "a cold-looking blonde . . . beautifully and expensively dressed."

Sylvia is looking for Mr. Julian Cadman. Julian, Edna tells her, is in conference. "I'm Mrs. Cadman," says Edna. Perhaps, suggests Nan, if she will come back a little later—

"So you're Mrs. Cadman?" says Sylvia, fixing her eyes on Edna. "I didn't know that Julian had been divorced."

"Er—er—you—er—didn't?"

"No, I didn't."

"Er—er—you're a friend of Julian's?"

"A very old friend."

"Are you from Wisconsin, too?"

"Madison."

"Julian's often mentioned the Senator from Wisconsin—you wouldn't be his wife?"

"No, I wouldn't."

"Won't you sit down?"

"Thank you, Mrs. Cadman." Sylvia has taken a cigarette from her bag and lighted it nonchalantly.

"Edna!" Nan is being overlooked.

"I'm awfully sorry—allow me to present Mrs. Thomas Dillon."

"How do you do—Mrs. Dillon?"

"Excuse me, I don't mean to be rude, but I didn't catch *your* name."

"I'm Mrs. Julian Cadman."

The situation is pretty confusing. At first Edna and Nan try to brazen it out, but not very successfully. Then Julian appears and is also slightly flabbergasted. Only Sylvia remains entirely calm.

"Julian, I don't quarrel with the way you're living," she is saying. "Ten years ago we agreed that we'd each go our own way . . ."

"Yes, and I've abided by that faithfully. I've gone mine."

"I see you have. But now the situation has changed. You're in Washington, and doing very well, and I feel that it's my place to be here with you."

"What?"

"I'm taking over from now on, Julian. I'm Mrs. Julian Cadman, and if there's any prestige attached to that, I'm going to get it. After all, I hung on all those years that you were dishing out Vick's Vapo-Rub at the Eagle Pharmacy, so now if you're meeting Paul McNutt I intend to be in on that too."

"You won't meet McNutt through me. I don't know him."

"But you must know someone more glamorous than Oscar Shumac, who delivers the groceries from the A & P and is the only man left in Madison. . . . Now, where are you living, Julian, because I'm moving in."

"At the Potomac Baths. Do you want to move in there?"

"Just a minute," Edna interrupts. "Everybody in Washington knows *me* as Mrs. Cadman."

"Oh, I'll find a way of explaining that. After all, I *am* Mrs. Cadman, so what does that make you?"

"But if they think *I'm* Mrs. Cadman, as all of them do, that makes a tramp out of *you*. Confusing, isn't it?"

"Yes, but not confusing enough, because if I have to I'll take a full-page ad in the *Washington Post* and publish my marriage certificate. And I mean it."

There does not seem to be very much to do about that. Sylvia assures them that she is not a hard woman, but she is determined. Either she will come and live with Julian, or he will come and live with her. It is for Julian to decide. With this she leaves them.

Sylvia, Edna agrees, has "certainly opened up a new can of tomatoes." Nor does Edna know what she can do about it, except to leave town, and Julian will not hear to that. . . .

Tom has arrived with Chaplain Stevens. For a moment they are all happy to meet each other. The Chaplain is fond of Tom and is going to fly with him on his new assignment. Now he is ready to go ahead with the wedding whenever they are ready. Everything is all right, Nan agrees weakly, except—the divorce decree hasn't arrived. Tom is distressed. Nan knows she is divorced, and she has been trying all morning to get a line to New York to confirm the decree, but there are no lines.

Chaplain Stevens is worried. How can he marry a girl until he knows that she is divorced? At that moment word comes from the office that there is a letter there for Mrs. Thomas Dillon. That undoubtedly is the missing decree. Again the wedding party is arranged. Edna hums a few bars of the wedding march and Chaplain Stevens has just begun—"Dearly beloved, we are gathered here—" when a bellboy appears at the door with Nan's letter. Feverishly she opens it, that the Chaplain may see the decree for himself, and finds—not the divorce decree but a report from the Wordsworth Chemical Laboratory on tests Judge Blake had made her take for the War Wives' Relief Corps. So the wedding's off again.

Tom is pretty mad. Mad at Nan's stupid attorney; mad at the confusion Nan's friends are causing. Finally Nan gets a little mad herself—

". . . It's fine for you," she charges, facing Tom; "hop off to China with bands playing and flags waving, and all that excitement and glamor, but what becomes of me! I sit at home on my tail, listening to H. V. Kaltenborn and André Kostelanetz."

Now a compromise is suggested. If they can all honestly assure him that Nan surely has been divorced, Chaplain Stevens feels that he will be justified in breaking a rule and going ahead with the wedding. The party resumes its places. Tom and Nan join hands. Then Natalia breaks in. She is back from the pawnbrokers with six hundred fifty dollars and a ticket.

This announcement renews the confusion. What was it that Natalia had pawned? Harry Halsted is particularly interested. If it happens to be those clips of Vivian's Harry is through. He'll never marry Vivian now.

Chaplain Stevens is puzzled. Aren't Harry and Vivian married? "No, and we're not going to be!" shouts Harry, turning to Vivian. "I've taken those clips out for the last time, and that goes for you, too." One last burning look at Vivian and Harry has again slammed the door behind him.

Nan and Tom are apologetic about the interruption, but time is pressing. They would urge Chaplain Stevens to hurry. The Chaplain is eager to please, but— And then Sylvia Cadman comes back. She is looking for her husband, and— This is a little too much for Chaplain Stevens. He starts looking for his hat.

"Chaplain, you're not going to leave?" wails Nan. "We've got to get married!"

"*You've* got to get married?" shouts the Chaplain. "Everybody in this room has got to get married." And he is gone.

"Fine bunch of vouchers you picked out!" Tom is disgusted.

"But, Tom, we can find somebody else, can't we?" Nan is still hopeful.

"In ten seconds?" Tom has recovered his hat and is on his way. "I'm going to the Orient and I hope to God I never come back!" he calls from the door.

"I seem to be causing no end of trouble," quietly ventures Sylvia. "However, I'll get right out. Shall we be on our way, Julian?"

Julian is trapped. Warren Buckley, coming from the bedroom, is considerably surprised to be introduced to a second Mrs. Cadman, but manages finally to adjust matters. The three of them, just Mr. Buckley, Julian and she—Sylvia thinks—might have tea in the lounge. With a little prodding Julian thinks so, too, but he is not very happy about it.

Perhaps the ersatz brides would now like to join her in a cup of hemlock, Edna suggests. They would. She proposes a toast: To our vanishing Americans! . . .

There is a buzz at the door and Admiral Owens arrives, followed by Manager Jordan and an assortment of bellboys bearing valises and a sea bag. "The Admiral is a stalwart man of sixty.

He wears rows of campaign ribbons and carries himself in the best Annapolis manner."

Manager Jordan has assigned the ladies' suite to Admiral Owens. The fact that they now have the money to pay their bill, and press it upon him, makes no difference. He had given them due warning and they will have to get out.

"But, Mr. Jordan, that isn't fair," protests Vivian. "We won't have any place to sleep." She smiles sweetly at the Admiral.

"Sorry, ladies," suavely mutters the manager.

ADMIRAL—Now hold on, Jordan. Let's think this thing over. (VIVIAN *smiles at him again.*) I don't see why these young ladies should be compelled to leave. Perhaps we can come to some compromise.

JORDAN (*concealing his annoyance*)—But the ladies have overstayed their time, Admiral.

ADMIRAL—Suppose you just go on your way, Jordan. You bore me.

JORDAN (*flustered*)—Uh—yes. Yes. Certainly, sir.

NATALIA—Admiral, you are a credit to the ocean.

ADMIRAL—Thank you . . . I'm sorry that this had to happen, ladies. But I'll not disturb you. I'll only be here a few days.

VIVIAN (*with one of those smiles*)—Oh, that'll be wonderful.

ADMIRAL—And now if you'll excuse me . . . (*Going toward bedroom.*)

GENERAL (*entering from the other bedroom; angrily*)—Vivian, I've been in here for— Why, Admiral Owens!

ADMIRAL—General Slade! To think of meeting you here!

GENERAL—Uh—yes. Yes.

ADMIRAL—Are you, living in that room?

GENERAL—No. Are you living in that one?

ADMIRAL—Yes!

GENERAL (*testily*)—Well, I suppose I'll be running into you from time to time.

ADMIRAL—Yes. Yes. Drop in.

GENERAL—Yes, yes. (*For a moment they glare at each other. Then the* GENERAL *wheels and goes into the bedroom, slamming the door. The* ADMIRAL *slams his.*)

EDNA (*looking from one door to the other*)—The Army—the Navy—all we need are the Marines! (*The door opens and six Marines enter.*)

MARINE—The U.S.O. sent us over. They said you wanted
some Marines for dinner.
The curtain falls.

ACT III

It is a Sunday morning four weeks later. The Admiral is folding up his blanket and straightening up the sofa. His sea bag
is practically packed and he is ready to shove off. Cheerily he
calls the girls to tell them good-by.

They come lazily in. Vivian and Edna have sections of the
Sunday papers; Nan is finishing a cup of coffee. They are sorry
to see the Admiral go, though Edna imagines that his hammock
will feel pretty good to him after four weeks on the couch. To
the contrary, the Admiral assures her, these have been the pleasantest four weeks he has ever spent on shore.

Now the Admiral has a little souvenir for each of them. To
Nan he gives a shoulder epaulette that he had worn to an Army-
Navy football game in 1902. For Edna he has saved a jagged
piece of wood from the stern of the first ship he ever commanded.
And to Vivian he gives his prize stamp collection, "the work of
half a century."

The girls are duly impressed with the Admiral's thoughtfulness,
but Vivian is sorry she did not know he was saving stamps. She
could have given him some of those she has been throwing away.

"I hate to think of your going, Humphrey," sighs Vivian.
"Where can I get in touch with you?"

"The Navy. Where can I get in touch with you?"

"The Army."

"Well, anchors aweigh!" The Admiral leaves them.

The girls go back to their papers. Edna is looking for the
society section, hoping she may discover where Julian has been
going with his wife. Vivian can't understand why the papers
don't have a Sex section. That's what people are really interested in.

Presently Manager Jordan appears. His welcome is not too
cordial, but he has come with a message—

"I wonder if I might speak to you ladies quite frankly?" he
wonders, as they all turn to look at him. "When you first took
over this suite, some weeks ago, it was to be occupied by you,
Mrs. Halsted, and your husband, the Colonel. I now find, however, that in some mysterious way, the successive steps of which
I have been quite unable to follow, the Colonel has disappeared

and has been replaced by you ladies, to say nothing of your house guest, Sergeant York. Ordinarily I would regard this as a most charming substitution, but—who is going to pay the bill?"

"But we did give you an awful lot of money, Mr. Jordan."

"That was four weeks ago yesterday, Mrs. Halsted."

"But you know it'll be paid, Mr. Jordan."

"That is my fond hope," admits Mr. Jordan, as he carefully puts the bill on the table. "Meanwhile I shall leave this here." His voice hardens. "And don't try to take your luggage out!"

Julian Cadman, "very pale and very haggard, as though he had been through the wars," lets himself in quietly. His greeting for Edna is affectionate and apologetic. He has been having a terrible time keeping up with parties. Six nights in a row they happen. And no one is expected to leave until the guest of honor, the highest-ranking dignitary, leaves. If the dignitary gets hooked into a bridge game it is sometimes five in the morning before he quits.

Julian has left Mrs. Cadman downstairs having breakfast with Warren Buckley. He had told her he was going to the barber shop to be shaved. Then he had sneaked up to the girls' suite. If they don't mind he will plug in his electric razor and shave there. He would like to come back and take a nap, too, but he can't. This is Sunday, and every Sunday Buckley takes a walk in Rock Creek Park and he and Sylvia have to go along.

"Rock Creek Park—that sounds promising," mutters Edna. "If you miss her with a rock you've still got the creek."

Edna is discouraged, and a little tearful. "I wouldn't care a damn if I didn't love you," she sniffles. "She's never going to let you go . . . Julian, I want to go home."

Julian is sympathetic and hopeful. He is sure everything is going to be all right. If he makes his deal with Buckley, as he expects to do, he has a way of handling Sylvia.

Julian has gone, leaving Edna at least a little cheered. She is happier than Nan, who can't understand why she doesn't hear from her Tom. Or Vivian, who is about to break down and call her Harry. . . .

Natalia, who has not been home all night, is back. She had been taking a walk. She had walked to Baltimore and back, with Vivian's dog, Duke. It was pretty hard on Duke. "He couldn't took it—he goes tired on me—I have to carry him half-way home," Natalia reports.

Harry telephones. All the mean things Vivian was prepared to call him fade into a happy greeting. Harry is coming over, and Vivian will be right there, waiting.

She is waiting when General Slade appears. Vivian hadn't expected the General and it is pretty disconcerting when he asks to speak to her alone. Natalia decides to lie down; Edna and Nan find other excuses.

"I hope it won't take long, Stanley . . ." hopes Vivian.

GENERAL—Vivian dear, I was in the steam room of the Officers' Club just now—I always steam myself out on Sunday mornings— when a visitor was announced. My half hour wasn't up and I couldn't come out, so he took off his clothes and came in to see me. It was an FBI man.

VIVIAN—It—was?

GENERAL—Of course he didn't have his credentials on him, under the circumstances, but—Vivian, the FBI cannot find any trace of your marriage to Colonel Halsted.

VIVIAN—They can't?

GENERAL—And furthermore both Mrs. Dillon and Mrs. Cadman have registered for Government work, and the FBI has failed to find any record of their marriages either.

VIVIAN—They can't be—very thorough. The FBI.

GENERAL—Now I need hardly tell you, Vivian, that this is very embarrassing. I don't like the idea of the FBI coming around asking me questions about you. I don't like it at all. Besides, they might find out about me.

VIVIAN—Find out—what about you?

GENERAL (looking around cautiously to make sure he is not overheard)—I have a floating kidney.

VIVIAN—You have?

GENERAL—Yes, I have. I got it in '29. When Columbia Gas went down to seven, it hit me in my weakest spot. Of course as a General I don't have to use it for anything, but—still . . .

VIVIAN—But nobody'll ever know it, Stanley.

GENERAL—Thank you! Thank you very much. But the point is—what am I going to tell the FBI about you?

VIVIAN—But, Stanley, you believe Harry and I are married, don't you?

GENERAL (pausing and looking at her)—No, Vivian. I don't, and I never have.

VIVIAN—You don't? Then what kind of a woman do you think I am?

GENERAL—You're an adorable woman, a beautiful woman. (Holds her.) I love you and I want to marry you myself.

VIVIAN—Stanley, you mustn't talk to me that way. And you mustn't stay here. Harry's on the way over—he'll be here any minute.

GENERAL—Harry! Harry! Harry! Hell! Harry hasn't bothered us for the past month! Why should he now?

VIVIAN—But that's only because he's been mad at me. It's because he came in that night and found you dictating to me at one o'clock in the morning.

GENERAL—Why don't you be honest with me, Vivian! You know I love you! I've been walking around with this . . . (*He takes a ring out of his pocket.*) I was afraid to give it to you. But now—I'm no longer afraid.

Protesting weakly, Vivian lets General Slade slip the ring on her finger. "Stanley, it's a dream," she admits. But she wouldn't think of keeping it—not until he tells her that he had wished it on. If she were to take it off now it would bring them both very bad luck—

"It would?" Vivian is quite willing to be convinced. "That's bad! I've still got two years to go on a mirror I broke."

"Let me share those two years with you, and all the years to come," the General is saying. He is putting his arms around her just as the door opens and Harry Halsted appears.

With a formal "Good morning, General," and a "Good morning, Colonel," the greetings are very military. The tone in which they are spoken, however, is acid. The General is quick to declare that he has reason to believe that Colonel Halsted and Vivian are not married. Nor is he willing to take the Colonel's word that they are, seeing that now he has a personal reason for investigating the case. He has just given Vivian a ring.

Repressing his anger with some effort, Col. Halsted regrets that Vivian has permitted herself to accept the ring, and if Gen. Slade were not his superior officer there are things he would like to say to him.

Gen. Slade has no wish to take advantage of his rank, and begins quickly to unbutton his coat. He gallantly begs Vivian to excuse the appearance of his suspenders. Harry is also quickly out of his coat—

GENERAL—Now, Halsted, we are on an equal footing. Go ahead.

HARRY—Slade, where the hell do you get off to give Vivian a ring?

VIVIAN—Please, Harry, it's only three carats!

GENERAL *(fuming)*—Four carats!

HARRY—I don't give a damn what it is! You send me away to Camp Dix on a lousy assignment for two weeks, just so you could hang around here.

GENERAL—You were right here for the other two weeks. You never came near her—she said so herself.

VIVIAN—I did not—not exactly.

HARRY—What I do is none of your damned business!

GENERAL—Is that all you have to say?

HARRY—No! Get the hell out of here before I throw you out!

GENERAL—Is that all?

HARRY—That's all!

GENERAL—Give me my coat. (*In silence the two men get into their army coats.*)

VIVIAN—I'm awfully sorry this had to happen.

GENERAL—That's all right, Vivian, don't worry about me.

HARRY *(saluting)*—I believe, sir, that I am supposed to report to you at eight o'clock tomorrow morning, sir.

GENERAL *(pointedly)*—That's right, Colonel. Unless you are suddenly called back to Camp Dix tonight.

Three different times their coats come off, insults are passed and the coats are replaced. In between the verbal assaults Vivian suggests that, in place of her having dinner with the General the next night, as he has proposed, they all three have dinner together.

The General looks inquiringly at the Colonel. "I would consider it an honor, sir," says the Colonel.

The next minute the coats are off again. "I wouldn't eat dinner with you if I have to starve to death!" shouts Col. Halsted.

At which point the General, resuming his coat, decides that he will have to go to the steam room. His pores are all open.

"Attention!" the General commands. Col. Halsted snaps to attention. "Col. Halsted, you have just twenty-four hours to submit proof of your marriage. If you don't you'll face an army court-martial . . . At ease!"

With this the General storms into the hall. A moment later he storms back into the room. In the confusion the angry militarists had exchanged coats.

With the General gone, Harry's anger is switched quickly to Vivian. It is a curious fact, he thinks, that every time he comes to the hotel he finds the General dictating to her, though she has

never had either a pad or pencil. And as for the damned ring:
Let her take that off right now.

But Vivian begs to be allowed to wear the ring—just around
the house—until she has had a chance to show it to Edna and
Nan, who never get anything.

"I should have known that you didn't give a damn about me
when you pawned those clips again!" storms the angry Harry.

"If you gave a damn about me you'd take them out again!"
counters Vivian.

"All the way over here I knew this wasn't going to work."

"Harry Halsted, do you mean to say that just because I'm
wearing this ring for a few minutes . . . I *was* going to take
it off, but now I won't!   After all, a person has some pride!"

"That's the one thing we agree about!" he shouts, and again
the door slams after him.

"I can always tell when Harry leaves," observes Edna, as she
and Nan come back into the room.

Now Vivian has a new idea: She will send Natalia back to the
pawnbrokers with the General's ring (which she displays with
frank satisfaction to Nan and Edna) and get Harry's clips out.
That will show Harry whether she loves him or not.

Julian is back and this time with good news.   The deal with
Warren Buckley is practically closed and the papers are going
to be signed right there in the girls' room.   More than that, as
soon as he gets Buckley's check Julian is going to give it to
Sylvia and Sylvia is going to Reno.

"The minute I sign that contract we're as good as married,"
gloats Julian.

"Nothing's as good as married," ruefully adds Nan.

A few minutes later Buckley has arrived with the papers.   He
is in an expansive mood as he borrows Julian's fountain pen.

"You don't know what this is going to do for me," Julian says
to him, as he turns to put his arm around Edna.

"I can guess."   Buckley is smiling benignly.   "Cadman, you
want to know why I'm taking your process?   Because I pride
myself that I know how to judge men.   Always have known.
Twenty-five years ago a man came around to my house, wanted
to know if he could clear away the snow.   I gave him a shovel
and said 'Go ahead.'   Then he told me he was an ex-convict.
Lot of men would have taken the shovel away from him, but I
formed my judgment of that man, and I believed in him.   So I
let him shovel that snow.   And do you know where he is today?
Right here in this town—one of the biggest men in Washington."

General Slade has returned, and is somewhat perturbed. He had left something with his secretary that he wants back, he explains to the others. Turning to Vivian he suggests that she return what she has of his and he will be on his way. Vivian is worried. It will be practically impossible to do that, seeing that she has sent it out to be cleaned. Evidently, suggests the General, she doesn't know what he is talking about. Let them go into the next room and talk it over, officially.

The General and Vivian have no sooner disappeared than Harry is back, this time with a cellophane box enclosing a couple of orchids. He, too, would like to know where Vivian is. She's there, Nan tells him, but she's pretty busy. At which moment the General emerges from the bedroom, red-faced and shouting:

"And if I don't get it back you'll be a mighty sorry little lady!"

With that the General stalks out, just as Vivian appears. "Harry!" she shouts gleefully. In answer Harry throws his orchids angrily at her and follows the General. Vivian bursts into tears and Nan, the comforter, follows her back into the bedroom.

Again Buckley, the Rubber Chief, and Julian return to their contract. Julian has been looking the contract over and is ready to approve it. With a flourish Buckley is about to sign and make a little more history.

There is a buzz at the door. A messenger from Mr. Buckley's office has a paper for the Chief. Proudly commenting on the efficiency of his staff, which is always able to find him wherever he is, Buckley tears open the envelope. He glances at the contents, and with a startled exclamation of "I'll be damned!" grows florid with excitement.

"Those blasted dunderheads! I knew they were out to get me!" he shouts. And when they would know what has happened he adds: "I'm not the Rubber Chief anymore! I'm fired! I'll bust this thing wide open! I'll take it to the President! I know the two-timing rat that did it!"

"Then the whole thing is off?" weakly inquires Julian.

"Off? What do you think, you thick lug!"

Out he goes and the door slams so violently after him that Vivian comes from the bedroom thinking that Harry has come back.

A moment later "a stocky young man with a good solid face" has appeared at the door. His name is Timothy Walsh and he is inquiring for Vivian Marsden, Nan Curtis and Edna Stokes. He comes from the Federal Bureau of Investigation—

"It's this way. You three are a little rich for our blood. We've had about eight operatives trying to check up on you girls. Two of them have enlisted as parachute jumpers and another one's having a nervous breakdown. So we figured it would free the department for other work if you girls were to sort of start packing."

"Packing?"

"Now, there's a lovely train goes out of here at one o'clock, and I've got priorities on three parlor chairs. Compliments of the United States Government."

"But I can't leave!" wails Nan, a little frantically.

"We haven't done anything," protests Vivian.

"Just what are we charged with?"

"Let's not go into that. That's what got us crazy. We've rounded up spies, saboteurs, kidnapers and blackmailers, but the case of 'The Three Groomless Brides' has got us completely stopped. (*Looks at his watch.*) One o'clock. I'll be waiting in the corridor if there's any questions."

In the midst of this depression Natalia reappears, humming the Volga Boat Song. She has Vivian's clips and six dollars left over. "*He* teach *me* Russian bank!" mutters Natalia, contemptuously. . . .

There is another stranger at the door. He is Stephen Forbes and he is a presidential secretary. He has come in search of Mrs. Thomas Dillon. With some little excitement the girls call Nan, who appears from her bedroom carrying her shoes in her hand.

"I have a signal honor to confer upon you," reports Mr. Forbes, following the introductions. "I have come to extend an invitation for luncheon at the White House today—you are to be the guest of the President and Mrs. Roosevelt."

"Uh—what?" Nan is startled.

"The—the White House?" exclaims Edna.

"Are you sure you've got the right Mrs. Dillon?"

"Is it permissible to tell them a little more?" asks Julian.

"Well, it was supposed to be the President's little secret, but— (*He turns to* NAN.) your husband, Lieutenant Dillon, is with the President now."

"Tom! In America!"

"He landed this morning. . . . You'll hear all the details at luncheon, and you'll also have the pleasure of pinning the Distinguished Flying Cross on him."

Nan starts to cry softly, but recovers enough to insist to Mr.

Forbes that it will be absolutely necessary for her to see Tom, for a few minutes at least, before luncheon. It is Mr. Forbes' idea that Mr. Dillon will be rushing to see his wife as soon as he is free.

"I've got to get married!" announces Nan, the minute Mr. Forbes has disappeared through the door. "I won't be introduced to the President and Mrs. Roosevelt as Mrs. Thomas Dillon until I *am* Mrs. Thomas Dillon!"

"You're right!" Edna agrees. "Julian, we've got to get someone to marry them! You've got to dig up a minister."

But it is Sunday morning. The ministers are all in their pulpits. How about Judge Blake? That's an idea. The Judge is at the Nursery Home, just around the corner. Julian is off with a rush to fetch the Judge.

A moment later Tom Dillon is at the door. A second after that Nan is in his arms and holding the embrace. Vivian and Edna discreetly withdraw.

"Darling, you look marvelous," Nan is saying.

"I feel great."

NAN—So you're a hero—what did you do?

TOM—It seems I sank an aircraft carrier.

NAN—You mean I inspired you to do that?

TOM—Well—it wasn't exactly that way . . . It was a beautiful Sunday morning—I was feeling fine and beginning to forget everything—when a motor launch pulled up and Chaplain Stevens stepped out.

NAN—Wasn't he the one you brought up here?

TOM—The same. They'd sent him over from the mainland to conduct the services. He handed me your cable—and during his sermon he kept staring right at me.

NAN—You must have imagined it.

TOM—Imagine? Hell! Do you know what his text was? "Thou shalt not covet thy neighbor's wife."

NAN—But he couldn't have meant you.

TOM—No? Everybody was staring at me— I crawled out on my hands and knees during the meditation. I got in my plane and went out looking for trouble. I was jay-flying over the Coral Sea when suddenly I spotted a carrier.

NAN—A Jap carrier?

TOM—Darling. I think so or they wouldn't be having us at the White House.

NAN—Yes, of course—go on . . .

Tom—At that point I took one last look at your cable and then I thought of our last few minutes together, and I got so mad at that lawyer of yours. Well, you'll hear the rest at the White House.

Nan—Tom, I'm so proud of you. It was heroic.

Tom—The hell it was. It was just my lousy disposition.

Julian has found Judge Blake and practically dragged her back to the hotel. Nan explains to the Judge that she and Tom have to get married right away, whatever the Judge may think of them. The Judge evidently is ready to forget whatever she may think, but she isn't a Judge—not a real Judge. In Montana she was the Judge of an annual pie-eating contest. That is how she came by the title.

Now the excitement starts all over. It is ten minutes to one and no minister. There is also a huge bunch of roses for Nan with a card from Mr. and Mrs. Franklin D. Roosevelt, which emphasizes the crisis. Mr. Walsh, the FBI man, sticks his head in the door just in time to hear the reading of the Roosevelts' card. That is enough for him. "This is the damnedest case I ever saw," mutters Mr. Walsh, as he sneaks back down the hall.

Suddenly Natalia appears at the door. She is dragging an enormous Russian priest by the hand—"long black mustache, beard, robe and everything."

"Father Nicolai! I happen to remember! Every Sunday he come downstairs to get shave!" Natalia is explaining.

The next minute she is arranging the wedding party in front of the mantel, and serving at the same time as interpreter for Father Nicolai.

"He wants you should kneel down in front of him on both sides and give him the ring," instructs Natalia.

They kneel. Father Nicolai goes into the Russian wedding service, "which is exceedingly long and exceedingly Russian."

The phone rings, but the ceremony goes on and on. Julian answers the phone. He is immediately filled with excitement. He whispers excitedly to Edna. Sylvia is going to Reno to get her divorce! She is going to marry Warren Buckley! What a break!

Father Nicolai has got to the singing stage in the wedding ceremony about the time Harry comes through the door, carrying more flowers than before. Vivian sees Harry. Harry sees the recovered clips on Vivian's shoulders. So she does love him after all! They fly to each other's arms.

Father Nicolai is still singing. Soon he is through. "That's all. Get up! You're married!" calls Natalia. Nan and Tom get to their feet. In the corridor a bugler is blowing a fanfare.

Suddenly the double doors swing open. Six sailors in white enter, group themselves on the two sides of the door, forming an arch. Tom and Nan, arm in arm, walk through the double lane.

"Lunch with the President!" cries Natalia, expansively. "Dis America's a hell of a nice country!"

THE CURTAIN FALLS

THE DAMASK CHEEK

A Comedy in Three Acts

By John Van Druten and Lloyd Morris

IN an interesting introduction to the printed version of "The Damask Cheek" John Van Druten, who wrote the play with Lloyd Morris as his collaborator, tells of the comedy's genesis. He had long wanted to write a play for Flora Robson, the English actress who had been kept on rather a strict diet of serious dramas the last several seasons, and who had recently established herself in America as the star of a fascinating bit of horror called "Ladies in Retirement."

"It all began with the Hotel Ansonia in New York City," reports Mr. Van Druten. "I was walking up Broadway on a blue and gold morning in late September of last year, when I saw its rococo shape rising before me like something out of my childhood. I did not know what it was, but I had an odd sense that it was somehow important to me, and I decided to go on and find out. . . . I wandered around the hotel and its lobbies, seeing visions of hansoms and the early taxicabs, gentlemen in silk hats and capes squiring ladies with piled hair and satin opera cloaks. I remembered the shiny illustrated advertisements of supper-rooms at London hotels and restaurants in my childhood, and I thought, too, of an aunt of mine, a younger sister of my mother's, who lived in New York and came to visit us each summer, bringing with her what I once heard a movie producer call an 'aurora of romance,' in her clothes, her jewelry, her Innovation trunks and the touches of American idiom in her speech. Suddenly the initial idea of 'The Damask Cheek' was born in the figure of Miss Robson as an English girl visiting her family of cousins in the New York of a past generation."

It was then he realized that he was not himself as familiar with old New York as he should be to use it as the background for a drama. He did not come to America until 1926, the year of his first success with "Young Woodley." And it was after he had confessed this to his friend, Morris, who was at the time at work on a volume of his own childhood memories of New York, that the collaboration was agreed upon.

Thereafter Mr. Van Druten went back to California and much

of the work on the play was done by correspondence. There were frequent changes of story and characters, a common experience with the building of a play, and the script was not finished until April, 1942. Then Miss Robson approved it and Mr. Wiman bought it. Rehearsals were started early in the Fall, and production was achieved at the Playhouse in New York in late October, after a Boston tryout earlier that month.

The library in Mrs. Randall's house in New York's East Sixties, which is the scene of "The Damask Cheek," is on the second floor front. It is a handsomely furnished room, with a backwall alcove of books, a grand piano, and large, deepset windows looking out upon the street. There are two couches, one with a long table back of it; a variety of end tables and a number of comfortable chairs. It is the afternoon of a mid-December day in 1909.

As we come into the room Rhoda Meldrum is writing letters at a desk. "She is an English girl of about thirty, pleasant, good-natured and instantly likeable. She is not pretty, but has what is called a 'very sweet face,' and is often described as 'interesting.' There is an expensive quality about her clothes, and her hair is rather elaborately dressed."

Presently Miss Pinner appears. She is "a faded, birdlike little old maid of fifty-odd, dressed in street clothes and hat and she carries a manicuring case." Miss Pinner has been getting the Randall ladies fixed up for a dance that night, and is anxious that they shall remain as fixed. If Miss Meldrum were to get ink on her fingers that would be quite terrible.

Mrs. Randall, "in her early fifties, gray-haired and handsome, dominant and a little fretful and peevish," having been dismissed by Miss Pinner, is carrying on preparations for the dance. There are florists' boxes of corsage size to be emptied and there is no room for their contents in an icebox already bursting with food. The flowers will have to be put outside, on the window sill of Mrs. R.'s room.

Daphne Randall, seventeen and very pretty, arrives in time for tea. Miss Pinner has put Daphne's hair up for the first time, and Daphne is quite impressed with the importance of that event.

Now Jimmy Randall, the man of the family in this fatherless home, has arrived. "He is about thirty-two, easy, engaging and rather selfishly casual." Jimmy comes with a bucket of ice. Tea is all right in its way, but he, having just come from a squash court, wants a highball. Also his friend, Neil Harding, who is to follow, will want a highball. Mr. Harding, Rhoda gathers from the enthusiasm aroused by the mention of his name, must be an exciting person. All the girls Miss Pinner knows are crazy about him, and even Daphne has had a teentsy crush on Neil.

"How does such a wonder come to be around loose?" Rhoda would know. "I gather he isn't married."

"He had too much sense," ventures Jimmy.

"Now, Jimmy, that's no talk from an engaged man," protests Miss Pinner.

Which reminds Jimmy that he hasn't checked on his Calla recently. Where can she be? Mrs. Randall hasn't seen Calla since they had luncheon at Maillard's. Rhoda suggests that perhaps Calla is having her hair done outside, knowing that Miss Pinner would have her hands full.

Rhoda goes to see about the flowers, at Mrs. Randall's suggestion, which gives Jimmy the impression that his mother is rather making use of Rhoda. "She might be a poor relation instead of belonging to the one rich branch of our family," protests Jimmy. ". . . Honestly, do you think Rhoda is having any kind of a good time here?"

"I hope so," answers his mother, a little testily. "I had a tea for her. She's been to the opera and the theatre—Sothern and Marlowe. Calla took her shopping. She went with Michael to the Bioscope. And the Judge took her to hear Burton Holmes."

"Well, maybe that's all she wants."

"I don't know what more I can do. She's not the kind who expects a lot of fuss made over her, fortunately. She's a very sensible girl."

"Yes, there's never been any nonsense about Rhoda."

"*You* never were interested in her, were you, Jimmy? *That* way, I mean?"

"Good God, no!"

"I don't see why you shouldn't have been. She's a very nice girl. There's nothing wrong with her."

"I know, Mother. My trouble is that I've always liked girls— *that* way—who *had* something wrong with them."

"Yes, you have. Oh, I'm not thinking of Calla. You know I'm very fond of Calla."

Rhoda has come back into the room and settled down with a bit of tapestry work. Jimmy and his mother continue their discussion, which is now concerned with the question of who is to make the announcement of Jimmy and Calla's engagement at the dance. Jimmy favors his friend Neil. Mrs. Randall thinks

that Judge Hazeltine, an old family friend, would be better—
seeing he has always been devoted to the family. "When you
get older you'll learn to value affection," Mrs. Randall assures
her son.

"I do, if it's mutual," protests Jimmy. "It's just one-sided
affection that I can't deal with. I think having people thrust it
on you can be the most awful burden. Don't *you*, Rhoda?"

"It's all very well for *you*. You're a man. Men can choose
their friends; girls have to take what they can get. If *you* meet
someone you like, you can go after them. A poor girl has to
wait to be gone after."

Jimmy has gone to dress and Rhoda is back. This gives Mrs.
Randall a chance to return to the subject of Calla. "Tell me,
Rhoda, are actresses looked upon the same way in England as
they are here?" she asks.

"How is that?" Rhoda is slightly puzzled.

Mrs. Randall—Well, I don't know what the word is, quite—
but—when Jimmy first told me Calla was an actress—I was—
well—a little worried about it. Perhaps it was unfortunate that
I'd been to see "The Easiest Way" only the week before.

Rhoda—What is "The Easiest Way"?

Mrs. Randall—Oh, it's a play that's been a great success.
Although a lot of people think it should never have been put on.

Rhoda—Oh, then I must see it. Is it really so bad?

Mrs. Randall—Well, no. It's a very *strong* play, really, if
you look at it in the right light. It's about an actress and her . . .
difficulties. Oh, of course I know Calla isn't like that. She's
told me all about her life, and how hard it is for a girl to keep
straight in the theatre. She says the other girls used to make
fun of her, because she *did*—keep straight, I mean. But all the
same— And then there are the children—Daphne and Michael.
I was very worried about *them*, with Calla, in the beginning.

Rhoda—How worried?

Mrs. Randall—I was afraid they might find her romantic or
attractive, and get ideas. Of course, she isn't famous or anything. She's never played any parts of consequence. But, all
the same—an actress. Fortunately, though, they didn't. They
still seem to be more impressed with *you*.

Rhoda—With me?

Mrs. Randall—Oh, you've always been a heroine to the children.

Rhoda—I can't imagine why.

Mrs. Randall—Well, in the first place, they don't know you very well. But they've always remembered you from the times we went to Europe. And then, being English, and seeing your picture in the *Sketch* and *Tatler*.

Calla Longstreth has come in. "She is twenty-two, and very pretty. She wears outdoor clothes, of a kind that in that period might have been regarded as slightly 'fast.'" Calla has, as Rhoda had suggested, been to her old hairdresser in the Astor to have her hair done. She knew that Miss Pinner would be waiting for her, but—

"I'm sorry, Mrs. Randall, but I haven't really liked the way Miss Jessie has been doing me, and I thought as tonight was a special occasion, I'd like to look nice. (*A dead silence. She looks at herself in a mirror.*) And I think I do."

Mrs. Randall is convinced that curls and clusters aren't very fashionable any more, though there doesn't seem to be anything she can do about that. Now she would like to know what Calla had done with Michael, the Randalls' younger son. Calla had not done anything with Michael, except give him money to go to a matinee. She had left him at Times Square. . . .

When Calla and Rhoda are alone, Calla is free to express a few opinions about life at the Randalls' that have been troubling her for a long time. First she pours herself a drink. Rhoda may have heard that nice girls don't drink whiskey. But, what the hell? "You don't mind all this, do you? This house? This kind of life?" Calla asks.

"It's what I'm used to."

Calla—That's not what Jimmy says. He says your home's much sweller than this. Your family's much richer than his, aren't they?

Rhoda—A little, perhaps.

Calla—You have a home in the country, as well as your one in London, and it can't really be as stuffy as this. You don't know how this has all got me down. First of all living here, in the house, for three months, till you came, and then being pushed off to that plaguey boarding-house, right around the corner.

Rhoda—I'm sorry I turned you out.

Calla—Oh, it's better than it was here, even if it does close its doors at one in the morning. You know I'm having to sleep here tonight, don't you? I'm sharing your room.

Rhoda—Yes, I know.

CALLA—Well, it won't be like this when we're married, and that's going to be sooner than Mrs. Randall thinks.

RHODA—Oh?

CALLA—A year's engagement! Why? I've been on approval for three months. No, just as soon as it's been officially announced—and that'll be tomorrow—then we can go right to it. And if it means a showdown, well, I'm ready for it.

RHODA (*warily*)—Is that Jimmy's idea, too?

CALLA—We haven't talked about it yet. But, listen, if you want to get married, you want to get married. . . .

RHODA—Yes, I see that. But . . . (*Tentatively.*) I'd try and do it without the—showdown, did you call it?—with Aunt Lucy.

CALLA—Why?

RHODA—For Jimmy's sake—and your own. He's fond of his mother . . .

CALLA—Yes, I know he is. I can't think why. She rides him, too, as much as she dares.

RHODA—Well, he's used to her. And if you have a row, that'll mean unpleasantness—and a lot of unhappiness for him. You can manage it tactfully, I'm sure. Why don't you tell her you're sorry about this afternoon?

CALLA—Why should I? I already brought her violets!

RHODA—Yes, but I'm afraid she saw through that! But if you say you're sorry, then it'll all be smooth, and we can have a nice time tonight. After all, it's your engagement party.

CALLA—It isn't. She's giving this dance for you.

RHODA—Well, I think she's killing two birds with one stone. And she's gone to a lot of trouble about it.

Calla finds Rhoda a little difficult to understand. Sometimes she seems quite as though she were of Jimmy's generation, and at other times she acts as if she were his spinster aunt. Rhoda's a good sport, Calla knows that, from what Jimmy has told her, but why should she be so quick to take Mrs. Randall's side about things?

"I'm not taking anyone's side," insists Rhoda, with a touch of suppressed temper. "I just said I thought it would be nice if you'd—well, not apologize—because it isn't as important as that —but if you'd say you were sorry you'd hurt her feelings, or been thoughtless. I just thought it might make it pleasanter all round, for everybody. But if you don't want to, it really doesn't matter a damn."

Calla decides she can afford to be nice this time. She will tell Mrs. Randall she is sorry. She is feeling expansive right now. She has been to see a fortune teller, and that lady has assured her that everything is going to work out to her advantage, even though nothing happens as she (Calla) had planned.

When Mrs. Randall comes back Calla assures her that she is sorry about the hairdresser. Mrs. Randall accepts the explanation gracefully, but with mental reservations. She suspects Rhoda prompted it, and when, after Calla leaves them, she discovers that the glass from which her prospective daughter-in-law had been sipping "charged water" smells of whiskey, her conviction that Calla is deceitful at heart is strengthened.

"Oh, Rhoda, I'm so worried," Mrs. Randall confesses, coming to sit beside Rhoda. "I've *prayed* that something would happen to stop it before it is too late. That's why I insisted on this three months' trial, and on her living here. I hoped that if Jimmy saw her in his own surroundings, he might realize—how unsuitable it was."

RHODA—Jimmy doesn't know you don't approve?

MRS. RANDALL—No. No. It was obvious that he was very— infatuated with her, and he isn't a boy to brook opposition. And since his father died . . . (*She breaks off tearfully.*) But it's been a dreadful strain pretending I was fond of her and pleased about it. I've pretended to everyone. Oh, why couldn't Jimmy have wanted to marry *you?* (RHODA *laughs.*) Why do you laugh? I think you'd be an ideal daughter-in-law.

RHODA (*laughing*)—Oh, no, I wouldn't. You don't really know me a bit, Aunt Lucy. I'm awful, underneath.

MRS. RANDALL—I don't believe that. You seem to me to have all the right qualities for Jimmy. You'd make a wonderful mother. You're very good style. You're sensible, practical, good-tempered . . .

RHODA—That's where you're wrong, Auntie. I've got a filthy temper when I let go. Don't you remember how I cut poor little Lily Mandeville's head open just in a quarrel in the nursery?

MRS. RANDALL—That was when you were tiny.

RHODA (*lightly*)—I still get impulses that way.

MRS. RANDALL—So does everyone. The trouble with you is that you're *too* good-natured. At least, that's what your mother says.

RHODA—Yes, she's talked to me about it.

MRS. RANDALL—You know, *men* like a little mystery in a girl.

RHODA—Well, I think it's a bit late for me to manage that.

MRS. RANDALL—We'll have to see what we can do.

RHODA—Aunt Lucy, did Mother send me over here for you to find someone for me?

MRS. RANDALL—Of course not. She thought it was a little lonesome for you at home, with both your sisters married, and all the girls you came out with, too. She said you were spending all your time with married couples and suffragettes. Naturally, she'd like to see you married. And in a new country, where nobody knows you . . .

RHODA (teasingly)—You think I might seem more mysterious? The way French actresses always succeed in England, no matter how bad they are?

MRS. RANDALL (offended)—Of course, if you're going to make fun of the whole thing . . .

RHODA—Well, that's better than taking it too seriously, don't you think? (Taking her hand.) I'm all right, Aunt Lucy. I'll surprise you all yet.

MRS. RANDALL—Well, you haven't a great deal of time.

Jimmy has changed to his white tie and tails and is back with a cocktail shaker and the proper ingredients. He is in very good spirits, too. When Mrs. Randall has gone to her room he suggests to Rhoda that he thinks he will bring a couple of bottles of *good* champagne—not the kind his mother buys at Bloomingdale's—to the library so that he and she can have it for a sort of sitting-out room during the party. That, agrees Rhoda, would be fine.

It develops, too, that Jimmy and Rhoda had eluded the family that afternoon and had gone skating at the St. Nicholas rink. That was quite an adventure for Rhoda, and fun for Jimmy. It brought back to them days they had enjoyed when Jimmy was visiting in England, when Rhoda used to talk Cockney for him. She still can do that, and does. That's fun, too.

Jimmy is still possessed of the idea that Rhoda has been having a dull time at the Randalls'. He would have liked to do more for her, but, of course, with Calla—

Rhoda understands. She has taken up her tapestry and is working industriously at that. Yes, she confesses, she has occasionally felt a desire to "break out," as she puts it. But where would be the point to that, except "for the sheer satisfaction of having done it—*once*. Like a kind of wild oat."

"I believe in wild oats. Moderately wild," admits Jimmy.

Rhoda knows about that, too. She remembers the time Jimmy got into a little mixup with Thérèse, her French governess, on one of his London visits. Jimmy remembers, too. "You were a grand scout over that," he tells her.

"I gather you've told Calla all about it."

"Oh, sure. Calla likes to hear about my adventures. It's funny."

"But you like telling about them, don't you?"

"Stop kidding me. I'm not a ladies' man, really."

"No?"

"Not the way Neil is, for example."

"Neil? Oh, the fascinating Mr. Harding."

"Neil's always knee-deep in half a dozen affairs at the same time. Girls fall for him so violently and throw themselves at him."

"And he always picks them up?"

"Well, he takes what the gods give."

Jimmy is mixing them a cocktail. As he works there is a little something more that Rhoda would like to know. Does Jimmy intend going on sowing wild oats after he is married?

"Good Lord, no. Why?"

"I just wondered."

JIMMY—No, I believe in putting that kind of thing completely behind one. Where would be the point in getting married, otherwise?

RHODA—I agree.

JIMMY (*handing the cocktail*)—Well—having disposed of that question— Here's how! (*They drink.*) It's funny, having you here. You know, coming in here this afternoon and finding you behind the tea-table, reminded me so much of England and your place down in Hatfield. I felt I was right back there. We did have fun, didn't we?

RHODA—Yes.

JIMMY—It's strange, you know, that all of that appeals to me so much. It's not the kind of life I'll ever lead. It's not Calla's dish, by any means.

RHODA—No. I suppose not.

JIMMY—And that's funny, too. Calla, I mean. She's the last sort of girl I'd ever imagined myself marrying. I always thought I'd marry—oh, a sort of girl of good family—one of Boston's best —someone like Neil's sister.

RHODA—What's she like?

JIMMY (*reflectively*)—Well—she's not exactly pretty, but she's —good style. Sensible, practical—you know, not a bit mysterious or anything . . .

RHODA (*parenthetically*)—Poor girl!

JIMMY (*continuing*)—But she's a wife that anyone would be proud of. You know, living in the country and having slews of kids. I've always wanted kids. . . .

RHODA—Yes, you ought to have them. You've always been good with children. Is—Calla fond of children?

JIMMY (*slowly*)—I don't really know. I don't think, very. (*Then quickly.*) Well, as I say, that's what I'd always seen myself marrying. But when it came to falling in love . . . Well, I guess there's some kind of a streak in me that makes me fall for girls who are a bit—tarnished. No, I don't mean that. That's a hell of a thing to say.

RHODA—I know what you mean. You've always been like that. When you were small you always used to like—sparkly things. There was a children's fancy-dress party we gave in Cumberland Terrace, and you were frightfully fascinated by a girl in a dress all made out of tinsel. You followed her about all the evening.

JIMMY—Good Lord, yes, I remember. And you were . . . ?

RHODA (*grimly*)—A snowflake.

Michael has come from the matinee. He had seen "The Easiest Way," but he hopes they won't tell his mother. The play was wonderful. And it was awfully interesting the way people gasped at the last line.

Daphne has come in, too. She also has her adolescent problem, which comes out in her talk with Rhoda after Michael has gone to dress. Daphne is in love with Neil Harding. Neil doesn't know it, though once he had taken her to the Hippodrome, and to tea at the Plaza afterward. "He always said he'd take me out again—but he never did," confesses Daphne. "He was just being kind that time to Jimmy's kid sister."

"Are you really unhappy about him?"

"I've been unhappy—only sort of happily unhappy, if you know what I mean. . . ."

"I do."

"I mean, it's all right, if you know there's no chance. You can sort of accept that and almost—well—enjoy it. I mean, if I thought that he was in love with someone else, for instance. Well, I could stand that—and feel like Viola in 'Twelfth Night,' or something. You know . . ."

" 'She never told her love . . .' "

" 'But let concealment, like a worm i' the bud . . .' "

" 'Feed on her damask cheek,' " finishes Rhoda.

Daphne hasn't given up hope. She has discovered that Neil isn't in love with anyone else, so she feels she still has a chance. If he just wouldn't think of her always as a kid. But men are like that. They get an idea of you as one thing and never can see you as anything different.

Rhoda agrees to that, but she thinks, too, that Daphne is much too young to generalize about men, and much too young for Neil Harding. She'll get over it.

"Did you have anything like this happen to you? When you were my age?" asks Daphne.

"Yes."

"Was it the same? Was he a lot older than you?"

"No. Not a lot."

"Well, why didn't you get married, then?"

"He didn't think of me that way."

"Was he—wonderful?"

"I don't know. No, not in the sense you mean, I think."

"What was he like?"

"Oh, he was sweet, and selfish, and jolly, and sort of—dependent. Though *he* never thought he was. He was very good at games, and wonderful with children. I think he was the sort of man who never quite grows up, himself, and that's always the hardest kind to get over."

Jimmy has brought Neil Harding. "He is about Jimmy's age, and very handsome." Neil has been upstairs talking with Michael and hearing a lot about Miss Meldrum, he admits, after the introductions. "He painted a most dashing portrait," says Neil.

"Michael's prejudiced," laughs Jimmy. "She took him to Rumpelmayer's in London when he was seven, and let him eat himself sick with cream cakes. Memories like that color a whole lifetime. Now, *my* earliest memories of Rhoda are getting a black eye, a nosebleed, and sharing our first cigarette."

NEIL—Weren't *you* sick?

JIMMY—We were sick together. That's what makes the difference.

RHODA (*lightly*)—So you see, I haven't much to hope from Jimmy.

JIMMY (*putting a brotherly arm around her shoulder*)—But

we've been very good friends, all the same!

RHODA (*smiling at him*)—Memories that color a whole lifetime.

JIMMY (*smiling back*)—Sure! (*He moves away to put his cigarette ash in the wastebasket. Her eyes follow him for just a moment too long.*)

NEIL (*opening his cigarette case*)—May I be allowed to smoke?

RHODA (*catching herself, and bringing her attention back to him with a start*)—Oh, of course.

NEIL—Will *you?* Michael tells me that you do. Still do, I should say, after Jimmy's story.

RHODA (*smiling*)—Thank you. (*She takes a cigarette.*) Michael seems to have told you a great deal.

NEIL—Well . . . (*He lights her cigarette for her.*)

RHODA—You know, Mr. Harding, I've heard a lot about *you,* too—from Jimmy.

NEIL—Also a dashing portrait, I hope?

RHODA (*smiling*)—Oh, yes, quite. (*She glances at* JIMMY, *and then back again at* NEIL.) Quite!

The curtain falls.

ACT II

It is about nine o'clock the same evening. Michael, wearing a new dinner jacket a little awkwardly, is in the middle of a long recital to Rhoda, who is working on her tapestry. Rhoda is wearing a quite beautiful evening gown and listening patiently.

"No, she's not *bad,* exactly; she's just *weak,*" Michael is saying. "She does try to give up the old life for him, but she's been sapped by luxury. That's what the other man tells him in the first act. He says, 'Her simplest gown flirts with a hundred-dollar note.' Do dresses really cost that much?"

"A hundred dollars? That's twenty pounds. Some, yes. Smart ones. You can get them for less."

"So, you see, she never mails the letter. She just burns it. It's the easiest way."

"Yes, I see."

Michael would go on, but Daphne bursts in and that forces an interruption. Her mother is very anxious about the others, Daphne reports, and wants Michael to telephone the hotel and find out if they've left. Michael doesn't want to telephone. He is telling Rhoda something that is none of Daphne's business.

Let Daphne telephone. Not for Michael, she won't, but for Rhoda she will. So the story goes on—

"Well, then in the next act, they're living together again, and it's all rich and everything, and a telegram comes to say that John's coming back."

"Oo!" Rhoda's pretended excitement is quite real.

MICHAEL—Well, then she's going to confess everything to him, only the other woman comes—the other—(*Choosing the lesser word*) actress. And she says that she's a fool to tell him. She says that all men lie to women, and that women like them are just the common prey of any man who comes along. She says that . . .

RHODA (*interrupting*)—Look, Michael, I don't think you'd better go into all the dialogue now. Your mother will be in any minute. Just tell me the story.

MICHAEL—Oh, well, then John comes and he wants her to marry him and go to Nevada with him that afternoon. He still thinks she's reformed, and he's reformed, too.

RHODA—What's he reformed from?

MICHAEL—Oh, he used to be sort of wild, but he says being in love with her has cured him. He says she's made him believe in God. Well, after that, she just can't tell him . . .

RHODA—No, I can see that.

MICHAEL—Only Brockton comes in—and he's got a latch key, and it's *her* apartment, so then John *knows!* Well, then there's a terrific scene where he tells her that she isn't any good. (*With some relish.*) He says she's not immoral, she's un-moral, and that with her it's the easiest way, and she'll just sink down and down to the very bedrock of depravity. So she says she'll shoot herself. She gets the revolver and everything, and he just stands there and dares her to do it, and she can't. So he goes away, and she's left all alone. And that's when it comes. The last line, I mean. She tells the maid to get out her prettiest dress. She says, "Dress up my body and paint my face. They've taken my soul away with them." And the maid asks her if she's going out, and she says, "Yes, I'm going to Rector's to make a hit, and—(*Dropping his voice.*) to hell with the rest." I think she means she's going to become a—well, a professional. And that's the end. It's wonderful. Oh, my stud's gone again. (*He busies himself with it.*)

RHODA (*amused*)—Well, you've had an afternoon, haven't you?

MICHAEL—It's awfully stark and true to life.

RHODA (*smiling*)—What makes you think that?

MICHAEL—Well, Jimmy's talked to me—about life, and about Calla, and how hard it is for a girl to go straight on the stage. The other women—and the men who prey on them and lead them astray. Rhoda, you don't think . . .

RHODA—What?

MICHAEL—Well, after the play this afternoon, I was sort of thinking about it, and you don't think that Calla could be like the girl in it, do you? And that she's marrying Jimmy to sort of get back?

RHODA (*really rather shocked*)—No, of course I don't. Michael, what absolute nonsense! Jimmy and Calla are in love with each other.

MICHAEL—The girl was in love with the man in the play. And he with her. That's why she was afraid to tell him the truth.

Rhoda will have no more of that. She is prepared to believe now that "The Easiest Way" is indeed a very improper play and that Michael should not have seen it.

Michael cannot understand that attitude. He had always thought Rhoda broad-minded. In fact he had just been telling Neil Harding how broad-minded she was, and Neil had said she certainly sounded fascinating.

The appearance of Mrs. Randall, in black velvet and old lace, halts the argument. She is worried about many things. About Jimmy and Calla; about Michael's shirt stud, which he seems to have broken; about Miss Pinner, who is going to stay on for the toasts and speeches and is resting in Daphne's room, and finally about the band, which has arrived and failed to bring "Yip-I-Addy-I-Aye." She must go and see about the band . . .

Jimmy, Neil and Calla have finally arrived. And now that they are there it appears to Calla that there is nothing for them to do but sit and twiddle their thumbs. Jimmy has a better idea. They can all have a little drink. He finds a bottle of champagne in an ice bucket and soon the party is under way.

Jimmy would have Rhoda sing a ballad she used to sing called "Mélisande in the Wood." Rhoda agrees to sing, if Jimmy will recite the "Little Boy Blue" that he used to do. Jimmy starts "Little Boy Blue" by Eugene Field—

> " 'The little toy dog is covered with dust,
> Yet sturdy and staunch he stands—' "

Calla remembers that. And so does Neil. So does Rhoda. They finish it in chorus. Then Jimmy's demand for "Mélisande in the Wood" is repeated and Rhoda goes to the piano.

"She's got a lovely voice, me cousin Rhoda, when she don't crack on the 'igh notes," says Jimmy, imitating Rhoda's Cockney speech.

"You'd crack on the 'igh notes yourself, if you'd been cleaning out the sink all day, like I 'ave, me boy," Rhoda tosses back at him.

They are all around the piano now, with their drinks, and Jimmy is interposing ribald comments from time to time. They have all joined in the song, too, with burlesque intensity, before it is finished.

Now Rhoda has drifted into the dance music from "The Dollar Princess," and Jimmy and Calla are dancing. Neil is content to stand at the piano studying Rhoda as she plays. A moment later Michael has dashed in, his shirt out, his suspenders down. More trouble with his shirt studs. They have to be screwed in. Jimmy must stop dancing and fix them.

The stud situation becomes more and more important. They just have to be fixed, because Mrs. Randall is waiting anxiously for Michael to get a taxi and go for the Religieuse. It sounds like a nun, Jimmy allows, but it really is the dessert for the party. Mazetti has it ready, but there is no one to deliver it. Finally, as Mrs. Randall's excitement grows and there seems no prospect of getting Michael dressed, Neil offers to go for the Religieuse. Daphne will go with him because she knows the Mazetti address. That fixes that.

Michael's shirt is finally adjusted, but Jimmy will have to go with him to tie his tie. Which reminds Mrs. Randall of something. "Michael, where did you go this afternoon?" she asks her son.

"To the Hippodrome," promptly answers Michael.

"Are you sure?"

"Yes. Why?"

"Then what's the program of 'The Easiest Way' doing on your bureau? (*Glances exchanged around.*) I'm very angry with you. You knew I didn't want you to see that."

"I don't see why not?"

"Never mind why not. I told you you weren't to go. And I don't like your telling me you'd been to the Hippodrome. Now, go on upstairs. I'll talk to you tomorrow."

With Michael gone it develops that practically everybody knew that he had been to see "The Easiest Way" except Mrs. Randall. She is extremely annoyed with them all for conspiring in deceiving her.

"Well, that makes a pleasant start to the evening," ventures Calla, as Mrs. Randall marches majestically out of the room.

"Oh, that'll soon blow over," promises Jimmy. "She and Father went on just like that about me and 'The Second Mrs. Tanqueray.'"

"Yes, but this time it's not going to blow over quite so easily."

"Why not?"

"Because *I'm* involved in it. Jimmy, I think it's about time you realized that your mother doesn't like me. In case you haven't realized it, let me point it out to you. She hates me like poison."

To Jimmy, Calla's idea is all nonsense, and when she appeals to Rhoda, it is Rhoda's opinion that the subject should be dropped, for the present, at least.

"Listen, I let you talk me into apologizing to her this afternoon," snaps Calla, turning to Rhoda; "and I've been mad at myself ever since. So, Jimmy, boy, with our engagement popping tonight, you might as well face it. *Your—mother—doesn't —like—me.* And Teacher's Pet, there, knows it perfectly well."

JIMMY—Calla!

CALLA—And all this fuss about "The Easiest Way" is because your mother thinks that's the story of my life!

JIMMY—Oh, don't be so silly!

CALLA (*to* RHODA)—I bet she's told you that.

RHODA (*whose temper is fraying out quickly*)—No, she hasn't. But if she did think it, don't you think that might be a little bit your fault?

CALLA—What do you mean?

RHODA—Well, I don't know, but it seems to me that I've heard an awful lot since I've been here about—the temptations of the stage, and what a hard time you've had resisting them . . .

CALLA—Are you insinuating . . . ?

RHODA—No, I'm not. But I just think you've talked a little too much about it—both of you, if you want to know—and if Aunt Lucy has got any such ideas, it's you who've put them there.

CALLA—It's easy enough for you to be smug. You've never known what it is to be up against it—not know where your next meal's coming from. . . .

RHODA (*heatedly*)—I'm not being smug, and that's no argument.

JIMMY (*worried, but trying to be light about it*)—Now, girls!

CALLA (*over-riding him*)—Why isn't it any argument?

RHODA (*fiercely*)—I might just as well say that you've never known what it is *not* to be up against it, and to know so damn well where your next meal's coming from that you could scream from the sheer boredom of life!

JIMMY (*shouting them down*)—What are you two talking about?

RHODA (*sitting again, rather huffily*)—I've no idea!

JIMMY—I don't know what's the matter with you both.

NORA (*entering from the bedroom, carrying two corsages*)—Mr. Jimmy, the mistress says will you please come down? Judge Hazeltine's here, and there are some other people just arriving.

JIMMY—Oh, all right, Nora. We'll be right down.

NORA (*looking at the corsages, uncertain as to which belongs to whom.* JIMMY *takes them from her*)—Thank you, Mr. Jimmy. Watch the pins.

JIMMY (*looking from* RHODA *to* CALLA *and back again*)—Now, will you two please make it up? Remember, you've got to share a bedroom tonight!

RHODA—I'm sorry, Jimmy. Sorry, Calla.

CALLA—Oh, all right. I'm sorry, too.

JIMMY (*giving them their flowers*)—Well, that's all right then. Let's go down. (*He holds the door open for them.*)—Oh, I've got to tie Michael's tie. You go ahead. I'll be right after you.

"The two girls go out. Jimmy stands for a moment in the doorway, thinking. Then he goes out" as the curtain falls.

Later that evening the party is in full swing below stairs. In the library Miss Pinner, with a glass of champagne in her hand, is listening to the sounds of revelry that float upward. The singing of "For He's a Jolly Good Fellow" makes her a little sad, but the champagne is cheering.

Presently Nora, the maid, joins Miss Pinner. Nora is willing to drink the health of Jimmy and Calla, but she never thought Jimmy would go through with the wedding. Nor did his mother. Mrs. R. had said as much to practically everybody—except Mr. Jimmy—says Nora.

When Mrs. Randall comes her attitude seems to bear out the reports of her lack of enthusiasm. But there's no turning back now, she admits, a little dolefully. She is glad no one except

Miss Pinner knows how she really feels about the engagement.

Anyway, the party has been going very well. Rhoda seems to be having a good time. Perhaps she has made herself a little conspicuous dancing so frequently with Mr. Harding, but of course there is nothing really to that. Rhoda isn't the kind that would interest Neil, even though she has money. The Hardings don't need money.

When Jimmy and Calla appear, Mrs. Randall is quick to wish them happiness and to kiss them both. She hopes they liked the party. For her part she thought Mr. Harding's speech was a little facetious, and she thought Jimmy should have said a little more than he did. But, she's satisfied.

With Jimmy's mother gone, Calla is free to admit that the party has been her idea of hell. Jimmy may have been used to this sort of thing all his life, but she hasn't. Who are all these people, anyway—

"The gink with a face like a kneecap, who thinks it's cute to squeeze you when you dance?" Who was he? "He's almost as bad as the Judge. I guess it's because I'm an actress," Calla concludes. "You can take liberties with actresses."

That would be Chuck Stebbings. Chuck had married Betty Henderson. "She's wearing blue—with a feather-brush thing in her hair," explains Jimmy; "a vinaigrette, or whatever you call it. Betty used to be considered fast. She got herself into quite a scandal a few years back."

"Oh—how?" Calla is interested in this one.

"She met a man at a dance, and the next day she was seen lunching with him at Claremont. She got into awful hot water. People stopped asking her out. . . ."

"My God—just for a lunch?"

"Oh, she had a hell of a time till Chuck married her, and that was considered pretty brave of him. Mother and her mother were at school together."

Calla is worried. Will she and Jimmy have to know people like Betty and Chuck after they are married? Jimmy thinks they will. After all, you can't just drop people you've always known.

"You know, there's a lot I can't make out about you," says Calla. "You don't really enjoy a party like tonight's. . . . You do enjoy the kind of party that—well, the kind of party that we met at. But you still cling to all this."

"It's my background," admits Jimmy.

They are pretty close to a quarrel when Rhoda comes upon

them a moment later. Jimmy is all for getting them a quick drink before the music starts again. Rhoda will have one, but Calla had rather take the time to go and freshen up a bit.

Jimmy and Rhoda have their drink together. Jimmy would also exchange confidences. Is it true that his mother doesn't like Calla? Rhoda is evasive. She thinks it probable that Mrs. Randall doesn't understand Calla. But that doesn't matter, Rhoda insists. If Jimmy likes her and wants to marry her, that's all that matters.

"I don't think you quite understand," Jimmy is saying. "After all, there is something in what Calla says. You've been brought up so differently. You've never known that world."

"No, I know."

"Besides, Calla's very attractive. To men. Even before she went on the stage—when she was quite a kid—she always had men after her."

"Yes, of course she did."

"Women like Mother don't understand that. I don't think you do, either. I mean, to anyone who's not always had that sort of thing, anyone who has, seems—oh, I don't know—*suspect*. It's not a girl's fault if she's attractive."

"Fault?"

"It's very easy to condemn if you've never had any temptations," snaps Jimmy, angrily.

Rhoda's mouth opens in amazement, but she has no chance to answer. Mrs. Randall has come back and wants to talk with her. Jimmy goes back to the dancing.

Is Rhoda having a good time, her aunt would know? Has she plenty of partners? Has she danced with the Judge? Isn't she, perhaps, favoring Mr. Harding a little too much? After all, Rhoda is a stranger, and people are apt to notice everything she does.

Rhoda is at some pains to preserve her temper, and quick to assure Mrs. Randall that everything is quite all right.

With Mrs. Randall returned to her party, it is Daphne who takes up the questioning. What does Rhoda think of Neil Harding? Rhoda thinks Mr. Harding is attractive, but also that he is quite well aware of that fact.

Neil, reports Daphne, talked a lot about Rhoda in the taxi. Thought she was most attractive. Otherwise, nothing happened during the ride. Daphne didn't think anything would happen, but wondered a lot about what she should have done. "Mother told me once no self-respecting girl lets herself be kissed by a man she isn't engaged to. Is that true?"

Rhoda thinks it all depends. Certainly a girl shouldn't let everyone kiss her. Daphne can understand that.

"He wanted to know a lot about you," Daphne rattles on.

"And what did you tell him?"

"Oh, I told him about you. I told him you said you weren't attractive to men."

"Daphne! You didn't!"

"He said you were joshing me. I told him you were serious."

"Daphne!"

"He thinks you're mysterious."

"What on earth made you tell him that?"

"Well, you said so. . . ."

"I might have said I had a spot on my back, or that my hair wasn't my own, but you don't have to tell other people that. Really!"

Daphne is a little ashamed of herself now. "No, I guess it was silly of me," she admits. "It was just that . . . well, talking to him, I didn't think. But I am sorry. I know it was silly of me now."

Daphne has Rhoda's forgiveness and runs back to the dance. But Rhoda has a bit of a headache and decides to stay where she is for a little. For a minute she remains slumped in her chair, "near the end of her tether with depression, nerves and irritation." She finishes her champagne and, with some decision, pours herself another glass. She is at the window looking out at the falling snow when Neil Harding comes for his dance.

If Rhoda has never seen New York under snow, he tells her, it is really quite beautiful. Especially in Central Park. Driving around in a hansom at night, when it has been snowing, is one of Neil's hobbies.

Would he mind if they sat the dance out? Rhoda asks. He'd like it. And a bit of champagne, too, if he may join her. Has she been very bored? She has been looking as though she might be, a little, Neil has noticed. But, of course, "in the nicest, and politest, and most English way possible."

Rhoda thinks perhaps he would understand, if he had tried dancing with Judge Hazeltine—and checks herself immediately. She shouldn't have said that. Still, Neil is understanding.

Neil would like to have Rhoda tell him about girls who have been presented at court. He had never known any, and is really a little scared at the thought of them—a little scared of Rhoda, in fact.

"I don't know what you're thinking," says Neil. "I know you're thinking something, and I don't know what it is."

"You don't know what I'm thinking about what?"

"Anything. The dance—America—me . . ."

"I'm enjoying them all a great deal."

"Well, that's encouraging if you mean it. But, you see, I don't know if you mean it. I've danced with you three times. . . . We've talked about nothing . . . I heard you sing in here this evening—but I don't know whether any of that is really you. I don't think it is. I think somewhere deep down, you're quite, quite different."

Rhoda would like to know what Neil thinks she is—deep down. He doesn't know. That is what fascinates him. He has heard so many conflicting reports. Michael, for instance, thinks she may be fast, though Michael meant that as a compliment. And why did she tell Daphne that she was not attractive to men?

"I can't think of an answer to that, that wouldn't sound like—fishing," admits a plainly flustered Rhoda.

NEIL—You know it isn't true.

RHODA—Do I?

NEIL—You've got a kind of—light inside you. It's only just beginning to come on. I've known all evening it was there, if only one could find the switch. You're quite different now it's on. Has anyone ever told you that you look like the Sphinx?

RHODA—No, but I've seen the Sphinx, and it isn't really a compliment.

NEIL—No?

RHODA—No, it's very battered with a broken nose.

NEIL—Oh, I'm sorry. But you see, I haven't seen it. Isn't it—mysterious and inscrutable, the way it's written up?

RHODA—I think it's more—the idea of it.

NEIL—Well, that's what I meant about you. I think you could be dangerous, too. If you weren't being English, and would let yourself. You know, we're in America. (*His hand touches hers for a moment and she withdraws it.*)

RHODA (*in an odd voice*)—What did Jimmy say about me?

NEIL—Jimmy's a fool. He doesn't know anything about women. (*There is a pause. Disturbed, she rises and moves away from him, walking to the window.*)

RHODA—It's still snowing.

NEIL (*coming close behind her to look*)—It's still beautiful.

RHODA (*more because she is at a loss for what to say, than for any other reason*)—There's a poem about London snow . . .

NEIL (*very quietly*)—What is it?

RHODA (*quoting*)—"When men were all asleep, the snow came flying,
              In large white flakes upon the city brown,
              Stealthily and perpetually settling and loosely lying,
              Hushing the latest traffic of the drowsy town . . ."

NEIL—I like that. (*She turns from the window. They face each other and he kisses her. They hold the kiss for a moment, then, as they separate, he catches her hands.*) Let's go out and look at it.

RHODA—We can't.

NEIL—Why not? Come out and look at Central Park in the snow.

RHODA—We can't leave the dance.

NEIL—We can if we want to. And I want to. Don't you?

RHODA—We can't.

NEIL—It won't take more than half an hour. No one will notice.

RHODA—Yes, they will.

NEIL—Then let them. What do you care? Listen, down there, there's a bad band playing bad music, and a lot of people dancing badly on a crowded, bad floor. They're people you've never seen in your life before, and will probably never see again. Out there is something else that you may never see again. New York in the snow. Please let me show it to you.

RHODA—But how can we?

NEIL—Just get a coat and something to put over your head. If anyone sees you, you can say you're going to get a breath of air for your headache. I'll slip out first. I'll meet you at the corner. We'll drive down to the Plaza, and then get a hansom. Won't you? Won't you?

RHODA—I shouldn't.

NEIL—But you will?

RHODA—All right. For just half an hour.

NEIL—Good. I'll go down first. You will come?

RHODA (*gaily*)—Yes.

"He smiles at her and goes out, leaving the door open. The music swells up from below. Rhoda stands for a moment, and then moves happily across the room. She stops halfway for an instant to look back at the window, her face radiant, and then starts quickly for the door."

The curtain falls.

ACT III

Around noon the next day Miss Pinner arrives. She has dropped in for a box of goodies from the party Mrs. Randall had promised to save for her, and she finds Mrs. R. in a state of mind. This time it isn't Calla who has upset her. It's Rhoda. For two hours during the party Rhoda had disappeared with Neil Harding and no one knew where they were. They had, it appears, gone for a ride in the park!

So far there has been no explanation, reports Mrs. Randall. Rhoda was up at 8 o'clock and went for a walk. Of course everybody is, or will be, talking about it. Judge Hazeltine has already called, and so has Betty Henderson's mother. It'll be all over New York by lunchtime!

When Rhoda returns from her walk she is quite calm and collected. Miss Pinner is quick to sense the atmosphere and to excuse herself, and Mrs. Randall loses no time in demanding an explanation from Rhoda.

Rhoda is sorry for what happened, but there is nothing she can say. She can understand Mrs. Randall's anxiety about her, but still there is nothing she can offer by way of explanation. She and Mr. Harding had gone for a ride around the park—

"Did he make love to you?" her aunt would know.

"Aunt Lucy, that is a question I have no intention of answering," says Rhoda.

"That means he did."

"I don't see why you think that. It might equally well mean that he didn't."

Letting the matter pass, Mrs. Randall's chief concern now is what she is going to do with her niece. Rhoda certainly will be thoroughly compromised; everybody is already talking about what she has done. What her (Rhoda's) mother will say when she gets Mrs. Randall's letter is quite beyond Mrs. R.

"I've had to explain why I can't do anything about you," Mrs. Randall explains. "Because I can't, you know. Any chances you may have had are completely ruined. I should have thought, if you had nothing else to restrain you, that at least might have occurred to you."

"It never occurred to me that I had any chances to ruin."

"Well, that's what you came over here for, wasn't it?"

"No!"

"Well, why did you come?"

"I came because I wanted to."

"That seems to be the only reason you can give for anything."

"It seems to me a good one."

"If you think you can go through life doing everything you want to . . ."

"I don't. I've spent almost my entire life not doing *anything* I wanted to. Or not being able to."

It seems that there is nothing for Mrs. Randall to do but to wash her hands of Rhoda from now on. Probably the best thing for Rhoda to do would be to go to her Aunt Bessie, in Indianapolis, until her New York escapade has blown over, if it ever does.

Mrs. Randall has left her with the suggestion that if she would prefer to have her luncheon on a tray at home, if the family goes out, it probably can be arranged. Then Jimmy arrives. He is taking the morning off, and he, too, has been out for a walk.

Hearing of his mother's feeling about Rhoda's leaving the party the night before, and of her sentence to Indianapolis, Jimmy's reaction is that the whole thing is a lot of nonsense. That his mother should think that Rhoda has compromised herself by going for a drive with Neil is, to Jimmy, a little lunatic. But Rhoda doesn't agree. "She's quite right," says Rhoda. "It was an idiotic thing for me to have done, and I must have been quite mad."

"You mean—you really think you've—blotted your copybook?"

"Yes, I know I have."

"Oh, it's ridiculous. You're all behaving as if he'd seduced you."

"The conventions of Society are that if a man and woman are in a position where he could have seduced her, it doesn't make any difference whether he did or not."

Jimmy had never thought of it like that, but he's sure the whole thing will blow over, like everything else. Or nearly everything. Which brings Jimmy to his own particular problem. He's the one who has been the fool—about Calla—

"I don't want to marry her," explodes Jimmy. "There, now I've said it. At last I've said it—out loud and to someone else. I've been saying it to myself all morning. I've been spending the last three months trying not to say it to myself."

RHODA—You mean—from the beginning . . . ?

JIMMY—Almost from the beginning. Only I wouldn't face it.

I think it was only here last night when she said Mother didn't like her that I faced it properly.

RHODA—But—why should that have made a difference?

JIMMY—Oh, it wasn't that it was Mother. It could have been anybody. But haven't you ever noticed how you can go on saying that you like something—kidding yourself you like it— and then someone comes along and says they *don't* like it, and quite suddenly you know that you don't either, and that you've always known you didn't?

RHODA—Yes—with a book or a play or something to eat . . .

JIMMY—Well, it was just like that with Calla. And I had to wait till last night before I was able to admit it. A couple of hours before our engagement was announced. You can imagine how I felt. I'm afraid I took it out on you.

RHODA—That's all right.

JIMMY (*patting her shoulder*)—Good old Rhoda. You're always there, aren't you?

RHODA (*after a moment*)—What are you going to do?

JIMMY—Nothing. What can I do?

RHODA—An engagement isn't a marriage.

JIMMY—I can't let her down. I've promised her marriage. Security, and permanence. They're things she's never had. She's been up against it all her life. (*Hastily.*) Oh, I don't only mean the way we talked about last night. Though that, too. And then, there again . . .

RHODA—What—there again?

JIMMY—Well, that's another reason why I can't do anything.

RHODA—Do you mean that—you and she . . . ? (JIMMY nods.) Oh, I see. (*She seems to retreat into herself somewhat.*)

JIMMY—So there you are.

RHODA—Then all this talk about her being a good girl . . .

JIMMY—She was.

RHODA—She's not going to have a baby?

JIMMY (*with a laugh*)—No! I almost wish she were, in a way. But it just makes it more impossible, that's all. Oh, it's no good talking about it. But I just wanted to say it once—to someone. And I always have confided in you.

RHODA—You mean, you're really going to marry her, feeling like that?

JIMMY—I can't do anything else. Oh, don't look so tragic. I daresay it won't be any worse than most marriages. Only it seems so silly to have waited until my age for this. If I'd been nineteen, there might have been some excuse. I guess I've just never grown up, or I'd have learned about . . . tinsel before now. (*He gives her a sad, rueful little smile.*) It is silly, isn't it?

RHODA—I wish I could do something to help you.

Calla has come for a cigarette. She is wearing a wrapper and looks rather tousled. Mrs. Randall, finding her there, is not pleased with the wrapper. Neither was she pleased to hear from Judge Hazeltine that Calla had promised him two dances and then danced them with someone else. Calla admits the charge. She didn't dance with the Judge because she didn't like being pinched. The Judge, says Calla, is a nasty old man.

"He's been trying to paw me ever since he first met me," insists Calla. "I know his type well."

"Calla, that is a deliberate and disgusting lie!" charges Mrs. Randall. "Judge Hazeltine is one of the most respected men in New York."

"Yes, they always are!" answers Calla, and her classification is confirmed a moment later by Rhoda, who had also been pinched by the Judge.

Mrs. Randall is outraged. She refuses to believe them. This is something they have made up. And if it isn't, then they brought it on themselves. "No gentleman is ever familiar with a lady unless she has cheapened herself with him," declares Mrs. Randall. "Perhaps he had reason to believe that it was—what you were accustomed to!" With that parting shot Aunt Lucy leaves them.

There's something that Rhoda would know. Why did Calla tell Jimmy that his mother did not like her? Calla is perfectly frank. She plans to break up the hold that Jimmy's mother has on him. It may hurt Jimmy, but he will get over it.

Is Calla in love with Jimmy? Rhoda would like to know. Calla isn't sure. It's a question she has been asking herself for several weeks. Nor is she sure she is going to be happy with Jimmy. But why is Rhoda interested?

"Do you think I'm a fool to go through with it?" demands Calla.

RHODA—From your point of view? I don't know. I don't know what you expect from it.

CALLA—I'll tell you. I expect exactly what I'll get. Security. Enough money to live on. Not having to worry about the rent, or whether I get a job for the next three months or not. Not having handkerchiefs drying all over the mirrors, or going without lunch to get my gloves cleaned, or my shoes fixed.

Rhoda—Yes, you'll get that.

Calla—The trouble is that for the last three months, I've had it, and it bores the hell out of me. You see, he isn't really rich. That's the snag. I didn't realize it at first. It looked like riches to me. But it isn't. He's just—comfortably off. And that's not good enough. You're really rich. You know.

Rhoda—Do you mean you want to get out of it?

Calla—I mean, I'd like to, but I think I'd be a fool. In six months' time, I'd be back exactly where I am. I'd thought of driving *him* to breaking it off. For what I could get out of it. But it wouldn't be enough. I wouldn't settle for less than twenty-five thousand. I could get that in court. But he couldn't pay it. Nor could his mother. I know that.

Rhoda (*quietly*)—I could.

Calla—What did you say?

Rhoda—I said I could.

Calla—What do you mean?

Rhoda—I mean that if you'll take twenty-five thousand dollars to break off your engagement, I'll give it to you.

Calla—What for?

Rhoda—Because I think the whole thing is a horrible mistake. You don't want to marry Jimmy, and he doesn't want to marry you.

Calla—Did he tell you so?

Rhoda—I've got eyes of my own.

Calla—But why should *you* fork over?

Rhoda—Because I'm fond of him, and I don't want to see him unhappy.

Calla—Are you in love with him?

Rhoda—Don't be so silly.

Calla—Well, I knew you were rich, but . . .

Rhoda—Look, you said you'd take twenty-five thousand. If you will, I'll give you a check on my bank in London. I'll give it to you now. (*She goes for her pocketbook.*) I've got my checkbook here. Will you take it?

Calla—Wait a minute. I've got to think this over.

Rhoda—All right, but in that case, I can think it over, too. You'd better take it while you can.

Calla thinks quickly and decides that if Rhoda will make it thirty thousand she'll take it. Rhoda writes the check. Now there is one other thing Rhoda would know. "Had you really always been straight, till you met Jimmy?"

"Yes. That is—at least . . ."

"That's all. That's all I wanted to know. I thought you hadn't—quite." And Rhoda hands over the check.

"What do I do now?"

"You tell Jimmy that you've changed your mind, and that you want to break off the engagement. And you don't tell him about *that*. Naturally."

"No. Naturally."

"That's all."

But Calla isn't satisfied. There is something back of Rhoda's action, she knows that. And now she has it. Rhoda is herself in love with Jimmy and has been all this time.

CALLA—That's why I've never been able to make you out! That's why you've nursed him through all his affairs! It's true, isn't it?

RHODA (*after a moment*)—All right, then. It's true. I've always been in love with him. I've known it never could come to anything, but—if he's unhappy with you, at least I can get him out of it. That's all.

CALLA—Don't try and pull the wool over my eyes! Well, I've heard of American girls going to England and buying husbands for themselves but . . .

RHODA (*appalled and aghast*)—What? Is that what you think? (*Reaching for the check, in an access of horror.*) Give me that back!

CALLA (*retreating*)—You're just paying me off to leave the coast clear for yourself! And what a hope you've got!

RHODA (*starting after her*)—You nasty little demi-rep!

CALLA (*dodging her round the couch*)—Me? And what do you think you are? Spooning in hansom cabs with men!

RHODA (*chasing her; murderously*)—If I get my hands on you . . .

CALLA (*still dodging*)—So this is the famous temper that I've heard about!

RHODA—You'll do more than hear about it in a minute! (*The chase continues. A table goes over. RHODA catches her.*) Now, then (*Shaking her.*), you'll take back what you said!

CALLA—I won't! (*She pulls her hair.*)

RHODA (*grabbing at CALLA's hair*)—Let go! Let go! (*She bites her. CALLA screams and lets go of her hair. They go into a clinch, and wrestle. Another piece of furniture goes over, and*

*they go with it, rolling on the floor, struggling with each other.
Banging* CALLA'S *head on the floor.*)   Now then.   Take it back!
Take it back!   (*The door opens and* JIMMY *appears, his coat off
and shaving soap on his face.*)

JIMMY—Hey, what's going on?   Rhoda!   Calla!   What are
you doing?   (*He rushes forward and starts to separate them.*
RHODA *leaps up, staring at him for a moment, wide-eyed and
stricken.   He lays his hand on her arm.*)   Rhoda, what's the
matter?   Rhoda!   (*She shakes him off.   Again he touches her.*)
Rhoda!   What is it?

RHODA (*flinging him off, violently*)—Oh, go to hell!   (*She
dashes out of the room, leaving him staring after her.   CALLA is
sitting up on the floor.   In the doorway, as* RHODA *rushes out,*
MRS. RANDALL *appears, also staring after her.*)

The curtain falls.

It is mid-afternoon when Jimmy finds his little brother Michael
absorbed in H. G. Wells' "Ann Veronica" in the living room.
Michael has found the novel fairly dull until Jimmy intimates
that he'd better not let his mother catch him reading it.   That
gives him the idea that it may yet turn out to be "hot stuff" and
his search for "the bad part" is stimulated.

Michael is also curious about what has happened to Rhoda.
He had heard his mother tell Daphne that Rhoda had compromised herself.   If that is true, what does it mean, exactly?   Is it
worse than being—fast?   Would it, in this instance, mean that
Neil had seduced Rhoda?

"Good God Almighty, no!" thunders an outraged Jimmy.
"Whatever put that into your head?"

"I just thought . . ."

"You really are a little idiot.   What opportunity did he have
to seduce her, anyway?"

"I thought perhaps they went to a hotel."

"Really, what do you think people are?   . . . And Rhoda,
of all people!   One of the things you've got to learn as you grow
up, my boy, is the difference between a good woman and a bad
one, or you'll get yourself into the most awful messes."

"How does one tell?"

"One doesn't tell.   One knows."

"How?"

"I don't know.   One does."

Michael would also like to know what had caused all the
racket in the living room that morning.   It sounded like a fight.

Jimmy doesn't know anything about that, either. If he did, he wouldn't tell Michael. All he is willing to divulge is the fact that he and Calla are not engaged any more. With that he is gone.

Michael tries to piece out his information by quizzing Daphne, but she doesn't know anything, either. Probably Calla broke off her engagement to Jimmy at lunch. At least they had gone to lunch together.

Now Neil Harding has arrived. He has come to see Rhoda, and he is prepared to wait until she appears. Michael needn't bother to tell Jimmy that Neil's there. Daphne will keep him company.

Daphne is worried. She is perfectly willing to entertain Neil, but there is something she must know. Is he in love with Rhoda? Considering that he has known Rhoda only for a day, Neil considers Daphne's question ridiculous. The fact that they had been together the night before means nothing. Very well, if Neil is not in love with Rhoda, and doesn't want to marry her—that leaves the way clear for Daphne.

"I'm in love with *you*," says Daphne, in a tight, determined little voice.

"What? Daphne!"

"I am."

"Daphne, you can't be!"

"Yes, I can. I have been—for a long time."

"But you don't know what you're saying."

"Yes, I do. I'm in love with you. That's why I asked you about Rhoda. If you'd said yes, I wouldn't have told you. But if you're not in love with her . . ."

"I'm not in love with anyone."

"That's what I thought. That's why I told you."

"Yes, but, Daphne—it's very, very sweet of you, but it's crazy."

Very kindly, Neil undertakes to correct Daphne's adolescent impressions of love, and presently, after she had tried to act a little like the heroine of a novel, Daphne is convinced suddenly that she has been a little silly. She would run away, now, embarrassed and ashamed, but Neil restrains her—

"Daphne, listen. I'm very, very touched at your feeling like this, but—it's all wrong."

"I know. Please let me go," pleads Daphne.

"Not for a minute."

"Please. Please. I've been a fool. Don't make me stay here."

"But, Daphne . . ."

Rhoda has come into the room and Daphne has bolted. Rhoda thinks she understands why. The thought distresses her momentarily, but Neil quickly sweeps it away. She has no sooner laid aside her furs than he goes to her, puts his arms about her and tries to kiss her. She quickly releases herself and moves away.

"You let me last night," pleads Neil.

"Last night was last night. This is this afternoon."

"Do I have to wait till six o'clock—like the first drink?"

Rhoda's answer is quick and positive. She does not know what he is thinking—or expecting—but this sort of thing cannot go any further. Not because of last night—not, at least, in the sense he means—but rather because of something that had happened that morning, Rhoda is returning to England.

"There's nothing the matter," she assures him. "At least, not to do with you. I'm very grateful to you. Really I am."

"For what, for God's sake?"

"For last night. You were very flattering. You said very charming things, and I wanted to hear them. You gave me an adventure that I shall always remember. Driving round Central Park in the snow with you, and being made love to—very charmingly. You do make love charmingly."

"Are you kidding me?"

"Indeed, no. I'm saying thank you."

"Then why won't you see me again?"

"Because one glass of champagne is enough."

Neil is still at a loss to understand, and his vanity is plainly hurt, but Rhoda is quite convinced he will recover.

Jimmy has come and Rhoda has left the men together. Neil is still disturbed. He never has been able to understand English women. What is Rhoda?

"Well, in Mother's phrase, she's a very nice girl," says Jimmy. "There's nothing wrong with her. (*With a thought.*) Although I think Mother's revised that opinion since last night. *And* this morning. I'm even beginning to revise it a bit, myself. What was the idea of you and her going off last night, by the way?"

NEIL—An impulse.

JIMMY—Damn fool one.

NEIL—Have you never had an impulse to whirl a girl away from a ballroom?

JIMMY—Sure. Not Rhoda, though.

NEIL—You think of her the way I do about my sister, don't you?

JIMMY—Yes, I think I do—from that point of view.

NEIL—Well, that's where you're wrong. Alice would never behave the way she did last night.

JIMMY (*astonished*)—You mean . . . ?

NEIL—I mean.

JIMMY (*incredulous*)—Rhoda?

NEIL—Rhoda.

JIMMY—You mean you made love to her? (NEIL *nods.*) And she let you? (NEIL *nods again.*) What do you mean—"making love"?

NEIL—I mean "making love." Romantic love, in a hansom. You've done it yourself. You know. And then this afternoon when I expect some kind of follow-up, she quietly tells me that "That's all there is, there isn't any more." Not that it was all a mistake, and should never have happened, and that she can't think what she was doing . . .

JIMMY (*exploding somewhat*)—Well, *I* can't think what she was doing. Or you, either.

NEIL (*astonished*)—Hey!

JIMMY (*rather pompously*)—No, damn it, I mean it. You don't do that sort of thing with decent girls in decent houses. And decent girls don't let you.

NEIL—Jimmy, what's happened to your sense of humor?

JIMMY—What's my sense of humor got to do with it?

NEIL—Everything. You've never gone self-righteous like this before.

JIMMY—You've never pulled a trick like this before.

NEIL—Jimmy, she's not a kid of eighteen. She knows how many beans make five.

JIMMY (*as before*)—And that's no way to talk about her, either.

NEIL—Oh! Sorry!

JIMMY (*coming out of it a little*)—No, but honestly, can't you see the difference between a girl like Rhoda, and—the kind of girl you can do that sort of thing with?

NEIL—Jimmy, you won't hit me if I repeat that the whole point is that she turns out to *be* the kind of girl you can do that sort of thing with?

JIMMY—You don't mean . . . ?

NEIL—I wouldn't know. If I'd had an apartment in New York that we could have gone to, instead of driving round Central

Park, I might be able to answer you.

JIMMY—Rhoda would never go to a man's apartment.

NEIL—Not this afternoon. But last night . . . Well, as I say, I don't know. And I guess I never shall. Oh, well . . .

JIMMY—Well, I'm certainly seeing a lot of new sides to her, all of a sudden.

Neil suggests that perhaps Jimmy feels like making love to Rhoda himself now. There are people who don't find anyone attractive until someone else tells them they are. As for Rhoda? Who knows? Perhaps any girl is potentially a bad girl—anyway, Rhoda's going back to England—

Jimmy can't believe that. Rhoda is going to Indianapolis. Even if she said England, she meant Indianapolis. . . .

Neil has gone and Rhoda, having changed to an afternoon frock, is back. She has taken up her tapestry work. For a moment Jimmy stands staring at her, "as though seeing her suddenly anew and for the first time."

He starts to speak, but she stops him. She wants to apologize, both for what happened last night and this morning. That's all right, insists Jimmy, lightly. But he would like to know what it was all about—

"Didn't Calla tell you?" asks Rhoda, in some surprise.

"She said you'd had a row. She said you'd made it up afterwards, upstairs. She wouldn't tell me what it was about."

In that case, Rhoda also prefers to keep quiet. Now Jimmy has something to tell Rhoda. Calla has broken off their engagement. Rhoda is not surprised. It was, she thinks, quite obvious that it would not have worked out.

"I asked her what she was going to do—how she was going to live . . ." Jimmy is saying.

"And she said?" Rhoda is holding her breath.

"She said she'd be all right. She'll go back on the stage. I wanted to make some sort of—settlement or something, but she wouldn't take it."

"I like her for that."

"Oh, Calla's all right in lots of ways. It's just that—as a wife, she wouldn't do. For me, anyway. It was just the wrapping I liked. It's the most extraordinary feeling to be free again. I can't believe it. It's such luck!"

Rhoda is glad that Jimmy is glad. And now, what is this about Rhoda's going back to England, when she's just come? Rhoda is a little evasive. After the way she has behaved—

It may not mean anything to Jimmy, but it does to Rhoda. "I feel horrible about it," she says. "Dirty and ashamed—"

"Is that why you want to go home?"

RHODA—That on top of everything else. It's all turned out all wrong. My whole visit here.

JIMMY—Has this anything to do with Neil?

RHODA—No. It hasn't anything to do with anyone—except myself. I'm disgusted with myself from every point of view. I'm nothing like the kind of person that I thought I was, and I don't like what I turn out to be—*at all*. I'm not even a lady!

JIMMY (*impatiently*)—Oh, what rubbish!

RHODA—No, it's true. I can't stay here. I booked my passage this afternoon—sailing next week on the *Baltic*. I'll get around to all the necessary lies and arrangements with Aunt Lucy later. I shall probably have a bad cold between now and leaving.

JIMMY—Mother's not sending you home?

RHODA—No, but she won't stop me going.

JIMMY—But it's ridiculous. I don't want you to go. God knows when we'll meet again. And just now when I'm suddenly seeing you quite differently for the first time . . . (*She looks up.*) You know it's crazy the way we've always been brought up as—brother and sister, almost . . . It's stopped our ever seeing each other as anything else. At least, it's stopped me— till now.

RHODA—Why now?

JIMMY—I don't know. I guess because—the wrapping's changed.

RHODA (*bewildered*)—What?

JIMMY—I've always taken you so completely for granted. But now, if you wouldn't go . . .

RHODA—What do you mean—"If I wouldn't go?"

JIMMY—Well, I'd kinda like to start off on a different foot, if that wouldn't seem too silly to you. Oh, I know you've never thought of me that way. I wouldn't know how to make myself romantic to you, but—that's what you've become to me. (*Looking at her and speaking with a kind of surprised puzzlement.*) I've always known you had all the other things, but I never realized before that you're really very attractive, too. You're the kind of girl I want to marry.

RHODA (*suddenly, after one perfect moment*)—Jimmy, who put you up to this?

JIMMY—No one. I just think I've been completely blind, that's all.

RHODA—No one's said anything?

JIMMY—Do you mean Mother? Oh, she's often hinted . . . I know she'd like us to get married.

RHODA—Not any more.

JIMMY—Oh, she'd get over that, if we did. (*Solemnly.*) I'll help you live the scandal down.

RHODA (*with a mild case of hysterics, half-laughing, half-crying*)—Oh, Jimmy.

JIMMY (*alarmed*)—What's the matter?

RHODA—You've such a passion for tarnished women!

JIMMY—That's a hell of a thing to say—now. (*He turns away, a little hurt and sulky.*)

RHODA (*coaxingly*)—Jimmy, I don't mind. It's rather nice to be . . . tinsel, for once. (*He starts back toward her, but is stopped by the entrance of* NORA, *with the lace teacloth. She goes over to the table, places it and lays the cloth.*) Oh, here's tea. Good! (*She resumes her tapestry.*)

JIMMY (*in Cockney tones, referring to the tapestry*)—'Ow's Grandma Meldrum coming on?

RHODA (*also Cockney*)—Well, I was thinking. 'Er eyesight ain't what it used to be. If I was to buy 'er a piece, I don't think she'd know no different. And (*in her own voice*) I could give this up—if you really hate it.

NORA—Will Miss Longstreth be here for tea, Mr. Jimmy?

JIMMY—Oh—er—no, Nora. No, she won't.

NORA—It'll be just five cups, then. (*She goes out for the tray.*)

JIMMY—I do wish I knew what your row with Calla was about.

RHODA—That, Jimmy, is something that I'll never tell you.

JIMMY—Not even when we're married?

RHODA (*smiling at him*)—Not even when we're married!

THE CURTAIN FALLS

KISS AND TELL

A Comedy in Three Acts

By F. Hugh Herbert

THERE is always something exciting about an overnight hit on Broadway. It is the sort of theatre-going adventure that expands the somewhat romanticized legend of the first night and its brilliant audience. There are dozens of first nights that are no more exciting in the Broadway theatre than they would be anywhere else in the country; dull performances of dull plays, from which both the paying patrons and the invited critics exit wearily.

But two or three, or four or six, times a season the play is right, the cast is right, the audience is right and all is right as right can be. Then the lobby and sidewalk chatter takes on an exuberant tone; eyes sparkle with a happy enthusiasm, and the meanest critics dash away to tell gustily their versions of the felicitous event.

The F. Hugh Herbert comedy, "Kiss and Tell," gave such an evening to this season of 1942-43, when George Abbott brought it to production in mid-March. In fact, before that there was no doubt in the minds of any who had had close association with the play of its ultimate success.

"I couldn't tell what some of the critics might think of it," said Jessie Royce Landis, who was one of the first to read the script and was quick to accept an invitation to play a leading part. "There might be critics who would not like it. But I was as sure the public would like it as I was sure of anything in this world."

So sure was Miss Landis, in fact, that she insisted on buying a small interest in the play, which Mr. Abbott obligingly sold her. There will be three companies playing "Kiss and Tell" the season of 1943-44, so Miss Landis is quite happy. A fortune teller promised her she would be, she admits.

The production of this comedy was also a pleasantly different experience for the author, F. Hugh Herbert. He had been in Hollywood writing scenarios and radio scripts. It was from one of the latter that the character of Corliss Archer, the heroine, emerged. Mr. Herbert wrote the comedy, sent it on to Mr.

Abbott and prepared to wait at least a reasonable two or three months before hearing anything from it.

Mr. Abbott read the script the night it came in; wired his acceptance next day and asked Mr. Herbert when he thought he could be in New York. Mr. Herbert thought it might take him a week but not longer. Which is how it happens once in a blue moon. Now to the play:

The Harry Archers' back porch has grown from a deck with an awning into what is practically a large, irregular room. There is a substantial roof over it and a high wall of large clapboards extends around it. The outside stairs lead to the upper floor, and the door from the back of the house serves as a general entrance. There is a screen door letting into a garden at the side. The room is comfortably furnished with leftover things from the main house. These include a glider, a large sofa, two large wicker chairs and a wicker table. Back of the sofa there is a ping-pong table, with the paddles and balls in a rack on the house wall.

It is about 5 in the afternoon of a Summer's day and warm sunlight streams in from the garden. As we enter, Mr. Willard, a house painter, "about sixty-five and in need of a shave," is at the top of a stepladder painting the ceiling.

Louise, "a stocky, forthright woman who has been in the employ of the Archers for seventeen years," leaves the kitchen long enough to suggest that the color Mr. Willard is using is too light, but Mr. Willard is in no way disturbed by the criticism. He is used to criticism. Neither is he worried when Louise finds a speck of paint on the sofa. "Anything short of a nest of field mice in that sofa is so much velvet," in Mr. Willard's estimation.

Corliss Archer, "a slim, very pretty girl, quite mature for her fifteen and a half years," comes from the house. She, too, has a shot at Mr. Willard's job. It seems to her that the shade is a trifle dark. Mr. Willard doesn't think much of that criticism, either.

Corliss has run upstairs when Raymond Pringle appears from the garden. Raymond is "about twelve, neatly dressed, well-groomed and intelligent." He comes from down the street a couple of blocks, he tells Mr. Willard, and while he has no criticism to offer of the shade being applied to the porch ceiling, he does think it will need another coat to cover the stain. Neither does Raymond approve of the kind of paint being used. "It has a very poor rating by *Consumer's Digest*," he says.

"By what?"

"Consumer's Digest. That's a wonderful magazine that tells you what stinks and what doesn't."

Raymond has come to make sure that the Archer coast is clear before he signals to his sister Mildred to follow. Now Mildred comes through the garden. She is an attractive young woman of eighteen, and anxious to see Corliss. The cause of her anxiety appears as soon as they are able to get rid of the pestiferous Raymond. Mildred wants to know what Corliss knows about Corliss' brother Lenny.

"He'll be here tomorrow," reports Corliss.

"Gosh, how wonderful! Aren't you thrilled to tears?"

"Uh-huh. You know it's funny. I suppose it's the war. If anyone had suggested to me a year ago that I'd be thrilled to death to see my own brother—I'd have said they were nuts."

"What about me? He isn't even my brother."

"I wonder what Lenny'll think about this family feud?" Corliss wonders.

"Does he have to know?"

"He'll find out, won't he? Your parents won't be invited to dinner—and we won't be invited to your house."

"My goodness, we didn't do anything so terrible."

"Well—my parents thought it was. It's different with you—after all, you're practically eighteen—and you're allowed to smoke and everything, but I'm not sixteen yet—even though I do look much older than you, sometimes."

"Gosh, can't they see it was only patriotism made us do it? After all, we did raise gobs of dough—more than any of the other concessions."

"I know—but Mother said it was simply outrageous for a girl my age to be selling kisses at a Red Cross Bazaar—and Daddy hit the ceiling—and so now, of course—(*Looking at* Mildred.) —you're a bad influence."

"Do your parents really think I'm a bad influence?"

"They think you put ideas in my head. Ever since I had to wear brassières my family's been watching me like a couple of hawks. (*Thoughtfully.*) Mildred, isn't it amazing how things happen? One minute Lenny's just my big brother and a pain in the neck—and then suddenly—boom—we're all grown up, and he's a lieutenant in the Army Air Corps and smokes a pipe without looking silly—and writes the most beautiful letters."

There is a call for Corliss from a garden two backyards removed from the Archers'. It comes from Dexter Franklin, and irritates Corliss considerably. "Honestly, the way that boy pesters me!" She sighs heavily, and would send Dexter away. But it's no use. Dexter is there before she can say anything. Dexter "is about seventeen, freckled, gawky, but a rather engaging youth." He is carrying a lug of vegetables and is extremely dirty.

The girls would go on with their talking, suggesting that Dexter run along, but Dexter is not impressed. "Thinking up some other ways to sell more kisses?" he sneers. "I never was so humiliated in my life."

"You? What's it got to do with you?" demands Mildred.

"When you've lived next door to a person all your life and seen them grow up, you don't like to see them exposed to evil influences."

"Tell the repulsive little drip to go away," insists Mildred.

"Uniform crazy—that's what you are—and you're doing your best to make Corliss that way, too. I agree with the Archers one hundred per cent," Dexter adds, pontifically. "I think you're a very bad influence."

Mildred and Raymond have gone home. Dexter is relieved. He doesn't like Mildred's snooping around, and Corliss resents Dexter's saying such things. Furthermore he is not to say one thing to Lenny about what has happened. "It is absolutely imperatable that he doesn't know," insists Corliss, dramatically.

"You mean imperative."

CORLISS—I mean you're to shut up!

DEXTER—I shall make a point of telling him personally.

CORLISS—Dexter Franklin! You're about as low and vile a person as ever I laid eyes on. I'll thank you to just get up and go home and stay home! And I'll thank you to never show your silly face here again.

DEXTER—Tut—Tut! You get that from Mildred, too. She's got a temper like a fishwife.

CORLISS (*realizing her rage is getting her nowhere and trying another tack*)—Dexter—don't say things like that. It hurts me. I can't bear it when my friends don't like each other.

DEXTER—I've got nothing against Mildred personally except that she's a lousy influence.

CORLISS—Dexter—would you like to do me a great favor?

DEXTER (*soulfully*)—I'd do anything for you, Corliss. You know I would.

CORLISS—Do you mean that, Dexter?

DEXTER—Holy cow, haven't I always? When you put that dead fish in my mother's lingerie drawer—who took the blame?

CORLISS—That was when we were just kids.

DEXTER—Well—don't you believe I'd do more for you now —the way I feel about you now?

CORLISS (*wistfuly*)—How could I be sure?

DEXTER—Just ask me. There's nothing I wouldn't do for you.

CORLISS—Then will you promise not to tell Lenny? I know it was silly of us, Dexter—but, my goodness, there's been such a stink about it already, we don't want to spoil Lenny's leave, do we? Please, Dexter—promise you won't tell?

DEXTER—Okay. I promise.

CORLISS (*patting his cheek*)—You're nice.

DEXTER—On one condition.

CORLISS—What's that?

DEXTER (*vaguely*)—Oh, it's nothing you've got to do right now—immediately. It's just—just what we've been talking about. You know what I mean.

CORLISS (*turning to him*)—Well, is there any harm in telling me?

DEXTER (*wailing*)—Don't make me go through it all again, Corliss. You know what I mean. After all, I will be eighteen some day.

CORLISS (*enjoying herself*)—Are you proposing to me, Dexter?

DEXTER—Don't kid about it, Corliss. I know it sounds funny when all I've got is an allowance of fifty cents a week—but it isn't funny to me. (*Soberly.*) I'm only asking you to wait for me.

CORLISS (*very sweetly*)—All right, Dexter. I'll wait.

DEXTER—Gosh, Corliss—you're swell. (*A deep gulp.*) And look, Corliss—I don't want to bring up a sore subject—but will you promise me something else?

CORLISS—What?

DEXTER—Well—I know how patriotic you really are, and all that—and guys in uniform probably do look romantic to a girl —but—well, I wish—

CORLISS—Dexter—you're crazy. A uniform means nothing to me. I can take it or leave it.

DEXTER—Well, just as a favor to me—leave it, will you?

CORLISS—I'm used to uniforms in my family. I mean—look at Uncle George—he was in the Navy before I was born.

DEXTER—Believe me, I'm not worrying about Uncle George. (*He kisses her on the cheek—she draws away and giggles.*)

CORLISS (*as the front door slams*)—That's Mother and Daddy.

Do you want them to find us necking?

DEXTER (*making for the screen door*)—Gosh, no, don't forget we're going to a movie tonight after dinner—

CORLISS—Okay.

Mrs. Archer comes through the house, her arms filled with bundles. "She is in her early forties and quite attractive." She greets her daughter affectionately, puts her parcels on the table and announces that there is to be company for dinner. The Archers had picked up a young soldier who was thumbing a ride and, out of a clear sky, Mr. Archer had invited him to dinner. He turned out to be Pvt. Earhart of the Tank Corps.

Corliss is all excitement. What's the soldier like? Is he good-looking? Is he— Mr. Archer and Pvt. Earhart are there. "Archer is in his late forties. Earhart is a handsome-looking boy of about twenty-four. He wears a fairly well-fitting G.I. uniform. He is well educated, has great charm and is thoroughly at ease."

"Yes," Archer is saying, "this used to be just a deck with an awning but we've built on to it in dribs and drabs over a period of years—and now we like it so much, we practically live out here."

Corliss has looked the soldier over and is thoroughly satisfied. She greets her father with an excess of affection that might easily be interpreted as an act for the stranger's benefit, and she accepts the introduction demurely.

"You don't have to call her Miss Archer. She's only—"

But Corliss stops that. "Daddy, darling, you don't have to give him my life history. (*To* PVT. EARHART.) Aren't parents a scream, though? No matter how old you get, they still treat you like you were an infant."

"They're all the same," confides Pvt. Earhart, flatteringly. "It was all I could do to prevent my mother from writing to the top sergeant in my outfit telling him to be sure and see that Jimmy didn't get his feet wet."

"Oh, is your name Jimmy? That's one of my favorite names."

"I like the name Corliss, too."

Mr. and Mrs. Archer have exchanged amused glances, and Archer has taken Pvt. Earhart by the arm to lead him into the garden. "Oh, Mother, I like him!" Corliss announces, almost before the men are out of hearing. "He's so good-looking. He has eyes like Tyrone Power."

Furthermore it is Corliss' opinion that it is nothing short of a crime for her mother to feed leftovers to a man like that. Mrs. Archer is sure that what they have to offer will be better than sandwiches and coffee at the U.S.O., and that gives Corliss another idea. If Pvt. Earhart was going to the U.S.O. it would indicate that he hasn't a girl. And if he hasn't a girl— Look at her slacks! Aren't they awful! No shape left—

"Mother, have you told him how old I am?"

"No."

"Did Daddy tell him?"

"No—but he can see for himself, can't he?"

"Oh, Mother, you know very well I look at least two years older—but as a rule you and Daddy can never wait to tell people that I'm not sixteen yet and still a ninfant."

"An infant, Corliss, not a ninfant. I wish you wouldn't always run your words together."

Corliss ignores the correction and moves closer to her mother. "Does he have to know?" she asks, a little pleadingly.

"Darling—what difference does it make if he does know?"

"Oh, Mother, knowing a girl's right age affects a man's entire physiology."

"I think you mean psychology, don't you?"

"All right—but it makes all the difference in the world the way a man treats you—the way he even looks at you. Once in a while I like at least to be looked at as if I wasn't an infant."

"Oh, darling!" Mrs. Archer affectionately brushes the hair out of her daughter's eyes. "I wish you weren't in such a desperate hurry to grow up. You've got all your life ahead of you to do that in."

Then there is the question of cocktails. If her mother serves cocktails—Corliss realizes that she is too young to have one— but can't Louise pass them to her, so she can say she doesn't care for one? That, thinks Mrs. Archer, will be all right.

And that little bottle of perfume— "The answer is *no!*" announces Mrs. Archer before Corliss can finish.

"But gosh, Mom—that's a very girlish smell, honestly it is."

"Soap smells even more girlish," declares Mrs. Archer.

Mr. Archer and Pvt. Earhart are back from their tour of the garden, and Mr. Archer has gone into the house. Pvt. Earhart wants Corliss to know how grand he thinks her parents are. "I think it's simply swell of them to pick up a perfect stranger and bring him home to dinner."

"Oh, I do, too," agrees Corliss, offering him a cigarette. "I mean, I think it's swell they brought you."

No, Corliss will not smoke with him. She has been sort of tapering off since the doctor told her it was affecting her sinuses.

"I hear you have a brother in the service," Pvt. Earhart is saying.

"Yes. He's coming home on leave tomorrow. He's in the Air Corps. He's a lieutenant."

"That's swell. How old is he?"

"Oh—Lenny's in his twenties. He's just a few months older than I am."

"How few?"

"Oh, I forget. Three or four."

With an effort Pvt. Earhart suppresses his amusement. "I have a kid sister just going on fourteen," he says.

"Oh, my! They're cute at that age. I mean, you know, all legs and elbows." She is sprawling clumsily on the sofa. "We still have some faded old snapshots of me at that age and I'm a scream."

Pvt. Earhart grows expansive. Home atmosphere is the thing that soldiers miss most. No, he doesn't know many people in town. Not a soul in fact.

"That's terrible," sympathizes Corliss. "How do you spend your leaves?"

"I don't know. Mooch around. Go to the library. Go to a show."

"Alone?"

"Mostly. Sometimes with other fellows."

"Don't you have a girl?"

"Nope. Not even back home."

"Don't you like girls?"

Before he can answer, Mr. and Mrs. Archer are back and Jimmy is being taken to where he can wash up. Dinner is about ready.

"Mother, you know what that poor man said?" Corliss is greatly concerned. "He doesn't know a single girl in town that he can take to the movies. Isn't that pathetic?"

"Yes, dear—I know how your heart must bleed for him, but no dates until you're at least sixteen. That's final."

"My gosh! No perfume—no rouge—no cocktails—no dates— I might as well be living in a monastery."

"God help the monastery that takes you in!" This from Mr. Archer, who is promptly rebuked by Mrs. Archer.

Louise has called them in. "Go easy on the celery," she cautions as the Archers pass her in the doorway.

The curtain falls.

An hour and a half later, Corliss and Pvt. Earhart are back on the porch and in the midst of a furious game of ping-pong. Corliss, as Pvt. Earhart admits, is beating the pants off him. Nineteen-four the game stands, in her favor.

Presently the Archers, carrying their demi-tasse cups, come from the dining room. Between volleys Corliss archly suggests that the porch is much too drafty for her mother and, as for her father, it is plain to see that he isn't at all comfortable. But Father and Mother insist on sticking it out.

"Your serve, honey," Jimmy is saying. "Nice try, Jimmy," Corliss counters, gaily, as she puts across the winning shot.

They decide to change ends for the next game. Corliss is more used to avoiding the stairs on which Jimmy constantly bumps his head. There is a whispered conference between the Archers, and this is followed by a suggestion from Mrs. Archer that, seeing it is Saturday night, Pvt. Earhart doubtless has other things to do in town.

"You don't have to be polite, Earhart," adds Mr. A. "Don't feel obligated because you shared our meat loaf and lamb chops."

But Pvt. Earhart is perfectly comfortable. "You're both awfully kind," he tells them. "But honestly I'm having a swell time here. If I did go to town, I'd only bum around with nothing to do."

"You see?" Corliss is a little exultant. "All right, Jimmy, here we go." As she picks up a ping-pong ball from the floor and hands it to Jimmy "she lets her hand linger on his longer than a young gal should."

The game goes on, but not for long. Mrs. Archer decides suddenly that it *is* a little chilly on the porch and asks Corliss to run upstairs and get her a scarf or something. Corliss doesn't want to run anywhere, except around the ping-pong table. Mr. Archer offers to go, but Mrs. Archer is insistent. Corliss is the only one who knows where the scarfs are. It is a contest, but Corliss gives up finally and dashes up the stairs.

"Your daughter plays a swell game," admits Pvt. Earhart.

"Yes. We think she does—for a youngster of fifteen," gently agrees Mrs. Archer.

"Oh, come—give her a break—she is going on sixteen." This from Mr. Archer.

"They're so funny at that age. My kid sister's about eighteen months younger than Corliss, but she tries to be just as grown up, too."

"Really."

"Lipstick, scarlet nails, permanents—all the works."

"Corliss' one ambition is to be taken for nineteen and considered sophisticated."

"I know—she's cute."

"Don't tell her you know how old she is. We're supposed to be under oath not to reveal it."

"I'll treat her as if she were all of twenty."

Corliss comes bounding down the stairs with her mother's scarf. She has taken time to change her slacks for a pair of bright shorts. A suspicious sniff of her mother's nostrils convinces her that her child has also been dipping into the perfume.

Corliss and her soldier have just resumed their game when there is a wild call from the next yard. That would be Dexter, but Corliss pretends not to hear. Not until the family and Pvt. Earhart as well call her attention to what her father describes as Dexter's mating call does Corliss acknowledge it. Even after Dexter follows the call she would suppress him with a look if she could. Certainly she has no recollection of a date to go to the movies with Dexter—

"My gosh, why do you have to put on a corny act all the time?" Dexter is quite disgusted.

"I'll thank you to go home and leave people alone," says Corliss, with dignity.

"Don't be a drip!"

Mr. Archer has a solution. Why shouldn't they all go to the movies? They should and do. The Archers and Pvt. Earhart go on ahead. Dexter waits for Corliss to change back to slacks.

"Fine thing!" exclaims Dexter as Corliss starts up the stairs. "The moment my back is turned and there's a uniform around—"

"I hate you. I hate you with all my heart and soul." Corliss' voice is cold with venom. "I shall hate you until the day I die."

"Don't be a drip! Who is he anyway?"

"He's just a soldier that Mother picked up."

"Holy cow! I didn't think she'd do things like that." Corliss has disappeared up the stairs.

Raymond Pringle comes through the garden. He isn't supposed to be there, he explains to Dexter, on account of the Pringle-Archer feud, which Raymond thinks is dumb. But he would like to do a little business with Louise. Raymond has a new cleaning fluid, which he is prepared to sell at bargain prices, if Louise is interested. Louise isn't.

It's all right about their going to the movies. Raymond wouldn't be interested in a picture with Hedy Lamarr and Veronica Lake in it. "I'm afraid I'm still too young to get a kick out of glamor," says Raymond. "Give me a good documentary film any time. . . ."

Lenny Archer has arrived unexpectedly. "He is a very good-looking boy of twenty-one, wearing the uniform of a lieutenant in the Army Air Corps." Lenny had flown in and had had a snack on the plane. But he could still do with a cup of coffee and some of Louise's cookies. He would also like to know the family news. How's Mildred? Is she home?

RAYMOND—I haven't the foggiest idea.

LENNY—Well, was she home for dinner?

RAYMOND—Probably. I took pot luck with some friends.

LENNY—Well, don't you know where she is?

RAYMOND—Nope. Live and let live—that's my motto.

LENNY—I think I'll run over and say hello to your folks.

RAYMOND—Well, Lenny, you can suit yourself, of course, but I'd advise you to check with your folks first.

LENNY (*puzzled*)—What do you mean?

RAYMOND—Well, if you must know—Corliss and Mildred aren't even allowed to see each other.

LENNY—Why?

RAYMOND—Maybe they'd better tell you. I think it's too dumb for words.

LENNY—Are your parents home?

RAYMOND—Yes.

LENNY—Then I'll go right down and ask them what it's all about.

RAYMOND—Look, Lenny—you're a very fine pilot and all that, but I know more about family quarrels than you do.

LENNY—But what's it all about? There must be some reason.

RAYMOND—There is—and it's dumb.

LENNY—But I can't understand it. I've been writing to Mildred nearly every day and—

RAYMOND—Oh—are those letters from you? She sleeps with them under her pillow.

Lenny—She does?

Raymond—And she's the girl who ground up some glass to put in your cereal one time. (*Holding his hands up.*) Time marches on!

Lenny—Listen, kid—call up your house and see if she's home.

Raymond (*dialing*)—Okay.

Lenny—And if she is—don't tell her I'm here—but tell her to— Wonder where I'd better meet her?

Raymond—Oh, it's all right. She can come here when there's nobody home. Louise thinks it's dumb, too.

Lenny—Okay—but don't tell her I'm here, see? I want to surprise her.

Raymond—Have you really got a case on Mildred?

Lenny—More than that.

Raymond—Well, she is pretty, I admit—but intellectually, she's a goon.

Lenny—Look, Raymond—I don't want any trouble with you because of what I told you.

Raymond—You mean kid brother stuff? You've been seeing too many B pictures. (*Into the phone.*) Hello. Hello, Mildred.

Lenny—Don't tell her I'm here.

Raymond (*whispering*)—Go away. Let me handle this. (*Into phone.*) I'm over at the Archers'. Corliss wants to talk to you. No—they're all out. What? Oh, my gosh—tell Mother you're going out to mail a letter. Do I have to think of everything? All right. Well, make it snappy. (*Looks at* Lenny *and hangs up.*)

Lenny (*taking coin from pocket*)—Is she coming?

Raymond—She'll be here in a minute. (*Bluntly.*) I suppose you want me to leave.

Lenny (*grinning*)—That's not a bad idea. (*He flips the half dollar up and down.*)

Raymond (*calmly*)—Are you flipping that just because you're nervous, or do you want to give it to me? (*With a laugh* Lenny *tosses it to him.*) I was going anyway, but it's very nice of you all the same. Thanks, Lenny.

Mildred Pringle has come quickly through the garden. Lenny is hiding back of the sofa. She calls Corliss and then turns to find Lenny standing before her. The next minute they are in each other's arms. Their greeting is ardent. Why hadn't he let them know he was coming? And why does he fly when the train is safer?

"I'll take it up with General Arnold," Lenny promises. "He's an old-fashioned man, though—he thinks pilots should fly."

And now Lenny must know all about the feud and what started it. "Well, darling," Mildred begins, "Corliss and I cooked up a nice white lie for you—but maybe I'd better tell you the truth. It's all very silly—and very simple. We had a Red Cross Bazaar here about a month ago—and we sold kisses at a dollar each for the Red Cross—Corliss sold more than I did and when your parents found out about—you see, we told them we were going to sell embroidered guest towels—well, when they found out about it, they threw fifteen different kinds of fits— and they decided I was a very bad influence on Corliss—and that made my parents sore—and that's all."

"Well, I'll be damned!"

"Are you shocked?"

"No. Of course not—but it's a strange feeling to realize that men would actually pay good money to kiss your kid sister. (*Skeptically.*) Did she really sell more than you? At a dollar?"

"Yes, but she was letting them have a second one at fifty cents. Well, you see, I didn't know about that cut-rate business. Honestly, Lenny, we cleaned up."

"You beautiful screwball!"

"Try and patch things up, Lenny, will you? The way it is now your parents think I contaminate Corliss."

Lenny laughs at that. "Just one minute and you can contaminate *me*," he says, taking her in his arms and kissing her good and hard.

Everything's wonderful, but there is bad news to come. Lenny's leave has been cut to seventy-two hours. For a little Mildred is stunned. That might mean that the army is planning to send Lenny overseas. Mildred just can't let him go—

"That's what millions of girls all over the world are saying and there isn't a thing they can do about it, Baby. (*Grinning.*) Correction. I take that back. There *is* something they can do about it."

"What?"

LENNY (*walking over to her and taking her by both hands*)— Darling—do you know of any good reason why two people who are nuts about each other should wait? Let's get married right away.

MILDRED—You mean—now?

LENNY (*laughing*)—Well, no, not this second. I'd imagine we'd have to find a justice or something on that order. (*Kissing her.*) How about it? Let's get married right away. Huh?

MILDRED—Oh, Lenny—I'd love to more than anything, but they'd never let me. My parents, I mean. They don't even dream that we feel this way about each other. Or that we've been writing so often—or anything.

LENNY—Honey, I'm not suggesting a formal wedding with engraved invitations and rice. I—

MILDRED—But, Lenny—

LENNY—I've got just 72 hours left, darling. I'm suggesting an immediate Grade A Number One elopement.

MILDRED—But what about my parents?

LENNY (*eagerly*)—Let's not tell them.

MILDRED—But what about your parents, Lenny?

LENNY—Have you got a parent complex or something? After all, it's nobody's business but ours, is it?

MILDRED—Oh, Lenny—I'd love to—but your mother and father think I'm terrible.

LENNY—They're not marrying you. I am.

MILDRED—I'm afraid they won't want me as an in-law. Honestly, Lenny, it's tough enough for a girl when a boy's parents like her. There's always a little resentment.

LENNY (*embracing her*)—Darling, you're nuts. They'll be crazy about you—and we'll keep it a secret until they've forgotten all about this silly row. (*Urgently.*) Will you, Mildred? Then, no matter what happens, we'll at least have belonged to each other for a little while. Will you, Mildred?

MILDRED (*gravely*)—All right, Lenny. Let's. (*With a whoop of joy he practically picks her up in his arms and loves her.*) I think we're both a little crazy—but it's wonderful.

Raymond has appeared outside the screen door. For a moment he observes closely, then he coughs loudly. Mildred and Lenny jump apart. What does Raymond mean? He promised to stay away. Raymond can't help himself. Mrs. Pringle is on the war path. Raymond had told her that Mildred was at the Red Cross rolling bandages, and she had insisted that he should bring her home right away.

"If you two want to say good night—it's nice and dark in the garden," suggests Raymond. "I've no objection to waiting a minute or two."

Louise has come to clear the table. Raymond explains about Lenny and Mildred. "They're both all a-twitter," he sneers. "I think it's dumb."

"You'll think different when you're a little older," ventures Louise.

"I suppose. That's what often depresses me. (*Drinks coffee in cup.*) Louise, I'll be glad when I get old enough to drink coffee. I'm very fond of it. Maybe it's because I'm her brother, Louise, but I don't know what he sees in that girl. (*Barging into the garden.*) Okay. Break it up!"

The curtain falls.

ACT II

The next day is Sunday. The Archers are variously disposed. Corliss is washing Marchbanks, the family spaniel. Mr. Archer, with a couple of Sunday papers, has come to the porch to make himself a drink. It would be a good thing for them both if he would take Marchbanks for a walk, thinks Corliss, but nothing is farther from Mr. Archer's intention.

Lenny, it appears, has been away all day. He may be seeing friends, but so many of them have phoned to ask for him that that doesn't seem likely to Mrs. Archer.

"I had breakfast with Lenny, Mother—and he knows all about that silly Pringle feud," Corliss is saying. "He only laughed. He didn't think it was anything grisly."

"Some day he'll have a fifteen-year-old daughter—and then he won't laugh."

Outside there is the honk of a jeep. A moment later Pvt. Earhart has appeared in the door, a large box of candy under his arm. Corliss is quick to spy both Jimmy and the candy.

Pvt. Earhart is on his way back to camp with a jeep full of men. He couldn't withstand the temptation to drop in and again thank them for the swell time they had given him. Neither he nor the others could possibly stay to Sunday dinner, as Mr. Archer suggests, a little to Mrs. Archer's dismay; they have to be in camp by 7 P.M. sharp. But, personally, Pvt. Earhart would like to take a rain check on the invitation. "Any time you're in town just give us a ring," beams Mr. Archer. And when Corliss has gone to the door with the soldier, he adds: "Nice boy, that."

"Yes. I wonder if he came by just to say thank you—or to see Corliss?" ponders Mrs. Archer, thoughtfully.

MR. ARCHER—Don't be silly—she's just a child and he knows it. She probably reminds him of his kid sister.

MRS. ARCHER—Possibly. But they *were* holding hands at the movie last night.

MR. ARCHER—They were? Why—the little devil. Are you sure? I know she was holding hands with Dexter, because I saw them. I sat next to Dexter. (*Rather smugly.*) I'm beginning to suspect that our dear little daughter has a streak of bitchiness in her that's all wool and a yard wide.

MRS. ARCHER—I wouldn't be so proud of it if I were you. Besides, that's a terrible word.

MR. ARCHER—Okay. Let's call it femininity, then. Like that better?

MRS. ARCHER—I wasn't going to say anything about it to you —but since the little return visit—I'm rather worried. (*She puts her paper down.*) Corliss is—well, she's really very pretty, and quite mature for her years—and I'd hate to have her start a silly flirtation with this boy.

MR. ARCHER—That's simple enough. The next time he calls —you just tell him Corliss is out.

CORLISS (*coming from hall*)—Look, Mother—isn't he a lamb? He brought this for me! (*Opening candy-box.*) Oh, boy— chocolate-covered nuts! Two pounds! (*Offers candy to her mother.*)

MRS. ARCHER—No, thanks.

CORLISS—Wasn't that darling of him? (*She offers the box to her father and munches a large piece of candy happily.*) And he said the loveliest things about you two. He thought you were awfully pretty, Mother, and could easily be my older sister. And he said Daddy was very distinguished looking.

MRS. ARCHER—Darling—don't ruin your appetite for supper.

CORLISS—I won't. You know, Mother—we really should have offered to put Jimmy up for last night. D'you know where that poor boy slept? At the Y.M.C.A.

MR. ARCHER—Why not? He's young, manly and Christian, isn't he?

CORLISS—He said he was very lonely.

MRS. ARCHER—He did!

CORLISS—Mother—when he gets leave again, will you ask him to spend the night?

MR. ARCHER—Maybe you'd like us to adopt him?

CORLISS (*rolling her eyes*)—Oh, boy!

MRS. ARCHER—Corliss—don't be vulgar. Harry, must you encourage her?

CORLISS—You know—when he smiles his eyes twinkle just like Don Ameche's.

Mary Franklin, Dexter's mother, has dropped in from next door, followed shortly by Mr. Franklin. Mrs. Franklin brings her knitting and Mr. Franklin brings a bit of gossip that has turned out to be true. He has to wait until Corliss goes to tell Dexter his mother wants him before he can tell it.

"Listen! Know what we just heard? It's true about the little Hoffman girl," says Mr. Franklin. When they have absorbed that shock he continues: "She's going to have a baby—and the only thing they can do is get her married to the boy right away. He didn't know how young she was. She swore she was eighteen and he believed her, or says he did."

"You see?" Mrs. Archer is looking intently at her husband. "You see how frightfully—(*Moves closer to* MR. ARCHER)—important it is to see that Corliss is held down? Janie Hoffman's younger even than Corliss. She was a grade lower in school."

"Yes—but she was always kind of wild."

"Background's got something to do with it, too," says Mrs. Franklin.

"Boy—am I glad Dexter isn't a girl!" explodes Dexter's father.

"There are times these days when I wish he were."

"If Dexter were a girl—sentimental sap that he is—you'd be an illegitimate grandmother right now."

"That's a fine thing to say about your own son."

Corliss is back and Dexter is with her. It doesn't take Dexter long to spy Corliss' chocolate-covered nuts, but the joy of the discovery vanishes when he learns who had given them to Corliss. Pvt. Earhart, eh?

"Well, all I can say is that you should've flung 'em in his face," declares Dexter, putting back those he had taken. "Don't you know anything about life?" His voice is breaking with emotion. "You accept a huge box of candy like this from a perfect stranger—a soldier who is supposed to respect womanhood—and what happens next?"

"Don't get so excited, Dexter," warns Mr. Franklin.

"Holy cow, Dad—wouldn't you get burned up if Mother took valuable gifts from strange soldiers?"

"Jimmy spoke very nicely about you, Dexter," purrs Corliss, starting up the stairs. "Yes—he said, 'Please remember me to that amusing little boy from next door.'" With that she darts up the stairs, leaving Dexter seething with rage.

"Dexter—if you ever want to throttle her with your bare hands, I'll defend you free of charge," promises Mr. Archer.

"Yeah, and I'd be acquitted," declares Dexter, barging into the garden.

Corliss and Dexter are sweet, their mothers are agreed. Dexter is crazy about Corliss, and Corliss torments the life out of him. But they can be nice to each other, too. Mrs. Franklin can remember the time when they were always fighting whenever she came suddenly upon them. Now she frequently catches them holding hands and kissing. Which worries Mrs. Archer a little.

Lenny is home. He has, he admits non-committally, been driving the car all over the map. Called on one or two friends. Ran into Mr. and Mrs. Pringle among others. Invited them over, but they suggested that he had better check with his mother before he started issuing invitations. The whole thing is pretty silly to Lenny, a sentiment with which Corliss agrees when she rejoins them.

But now there is some disturbance outside and Louise is in to announce that Mrs. Pringle herself is calling. She would like to see Mrs. Archer. The next minute Mrs. Pringle comes briskly in, followed by a protesting Raymond. Mrs. Pringle "is a smartly dressed, pretty woman, and is in a towering rage."

"I'm sorry to come barging in like this, Janet, in view of everything—but there are some things that I cannot ignore." It is plain Mrs. Pringle is making an effort to control herself.

The Franklins think that perhaps they should be going, but Mrs. Pringle insists that they should stay. She wants the whole thing thrashed out. "I am just so furious I could chew nails," Mrs. Pringle admits, pushing Raymond in front of her and demanding that he tell them all that he had told her. Raymond would have preferred not to speak, but does get as far as a visit to the Campbells', where he was trying to sell the cook a magazine subscription. At this point his impatient mother takes the story away from him—

"According to Raymond, who distinctly overheard it from the kitchen," charges Mrs. Pringle, "Marjorie Campbell was telling her bridge club that you (*An accusing finger at* Mrs. Archer) had said to her that Mildred, *my daughter*, was nothing better than a little tramp."

"How ridiculous!" answers Mrs. Archer, indignantly. "I never said anything of the sort. It's a word I never use."

Mrs. Pringle—Raymond—was that the word you heard?

Raymond (*uneasily*)—Well—it sounded like—(*A happy thought.*)—but it could have been scamp.

Mrs. Pringle—Don't quibble, Raymond. You told me it was tramp, and you even asked me whether I thought Mildred was a tramp.

Mrs. Franklin—Dorothy, I'm surprised at you. Listening to garbled gossip. I'm quite sure Janet would never say such a thing.

Mrs. Pringle—Kindly keep out of this, Mary. I'm talking to Janet.

Mr. Franklin (*angrily*)—Wait a minute—we wanted to beat it, and you asked us to stay. Seems to me she's got a right to put in her two-bits worth.

Raymond—I think it's very dumb.

Mrs. Pringle (*turning on him*)—You keep quiet. You think everything's dumb.

Raymond—It's my experience that most things are.

Mrs. Pringle—And furthermore, Amy Barker's laundress overheard a long conversation—

Raymond (*interrupting*)—Mother—that laundress is not reliable.

Mrs. Pringle—What do you know about it?

Raymond—She signed an order for some soap and then welshed on the deal, and I got stuck.

Lenny (*amiably*)—May I make a suggestion?

Mrs. Pringle (*coldly*)—By all means.

Lenny (*lightly*)—This whole feud is too silly for words—and you're never going to get anywhere by hashing the whole thing over. Bury the hatchet—and forget it.

Corliss—I think that's a wonderful idea. Don't you, Dexter?

Dexter (*thoughtfully*)—Well—I'd never go so far as to say Mildred's exactly a tramp—but I do think she's a bad influence.

Mrs. Pringle (*gasping*)—Well!

Raymond—Here we go again.

Corliss (*to* Dexter—*furiously*)—Why can't you keep your big trap shut?

Dexter—You asked me, didn't you? I only—

Mrs. Pringle (*icily*)—You've said quite enough. I can see where the entire neighborhood is being influenced and prejudiced against Mildred—and that's perfectly all right with me. I can only say that I'm very sorry that a friendship of so many years should come to an end like this.

LENNY (*anxiously*)—Don't fly off the handle, Mrs. Pringle. You were laughing about it this morning when I—

MRS. PRINGLE—That was before Raymond had repeated to me the outrageous things your mother—had said.

MRS. ARCHER—Now wait a minute, Dorothy.

MRS. PRINGLE—It's no use, Janet. I'm never going to set foot in your house again, and I shall forbid both Mildred and Raymond to do so. And Corliss will no longer be welcome at my house, nor will Lenny. Come, Raymond.

In the recapitulation, after Mrs. Pringle and Raymond have disappeared, Mrs. Archer again is sure that she said nothing like what she is charged with. "I said—and I'm perfectly willing to repeat it—that with so many silly, uniform-crazy girls around these days—a great many of them turning into little tramps— I'd be just as happy if Corliss saw as little as possible of Mildred."

"You seem to have said quite a mouthful," ventures Mr. Franklin.

Now the Archers and the Franklins have gone and Lenny has sent Dexter home. That attended to, he turns on Corliss. She certainly has helped to gum things up. Corliss would tearfully explain that she's done nothing wrong, when Raymond comes stealthily back, hoping to straighten things out

"Get out of here—you filthy, sneaking little spy," Corliss shouts at him.

"Mother's having hysterics, too," calmly reports Raymond. "Mildred's also crying her eyes out; and Pop's swearing to beat the band, words even I never heard before. (*Smugly.*) Yes, sir, over at the Pringles' hell's a'-poppin'."

"What's Mildred crying for?" Lenny is disturbed.

"Oh, they're picking on her."

"What about?"

"Well, it's really very funny. She was gone all day—and she won't say where she was—and now Pop's beginning to think maybe she *is* a little tramp after all."

Raymond suddenly remembers that he has brought Lenny a note from Mildred. "I doubt if it'll be very legible," he says. "She wrote it with purple ink and wept all over it."

The letter makes it imperative that Lenny should see Mildred. Raymond thinks perhaps he can fix that, too. He can get his people out of the house any time Lenny suggests.

"I'm an air raid messenger," Raymond explains, "and I'm on very good terms with the senior warden. I can have him call an 'incident' if you like."

" 'Incident?' "

"Yes. You know. We have 'em every now and then. An incendiary bomb is supposed to have fallen at the corner of Walnut and Main—that sort of stuff. Then all the wardens and first aiders have to troop out and rope off streets. Pop puts on his helmet and gas mask—blows his whistle and stops traffic. . . . Pop gets quite a kick out of it. (*Patronizingly.*) What time do you want me to fix it for you?"

"How about eight-thirty?"

"You can rely on it."

"Raymond—you're terrific."

"Oh, that's all right. I like 'incidents' myself. I buzz around on my bike and get a chance to boss people. Half the wardens in our zone are dopes, anyway. Well—so long."

Another complication arises. Corliss must know whether Lenny did spend the day with Mildred or not. Lenny wants to tell her, but doubts if she can keep a secret.

"I'll take an oath in blood—like we did when we were kids," promises Corliss, excitedly. "Will that satisfy you, Lenny? You know I never went back on that."

Lenny agrees to the oath and Corliss, finding a pin in her mother's work basket, pricks her finger and, with a few solemn passes, intones: "I swear in blood by everything I hold sacred that I will never reveal this secret." That done, she turns excitedly to her brother. "What is it, Lenny? Tell me."

LENNY—Mildred and I were married this morning.

CORLISS (*thrilled*)—Oh, Lenny! Does anyone know?

LENNY—Not a soul. We drove across the state line to Wyndham Ferry—dug up a justice of the peace—and he and his wife are the only ones who know—except you.

CORLISS—Aren't you going to tell Mother and Dad?

LENNY—Not until this row blows over. (*Producing the note from his pocket.*) We had planned to break it to them gently tonight—but now Mildred feels that her folks would move heaven and earth to get it annulled.

CORLISS—Could they?

LENNY (*ruefully*)—I guess they could. She lied about her age on the license. She won't be eighteen until next month.

CORLISS—Golly. Annulled. That'd be awful.

LENNY (*quietly*)—Awful is right.

CORLISS (*wonderingly*)—Gosh! That makes Mildred my sister-in-law.

LENNY (*indulgently*)—Uh huh.

CORLISS (*a sudden pleased smile*)—Oh, boy, now I won't have to pay her the forty-five cents I owe her. Relatives never pay up. Lenny, may I see what Mildred wrote?

LENNY—You may not.

CORLISS (*stroking his hair*)—Are you terribly in love?

LENNY—Well—we didn't get married just for the hell of it. This is for keeps.

CORLISS (*soberly*)—It oughtn't to be a secret, Lenny. Mom and Dad ought to know. Oh, they'd forget all about this row.

LENNY—Maybe. But that wasn't really what I was thinking about. What I mean is this—they always came first in everything, see—and now—well, it's only natural that if I go overseas, I'll be thinking of—(*A little hesitation—and then with great pride.*)—of my wife first—and it's only human for them to feel it. Know what I mean, Corliss?

CORLISS—I know what you mean, Lenny—but don't you think perhaps their feelings will be hurt more if you don't tell them about a terrific thing like getting married?

LENNY (*troubled*)—I don't know.

CORLISS (*sighing*)—Gosh, loving people makes life frightfully complicated, doesn't it?

LENNY (*putting his arm around her shoulder*)—You're not a bad little egg at that. I'm glad I told you.

CORLISS—I am, too. And very proud. That you trusted me, I mean.

LENNY—I'll see Mildred later this evening, and I'll tell her that you know. Then maybe between the three of us we can work out some way to let the others know before my leave is over.

CORLISS—Oh, I hope so, Lenny. It's such a tremendously important thing that I—

LENNY (*warningly*)—You took an oath in blood.

CORLISS—They could torture me and I wouldn't tell.

Now there is a further disturbance in the house, with the voices of Mr. and Mrs. Archer raised above normal pitch. Mrs. Archer keeps advising Mr. Archer to hold his handkerchief to his nose, while Mr. Archer continues to shout that he'll sue somebody, and have him arrested as well.

Presently the Archers come from the house. "Mr. Archer holds a bloody handkerchief to his nose and is extremely disheveled. There is a wide rip in one trouser leg. One eye is already beginning to close with the beginning of a magnificent shiner."

Mrs. Archer, and then the children, are excitedly solicitous. Let Corliss fetch ice cubes from the kitchen. Mrs. Archer will get him a drink. And let Mr. Archer try not to bleed on the Navajo rug!

"Mom, was he hit by a car?" Lenny would know.

"No! I was hit by Mr. Pringle—the dirty, cowardly rat! And I'll sue him if it's the last thing I do!" shouts Mr. Archer.

Corliss is back with the ice, followed by Louise. The excitement and the questions increase.

"Will someone please tell me what happened?" wails Corliss.

MRS. ARCHER (*to* CORLISS)—We were walking home past the Pringles' house, and they were in front—and we got into an argument—

MR. ARCHER—And without any warning the yellow coward socked me right in the nose.

MRS. ARCHER—You started it, Harry. You called him a vile name.

MR. ARCHER (*truculently*)—I did not. I called him a stupid son of a (MRS. ARCHER *tries to hush him.*) bitch—because he is a stupid son of a bitch.

MRS. ARCHER (*shocked, massages her neck*)—Harry! Please!

LOUISE (*grinning*)—That's telling 'em, Mr. Archer.

MR. ARCHER—Stop rattling that dishpan under my chin for God's sake—let me get to the phone.

LENNY—Wait until your nose stops bleeding, Dad.

MRS. ARCHER—What do you want the phone for? (CORLISS, *back of sofa, tries to put ice on his eye.*)

MR. ARCHER—I'm going to call the D.A.'s office and have him arrested for disturbing the peace and causing a riot.

CORLISS—Put this under your eye.

MR. ARCHER—He's not going to get away with this. No wonder Mildred's a bad influence on Corliss when her father's a homicidal maniac. (CORLISS *puts ice to his eye.*) That's my good eye.

Louise—Keep your head still, Mr. Archer. (RAYMOND *enters from the garden.*)

RAYMOND—Psst! Lenny! (*Amiably.*) Hi, Mr. Archer.

MR. ARCHER (*wheeling around in chair, brushing women aside, pointing dramatically at* RAYMOND)—Get that spawn of Robert Pringle's out of this house!

RAYMOND (*soothingly but promptly backing towards the door*) —Okay, Mr. Archer, okay. I'm going. I just thought you might be interested to know that Pop's in far worse shape than you are.

The curtain falls.

Two months later, on a bright Saturday morning, Dexter finds Mrs. Archer on the porch sewing on a dress for Corliss. It is a good time, thinks Dexter, to ask Mrs. Archer a serious question. It's about the facts of life. Not, he is quick to explain, the facts of his life, but of Corliss'. For one thing, has Mrs. Archer ever been whistled at on the street? Yes—once—Mrs. A is pleased to confess. But, Corliss, unhappily, Dexter feels, hasn't got her mother's strength of character, and whistling just naturally goes to her head. "I think it's a great mistake that the Army gives the soldiers any spending money," Dexter concludes, grimly. Before he can add anything to that conclusion Corliss has come with the mail. Her casual greeting, "Hi, Droopy!" temporarily discourages further comment.

There is nothing from Lenny in the mail. "I guess he's so busy mopping up in Tunisia that he doesn't have much time to write," guesses Corliss.

"In high school he nearly flunked in geography and history— and now he's helping to make both," notes Mrs. Archer, a little sadly.

It is while Corliss is trying on the dress her mother is making that it becomes evident that she has grown a lot lately. It is Dexter's opinion that she is getting fat, but Corliss brands that as a dirty lie. She really is as flat as a board, when she holds in.

It is when Louise comes from the kitchen to demand to know what Corliss has done with her pastry cutter that the truth comes out about Mildred's having been over there the night before. At first Corliss would lie out of the Mildred charge, but finally she confesses—

"Well—you and Daddy were at the movies and it seemed like a good opportunity," Corliss explains, and adds, with spirit: "Oh, Mother—honestly—you don't know how—how crazy this silly family squabble is."

"Corliss—in many ways I agree—but your father and Mr. Pringle are suing and counter-suing each other right now for ten thousand dollars damages and we—"

"Yeah, Mr. Pringle won't forget in such a hurry," chips in Dexter. "Their cook told our cleaning woman that his dentist's bill's over three hundred bucks already."

Now Pvt. Jimmy Earhart is on the phone and would speak with Miss Corliss Archer. Mrs. Archer is quick to answer the phone before Corliss can get to it. She informs Pvt. Earhart that Corliss is away for the week-end.

"Mother—how could you?" Corliss is terribly upset.

"He's been here three times now, Corliss. That's quite enough. You're much too young to— Come here."

"All right—but why did you have to lie to him? He'll know you were lying."

"Nonsense. How can he possibly know?"

"Because I just—"

And then, after Dexter has been sent home to save Corliss' feelings, the truth is told.

"Darling—have you been meeting this boy?" asks Mrs. Archer.

CORLISS—Only once, Mother—yesterday—and that was just by accident, honestly. I swear. I'd had my music lesson—and I was waiting for the bus—and suddenly I saw Jimmy, and so we said hello and he took me to the Owl Drug for a coke and a snack —and that's all. Surely there's nothing wrong with that.

MRS. ARCHER—Are you sure you didn't meet him by appointment?

CORLISS—No, Mother. Honestly.

MRS. ARCHER—Why didn't you tell us about it last night at dinner?

CORLISS—I don't know, Mom. You're so strict and everything. I don't know. I was going to—

MRS. ARCHER—Is that why he called just now? Did you make a date for tonight?

CORLISS—Well—no, not a date—I'm not allowed to make dates, but I told him we'd be home, and I said I was sure you'd be glad to have him come. Oh, Mother—he's so cute! He's a corporal now. And I was wrong about his eyes. They're not like Tyrone Power's or Don Ameche's. They're like Charles Boyer's. You know—sort of sleepy and noble and tender.

MRS. ARCHER—Oh, darling—I used to think when you were five that you couldn't be more trouble—and now look at you!

Here—take this off now. (*She takes the dress off* CORLISS *and is busy with pins and scissors.*)

CORLISS—If you'd just resign yourself to the fact that I'm no longer an infant, you wouldn't worry so much. (*A pause.*) Did Jimmy sound miffed over the phone?

MRS. ARCHER—Never mind about Private Earhart—

CORLISS—Corporal Earhart.

MRS. ARCHER—I'm afraid Dexter's right. You're fickle. You're definitely flirting with that soldier—and I think it's terrible.

CORLISS—You can't fight against nature, Mother.

MRS. ARCHER (*amused*)—You keep nature out of this, if you please.

CORLISS (*answering the telephone eagerly*)—Hello! Oh, hello, Daddy—yes—yes— (*Laughs.*) Oh, you poor darling—hold the wire a sec. (*Turning to* MRS. ARCHER.) He's at the corner of Washington and Fourth, and he wants to know if you'll devote a quart of gasoline to picking him up. He says he's exhausted and in tears.

MRS. ARCHER (*busy sewing*)—Washington and Fourth? Why doesn't he take the bus?

CORLISS (*into phone*)—Mother says why don't you take the bus? (*A pause—and then, giggling.*) He says he's got a hundred pound sack of fertilizer with him and they won't let him on the bus and even the pedestrians are avoiding him.

MRS. ARCHER (*laughing*)—All right. I'll pick him up.

CORLISS (*into phone*)—All right, Daddy. Rescue is at hand. Mother's just leaving. (*She blows a couple of kisses into the phone.*) By, Angel.

With her mother out of the house, Corliss loses no time in calling Dexter. Finding him talking to Mildred she asks them both to come over. Dexter is still sore about the drug store incident. There he was, buying a coke for Betty Campbell, he is telling Mildred, when he looks over and there in a corner booth was Corliss, looking at this soldier with gooey eyes.

So he was treating Betty Campbell, was he? That's enough for Corliss. "There's one thing that I'll not stand for," she says, majestically; "and that's fragrant infidelity."

"The word is flagrant, Corliss," corrects Mildred, laughingly.

"What did I say?"

"You said fragrant."

"Well, I meant it. Your behavior stinks. Now get out!"

With this Corliss starts to push Dexter through the door. The next minute they are in a scuffle. When they come out of it Dexter has given Corliss a pretty hard push in the shoulder.

Corliss is both angry and resentful. Dexter has struck her and she is going to tell her father. "You've been warned before that you're getting much too big to slug me. I'm going to tell Daddy, and he'll forbid you to come to this house. Now—get out!"

"Holy cow—I'm sorry!" protests Dexter, contritely, as he goes on into the house. In a minute he is back, scratching on the screen. "Corliss—don't tell your old man— He might get sore." But Corliss is firm.

Mildred has had a letter from Lenny—a sweet letter, signed "Your adoring husband." That's the way he signs all his letters.

"I can't wait to see what he says when he knows. He'll be so thrilled," says Mildred, gently.

"Did you write and tell him?"

MILDRED—Uh huh. Last night. I had to.

CORLISS—What did you say?

MILDRED (laughing)—I said, "Darling—I'm going to have a baby and pretty soon I'm going to have to tell them all that we're married."

CORLISS—Golly! Poor Lenny—he'll go nuts! Maybe you shouldn't have told him yet.

MILDRED—Well— I didn't tell him the first time we saw Doctor Fabling, although he was sure then—I waited a week.

CORLISS—He's nice, isn't he? Doctor Fabling, I mean.

MILDRED—Do you suppose he really believes my name is Mrs. William Smith? I think maybe we should have picked a less obvious name.

CORLISS—Even if he does suspect—he can't say anything.

MILDRED—You mean because he's a doctor?

CORLISS—Sure. They all have to take a hypocritical oath.

MILDRED (worried)—I hope nobody saw us go there.

CORLISS (sitting up)—My dear girl—why do you suppose I snooped up and down that corridor for hours before you went in or came out?

MILDRED—Yes, but—

CORLISS—Stop worrying, Mildred. My gosh, I stood in the doorway of his office like Horatious holding the bridge before I gave you the high sign.

MILDRED—But suppose we were seen going into the building?

CORLISS—Don't be a dope. The Reeves Building's got hundreds of offices. Everyone who goes in there isn't going to have a baby.

MILDRED—I wish your Dad hadn't ruined my father's bridgework. Honestly, when I hear my Pop ranting about what he's going to do to your father—it's awfully hard not to tell him he's talking about the grandfather of my child.

They are interrupted by Raymond Pringle, who rushes in breathlessly to report that his mother is on the way over. She had been on the phone for half an hour and seemed awfully pleased about something. Raymond had heard her say that she would go right over and see Mrs. Archer.

"Better not let her catch you here, that's all I can say," Raymond advises his sister.

"Corliss—swear you won't tell," pleads Mildred, hurrying home.

"I swear. I already swore in blood."

Mrs. Pringle arrives, looking smugly satisfied. She is in no hurry. She will wait for the Archers. Meantime Corliss would entertain her if she could.

"Aren't you putting on a little weight, dear?" Mrs. Pringle asks, cattily.

"No."

"Well—maybe it's because I haven't really seen you properly for several months."

"How's Mildred?"

"Darling—you did that very well—but you don't have to pretend with me. I know that you and Mildred are seeing each other all the time—despite all our strenuous objections."

"Do you have objections, too? At first, you thought it was absurd."

"For a time, yes. But—now—well—the shoe's on the other foot."

"I don't know what you mean."

"You'll find out, my dear—you'll find out soon enough."

When the Archers arrive, Mrs. Archer apprehensive, Mr. Archer profanely curious, Corliss is sent to her room. Then Mrs. Archer turns to Mrs. Pringle and would have a reason for the visit.

"I have just learned something that I feel it my duty to tell you," begins Mrs. Pringle, with a little snort of relish. *"You* were the people who felt my daughter was a bad influence on yours."

Mr. Archer (*angrily*)—If you have come over here to—

Mrs. Archer—Harry, please. Let's try to remember that we're gentlepeople.

Mrs. Pringle—Too bad you didn't think of that when he knocked four of Bob's teeth down his throat.

Mrs. Archer—All right, Dorothy. What is it?

Mrs. Pringle—I thought you might be interested to know that your precious little Corliss—who might be contaminated by associating with Mildred—is having a sordid affair with a soldier.

Mr. Archer (*raging*)—Get out of my house! Get her out of here before I forget myself and smash her bridgework!

Mrs. Archer—Harry!

Mrs. Pringle—I don't blame you for being upset. I was shocked myself.

Mr. Archer—Just what do you mean, Dorothy?

Mrs. Pringle—I mean just what I say. She's been having an affair—with the usual consequences.

Mr. Archer (*grimly*)—What consequences?

Mrs. Pringle (*triumphantly*)—She's pregnant—that's all!

Mrs. Archer—How dare you—

Mrs. Pringle—You don't think I'm making it up, do you?

Mrs. Archer—Making it up! I say you're a God damned liar.

Mrs. Pringle—Then suppose you ask Corliss why she has been visiting Doctor Fabling in the Reeves Building?

Mr. Archer—Corliss!

Mrs. Pringle—In case you don't know already he only takes obstetrical cases.

Mr. Archer—Corliss!

Corliss (*coming down the stairs*)—Yes, Daddy.

Mr. Archer—Come here, Corliss. This—this woman has just had the—the gall to say—

Corliss—Yes, Daddy. I heard. I wasn't listening—honestly —but I couldn't help hearing.

Mr. Archer—Then tell her she's a liar.

Corliss—Well, I—er—

Mrs. Pringle (*triumphantly*)—If I ever saw guilt written on a face—that's it.

Mrs. Archer (*quickly*)—Corliss—sit down. (*Very gingerly* Corliss *does so.*)

MRS. PRINGLE—If you want to lead up to it gently—ask her if she was at the corner of Jefferson and Fifth yesterday with her soldier friend having a cocktail—

CORLISS (*yelping with indignation*)—It was a shrimp cocktail! I'll murder Betty Campbell!

MR. ARCHER (*grimly*)—What soldier?

MRS. ARCHER—I know about it, Harry. It was Private Earhart.

CORLISS—Corporal Earhart.

MRS. ARCHER—Be quiet, Corliss.

MR. ARCHER—What's this about Doctor Fabling in the Reeves Building?

CORLISS (*cornered*)—Well—I—

MRS. PRINGLE—It's no use trying to deny it. You were seen coming out of his office yesterday—and the week before. Sneaking out—very furtively, according to my information.

MRS. ARCHER—Corliss—look at me. Is that true, Corliss.

CORLISS (*looking down*)—Yes, Mother.

MRS. ARCHER (*appalled*)—Oh!

MRS. PRINGLE (*this is her great moment*)—In future, Janet, perhaps you'll be a little bit more careful who you call a tramp.

Mrs. Pringle sweeps out of the room. For a moment the Archers are stunned. Then Mr. Archer leaps to the telephone. He will talk with the commanding officer at Camp Morningside. He will have this Earhart court-martialed and shot. "He knows that you're not sixteen yet. He—"

"Yes, Daddy—but—but—well—it isn't *him!*"

Slowly Mr. Archer hangs up the phone, an expression of utter defeat spreading over his face. In a voice of doom he asks, weakly: "Then who is it?"

From next door Dexter can be heard faintly calling Corliss. Her face takes on an expression of resignation. "Dexter!" she murmurs with a sigh.

"My God! Dexter!" Mr. Archer is beside himself with rage. "I'll kill him! I'll kill him!" he is shouting when Dexter, grinning amiably, walks in from the garden.

"Hi, everybody!" Dexter is cordiality itself.

MR. ARCHER (*trying to slip from MRS. ARCHER's hold*)—Get out of my sight—you vile, unspeakable, shameless, filthy little swine!

DEXTER (*alarmed*)—Huh? Gee whizz, Mr. Archer, I'm sorry

—it will never happen again. (MR. ARCHER, *snorting with rage, is trying to shake off his wife, who hangs on to him sobbing.*)

MRS. ARCHER (*still holding*)—Harry! I implore you! Please control yourself. Murdering him isn't going to help— Please.

DEXTER—Huh? Holy cow, Mr. Archer—it was Corliss' fault as much as mine.

MR. ARCHER (*panting*)—You filthy little cad.

CORLISS—Dexter—you don't know what you're saying.

DEXTER—But, Mr. Archer—it was all in fun.

MRS. ARCHER (*pulling* MR. ARCHER *toward the hall*)—Please, Harry! Please. Let's go and sit down calmly and think what we can do. Please.

DEXTER—He was livid. I didn't sock you that hard.

CORLISS—Oh, gosh, Dexter—I'm in an awful jam.

DEXTER—*You?* He was sore at *me.* I didn't do anything so terrible.

CORLISS—No, Dexter—but—but—well—he seems to think you did.

DEXTER—Gee whizz—what did you tell him?

CORLISS—Dexter—you've got to take an oath—in blood—not to breathe a word if I tell you the truth.

DEXTER—I swear in blood. Look, there's blood on my chin. I just shaved.

CORLISS (*impressively*)—Well—in the first place—Lenny and Mildred are married.

DEXTER (*amazed*)—What? Married?

CORLISS—Shhh!

DEXTER—Holy cow!

CORLISS—And in the second place—Mildred's going to have a baby!

DEXTER—She is?

CORLISS—But my parents and her parents don't dream that they're married— So, of course, they can't know she's going to have a baby, see? I'm the only one who knows.

DEXTER (*still puzzled*)—Well—go on.

CORLISS—And I've been going with Mildred to see her doctor—Doctor Fabling in the Reeves Building.

DEXTER—Yes.

CORLISS—Well—evidently somebody saw me leaving his office —and must've phoned Mrs. Pringle—so she came tearing over here—and—well—well—they all seemed to jump to the conclusion that I'm going to have a baby—and—well—I swore in blood I'd never tell about Mildred—so I let 'em think it.

Dexter—Oh, boy—you are in a jam—

Corliss—Yes, Dexter—and—well—for a moment they thought Jimmy was to blame—and Daddy was already calling the C.O. to have him executed.

Dexter—Gee whizz!

Corliss—And Daddy was just demanding to know who it was—and then you came in—and now they seem to think it's you.

Dexter (*appalled*)—No *wonder* your father was miffed.

Corliss (*urgently*)—Dexter—would you mind not denying it for a little while? I've got to have time to think!

Dexter (*horrified*)—Holy cow—they've probably gone next door.

Corliss (*imploringly*)—You said you'd do anything for me, Dexter.

Dexter—What's *my* father going to say? Holy cow!
The curtain falls.

ACT III

It is about eight o'clock that night. It is dark outside and the lamps are lighted on the Archer porch. Mr. Archer is at the phone, dialing furiously. He has been trying to get Dr. Fabling for hours, but with no success. This time the girl in the office hangs up on him. Archer is furious. What right has an obstetrician to play golf, anyway. Especially at night.

Louise has appeared with a tray of food for Corliss, and would take it to her room. Mr. Archer stops that, too. Corliss has been locked in her room and is to stay there, incommunicado, until her father orders differently.

With some difficulty Mrs. Archer gets Mr. Archer calmed down. He gives in about the food for Corliss, too, finally, and goes for a walk around the block.

"Don't walk past the Pringles'," cautions Mrs. Archer.

"God forbid! They've probably got the place lit up with neon lights and are dancing on the lawn."

With her father gone, Corliss appears at the top of the stairs. She wants to talk with her mother. "Mother, do you think I'm awful?" she asks, a little plaintively.

"I've already told you what I think," Mrs. Archer answers. "For over an hour—and it seemed to make no impression, Corliss. You don't seem to realize what a dreadful thing it is. I can't understand you."

"Mother—do you hate me? Please don't hate me."

With a suppressed cry Mrs. Archer runs up the stairs and puts her arms around her daughter. She is weeping a little. "Oh, darling, don't be silly. Of course I don't."

"You know—I think Daddy'd like to break my neck."

"Yes, but only because he loves you—you little idiot—" She is weeping again.

"Oh, Mom—please don't feel so awful—it— Oh, Moms, please don't cry. (*In anguish.*) Oh, if only I could explain."

"I'm so ashamed, Corliss. I feel it must be my fault."

"Oh,—Mother, no."

"You were always— Let's not talk."

"Boy, you should hear what the Franklins are saying to Dexter," exclaims Corliss, as her mother gains control of her emotions. "I've been leaning out my bedroom window listening. Poor Dexter. They're bawling him out like nobody's business and there hasn't been a peep out of him."

"Well, I should hope not."

"You don't understand, Mother."

Mildred is on the phone, but Mrs. Archer recognizes the phoney voice and hangs up on her. Corliss is distressed. She wishes her mother could understand Mildred is her best friend; that she feels almost like a sister to her. And Lenny is very fond of Mildred. But Mrs. Archer is firm and again a little mad. She sends Corliss back to her room.

Mr. Archer is back and still excited. He can't get Dr. Fabling. He can't understand how Mrs. Archer can sit calmly knitting at a time like this. And when he hears her hoping that Corliss' baby will be a girl, he is practically undone. Of course they will have to leave town. Why? Mrs. Archer would know—

MR. ARCHER—For God's sake, Janet—who's going to give their legal business to me when I'm the grandfather of an illegitimate child?

MRS. ARCHER—Don't be silly, Harry. It won't be illegitimate. They'll naturally have to get married at once.

MR. ARCHER—I am not going to become the father-in-law of that—that holy cow!

MRS. ARCHER—Harry, please try and be sensible. We've discussed it all with the Franklins already, and we're all agreed that it's the only thing they can do.

MR. ARCHER (*growling*)—I suppose it is—dammit.

MRS. ARCHER—It'll all work out all right, dear. Dexter's

really a very nice boy, and—

Mr. Archer (*this is too much*)—A nice boy! You call the little swine, who—

Mrs. Archer—Harry—you're not helping the situation. We've got to try to be tolerant. At least we do know they're in love with each other.

Mr. Archer (*disgusted*)—In love! They're both practically still in their swaddling clothes.

Mrs. Archer—Harry—do you remember 1918?

Mr. Archer—What about 1918?

Mrs. Archer—Do you remember the flivver you had, Harry?

Mr. Archer (*dubiously*)—Yes. What of it?

Mrs. Archer (*watching him with a mischievous smile*)—Do you remember the night we parked under the trees by the river?

Mr. Archer—My God, Janet, we were engaged. We were in love. We knew we were going to be married.

Mrs. Archer—Ever since Corliss and Dexter were adolescent they've known, too.

Mr. Archer—At the time to which you refer I was nearly twenty-two—and earning my own living. Dexter is only just seventeen and gets fifty cents a week.

Mrs. Archer—Well—between us and the Franklins we'll have to increase that.

Mr. Archer (*with a bit of difficulty*)—Janet—since you brought up the subject of 1918—and the flivver—may I remind you that we never—actually—

Mrs. Archer (*gently interrupting*)—This generation is a little less inhibited.

Mr. Archer—That's what I'd call a magnificent understatement.

A buzz at the hall door is followed by a good deal of racket in the hall. This would be Mr. Archer's brother, Uncle George, a Commander in the Navy. Uncle George is "a hearty, jovial man, nearing fifty," and he has flown in from his Eastern station with an idea. He would like to have Corliss, his favorite niece, go back with him.

"She doesn't know it, but she's going to take part in a christening," chortles Uncle George, while the Archers exchange frightened stares. "If it's okay with you two, I'm going to fly back with Corliss to the Navy Yard—and let her christen a destroyer."

While the Archers are recovering, Uncle George has gone to the foot of the stairs and is calling lustily for Corliss. The next minute Corliss has come bounding down the stairs and thrown herself into her uncle's arms. "Uncle George—you darling! How super!"

After a bear hug, Uncle George would make a fairly elaborate examination of his niece. How good is her right hand? How's her grip? Are her muscles under good control?

"I can beat Dexter at tennis!" declares Corliss.

"Wish to God she could outrun him!" mutters her father.

"Even he says I've got a good backhand drive," Corliss goes on.

"Tennis and smashing bottles are two very different things," Uncle George insists, sitting down and pulling Corliss onto his knee. "Corliss—how would you like to christen a destroyer?"

"Me? Oh, you're kidding. Me? Christen a destroyer? (*She hugs him enthusiastically.*) Oh, Uncle George, you're wonderful! Would I be in the newsreels? Oh—how perfectly super!"

Then a difficulty arises. The Archers are forced to tell Uncle George that, because Corliss has done something that has upset them very much, they have been forced to deny her all privileges as a punishment.

"Well, in this case I am going to ask for a special dispensation," announces Uncle George, his arm around Corliss. "It's for Uncle Sam."

"She's done her bit," growls Archer.

Now there is a commotion approaching through the garden. The Franklins are coming over, herding a protesting Dexter before them. "One more word out of you, Dexter, and I'll knock your block off, so help me God!" an angry Mr. Franklin is saying. They spy Uncle George and, with obvious difficulty, change their attitude to one of friendly greeting. Uncle George is especially glad to see Dexter again. The Franklins should, he thinks, be proud of their kid. The Franklins are not quite sure about that.

Uncle George has gone to freshen up. The Archers and the Franklins go into a family conference, shunting Corliss and Dexter to the sidelines and warning them to keep their mouths shut.

It is a little unfortunate, Mrs. Archer thinks, that Uncle George should choose this particular time for a visit, but perhaps if they were to let Corliss go back with him—

"Can you imagine, Dexter, he wants me to christen a destroyer. Wouldn't that be neat?"

"Holy cow—what a break!"

"Will you shut up!!" shout Mr. Archer and Mr. Franklin, as one voice.

"And then," continues Mrs. Archer to Mrs. Franklin, "I thought you and I could follow by train with Dexter—and they could be married back East—very quietly.   And then, I thought—"

Mrs. Archer doesn't finish her thought.   Louise is in and out (deliberately, if you ask Mr. Archer) and the two families decide to go over to the Franklins' to finish their talk.

Left alone, Corliss and Dexter have a chance to check on their situation.   "Oh, Dexter, I think you're behaving simply wonderfully," exclaims Corliss, with real enthusiasm.   "I'll never forget it."

DEXTER (*ruefully*)—Nor will I.   You should have heard what my father said to me!

CORLISS—I did.   They locked me in my room, but I could hear clear as anything.

DEXTER—Did you hear him say that if a mob came to lynch me, he'd turn me over to 'em without a qualm?

CORLISS—Golly, we are in a mess, aren't we?

DEXTER—Yeah—but it has its bright side, too.

CORLISS—Where?

DEXTER—Well—they're arranging for us to be married right away.

CORLISS—I know but—

DEXTER (*sitting beside her on the sofa*)—In my rosiest dreams I figured we'd have to wait at least until I was drafted.   So, in a way, this is quite a break.

CORLISS—Dexter Franklin—you don't think for a moment I'm going to let you go as far as that?

DEXTER—Holy cow, why not?   It's perfect!

CORLISS—I'm only stalling for time.   As soon as I can check with Mildred, we'll just have to tell them the truth, that's all.

DEXTER—Why don't you wait until they've got us safely married and then tell?   Holy cow, you dragged me into this.   I deserve some consideration.

CORLISS—All right—maybe I will.   Oh, boy, if I was married they couldn't stop me making dates with soldiers.

DEXTER—Listen—if I ever catch you even looking at a soldier—

Raymond Pringle has arrived, looking for Mildred.   She isn't home and Raymond thinks it important that she should be found. There's a telegram home for her. That news is exciting also to Corliss—

"Didn't your mother open it?" she asks.

"Fortunately she didn't get a chance. I took it at the door and hid it under the mat. I know my family."

With that Raymond is gone. Louise comes from the kitchen, bearing a snack on a tray for Uncle George. Corliss stops her: "Louise—if anything happens to—soldiers or sailors—who gets notified first?"

"The next of kin, dear."

"Would that be their wives—or their parents?"

"The wife hears first, I guess."

"By telegram?"

"Usually."

Corliss is worried. She is leaning sorrowfully against the stair post when her father and mother and the Franklins come back, marching in a little dolefully. Dexter, she tells them, is with Uncle George. Maybe Uncle George will get him in the Navy.

"Did you decide anything?" Corliss would know.

"Yes. We'll tell you about it later," her mother answers.

"And don't look so smug," barks Mr. Archer. "It isn't a picnic."

Mrs. Franklin objects to the Archer tone. "Really, Harry, you shouldn't pick on her all the time. Corliss, dear, you look a little pale. Come over here on the couch next to me and get all comfy."

"There's no need to coddle her, Mary," protests Mrs. Archer.

"Now, Janet—we all agreed we weren't going to be bitter any more. It's going to be as much my grandchild as yours."

"Sure. By all means. Let's celebrate. Let's invite the neighbors for a baby shower."

"I've always loved Corliss and hoped this would happen— Not in this way, I mean. But it doesn't make any difference in my affection for her."

"You'll forgive me if I don't clasp Dexter to my bosom immediately."

Uncle George is just finishing one about the sailor who was picked up on a rubber life raft ten days after the torpedoing when he and Dexter come in. Uncle George has his arm around Dexter's shoulder.

"This kid of yours, Franklin, is quite a lad—quite a lad," beams Uncle George.

"I—er—I'm glad you think so, Commander."

"Yes, sir—he's just been telling me all about his latest achievement."

"He has?"

"For a boy of his age, I'd say that's quite remarkable."

"You would?"

"Yes, sir! And he's modest— Doesn't boast about it the way a lot of kids would."

"Huh?" This from Mr. Archer.

"What did you say?"

"Listen—collecting nine hundred pounds of scrap iron all by yourself—"

"Oh, oh—that. Oh, yeah, sure." Mr. Franklin is greatly relieved.

"That's the spirit and the brawn we need in the Navy."

Dr. Fabling is on the phone, but with a quick glance at Uncle George, Mr. Archer assures the doctor he must have the wrong number. A moment later another small riot breaks out in the house. Raymond, with a whoop, comes flying in on his roller skates, shouting a wild "Wow! Whoopee! Oh, boy, oh, boy, oh, boy! And to Mr. Archer he adds: "Hi, Grandpapop! I just heard the news. Wow!"

Mildred, it is soon told, has her telegram and has told the truth to the family. The family, according to Raymond, has gone completely nuts. Mr. Pringle is even then in the house, kissing Louise.

"That's nothing!" insists the exuberant Raymond. "On the way over he kissed a cop!"

Now the Pringles, wildly calling for Janet and Harry, are raising all sorts of a row in the Archer house. "Holy cow! They've all gone nuts!" insists Dexter, as the family surges into the house to investigate.

Mildred and Corliss are alone for a minute. "Oh, Corliss— it's about Lenny— Isn't it wonderful! It says he shot down three Nazi bombers and he's going to get a medal!"

"Oh, Mildred— How wonderful."

"Corliss! Can you ever forgive me! Why didn't you say something?" Mrs. Pringle has thrown her arms around Corliss.

"I was dying to— I knew all along!"

And now Mr. Pringle appears. He is a little drunk, has a highball glass in his hand and has his arm around Louise. Mr. Pringle is very, very happy.

"Louise—you gorgeous creature—we crave ice—gobs of ice—

and glasses—millions of glasses—and more liquor."

"All right—then let go of me!" giggles Louise, pulling herself away and starting for the kitchen. Mr. Pringle turns to Corliss, who is still being embraced by the contrite Mrs. Pringle.

"Corliss—you poor sweet little thing! My God—she's kissing the woman after all the terrible things she said about you!"

As Mrs. Archer comes from the house he raises his glass: "Here's to Lenny—the finest damned flyer ever come out of this town."

Mrs. Pringle—Bob—you've had enough.

Mr. Pringle—I'm going to be a grandfather and my son-in-law's a hero and I'm going to get stinking. (*Embracing* Mrs. Archer.) Janet—I adore you.

Mrs. Archer—Do you adore Harry, too—after what he did to your bridgework?

Mr. Pringle—I just kissed him, too—and he never said a word— Come on— Come on, Corliss—everybody.

Mr. Archer—Where's that telegram? I want to see it with my own eyes.

Corliss (*handing it to him*)—Here, Daddy—

Mr. Archer—That boy! Brings down three bombers and hasn't the nerve to tell us he's married.

Mildred—May I have it? It's mine. (Archer *gives her the telegram*.) And I'm not a little tramp, honestly.

Mr. Archer—Where is everybody? Got to keep an eye on Pringle—he's going berserk—

Raymond (*skating into* Mr. Archer)—Sorry, Grandpapop—

Mr. Archer—My God! I'm related to you!

Corliss—Raymond, you must try to be very nice to Daddy.

Raymond (*turning in kitchen door*)—He'll get the usual discount—that's all.

Corliss—Oh, Dexter! Isn't it all too wonderful?

Dexter (*leaning against the newel post*)—They're not going to let us get married now, you dope!

Corliss—I mean going to New York and the destroyer I'm going to christen!

Dexter—Yeah.

Corliss—Well—aren't you thrilled about that?

Dexter—Why should I be? Nobody's going to think I'm the father of a destroyer. (Louise *enters carrying a tray of liquor and glasses*.)

Mrs. Archer (*turning to* Corliss *and* Dexter)—And as for

you two sweet, quixotic, crazy little idiots!

RAYMOND—Listen to them! Mass hysteria—that's what it is.

MRS. ARCHER—I ought to smack you both.

CORLISS—I thought we put on a pretty good act.

MRS. ARCHER—Much too realistic—but I should've known that Dexter couldn't do a thing like that.

DEXTER—Holy cow—why not?

THE CURTAIN FALLS

OKLAHOMA

A Musical Comedy in Two Acts

BOOK BY OSCAR HAMMERSTEIN 2D; SCORE BY RICHARD RODGERS

(Adapted from Lynn Riggs' "Green Grow the Lilacs")

A PROPITIOUS joining of circumstances and the fates played a part in the production of "Oklahoma" this season. This musical comedy hit of the year, and of several years for that matter, did not arrive on Broadway until the last day of March, 1943, but its preparation had been actively in the hearts and minds of its creators for many months.

To go back to the beginning, "Oklahoma" is a musicalized version of Lynn Riggs' folk comedy, "Green Grow the Lilacs," which was produced by the Theatre Guild the season of 1930-31. Mr. Riggs at the time was a 32-year-old Oklahoma poet who had traveled a bit and decided on a playwrighting career. "Green Grow the Lilacs" was a straight folk comedy, as he wrote it. Theatre Guild producers suggested the inclusion of more cowboy songs and choruses, and these were added. The production proved no more than a subscribers' success, however, being withdrawn after sixty-four performances.

Guild producers never forgot their first enthusiasm for "Green Grow the Lilacs," and there has been talk of a revival from time to time. Last year the talk crystallized into determination. About this same time Oscar Hammerstein 2d, who was working in Hollywood, decided he would like to do a new libretto based on the "Lilacs" romance. When Hammerstein returned from California he approached Theresa Helburn of the Guild with his idea, only to find that she had already talked with Richard Rodgers about writing the music for such an adaptation. Hammerstein and Rodgers had long wanted to work on a musical play together, and here was their chance. They accepted it with enthusiasm.

To give the new work added distinction in the musical comedy field the inclusion of a dream ballet, conceived and staged by Agnes de Mille, was sheer inspiration. It not only gives definite stimulation to the story, but provides an original interlude of first importance to the opera as entertainment. Conceived in the spirit and form of Miss de Mille's "Rodeo" ballet, produced the season before by the Ballet Russe de Monte Carlo, the

"Laurey Makes Up Her Mind" ballet number adds both humor and character to "Oklahoma."

For their part, the Messrs. Hammerstein and Rodgers, working as collaborators for the first time, have been exceptionally faithful to the author of their source-material in their adaptation of "Oklahoma." They have kept it pretty consistently in the mood of "Green Grow the Lilacs;" they have preserved, at least in part, much of Lynn Riggs' poetic fervor and his devotion to the verities and the beauties of nature. They have let Mr. Riggs set the moods, but they have increased the pace of the succeeding scenes. The liberties they have taken with the Riggs characterization in the interests of cheaper, and therefore more popular comedy interludes, they have taken with a kind of decent reluctance that is, I think, to their credit.

The opening scene of "Oklahoma" is especially an expanded Riggs mood, so far as the background is concerned. The blue, cloud-flecked sky; the sweeping prairies; the sun-baked earth; the placid, neighborly, simple-minded home folk; the calicoed women and the checker-shirted cowhands are all in the cow-country tradition, or more particularly in the lightly exaggerated stage tradition of this and similar localities.

In the foreground Aunt Eller Murphy, "a buxom, hearty woman about fifty," is sitting behind a wooden, brass-banded churn, "looking out over the meadow [which is the audience], a contented look on her face, churning to the rhythm of a gentle melody."

"It is a radiant Summer morning several years ago," Author Riggs wrote in the original play; "the kind of morning which—enveloping the shapes of earthmen, cattle in the meadow, blades of the young corn, streams—makes them seem to exist now for the first time, their images giving off a golden emanation that is partly true and partly a trick of the imagination, focusing to keep alive a loveliness that may pass away."

The melody to the rhythm of which Aunt Eller is doing her churning, it presently appears, is that of a song being sung by Curly McLain, "a tall, waggish, curly-headed young cowboy."

"There's a bright, golden haze on the meadow," sings Curly. "There's a bright, golden haze on the meadow. The corn is as high as a elephant's eye, An' it looks like it's climbin' clear up to the sky—

"Oh, what a beautiful mornin',
Oh, what a beautiful day.

I got a beautiful feelin'
Everythin's goin' my way.

"All the cattle are standin' like statues,
All the cattle are standin' like statues.
They don't turn their heads as they see me ride by,
But a little brown mav'rick is winkin' her eye.

"Oh, what a beautiful mornin,'
Oh, what a beautiful day.
I got a beautiful feelin'
Everythin's goin' my way."

Curly comes into view now, apparently greatly interested in what effect his singing has had on the lady at the churn and, quite possibly, on another and younger lady who should be in the house.

"If I wasn't a ol' womern, and if you wasn't so young and smart-alecky—why, I'd marry you and get you to set around at night and sing to me," jokes Aunt Eller.

"No, you wouldn't neither," answers Curly, walking over to the steps of the house and trying hard to peek in the windows; "cuz I wouldn't marry you ner none o' yer kinfolks ef I could he'p it."

"Oh, none of my kinfolks, huh?"

"And you c'n tell 'em that—ALL of 'em, includin' that niece of yourn, Miss Laurey Williams." Curly has raised his voice so that Laurey will hear if she is inside the house. Now he comes back to Aunt Eller and speaks deliberately. "Aunt Eller, if you was to tell me whur Laurey was at—whur would you tell me she was at?"

"I wouldn't tell you a-tall. Fer as fur as I c'n make out, Laurey ain't payin' you no heed."

Curly just can't understand this. "Whur'd you git sich a uppity niece 'at wouldn't pay no heed to me?" he demands. "Who's the best bronc buster in this yere territory? . . . And the best bull-dogger in seventeen counties? Me, that's who? And looky here, I'm handsome, ain't I?"

"Purty as a pitcher."

"Curly-headed, ain't I? And bow-legged from the saddle fer God knows how long, ain't I?"

"Couldn't stop a pig in the road."

"Well, whut else does she want then, the damn she-mule."

It is wise Aunt Eller's opinion that Curly has come over to

ask Laurey to go to the box social with him, and Curly ain't prepared to deny that he has. Maybe he'll take Aunt Eller, too. But there is no indication on Laurey Williams' part that she even suspects such a thing, or even knows that anybody like Curly McLain is even in the yard.

True, she is humming Curly's song, "Oh, what a beautiful mornin'," when she comes from the house to hang up an apron on the clothesline, but she doesn't pretend to notice him for several minutes. Then she is deliberately disdainful. "Laurey is a fair, spoiled, lovely young girl of about eighteen."

"Is this all that's come a-callin', and it a'ready ten o'clock of a Sattiddy mornin'?" demands Laurey.

"You knowed it was me 'fore you opened the door," protests Curly, sullenly.

"No sich of a thing."

"You did, too! You heard my voice and knowed it was me."

"I heared a voice talkin' rumbly along with Aunt Eller. And heared some one a-singin' like a bullfrog in a pond."

"You knowed it was me, so you set in there a-thinkin' up sumpin' mean to say. I've a good mind not to ask you to the box social."

"If you did ast me, I wouldn't go with you. Besides, how'd you take me? You ain't bought a new buggy with red wheels onto it, have you?"

"If I was to ast you they'd be a way to take you, Miss Laurey Smarty."

"Oh, they would?"

Whereupon Curly proceeds to stagger Laurey with an idea, including a vision in song of a most wonderful "Surrey With the Fringe on the Top."

"Laurey doesn't let on at first how she is tuck up with it. Aunt Eller is the one who falls like a ton of bricks immediately, and helps Curly try to sell the idea to Laurey"—

"When I take you out tonight with me, Honey, here's the way it's goin' to be: You will set behind a team of snow-white horses in the slickest gig you ever see!"

"Chicks and ducks and geese better scurry
  When I take you out in the surrey,
  When I take you out in the surrey with the fringe on top!
  Watch thet fringe and see how it flutters
  When I drive them high-steppin' strutters!

Nosey-pokes'll peek through their shutters and their eyes will
    pop!
The wheels are yeller, the upholstery's brown,
The dashboard's genuine leather,
With isinglass curtains you can roll right down
In case there's a change in the weather—
Two bright side-lights, winkin' and blinkin'!
Ain't no finer rig, I'm thinkin'!
You c'n keep yer rig if you're thinkin' 'at I'd keer to swop
Fer that shiny little surrey with the fringe on top!"

Laurey would still pretend unconcern, but she is obviously slipping. Has Curly really got a team of white horses? "One's like
snow—the other's more like milk," boasts the imaginative Curly,
as he swings into the second chorus.

"Y'd shore feel like a queen settin' up in that carriage!" sighs
Aunt Eller, ecstatically.

But Laurey is still holding out. She doesn't believe much in
that fine rig, unless Curly went and spent all his money "h'arin'
a rig and now ain't got nobody to ride in it." If he made it
all up outa his head, as Curly intimates smilingly that he did, he
oughta be put right off the place, and she's one to help Aunt
Eller put him off.

Laurey has grabbed a fly-swatter and is chasing Curly around
the yard. He dodges her successfully, protesting as he does so
that just "makin' up a few purties ain't agin no law." She
tires now, turns her back on him and sinks into a chair. With
a wink for Aunt Eller, Curly sneaks up behind her and sorta
whispers: "Don't you wish they *was* such a rig, though? 'Nen
you could go to the play-party and do a hoe-down till mornin',
if you was a mind to. . . . 'Nen when you was all wore out,
I'd lift you onto the surrey and jump up alongside of you—
And we'd jist point the horses home. . . . I can jist pitcher the
whole thing—

"I can see the stars gettin' blurry
When we ride back home in the surrey,
  Ridin' slowly home in the surrey with the fringe on top—"

Curly has finished his song and is smiling contentedly. Laurey
is still doubtful and a little mad. "Why'd you come around here
with yer stories and lies, gittin' me all worked up that-a-way?"
demands Laurey. "Talkin' 'bout the sun swimmin' on the hill,

and all—like it was so. Who'd want to ride alongside of you anyway?"

"Whyn't you jist grab her and kiss her when she acts that-a-way, Curly. She's jist achin' fer you to, I bet," advises Aunt Eller.

"Oh, I won't even speak to him, let alone 'low him to kiss me, the braggin', bow-legged, wish't-he-had-a-sweetheart bum!" With this Laurey has flounced herself into the house and slammed the door.

"She likes you—quite a lot," muses Aunt Eller.

"Whew! If she liked me any more she'd sic the dogs onto me," explodes Curly.

It now appears that what Curly had really come for was to borrow Aunt Eller's big wagon to bring a crowd of folks down from Bushyhead for the box social. He'd forgotten about that. Now he will go and hitch up the horses, if she says it is all right, which she does. . . .

A crowd of cow hands has swarmed into the yard, nudging before them a big fellow with a smile as broad as his face, which is pretty broad. He is Will Parker. Will is excited because he has been up to the fair and won fifty dollars prize money in the steer-ropin' contest. The fifty dollars means a lot to Will, seeing that Ado Annie Carnes' father had told Will that if he was ever worth fifty dollars he could have Annie.

"If he don't keep his promise I'll take her right from under his nose, and I won't give him the present I brung for him," announces Will.

The present, which he shows to the fellers, is a "Little Wonder" novelty knife. If you hold it to your eye right you can see a pitcher in the handle. And when you get a good look and turn it around, the pitcher changes. Ike tries it. "Well, I'll be side-gaited!" exclaims Ike. Now, with their curiosity at fever-heat, the boys line up to take turns havin' a peek at the Little Wonder.

"Silly goats!" sniffs Aunt Eller. She would turn away if her own curiosity did not get the better of her. She yanks the smallest of the cow hands out of line and takes his place. When she gets hold of the Little Wonder she takes a good look.

"The hussy!" exclaims Aunt Eller, disgustedly. "Ought to be ashamed of herself! You, too," she shouts, glaring at Will. . . . "How do you turn the thing to see the other pitcher? . . . Wait, I'm gettin' it. . . ." When she gets it she takes the Little Wonder away from her eye quickly. "I'm a good mind to tell Annie on yer!" She hands the Little Wonder back and walks away in shocked surprise. Then she suddenly "busts out laughing."

"No tellin' what you been up to," opines Aunt Eller. "Bet you carried on plenty in Kansas City."

"I wouldn't call it carryin' on," protests Will. "But I shore did see some things I never see before."

Which, reasonably enough, reminds Will of a song called "Kansas City." In this he tells of his adventures and his discoveries. "They've gone about as fur as they c'n go in Kansas City," he assures them, and proceeds to enumerate the strings of gas buggies, the seven-story skyscrapers, and so forth, including—

"Y'c'n turn the radiator on whenever you want some heat.
With ev'ry kind of comfort ev'ry house is all complete.
You c'n walk to privies in the rain an' never wet yer feet!
They've gone about as fur as they c'n go."

He would add a few lessons in the new dance, the two-step, when the song is finished, and take Aunt Eller as his partner. But by the time the boys have finished one refrain Aunt Eller decides that that is as far as she c'n go, too. . . .

Will and the boys have gone to pick up Andrew Carnes, Ado Annie's father, deliver the fifty dollars and complete arrangements with Ado Annie herself. . . .

Now Curly is back and would also get his romance straightened out. First, he has got to know from Aunt Eller who is the "low, filthy, sneak 'at Laurey's got her cap set for?"

So far as Aunt Eller knows he is talking about himself. Of course there is Jace Hutchins, and a fine young farmer is Jace. Then there is that ol' widder man over at Claremore. And then there's "someone nearer home that's got her on his mind most of the time, 'til he don't know a plow from a thrashin' machine."

This someone would be Jud Fry, that "bullet-colored, growly man," as Curly calls him, who sleeps in the smokehouse. Jud is a good farmhand, Aunt Eller insists, and she won't hear nothing against him. She isn't saying that Laurey has taken up with Jud, but of course he is there all the time, as Curly charges; eats his meals with her and Laurey like one of the family.

At that moment Jud and Laurey come from the house. "Changed my mind about cleanin' the henhouse today," Jud tells Aunt Eller. "Leavin' it until tomorrow. Got to quit early cuz I'm drivin' Laurey over to the party tonight."

"You drivin' Laurey?" demands Curly.

"Ast her," challenges Jud. Laurey doesn't deny it.

"Well, wouldn't that just make you bawl? . . . Well, don't fergit, Aunt Eller. You and me's got a date together. And if you make up a nice box of lunch, mebbe I'll bid for it."

"How we goin', Curly? In that rig you made up? I'll ride a-straddle of them lights a-winkin' like lightnin' bugs!"

"That there ain't no made-up rig, you hear me. I h'ared it over to Claremore."

This news is a little stunning to Laurey. She looks as though she might burst out crying as Curly disappears gaily singing a refrain from the surrey song. Then she turns, a little frightened, to plead: "Aunt Eller, don't go to Skidmore's with Curly tonight. I'll have to ride with Jud all alone."

"That's the way you wanted it, ain't it?"

"No. I did it because Curly was so fresh. But I'm afraid to tell Jud I won't, Aunt Eller. He'd do sumpin' turrible. He makes me shiver ever time he gits clost to me. . . . Ever go down to that ole smokehouse where he's at?"

"Plenty times. Why?"

"Did you see them pitchers he's got tacked onto the walls?"

"Oh, yeah, I seed them. But don't you pay them no mind."

"Sumpin' wrong inside him, Aunt Eller. I hook my door at night and fasten my winders agin it. Agin it—and the sound o' feet walkin' up and down out there under that tree outside my room."

"Laurey!"

"Mornin's he comes to his breakfast and looks at me out from under his eyebrows like sumpin' back in the bresh some'eres. I know what I'm talkin' about."

"You crazy young 'un! Stop actin' like a chicken with its head cut off." . . .

Now they have company. Ali Hakim, a Persian peddler who makes periodical trips through the country, has driven up and with him is Will Parker's Ado Annie. Aunt Eller has been waiting for that Peddler. Once he had sold her an egg-beater that he promised would "beat up eggs, and wring out dishrags, and turn the ice-cream freezer." She's got something to say to him.

Ado Annie is a pretty, not too bright-looking, farm girl. She has been riding a piece with the Peddler and is planning to go on to the box social with him. Will Parker? Ado Annie hadn't counted on Will's being back so soon. Promised Will? No, she hadn't exactly promised. She'd just said mebbe.

"Don't you like Will no more?" demands Laurey.

" 'Course I do. They won't never be nobody like Will."

"Then what about this peddler man?"

"They won't never be nobody like him, neither."

"Well, which one d'you like the best?"

"Whutever one I'm with."

"Well, you air a silly!"

"Now, Laurey, you know they didn't nobody pay me no mind up to this year, 'count of I was scrawny and flat as a beanpole. 'Nen I kinda rounded up a little and now the boys act diff'rent to me."

"Well, what's wrong with that?"

"Nuthin' wrong. I like it. I like it so much when a feller talks purty to me I git all shaky from horn to hoof! . . . Don't you?"

"Cain't think what yer talkin' about."

"Don't you feel kinda sorry fer a feller when he looks like he wanted to kiss you?"

"Well, you jist cain't go around kissin' every man that asts you. Didn't anybody ever tell you that?"

"Yeow, they *told* me—"

Which reminds Ado Annie of a song. It might be called a problem song. The title is "I Cain't Say No."

"It ain't so much a question of not knowin' what to do," sings Ado Annie; "I knowed what's right and wrong since I been ten. I heared a lot of stories—and I reckon they are true—, About how girls're put upon by men. I know I mustn't fall into the pit, But when I'm with a feller I fergit—

"I'm jist a girl who cain't say no,
I'm in a turrible fix.
I always say Come on, le's go,
Jist when I orta say nix!
When a person tries to kiss a girl
I know she orta give his face a smack,
But as soon as someone kisses me
I somehow sorta wanta kiss him back!
I'm jist a fool when lights are low.
I cain't be prissy and quaint—
I ain't the type thet c'n faint—
How c'n I be whut I ain't?
I cain't say no!"

When Ado Annie completes her story of how she gits sorry for the men, she is still in a fix regarding Will Parker and the peddler. Right now she is especially sorry for the peddler, whose name is Ali Hakim, and who is being roundly cussed out by Aunt

Eller over that ole egg-beater. Ali Hakim wants to marry Ado Annie. She knows that because when they were drivin' along he had told her that he would like to drive with her to the end of the world. If they was to go that far it would mean they would have to stay somewhere at night, and that would mean that Ali would be wantin' a weddin', wouldn't it?

Not to a peddler, it wouldn't, Laurey is quick to tell her. But Ado Annie is still uncertain about it.

Ali Hakim is a small, swarthy Persian with beady eyes. He wears a red bandanna around his neck. "His speech is a blurred European tongue with Middle Western variations." At the moment he is trying to placate the still angry Aunt Eller. If her egg-beater doesn't work he will give her something else just as good. What would she like as a present? How about a pair of Persian silk garters?

"They look awful purty, with bows onto them and all," says Ado Annie.

Aunt Eller thinks she might try a pair on, but when Ali would slide one over her ankle she kicks him down.

"Funny woman," says Ali, turning to Ado Annie with a shrug. "Would be much worse if I tried to take her garters off."

"Yeh, cuz that ud make her stockin's fall down, wouldn't it?" reasons Annie.

Aunt Eller has turned her back, adjusted the garter, approved of it and is reaching for its mate. Ali would like to sell her that one for four bits—fifty cents. And that starts the Aunt Eller-Peddler feud all over again. Finally she grabs the garter out of his hand and that ends that.

"All right—all right," Ali submits. "Don't anybody want to buy something? How about you, Miss Laurey? Must be wanting something—a pretty young girl like you."

LAUREY—Me? Course I want sump'n. (*Working up to a kind of abstracted ecstasy.*) Want a buckle made outa shiny silver to fasten onto my shoes! Want a dress with lace. Want perfume, wanta be purty, wanta smell like a honeysuckle vine!

AUNT ELLER—Give her a cake of soap.

LAUREY—Want things I've heared of and never had before—rubber-t'ard buggy, a cut-glass sugar bowl. Want things I cain't tell you about—not only things to look at and hold in yer hands. Things to happen to you. Things so nice, if they ever did happen to you, yer heart ud quit beatin'. You'd fall down dead!

PEDDLER—I've got just the thing for you. (*He fishes into his satchel and pulls out a bottle.*)   The elixir of Egypt!

LAUREY—What's 'at?

PEDDLER—It's a secret formula, belonged to Pharaoh's daughter!

AUNT ELLER (*putting her nose to it*)—Smellin' salts!

PEDDLER (*snatching it away*)—But a special kind of smelling salts. Read what it says on the label: "Take a deep breath and you see everything clear." That's what Pharaoh's daughter used to do. When she had a hard problem to decide, like what prince she ought to marry, or what dress to wear to a party, or whether she ought to cut off somebody's head—she'd take a whiff of this.

LAUREY (*excited*)—I'll take a bottle of that, Mr. Peddler.

PEDDLER—Precious stuff.

LAUREY—How much?

PEDDLER—Two bits. (*She pays him and takes the bottle.*)

AUNT ELLER—Throwin' away yer money!

LAUREY (*holding the bottle close to her, thinking aloud*)—Helps you decide what to do!

PEDDLER—Now don't you want me to show you some pretty doodads? You know, with lace around the bottom, and ribbons running in and out?

AUNT ELLER—You mean fancy drawers?

PEDDLER (*taking a pair out of pack*)—All made in Paris.

AUNT ELLER—Well, I never wear 'em myself, but I shore do like to look at 'em. (PEDDLER *takes out a pair of red flannel drawers.*)

ANNIE—Yeah, they're all right—if you ain't goin' no place.

Aunt Eller and Laurey have gone in the house. Ado Annie is taking advantage of the moment to clear up that little matter of driving to the ends of the earth with her Persian. Just what did he mean when he made that suggestion?

Well, Ali didn't really mean the end of the world. What he really had in mind was a ride that would end, perhaps, in Claremore—at the hotel.

"Whut's at the hotel?" Ado Annie wants to know.

"In front of the hotel is a veranda," explains the peddler. "Inside is a lobby— Upstairs—upstairs might be Paradise."

"I thought they was jist bedrooms."

"For you and me, baby—Paradise."

"Y'see! I knew I was right and Laurey was wrong! You do want to marry me, don't you?"

"Ah, Ado Annie!" He has taken her in his arms and is embracing her impulsively. Suddenly her words sink in. He pulls away. "What did you say?"

"I said you do want to marry me, don't you? What did you say?"

"I didn't say nothing."

With a whoop, Will Parker arrives, and without more ado practically sweeps Ado Annie off her feet. "How's my honey-bunch? How's the sweetest little hundred and ten pounds of sugar in the territory?" That's Will's greeting.

He would apologize to Ali Hakim when Annie introduces them. He (Will) is a little excited because he is going to marry the girl.

"Marry her? On purpose?" Ali is both surprised and delighted.

But Ado Annie would deny the charge. She isn't sure. Even after Ali has left them and Will has told her about the fifty dollars and reminded her of her father's promise, she isn't sure. If he has already spent the fifty dollars on presents for her, as he says he has, he hasn't got the cash—

"Whut I got is worth more'n the cash," cries Will. "Feller who sold me the stuff told me."

"But, Will . . ."

"Stop sayin' 'But, Will!' When do I get a little kiss? . . . Oh, Ado Annie, honey, y'ain't been off my mind since I left. All the time at the fair grounds, even, when I was chasin' steers. I'd rope one under the hoofs and pull him up sharp, and he'd land on his little rump. . . . 'Nen I'd think of you."

"Don't start talkin' purty, Will!"

But Ado Annie can't stop Will. First thing she knows he has grabbed her up in his arms again, and that puts him right into a singing mood—a soft, seductive singing mood that simply gets Ado Annie—

"S'posin' 'at I say 'at yer lips're like cherries, er roses, er berries?" sings Will. "Whut you gonna do?" He puts her hand on his heart. "Cain't you feel my heart palpatatin' an' bumpin', awaitin' fer sump'n nice from you? I gotta git a kiss an' it's gotta be quick, er I'll jump in a crick an' die."

"What's a girl to say when you talk that-a-way?" pleads Ado Annie, and Will gets his kiss. . . .

All the girls and boys come rushing in now with their lunch hampers. There is much laughing and shouting and before anyone knows it a dance is organized. Laurey, coming out on the porch, can't help but see that Curly is sticking pretty close to a girl named Gertie. Now Gertie is waltzing with him and they have begun to sing, "Oh, what a beautiful mornin' " and dancing to it. And now, at Aunt Eller's suggestion, Curly and Gertie have gone down to the barn to water the horses—

"Looks like Curly's tuck up with that Cummin's girl," says someone.

"Whut'd I keer about that?" pouts Laurey, and while Aunt Eller and the others are getting the hampers together Laurey sings a little song just to show how little she does keer— "Many a New Day" is the title, and it goes—

"Why should a womern who is healthy and strong
Blubber like a baby if her man goes away?
A-weepin' and a-wailin' how he's done her wrong—
That's one thing you'll never hear me say!
Never gonna think that the man I lose
Is the only man among men.
I'll snap my fingers to show I don't care.
I'll buy me a brand new dress to wear.
I'll scrub my neck and I'll bresh my hair
And start all over again.

"Many a new face will please my eye,
Many a new love will find me.
Never've I once looked back to sigh
Over a romance behind me.
Many a new day will dawn before I do!
Many a light lad may kiss and fly,
A kiss gone by is bygone.
Never've I asked an August sky,
'Where has last July gone?'
Never've I wandered through the rye,
Wonderin' where has some guy gone—
Many a new day will dawn before I do!"

. . . . . .

Ado Annie has come to give Ali Hakim the sad news. She has got to marry Will. Ali takes it manfully, even cheerfully. If Ado Annie is sartin sure that she will have to marry Will, and there is no chance for her to change her mind—then his heart is broken. Ado Annie is sorry, but grateful.

Then along comes Ado Annie's father. He is a scrappy little man and he carries a shotgun. He wants to know about this story of Will Parker's fifty dollars, and he wants to advise Ado

Annie to get it away from Will before he loses it.

"But, Paw—he ain't exackly kep' it. He spent it all on presents—"

"See? Whut'd I tell you? Now he cain't have you. I said it had to be fifty dollars cash!"

"But, Mr. Carnes, is that fair?" Ali Hakim is worried.

"Who the hell are you?"

"This is Ali Hakim," explains Annie.

"Well, shet your face, or I'll fill yer behind so full of buckshot you'll be walkin' around like a duck the rest of your life."

"Ali, if I don't have to marry Will, mebbe your heart don't have to be busted in two like you said."

"I did not say that."

"Oh, yes, you did."

Naturally, Mr. Carnes can't stand around letting any man call his daughter a liar. He decides to investigate. Just what has this peddler been saying to Ado Annie? And where? And when?

Ado Annie remembers. Last night, in the moonlight, alongside a haystack, Ali had called her his Persian kitten. "He said I was like a Persian kitten cuz they was the cats with the soft, round tails," confesses Ado Annie.

"That's enough," explodes Carnes. "In this part of the country that better be a proposal of marriage."

"That's what I thought," agrees Ado Annie.

"Look, Mr. Carnes . . . I'm no good," pleads Ali. "I'm a peddler. A peddler travels up and down and all around and you'd hardly ever see your daughter no more."

"That'd be all right. Take keer of her, son. Take keer of my little rosebud."

With that Carnes takes a firmer grip of his shotgun and leaves them. "Oh, Ali Hakim, ain't it wonderful, paw makin' up our mind for us?" purrs Ado Annie. "He won't change, neither. Onct he gives his word that you c'n have me, why, you *got* me."

"I KNOW I got you!"

"Mrs. Ali Hakim . . . the Peddler's Bride! Wait till I tell the girls!" And Ado Annie has run happily away to spread the news.

It is obviously time for Ali to express his indignation in song. And he does. "It's a Scandal! It's a Outrage!" protests the peddler. He's been Trapped! Tricked! Hoodblinked! Hambushed! As the cowboys trickle in he takes them into his confidence—

"Twenty minutes ago I'm free like a breeze.
Free like a bird in the woodland wild,
Free like a gypsy, free like a child,
I'm unattached!"

Several of the men jump over the fence and gather closer, the better to hear this burning lament—

"Twenty minutes ago I can do what I please,
Flick my cigar ashes on a rug,
Dunk with a doughnut, drink from a jug—
I'm a happy man."

The men find themselves comfortable places to sit. This is evidently going to be quite a story—

"I'm minding my own business like I oughter,
Ain't meaning any harm to anyone,
I'm talking to a certain farmer's daughter,
Then I'm looking in the muzzle of a gun!"

The men are in perfect agreement: "It's gittin' so you cain't have any fun," they sing. "Every daughter has a father with a gun!" . . .
"It's a scandal! It's a outrage! How a gal gits a husband today!"

"If you make one mistake when the moon is bright,
Then they tie you to a contract so you'll make it every night."

By the time the peddler is finished with his song, the men are ready to announce their independence, if not to start a revolution. But just then the girls appear and they are completely cowed. Each girl picks her a man and holds him. They may have come in one by one. They go out two and two—and like it. . . .
Curly and Gertie are back. Laurey is packing her lunch hamper on the porch. There is a good deal of glaring. Remarks are passed. Then Aunt Eller calls Gertie in the house. Gertie would have Curly go in with her, but he isn't ready jist yet.
"Well, don't be long," cautions Gertie. "And don't fergit when the auction starts, mine's the biggest hamper!"
Gertie is laughing when she disappears. But Laurey isn't laughing. So that is the Cummin's girl she has heared so much about! My, how old she's got! "Never did see anybody git so peeked lookin' in so short a time," muses Laurey.

Is she really goin' to drive to the box social with that Jud feller? Curly would know. Laurey doesn't see why she shouldn't. No reason, Curly admits, except everybody seems to expect her to go with him. In that case it is probably just as well she isn't. People might talk about them.

"You know how they air—like a swarm of mud wasps," says Laurey. "Always gotta be buzzin' 'bout sump'n."

"Well, whut're they sayin'?" Curly would know. "That you're stuck on me?"

"Uhn-uh. Most of the talk is that you're stuck on me."

"Cain't imagine how these ugly rumors start."

"Me, neither."

Laurey is singing now. "Why do they think up stories that link my name with yours?" she asks, melodiously.

"Why do the neighbors gossip all day behind their doors?" joins in Curly.

"I have a way to prove what they say is quite untrue," warbles Laurey. "Here is the gist, a practical list of 'don'ts' for you:

> "Don't throw bouquets at me—
> Don't please my folks too much,
> Don't laugh at my jokes too much—
> People will say we're in love.
> Don't sigh and gaze at me,
> Your sighs are so like mine—
> Your eyes mustn't glow like mine—
> People will say we're in love.
> Don't start collecting things—
> Give me my rose and my glove;
> Sweetheart, they're suspecting things—
> People will say we're in love."

"Some people claim that you are to blame as much as I," counters Curly. "Why do you take the trouble to bake my fav'rit pie? Grantin' your wish, I carved your initials on that tree. . . . Jist keep a slice of all the advice you give so free—

> "Don't praise my charm too much,
> Don't look so vain with me—
> Don't stand in the rain with me,
> People will say we're in love:
> Don't take my arm too much,
> Don't keep your hand in mine,
> Your hand feels so good in mine—

> People will say we're in love.
> Don't dance all night with me,
> Till the stars fade from above,
> They'll see it's all right with me,
> People will say we're in love!"

The song finished, they are back on that old Jud topic. Curly thinks maybe Laurey could tell Jud that she couldn't go with him, but Laurey is afraid she couldn't. In that case Curly thinks he will go down to that smokehouse to see what's so attractive about that Jud. And off he goes, angrily.

Laurey watches him go. She is sitting in the rocker, softly repeating a refrain of the song: "Don't sigh and gaze at me; your sighs are so like mine, your eyes mustn't glow like mine—"

She is crying softly when Aunt Eller comes out and offers her a hanky.

"Whut'd I want with a ole hanky?" snaps Laurey.

"Y'got a smudge on yer cheek—jist under yer eye."

Laurey dries her eyes and starts toward the house. Suddenly she remembers her bottle of " 'Lixir of Egypt" and goes back to get it. She looks at Aunt Eller and then runs out through the gate. Aunt Eller is rocking contentedly. She is smiling and humming a refrain of "People Will Say We're in Love" as the lights dim.

Scene Two

The smokehouse is "a dark, dirty building where the meat was once kept. The rafters are smoky, covered with dust and cobwebs." A low loft is a catch-all for many things: horse collars, plowshares, binder twine, a keg of nails. Under the loft Jud's bed "is grimy and never made. On the walls tobacco advertisements; an enlistment poster; covers off the Police Gazette." Two chairs, a table and a spittoon comprise the furniture.

Jud Fry "is about thirty-five, with a curious earth-colored face and hairy hands." He comes slouching in the door now, and is no sooner seated at the table than there is a knock on the door. Jud goes quickly on tiptoes to the window and peeks out. He glides swiftly back to the table, takes a pistol from the drawer and starts to polish it. At a second knock he yells: "Well, open it, cain't you?"

With a genial "Howdy," Curly strolls in. He has come, he explains, just to make a call. He takes note of Jud and the gun and starts a casual inspection of the room. Notices the pink pictures especially. One is of a "naked womern." At least she is almost naked. Jud is interested. That one ain't a thing to what he's got in the drawer. He pulls out a greasy pack of postcards to prove it. They's some humdingers among those.

"I'll go blind," protests Curly, covering his eyes and tossing the cards back on the table. "That's a good-lookin' rope you got there." He takes the rope off its peg and begins to spin it. "Spins nice. You know Will Parker? He can shore spin a rope." He tosses the rope over a rafter and pulls down on both ends tentatively. "You could hang yerself on that, Jud."

"I could what?"

"Hang yerself. It ud be as easy as fallin' off a log! Fact is, you could stand on a log—or a cheer if you'd rather—right about here—see? And put this here around your neck. Tie that good up there first, of course. Then all you'd have to do would be to fall off the log—or the cheer, whichever you'd rather fall off of. In five minutes, or less, with good luck, you'd be dead as a doornail."

"Whut'd you mean by that?" Jud is suspicious, but a little fascinated, too.

" 'Nen folks ud come to your funril and sing sad songs."

"Yamph!"

"They would. You never know how many people like you until you're daid. Y'd probably be laid out in the parlor— Y'd be all diked out in yer best suit with yer hair combed down slick, and a high starched collar."

Jud's interest mounts as Curly's imagination leads him on. There would be flowers, and palms all around the cawfin; the men ud bare their heads and the womern would sniffle softly. Some might even faint, especially those that had taken a shine to him.

"Whut womern have tuck a shine to me?" demands Jud.

"Lots of womern. On'y they don't never come right out and show you how they feel less'n you die first. They'd shore sing loud, though, when the singin' started—sing like their hearts ud break."

Curly has decided to sing the rest of it. "He starts earnestly and solemnly, improvising the sort of thing he thinks might be sung:

> "Pore Jud is daid,
> Pore Jud Fry is daid!
> All gether 'round his cawfin now and cry,
> He had a heart of gold

And he wasn't very old—
Oh, why did sich a feller have to die?
Pore Jud is daid,
Pore Jud Fry is daid!
He's lookin', oh, so peaceful and serene."

JUD (*touched and suddenly carried away, takes off his hat, sings soft response*)—And serene!
CURLY—He's all laid out to rest
        With his hands acrost his chest,
        His fingernails have never b'en so clean!

(JUD *turns slowly to question the good taste of this last reference, but* CURLY *plunges straight into another item of the imagined wake.*) " 'Nen the preacher'd git up and he'd say: 'Folks! We are gathered here to moan and groan over our brother Jud Fry who hung hisse'f up by a rope in the smokehouse.' 'Nen there'd be weepin' and wailin'— (*Significantly.*) From some of those womern. (JUD *nods his head understandingly.*) 'Nen he'd say, 'Jud was the most misunderstood man in the territory. People useter think he was a mean, ugly feller. (JUD *looks up.*) And they called him a dirty skunk and a ornery pig-stealer. (CURLY *switches quickly.*) But—the folks 'at really knowed him, knowed 'at beneath them two dirty shirts he alw'ys wore, there beat a heart as big as all out-doors.' "

JUD (*repeating reverently, like a negro at a revivalist meeting*)—As big as all out-doors.

The lament continues for another verse, but Curly finally winds it up.

"Pore Jud is daid,
    A candle lights his haid.
    He's lookin', oh, so purty, and so nice.
    He looks like he's asleep,
    It's a shame that he won't keep,
    But it's summer and we're runnin' out of ice . . ."

Curly's sympathy is too much for Jud. He sits at the table and begins to weep. But he's up again in a minute, his eyes narrowing. Mebbe it won't be his funeral. Mebbe it'll be Curly who'll go first. Could be, Curly admits.

Now Curly would know more of Jud's background. Didn't he used to work up at Quapaw? He did, Jud admits. And before that he worked over by Tulsa. They treated him lousy there; treated him like dirt. Did he git even? Curly is curious. That startles Jud. Who said anythin' about gittin' even? But if he ever did want to git even, he'd know how to do it.

With a gun? Curly wants to know. Naw! There's safer ways than that, if you use your brains. Does Curly remember the f'ar at the Bartlett farm over by Sweetwater? Curly remembers. Turrible accident. Burnt up father and mother and daughter.

"That warn't no accident," sneers Jud. "A feller told me— the h'ard hand was stuck on the Bartlett girl, and he found her in the hayloft with another feller."

"And it was him that burned the place?"

"It tuck him weeks to git all the kerosene—buying it at different times. Feller who told me made out it happened in Missouri, but I knowed all the time it was the Bartlett farm— What a liar he was."

"And a kind of a—a murderer, too. Wasn't he?" asks Curly. He opens the window to let in a little air.

Jud's suspicions begin to stir. Curly hasn't told him yet what business has brought him there. They haven't got any cattle or cow ponies to sell, and the oat crop is already spoken for. That would leave only one other thing on the farm that Curly might want, and it better not be that.

But it is, Curly is quick to admit, with some defiance, as he rises to face Jud. Jud's threats mean nothing to him. "A feller wouldn't feel very safe in here with you . . . if he didn't know you. But I know you, Jud," says Curly, firmly.

"In this country they's two things you c'n do if you're a man. Live out of doors is one. Live in a hole is the other. I've set by my horse in the bresh some'eres and heared a rattle snake many a time. Rattle, rattle, rattle! he'd go, skeered to death. Somebody comin' clost to his hole! Somebody gonna step on him! Get his old fangs ready, full o' pizen! Curl up an' wait! Long's you live in a hole yer skeered; you got to have pertection. You c'n have muscles—oh, like arn—and still be as weak as a empty bladder—less'n you got things to barb yer hide with."

Curly has taken a step nearer Jud; his voice suddenly becomes harsh and distinct. "How'd you git to be the way you air, anyway—settin' here in this filthy hole—and thinkin' the way you're thinkin'? Why don't you do sump'n healthy onct in awhile, 'stid of stayin' shet up here a-crawlin' and a-festerin'."

With an angry grunt Jud has reached for the pistol. "In a kind of reflex, a kind of desperate frenzy, he pulls the trigger.

Luckily the gun is pointed toward the ceiling."

Curly, "actually in a state of high excitement, but outwardly cool and calm, draws his own gun. "You orta feel better now," he says. "Hard on the roof, though. I wisht you'd let me show you sump'n."

Jud doesn't move, but Curly proceeds to show him how easy it is for him to shoot a bullet through a knothole no bigger'n a dime, without even techin' the edges. "I knowed I could do it. You saw it, too, didn't you?"

Before Jud can answer there is a racket outside. The folks at the house have heard the two shots and come hurrying over. Aunt Eller arrives gasping for breath. Who f'ared off a gun and why? Curly points to the knothole. He had fired onct.

"Well, ain't you a pair of purty nuthin's, a-pickin' away at knotholes and skeerin' everybody to death!"

Aunt Eller is disgusted. She calls to the others that everything is all right and goes back to the house.

Ali Hakim stays on. He'd like to visit with men for a little. It's good to get away from the women. But Curly can't stay, either. He has to pick up the surrey he's h'ared. He's still hoping Laurey will decide to ride with him and Aunt Eller. Mebbe she will, too.

"She promised to go with me, and she better not change her mind," Jud calls after him. "She better not!"

The peddler would like to do a little business with his postcards, but Jud is in no mood for dickerin' today. He might buy one of those Little Wonders, though—one with a spring that when you press it 't releases a long, sharp blade. You could give it to a feller to look through, snap out the blade, which would be just above his chest, and then Bang! Down you come!

Ali doesn't carry anything like that. Too dangerous. But he has got a new line of postcards. Again Jud puts him off. He's through with pictures. He's going to get him a real woman.

Ali can't understand that. Always he is in trouble because of women. With pictures it's different. You get tired of them, all right. Throw them away and get some new ones. "You get tired of a woman, and what can you do? Nothin'! Just keep gettin' tireder and tireder!"

"So you want a real woman— Say, do you happen to know a girl named Ado Annie?"

"I don't want her." Jud is positive.

"I don't want her, either. But I got her."

Ali has packed his bag and started off. Jud watches him crossing the yard. "Don't want nuthin' from no peddler," he mutters. "Want real things! Whut am I doin' shet up here—like that feller says—a-crawlin' and a-festerin'. Whut am I doin' in this lousy smokehouse?"

The mood starts Jud singing lugubriously of his "Lonely Room." "The floor creaks, the door squeaks, there's a field mouse a-nibblin' on a broom. And I set by myself like a cobweb on a shelf, by myself in a lonely room."

But there are times, Jud sings, when he dreams of all the things he wishes for and sometimes they turn out like he wants them to be: Then he's better than any smart aleck cow hand—

"And the girl that I want ain't afraid of my arms, and her own soft arms keep me warm. And her long yaller hair falls acrost my face jist like the rain in a storm—"

> "I ain't gonna dream 'bout her arms no more!
> I ain't gonna leave her alone!
> Goin' outside,
> Git myself a bride,
> Git me a womern to call my own!"

Jud's wicked face has settled into an expression of evil determination. He is making ready to carry out his threat as the lights dim and the scene is changed.

SCENE THREE

The singing girls and Gertie have gathered under a tree at the edge of a beautiful clearing in the wood. A girl named Vivian is telling Gertie's fortune. The others are listening and giggling at the revelations.

Now Laurey has come upon them, walking a little wistfully, as though she were in a dream. She is carrying the bottle of "Egyptian Elixir" she had bought from the peddler, and this amuses the girls. Laurey is serious. The elixir is going to help her make up her mind, which is already clearing a little. Couldn't they go some other place to tell fortunes?

"Hey, Laurey, is it true you're lettin' Jud take you tonight 'stid of Curly?"

"Tell you better when I think everythin' out clear. Beginnin' to see things clear a-ready," she says. She has taken a long whiff of the elixir and closed her eyes tight.

By ones and twos the girls leave her, calling back suggestions for her dream-wishes—"Out of your dreams and into his arms

you long to fly." . . . "You don't need Egyptian smellin' salts
to tell you why." . . . "Out of your dream and into the hush
of falling shadows." . . . "When the mist is low and stars are
breaking through." . . . "Then out of your dreams you'll go
. . . Into a dream come true."

"Make up your mind, make up your mind, Laurey."

The girls have drifted off. The lights are dimming. Laurey is
picked out by a single ray. She is singing softly—

"Out of my dreams and into your arms I long to fly,
I will come as evening comes to woo a waiting sky.
Out of my dreams and into the hush of falling shadows,
When the mist is low, and stars are breaking through,
Then out of my dreams I'll go,
Into a dream with you."

The Ballet

In the fading light Curly appears at the other side of the
clearing. He stands for a moment looking across at Laurey. She
has risen and is facing him. Then out of the mists Curly's ballet
counterpart comes and stands beside him, and Laurey's ballet
counterpart is standing beside her. These are figures fading into
Laurey's dream. Now the real Curly and the real Laurey back
away into the grove and their ballet counterparts move toward
each other and into an embrace.

They are dancing ecstatically when a young girl appears,
sees them and rushes off to spread the news. Soon a crowd of
boys and girls have danced into the scene. Two of Curly's
cowboy friends stroll in and attract his attention. He kisses
Laurey and follows them.

Now the little girl has brought Laurey a nosegay and broken
into tears as she presents it. A bridal veil comes floating down
from the skies and groups of girl friends dance on to kiss Laurey
and help her arrange the veil. Now Curly and the cowboys gal-
lop in and dance gaily about Laurey. Curly takes his place
and awaits his bride, as she marches down an aisle the girls
have formed.

But now the ballet counterpart of Jud walks in and grabs the
veil from Laurey's head. When she looks up, expecting to see
Curly, it is Jud who is staring down at her. Horrified she backs
away. Her friends and Curly, too, their faces set and hard, walk
away from her. She is alone with Jud.

Jud starts to dance with Laurey, but his attention is soon diverted by the appearance of three dance hall girls who look very much like the Police Gazette pictures on the walls of the smokehouse. A few of the cowboys stroll in and whistle at the girls, who have broken into an amusing and satirically bawdy dance.

When the Police Gazette girls have danced away Laurey and Jud are again alone. Curly comes back. "The long-awaited conflict with Jud is now unavoidable. Curly, his hand holding an imaginary pistol, fires at Jud again and again, but Jud keeps advancing slowly upon him, immune to bullets. Jud lifts Curly in the air and throws him to the ground. A fierce fight ensues.

"The friends of Laurey and Curly run helplessly from one side to the other. Just when the tables seem to have turned in Curly's favor Jud gets a death grip on his throat! He is killing Curly! Laurey runs up to him and begs him to release her lover! It is clear by her pantomime that she will give herself to Jud to save Curly. Jud drops Curly's limp body, picks up Laurey and carries her away. Over Jud's shoulder she blows a feeble, heart-broken kiss to Curly's prostrate form on the ground. The crowd surrounds Curly and carries him off in the dark."

Now the lights are up again. The real Jud is shaking the real Laurey out of her dream.

"Wake up, Laurey," he calls. "It's time to start for the party."

Laurey awakens mechanically and starts to go with Jud. Just then the real Curly appears and waits expectantly. Laurey hesitates, but, remembering her dream, "she avoids its reality by taking Jud's arm and going with him, looking back wistfully at Curly with the sad eyes of her ballet counterpart."

Curly is standing alone, puzzled, dejected and defeated. The curtain falls.

ACT II

The box party is in full swing at Skidmore's ranch house. The guests are dancing a set. This doesn't go on for long. Andrew Carnes wants to sing. His is a practical sort of song with which the neighbors are familiar. This permits them all to join the choruses and the dance that goes with them.

"The farmer and the cow man should be friends," sings Carnes in a husky baritone. "Oh, the farmer and the cow man should be friends. One man likes to push a plow. The other likes to chase a cow. But that's no reason why they cain't be friends!

"Territory folks should stick together,
Territory folks should all be pals,
Cowboys, dance with the farmers' daughters!
Farmers, dance with the ranchers' gals."

The dance, however, doesn't bring them closer together. Shortly familiar arguments are flying back and forth. "I'd like to say a word for the farmer," shouts Andrew Carnes. "He come out West and made a lot of changes."

"He come out West and built a lot of fences!" counters Will Parker, scornfully. "And built 'em right acrost our cattle ranges," chimes in Curly.

Something is about to be started when Carnes steps in, quiets the argument, and goes on with his song. There are a lot of verses and a lot of threatened fights. When one of the brawls gets a good start and the women can't stop it, Aunt Eller grabs a gun, fires it in the air.

"They ain't nobody goin' to slug out anythin'," she announces. "This here's a party! Sing it, Andrew!" And Andrew sings.

Soon the dance is resumed, gay and unrestrained. Then it is announced that it is time to start the box social. Aunt Eller, by popular vote, must be the auctioneer.

"All right, then," Aunt Eller agrees, taking her place at the head of the crowd. "Now you know the rules, gentlemen. Y'got to bid blind. Y'ain't supposed to know whut girl goes with whut hamper. Of course if yer sweetheart has told you that hers'll be done up in a certain kind of way with a certain color ribbon, that ain't my fault. Now we'll auction all the hampers on t'other side of the house and work around back here. Follow me."

The crowd has followed Aunt Eller when the peddler strolls in and stops Will Parker. He feels that he and Will should have a talk. Will is pretty mad at Ali's having gone and gotten himself engaged to Ado Annie.

"I don't know what to call you," sneers Will. "You ain't purty enough for a skunk. You ain't skinny enough for a snake. You're too little to be a man and too big to be a mouse. I reckon you're a rat."

"That's logical," admits Ali.

Will would also like to be sure the peddler loves Ado Annie—loves her enough to spend his last cent on presents for her. That's how Will loved her, and he has the presents to show for it.

It is the bag of presents that gives Ali an idea. If Will had the fifty dollars they cost in cash, would he take Ado Annie back? Of course he would. With that assurance the peddler goes into the bag and begins offering Will fabulous prices for what he finds—eight dollars for a hot water bag that only cost three-fifty; twenty-two dollars for a nightgown with ribbons and bows on the neck line. That was to be Will's wedding nightgown, but not for twenty-two dollars. All right. Ali will pay twenty-two fifty—but not a cent more.

A pair of corsets is bought for fifteen dollars—that makes a total of forty-five fifty—and Will begins to get the idea. If he can get another three-fifty! He offers the peddler his Little Wonder, but the peddler is afraid of those contraptions since he found out about the knife attachment.

At that moment Laurey comes running in, a frightened look in her eyes. She is looking for Aunt Eller and the others and goes on around the house to find them. A second later Jud Fry appears, calling to Laurey. He is carrying her lunch basket. Will offers him the Little Wonder. It happens to be something Jud is interested in having. He buys it for three-fifty.

Now Will is excited. He closes his eyes and begins struggling with a deep mathematical problem. "Let's see—three fifty from him and forty-five fifty from you—'at makes fifty dollars, don't it?"

He's still a dollar short, Ali is obliged to tell him. For a second Will's face is clouded with disappointment, then he thinks of such presents as are left. "How much for all the resta the stuff in this bag?" he asks.

"One dollar!" bids Ali.

"Done! . . . Now I got fifty dollars, ain't I? Know what that means?" He turns on the peddler. "Means I'm goin' to take Ado Annie back from you!"

"You wouldn't do a thing like that to me!"

"Oh, wouldn't I? And when I tell her Paw who I got mosta the money offa, mebbe he'll change his mind 'bout who's smart and who's dumb!"

The crowd is coming back. Jud is snapping the blade in and out of the Little Wonder and winking at the peddler. Aunt Eller has brought the last two hampers with her. "Who's they are I ain't got no idy," says she.

"The little one's mine! And the one next to it is Laurey's!" proudly proclaims Ado Annie.

"Well, that's the end of *that* secret," admits Aunt Eller. "Now whut am I bid fer Annie's hamper?"

The bidding starts at two bits and goes to four. Won't the peddler man pay six? Naw! At least he won't until he feels the barrel of Annie's father's gun in his ribs. Then he goes first to six bits and finally to ninety cents. It might have been awkward for the peddler if Will hadn't stepped in to bid his whole fifty dollars at this point. That causes a good deal of excitement.

Father Carnes doesn't believe Will has got fifty dollars, and when Will produces the money Carnes insists he has already given it to the schoolhouse by his bid. Ado Annie still belongs to the peddler.

This worries Ali. Finally, with a gulp, he raises the bid to fifty-one dollars. This leaves Will with fifty in cash. He gets Ado Annie and the peddler gets the lunch.

Now Aunt Eller puts up Laurey's basket. "I took a peek inside awhile ago and I must say it looks mighty tasty," promises Aunt Eller. "Whut do I hear, gents?"

The bidding has gone to a dollar when Jud booms in with a dollar and a quarter. Cord Elam and Andrew Carnes start pushing the bidding up until Jud is forced to say four dollars and two bits to stay in the contest. Then they run it up to six dollars and two bits. Jud is about to pay the money and take the hamper, but Aunt Eller stops him—

"Hold on, you! I ain't said goin', goin', gone yit! . . . Goin' to Jud fer six dollars and two bits! Goin—"

Curly has come in with a saddle on his arm. "Who'd you say was gittin' Laurey?" he asks.

"Jud Fry."

"And for how much?"

"Six and a quarter."

"I don't figger 'at's quite enough, do you?"

"It's more'n you got!" snaps Jud, angrily.

Curly's saddle cost thirty dollars. He sells it for ten and bids the ten. When Jud adds his usual two bits, Curly turns to the cowboys—

"Most of you boys know my horse, Dun. She's a—" He swallows hard. "—a kind of nice horse—gentle and well broke."

"Don't sell Dun, Curly," cries Laurey; "it ain't worth it."

"I'll give you twenty-five fer her," says Cord Elam.

"I'll sell Dun to you." He turns to Aunt Eller. "That makes the bid thirty-five, Aunt Eller."

"Curly, yer crazy!" beams Aunt Eller. "But it's all fer the

schoolhouse, ain't it? All for educatin' and larnin'. Goin' for thirty-five. Goin'—"

"Hold on! I ain't finished biddin'!" shouts Jud, grinning fiercely at Curly. "You jist put up everythin' y' got in the world, didn't yer? Cain't bid the clothes off yer back, cuz they ain't worth nuthin'. Cain't bid yer gun cuz you need that— Yes, sir! You need that bad!" He is looking at Aunt Eller. "So, Aunt Eller, I'm jist as reckless as Curly McLain, I guess. Jist as good at gittin' whut I want. Goin' to bid all I got in the world—all I saved fer two years, doin' farm work. All fer Laurey. Here it is! Forty-two dollars and thirty-one cents." And he pours the money out onto Laurey's hamper.

"Anybody want to buy a gun?" asks Curly. "You, Joe? Bought it brand new last Thanksgivin'. Worth a lot."

"Curly, please don't sell your gun!" Laurey's lips are trembling.

Joe offers eighteen for the gun. Curly takes it; that makes his bid fifty-three dollars and Laurey's hamper goes to Curly.

There is an ugly look on Jud's face as he starts to move toward Curly. Urged on by a watchful Aunt Eller, the crowd breaks into "The Farmer and the Cow Man."

"That's the idy. The cow man and the farmer shud be friends," calls Skidmore, his hand on Jud's shoulder. "You lost the bid, but the biddin' was fair." He turns to Curly. "C'mon, cow man—shake the farmer's hand!"

Jud puts out his hand. Curly hesitates, but finally takes it. Jud takes his Little Wonder out of his pocket. He wants Curly to look at it. The peddler is whispering furiously to Aunt Eller. Curly has taken the gadget and is putting it up to his eye when Aunt Eller calls excitedly: "Curly! Curly, whut you doin'?"

"Doin'? Nuthin' much. Whut you want to squeal at a man like 'at fer? Skeer the liver and lights out of a feller."

"Well, then, stop lookin' at those ole French pitchers and ast me fer a dance. You brung me to the party, didn't you?"

"All right then, you silly ole womern, I'll dance 'ith you. Dance you all over the meadow, you want! Pick 'at banjo to pieces, Sam!" And they have danced wildly away.

A moment later Will and Ado Annie have danced in. They stop to check up. Will has the fifty dollars and it is up to Ado Annie to set the day. She wants to be married on August 15. That was the first day she was kissed. "Was it? I didn't remember that," says Will, smiling. "You wasn't there," frankly admits Ado Annie.

Which reminds Will that now that they are going to be engaged, Ado Annie will have to stop having fun with other fellers. It's going to be "All Er Nuthin'" with Will.

Annie isn't so sure she can live up to Will's standards, but she promises, in song, to do her best—

"With you it's all er nuthin'— All fer you and nuthin' fer me!" Ado Annie concludes. "But if a wife is wise she's gotta realize that men like you are wild and free. So I ain't gonna fuss, ain't gonna frown; have your fun, go out on the town; stay up late and don't come home 'til three, and go right off to sleep if you're sleepy—there's no use waitin' up fer me!"

Will has grabbed and is kissing her as the scene changes.

SCENE TWO

Jud Fry has danced Laurey out of the dance and onto the Skidmores' kitchen porch. There he stops dancing and insists on having a talk. There's several things he'd like to know about Laurey. Principally he would like to know why she is so determined to avoid him. He can remember the time she was so kind to him—when he was sick. He can remember the hot soup she brought him, and the feel of her hand on his brow when she thought he had a fever.

Frightened, Laurey moves away. Jud would hold her if he could. He's never forgot a thing she's said to him, a thing she's done fer him—and now—

"I ain't good enough, am I? I'm a h'ard hand, got dirt on my hands, pig-slop— Ain't fitten to tetch you. You're better, so much better. Yeah, we'll see who's better—Miss Laurey. 'Nen you'll wisht you wasn't so free 'th yer airs, you're sich a fine lady—"

Laurey becomes suddenly angry and loses her fear. "Air you making threats to me?" she demands, facing him. "Air you standin' there tryin' to tell me 'f I don't 'low you to slobber over me like a hog, why, you're gonna do sump'n about it? Why, you're nothin' but a mangy dog and somebody orta shoot you. You think so much about bein' a h'ard hand. Well, I'll jist tell you sump'n that'll rest your brain, Mr. Jud. You ain't a h'ard hand fer me no more, you c'n jist pack up yer duds and scoot. Oh, and I even got better idys'n that. You ain't to come on the place again, you hear me? I'll send yer stuff any place you say, but don't you so much 's set foot inside the pasture gate or I'll sic the dogs onto you!'"

"Said yer say! Brought it on yerself," growls Jud, his looks dark, his voice low and harsh with an inner frenzy. "Cain't he'p it. Cain't never rest! Told you the way it was. You wouldn't listen—"

He has gone past the corner of the house and disappeared. Laurey has sunk down on the bench, a frightened little girl again. Will Parker comes in. He's looking for Ado Annie. She's gone again. Laurey would send him to find Curly. "I wanta see Curly awful bad," she says. "Got to see him."

And, before Will can turn, there is Curly, standing right behind her. She is leaning against him now, crying softly. "Curly— I'm afraid, 'fraid of my life—!"

CURLY (*in a flurry of surprise and delight*)—Jumpin' toadstools! (*He puts his arms around* LAUREY, *muttering under his breath.*) Great Lord!

LAUREY—Don't you leave me—

CURLY—Great Godamighty!

LAUREY—Don't mind me a-cryin', I cain't he'p it—

CURLY—Cry your eyes out!

LAUREY—Oh, I don't know what to do!

CURLY—Here. I'll show you. (*He lifts her face and kisses her. She puts her arms about his neck.*) My goodness! (*He shakes his head as if coming out of a daze, gives a low whistle, and backs away.*) Whew! 'Bout all a man can stand in public—! Go 'way from me, *you!*

LAUREY—Oh, you don't like me, Curly—

CURLY—Like you? My God! Git away from me, I tell you, plumb away from me! (*He backs away and sits on the stove.*)

LAUREY—Curly! You're settin' on the stove!

CURLY (*leaping up*)—Godamighty! (*He turns around and puts his hand down gingerly on the lid.*) Aw! 's cold's a hunk of ice!

LAUREY—Wisht it ud burnt a hole in yer pants.

CURLY (*grinning at her, understandingly*)—You do, do you?

LAUREY (*turning away to hide her smile*)—*You* heared me.

CURLY—Laurey, now looky here, you stand over there right where you air, and I'll set over here—and you tell me whut you wanted with me.

LAUREY (*grave again*)—Well—Jud was here. (*She shudders.*) He skeered me—he's crazy. I never saw nobody like him—

He talked wild and he threatened me. So I—I f'ard him! I wisht I hadn't a! They ain't no tellin' whut he'll do now!

CURLY—You f'ard him? Well then! That's all they is to it! Tomorrow I'll get you a new h'ard hand. I'll stay on the place myself tonight, 'f you're nervous about that hound-dog. Now quit yer worryin' about it or I'll spank you. (*His manner changes. He becomes shy. He turns away unable to meet her eyes as he asks the question.*) Hey, while I think of it—how—how 'bout marryin' me?

LAUREY (*as they stand back to back*)—Gracious, whut'd I wanta marry you fer?

CURLY—Well, couldn't you mebbe think of some reason why you might?

LAUREY—I cain't think of nothin' right now, hardly.

CURLY (*following her*)—Laurey, please, ma'am—marry me. I—don't know what I'm gonna do if you—if you don't.

LAUREY (*touched*)—Curly—why, I'll marry you—'f you want me to—

CURLY (*kissing her*)—I'll be the happiest man alive soon as we're married. Oh, I got to learn to be a farmer, I see that! Quit thinkin' about th'owing the rope, and start in to git my hands blistered a new way! Oh, things is changin' right and left! Buy up mowin' machines, cut down the prairies! Shoe yer horses, drag them plows under the sod! They gonna make a state outa this, they gonna put it in the Union! Country a-changin', got to change with it! Bring up a pair of boys, new stock, to keep up 'th the way things is goin' in this here crazy country! Now I got you to he'p me—I'll mount to sump'n yit! . . .

Curly is so excited he'd like to shout loud enough for everybody in the county to hear that Laurey Williams is his girl; that she's went and got him to ast her to marry him! He has kissed Laurey again. And again. And now they are happily singing a refrain of "People Will Say We're in Love." Let people say it! Who cares now?

The scene has changed. The peddler has come to say good-by to Ado Annie. The lonely gypsy must go back to the lonely road. He's glad he's leaving Annie with a man who loves her "like nothing ever loved nobody. . . . A man who will stick to you all your life and be a regular Darby and Jones."

Now he would show her how they say good-by in Persia. He

draws her tenderly to him and plants a long kiss on her lips. "That was good-by?" asks Ado Annie, wistfully. So there is another long kiss—and in walks Will Parker. "I am glad you will marry such a wonderful man as this Will Parker," the peddler is quick to say, as he catches a sight of Will. "You deserve a fine man and you got one."

"Hello, Will. Ali Hakim is saying good-by," Ado Annie explains.

Ali continues his leave-taking. He is a friend of the family now. He has an arm around Annie and a hand on Will's shoulder. "Back to the open road. A poor gypsy. Good-by, my baby." He is smiling at Will as he reaches for Ado Annie. "I show you how we say good-by in my country." Ado Annie is set and willing. He releases her finally. "Persian good-by," he repeats. "Lucky fellow! I wish it was me she was marrying instead of you."

"It don't seem to make no difference hardly," says Will.

Ado Annie would like to be sure that occasionally Will would remember, even if he never goes traveling, to give her one of those Persian good-bys. But she has much to learn, Will assures her. A Persian good-by ain't nuthin' compared to a Oklahoma hello! Which he proceeds to demonstrate. And he's right.

SCENE THREE

At the back of Laurey's house the wedding party is going great guns. The shouting and cheering comes from beyond the barn. In the yard Carnes is worried. He has been afraid Jud Fry would be making trouble. Jud has been away for three weeks, but he is back now. Carnes had seen him drunk in Claremore.

The crowd comes pouring in. Laurey is wearing her mother's wedding dress and is very lovely. The boys and girls are singing—

"They couldn't pick a better time to start in life!" . . . "It ain't too early and it ain't too late!" . . . "Startin' as a farmer with a brand new wife—" . . . "Soon be livin' in a brand new state!"

The brand-new state, it soon appears, is Oklahoma. It is Curly who sings about that—

"Oklahoma!
Where the wind comes sweepin' down the plain,
And the wavin' wheat
Can sure smell sweet

When the wind comes right behind the rain.
Oklahoma!
Every night my honey lamb and I
Sit alone and talk
And watch a hawk
Makin' lazy circles in the sky.
We know we belong to the land,
And the land we belong to is grand!
And when we say:
Ee—ee—ow! A-yip-i-o-ee-ay!
We're only sayin',
'You're doin' fine, Oklahoma!
Oklahoma. O.K.!' "

It is a stirring song, repeated now by all the cow men and the farmers and all their womenfolk. . . .

It's time for Laurey to be dressin', and time for Curly to be gettin' his things out of Aunt Eller's room. The bride and groom have no sooner disappeared in the house than conspiracy is hatched among the men. Of course there's goin' to be a shivoree, says Carnes. It's a good old custom and never hurt nobody. Ado Annie is hopin' it ain't goin' to be rough.

Now Gertie Cummings joins the party. She missed Laurey's wedding, but she had one of her own. And who do you think she married? Ali Hakim, the lonesome gypsy! Ado Annie can hardly believe it.

"Did you see my ring, girls?" Gertie is giggling, ecstatically. The girls have surrounded her.

"How long you been married?" Ado Annie asks the peddler. Ali appears "dejected, sheepish and a ghost of the man he was."

"Four days." Gertie's laugh rings out from the group. Ali winces. "Four days with that laugh should count like a golden wedding," he wails.

"But if you married her, you musta wanted to," persists Ado Annie.

"Sure I wanted to. I wanted to marry her when I saw the moonlight shining on the barrel of her father's shotgun! . . . I thought it would be better to be alive. . . . Now I'm not so sure." . . .

The shivoree has started. The men have come sneaking back one at a time. One climbs up the trellis for a peek in a second story window. What he sees sets him snickerin'. He comes down and reports to the others and there is a smothering of giggles and snorts.

At a signal they all start pounding on tin pans with spoons. The din is terrific.

"Come on down, peaceable, Laurey, sugar!" yells one.

"And you, too, you curly-headed cowboy," calls another.

Three of the men have run into the house. The others are tossing up rag dolls and shouting: "Hey, Laurey! Here's a girl baby fer you!" . . . "And here's a baby boy!" . . . "Here's twins!"

Curly is pulled out of the house and hoisted on the shoulders of the men. Laurey and Aunt Eller are on the porch, enjoying the good-natured hazing.

Suddenly Jud Fry appears. Everyone becomes quiet and still, sensing trouble. "Weddin' party still goin' on? Glad I ain't too late. Got a present for the groom! But first I wanta kiss the bride!"

Jud grabs Laurey, but Curly pulls him off. "An' here's my present fer you!" With that he hits Curly. The fight starts, with the crowd milling around the two men. Jud pulls out a knife and starts for Curly. Curly grabs him by the arm and throws him. Jud falls on his knife, groans and lies still. The men are bending over him, offering advice freely as to what should be done.

Laurey is clinging desperately to Curly. "Cain't be! Like that—to happen to us!" she weeps. Curly has slumped back from the crowd like a sick man.

They have carried Jud to a rig to be driven to a doctor's. Curly has kissed Laurey and turned her over to Aunt Eller. He will have to go along and see if anything can be done. "I don't see why this had to happen when everythin' was so fine," weeps Laurey.

"Don't let yer mind run on it," advises a comforting Aunt Eller. "If you cain't fergit jist don't try to, honey. Oh, lots of things happens to folks. Sickness, er bein' pore and hungry. Even—bein' old and afeared to die. That's the way of it, cradle to grave. And you can stand it. They's one way. You gotta be hearty, you got to be. You cain't deserve the sweet and tender things in life less'n you're tough."

Curly is back. Cord Elam, who is a fed'ral marshal, thinks he orta give himself up—tonight, he reports. "Tonight!" echoes Laurey, miserably.

"Why, yer train leaves Claremore in twenty minutes!" protests Aunt Eller.

"Best thing is for Curly to go of his own accord and tell the Judge," insists Elam.

But Andrew Carnes is the Judge, ain't he? Why not tell him now and git it over with? It wouldn't be proper outside a court, Elam thinks. That would be breakin' the law.

"Well, let's not break the law. Let's just bend it a little," suggests Aunt Eller. "Come on, Andrew. Start the trial. We ain't got but a few minutes."

"Andrew—I got to protest!" Cord Elam is worried.

"Oh, shet yer trap," says the Judge. "We can give the boy a fair trial without lockin' him up on his weddin' night." He turns to Curly. "Here's the long and short of it: First I got to ask you: Whut's your plea?" When Curly doesn't answer he adds: "That means why did you do it?"

"Why'd I do it? Cuz he's been pesterin' Laurey and I'd always said some day I'd—"

"Jist a minnit! Jist a minnit! Don't let your tongue wobble around in your mouth like 'at. . . . Listen to my question. What happened tonight 'at made you kill him?"

"Why, he come at me with a knife—and—and—"

"And you had to defend yerself, didn't you?"

"Why, yes—and furthermore—"

"Never mind the furthermore—the plea is self-defense—" The women start to chatter. "Quiet! . . . Now, is there a witness who saw this happen?"

Several of the men speak up. "I seen it." . . . "Self-defense all right." . . . "Tried to stab him 'ith a frog sticker!"

Again there is some objection on Marshal Elam's part, but this time Skidmore shuts the Marshal up. "We ain't goin' to let you send the boy to jail on his weddin' night. We jist ain't goin' to *let* you. So shet up!"

The boys are for pulling the happy couple to the train in Curly's surrey but Carnes stops them. "Hey, wait! I ain't even told the verdick yet."

"Well—the verdick's not guilty, ain't it?" asks Curly.

" 'Course, but—"

"Well—then say it!" pleads Laurey.

"NOT GUILTY!" shouts the crowd.

"Court's adjourned!" laughs Carnes.

Aunt Eller has sunk into a chair to recover from the excitement. Ado Annie and Will Parker wander in holding hands. "Where on earth you been?" Aunt Eller wants to know.

"Will and me had a misunderstandin'. But he explained it

fine," says Ado Annie. There are wisps of straw clinging to Ado Annie's back as she turns to go.

"Hey there, bride and groom, y' ready?" calls one of the boys as the surrey is wheeled out into the yard.

"Here we come!" yells Curly, dashing from the house with a happy Laurey. She runs over to kiss Aunt Eller. Curly climbs into the surrey and Laurey is lifted up beside him. Aunt Eller and three of the girls are crying a little. Everyone else is singing "Oh, what a beautiful mornin'" gaily and loudly. "Oh, what a beautiful day—"

The men have started to pull the surrey. Everybody is waving and shouting.

THE CURTAIN FALLS

THE PLAYS AND THEIR AUTHORS

"The Patriots," a drama in a prologue and three acts by Sidney
Kingsley. Copyright, 1943, by the author. Copyright and
published, 1943, by Random House, Inc., New York.

Sidney Kingsley made his first appearance in these volumes
as the author of "Men in White" the season of 1933-34. Again
in 1935-36 he scored a notable success with "Dead End," and
in 1939-40 one of his minor successes, "The World We Make,"
produced by the Theatre Guild, was included. Mr. Kingsley is
a native New Yorker, born in 1906, and graduated from Cornell
in 1928. He was prominent in the activities of the Cornell Dramatic Club, has done a bit of professional acting, and recently
received a lieutenant's commission in the Army.

"The Eve of St. Mark," a drama in two acts by Maxwell Anderson. Copyright, 1942, by the author. Copyright and published, 1942, by Anderson House, Washington, D. C. Distributed by Dodd, Mead & Co., New York.

Maxwell Anderson consistently maintains his record as a regular contributor to this year book of the drama in America. We
began printing Anderson plays in the issue of 1924-25, when he
was co-author of "What Price Glory?" with Laurence Stallings.
We followed with his "Saturday's Children" in 1926-27, his
"Gypsy" in 1928-29, "Elizabeth the Queen" in 1930-31 and his
Pulitzer prize-winning political satire, "Both Your Houses," in
1932-33. "Mary of Scotland," "Valley Forge," "Winterset,"
"High Tor," "The Star Wagon" followed the succeeding five seasons in a row. "Key Largo," 1939-40, and "Candle in the Wind,"
1941-42, have been his most recent entries. Mr. Anderson is a
native of Atlantic, Pa., where he was born in 1888, and his early
writing career was devoted to newspapers and magazines.

"The Skin of Our Teeth," fantastic drama in three acts, by
Thornton Wilder. Copyright, 1943, by the author. Copyright and published, 1943, by Harper & Brothers, New York
and London.

Thornton Wilder made his debut as a "Best Plays" author in the 1937-38 volume with his widely popular "Our Town." That production was definitely on the novelty side, and with "The Skin of Our Teeth" Mr. Wilder certainly clinches his standing as a creative dramatist. He was born in the Middle West, at Madison, Wis., in 1897, while his father, Amos Porter Wilder, was editing a newspaper there. He spent a good deal of his youth, however, in China, when his father was sent to the East as an American Consul General. He was sent home to school and studied at both Oberlin and Yale Universities. He wrote a first play, "The Trumpet Shall Sound," didn't care for it, and turned to novels. He won a Pulitzer award with "The Bridge of San Luis Rey." He came back to the theatre with an adaptation of "Lucrece" for Katharine Cornell. Following "Our Town" he wrote a comedy called "The Merchant of Yonkers" which was not quite good enough to last, even with Jane Cowl playing the heroine. "The Skin of Our Teeth" was this season given the Pulitzer prize as the best play by an American author produced in New York the season of 1942-43.

"Winter Soldiers," drama in two acts by Dan James. Copyright, 1943, by the author.

Dan James was born in Kansas City, Mo., in 1911, and graduated from Yale in 1933. He earned the distinction of being the only graduate majoring in classic Greek. This, to Mr. James, is still something of a mystery. The next three or four years he tried being a traveling salesman, a clerk, and a truck swamper in the Oklahoma oil fields. After these adventures he took to writing plays. They were, those that he finished, and again according to Mr. James, all bad. In 1938 he went to Hollywood and for two years worked as an assistant writer and director for Charles Chaplin, who at the time was working on and worrying about "The Great Dictator." In 1940 Mr. James married Lilith Stanward, who thereupon quit a career as a ballerina. He spent 1941 recovering from the Chaplin influence, and in 1942 he wrote "Winter Soldiers." He sent the script to Shepard Traube, who took it to the Playwrights Company. The Messrs. Robert Sherwood, Maxwell Anderson, Elmer Rice and S. N. Behrman of that company decided that a production of "Winter Soldiers" would cost more than the experiment would be worth, and handed the script back—together with their Sidney Howard Memorial Award for 1942, the same being $1,500 in cash, paid annually to the most promising young American playwright whose work is brought to their attention. "Winter Soldiers" was later produced off Broadway at the Studio Theatre of the New School for Social Research, Mr. Traube directing. At the moment Mr. James is back in Los Angeles working with his wife on a musical play for Broadway. It is not, he insists, about Oklahoma.

"Tomorrow the World," a drama in three acts by James Gow and Arnaud d'Usseau. Copyright, 1943, by the authors. Copyright and published, 1943, by Charles Scribner's Sons, New York.

The authors of "Tomorrow the World" are fellow scenarists of Hollywood. Mr. Gow was born in Iowa and educated at the Universities of Iowa and Colorado. Mr. d'Usseau is a native of Los Angeles and had his schooling in both Los Angeles and New York. The two met at the RKO studios and worked together on a picture called "Repent at Leisure." Since then they have joined their talents frequently, and have recently written a second play which will probably pop up in next season's list.

Both were former newspaper men. Gow worked on the old morning *World* in New York for three years, being the film critic the last eight weeks of the paper's life. Before that he had been both a church and theatre organist. After the *World* was discontinued he went to Hollywood, and had a hand in shaping "One Night of Love" for Grace Moore. He has had two plays, written with Edmund North, tried out in California.

D'Usseau was working as a United Press reporter in Arizona when he decided to try Hollywood. His first job was that of a scene dresser and then he switched to the writing department. Success with a mystery story kept him tied to that type of work for months.

"Harriet," a drama in three acts by Florence Ryerson and Colin Clements. Copyright, 1943, by the authors. Copyright and published, 1943, by Charles Scribner's Sons, New York.

Florence Ryerson and Colin Clements were Western-born, but Eastern-educated, she finishing at Radcliffe and he at Harvard. They both studied with George Pierce Baker in his 47 Workshop. Since graduation, operating as a family writing team, they have probably produced more short stories, novels, scenarios and plays than any other pair in America. Ask Mr. Clements, as I did, about Miss Ryerson, and this is what you get:

"Ryerson is the third generation in her family to earn a living by writing. Her earliest contact with the profession was when she was planted in the wastebasket under her newspaper editor father's desk to keep her out of the presses. It is impossible for her to remember when she first started writing, but there was, for many years, a crisp five-dollar bill in the family safety-deposit, payment for a story written and published at the age of eight."

And then, if you turn about and ask Miss Ryerson about Mr. Clements she responds enthusiastically with this:

"Clements was adventurous. After a period of stage work in New York, both as actor and stage manager, he went abroad, managed to get involved in the Mesopotamian campaign, from which he barely escaped with his life, lived in Roumania long enough to dramatize one of Queen Marie's novels for the State Theatre, then returned to Paris, where he wrote his first book of short plays. Later he directed theatres in various parts of America."

When not in New York, they live at Shadow Ranch, in the San Fernando Valley, in California, with their son. For the last few years they have almost entirely given up studio work for the writing of plays. "June Mad" and "Ever Since Eve," written for young people, are steady best sellers in the high-school and little-theatre field. " 'Through the Night,' a mystery play, was blitzed out of London and into the provinces by the Huns," admits Mr. Clements. " 'Glamour Preferred,' a Hollywood comedy, was blitzed out of New York by the critics."

"The Doughgirls," a comedy in three acts by Joseph Fields. Copyright, 1943, by the author. Copyright and published, 1943, by Random House, New York.

Mr. Fields became a "Best Plays" author in the volume covering the season of 1940-41, when he and Jerome Chodorov co-authored the popular comedy, "My Sister Eileen." Last season the same two wrote the immensely successful "Junior Miss." Both plays stemmed from short stories featured in the *New Yorker* magazine, "My Sister Eileen" being a creation of Ruth McKenney and "Junior Miss" a child of Sally Benson's imagination. This year Mr. Fields' first solo work, "The Doughgirls," has no other inspiration than that furnished by his own recent visits to wartime Washington. Mr. Fields is the eldest son of the late Lew Fields, comedian. He was born in New York in

1895 and educated in New York schools. He expected to be a lawyer, but found writing more to his liking. In the Navy in the First World War he wrote many sketches for the gobs. Out of the Navy he did sketches for several Ziegfeld Follies.

"The Damask Cheek," a comedy in three acts by John Van Druten and Lloyd Morris. Copyright, 1943, by the authors; copyright and published, 1943, by Random House, New York.

John Van Druten, born in London, England, in 1901, took to play writing when he got fed up with lecturing on law to the students of various universities, including one at Aberystwyth, Wales. His first play to register solidly was "Young Woodley," (1925), which was a story of undergraduate life in England and was barred by the English censor as reflecting discreditably upon the English school system. The play, however, proved a great success in America. Mr. Van Druten has stuck pretty closely to playwriting since then. His best-known successes in America have been "There's Always Juliet," "The Distaff Side," and "Old Acquaintance," which Jane Cowl and Peggy Wood played through the season of 1940-41.

Lloyd Morris, Mr. Van Druten's collaborator in the writing of "The Damask Cheek," is a native New Yorker, born in 1893. His life has been devoted to literary pursuits. He was a lecturer in literature at Columbia University from 1922 to 1932. He has done a good deal of magazine editing and book reviewing and is the author of "The Celtic Dawn," "The Poetry of E. A. Robinson," "The Rebellious Puritan—a Portrait of Mr. Hawthorne," and "This Circle of Flesh."

"Kiss and Tell," a comedy in three acts by F. Hugh Herbert. Copyright, 1943, by the author. Copyright and published, 1943, by Coward, McCann, Inc., New York.

The author of the most typically American domestic comedy of the season is English-born. F. Hugh Herbert was working in the advertising department of Selfridge's department store in London when, in 1920, he decided to spend a vacation in these United States and see what they were like. The visit satisfied and enthused him. He went back to England, applied for a place on the U.S.A. quota list, came back to America and is now a full-fledged American citizen. He served a term as a practicing scenarist at the Paramount Studio on Long Island. Since then he has worked for the lot of them at different times, and still found time to write four novels, "There You Are," "Vengeance," "A Lover Would Be Nice" and "Revolt of Henry." Also he has been a steady contributor to the magazines, and it was a contract to write twenty-four installments concerned with the life and activities of Corliss Archer that led, first to the radio program, "Meet Corliss Archer," and later to the play, "Kiss and Tell." He finished the play in four weeks, being so well acquainted with the characters it was easy for him to dictate the script. He sold it practically overnight to George Abbott. The Herberts include the author, his wife and their two daughters, Diana, 14, and Pamela, 12. It is from the daughters and their friends, admits Mr. Herbert, that he cribs lines and scenes for both stories and plays.

"Oklahoma," a musical comedy in two acts by Oscar Hammerstein 2d, music by Richard Rodgers. Copyright, 1943, by the authors.

Both Hammerstein and Rodgers are native New Yorkers; both were educated here; both attended Columbia University. Hammerstein was on the graduate committee the year Rodgers wrote his first varsity show, and they like to believe now that it was the Hammerstein vote that put the Rodgers show over, Rodgers being a freshman at the time. Before that no freshman's score had ever been accepted.

Hammerstein is a scion of the theatrical family of that name, having been named to carry on in the tradition of his famous grandfather, the first Oscar, who had a hand in reshaping the operatic history of the metropolis. Oscar 2d had no intention originally of taking to show writing. He expected to be a lawyer, and all his studying was directed to that end. But he "got to fooling around with the varsity shows," and that settled it. When he told his uncle Arthur of his decision to enter show business Arthur insisted that he should learn something of the practical side of play-producing before he tried to write. Oscar 2d started as an assistant stage manager. When he did finally get fully settled writing the books for musical comedies he turned out six hits in seven years—"Rose Marie," "Sunny," "The Desert Song," "Show Boat" and "New Moon."

Rodgers was four years old when his musical gifts became assertive, but he did not write a first song until he was fourteen. His father was a serious-minded physician, but his mother was musically inclined, so, naturally, Richard found inspiration in her encouragement. He and Lorenz Hart were fellow students at Columbia; did several of the varsity shows; got their real start when the Theatre Guild staged a "Garrick Gaieties" to raise funds with which to buy a pair of tapestries for the new Guild Theatre. Rodgers and Hart also turned out a series of hits, once they were started, including "Dearest Enemy," "A Connecticut Yankee," "On Your Toes," "Babes in Arms," "I'd Rather Be Right," "I Married an Angel," "The Boys from Syracuse" and "By Jupiter." The Theatre Guild brought Oscar and Richard together for the "Oklahoma" job.

PLAYS PRODUCED IN NEW YORK

June 15, 1942—June 15, 1943

(Plays marked with asterisk were still playing June 15, 1943)

THE CAT SCREAMS

(7 performances)

A drama in three acts by Basil Beyea, based on the novel of the same title by Todd Downing. Produced by Martha Hodge at the Martin Beck Theatre, New York, June 16, 1942.

Cast of characters—

Consuelo	Cecilia Callejo
Professor Parkham	Herbert Yost
Gwen Reid	Doris Nolan
Miss Giddon	Mildred Dunnock
Steven Tybalt	Lloyd Gough
Madame	Lea Penman
Carl Parkham	Gordon Oliver
Micaela	Osceola Archer
Oliver Reid	Harry Sheppard
Doctor Otero	Martin Wolfson
Soldier	George Spaulding
Soldier	Michael St. Angel

Acts I, II and III.—Lounge of a Pension in La Jorta, Mexico.
Staged by Arthur Pierson; setting by John Root; costumes by Mary Grant.

Madame is running a pension in La Jorta, Mexico. Many of her guests are American. Madame has a pet Siamese cat which can scent the approach of death, according to the superstition of Micaela, Madame's servant. When the cat screams and Micaela faints Dr. Otero is called. He immediately declares a quarantine and places guards around the house. Shortly thereafter an epidemic of suicides breaks out, in the pension and in the village. In the end the epidemic is tied in with a little job of dope-running the Madame was conducting on the side.

(Closed June 20, 1942)

LAUGH, TOWN, LAUGH!

(65 performances)

A vaudeville show assembled and produced by Ed Wynn at the Alvin Theatre, New York, June 22, 1942.

Principals engaged—

Ed Wynn	Jane Froman
Charles Dale	Carmen Amaya
Joe Smith	Anne Graham
Ken Davidson	Eleanore Schramm
The Herzogs	Hugh Forgie
Hermanos Williams Trio	Emil Coleman and Orchestra
Señor Wences	The Volga Singers
Volga Sisters	Hector's Dogs

Jerry Brannon

Staged and directed by Mr. Wynn, who served as his own master of ceremonies.

(Closed July 25, 1942)

THE CHOCOLATE SOLDIER

(24 performances)

An operetta in three acts by Rudolph Bernauer and Leopold Jacobson, based on George Bernard Shaw's "Arms and the Man"; American version by Stanislaus Stangé; music by Oscar Straus. Revived by Joseph S. Tushinsky and Hans Bartsch at Carnegie Hall, New York, June 23, 1942.

Cast of characters—

Nadina..Helen Gleason
Aurelia...Frances Comstock
Mascha..Doris Patston
Lieutenant Bummerli..Allan Jones
Capt. Massakroff...Detmar Poppen
Col. Popoff..A. Russell Slagle
Major Spiridoff..Michael Fitzmaurice

Act I.—Nadina's Sleeping Apartment in Popoff's House. Acts II and III.—Garden of Popoff's House.

Staged by John Pierce and José Ruben; settings by E. B. Dunkel Studios; costumes by Paul Dupont.

"The Chocolate Soldier" was first produced in New York by F. C. Whitney at the Lyric Theatre September 13, 1909, with Ida Brooks Hunt as Nadina, Jack Gardner the Bummerli. It ran for 296 performances. Its last previous revival was at the St. James Theatre, New York, May 2, 1934, when Charles Purcell and Donald Brian were the producers for a two weeks' run, Berenice Claire singing Nadina and Charles Purcell Bummerli.

(Closed July 12, 1942)

BROKEN JOURNEY

(23 performances)

A drama in three acts by Andrew Rosenthal. Produced by Martin Burton at the Henry Miller Theatre, New York, June 23, 1942.

Cast of characters—

Hale Thatcher.......................................Tom Powers
Essie..Helen Carew
Belle Newell.....................................Phyllis Povah
Rachel Thatcher Arlen............................Zita Johann
Dan Hardeen...................................Warner Anderson
Christina Landers.................................Edith Atwater
Trina..Joan McSweeney
Howard Newell....................................Gordon Nelson
    Acts I, II and III.—Living Room of Thatcher Home, Suburb of
City in Ohio.
    Staged by Arthur Hopkins; setting by Raymond Sovey.

Christina Landers and Dan Hardeen, war correspondents, radio
commentators and lecturers, come back from war-torn Europe
after having traveled and lived together through many adventures. Christina is a widow and her 10-year-old daughter travels
with her. Stopping over in Dan's old home town in Ohio, Dan
discovers that he still loves Rachel Arlen, who had once refused
to share his adventurous life. He stays on and marries her,
somewhat to Christina's deep hurt. Christina takes her daughter
and goes on. Comes Pearl Harbor. Christina broadcasts from
Manila, Dan hears the call and leaves Rachel wondering.

(Closed July 11, 1942)

*STAR AND GARTER

(408 performances)

A burlesque revue assembled by Michael Todd; music and
lyrics by Irving Berlin, Al Dubin, Will Irwin, Harold Rome,
Lester Lee, Irving Gordon, Alan Roberts, Harold Arlen, Frank
McCue, Doris Tauber, Dorival Caymmi, Jerry Seelen, Jerome
Brainin, John Mercer, Sis Wilner and Al Stillman. Produced by
Michael Todd at the Music Box, New York, June 24, 1942.

Principals engaged—

Bobby Clark	Gypsy Rose Lee
Prof. Lamberti	Georgia Sothern
Pat Harrington	Marjorie Knapp
Wayne and Marlin	Lynn, Royce and Vanya
Gil Maison	La Verne Upton
Richard Rober	Eppy Pearson
Joe Lyons	Kate Friedlich
Bill Skipper	Carrie Finnall
Frank Price	Letitia
Juanita Rios	Frank and Jean Hubert

The Hudson Wonders

    Staged by Hassard Short; dances directed by Al White, Jr.; music
by Raymond Sinatra; settings by Harry Horner; costumes by Irene
Sharaff.

* STARS ON ICE

(427 performances)

An ice skating revue assembled by Sonja Henie and Arthur M. Wirtz; music by Paul McGrane and Paul Van Loan; lyrics by Al Stillman. Produced by Sonart Productions at the Center Theatre, New York, July 2, 1942.

Principals engaged—

Carol Lynne	Skippy Baxter
Twinkle Watts	Dorothy Caley
Mary Jane Yeo	Helga and Inge Brandt
Fritz Dietl	Edwina and Cliff Thaell
Mayita Montez	Hertha Grossman
Alex Hurd	Paul Castle
Paul Duke	Bob and Peggy Whight
Fred Trenkler	Monte Stott
Jack Kilty	Vivienne Allen
A. Douglas Nelles	Neil Rose
Donald Arthur	Meryl Baxter
Charles Slagle	Rudy Richards
Edwina Blades	Buster Grace
Marta Dietl	Karen Lane
Sidney Spaulding	Geoff Stevens

Staged by William H. Burke and Catherine Littlefield; skating direction by May Judels; music directed by David Mendoza; choreography by Catherine Littlefield; settings by Bruno Maine; costumes by Lucinda Ballard; lighting by Eugene Braun.

(Closed May 16, 1943, for a month's vacation)

THIS IS THE ARMY

(113 performances)

A musical revue assembled by Irving Berlin; lyrics and music by Irving Berlin; dialogue by James McColl. Produced by Uncle Sam for the benefit of the Army Emergency Relief Fund at the Broadway Theatre, New York, July 4, 1942.

Principals engaged—

Staff Sgt. Ezra Stone	Sgt. Irving Berlin (1917)
Pvt. Stewart Churchill	Cpl. Earl Oxford
Pvt. William Horne	Pvt. Jules Oshins
P.F.C. Fred Kelly	P.F.C. Leander Berg
P.F.C. Joe Cook, Jr.	Pvt. Anthony Ross
Pvt. Robert Moore	Cpl. Philip Truex
Pvt. Hayden Rorke	Pvt. William Pillich
Pvt. Juss Addiss	Pvt. Robert Sidney
Pvt. Robert Shanley	Pvt. Derek Fairman
Pvt. Gary Merrill	Pvt. Louis de Milhau
Pvt. Ralph Margelsson	Pvt. Ray Goss
Pvt. Alan Manson	Pvt. Larry Weeks
Sgt. Dick Bernie	Pvt. Hank Henry
Pvt. Pinkie Mitchell	Sgt. John Mendes
P.F.C. James McColl	Pvt. Ross Elliott
Pvt. Leonard Berchman	The Allon Trio
P.F.C. Louis Salmon	Sgt. Arthur Steiner
Pvt. Samuel Carr	Pvt. Belmonte Cristiani

Pvt. Claude Watson	Cpl. James A. Cross
Pvt. Richard Irving	Pvt. William Wykoff
Pvt. Tileston Perry	Pvt. Marion Brown
Pvt. Joe Bush	Pvt. Arthur Atkins
Sgt. Alan Anderson	Pvt. Richard Reeves
Pvt. Howard Brooks	Pvt. Norman Van Emburgh
Pvt. William Roerich	Pvt. Burt Ives

Pvt. Robert Kinne

Yip, Yip Yaphankers—Peter O'Neill, Peter J. Burns, Dan Healy, John Murphy, Jack Riano, Harold Kennedy

Staged by Staff Sgt. Ezra Stone; dances directed by Pvt. Robert Sidney and Cpl. Nelson Barclift; music directed by Cpl. Milton Rosen stock; military formations by Cpl. Chester O'Brien; settings and costumes by Pvt. John Koenig.

(Closed September 26, 1942)

YOURS, A. LINCOLN

(2 performances)

A drama in two acts by Paul Horgan, inspired by Otto Eisenschiml's book, "Why Was Lincoln Murdered?". Presented by the Experimental Theatre, Inc., at the Shubert Theatre, New York, July 9 and 12, 1942.

Cast of characters—

Young Roundhill	Del Hughes
Lincoln	Vincent Price
Doctor	David Koser
Orderly	Tony Mannino
Orderly	Stephen Haddon
First Senator	Homer Miles
Second Senator	Watson White
Third Senator	Robert Toms
Stanton	Sherman A. MacGregor
Mrs. Lincoln	Mary Michael
Major	Gibbs Penrose
Booth	Donald Randolph
Herold	Tom McDermott
Tad	Robert Lee
Sherman	Bill Johnson
Grant	Harry Bellaver
Aide	Harry Townes
Boarding House Keeper	Ruth Hermanson
Crook	Wendell K. Phillips
Workman	Don Valentine
Roundhill	Parker Fennelly

Act I.—Scene 1—Military Hospital, Washington, D. C. 2—Office of Secretary of War. 3—Stage of Ford's Theatre. 4—Cabin of Presidential Yacht, "River Queen," City Point, Va. 5—Porch of White House. Act II.—Scene 1—Parlor of Washington Boarding House. 2.—At President's Bedroom Door, White House. 3—President's Box at Ford's Theatre. 4—Sitting Room in the White House.

Staged by Robert Ross.

Lincoln, near the close of the Civil War, is striving mightily to bring the struggle to an end; favoring every possible concession that will get the fighting men back to their homes and farms. Secretary Stanton is the chief opposition, blocking all Lincoln's peace moves and being finally connected, by inference and circumstantial evidence, with at least guilty knowledge of the John Wilkes Booth plot to assassinate the President.

THE MERRY WIDOW

(39 performances)

An operetta in three acts by Victor Leon and Leo Stein; English lyrics by Adrian Ross; music by Franz Lehar. Revived by Joseph S. Tushinsky and Hans Bartsch at Carnegie Hall, New York, July 15, 1942.

Cast of characters—

St. Brioche	Michael Fitzmaurice
Natalie	Elizabeth Houston
Camille de Jolidon	Felix Knight
Cascada	George Mitchell
Olga	Elaine Ellis
Novakovich	Neil Fitzgerald
Khadja	Roy M. Johnston
Nish	John Cherry
Baron Popoff	Eddie Garr
Sonia	Helen Gleason
Prince Danilo	Wilbur Evans
Madam Khadja	Harriet Borger
Head Waiter	Carl Nelson
Zo Zo	Diana Corday
Premier Dancer	Peter Birch

Act I—The Marsovian Embassy in Paris. Ace II.—Garden of Sonia's Residence in Paris. Act III.—Café Maxim, Paris.

Staged by John Pierce and Felix Brentano; artistic supervision by Richard Eichberg; music directed by Joseph Tushinsky; costumes and gowns designed by Eaves Costume Company.

Recent revivals of "The Merry Widow" in New York were those of December, 1929, with Beppe De Vries in the name part, Evan Thomas as Danilo, Roy Cropper the Jolidon and Richard Powell as Popoff. The Civic Light Opera Co. sang the operetta at the Erlanger Theatre in September, 1931, with Alice McKenzie as Sonia, Donald Brian the Danilo, Hal Forde the Popoff, Roy Cropper the Jolidon.

(Closed August 16, 1942)

LET'S FACE IT

(547 performances)

A musical comedy in two acts by Dorothy and Herbert Fields, based on "The Cradle Snatchers"; music and lyrics by Cole Porter. Returned by Vinton Freedley to the Imperial Theatre, New York, August 17, 1942.

Cast of characters—

Polly Lee	Janice Joyce
Madge Hall	Marguerite Benton
Helen Marcy	Frances Tanner
Dorothy Carlton	Helen Devlin
Anna	Kalita Humphreys
Winnie Potter	Mary Jane Walsh
Mrs. Fink	Lois Bolton
Mrs. Wigglesworth	Margie Evans
Another Maid	Sally Bond
Maggie Watson	Carol Goodner
Julian Watson	Joseph Macaulay
Nancy Collister	Vivian Vance
George Collister	James Todd
Cornelia Abigail Pigeon	Edith Meiser
Judge Henry Clay Pigeon	Fred Irving Lewis
Molly Wincor	Marion Harvey
Margaret Howard	Beverly Whitney
Ann Todd	Sondra Barrett
Phillip	Henry Austin
Jules	Toni Caridi
Eddie Hilliard	Jack Williams
Frankie Burns	Benny Baker
Muriel McGillicuddy	Sunnie O'Dea
Jean Blanchard	Nanette Fabray
Lieutenant Wiggins	Houston Richards
Jerry Walker	Danny Kaye
Gloria Gunther	Betty Moran
Sigana Earle	Miriam Franklin
Master of Ceremonies	William Lilling
William	Fred Nay
Dance Team	Mary Parker and Billy Daniel
Mrs. Wiggins	Kalita Humphreys

The Royal Guards: Tommy Gleason, Ollie West, Roy Russell, Ricki Tanzi, Henry Austin, Toni Caridi.

Staged by Edgar MacGregor; dances directed by Charles Walters; music directed by Max Meth; settings by Harry Horner; costumes by John Harkrider.

"Let's Face It" opened at the Imperial Theatre, New York, October 29, 1941, and ran until July 18, 1942, when it vacationed for a month, returning August 17, 1942. In the above cast Frances Turner substituted for Helene Bliss, Carol Goodner for Eve Arden and Sondra Barrett for Jane Ball.

(Closed March 20, 1943)

THE NEW MOON

(24 performances)

An operetta by Oscar Hammerstein 2d, Frank Mandel and Laurence Schwab; music by Sigmund Romberg. Revived by Joseph Tushinsky at Carnegie Hall, New York, August 18, 1942.

Cast of characters—

Julie	Doris Patston
Beaunoir	George Leonard
Capt. Duval	Gene Barry
Vicomte Ribaud	Marcel Journet
Fouchette	Carl Nelson

```
Robert Misson.....................................Wilbur Evans
Alexander............................................Teddy Hart
Besac...............................................Paul Reed
Jacques.........................................George Mitchell
Marianne Beaunoir................................Ruby Mercer
Phillippe..........................................Everett West
Spanish Dancer..................................Viola Essenova
Clotilde.........................................Hope Emerson
Première Danseuse..................................Viola Essen
Premier Dancer....................................Peter Birch
```
    Act I.—Scene 1—Grand Salon of Monsieur Beaunoir's Mansion Near
New Orleans. 2—Chez Creole. Act II.—Scene 1—The Deck of
"The New Moon." 2—On an Island.
    Staged by John Pierce; music directed by Joseph Tushinsky.

"The New Moon" was first sung in New York at the Imperial
Theatre September 19, 1928. Evelyn Herbert and Robert Halliday were the Marianne and Robert.

(Closed September 6, 1942)

ACROSS THE BOARD ON TOMORROW MORNING
and
TALKING TO YOU

(8 performances)

A fantasy and a short drama by William Saroyan. Presented
by The Saroyan Theatre at the Belasco Theatre, New York,
August 17, 1942.

ACROSS THE BOARD ON TOMORROW MORNING

Cast of characters—

```
Harpist.......................................Lois Bannerman
Thomas Piper.....................................Canada Lee
Jim..............................................Bill Challee
John Callaghan..............................Edward F. Nannary
Harry Mallory..................................Irving Morrow
Helen............................................Jane Jeffreys
Peggy...........................................June Hayford
Lois............................................Carol Marcus
R. J. Pinkerton................................Arthur Griffin
John Callaghan's Grandson..........................Jules Leni
Pablo....................................C. Gilbert Advincula
Pancho...........................................Sam Sotelo
Sammy...........................................Larry Bolton
Rhinelander 2-8182..........................Lillian McGuinness
Fritz...........................................Lewis Charles
The Poet....................................Maxwell Bodenheim
Callaghan Mallory...............................William Prince
```
    Scene—Callaghan's, on East 52nd Street, New York City.

TALKING TO YOU

Cast of characters—

```
The Crow.......................................Peter Beauvais
The Tiger......................................Irving Morrow
```

Blackstone Boulevard................................Canada Lee
The Deaf Boy..Jules Leni
Fancy Dan............. ....Lewis Charles
Maggie......................................Lillian McGuinness
The Midget................................Andrew Ratousheff
   Scene—A Spacious Basement Room on O'Farrell Street in San Francisco, California.
   Staged by William Saroyan; settings by Cleon Throckmorton.

Thomas Piper is a philosophic waiter in Callaghan's, a night club in New York. He plays a race horse named Tomorrow Morning across the board. He also watches life flow through Callaghan's, and jam, and flow again. He ponders the mysteries; changes personalities with a guest; assists in the birth of a premature baby delivered by the Filipino cooks in the kitchen; sees all the realities of living fade as in a mist and is still wondering at curtain time.

In "Talking to You" Blackstone Boulevard is a colored prize-fighter who is instinctively inhibited from hurting people whose spirits he senses as being good, a complex that interferes with fighting. He adopts a deaf white boy as his brother, and listens to a blind white man as to a spiritual father.

(Closed August 22, 1942)

I KILLED THE COUNT

(29 performances)

A drama in prologue and three acts by Alec Coppel. Produced by Messrs. Shubert in association with Frank Carrington and Agnes Morgan at the Cort Theatre, New York, August 31, 1942.

Cast of characters—

Count Victor Mattoni...............................Rafael Corio
Polly..Ethel Morrison
Divisional Inspector Davidson.......................Louis Hector
Detective Raines...............................Bertram Tanswell
Martin...Le Roi Operti
Police Constable Clifton......... ....James Ganon
Louise Rogers......................................Doris Dalton
Renee La Lune......................................Ruth Holden
Samuel Diamond..............................Clarence Derwent
Johnson..Edgar Kent
Mullet...A. J. Herbert
Bernard K. Froy....................................Robert Allen
Viscount Sorrington................................Guy Spaull
   Acts I, II and III.—Living-Room of Count Mattoni's Flat, London, England.
   Staged by Frank Carrington and Agnes Morgan; setting by Emil Holak.

Count Victor Mattoni is found murdered in his flat in London. Inspector Davidson of Scotland Yard takes on the investigation. One by one he calls in the suspects and three of them confess individually to the crime, each offering circumstantial evidence to prove that he did it. Later the three confessions are revealed as a part of a scheme to get rid of the count and so befuddle the authorities that no conviction is possible.

(Closed September 26, 1942)

TOBACCO ROAD

(34 performances)

A play in three acts by Jack Kirkland, based on a novel by Erskine Caldwell. Revived by Jack Kirkland at the Forrest Theatre, New York, September 5, 1942.

Cast of characters—

Dude Lester	Norman Budd
Ada Lester	Sara Perry
Jeeter Lester	John Barton
Ellie May	Sheila Brent
Grandma Lester	Lillian Ardell
Lov Bensey	Joe Silver
Henry Peabody	Fred Sutton
Sister Bessie Rice	Vinnie Phillips
Pearl	Sondra Johnson
Captain Tim	Harry Townes
George Payne	Edwin Walter

Acts I, II and III.—Farm of Jeeter Lester, on a Tobacco Road in the Back Country of Georgia.

Staged by Anthony Brown; settings by Robert Redington Sharpe.

John Barton in the above cast was the sixth Jeeter Lester to appear in "Tobacco Road" on Broadway. Henry Hull was the original and played 233 performances beginning December 4, 1933. The others were James Barton, James Bell, Eddie Garr and Will Geer who played in the 3,182nd and last performance, May 31, 1941, topping the list of long runs on Broadway.

(Closed October 3, 1942)

* JANIE

(321 performances)

A comedy in three acts by Josephine Bentham and Herschel Williams. Produced by Brock Pemberton at the Henry Miller Theatre, New York, September 10, 1942.

Cast of characters—

Charles Colburn	Maurice Manson
Elsbeth Colburn	Clare Foley
Lucille Colburn	Nancy Cushman
Rodney	John Marriott

```
John Van Brunt..................................Howard St. John
Janie Colburn.....................................Gwen Anderson
Bernadine Dodd................................Betty Breckenridge
Paula Rainey....................................Margaret Wallace
Scooper Nolan.........................................Frank Amy
Thelma Lawrence..................................Linda Watkins
Dick Lawrence.....................................Herbert Evers
Tina...........................................Artiebell McGinty
Andy..........................................Michael St. Angel
Frank...........................................Franklin Kline
Oscar..............................................Paul Wilson
Hortense Bennington............................Gertrude Beach
"Dead-Pan" Hackett..............................Blaine Fillmore
Carl Loomis...................................J. Franklin Jones
Joe Jerome.......................................Nicky Raymond
Mickey Malone....................................Kenneth Tobey
Uncle Poodgie..................................W. O. McWatters
          Soldiers from Camp Longstreet.
  Acts I and II.—The Colburns' Living-Room.  Hortonville, a Small
City in the United States.  Act III.—Scene 1—Mrs. Colburn's Up-
stairs Sitting-Room.  2—Living-Room.
    Staged by Antoinette Perry; settings by John Root.
```

Janie Colburn was going on 17 when her mother's old friend, Thelma Lawrence, came to visit and brought her 19-year-old son, Pvt. Dick Lawrence, with her. Dick proceeded to take Janie over, though Janie tried desperately to remain true to Scooper Nolan, her High School pal. When the old folks go to the country club for a Saturday night dance Janie decides to give a party for a couple of Dick's friends in camp. Practically Dick's whole company accepts and overruns the house. The boys eat all the food in the ice box, and drink up a lot of papa's liquor. The only thing that saves Janie is the fact that papa meets a man as a result of the party who helps him with his priorities.

THE MORNING STAR

(24 performances)

A drama in three acts by Emlyn Williams. Produced by Guthrie McClintic at the Morosco Theatre, New York, September 14, 1942.

Cast of characters—

```
Mrs. Lane.........................................Brenda Forbes
Mrs. Parrilow....................................Gladys Cooper
Alison Parrilow.....................................Jill Esmond
Dr. Datcher (S.D.)............................ Cecil Humphreys
Brimbo Watkyn...................................Rhys Williams
Cliff Parrilow.....................................Gregory Peck
Wanda Baring....................................Wendy Barrie
Sir Leo Alvers...................................Nicholas Joy
    Acts I, II and III.—Drawing-Room of Mrs. Parrilow's House in
Chelsea, London, S.W.
    Staged by Guthrie McClintic; setting by Steward Chaney.
```

Cliff Parrilow, a brilliant student of medicine in London in the summer of 1940, was about to receive his degree and to give to the world certain discoveries he considered of great importance. Came the war and Cliff temporarily lost control of his reason. Being put at menial tasks in hospital work he rebelled, lost interest in living, left his wife and took up with a blonde trollop named Wanda. When his mother opened her home to victims of the blitz Cliff found his work again, came to see everything in its true light and returned to the missus.

(Closed October 3, 1942)

NEW PRIORITIES OF 1943

(54 performances)

A variety show assembled by Clifford C. Fischer; ensemble music and lyrics by Lester Lee and Jerry Seelen. Presented by Clifford C. Fischer by arrangement with the Messrs. Shubert at the 46th Street Theatre, New York, September 15, 1942.

Principals engaged—

Harry Richman	Carol Bruce
Bert Wheeler	Sally Keith
Hank Ladd	Imogene Carpenter
Henny Youngman	Francetta Malloy
Ted Adair	Dorothy Partington
Johnny Burke	Harrison and Fisher
The Bricklayers	Radio Aces
The Acromaniacs	The Priorettes

Staged by Jean Le Seyeux; dances directed by Truly McGee; music directed by Lou Forman.

The first "Priorities of 1942" started in March of the year it aimed to glorify and continued for 353 performances. Its chief performers were Lou Holtz, Willie Howard, Phil Baker and Paul Draper. Joan Merrill and Hazel Scott were also in the lineup.

(Closed October 11, 1942)

SHOW TIME

(342 performances)

A vaudeville show assembled and presented by Fred F. Finklehoffe at the Broadhurst Theatre, New York, September 16, 1942.

Principals engaged—

George Jessel	Ella Logan
Jack Haley	Lucille Norman
Bob Williams	Con Colleano
The DeMarcos	The Berry Brothers

Olsen and Shirley

"Show Time" was organized on the Pacific Coast by the Fred F. Finklehoffe who was co-author with John Monks, Jr., of the successful comedy, "Brother Rat." Headed by George Jessel and Jack Haley, who revived the best of their old vaudeville routine, the combination was highly successful, achieving a record run for vaudeville bills.

(Closed April 3, 1943)

VICKIE

(48 performances)

A farce in three acts by S. M. Herzig. Produced by Frank Mandel at the Plymouth Theatre, New York, September 22, 1942.

Cast of characters—

Vickie Roberts	Uta Hagen
George Roberts	Jose Ferrer
Mr. Dunne	Taylor Holmes
Blanche	Evelyn Davis
Mr. Noonas	Frank Conlan
Mrs. Dunne	Mildred Dunnock
Amy	Colette Lyons
Private Cootes	Edmund Glover
Private Carter	Red Buttons
Karen	Gerry Carr
Sandra	Lynne Carter
Greta	Mme. Margaret Matzenauer
Taxi Driver	George Spelvin
Kay Hackett	Wynne Boze
Mr. Corliss	Charles Halton
Mrs. Frye	Eleanor Gifford
Mrs. Arthur	Marcella Markham
Mr. Hatch	Del Hughes
Mrs. Corliss	Sara Seegar

Acts I, II and III.—Living-Room of the Roberts' Apartment in a Suburb of New York.

Staged by José Ferrer and Frank Mandel; setting by Ernest Glover.

Vickie Roberts is the wife of George Roberts, an inventor who has been trying to sell a war machine to the government. In the excitement of organizing women war workers Vickie joins a local group of emergency godmothers, gets herself a uniform and largely forgets her domestic obligations. When a government representative comes to inspect George's war machine Vickie's pals take him for a spy. Vickie goes Mata Hari to hold him captive with her lure, while her pals send for the F.B.I. Then Vickie blackmails the innocent into buying George's machine.

(Closed October 31, 1942)

WINE, WOMEN AND SONG

(150 performances)

A revue-vaudeville-burlesque show. Produced by Lee Shubert, I. H. Herk and Max Liebman at the Ambassador Theatre, New York, September 28, 1942.

Principals engaged—

Margie Hart	Jimmy Savo
Ruth Mason	Herbie Faye
Isabel Brown	Murray White
Marian Miller	Eugene and Richard Wesson
Evelyn Farney	Noel Toy
Pinkie Lee	Murray Briscoe
Don Ritz Favorettes	Billy and Buster Burnell

Supervised by Max Liebman; ensembles by Truly McGee; music directed by Murray Friedman; setting by Frederick Fox.

(Closed December 3, 1942)

MAGIC

(47 performances)

A comedy in two acts by G. K. Chesterton. Revived by Eddie Dowling at the Belasco Theatre, New York, September 29, 1942.

Cast of characters—

Conjurer ....Eddie Dowling
Patricia Carleon...................................Julie Haydon
Hastings...Farrell Pelly
Rev. Cyril Smith...................................Bram Nossen
Dr. Grimthorpe....................................John McKee
The Duke......................................Stanley Harrison
Morris Carleon....................................Jess Barker
    Prelude: A Garden in a Misty Twilight. Acts I and II.—The Duke's Drawing-Room.

Followed by:

HELLO, OUT THERE

A drama in one act by William Saroyan. Produced by Eddie Dowling.

Cast of characters—

Photo Finish... ....Eddie Dowling
Ethel...Julie Haydon
The Man...John Farrell
Another Man......................................Farrell Pelly
The Woman...Ann Driscoll
    Scene: A Little Jailhouse in Matador, Texas.
    Both plays under the supervision of Elizabeth Miele; staged by Eddie Dowling; settings and costumes by Watson Barratt; lighting by Feder.

"Magic," written in 1913, produced in America in 1917, relates the adventure of Patricia Carleon, an Irish girl who believed in fairies, and the shock of her threatened disillusionment when a conjurer would convince her that all God's miracles are nothing more than man's magic.

"Hello, Out There" reveals the adventure of Photo Finish, an itinerant gambler, who is arrested and jailed in a small Texas town and charged with rape. The charge is a lie, but the only one who hears Photo's call for justice and understanding is Ethel, a young girl who cooks for the prisoners. Photo gives all his money to Ethel before a mob breaks into the jail and the lying woman's husband shoots him.

(Closed November 7, 1942)

STRIP FOR ACTION

(110 performances)

A comedy in two acts by Howard Lindsay and Russel Crouse. Produced by Oscar Serlin, Lindsay and Crouse at the National Theatre, New York, September 30, 1942.

Cast of characters—

Brooklyn	Coby Ruskin
Jeff	Wylie Adams
Tony	Richard Sanders
Mitch	Owen Martin
Buzz	Kenny Forbes
Dan	Bert Freed
Eddie	Jack Albertson
Hollenbeck	Jerry Thor
Tex	Don Kohler
Snag	Richard Clark
Gus	James McMahon
Clint	Charlie Kaye
Mike	Will J. Ward
Virginia	Jacqueline Paige
Warts	Joseph Haworth
Sally	Olga Brace
Pinky	Howard Blaine
Kitty	Kitty Voss
Duchess	Gary Myles
Garbo	Jeraldine Dvorak
Irene	Evelyn Russell
Jonesy	Harold Abbey
Farmer	Wendell Corey
Billy Miller	Billy Koud
Anita	Toni Crane
Wolf	John Deshay
Ruthie	Eleanor Boleyn
Dracula	Betty Noonan
Sam	Milton Bronson
Judy	Gloria Ingles
Hazel	Boo La Von
Maizie	Marji Beeler
Dottie	Pat Flynn
Shirley	Doris Faye
Doris	Helen Barrie
Gladys	Anita Arden

Joey...Joey Faye
Nutsy...Keenan Wynn
Harry...Murray Leonard
Florida...Jean Carter
Traps..Tommy Farrell
Mess Sergeant.....................................Barry Kelley
Squee..Eleanor Lynn
Capt. Adams......................................Gordon Nelson
Major Daniels.....................................David Kerman
Lieut. Nelson...................................Leonard Patrick
Commissioner Ainley..............................Leslie Barrie
Chief of Staff..................................Harry Bannister
Gen. McPhelan......................................Paul Huber
        Act I.—Stage of Bijou Theatre in Small Town in Maryland. Act
II.—Scene 1—Office in War Department, Washington, D. C. 2 and
9—Stage of Bijou Theatre. 3—The Show—Opening Number. 4—The
Show—The Comics. 5 and 7—Backstage in the Wings. 6—The Show
—Bed-Room Scene. 8—The Show—The Strip-Tease.
        Staged by Bretaigne Windust; settings by Raymond Sovey.

Nutsy, a burlesque comic before he was drafted, decides it
would be fun for his buddies if his old burlesque troupe were invited to give a show for them in the village theatre near camp.
With the aid of Squee, daughter of Za-Za, the greatest tease-
stripper of her day, whose father had been batman to a General
in the Philippines during the Spanish-American War, army permission is obtained and the show arrives. Rehearsals, riots, and
fun.

(Closed January 2, 1943)

LET FREEDOM SING

(8 performances)

A musical revue in two acts by Sam Locke; music and lyrics
by Harold Rome, Earl Robinson, Marc Blitzstein, Lou Cooper,
Roslyn Harvey, Walter Kent, John Latouche, Hy Zaret and
Lewis Allan.   Produced by Youth Theatre at the Longacre
Theatre, New York, October 5, 1942.

Principals engaged—

Berni Gould	Mitzi Green
Lee Sullivan	Joan Dexter
Phil Leeds	Betty Garrett
Mordecai Bauman	Jane Johnstone
Jack Baker	Margie Jackson
Bob Davis	Marion Warnes
Jules Racine	Ethel Sherman
Bill Randall	Lois Girard
Harry Mack	Sally Gracie
Remi Martel	Ruth Cavanaugh
Pat Shibley	Buddy Yarus

Molly Hoban

        Staged by Joseph Pevney and Robert H. Gordon; settings by Herbert
Andrews; costumes by Paul DuPont; choreography by Dan Eckley;
music directed by David Mordecai.

(Closed October 10, 1942)

* THE EVE OF ST. MARK

(291 performances)

A drama in two acts by Maxwell Anderson. Produced by The Playwrights' Company at the Cort Theatre, New York, October 7, 1942.

Cast of characters—

Deckman West	Matt Crowley
Cy	Grover Burgess
Nell West	Aline MacMahon
Neil West	Carl Gose
Zip West	Clifford Carpenter
Ralph West	Edwin Cooper
Pete Feller	Stanley G. Wood
Janet Feller	Mary Rolfe
Private Quizz West	William Prince
Private Thomas Mulveroy	Eddie O'Shea
Private Shevlin	David Pressman
Corporal Tate	Charles Mendick
Private Francis Marion	James Monks
Private Glinka	Martin Ritt
Sergeant Ruby	George Mathews
Sergeant Kriven	Robert Williams
Lill Bird	Joann Dolan
Sal Bird	Toni Favor
Waiter	Charles Ellis
Flash	Dorothea Freed
Dimples	Beatrice Manley
A Guard	Kent Adams
Pepita	Joven E. Rola

Act I.—Scenes 1 and 5—Nell West's Kitchen. 2—The Barracks at Fort Grace. 3—Janet's Room. 4—The Moonbow Restaurant. Act II.—Scene 1—A Gangplank. 2—A Field. 3 and 6—The Cave on the Island. 4 and 5—A Corner of the Cave. 7—Nell's Kitchen.
Staged by Lem Ward; settings by Howard Bay; Lighting by Moe Hack.

See page 68.

COUNT ME IN

(61 performances)

A musical comedy in two acts by Walter Kerr, Leo Brady and Nancy Hamilton; music by Ann Ronell and Will Irwin; orchestrations by Russell Bennett. Produced by the Messrs. Shubert, Ole Olsen and Chic Johnson in association with Richard Krakeur and W. Horace Schmidlapp at the Ethel Barrymore Theatre, New York, October 8, 1942.

Principals engaged—

Charles Butterworth	Luella Gear
Hal LeRoy	June Preisser
Milton Watson	Mary Healy
John McCauley	Melissa Mason
Joe E. Marks	Alice Dudley
Alfred Latell	Jean Arthur

Don Richards   Gower and Jeanne
The Rhythmaires   The Ross Sisters
Staged by Robert Ross; supervised by Harry Kaufman; dances directed by Robert Alton; settings by Howard Bay; costumes by Irene Sharaff.

(Closed November 28, 1942)

THREE MEN ON A HORSE

(28 performances)

A comedy in three acts by John Cecil Holm and George Abbott. Revived by Alex Yokel at the Forrest Theatre, New York, October 9, 1942.

Cast of characters—

Audrey Trowbridge	Kay Loring
The tailor	J. Ascher Smith
Erwin Trowbridge	William Lynn
Clarence Dobbins	Fleming Ward
Delivery boy	Don D'Arcy
Harry	William Foran
Charlie	Horace McMahon
Frankie	Teddy Hart
Patsy	Sid Stone
Mabel	Jean Casto
Moses	Richard Huey
Gloria	Iris Hall
Al	James Truex
Mr. Carver	William Balfour
Hotel maid	Gay Seabrook

Act I.—Scene 1—Living Room of Trowbridge House, Ozone Heights, New Jersey. 2—Bar-Room in Basement of Lavillere Hotel, New York City. Acts II and III.—Scene 1—Ozone Heights. 2—A Room in the Lavillere Hotel.

Staged by John Cecil Holm; music directed by Alexander Haas; settings by Perry Watkins.

"Three Men on a Horse" played on Broadway from January 30, 1935, to January 9, 1937, with a score of 835 performances.

(Closed October 31, 1942)

OY IS DUS A LEBEN!

(139 performances)

A musical cavalcade in two acts by Jacob Kalich; lyrics by Molly Picon; music by Joseph Rumshinsky. Produced by Edwin A. Relkin at the Molly Picon Theatre, New York, October 12, 1942.

Cast of characters—

Theater	Leon Gold
Achashverosh	David Lubritsky
Vaschti	Jennie Casher
Vaizuso	Esta Saltzman

Jacob P. Adler....................................Boris Auerbach
David Kessler.......................................Izidor Casher
Sigmund Mogilesco...................................Sam Kasten
Boris Thomashefsky............................Michael Welinski
Bessie Thomashefsky..........................Tillie Rabinowitz
Keni Lipzin...Celia Pearson
Molly..Molly Picon
Mr. Kay..Jacob Kalich
Mrs. Picon.......................................Dora Weissman
Ziggie...Izidor Casher
Rosalia..Anna Appel
Misha..Leon Gold
A Comedian..Sam Kasten
Sylvia...Esta Saltzman
Nadya..Jennie Casher
Zelda..Tillie Rabinowitz
Rebbitzen.......................................Rosa Greenfield
Schlome...Charles Cohan
Zalmyn...David Lubritzky
Getzel...Boris Auerbach
Chayeh-Sura...................................Rebecca Weintraub
Bailtsche..Miss Springer
Rivtche..Miss Klinger
Chavtsche..Miss Spiegel
Tsivtshe...Miss Bella
Romanian student................................Boris Auerbach
Romanian policemen..................Mr. Friedman, Mr. Samuels

Act I.—Stage of Arch Street Theatre, Philadelphia, 1912. 2, 3 and 4—Grand Opera House, Boston, 1918. Act II.—Royal Theatre, Bucharest, Romania, 1923. 2—A Little Town in Galicia, Poland. 3—Home of Mr. Kay's Mother. 4 and 5—The Molly Picon Theatre.

Staged by Jacob Kalich; dances directed by David Lubritzky and Lillian Shapero; settings by Harry Gordon Bennett.

The story of Molly Picon's life from the time she went on the stage in Boston, met and married Jacob Kalich, traveled to Europe to improve her Yiddish and broaden her technique, down to the day she arrived back in New York and became the idol of the lower East Side and the most popular soubrette in the Yiddish theatre.

(Closed February 6, 1943)

BEAT THE BAND

(68 performances)

A musical comedy in two acts by George Marion, Jr., and George Abbott; music by Johnny Green. Produced by George Abbott at the 46th Street Theatre, New York, October 14, 1942.

Cast of characters—

Buster da Costa...................................Romo Vincent
Veronica...Joan Caulfield
Hugo Dillingham....................................Jerry Lester
Willow Willoughby...................................Toni Gilman
Mr. Pirosh...Ralph Bunker
Princess...Eunice Healey
Damon Dillingham...................................Jack Whiting
Doorman..James Lane
Drummer...Leonard Sues
Trumpet Player....................................Johnny Mack

Band Girl...Evelyn Brooks
Mamita..Juanita Juarez
Querida...Susan Miller
Don Domingo....................................Averell Harris
1st Detective....................................Brian Connaught
2nd Detective...Marc Platt
Hotel Manager....................................Cliff Dunstan
Bell Girl..Doris Dowling
Hotel Owner...John Clarke
   Dancing Girls: Dorothy Barrett, Tessie Corrano, Eileen Devlin, Doris
     Dowling, Marilyn Hightower, Rhoda Hoffman, Muriel Hunt, Terry
     Kelly, Margaret Long, Mary MacDonnell, Frances Martone, Judy
     O'Brien, Ellen Taylor, Mimi Walthers, Doris York.
   Singing Girls: Kathleen Canes, Anita Dillon, Dolores Gaylord, Rosa-
     lind Madison, Leonore Rae, Roberta Welch, Nellilew Winger,
     Beverly Whitney.
   Dancing Boys: Jack Allen, Richard Andre, Larry Baker, Bob Copsey,
     Stanley Donen, Sidney Gordon, Harold Haskin, Herb Lurie, Robert
     McKernan.
   Damon Dillingham's Band: Johnny Mack, Drums; Leonard Sues,
     Steady Nelson, Clarence Willard, Trumpets; Ford Leary, Spud
     Murphy, Trombones; Pete Pumiglio, Clarinet; Dave Harris, Tenor
     Sax; Dick Kissinger, Bass; David Le Winter, Piano.
   Act I.—Scenes 1 and 4—Theatrical Agent's Office. 2 and 5—The
  Terrace. 3 and 6—The Apartment. Act II.—Scene 1—A Corridor.
  2—The Apartment. 3, 5 and 7—Lobby of Savoy-Perkins Hotel,
  Washington, D. C. 4 and 8—Boiler-Room of Hotel. 6—A Peach
  Orchard Outside of Washington.
   Staged by George Abbott; dances by David Lichine; settings by
  Sam Leve; costumes by Freddy Wittop.

Querida comes from the Caribbean to New York in search of
her godfather. She meets Jack Whiting, a jive band leader, who
has rented her godfather's apartment. Romance and song cues
ensue.

(Closed December 12, 1942)

BIRD IN HAND

(8 performances)

A comedy in three acts by John Drinkwater. Revived by
Ronald T. Hammond at the Morosco Theatre, New York, October 19, 1942.

Cast of characters—

Joan Greenleaf....................................Frances Reid
Alice Greenleaf...................................Viola Roache
Thomas Greenleaf..................................Harry Irvine
Gerald Arnwood...................................Henry Barnard
Mr. Blanquet.....................................Harry Sothern
Cyril Beverly....................................Romney Brent
Ambrose Godolphin, K.C.............................Nicholas Joy
Sir Robert Arnwood... ....J. W. Austin
Barmaid..Elizabeth Sutton
   Acts I and III.—The Bar Parlor, "Bird in Hand" Inn, Gloucester-
  shire, England. Act II.—Beverly's Bedroom.
   Staged by Ronald T. Hammond; settings by Holak Studios.

Joan Greenleaf, daughter of a Gloucestershire innkeeper, being
an attractive young girl of a new generation, is interested in
Gerald Arnwood, son of Sir Robert Arnwood, squire of the county.

Joan's father, Thomas, is of the old stock that believes in proper class distinctions. Thomas puts his foot down, denying Joan the privilege of going for a ride with Gerald. Joan goes anyway. Three guests at father's inn, the Bird in Hand, are called into council to decide whether Joan or her father is to be upheld. Finally Sir Robert is consulted and he decides for Joan and Gerald. "Bird in Hand" was played originally in New York in April, 1929, with an English cast headed by Jill Esmond, Herbert Lomas and Frank Petley.

(Closed October 24, 1942)

THE TIME, THE PLACE AND THE GIRL

(13 performances)

A musical comedy in two acts by Will Morrissey, John Neff and William B. Friedlander; music by Joe Howard; based on original version by Will M. Hough, Frank R. Adams and Joe Howard. Produced by Georges D. Gersene at the Mansfield Theatre, New York, October 21, 1942.

Cast of characters—

Mrs. Talcott	Evelyn Case
Molly Kelly	Vickie Cummings
Hjalmar Swenson	Clarence Nordstrom
Bud Swenson	Bert Lawrence
A Guide	James Phillips
A Patient	Robert Douglas
Tom Cunningham	Paul L. Wendel
Johnny Hicks	"Red" Marshall
Mr. Spree	Rolfe Sedan
An Attendant	Fred Kuhnly
Lawrence Farnham	Richard Worth
Margaret Swenson	Irene Hilda
Willie Talcott	Duke Norman
A Policeman	James Phillips
Joe Howard	Joe Howard
Ballerina	Rae McGregor

The Buccaneers: James Phillips, Wilson Lang, Fred Kuhnly, Robert Douglas.
The Girls: Olga Alexandrova, Irene Carrol, Kay Dowd, Rhoda Gerard, Sheila Herman, Marion Lulling, Peggy Lynn, Ruth Mitchell, May Muth, Dorothy Ostrander, Doris Pape, Terry Saunders, Connie Sheldon, Dot Sloane, Fanette Stalle, Dorothy Stirwalt, Helen Zurad.
The Boys: Jimmy Allison, Ray Cook, Kendrick Coy, Alfred Weber, Gene Stearn, Andrew Thurston.
Act I.—Grounds of the Sanitarium and Hotel of Famous Keeley Cure in the Mountains of Virginia. Act II.—Scenes 1 and 3—Grounds of Sanitarium. 2—Main Gate.
Staged by William B. Friedlander; dances directed by Carl Randall; music directed by Louis Katzman; settings by Karl Amend; costumes by Paul DuPont.

A slightly altered version of "The Time, the Place and the Girl" that was produced in Chicago in 1906. The plot concerns a day's adventures at a Keeley Institute when hard liquor was cheap and delirium tremens common.

(Closed October 31, 1942)

THE DAMASK CHEEK

(93 performances)

A comedy in three acts by John Van Druten and Lloyd Morris. Produced by Dwight Deere Wiman at the Playhouse, New York, October 22, 1942.

Cast of characters—

Rhoda Meldrum	Flora Robson
Miss Pinner	Ruth Vivian
Mrs. Randall	Margaret Douglass
Nora	Mary Michael
Jimmy Randall	Myron McCormick
Daphne Randall	Joan Tetzel
Calla Longstreth	Celeste Holm
Michael Randall	Peter Fernandez
Neil Harding	Zachary Scott

Acts I, II and III.—Living-Room of Mrs. Randall's House in the East Sixties, New York City, 1909.

Staged by John Van Druten; settings and costumes by Raymond Sovey.

See page 300.

(Closed January 9, 1943)

NATIVE SON

(84 performances)

A drama in a prologue and ten scenes by Paul Green and Richard Wright from Richard Wright's novel of the same name. Revived by Louis and George Brandt at the Majestic Theatre, New York, October 23, 1942.

Cast of characters—

Buckley, D. A.	Alexander Clark
Bigger Thomas	Canada Lee
Hannah Thomas	Evelyn Ellis
Vera Thomas	Helen Martin
Buddy Thomas	Rudolph Whitaker
Miss Emmett	Eileen Burns
Jack	Thomas Anderson
Clara	Rena Mitchell
G. H. Rankin	Rodester Timmons
Gus Mitchell	Wardell Saunders
Ernie Jones	C. M. Bootsie Davis
Mr. Dalton	Graham Velsey
Mrs. Dalton	Nell Harrison
Britten	Ralph Bell
Peggy	Frances Bavier
Mary Dalton	Anne Burr

Jan Erlone...Herbert Ratner
A Reporter..John Ireland
Judge...William Malone
Paul Max..John Berry
  Prologue.—Courtroom. Scene 1—The Thomas Room. 2—A Street.
3 and 5—The Dalton Study. 4—Mary Dalton's Bedroom. 6—Clara's
Room. 7—Basement of Dalton House. 8—Room in a Deserted House.
9—A Courtroom. 10—A Prison Cell.
  Staged by Orson Welles; settings by James Morcom.

"Native Son," as originally written by Paul Green and Richard
Wright, and taken from Mr. Wright's novel of the same title, was
first produced by John Houseman and Orson Welles at the St.
James Theatre, New York, in March, 1941. Following its original run it was taken over by other producers, reduced to the
proportions of a popular-priced drama, and sent on tour. A
second New York engagement was played at the Majestic Theatre, starting in October, 1942, with Canada Lee and many of
the original cast.

(Closed January 2, 1943)

LITTLE DARLING

(23 performances)

A comedy in three acts by Eric Hatch. Produced by Tom
Weatherly at the Biltmore Theatre, New York, October 27, 1942.

Cast of characters—

Katherine Wilson..................................Karen Morley
Wong...Peter Goo Chong
Kenneth Brown....................................Leon Ames
Cynthia Brown............................Barbara Bel Geddes
Teddy Graves.....................................Arthur Franz
Doctor Jarvis....................................Gerald Cornell
Miss Fairchild...................................Betty Kelley
Alice Buchfelter.................................Phyllis Avery
Sully Peters.....................................James J. Coyle
Ralph Pabst......................................Erik Martin
Danny..Dick Landsman
  Acts I, II and III.—Living-Room of Kenneth Brown's House in
Connecticut.
  Staged by Alfred de Liagre, Jr.; setting by Watson Barratt; lighting
by William Richardson.

Kenneth Brown is a writer of women's fiction, grown stodgy
and housebound. His daughter, Cynthia, comes to live with him
after having lived some years with her mother, from whom
Kenneth was separated. Neither Cynthia nor Kenneth's secretary, Katherine Wilson, approve of his way of life and twit him
about it. Cynthia's college room-mate, Alice Buchfelter, a knowing child, comes to visit Cynthia. Kenneth fastens upon Alice
as one to take him out of the rut. Together they explore the hot

spots. Kenneth becomes increasingly gay. It is a job to get him back to normal and engaged to Katherine.

(Closed November 14, 1942)

* ROSALINDA

(265 performances)

An operetta in a prologue and three acts adapted from the Max Reinhardt version of the Johann Strauss "Die Fledermaus" by Gottfried Reinhardt and John Meehan, Jr.; lyrics by Paul Kerby. Produced by Lodewick Vroom for The New Opera Company at the 44th Street Theatre, New York, October 28, 1942.

Cast of characters—

Alfredo Allevanto	Everett West
Gabriel Von Eisenstein	Ernest McChesney
Adele	Virginia MacWatters
Rosalinda Von Eisenstein	Dorothy Sarnoff
Falke	Gene Barry
Dr. Frank	Paul West
Fifi	Shelly Winter
Prince Orlofsky	Oscar Karlweis
Aide de Camp	Edwin Fowler
Frosch	Louis Sorin
Premier Dancer	Jose Limon
Première Danseuse	Mary Ellen

Ladies of the Ensemble: Nina Allen, Thelma Altman, Betty Baker, Xenia Bank, Nancy Baskerville, Jeanne Beauvais, Lillian C. Bennett, Betty Billings, Diana Corday, Anne Dawson, Camille Fischelli, Lucy Marshall, Frances McCann, Joan O'Neill, Dorothy Ramsey, Loretta Schere, Joan Wheatley, Jane Whyte.

Gentlemen of the Ensemble: Marden Bate, Edwin Fowler, David Goldstein, Harold Gordon, William Hearne, Alfred Kunz, Lawrence Lieberman, Alfred D. Morgan, Benjamin Siegel, Robert Tower, Bernard Tunisse, George V. Vincent, Alan Winston.

Ballet: Lillian Lanese, Yvonne Patterson, Phyllis Hill, Joyce Hill, Elise Reiman, Betty Lou Reed, Yvonne Tibor, Anne Wiman, Julia Horvath, Sonya Orlova, Douglas Caudy, Todd Bolender, Herbert Bliss, Jack Gansaert, Edward Bigelow, Jean Faust, Simon Sadoff, and William Dollar, ballet master.

Prologue—Outside Von Eisenstein's House. Act I.—Living-Room of Von Eisenstein's House. Act II.—Ballroom at Prince Orlofsky's Palace. Act III.—The Warden's Office at Local Jail.

Staged by Felix Brentano; music directed by Erich Wolfgang Korngold; dances by George Balanchine; settings by Oliver Smith; costumes by Ladislas Czettel; lighting by Jean Rosenthal.

"Die Fledermaus" was first sung in America, according to the George C. D. Odell "Annals of the New York Stage" in October, 1879, at the Thalia Theatre in Brooklyn, N. Y. The McCaull Opera Company, with DeWolf Hopper and Irene Perry, revived it in April, 1885. As "The Merry Countess" it was sung for 135 performances in 1912, with Fritzi Von Busing, Maurice Farkoa and the Dolly Sisters in the cast. In 1929 it was called "A Wonderful Night" in a version by Fanny Todd Mitchell. An adaptation by Lawrence Langner and Robert A. Simon called "Champagne Sec" was given in October, 1933, with Peggy Wood, Helen Ford, Kitty Carlisle and George Meader in the leads.

WITHOUT LOVE

(113 performances)

A comedy in three acts by Philip Barry. Produced by The Theatre Guild at the St. James Theatre, New York, November 10, 1942.

Cast of characters—

Patrick Jamieson	Elliott Nugent
Quentin Ladd	Tony Bickley
Anna	Emily Massey
Martha Ladd	Ellen Morgan
Jamie Coe Rowan	Katharine Hepburn
Kitty Trimble	Audrey Christie
Peter Baillie	Robert Shayne
Paul Carrel	Sherling Oliver
Richard Hood	Robert Chisholm
Robert Emmet Riordan	Neil Fitzgerald
Grant Vincent	Royal Beal

Acts I, II and III.—Living-Room of the Late Senator Owen Coe's House in Washington, D. C.

Staged by Robert Sinclair; setting by Robert Edmond Jones.

Jamie Coe Rowan, with a puritan and political background, is a widow living in a large house in Washington. Patrick Jamieson, whose father was in the diplomatic service abroad, is back in America hoping to do something to bring the British and the Irish together in the fighting of the war for liberty. In view of the difficulty Patrick finds getting living quarters in Washington, Jamie suggests that he stay at her house. To avoid gossip they will marry, but retain their single status. Both have had experiences, and both are through with love. For three acts they hold to their agreement. Then come capitulation, understanding and sleeping readjustments.

(Closed February 13, 1943)

MR. SYCAMORE

(19 performances)

A comedy in eight scenes by Ketti Frings based on a story by Robert Ayre. Produced by The Theatre Guild, Inc., at the Guild Theatre, New York, November 13, 1942.

Cast of characters—

Tom Burton	Harry Townes
Ned Fish	Harry Sheppard

John Gwilt...Stuart Erwin
Myrtle Staines....................................Leona Powers
Abner Coote......................................John Philliber
Estelle Benlow....................................Enid Markey
Julie Fish.......................................Louise McBride
Albert Fernfield...................................Buddy Swan
Mr. Fernfield....................................Walter Appler
Fletcher Pingpank................................Franklyn Fox
Reverend Doctor Doody..........................Russell Collins
Jane Gwilt..Lillian Gish
Fred Staines.......................................Otto Hulett
First Milkman...................................Ernest Theiss
Second Milkman.................................Kenneth Hayden
Third Milkman.....................................Rupert Pole
Mr. Oikle..Albert Bergh
Emily..Mary Heckart
Mr. Hammond.......................................Jed Dooley
Daisy Staines.....................................Pearl Herzog
Mr. Hoop..Ray J. Largay
Mr. Fink.......................................Harry Bellaver
      People of Smeed: Peggy Opdycke, Helen Brown, Albert Vees, and
      The Koralites: Kenneth Hayden, Rupert Pole, Mary Heckart,
      Ernest Theiss, Barbara Dale, Louise McBride.
      Scene 1.—A Street in Smeed. 2—Reverend Dr. Doody's Study.
3, 4, 5, 7 and 8—John's Back Yard. 6—Outside the Church.
      Staged by Lester Vail; supervised by Theresa Helburn and Lawrence
Langner; settings by Samuel Leve.

John Gwilt, tired of vegetating as a mailman, tired of tramping
his route day after day, and being influenced by the poetic
flights of fancy expressed by Estelle Benlow, the village librarian,
longs ardently to be a tree. As an experiment John plants himself in his own back yard, and, almost before he knows it, he *is*
a tree. Everybody happy, including John, who waves his limbs
and rustles his leaves in salute.

(Closed November 28, 1942)

* THE SKIN OF OUR TEETH

(239 performances)

A fantastic comedy in three acts by Thornton Wilder. Produced by Michael Myerberg at the Plymouth Theatre, New
York, November 18, 1942.

Cast of characters—

Sabina...Tallulah Bankhead
Mr. Fitzpatrick...................................E. G. Marshall
Mrs. Antrobus.................................Florence Eldridge
Dinosaur...Remo Buffano
Mammoth......................................Andrew Ratousheff
Telegraph Boy................................Dickie Van Patten
Gladys..Frances Heflin
Henry...Montgomery Clift
Mr. Antrobus...................................Fredric March
Doctor...Arthur Griffin
Professor...Ralph Kellard
Judge..Joseph Smiley
Homer...Ralph Cullinan
Miss E. Muse...................................Edith Faversham

```
Miss T. Muse.....................................Emily Lorraine
Miss M. Muse...................................Eva Mudge Nelson
Usher..........................................Stanley Prager
Usher...........................................Harry Clark
Girl...........................................Elizabeth Scott
Girl..........................................Patricia Riordan
Fortune Teller..................................Florence Reed
Chair Pusher......................................Earl Sydnor
Chair Pusher...................................Carroll Clark
Conveener.......................................Stanley Weede
Conveener.......................................Seumas Flynn
Conveener......................................Aubrey Fassett
Conveener......................................Stanley Prager
Conveener.......................................Harry Clark
Conveener.......................................Stephan Cole
Broadcast Official............................Morton Dacosta
Defeated Candidate...............................Joseph Smiley
Mr. Tremayne...................................Ralph Kellard
Hester.......................................Eula Belle Moore
Ivy..............................................Viola Dean
Fred Bailey....................................Stanley Prager
```

Acts I and III.—Home, Excelsior, New Jersey. Act II.—Atlantic City Boardwalk.

Staged by Elia Kazan; settings by Albert Johnson; costumes by Mary Percy Schenck.

See page 105.

ONCE OVER LIGHTLY

(6 performances)

A musical play in prologue and two acts. Americanized from Beaumarchais' "The Barber of Seville" by Laszlo Halasz; dialogues and solos by Louis Garden and Robert Pierpont Forshaw; ensembles by George Mead; original music of G. Rossini. Produced by Saul Colin in association with Henry Leiser at the Alvin Theatre, New York, November 19, 1942.

Cast of characters—

```
Figaro.............................................Igor Gorin
Rosina...........................................Grace Panvini
Almaviva..........................................Felix Knight
Don Basilio....................................Carlos Alexander
Dr. Bartolo.................................Richard Wentworth
Bertha..........................................Ardelle Warner
Fiorella...................................Myron Szandrowsky
```

Musicians and Soldiers: Van Atkins, Max Birnbaum, Dick Bracken, Anthony Musarra, Frank E. Price, Martin Stewart.

Prologue.—Street in Seville. Acts I and II.—Room in Dr. Bartolo's Home.

Staged by Robert H. Gordon; settings by Richard Rychtarik.

An Americanized version of "The Barber of Seville," with new dialogue by Louis Garden and Robert Forshaw. No change in story and few alterations in the Rossini score.

(Closed November 22, 1942)

YANKEE POINT

(24 performances)

A comedy in three acts by Gladys Hurlbut. Produced by Edward Choate and Marie Louise Elkins at the Longacre Theatre, New York, November 23, 1942.

Cast of characters—

Miz Bekins	Elizabeth Patterson
Jeremy Adams	Dorothy Gilchrist
Bob Adams	John Cromwell
Mary Adams	Edna Best
Doctor Nickerson	James Todd
Miss Higgins	Ann Dere
Ruth Lapo	Dora Sayers
Captain Trueman	Donald McClelland
Coast Guard	John Forsythe
Sandy Martin	K. T. Stevens
Uncle Pete	Arthur Aylsworth
George Fitch	Richard Rudi

Acts I and III.—The Living-Room. 2—The Observation Post, Eastern Sea Coast.

Staged by John Cromwell; settings by Frederick Fox.

Bob and Mary Adams are living at an exposed point on the Eastern seacoast. Mary is an air raid warden. Bob, having conquered the trend toward pacifism that had afflicted him after he came out of the First World War, is back in service in Washington, and anticipating being sent overseas. Sandy, the older daughter, is trying to adjust her thought to war, after resenting her father's change of viewpoint. Dorothy, the younger daughter, is having a time getting married to an aviation cadet training in Texas. Mary uncovers a German saboteur hiding near her watch tower and helps to turn him in. The Adamses are still standing four square as loyal Americans when Germany sends over a few test bombs.

(Closed December 12, 1942)

* COUNSELLOR-AT-LAW

(227 performances)

A drama in three acts by Elmer Rice. Revived by John Golden at the Royale Theatre, New York, November 24, 1942.

Cast of characters—

Bessie Green	Ann Thomas
Henry Susskind	Leslie Barrett
Sarah Becker	Clara Langsner
A Little Man	Edwin Hugh
A Large Man	Jay Velie

```
Zedorah Chapman.................................Betty Kelley
Goldie Rindskoff................................Freida Altman
Charles McFadden................................Jack Sheehan
John P. Tedesco.................................Sam Bonnell
A Bootblack....................................William Vaughan
Regina Gordon..................................Olive Deering
Herbert Howard Weinberg........................Kurt Richards
Arthur Sandler.................................John McQuade
Lillian Larue.................................Frances Tannehill
A Boy..........................................Caleb Gray
Roy Darwin.....................................Alexander Clark
George Simon...................................Paul Muni
Cora Simon.....................................Joan Wetmore
A Woman........................................Jane Hamilton
Lena Simon.....................................Jennie Moscowitz
Peter J. Malone................................John L. Kearney
Johann Breitstein..............................Barrie Wanless
David Simon....................................Philip Gordon
Harry Becker...................................Joseph Pevney
Richard Dwight, Jr.............................Buddy Buehler
Dorothy Dwight.................................Norma Clerc
Francis Clark Baird............................Elmer Brown
```
    Act I.—Scenes 1 and 3—Reception Room, Midtown Section of New
York.   2 and 4—Simon's Office.   Act II.—Scenes 1 and 3—Simon's
Office.   2—Reception Room.   Act III.—Scene 1—Simon's Office.   2—
Reception Room.
    Staged by Elmer Rice; settings by Raymond Sovey.

Paul Muni first played "Counsellor-at-Law" in New York
November 6, 1931.   When he was called back to Hollywood
for picture commitments Otto Kruger, who had played the part
of George Simon in the West, took over in New York.   Later
Muni returned, and the play totaled 412 performances before it
was finally withdrawn.   The story will be recalled as that of an
East Side boy who pulled himself up to a position of importance
in the legal fraternity and is then threatened with disbarment
because of a phony alibi he had endorsed during his climb.   He
is able in the end to defeat those who would pull him down.

THE PIRATE

(177 performances)

A comedy in three acts by S. N. Behrman, suggested by a
play by Ludwig Fulda; music by Herbert Kingsley.   Produced
by The Playwrights' Company and The Theatre Guild at the
Martin Beck Theatre, New York, November 25, 1942.

Cast of characters—

```
Pedro Vargas...................................Alan Reed
Manuela........................................Lynn Fontanne
Isabella.......................................Lea Penman
Mango Seller...................................Juanita Hall
Ines...........................................Estelle Winwood
Capucho........................................James O'Neill
Fisherboy......................................Albert Popwell
Trillo.........................................Maurice Ellis
Don Bolo.......................................Walter Mosby
```

```
Estaban.........................................Robert Emhardt
Serafin..........................................Alfred Lunt
The Hermit...............................William Le Massena
Lizarda...........................................Muriel Rahn
Viceroy.......................................Clarence Derwent
Maid to Isabella..................................Inez Matthews
Viceroy's Guards..................Guy Moneypenny, Peter Garey
Maids to Manuela........Ruby Greene, Anna Jackson, Lavinia White
    Members of Serafin's Troupe, Soldiers and Townspeople: David
    Bethea, Bruce Howard, Martha Jones, Jules Johnson, Clare Keith,
    Fredye Marshall, Charles Swain, Elois Uggams, Joseph Wash-
    ington, Carol Wilson, Jeffrey Etheridge.
    Musicians: Emilio Denti, Emmet Matthews, John Dixon, Adolphus
    Cheatham, Wilbur De Paris, Eddie Gibbs, John Brown, Max Rich,
    Herbert Cowens.
    Act I.—Scene 1—The Patio of Pedro Vargas' House in a Small
Village in West Indies.  2—A Mountain Road.  3—Public Square.
Act II.—Manuela's Bedroom.  Act III.—The Public Square.
    Staged by Alfred Lunt and John C. Wilson; dances directed by
Felicia Sorel; settings by Lemuel Ayers; costumes by Miles White.
```

Serafin takes his traveling mountebanks to a small village in the West Indies and asks the mayor for a license to perform. The mayor refuses, but, having been recognized by Serafin as a reformed pirate, later issues the license. Manuela, the mayor's wife, being highly romantic, is impressed by Serafin's story that he really is the pirate in question. When she learns of Serafin's deception she will have none of him, even though he walks a tightrope to get into her boudoir. At his show Serafin mesmerizes the lady and bids her reveal to the viceroy in the audience the fact that her husband is the pirate on whose head a price has been set. This puts him back in Manuela's good graces.

(Closed April 27, 1943)

THE GREAT BIG DOORSTEP

(28 performances)

A comedy in three acts by Frances Goodrich and Albert Hackett from a novel by E. P. O'Donnell. Produced by Herman Shumlin at the Morosco Theatre, New York, November 26, 1942.

Cast of characters—

```
Evvie Crochet....................................Joy Geffen
Topal Crochet........................Jeanne Perkins Smith
Mrs. Crochet.....................................Dorothy Gish
Gussie Crochet.................................Dickie Monahan
Paul Crochet..................................Gerald Matthews
Arthur Crochet..................................Jack Manning
Mr. Tobin..........................................John Morny
Commodore.......................................Louis Calhern
Mr. Dupre.........................................Nat Burns
Tayo Delacroix....................................Ralph Bell
Dewey Crochet...................................Clay Clement
Beaumont Crochet..............................Morton Stevens
```

Ed...Robert Crawley
    Acts I, II and III.—The Crochet Home, Grass Margin, Louisiana.
    Staged by Herman Shumlin; setting by Howard Bay.

The Crochets, Cajun folk in the deep south, are living from hand to mouth. Commodore Crochet is too lazy to work. Mother Crochet does her best to keep her family together. The floods wash a handsome doorstep down the river. The Crochets recover it, set it against their cabin door and hope to raise enough money to get a house to go with it. They never quite make it.

(Closed December 19, 1942)

WINTER SOLDIERS

(25 performances)

A drama in two acts and eleven scenes by Daniel Lewis James. Presented by Erwin Piscator at the Studio Theatre of the New School of Social Research, New York, November 29, 1942.

Cast of characters—

General Kessel	Ross Matthew
Marshal von Seldte	Lothar Rewalt
Tieck	Herbert Berghof
Marshal von Falken	Ronald Alexander
Colonel Gerhardt	John Altman
Colonel Kranz	Hanns Kolmar
General Holz	Theo Goetz
Colonel Schreiber	Alfred L. Linder
Janez	Vaughn George
Sentry	Michael Carter
Major Bauer	Paul Jones
Lieutenant Tilsen	Sterling Mace
Professor Hoffman	Paul Marx
Maxo	Max Leavitt
Franke	Rolf Bayer
Austrian Soldier	Paul Wagner
Girl	Dolly Haas
Gestapo Officer	Alexander Day
Berlin Announcer	Theo Goetz
Marya	Miriam Goldina
Antonin	Daniel Schatt
Jan	Geza Korvin
Karel	Boris Tumarin
Railroad Commissioner	Fred Lorenz
First German Soldier	Jack Lloyd
Second German Soldier	Frederick Tappen
Third German Soldier	Joe Bernard
Stefan	Guy Sorel
Nikolai	Boris Marshalov
Masha	Sara Strengell
German Captain	A. Horton Henderson
Sergeant	Charles A. Bastin
Katya	Paula Bauersmith
Grigori	R. Ben Ari
Red Army Lieutenant	George Andre
Hauser	Gilbert Leigh
Weiskopf	Mason Adams
German Lieutenant	John Stephens
Russian Commissar	David Alexander

Russian Gunner....................................Orin Jannings
Sergei..Nick Perry
Marshal Lechner..................................Robert G. Lance
    Act I.—Scene 1—German Staff Headquarters in Russia, End of
November, 1941.   2—Yugoslav Peasant Hut.   3—Mountain Cave.
4—Vienna.   5—Prerau, Czechoslovakia.   6—Polish Railroad Station.
Act II.—Scenes 1 and 5—German Staff Headquarters.   2—Russian
Collective Farm.   3—German Front Lines Before Moscow.   4—Russian Front Lines.
    Staged by Shepard Traube; settings by H. A. Condell; costumes by
Eaves; lighting by Hans Sondheimer.

See page 143.

(Closed December 20, 1942)

LIFELINE

(8 performances)

A drama in three acts by Norman Armstrong. Produced by
Gilbert Miller at the Belasco Theatre, New York, November 30,
1942.

Cast of characters—

Casey, Steward...................................Dudley Digges
Ronnie, Apprentice................................Bob White
Larry Oulton, 2nd Mate..........................Stanley Phillips
Peter Launder, 1st Officer.....................Colin Keith-Johnston
Dennis Comber, 3rd Mate..........................George Keane
Fred Judd, Wireless Operator.....................Everett Ripley
Captain J. McGrath, Master.......................Rhys Williams
Jim Lloyd, 1st Engineer..........................Whitford Kane
Ed Murgess, Bosun................................Edward Hunt
'Oppy Parker, Able Seaman........................Victor Beecroft
    Act I.—Scene 1—Salon of 5,000 ton Tramp Ship, the Clydesdale.
In Port, Canada.   2 and 3—At Sea, Atlantic.   Act II.—Scene 1—In
Convoy.   2—Out of Convoy.   Act III.—Scene 1—Out of Convoy.
2—Approaching the British Isles.   3—In Port.
    Staged by Dudley Digges; setting by Lemuel Ayers.

Captain J. McGrath, and a crew of Britain's merchant marine
navy, attempts to take the tramp steamer Clydesdale from Canada
to Liverpool with a cargo of petrol. Because her engines are
weak the Clydesdale drops behind the convoy, is attacked by a
submarine, which is sunk. A day later dive-bombers get after the
Clydesdale and set her afire. The crew takes to the boats and,
three days later, one boat discovers the ship adrift and still burning. Climbing aboard the men are able to put out the fire and
make port. A second boat is lost.

(Closed December 5, 1942)

R.U.R.

(4 performances)

A drama in three acts and an epilogue by Karel Capek, English version by Paul Selver. Revived by David Silberman and L. Daniel Blank at the Ethel Barrymore Theatre, New York, December 3, 1942.

Cast of characters—

Harry Domin	Gordon Oliver
Sulla	Gudrun Hansen
Marius	Lewis Wilson
Helena Glory	Edith Atwater
Dr. Gall	Horace Braham
Mr. Fabry	Hunter Gardner
Dr. Hallemeier	Louis Hector
Mr. Alquist	Hugo Haas
Consul Busman	Reginald Mason
Nana	Marie Louise Dana
Radius	Sydney Smith
Helena	Katharine Balfour
Primus	Wendell K. Phillips
Robot	Loy Nelson

Robots: Lewis Steele, Jay Williams, Robert Law, Dave Tyrrell, Denis Dengate, Clement Brace, Tom Knight, Doug Alexander, Miles Dickson, George Lambrose, Allen Stevenson, Carl Rapp and Bill Lazarous.

Act I.—Central Office of the Factory of Rossum's Universal Robots. An Island in the Future. Acts II and III.—Helena's Drawing Room. Epilogue.—A Laboratory.

Staged by Lee Strasberg; settings by Boris Aronson.

"R.U.R." (Rossum's Universal Robots) was first produced by the Theatre Guild in New York October 9, 1922, achieving a run of 184 performances. The story is of a group of scientists who perfect a mechanical man and reproduce his kind in batches of thousands. Continuing their experiments in the hope of peopling the world with robots that will take over all labor and leave humans to devote their lives to pleasure, the scientists supply their robots with synthetic hearts and minds, whereupon the robots turn and wipe the humans from off the face of the earth.

(Closed December 5, 1942)

THE SUN FIELD

(5 performances)

A comedy in three acts by Milton Lazarus, from a novel by Heywood Broun. Produced by Howard Lang at the Biltmore Theatre, New York, December 9, 1942.

Cast of characters—

Lefty Hendricks.....................................Jay Brassfield
Bill Doyle..Robert Lynn
Carl Randolph......................................Karl Malden
Jack Kennelly......................................Frank Otto
Whacky Cassatt.....................................Fred Sherman
Mrs. Doyle...Betty Kean
Jim Rocco..Lewis Charles
Mrs. Rocco...Katherine Meskill
George Wallace.....................................Donald Randolph
Warren Yost..Tom Tully
"Tiny" Tyler.......................................Joel Ashley
Karyl Dumont.......................................Florence Sundstrom
Judith Winthrop....................................Claudia Morgan
Bell Captain.......................................Regis Joyce
Hugh Coler...Richard Gordon
Mildred Deagon.....................................Fay Baker
Bessie...Georgia Burke
Waitress...Dorothy Eaton
Samuel Dickerman...................................Herbert Duffy
Rookie...Richard Midgley
Radio Voice..Bill Stern

    Act I.—Scene 1—Tiny Tyler's Suite in the Pilgrim Hotel. 2—Judith's Apartment. Act II.—Scenes 1 and 6—Restaurant Table on the Road. 2—Hotel Lobby. 3—The Tylers' Hotel Room. 4—Tiny Tyler's Suite. 5—Judith's Apartment. Act III.—Scene 1—Back Porch of Hotel Lee, Coldhaven, Florida. 2—Tyler's Room.

    Staged by Edward Clarke Lilley; settings by Ernest Glover; costumes by Kenn Barr.

Judith Winthrop is a writer for the slick paper magazines. Being sent to interview "Tiny" Tyler, a home-run king in baseball, she is fascinated by his forthright unaffectedness and his salty talk. "Tiny" is practically bowled over by Judith's class. After they are married "Tiny" gives up all his bad habits, including liquor and the dames, and sinks into a batting slump that loses his team the pennant. Judith leaves him for his own good, but comes back in time to rescue him from the camp follower to whom he has gone back.

(Closed December 12, 1942)

THE WILLOW AND I

(28 performances)

A play in three acts by John Patrick. Produced by Donald Blackwell and Raymond Curtis in association with David Merrick at the Windsor Theatre, New York, December 10, 1942.

Cast of characters—

Bessie Sutro.......................................Barbara O'Neil
Tinny..Amanda Randolph
Mara Sutro...Martha Scott
Bailey...Edwin Lewis
Theodore Sutro.....................................Edward Pawley

```
Millie Sutro..................................Cora Witherspoon
Dr. Oliver....................................Robert Harrison
Robin Todd....................................Gregory Peck
Duke Todd.....................................Alec Englander
Mabel.........................................Pauline Myers
Kirkland Todd.................................Gregory Peck
Dr. Trubee....................................Francis Compton
```
    Acts I, II and III.—Sutro Living-Room.
    Staged by Donald Blackwell; setting by Lemuel Ayers; costumes by
Aline Bernstein.

Mara Sutro, in her twenties and unmarried, meets and loves
Robin Todd, who comes to her town to practice medicine. Bessie
Sutro, Mara's youngest sister, also loves Robin, and is ready to
shoot herself on Mara's wedding day. Mara, finding Bessie in
tears, and also finding a revolver and an unexplained check of
Robin's made out to Bessie, tries to get at the bottom of the
affair. There is a struggle for the gun, which is discharged.
Mara, thinking she has killed Bessie, faints and when she recovers
her mind is a blank. For thirty years she is a living automaton,
cared for by Bessie and Robin after they married. Then Mara
recovers her mind, thinks Robin's son is Robin, who has died
years before, and has a difficult time readjusting her life.

(Closed January 2, 1943)

THE THREE SISTERS

(123 performances)

A drama in three acts by Anton Chekhov. Revived by Katharine Cornell at the Ethel Barrymore Theatre, New York, December 21, 1942.

Cast of characters—

```
Olga..........................................Judith Anderson
Masha.........................................Katharine Cornell
Irina.........................................Gertrude Musgrove
A Maid........................................Patricia Calvert
Baron Tuzenbach...............................Alexander Knox
Captain Solyony...............................McKay Morris
Doctor Chebutykin.............................Edmund Gwenn
Nurse.........................................Alice Belmore Cliffe
Feraport......................................Arthur Chatterton
An Orderly....................................Kirk Douglas
Colonel Vershinin.............................Dennis King
Andrey Prozorov...............................Eric Dressler
Kuligin.......................................Tom Powers
Natasha.......................................Ruth Gordon
Lieutenant Fedotik............................Stanley Bell
Lieutenant Roddey.............................Tom McDermott
Another Officer...............................Walter Craig
A Maid........................................Marie Paxton
```
    Act I.—The Home of the Prozorovs in a Russian Provincial Town,
1900.   Act II.—The Bedroom of Olga and Irina.   Act III.—The
Prozorov Garden.
    Staged by Guthrie McClintic; settings and costumes by Motley.

"The Three Sisters" was played in New York by the Moscow Art Theatre in February, 1923. It was revived by Eva Le Gallienne at the Civic Repertory Theatre in November, 1926, and by the Surry Theatre Company under the sponsorship of Dwight Deere Wiman in October, 1939.

(Closed April 3, 1943)

NEW FACES OF 1943

(94 performances)

A musical revue in two acts by John Lund with additional lyrics and sketches by June Carroll and J. B. Rosenberg. Produced by Leonard Sillman at the Ritz Theatre, New York, December 22, 1942.

Principals engaged—

Leonard Sillman	Diane Davis
Irwin Corey	Dorothy Dennis
Kent Edwards	Laura Deane Dutton
Tony Farrar	Doris Dowling
Ralph Lewis	Ilsa Kevin
John Lund	Marie Lund
Robert Weil	Alice Pearce
Hie Thompson	Ann Robinson

Staged by Leonard Sillman; sketches directed by Laurence Hurdle; choreography by Charles Weidman and John Wray; lighting by Carlton Winkler; music directed by Lee Wainer.

Counting "Fools Rush In" (1938) as one of the "New Faces" series, that also having been a Leonard Sillman revue, this 1943 edition is the fourth. The first came in 1934, the second in 1936.

(Closed March 13, 1943)

FLARE PATH

(14 performances)

A drama in three acts by Terence Rattigan. Produced by Gilbert Miller at the Henry Miller Theatre, New York, December 23, 1942.

Cast of characters—

Peter Kyle	Arthur Margetson
Countess Skrczevinsky (Doris)	Doris Patston
Mrs. Oakes	Cynthia Latham
Sergeant Miller (Dusty)	Gerald Savory
Percy	Jackie Kelk
Flying Officer Count Skrczevinsky	Alexander Ivo
Flight Lieutenant Graham (Teddy)	Alec Guinness
Patricia Graham	Nancy Kelly
Mrs. Miller (Maudie)	Helena Pickard
Squadron-Leader Swanson	Reynolds Denniston

Acts I, II and III.—Residents' Lounge of Falcon Hotel, Milchester, Lincs.
Staged by Margaret Webster; setting by Raymond Sovey.

Patricia Graham is a popular London actress who married Flight Lieut. Graham in London following an emotional upset during the London blitz of 1940. Months later, while she is visiting him at a hotel in rural England near a flying field, Patricia is hunted out by Peter Kyle, an actor lover with whom she had lived some years before and with whom she had quarreled. Still in love with Kyle, she is torn between the claims of both men upon her. Realizing, following a raid, how desperately her flier husband depends upon her moral support she gives the actor his dismissal.

(Closed January 2, 1943)

PROOF THROUGH THE NIGHT

(11 performances)

A drama in three acts by Allan R. Kenward. Produced by Lee Shubert at the Morosco Theatre, New York, December 25, 1942.

Cast of characters—

Cap	Ann Shoemaker
Smitty	Katherine Emery
Flo	Florence Rice
Pat	Thelma Schnee
Connie	Katherine Locke
Steve	Carol Channing
Sue	Margaret Phillips
Andra	Helen Trenholme
Nydia	Florence MacMichael
Helen	Julie Stevens
Grace	Muriel Hutchison
Sadie	Ruth Conley
Native Woman	Tevesa Teres

Acts I, II and III.—A Converted Gun Emplacement Adjacent to Bataan Peninsula, Early in 1941.
Staged by Allan R. Kenwood; supervised by Harry Kaufman; setting by Albert Johnson; lighting by Moe Hack.

Known as "Cry Havoc" in Hollywood, this is the story of a group of volunteer women aides shipped to Bataan some weeks before the fall of Corregidor. The girls suffer a series of emotional upsets during their tenancy of a "converted gun emplacement." One of their number is accused of being a spy. Another is suspected of Lesbian tendencies. They are all subject to attacks of nerves. In the end they are captured by the Japs and march out bravely to their deaths.

(Closed January 2, 1943)

SWEET CHARITY

(8 performances)

A comedy in three acts by Irving Brecher and Manuel Seff. Produced by Alfred Bloomingdale at the Mansfield Theatre, New York, December 28, 1942.

Cast of characters—

Mrs. Pat Mitchell, Secretary	Augusta Dabney
Mrs. Eva Ingersoll, President	Viola Roache
Nurse	Mildred Todd
Miss Beulah Ogilvie, Vice-President	Jane Seymour
Mrs. Laura Brindle, Treasurer	Enid Markey
Myron Mitchell	Whit Bissell
Mrs. Diane Martindale, Ways & Means	Mary Sargent
Jonathan Bates	Harlan Briggs
Sheriff Andrew Brindle	Calvin Thomas
Harry Trott	Philip Loeb
Photographer	Rollin Bauer
Trumpet Wilson	Dort Clark
Burton Sedgewick	John M. Kline
Mr. Hogarth	Leslie Litomy
Mr. Beasley	Hans Robert
Mr. Merritt	John Adair
John Dexter	John Kirk
Salvation Army Soldier	Clyde Waddell
The Family	With Liselotte Krumschmidt

Acts I, II and III.—Main Room of the "Friendly Hand" Clubhouse in a city several hundred miles from New York.

Staged by George Abbott; setting by Cirker and Robbins.

The ladies of the Helping Hand Society, officered by the Mesdames Ingersoll, Ogilvie, Brindle and Martindale, engage King Cole to bring his band to their Connecticut town and play for a bond-selling dance. They are to pay him $2,500 cash. They raise the money, but it is attached the day of the dance. The ladies are forced to resort to a series of minor swindles to replace it. At one of their meetings three of the club women find a box of marijuana cigarettes. Being innocent of the brand, they smoke them and become hilariously silly.

(Closed January 2, 1943)

THE RUSSIAN PEOPLE

(39 performances)

A drama in three acts by Konstantin Simonov; American acting version by Clifford Odets. Produced by The Theatre Guild, Inc., at the Guild Theatre, New York, December 29, 1942.

Cast of characters—

Martha Safonova	Margaret Waller
Maria Kharitonova	Eleonora Mendelssohn

Kozlovsky..Eduardo Franz
Valya..Elisabeth Fraser
Morozov..Robert Simon
Wounded Man..Ernest Graves
Safonov..Leon Ames
Borisov..Randolph Echols
Shura..Anna Minot
Vasin..Victor Varconi
Panin..Herbert Berghof
Lieut. Vasilyev....................................Peter Hobbs
Globa..Luther Adler
Old Man..Joseph Shattuck
Second Old Man.....................................Jefferson Coates
Rosenberg..Rudolph Anders
Werner...Harold Dyrenforth
Kharitonov...E. A. Krumschmidt
Unknown Man..Harro Meller
Red Army Man.......................................Ad Karns
Sentry...Jon Dawson
Captain Gavrilov...................................Roger Beirne
Krause...Walter Kohler
German Soldier.....................................David Koser
Semyonov...Mark Schmeid
Major General Lukonin..............................Robert Simon
   Red Army Men, German Soldiers: David Koser, Ad Karns, Ernest
Graves, Harro Meller, Jon Dawson, Michael Strong.
   Russian Singers: David Tuchinoff, Leo Resnik, Boris Belostozky,
Michael Greben, Lucien Arnold Ruttman, Seymour Osborne.
   Act I.—Scene 1—Home of Martha Safonova in Occupied Part of
Town in Russia. 2 and 3—A Railway Station used as Headquarters.
Act II.—Scene 1—The Kharitonov Home in Occupied Part of Town.
2—The Riverbank. 3—The Headquarters. Act III.—Scenes 1 and 3—
The Kharitonov Home. 2—The Riverbank.
   Staged by Harold Clurman; production under supervision of Law-
rence Langner and Theresa Helburn; settings by Boris Aronson.

A story of the little people back of the Russian lines who are
fighting with whatever means comes to their hands for the saving
of the motherland and the confusion of the Nazi invaders. Nine
episodes in which a quisling mayor of a Russian town plays with
the Nazis and is tortured when he fails them. His wife poisons
their chief tormentor and goes to her death triumphantly with
her husband. A happy, carefree doctor sacrifices himself as a
spy. Valya, a Russian girl, loves and serves Safonov, the Soviet
captain, as chauffeur and messenger, losing her life.

(Closed January 31, 1943)

YOU'LL SEE STARS

(4 performances)

A musical revue in two acts by Herman Timberg; music by
Leo Edwards. Produced by Dave Kramer at the Maxine Elliott
Theatre, New York, December 29, 1942.

Cast of characters—

Eddie Cantor.......................................Jackie Green
George Jessel......................................Jackie Michaels

Gus Edwards..Alan Lester
Walter Winchell..................................Irving Freeman
Groucho Marx.....................................Lou Dahlman
Herman Timberg....................................Fene Bayliss
Willie Hammerstein..................................John Briter
Harpo Marx.......................................George Lyons
Chico Marx..Sal La Porta
Zeppo Marx......................................Eugene Martin
Bob...Ronny Carver
Johnny Boston Beans..............................Gordon King
Biff Dugan..Jack Matis
Pisha Pasha.....................................Maurice Dover
Georgie Price......................................Buddy Simon
Mary...Norma Shea
Hildegarde.......................................Patricia Bright
Lola Lane..Reni Rochelle
Sassy Little......................................Honey Murray
School Teacher.....................................Joan Barry
Cuddles...Phyllis Baker
Vera Nulty..Pat Marshall
Jane Nulty.......................................Dorothy Dale
Ann Little.......................................Harriet Greene
Hazel Nulty......................................Betty May Lee
Specialty by......................................Jimmy Smith
    Act I.—Scene 1—Gus Edwards' Music Co.   2 and 5—Hammer-
stein's Stage Door.   3—Hammerstein's Victoria Stage.   4—Roof
Garden.   6—Hotel Astor.   Act II.—Scene 1—Walgreen's Drug
Store.   2 and 4—Madison Square Garden.   3—Backstage Madison
Square.
    Staged by Herman Timberg and Dave Kramer; dances directed by
Eric Victor.

Presumably an authenticated record of Gus Edwards' adventures as song writer and the promoter of genius. That it was authentic or authorized was vigorously denied by Mr. Edwards and his friends.

(Closed January 2, 1943)

* THE DOUGHGIRLS

(194 performances)

A comedy in three acts by Joseph Fields. Produced by Max Gordon at the Lyceum Theatre, New York, December 30, 1942.

Cast of characters—

Edna..Virginia Field
Julian Cadman......................................King Calder
Mr. Jordan..Sydney Grant
Colonel Harry Halsted..........................Reed Brown, Jr.
A Bellboy...George Calvert
Maids........................Mary Cooper, Mildred Haines
Vivian..Arleen Whelan
Another Bellboy....................................Jerome Thor
A Porter..Hugh Williamson
Another Porter....................................Kermit Kegley
Waiter...Walter Beck
Nan..Doris Nolan
Brigadier General Slade..........................William J. Kelly
Tom Dillon.......................................Vinton Hayworth
Judge Honoria Blake................................Ethel Wilson
Natalia Chodorov..................................Arlene Francis

A Stranger..Harold Grau
Orderly...Joseph Olney
Warren Buckley...............................Edward H. Robins
Sylvia..Natalie Schafer
Chaplain Stevens...............................Reynolds Evans
A Messenger......................................Hugh Williamson
Admiral Owens..................................Thomas F. Tracey
Timothy Walsh...............................James MacDonald
Stephen Forbes....................................Maurice Burke
Father Nicholai.................................Maxim Panteleieff
   Sailors, Marines, House Staff, Messenger, Etc.: George Davis, Joseph
Martin, Harold Murphy, Bernard Winter, Edward Joyce, Henry
Howell, Kermit Kegley, Hugh Williamson, Frank Taft, Theodore
Bryant.
   Acts I, II and III.—Washington Hotel Suite.
   Staged by George S. Kaufman; setting by Frederick Fox.

See page 268.

* SOMETHING FOR THE BOYS

(181 performances)

A musical comedy in prologue and two acts by Herbert and
Dorothy Fields; songs by Cole Porter. Produced by Michael
Todd at the Alvin Theatre, New York, January 7, 1943.

Cast of characters—

Chiquita Hart...................................Paula Laurence
Roger Calhoun.......................................Jed Prouty
Harry Hart...Allen Jenkins
Blossom Hart......................................Ethel Merman
Staff Sgt. Rocky Fulton............................Bill Johnson
Sgt. Laddie Green...............................Stuart Langley
Mary-Francis.......................................Betty Garrett
Betty-Jean..Betty Bruce
Micheala...Anita Alvarez
Lois, Lucille.......................................Barnes Twins
Lt. Col. S. D. Grubbs.............................Jack Hartley
Mr. Tobias Twitch...............................William Lynn
Corp. Burns.......................................Bill Callahan
Sgt. Carter...Remi Martel
Melanie Walker..................................Frances Mercer
Burke..Walter Rinner
Mrs. Grubbs.....................................Madeleine Clive
   Prologue.—Set 1—Chiquita's Dressing Room in Piccadilly Club,
Kansas City. 2—6th Ave. at 50th Street, New York City. 3—An
Assembly Line in Defense Plant, Newark, N. J. Act I.—Scene 1—
Alamo Plaza, San Antonio, Texas. 2—Near the P.X. at Kelly Field.
3—Patio of the Old Hart Estate, Near San Antonio. 4—A Crossroads.
5—Patio of New Hart Estate. Act II.—Scene 1—The Patio. 2—The
Terrace of Col. Grubbs' Home on the Post. 3—The Crossroads.
4 and 7—The Cadet Club at the Texas Hotel, San Antonio. 5—Corridor of Texas Hotel. 6—An Army Plane.
   Staged by Hassard Short; book directed by Herbert Fields; dances
by Jack Cole; settings by Howard Bay; costumes by Billy Livingston.

Chiquita Hart, a night club entertainer; Harry Hart, a carnival
pitch man, and Blossom Hart, a war worker, are found by the
Court of Missing Heirs and informed that they have inherited a
ranch in Texas. In Texas they discover their property abuts
Kelly Field and has been taken over by the army for maneuvers.

Which makes it nice for the boys when they invite their wives and girl friends down. Then the Army interferes.

NINE GIRLS

(5 performances)

A melodrama in two acts by Wilfred H. Pettitt. Produced by A. H. Woods at the Longacre Theatre, New York, January 13, 1943.

Cast of characters—

Jane	Maxine Stuart
Frieda	Ruth K. Hill
Alice	Barbara Bel Geddes
Eve	K. T. Stevens
Sharon (Glamor Pants)	Mary McCormack
Shirley	Marilyn Erskine
Betty (Tennessee)	Kayo Copeland
Stella (Shot-Put)	Irene Dailey
Mary	Adele Longmire

Acts I and II.—Front Room of Sorority Clubhouse in California's Sierra Nevada Mountains.

Staged by Reginald Denham; setting by John Root.

Mary was jealous of a certain girl and bashed in her head. The murdered girl had written a letter to Alice which might have placed suspicion on Mary, so Mary poisons Alice to protect herself. She would also have done away with a couple of others if she had not been uncovered as a homicidal maniac. The nine girls of the title are sorority sisters spending a week end in the Sierra Nevada Mountains.

(Closed January 16, 1943)

* DARK EYES

(174 performances)

A comedy in two acts by Elena Miramova and Eugenie Leontovich. Produced by Jed Harris at the Belasco Theatre, New York, January 14, 1943.

Cast of characters—

Larry Field	Carl Gose
Willoughby	Oscar Polk
Grandmother Field	Minnie Dupree
Pearl	Maude Russell
Helen Field	Anne Burr
Prince Nicolai Toradje	Geza Korvin
Natasha Rapakovitch	Eugenie Leontovich
Tonia Karpova	Elena Miramova
Olga Shmilevskaya	Ludmilla Toretzka
John Field	Jay Fassett

Act I.—Living Room of Field's Family Home on Long Island.
Act II.—Bedroom.
Staged by Jed Harris; settings by Stewart Chaney.

Natasha, Tonia and Olga are three Russian refugees adrift in New York. When they can no longer pay their rent they give the landlord a check drawn on a bank in which they have no money and are liable to arrest. In their dilemma they accept the invitation of their friend, Prince Nicolai, to spend a week-end at the home of his fiancée, daughter of an American industrialist. The industrialist, harassed with his work as a dollar-a-year man in Washington, comes home for a spell of peace and quiet and finds Natasha, Tonia and Olga. Even he succumbs to their charm and agrees to back a play they have written about three Russian actresses. Also he decides to marry one of them.

* THE PATRIOTS

(157 performances)

A drama in prologue and three acts by Sidney Kingsley. Produced by The Playwrights Company and Rowland Stebbins at the National Theatre, New York, January 29, 1943.

Cast of characters—

Captain	Byron Russell
Thomas Jefferson	Raymond Edward Johnson
Patsy	Madge Evans
Martha	Frances Reid
Doctor	Ross Matthew
James Madison	John Souther
Alexander Hamilton	House Jameson
George Washington	Cecil Humphreys
Sergeant	Victor Southwick
Colonel Humphrey	Francis Compton
Jacob	Thomas Dillon
Ned	George Mitchell
Mat	Philip White
James Monroe	Judson Laire
Mrs. Hamilton	Peg La Centra
Henry Knox	Henry Mowbray
Butler	Robert Lance
Mr. Fenno	Roland Alexander
Jupiter	Doe Doe Green
Mrs. Conrad	Leslie Bingham
Frontiersman	John Stephen
Thomas Jefferson Randolph	Billy Nevard
Anne Randolph	Hope Lange
George Washington Lafayette	Jack Lloyd

Prologue: 1790. Deck of a schooner. Act I.—Scene 1—The Presidential Mansion. 2—The Smithy of an Inn on the Outskirts of New York. Act II.—Scene 1—Hamilton's Home, Philadelphia. 2 and 3—Jefferson's Rooms. Act III.—Scene 1—Jefferson's Rooms at Conrad's Boarding House, Washington. 1800. 2—Interior of the Capitol.

Staged by Shepard Traube; settings by Howard Bay; costumes by Rose Bogdanoff and Toni Ward; lighting by Moe Hack.

See page 29.

THE BARBER HAD TWO SONS

(24 performances)

A war melodrama in three acts by Thomas Duggan and James Hogan. Produced by Jess Smith at the Playhouse, New York, February 1, 1943.

Cast of characters—

Customer	Steve Darrell
Mrs. Alta Hjalmer	Edit Angold
Lunke Hjalmer	Walter Soderling
"Ma" (Mrs. Mathieson)	Blanche Yurka
Hilda	Anita Vengay
Rudolph Bjorin Nilsen	J. Arthur Young
Karen Borson	Tutta Rolf
Christian Mathieson	Richard Powers
Johann Mathieson	Walter Brooke
Major Bowmann	Alfred Zeisler
Sergeant Brunnemann	Richard O'Connor
Corporal Heimer	James Darrell
Lars Tugar	Wolfgang Zilzer
1st German Soldier	Hanns Kolmar
2d German Soldier	Joseph Wiseman
Colonel Schmidt	Eddy Fields
Captain Ulmer	James Bass
Carl Nagel	Fairfax Burgher

Acts I, II and III.—Barber Shop of "Ma," Village of Aalesund.
Staged by Melville Burke; setting by Phil Raguel.

Mrs. Mathieson, the village barber of Aalesund, is helping with the wedding preliminaries of her artist son, Johann, when her sea captain son, Christian, returns home unexpectedly and recognizes in the musician who is to play for his brother's wedding a Nazi spy. Christian promptly strangles the fellow and tosses the body in the fjord. Later, when the Nazis have moved in, Christian is active as a patriotic saboteur, and thinks Johann is, too. But Johann is weak and selfish; he plots to elope with his fiancée and let the fight for liberty go. Discovering Johann's perfidy, and being forced to turn one son over to the Nazis, Mrs. Mathieson sadly sends Johann to the firing squad and shoots the fiancée who had been his fellow traitor.

(Closed February 20, 1943)

COUNTERATTACK

(85 performances)

A drama in three acts by Janet and Philip Stevenson, based on a Russian play by Ilya Vershinin and Mikhail Ruderman. Produced by Lee Sabinson at the Windsor Theatre, New York, February 3, 1943.

Cast of characters—

First German Soldier...............................Philip Pine
Second German Soldier.........................Douglas Hubbard
Third German Soldier.............................Richard Rudi
German Sergeant..................................Harold Stone
Emma Dahlgren.................................Barbara O'Neil
Weiler..Richard Basehart
Giltzparer..Karl Malden
Mueller...Richard Sanders
Huebsch...John Thomas
Stillmann.......................................Martin Wolfson
Ernemann......................................Rudolph Anders
Krafft...John Ireland
Kulkov.......................................Morris Carnovsky
Kirichenko....................................Sam Wanamaker
Lieutenant Petrov..............................Donald Cameron
Barsky..Orin Jannings
Generalov..Bert Freed

Acts I, II and III.—Cellar of a House on the Eastern Front, 1942.
Staged by Margaret Webster; setting by John Root.

Seven German soldiers and an Army Nurse are trapped in the cellar of a small town building on the Eastern front. Kulkov and Kirichenko, a Red guard, are left to interrogate them for later reports. Exploding bombs in the counterattack fill in all entrances to the cellar. For three days a battle of wits between the imprisoned Germans and their guards ensues. Threatened suffocation and loss of sleep all but do in the valiant Reds, but relief arrives in the well known nick of time.

(Closed April 17, 1943)

ASK MY FRIEND SANDY

(12 performances)

A comedy in three acts by Stanley Young. Produced by Alfred de Liagre at the Biltmore Theatre, New York, February 4, 1943.

Cast of characters—

Harold Jackson...................................Roland Young
Jane Brennan.......................................Kay Loring
Minnie Mae...................................Anna P. Franklin
Mrs. Jackson....................................Mary Sargent
Sandy..Norman Lloyd
Mary (Squeegee) O'Donnell......................Phyllis Avery
Li...Joseph Tso Shih
Christopher Dickson.............................Franklyn Fox

Acts I, II and III.—New York Apartment of Mr. and Mrs. Harold Jackson.
Staged by Alfred de Liagre; setting by Watson Barratt.

Harold Jackson, publisher, being bored with living and irritated by a frivolous wife, listens to the maunderings of a brash young soldier named Sandy, to whom Mrs. Jackson has taken a fancy. It is Sandy's idea that any man with money will do well to get rid of it against the time when the idealists begin making over the economic structure of the world after the war. With the inspiration of several highballs, Harold proceeds to dissipate his small fortune—first by doubling the salary of his hired help and then inviting them on a drinking party in Harlem. Within a few weeks the publisher is broke, or would be if an old book of his, "How to Live Better with Less Money," hadn't suddenly become a best seller, thanks to the build-up given it by his eccentric acts.

(Closed February 13, 1943)

FOR YOUR PLEASURE

(11 performances)

A dance vaudeville in four parts assembled and presented by George M. Gatts at the Mansfield Theatre, New York, February 5, 1943.

Principals engaged—

Yolanda Casazza	Frank Veloz
Susan Miller	Vicente Gomez
Bill Gary	Al and Lee Reiser
Golden Gate Quartette	Jerry Shelton

Staged by Frank Veloz; orchestra directed by Jerry Shelton.

Thirteen dance numbers by Veloz and Yolanda; guitar playing by Vincente Gomez; ballet-tap dancing by Bill Gary; accordion solos by Jerry Shelton; spirituals by the Golden Gate Quartette; songs by Susan Miller; piano duets by the Reisers.

(Closed February 13, 1943)

THE MOON VINE

(20 performances)

A comedy in three acts by Patricia Coleman. Produced by Jack Kirkland at the Morosco Theatre, New York, February 11, 1943.

Cast of characters—

Mrs. Meade ("Miss Eloise").........................Vera Allen
Strother Meade..Grace Coppin
Miss Lucy Telfair ("Aunt Lullah").................Kate McComb
Mrs. Sylvaine ("Miss Bessie")....................Agnes Scott Yost
Larkin..Robert W. Albury
Drop Dead...Drop Dead
Miss Francie Taylor...............................Phyllis Tyler
Uncle Yancey Sylvaine..............................Will Geer

```
Zack Meade.........................................Richard Tyler
Mattie.............................................Ruth Anderson
Ovid Carter.......................................Philip Bourneuf
Mariah Meade....................................Haila Stoddard
Ellen Hatfield..................................Mary Lou Taylor
Danny Hatfield....................................Arthur Franz
Porter...........................................Robert Crawley
Fane.............................................Michael Road
Andre..............................................Youl Brvner
Brother Walt Littlejohn.......................A. Winfield Hoeny
Rev. Dr. Randolph Hatfield..........................John McKee
Nic.................................................Biddy Fleet
Pic..............................................Elmer Snowden
```
　　　Acts I and III.—The Side Veranda. The Meade House, Manfield,
La. 1905. Act II.—Scene 1—The Veranda. 2—A Section of the
Revival Tent.
　　　Staged by John Cromwell; settings and costumes by Lucinda Ballard.

Mariah Meade got awfully tired of being engaged to a missionary who is saving souls in the Australian bush. When Danny Hatfield comes home from an experience as an actor, Mariah, who has always been stage-struck, induces her best girl friend to write her (Mariah) a letter announcing the death of the missionary in Australia and straightway thereafter sets her cap for Danny. But Mariah overacts her pretended grief over the death of the missionary, which sends Danny to a revival meeting with a confession that he is fearfully wicked himself and wants to reform so he can become a missionary. Mariah quits acting and takes Danny for better or worse.

(Closed February 27, 1943)

THIS ROCK

(37 performances)

A comedy in three acts by Walter Livingstone Faust. Produced by Eddie Dowling at the Longacre Theatre, New York, February 18, 1943.

Cast of characters—

```
Dannie.............................................Harlan Stone
Mary.............................................Joyce Van Patten
Joannie...........................................Joan Sheppard
Douglas MacMasters...............................Zachary Scott
Johnny MacMasters................................Alastair Kyle
Patton.............................................Roland Hogue
Margaret Stanley..................................Jane Sterling
Cecily Stanley.....................................Billie Burke
Malcolm Stanley....................................Nicholas Joy
Robert Duncan....................................Everett Ripley
Maid...............................................Lucia Victor
Cuthie..........................................Ethel Morrison
Angus............................................Malcolm Dunn
Sergeant Higgins...................................Gene Lyons
Mr. Harley.........................................John Farrel
Mrs. Proudie.......................................Mabel Taylor
Mr. Proudie.....................................Victor Beecroft
```

Little Daisy..Lorna Lynn
Little 'Arry.......................................Gerald Matthews
  Children: Suzzanne Johnston, Lois Volkman, Patsy Flicker, Buddy
    Millard, Dickie Millard, Richard Leone.
  Acts I, II and III.—A Room in the Stanley Home on the River Tyne,
England.
  Staged by Eddie Dowling; settings by Watson Barratt.

Twenty children from the London slums are billeted with the Malcolm Stanleys at their lovely home on the River Tyne. Cecily Stanley bitterly resents this action of the British government, but is shortly won over by the children, after she has had them scrubbed and outfitted with fresh linen. Johnny MacMasters, one of the young toughies and Cecily's particular favorite, is wounded in an air raid that destroys the Stanley gardens. Douglas MacMasters, Johnny's older brother, overcomes a class bitterness leveled at the blooming aristocracy when he rises in the ranks of the R.A.F. to a flier's rank, and finally marries Margaret Stanley, the Stanleys' lovely daughter and heiress as well.

(Closed March 20, 1943)

LADY IN THE DARK

(83 performances)

A musical play in two acts by Moss Hart; lyrics by Ira Gershwin; music by Kurt Weill. Revived by Sam H. Harris at the Broadway Theatre, New York, February 27, 1943.

Cast of characters—

Dr. Brooks.......................................Richard Hale
Miss Bowers.....................................Jeanne Shelby
Liza Elliott...................................Gertrude Lawrence
Miss Foster......................................Gedda Petry
Miss Stevens...................................Adrienne Moore
Maggie Grant...................................Margaret Dale
Alison du Bois......................................Ann Lee
Russell Paxton................................Eric Brotherson
Charley Johnson................................Hugh Marlowe
Randy Curtis...................................Willard Parker
Joe..Edward Browne
Tom...Walter Stane
Kendall Nesbitt....................................John Leslie
Helen...Helene Young
Ruthie......................................Rose Marie Elliott
Carol...Margaret Gigson
Marcia...Christine Horn
Liza's Father................................Nicholas Saunders
Ben Butler......................................Lee Bergere
Barbara...Jane Irving
Jack...Lynn Alden
  Soloists: Arthur Davies, Warren Jones, Byron Milligan.
  The Albertina Rasch Dancers: Rita Charise, Anne Helm, Joan Lee,
    June MacLaren, Christine Horn, Margaret Gibson, Alla Shishkina,
    Edward Browne, Richard D'Arcy, Nikolai Fatula, John Scott,
    Walter Stane. Scott Merrill, George Martin.

The Mapleton High Glee Club: Adelaide Abbot, Florence Wyman,
Ingeborg Bransen, Jean Cumming, Joyce Doncaster, Rose Marie
Elliott, Jane Irving, Lynn Alden, Ken Black, Jack Collins, Arthur
Davies, Warren Jones, Byron Milligan, Fred Perrone, Edwin
Ziegler, Matthew Ferrugio.
The Children: Bonnie Baker, Anne Bracken, Phyllis de Bus, Sally
Ferguson, Louise Pearl, Janice Smith, Edward Tappa, Robert
Allen, William Welch.
Act I.—Scenes 1 and 3—Dr. Brooks' Office. Scenes 2 and 4—Liza
Elliott's Office. Act II.—Scenes 1 and 3—Liza Elliott's Office. 2—Dr.
Brooks' Office.
Staged by Moss Hart and Hassard Short; choreography by Al-
bertina Rasch; musical direction by Maurice Abravanel; settings by
Harry Horner; costumes by Irene Sharaff; gowns by Hattie Carnegie.

"Lady in the Dark" was first produced in New York January
23, 1941. It ran for 162 performances, being withdrawn in June
so that Gertrude Lawrence might have a rest. Reopened September 1, 1941, with Eric Brotherson succeeding Danny Kaye,
Willard Parker following Victor Mature, Walter Coy replacing
Macdonald Carey and Paul McGrath taking over Bert Lytell's
job. An additional 305 performances were added before the play
was taken on tour.

(Closed May 15, 1943)

* HARRIET

(114 performances)

A play in three acts by Florence Ryerson and Colin Clements.
Produced by Gilbert Miller at the Henry Miller Theatre, New
York, March 3, 1943.

Cast of characters—

Auntie Zeb	Alberta Perkins
Henry Ward Beecher	Sydney Smith
Catharine Beecher	Jane Seymour
Harriet Beecher Stowe	Helen Hayes
Calvin Stowe	Rhys Williams
William Beecher	Guy Sorel
Edward Beecher	Geoffrey Lumb
Mary Beecher Perkins	Carmen Mathews
Charles Beecher	Hugh Franklin
Thomas Beecher	Gaylord Mason
Isabella Beecher	Harda Klaveness
James Beecher	Ronald Reiss
Dr. Lyman Beecher	Robert Harrison
Mr. Tuttle	Harrison Dowd
Mr. Wycherly	Victor Franz
Celestine	Mildred Taswell
Freddie Stowe (as a child)	Edmond Abel
Mrs. Hobbs	Helen Carew
Freddie Stowe (as a young man)	Jack Manning
Georgie Stowe	Joan Tetzel
Hatty Stowe	Betty Wade
Eliza Stowe	Lenore Wade
Jerusha Pantry	Seth Arnold
Lowell Denton	William Woodson
Sukey	Edna Thomas

Haley..Benedict MacQuarrie
Jane...Philippa Bevans
    Act I.—The Stowe Cottage, Cincinnati, Ohio. 1830. Act II.—The
Stowe House, New Brunswick, Maine. 1850. Act III.—The Stowe
Mansion, Andover, Mass. 1861.
    Staged by Elia Kazan; settings by Lemuel Ayers; costumes by Aline
Bernstein.

See page 224.

MEN IN SHADOW

(21 performances)

A drama in three acts by Mary Hayley Bell. Produced by
Max Gordon at the Morosco Theatre, New York, March 10, 1943.

Cast of characters—

Moy..Joseph De Santis
German Captain...............................Peter von Zerneck
German Lieutenant............................Peter Knego
Cherie.......................................Michelette Burani
Kenny..Everett Sloane
Polly..Francis De Sales
Lew..Roy Hargrave
Mordan.......................................Dean Harens
Enshaw.......................................Ernest Graves
German Sergeant..............................Martin Brandt
German Corporal..............................Michael Ingram
German Soldier...............................Wesley Adams
    Acts I, II and III.—Loft of Old Unused Mill, Adjoining Farmhouse
Somewhere on the French Coast.
    Staged by Roy Hargrave; setting by Frederick Fox.

Lew, Polly and Kenny are three American airmen shot down
in occupied France. Hiding out in the loft of an old mill hard
by a French farmhouse belonging to a sympathetic Cherie, their
adventures include frequent interruptions by investigating Nazis;
the taking in of Enshaw, who turns out to be a spy and gets his
neck cracked; the salvaging of Mordan, another American flier
who breaks both legs when he bails out of his plane, and their
final escape through a trapdoor in the roof through which they
have to hoist Mordan after his legs have been crudely set and
put in splints by the French farm woman.

(Closed March 27, 1943)

* KISS AND TELL

(103 performances)

A comedy in three acts by F. Hugh Herbert. Produced by
George Abbott at the Biltmore Theatre, New York, March 17,
1943.

Cast of characters—

Mr. Willard	James Lane
Louise	Francis Bavier
Corliss Archer	Joan Caulfield
Raymond Pringle	Tommy Lewis
Mildred Pringle	Judith Parrish
Dexter Franklin	Robert White
Janet Archer	Jessie Royce Landis
Harry Archer	Robert Keith
Private Earhart	John Harvey
Lieut. Lenny Archer	Richard Widmark
Mary Franklin	Paula Trueman
Bill Franklin	Calvin Thomas
Dorothy Pringle	Lulu Mae Hubbard
Uncle George	Walter Davis
Robert Pringle	Robert Lynn

Acts I, II and III.—Back Porch of Archers' Home.
Staged by George Abbott; setting by John Root.

See page 335.

APOLOGY

(8 performances)

A fantasy by Charles Schnee. Produced by Lee Strasberg at the Mansfield Theatre, New York, March 22, 1943.

Cast of characters—

The Lecturer	Elissa Landi
Albert Warner	Theodore Newton
Florrie and Laura	Thelma Schnee
Paul Vannon and William McCready	Ben Smith
Fortune Teller and Janitor	Harold J. Stone
Fraulein and Shoplifter	Merle Maddern
Betty	Erin O'Brien-Moore
Mr. Warner, Mr. Downing and E. B.	Clay Clement
Bingham and Lester Ballantine	James Todd
Manny	Lewis Charles
Evelyn	Peggy Allardice
Weber	Robert Simon

A variety of lighted scenes on a dark stage.
Staged by Lee Strasberg; setting and lighting by Samuel Leve; costumes by Paul Morrison.

Albert Warner, the son of the richest man in his village, might have married his childhood's chum, Florrie, who lived across the tracks. Being ambitious, he turned rather to Betty, whose father owned the biggest department store and was prepared to agree to take Albert in as a partner as the price of his marrying Betty. Albert continued to muss up his utterly selfish life until finally, in a crisis, he saw the light, found his soul and decided to devote the rest of his life to making the world a happier place for his own daughter to live in.

(Closed March 27, 1943)

RICHARD III

(11 performances)

A tragedy in two parts by William Shakespeare. Revived by Theatre Productions at the Forrest Theatre, New York, March 24, 1943.

Cast of characters—

Queen Margaret	Mildred Dunnock
King Henry VI	Harry Irvine
Richard, Duke of Gloucester	George Coulouris
King Edward IV	Tom Rutherford
Queen Elizabeth	Norma Chambers
Edward, Prince of Wales	Larry Robinson
George, Duke of Clarence	Harold Young
Sir Richard Ratcliff	John Parrish
Lord Hastings	Anthony Kemble Cooper
Lady Anne	Helen Waren
Earle Rivers	Norman Rose
Lord Grey	James Ganon
Duke of Buckingham	Philip Bourneuf
Lord Stanley	Stuart Casey
Marquis of Dorset	Eugene Struckmann
Casesby	Ralph Clanton
1st Murderer	John Ireland
2nd Murderer	Herbert Ratner
1st Citizen	Randolph Echols
2nd Citizen	Harold Young
3rd Citizen	Bertram Tanswell
4th Citizen	John Sylvester
Lord Mayor of London	Harry Irvine
Richard, Duke of York	Michael Artist
Messenger	Norman Rose
Scrivener	Bertram Tanswell
Page	John Sylvester
Sir James Tyrrel	Herbert Ratner
2nd Messenger	Eugene Struckmann
3rd Messenger	James Ganon
Sir James Blunt	John Ford
Duke of Norfolk	Randolph Echols

The Entire Action of the Play Is Laid in England from 1471-1485.

Staged by George Coulouris; settings by Motley; lighting by Jean Rosenthal.

The best-remembered of the "Richard III" revivals in New York was that which Arthur Hopkins made for John Barrymore in 1920. Walter Hampden played the tragedy as late as 1934 for eight performances, and before him Fritz Leiber and the Chicago Civic Shakespearean Company revived it in a repertory engagement in 1930.

(Closed April 3, 1943)

THE FAMILY

(7 performances)

A drama in three acts by Victor Wolfson based on the novel by Nina Fedorova. Produced by Oscar Serlin at the Windsor Theatre, New York, March 30, 1943.

Cast of characters—

Kahn	Joseph Tso Shih
Phillip Stowne	Lowell Gilmore
Dima	Alec Englander
Granny	Lucile Watson
Mme. Militza	Evelyn Varden
Professor Chernov	Arnold Korff
Mr. Sung	Yung Ying Hsu
Lida	Elisabeth Fraser
Tania	Marion Evensen
Anna Petrovna Chernov	Katherine Squire
Jimmy Bennett	Bill Lipton
Peter	Nicholas Conte
Chauffeur	Ronald Dexter
Mrs. Parrish	Carol Goodner
Amah	June Kim
Dog	Miranda
Dr. Isaacs	Boris Tumarin
Wah Gay	Kaie Deei
Chinese Gentleman Next Door	Ping Yuen Zi

Japanese Lodgers: Takashi Ohta, Nelson Kawate, Henry Takeuchi, P. C. Arenal, George Yamashige.

Acts I, II and III.—Living-Room of Number 11 Long Street in the British Concession, Tientsin, China.

Staged by Bretaigne Windust; settings by Boris Aronson; lighting by Moe Hack; costumes by Carolyn Hancock; sound by Saki Oura.

Forced out of Russia in the early days of the Kerensky revolution a family of White Russians lands in Tientsin, China. With Granny presiding as the matriarch of the group, the family opens a boarding house and attracts an assortment of guests. These include Prof. Chernov and his worried wife, who fears he is losing his mind; Mrs. Parrish, an English woman who is trying to drown in drink her sorrow over the loss of a small son; a Russian fortune teller; five Japanese spies; one Chinese secret agent. A series of exciting adventures ends in the return of Mrs. Parrish to London with the small son of the Russian family to comfort her and an older son, Peter, as her probable new romance.

(Closed April 3, 1943)

* OKLAHOMA

(86 performances)

A musical comedy in two acts by Oscar Hammerstein 2nd; music by Richard Rodgers; based on play, "Green Grow the Lilacs" by Lynn Riggs. Produced by The Theatre Guild at the St. James Theatre, New York, March 31, 1943.

Cast of characters—

Aunt Eller	Betty Garde
Curly	Alfred Drake
Laurey	Joan Roberts
Ike Skidmore	Barry Kelley
Fred	Edwin Clay
Slim	Herbert Rissman
Will Parker	Lee Dixon
Jud Fry	Howard da Silva
Ado Annie Carnes	Celeste Holm
Ali Hakim	Joseph Buloff
Gertie Cummings	Jane Lawrence
Ellen	Ellen Love
Andrew Carnes	Ralph Riggs
Cord Elam	Owen Martin
Mike	Paul Schierz
Joe	George Irving
Cowboy	Jack Harwood
Sam	Hayes Gordon

Act. I.—Scene 1—Laurey's Farm House. 2—The Smoke House. 3—Grove on Laurey's Farm. Act II.—Scene 1—The Skidmore Ranch. 2—A Meadow. 3—Stable Shed. 4—Laurey's Farm.

Staged by Rouben Mamoulian; dances directed by Agnes de Mille; music directed by Jacob Schwartzdorf; settings by Lemuel Ayers; costumes by Miles White; production under supervision of Lawrence Langner and Theresa Helburn.

See page 375.

* ZIEGFELD FOLLIES

(84 performances)

A revue in two acts; lyrics by Jack Yellen and Buddy Burston; music by Ray Henderson and Dan White; sketches by Lester Lee, Jerry Seelen, Bud Pearson, Les White, Joseph Erens, Charles Sherman, Harry Young, Lester Lawrence, Baldwin Bergensen, Ray Golden, Sid Kuller, William Wells and Harold Rome. Produced by Messrs. Shubert in association with Alfred Bloomingdale and Lou Walters, at the Winter Garden, New York, April 1, 1943.

Principals engaged—

Milton Berle	Ilona Massey
Arthur Treacher	Katherine Meskill
Jack Cole	Sue Ryan
Tommy Wonder	Nadine Gae

Dean Murphy	Christine Ayers
Jack McCauley	Imogene Carpenter
Jaye Martin	Mary Ganley
Manfred Hecht	Penny Edwards
Charles Senna	Patricia Hall
Ray Long	Dixie Roberts
Arthur Maxwell	Rebecca Lee
Virginia Miller	Ruth Rowan
Doris Brent	Marilyn Hightower
The Jansleys	Bil and Cora Baird
Yost's Vikings	The Rhythmaires

Ziegfeld Show Girls

Staged by John Murray Anderson; supervised by Harry A. Kaufman; dialogue directed by Arthur Pierson and Fred de Cordova; orchestra directed by John McManus; sets by Watson Barratt; costumes by Miles White; dances directed by Robert Alton.

* TOMORROW THE WORLD

(72 performances)

A drama in three acts by James Gow and Arnoud d'Usseau. Produced by Theron Bamberger at the Ethel Barrymore Theatre, New York, April 14, 1943.

Cast of characters—

Patricia Frame	Nancy Nugent
Jessie Frame	Dorothy Sands
Frieda	Edit Angold
Michael Frame	Ralph Bellamy
Leona Richards	Shirley Booth
Emil Bruchner	Skippy Homeier
Fred Miller	Richard Taber
Dennis	Walter Kelly
Butler	Richard Tyler
Tommy	Paul Porter, Jr.

Acts I, II and III.—Living-Room of Professor Michael Frame's Home in a Large University Town in the Middle West.
Staged by Elliott Nugent; setting by Raymond Sovey.

See page 180.

THE FIRST MILLION

(5 performances)

A comedy farce in three acts by Irving Elman. Produced by Jimmy Elliott at the Ritz Theatre, New York, April 28, 1943.

Cast of characters—

"Maw" Boone	Dorrit Kelton
Hoke Boone	Wendell Corey
Mink Boone	Dort Clark
Sank Boone	George Cotton
Emmy Lou	Lois Hall
Sheriff	Russell Collins
Tom Boone	Henry Barnard
Mr. Fairweather	John Souther
Lucius J. Beasel	Harlan Briggs
Pidgie	Louise Larabee

Acts I, II and III.—A Cabin in the Ozarks.
Staged by John Kennedy; setting by Wolfgang Roth.

"Maw" Boone and the morally and mentally defective Boone boys promised "Paw" that they would not begin spending their loot until they had accumulated their first million. The Boones were bank robbers and stick-up guys in the Ozarks. They still have $20,000 to gather when the play begins and kidnap the village banker, Lucius Beasel, to get it. In the end the youngest Boone boy turns honest, burns up the $980,000 hidden in the churn, thus forcing his depressed family to start all over.

(Closed May 1, 1943)

* THE CORN IS GREEN

(48 performances)

A drama in three acts by Emlyn Williams. Revived by Herman Shumlin at the Martin Beck Theatre, New York, May 3, 1943.

Cast of characters—

John Goronwy Jones	Tom E. Williams
Miss Ronberry	Esther Mitchell
Idwal Morris	Kenneth Clarke
Sarah Pugh	Gwyneth Hughes
A Groom	George Bleasdale
The Squire	Lewis L. Russell
Mrs. Watty	Eva Leonard-Boyne
Bessie Watty	Perry Wilson
Miss Moffat	Ethel Barrymore
Robbart Robbatch	Patrick O'Connor
Morgan Evans	Richard Waring
Glyn Thomas	Gene Ross
John Owen	Peter Harris
Will Hughes	Bert Kalmar, Jr.
Old Tom	J. P. Wilson

Boys, Girls and Parents: Julia Knox, Betty Conibear, Julia Carlson, Jane Van Duser, Josephine Capel, Gwilyn Williams.

Acts I, II and III.—Living-Room of a House in Glansarno, a Small Village in a Remote Welsh Countryside.

Staged by Herman Shumlin; setting by Howard Bay; costumes by Ernest Schrapps.

This was a return engagement of the touring company, played at a popular scale of prices. There had been numerous changes in cast since the first New York performance in November, 1940. Tom Williams had taken over the role of Goronwy Jones originally played by his brother, Rhys. Eva Leonard-Boyne succeeded Rosalind Ivan as Mrs. Watty, Lewis L. Russell followed Edmond Breon as the Squire, and Perry Wilson had taken on the role of Bessie Watty, played originally by Thelma Schnee. A few weeks later Donald Buka followed Richard Waring as the young miner, Morgan Evans, Waring having played the role from the first performance.

SONS AND SOLDIERS

(22 performances)

A drama in three acts by Irwin Shaw. Produced by Max Reinhardt, Norman Bel Geddes and Richard Myers at the Morosco Theatre, New York, May 4, 1943.

Cast of characters—

John Tadlock	Herbert Rudley
Victor Carnrick	Millard Mitchell
Rebecca Tadlock	Geraldine Fitzgerald
Andrew Tadlock	Gregory Peck
Andrew Tadlock, as a Child	Jack Willett
Dora Applegate, as a Child	Joan McSweeney
Lincoln Graves, as a Child	Bobbie Schenck
Ernest Tadlock, as a Child	Ted Donaldson
Lincoln Graves	Leonard Sues
Ernest Tadlock	Kenneth Tobey
Matthew Graves	Karl Malden
Marie	Sara Lee Harris
Anthony	Roderick Maybee
Miss Gillespie	Martha Greenhouse
Mr. Leverhook	William Beach
Mark Lowry	Edward Forbes
Dora Applegate	Audrey Long
Catherine Carnrick	Stella Adler
The Mailman	Edward Nannery
The Salesman	Jesse White
Catherine's Escort	Albert Bergh
Carol	Phyllis Hill
Alice	Harriet Jackson
Minister	Royal Dana Tracy

Acts I, II and III.—In a Small American City, Starting in 1916. Staged by Max Reinhardt; dances by Wally Jackson; setting by Norman Bel Geddes.

Rebecca Tadlock is going to have a baby. Her physician is fearful that if she does her chances of dying in childbirth are about 10 to 1. He recommends an operation. Rebecca suffers a temporary collapse during which she lives through the next twenty-five years of her life. In her sometimes happy, sometimes nightmarish visions, she follows the careers of herself and her children. She mothers two sons through their infancy, their school years and their young manhood. Then she gives them up to the war. Still, when Rebecca awakes from her dreams she decides to go through with the birth of her child. She will take the 10 to 1 chance. All lives, she says, are worth living.

(Closed May 22, 1943)

* THREE'S A FAMILY

(46 performances)

A comedy in three acts by Phoebe and Henry Ephron. Produced by John Golden at the Longacre Theatre, New York, May 5, 1943.

Cast of characters—

Sam Whitaker	Robert Burton
Irma Dalrymple	Ethel Owen
Adelaide	Doro Merande
Kitty Mitchell	Katharine Bard
Archie Whitaker	Edwin Philips
Hazel	Dorothy Gilchrist
Frances Whitaker	Ruth Weston
Delivery Man	Edmund Dorsay
Eugene Mitchell	Francis de Sales
Two Moving Men	Carl Judd, Earl McDonald
Another Maid	Gee Gee James
A Girl	Jean Bellows
Dr. Bartell	William Wadsworth
Joe Franklin	Richard Midgley
Marion Franklin	Virginia Vass

Acts I, II and III.—Living-Room of Sam and Frances Whitaker's Apartment on West 110th Street, New York.

Staged by Henry Ephron; setting by Stewart Chaney.

The Whitakers have a three-room flat on the upper West Side. Their maiden sister, Irma, lives with them. Their daughter, Kitty, quarrels with her husband and comes home, bringing her month-old baby with her. Things get pretty crowded. The Whitaker son, Archie, also appears with his wife, who is twelve days past her delivery date and can't find a room in any hospital. Kitty's husband, who has enlisted, returns with arms filled with presents for his baby and finds the baby has disappeared with a colored maid, who has been drinking the Whitaker liquor. The family obstetrician is a fumbling oldster who has been called from retirement to replace a younger doctor. He carries the farce to a confused but possible ending.

* THE STUDENT PRINCE

(7 performances)

An operetta in four acts by Dorothy Donnelly; music by Sigmund Romberg. Revived by the Messrs. Shubert at the Broadway Theatre, New York, June 8, 1943.

Cast of characters—

First Lackey	Howard Roland
Second Lackey	Dennis Dengate
Third Lackey	Fred Lane

```
Fourth Lackey....................................Ken Harlan
Prime Minister Von Mark.......................William Pringle
Dr. Engel......................................Everett Marshall
Prince Karl Franz.............................Frank Hornaday
Ruder..........................................Walter Johnson
Gretchen.......................................Ann Pennington
Toni...........................................Nat Sack
Detlef.........................................Roy Barnes
Von Asterberg..................................Lyndon Crews
Lucas..........................................Daniel De Paolo
Kathie.........................................Barbara Scully
Lutz...........................................Detmar Poppen
Hubert.........................................Jesse M. Cimberg
Grand Duchess Anastasia.......................Nine Varela
Princess Margaret.............................Helene Arthur
Captain Tarnitz................................Charles Chesney
Countess Leydon...............................Helena Le Berthon
Rudolph........................................Herman Magidson
Postillion.....................................Jimmy Russell
```

Act I.—Scene 1—Ante-Chamber in the Palace at Karlsburg. 2—Garden of the Inn of the Three Golden Apples. Act II.—Sitting Room of Prince Karl Franz at the Inn. Act III.—A Room of State in Royal Palace at Karlsburg. Act IV.—Garden of the Inn.

Staged by J. J. Shubert; choreography by Ruthanne Boris and Alexis Dolinoff; music directed by Pierre de Reeder and Fred Hoff; settings by Watson Barratt; costumes by Stage Costumes, Inc.

The first production of "The Student Prince" was made at the Jolson Theatre, 57th Street, New York, December 2, 1924, by the Messrs. Shubert. Howard Marsh was the Karl, Greek Evans the tutor, Ilse Marvenga the Kathie. It has been more or less continuously revived since then, breaking out every year or two in various parts of the country.

* THE MILKY WAY

(6 performances)

A comedy in three acts by Lynn Root and Harry Clork. Revived by Lucia Victor's New York Stock Company at the Windsor Theatre, New York, June 9, 1943.

Cast of characters—

```
Spider.........................................Max Leavitt
Speed McFarland...............................Stanley Phillips
Anne Westly....................................Lila Lee
Gabby Sloan....................................Lewis Charles
Burleigh Sullivan..............................Joey Faye
Mae Sullivan...................................Helen Gillette
Willard........................................Jerry Sylvon
Eddie..........................................Marshall Reid
Wilbur Austin..................................Bert Jeter
```

Acts I, II and III.—Speed's Room in Apartment Hotel in West Fifties in New York City.

Staged by Rodney Hale; setting by Cirker and Robbins.

"The Milky Way" was produced first May 8, 1934, at the Cort Theatre in New York. The late Hugh O'Connell played the milkman who becomes a champion fighter by accident. Gladys

George was the heroine, Brian Donlevy the defending champion and Leo Donnelly his manager. It ran for forty-seven performances.

THE ARMY PLAY-BY-PLAY

(1 performance)

The five one-act prize plays from the enlisted man's contest sponsored by John Golden in co-operation with the Special Service Branch Headquarters Second Service Command, Lt.-Col. William R. Bolton, Chief. Produced at the 46th Street Theatre, New York, June 14, 1943.

WHERE E'ER WE GO

By P.F.C. John B. O'Dea

Performed by Camp Wood. Cast of characters—

Tex	Pvt. Paul Tripp
Gentry	Sgt. Farris Brannan, Jr.
Sweeney	Sgt. Patrick F. Gallagher
Baxter	Pvt. Warren F. Hawkinson
Bonnelli	Pvt. Louis Menchel
Stover	Cpl. Pershing Dickinson
Joe	Cpl. Joseph Scollieri
Bliss	Sgt. Philip Kaplan
Silent Sam	P.F.C. Eugene Schoenig
Kenniston	Cpl. Daniel Jefferson
1st Sergeant	Pvt. Lawrence McGrath
Cpl. Black	Cpl. George Heffron

Scene—The Upper Story of a Wooden Barracks, Ft. Lewis, Washington.

Directed by Pvt. Paul Tripp.

FIRST COUSINS

By Cpl. Kurt S. Kasznar

Performed by Special Service Branch, Headquarters Second Command Service, New York City. Cast of characters—

Mack	Cpl. Ralph C. Geisler
Sam	Cpl. David N. Rieser
Clide	Pvt. Melvin Parks
Karl	Sgt. Gordon B. Thomson
Sailor	P.F.C. Leo H. Juditz
Commander	Cpl. Kurt S. Kasznar

Scene—The Hull of a Small German Submarine.

Directed by Sgt. Gordon B. Thomson.

BUTTON YOUR LIP

By P.F.C. Irving Gaynor Neiman

Performed by Fort Monmouth. Cast of characters—

Mack	Pvt. Daniel Millard
Smitty	Cpl. Herbert Greenhouse

Bernard..................................Cpl. Leonard A. Patrick
Corporal......................................Cpl. Phillip Pine
Brad.......................................Pvt. Eugene Erwin
Sergeant.......................................Cpl. Harold Gary
Joe.......................................Cpl. Erving J. Engelman
1st Rookie.................................Cpl. Homer Reynolds
2nd Rookie..............................P.F.C. Joseph Juliano
Weatherby............................Sgt. Abner Mendelsohn
Lieutenant..............................Cpl. Robert O. Wehling
Ryan......................................Cpl. Henry Brandon
Tester......................................Cpl. Clifford G. Kinkel
Captain......................................Cpl. Jack Arthur
3rd Rookie..............................Cpl. Michael P. Grace
Orderly..................................Sgt. Arthur J. O'Connell
    Scene—The Washroom of Barracks 3T, Camp Downey, 1333 Reception Center.
    Directed by Sgt. Arthur O'Connell.

MAIL CALL

By Air Cadet Ralph Nelson

Performed by Fort Hancock. Cast of characters—

Minnick..................................P.F.C. Joseph Sucarato
Spider.....................................Pvt. Charles Zimmerman
Johnson......................................Sgt. Tom Smith
Meitelbaum.................................Pvt. Edward Kramer
Luckadoo...............................Pvt. Joseph Ross Hertz
Mail Orderly..................................Sgt. Willis Taylor
    Scene—A Shelter in Some Almost Destroyed Village, Behind the Lines, Somewhere in the Theatre of Operations.
    Dircted by Pvt. Joseph Ross Hertz.

PACK UP YOUR TROUBLES

By P.F.C. Alfred D. Geto

Performed by Camp Upton. Cast of characters—

Cpl. Morelski..................................Pvt. Alfred Ryder
Elmer Benson..................................Pvt. George Petrie
Eddie Clark....................................Pvt. Sam Main
Cpl. Jones....................................Pvt. Edwin G. Milk
Sgt. Kelly....................................Pvt. Richard Kaplan
Capt. Stern..................................Pvt. Jules Munshin
M. P. ....Pvt. Erasmus Di Russo
    Scene—A Portion of a Warehouse at a Receiving Station.
    Directed by Cpl. Alan Wilson.
    Specialties during the evening by Pvt. Jules Munshin, Pvt. Erasmus Di Russo, Pvt. Vito Coppola.
    Music by the 369th Army Air Force Band of Stewart Field, New York. Production supervised by John Golden, assisted by Stuart Fox, Milton Stern and Sgt. Alex Kahn; musical arrangements by Capt. John J. Morrissey and Pvt. Jack Diamant; settings by Cirker and Robbins Studio; soldier art by Marc Brody. The prize judges included Elmer Rice, Russel Crouse, Kenyon Nicholson, Frederick Lonsdale and John Golden.

The single performance of "The Army Play-by-Play" netted the Soldiers and Sailors' Club of New York approximately $100,-000. Prizes were awarded all the contestants: First prize, $100, to P.f.c. John B. O'Dea for "Where E're We Go"; second, $80, to Lieut. Ralph Nelson for "Mail Call"; third, $60, to P.f.c. Irving Gaynor Neiman for "Button Up Your Lip"; fourth, $40 each, to P.f.c. Alfred D. Geto for "Pack Up Your Troubles," and to Cpl. Kurt Kasznar for "First Cousins" and fifth, $20 to Pvt. Arthur Vogel for "More Than We Know" which was not presented on the June 14 program. The judges were Russel Crouse, Kenyon Nicholson, Elmer Rice and John Golden, who contributed the prize money.

MAJOR CAST SUBSTITUTIONS

Many important changes were made in casts during the 1942-43 season. Among the most significant were:

"Arsenic and Old Lace"—Margaret Joyce replaced Helen Brooks as Elaine Harper June 15, 1942, and later in the month Laura Hope Crews became Abby Brewster in place of Josephine Hull; Herbert Ranson replaced Wyrley Birch as Rev. Dr. Harper; Forrest Orr played Teddy Brewster, previously played by John Alexander, and Erich Von Stroheim took Boris Karloff's role of Jonathan Brewster. In July Philip Bourneuf replaced Edgar Stehli as Dr. Einstein and in August Effie Shannon replaced Jean Adair as Martha Brewster and Joseph Sweeney took Edgar Stehli's role of Dr. Einstein. Ruth McDevitt replaced Laura Hope Crews as Abby Brewster in October and in December Henry Sharpe replaced Joseph Sweeney as Dr. Einstein, Mr. Sweeney replacing Erich Von Stroheim as Jonathan Brewster. In January, 1943, Walter Wagner replaced Philip Bourneuf as Mortimer and in May Henry Gribbon replaced Forrest Orr as Teddy Brewster.

"My Sister Eileen"—Joseph Buloff replaced Robert Bernard as Mr. Appopolous in June, 1942. In December Betty Furness took Shirley Booth's role of Ruth Sherwood and Peggy Knudsen Georgette Leslie's role of Eileen.

"Life with Father"—Richard Simon replaced John Devereaux as Clarence in July. Dorothy Gish replaced Dorothy Stickney as Vinnie and Louis Calhern played Howard Lindsay's role of Father Day late in August. In October Elaine Evans replaced Miss Gish and A. H. Van Buren took over Louis Calhern's role. Mr. Lindsay and Miss Stickney returned to the principal parts in November. In January, 1943, Jack Harrington took the part of Clarence, replacing Richard Simon. In April James Dobson replaced Jack Harrington. Michael Dreyfuss replaced Artie Quinn as John in April. In May Harry Bannister played Father, replacing A. H. Van Buren and Muriel Kirkland played Vinnie. Percy Waram and Margalo Gillmore played Father and Vinnie in the Fall of 1941.

"Sons o' Fun"—Wynn Murray replaced Ella Logan in early June, 1942, and Stella Clausen replaced Rosario the following January. Don Gautier replaced Frank Libuse and Jean Moorehead took Wynn Murray's role in March. Steve Olsen replaced Chic Johnson in April and Marty May replaced Ole Olsen in May, 1943.

"By Jupiter"—Nanette Fabray replaced Constance Moore in February, 1943.

"Priorities"—Romo Vincent replaced Phil Baker in July, 1942.

"Let's Face It"—Carol Goodner replaced Eve Arden in July, 1942, and the following February, Jose Ferrer replaced Danny Kaye.

"Claudia"—Phyllis Thaxter replaced Dorothy McGuire as Claudia in July, 1942. Later in the month the entire cast was changed, Beverly Bayne replacing Frances Starr as Mrs. Brown, Robert Shayne taking over the role of David Naughton; Elizabeth Newman, Bertha; Bruno Wick, Fritz; Robert Craven, Jerry Seymour; Susanne Caubaye, Madame Daruschka and Lila Lee, Julia Naughton. In October Richard Kendrick replaced Robert Shayne as David.

"Porgy and Bess"—In May, 1942, Etta Moten took the place of Anne Brown as Bess.

"Vickie"—John Forsythe took Edmund Glover's role of Private Cootes and Sallie Gracie became Sandra in place of Lynne Carter in October.

"Native Son"—In January, 1943, Patricia Palmer replaced Ann Burr as Mary Dalton.

"Eve of St. Mark"—Walter Burke replaced Eddie O'Shea as Private Mulveroy in November, 1942. Lyle Bettger replaced Charles Mendick as Corporal Tate in March and Stanley Prague replaced Martin Ritt as Pvt. Glinka. John Doll replaced William Prince as Quizz West early in June, 1943.

"Angel Street"—John Emery replaced Vincent Price early in December, 1942, and the following May Ferdi Hoffman replaced John Emery as Mr. Manningham. Jetti Preminger replaced Elizabeth Eustis as Nancy in May.

"Count Me In"—Fred and Elaine Parry replaced Gower and Jean early in November, 1942.

"Three Sisters"—Guthrie McClintic took Edmund Gwenn's role of Chebutykin for ten days in December, 1942.

"For Your Pleasure"—Mary Raye and Naldi substituted for Veloz and Yolanda in February, 1943.

"The Patriots"—Edwin Jerome took the part of George Washington soon after the play opened, taking the place of Cecil Humphreys. Mr. Humphreys resumed the part in May, 1943.

"Skin of Our Teeth"—Edith Faversham played the Fortune

Teller late in the season, replacing Florence Reed. Miriam Hopkins took Tallulah Bankhead's role of Sabina, Viola Frame replaced Florence Eldridge as Mrs. Antrobus and Conrad Nagel replaced Fredric March as Mr. Antrobus early in June, 1943.

"Ziegfeld Follies"—Sara Ann McCabe replaced Ilona Massey the last of May, 1943.

"Dark Eyes"—Tamara Geva replaced Eugenie Leontovich as Natasha Rapakovitch in June, 1943.

"Kiss and Tell"—Cyrilla Dorn replaced Judith Parrish as Mildred Pringle just before the season closed in June.

DANCE DRAMA

The Ballet Russe de Monte Carlo began the first of two three-day festivals at the Lewisohn Stadium celebrating the Silver Jubilee of that summer institution June 23, 1942. Balanchine's "Serenade," Alexandra Fedorova's version of "The Nutcracker" and Fokine's "Prince Igor" were danced by Alexandra Danilova, Igor Youskevitch, Frederic Franklin, Tatiana Orlova, Lubov Roudenko, Nathalie Krassovska and George Zoritch. Franz Allers conducted the Philharmonic-Symphony Orchestra. June 24 Leonide Massine danced with Alexandra Danilova, Nathalie Krassovska and Roland Guerard in "Beau Danube," Mia Slavenska danced the chief role of "The Magic Swan" and Tatiana Orlova danced the part of Zobeide in "Scheherazade."

The Season of Ballet in which S. Hurok presented the Ballet Theatre and the Ballet Russe de Monte Carlo alternate weeks at the Metropolitan Opera House, New York, opened October 6, 1942, with the Ballet Theatre in "Swan Lake," "Aleko" and "Princess Aurora." The première of "Aleko," created by Leonide Massine to a Tchaikovsky trio in A Minor, orchestrated by Erno Rapee and with scenery and costumes by Marc Chagall, inspired by Pushkin's poem, "Gypsies," was danced by Alicia Markova, Hugh Laing, George Skibine and others. "Swan Lake" was danced by Irina Baronova and Anton Dolin in the leading roles and "Princess Aurora" with Baranova, Dolan, Nora Kaye, Rosella Hightower, Sono Osato, Annabelle Lyon, Karen Conrad, Ian Gibson, Yura Lazovsky and others. Antal Dorati conducted the first two dance dramas and Mois Zlatin "Princess Aurora."

October 9 was devoted to a memorial program for Michel Fokine, introducing his newly staged "Petrushka," danced to Stravinsky music, with Irina Baranova and Yura Lazovsky in the leads supported by Richard Reed as the Moor and Rosella Hightower as the Street Girl. A children's program was presented October 10 and again October 24, including "Coppelia," "Peter the Wolf," "Les Sylphides," "Aleko" and "Naughty Lisette."

Eugene Loring's "Billy the Kid," with score by Aaron Copland, restaged by David Nillo, was performed October 25 with David Nillo as Alias and Ian Gibson as Billy. A world première was that of "Romantic Age," a burlesque by Anton Dolin with an arrangement from Bellini repertoire by Antal Dorati.

Other dance dramas presented by the Ballet Theatre during the season which closed November 1, were "Giselle," "Spectre de La Rose," "Lilac Garden," "Russian Soldier," "Afternoon of a Faun," "Baron Bluebeard," "Slavonika," "Pillar of Fire" and "Pas de Quatre." Among other dancers were Jean Hunt, John Kriza, Miriam Golden and Maria Karniloff.

The Ballet Russe de Monte Carlo replaced the Ballet Theatre from October 12 to October 20, 1942. The opening program included two new dance dramas by Bronislava Nijinska: "Snow Maiden" and "Chopin Concerto," and Leonide Massine's "Gaité Parisienne." "Snow Maiden" based on a Russian fairy tale, set to music of Glazunoff's "Seasons," with scenery and costumes by Boris Aronson, was danced by Alexandra Donilova and Nathalie Krassovska in the leading roles, with Igor Youskevitch and Frederic Franklin in support.

"Rodeo," by Agnes de Mille, based on American folk tunes, with score by Aaron Copland, settings by Oliver Smith and costumes by Kermit Love, was danced by Miss de Mille in the central role, supported by Lubov Roudenko, Frederic Franklin, Casimir Kokitch, Anton Vlasoff, Dorothy Etheridge and Milada Mladova.

Both Ballet Theatre and Ballet Russe de Monte Carlo returned in the Spring. The Ballet Theatre opened April 1 and continued until May 24 at the Metropolitan Opera House. The programs with a few exceptions were repetitions of the earlier engagement. David Lichine's "Helen of Troy" had its New York première with Vera Zorina in the name part April 3, 1943. Leonide Massine played the title role of his own "Aleko" for the first time in New York and added "Fantastic Toyshop" to the repertoire. "Romeo and Juliet," by Anthony Tudor, settings and costumes by Eugene Berman, set to music by Delius, was presented for the first time April 10 with Alicia Markova as Juliet and Hugh Laing as Romeo. Another production not presented in the earlier programs was the Stravinsky-Balanchine "Apollo." Michael Kidd restaged "Billy the Kid" and played the title role May 4, Janet Reed made her first appearance with the Ballet Theatre. Just before closing May 24, Argentinita, assisted by Pilar Lopez, Jose Greco and Manolo Vargas, was presented in a two-day Spanish dance festival. Sixty members of the Philharmonic Symphony Orchestra, conducted by Jose Iturbi, supplied the music for "Bolero," with Ravel music, and "Café de Chinitas," with Garcia Lorka music and décor by Salvador Dali.

The Ballet Russe de Monte Carlo reopened at the Broadway Theatre, May 19, 1943. Universal Art Inc. acted as sponsor and Fritz Allers directed the music. Among the dance dramas not presented in the earlier programs was "Igroushki," by Michel Fokine, using Rimsky-Korsakoff's "Fantasy on Russian Themes," with Joan Field playing the solo violin and décor and costumes by Nathalia Gontcharova. Another was "Les Elfes" set to Mendelssohn's "Midsummer Night's Dream," costumed by Christian Berard.

Argentinita appeared at Carnegie Hall, March 21, 1943, with a Spanish repertoire including "Triana," "Leyenda," "Zambrilla Gitana," "El Huayno," "Amor Gitano" and the Ravel "Bolero." Angna Enters opened her season at the Alvin Theatre, December 27, 1942, and Doris Humphrey opened the same night at the Studio Theatre, with Jose Limon as guest artist, devoting the opening program exclusively to Bach, dancing "Four Choral Preludes." Lotte Goslar appeared March 29, 1943, at Times Hall with Leon Varkas, Patricia Gardner and Betty Lind in her company. Felicia Sorel gave two performances at Labor Stage Theatre in June, 1943, assisted by Riccardo Sarroga, Wallace House and Frank Green.

The New Opera Company presented George Balanchine's "Ballet Imperial" in its first New York performance at the Broadway Theatre, November 4, 1942, as a curtain raiser to the Mussorgsky opera "The Fair at Sorochinsk." The dance drama was set to Tchaikovsky music directed by Emil Cooper, and the setting was designed by Mstislav Doboujinsky. The principal parts were danced by William Dollar, Mary Ellen Moylan and Gisella Cacialanza.

OFF BROADWAY

The Savoy Opera Guild, in its sixty-second week, started the season of 1942-43 on June 18, 1942, with "Patience" and "The Mikado," Lewis Denison directing. The Guild occupied the Cherry Lane Theatre. The Light Opera Theatre opened its fourth season June 18, 1942, with "The Mikado," directed by John Grahame and Alexander Maissel. The theatre suspended its production from November 15 until December 17. Costumes and settings were designed by Robert Feyti. The principals included Stanley Nabinger, Josephine Lombardo, Allda Mae Prigge, Robert Feyti, Florence Bauer, Ellie Krueger and Joseph Di Stefano.

The New York Light Opera Guild presented Franz von Suppé's operetta, "Fatinitza," at the Heckscher Theatre, June 24, 1942, staged by Bert Linger and conducted by John Hand. The principals included George Wagner, Hertha Sandig, Frank Murray, Charles Bergman, Lloyd Cole, Winifred Stewart, Helen Edwards and Arthur Silver.

At the Theatre Showcase "The Goldfish Bowl," by Vincent O'Connor, was presented and directed by William Boyman, July 15, 1942. Michael Artist, Daisy Bellmore, Zita Rieth, Doris Daniels and others were in the cast.

At the Cosmopolitan Opera House Gustav Kotaniji, who revived "The Gypsy Baron" in German earlier in the season, presented the Karl Milloecker operetta, "The Beggar Student," in a new English version by Don Wilson and Alix Szilasi, September 25, 1942, Robert Stolz, conductor. Donald Dame, Teresa Gerson, Ralph Herbert, John Garris, Margit Bokor and Kathryn Harvey were in the cast.

The Blackfriars' Guild opened the Blackfriars' Theatre, New York, October 29, with "Inside Story," a comedy by Peter Sheehan, directed by Dennis Gurney. In the cast were Elsbeth Hoffman, Dorothy Lambert, Douglas Keaton, J. Augustus Keogh, Julie Snow, Gene Lyons, Elsie Gustafson, June Meer, Alice Thomson, Albert Carroll, Robert James Hayward and Patsy O'Shea. A fantasy by Andrew Hawhe, with incidental music by Thomas H. F. Padrian, "Tinker's Dam," played from January 28 through February 14, 1943. The cast included Lawrence Fletcher, Gerald

Buckley, Peggy Wynn, James Ganon, Dort Clark, Eileen Heckert, H. E. Currier, Robert Hayward, Dorothy Steele, Marjorie Peggs, John Huntington, Alix Taran, John Rosene, Jackie Ayers, Patsy O'Shea and Selma Lewis. From April 1 through April 18, 1943, the Blackfriars presented John Drinkwater's Biblical play, "A Man's House," with Augustin Duncan, Cavada Humphrey, Frank Gibney, Royal D. Tracy, Charles Wallis, Dan Gallare, Sam Banham, Frank Lucas, Lawrence Tierner and Dennis Gurney in the cast. The season was concluded June 13, 1943, with "Moment Musical," a comedy by Charles Angoff. The players were Catherine Bradford, Eileen Heckert, Dayton Lummis, Joan Croydon, Jack Woods and Gene Lyons.

The second subscription season of the New Opera Company started at the Broadway Theatre, November 3, 1942, with "The Fair at Sorochinsk," a three-act opera by Moussorgsky, based on a Gogol short story, and "The Opera Cloak," by Walter Damrosch with libretto by Gretchen D. Finletter. The operas were staged by Michael Chekhov and the music conducted by Emil Cooper. The casts included Marina Koshetz (who alternated with Mary Henderson as Parrasia), Winifred Heidt, Michael Bartlett, Donald Dame, Mary Lida Bowen, Nathaniel Sprinzena, Virginia MacWatters and others.

Offenbach's "La Vie Parisienne" was presented November 10, 1942, Paul Breisach conducting the music and Felix Brentano directing the opera. The settings were designed by Marco Montedoro. Caroline Segrera, Virginia Card, Andzia Kuzak, Wilbur Evans, Hugh Thompson, Donald Burr, Paul Reed, Stanley Carlson, Paul Kwartin, Mary Davis, Cynthia Rose and Josephine Griffin made up the cast.

"The Queen of Spades," with libretto by Modeste Tchaikovsky, music by Peter I. Tchaikovsky, and a new English translation by Sumner Austin, opened November 27, 1942. Emil Cooper conducted, Ivan Ivantzoff directed. The season closed December 2, with Verdi's "Macbeth." Jess Walters, Florence Kirk and Roberto Silva were in the leading roles.

Late in January, 1943, Felix Brentano produced and staged "The Maid-Mistress" by Pergolesi, with an English version by Marion Farquhar and a prologue by Brentano, and "There and Return" by Paul Hindesmith. Both operas were conducted by Isaac Van Grove and the choreography was by Joan Woodruff. Virginia MacWatters (recruited from "Rosalinda"), James Pease and Arnold Spector were principals in "The Maid-Mistress" and Jean Merrill, George Rasely, Edward Kent and Roneo Rim played the leading parts in "There and Return."

At the Provincetown Playhouse, New Plays, Inc., produced "Homecoming," by Edward Peyton Harris, November 16, 1942. Staged by Augustin Duncan and Mr. Harris, the cast included Georgia Simmons, Augustin and Andrea Duncan, Elena Karam, Marguerita Sargent, Thurman Jackson, Scott Cooley and Immanuel Duval.

The American Actors used the Provincetown Playhouse for the production of Horton Foote's "Only the Heart," December 5, with Hilda Vaughn, Jeanne Tufts, Freeman Hammond, Constance Dowling, Jacqueline Andre and Richard Hart. March 19 the same company played Ben K. Simkhovitch's "The Playboy of Newark," with Russell Collins, Dona Keath, Dwight Marfield, Ad Karns, William Hare, Jane Rose and Peggy Meredith, Sanford Meisner directing.

"The Last Generation," a melodrama by David Millman, was produced by Max Malin and Mr. Millman at the Malin Theatre, December 15, 1942. Staged by Sibyl Ward, with settings by Patricia Reynolds, the cast included Sibyl Ward, John Young, Gertrude Ross, Mae Cooper, Will Wilson and Robert Kibbee. At the same theatre January 4, 1943, Script Clinic presented the Stage Guild Players in "Night Watch in Syria," a Biblical drama in modern dress, written and directed by Alexander King, acted by Regina Moor, John Young, Irving Palmer, David Tyrrell, Jay Weidenfeld, Melvin Davis and Angela Michael.

"Love Is No Heaven," a play by Paul Burton-Mercur, was produced and directed by the author at the Malin March 15, 1943. Cast included Anita Carroll, Elena Jordan, Dick Corbin, Joseph Hoar, Doris Deane, Lew Talkov and Arthur King. The American-Irish Theatre presented "War Wife," by the Rev. Will W. Whalen, at the Malin, April 29, 1943.

Ruth Draper began an eleven-day engagement December 25, 1942, at the New York Times Hall. Her program included "A Children's Party in Philadelphia," "In a Church in Italy," "A Dalmatian Peasant in the Hall of a New York Hospital," "On the Porch in a Maine Coast Vilage" and "A Class in Greek Poise."

"Doodle Dandy of the U.S.A.," a fantasy about the Four Freedoms, written and directed by Saul Lancourt, was presented by Junior Programs, Inc., in association with Gilbert Josephson, at the Belasco Theatre, December 26, 1942. Elie Siegmaster wrote the music and the choreography was by Ted Shawn. Among the performers were Sam Steen, Alfred Allegro, Leo Kahn, Barbara

Gaye, Mary Whitis Bell, Jacques Radunski, Beman Lord, John Hurdle and George Hoxie.

Sonja Henie's "Hollywood Ice Revue" started a ten-day run at Madison Square Gardens, January 18, 1943. Choreography and staging were by Catherine Littlefield, settings by Bruno Maine and costumes by Billy Livingston. In the cast were Dorothy and Hazel Caley, Fritz Dietl, James Hawley, Geary Steffen, Freddy Trenkler, Peter Killiam, John Flanagan and others.

At the Concert Theatre, February 26, "God Strikes Back," a drama by Paul Nord, was produced by the author and directed by Betty Kashman. The leading role was played by Yveli Aliki, a Grecian actress, her first English-speaking part. Others were Dorman Leonard, Pan Theodor, Ralph Clanton, Ludwig Roth, David Kernan, Kathleen Roland, Ernest Roberts, Thaddeus Suski, Irving Palmer and Michael Everett.

The Davenport Free Theatre presented "The Bells" through the holidays and "A Woman's Way" in March. In April, the Century Theatre Club presented the Davenport Theatre Company in the court scene from "The Merchant of Venice," Chekhov's "A Swan Song" and the quarrel scene from "The Taming of the Shrew" at the Commodore Theatre, the cast including Butler Davenport, Mary Mater, Edwin Wilson, Kay Goodman, Robert Sosman, Anthony Worth and Alan Zola, great-nephew of Emil Zola.

At the Dramatic Workshop of the New School for Social Research, where "Winter Soldiers," chosen as one of this season's ten best plays, was produced, five one-act plays were presented under the supervision of Erwin Piscator as part of John Gassner's and Paolo Milano's "March of Time" program, Château Dyer directing. They included "A Meeting," with Jack Bittner, Bob Elliott, Christina Soulias, Eddie Grove and Herbert Berghof; "The Cause of It All," by Leo Tolstoi, with Mimi Margo, Julie Follansbee, Erwin Kalser, Bob Elliott, Alfred Linder and George Bloostein, and "A Marriage Proposal," a comedy by Anton Chekhov, played by Nathan Rudich, Mae Cooper, Erwin Kalser and Ivan Lumov. Justine Rothschild assisted with the direction. A lecture on George Bernard Shaw by John Gassner, May 14, 1943, was illustrated by two of Shaw's plays: "Village Wooing" and "The Man of Destiny." "Kings in Nomania," by Percival Wilde, the first production of the Children's Theatre of the Dramatic Workshop, was presented January 30.

Three groups of blind actors performed a series of plays under the direction of Jane Rose at the Lighthouse, May 25, 1943. The plays were "The Old Lady Shows Her Medals," "Sparkin' " and "The Happy Journey."

Foreign Language Plays

The Committee for the Preservation of Austrian Art and Culture in the United States of America sponsored a presentation in German by Gustave Kotanyi of Johann Strauss's operetta "The Gypsy Baron" at the Cosmopolitan Opera House, June 19, 1942. Herbert Graf directed the performance, Robert Stolz the music, Walter Taussig the chorus and Etelka Serli the ballet. In the cast were Mario Berini, Margit Bokor, Ralph Herbert, Karl Farkas, Theresa Gerson, Annie von Hartman, Christina Carroll, John Garris, Frederick Destal, Helene Arden and Victor Franz.

A Spanish operetta, "La Leyenda del Beso," by Antonio Pasos, Enrique Reoyo and Silvo Aramburu, music by Soutello and Vert, was presented at the Cosmopolitan Opera House, November 19, 1942, by Evaristo Corredor and Hernando Silva. Carlos Morelli, Maria Robles and Fausto Alvarez headed the cast.

At the Heckscher Theatre, May 21, 1943, the Theatre of the Russian Drama presented Maxim Gorky's "The Lower Depths" in celebration of the 75th anniversary of Gorky's birth. The cast included Natalie Warren, Vladimir Zelitsky, Mme. M. Astrova, Mme. G. Tsehbetkava, V. Shaoupensky, Mme. E. Baliev and others.

"Be Happy," a musical comedy in Yiddish by Sholem Secunda and William Siegel, opened the season at the 2nd Ave. Theatre October 10, 1942, co-starring Menasha Skulnik, Michael Michalesko and Miriam Kressyn. Abe Gross staged the comedy, Isidor Lillian the lyrics, Lillian Shapiro the dances and Michal Saltzman designed the settings. At the same theatre on February 13, 1943, "The Rich Uncle," a musical play by Louis Freiman and Isidor Friedman, music by Sholem Secunda, was presented and staged by Menasha Skulnik and Abe Gross.

STATISTICAL SUMMARY

(Last Season Plays Which Ended Runs After June 15, 1942)

	Number	
Plays	*Performances*	
Best Foot Forward	326	(Closed July 4, 1942)
Blithe Spirit	657	(Closed June 5, 1943)
By Jupiter	427	(Closed June 12, 1943)
Claudia	722	(Closed January 9, 1943)
Guest in the House	153	(Closed July 4, 1942)
Let's Face It	547	(Closed March 20, 1943)
My Sister Eileen	864	(Closed January 16, 1942)
Porgy and Bess	286	(Closed September 26, 1942)
Priorities of 1942	353	(Closed September 6, 1942)
Top Notchers	48	(Closed June 20, 1942)
Uncle Harry	430	(Closed May 29, 1943)

"Claudia" opened February 12, 1941, and ran until March 7, 1942, with 453 performances; then took a ten-week vacation, returning May 24, 1942, and playing until January 9, 1943, making a total run of 722 performances.

LONG RUNS ON BROADWAY

To June 15, 1943

(Plays marked with asterisk were still playing June 15, 1943)

Plays	Number Performances	Plays	Number Performances
Tobacco Road	3,182	The Green Pastures	640
Abie's Irish Rose	2,327	Is Zat So	618
*Life with Father	1,510	Separate Rooms	613
Hellzapoppin	1,404	Student Prince	608
Lightnin'	1,291	Broadway	603
Pins and Needles	1,108	Adonis	603
*Arsenic and Old Lace	1,017	Street Scene	601
The Bat	867	Kiki	600
My Sister Eileen	865	Blossom Time	592
White Cargo	864	Brother Rat	577
You Can't Take It with		Show Boat	572
You	837	The Show-Off	571
Three Men on a Horse	835	Sally	570
The Ladder	789	Rose Marie	557
The First Year	760	Strictly Dishonorable	557
The Man Who Came to		Good News	551
Dinner	739	Let's Face It	547
Claudia	722	Within the Law	541
Seventh Heaven	704	The Music Master	540
Peg o' My Heart	692	What a Life	538
The Children's Hour	691	The Boomerang	522
Dead End	687	Blackbirds	518
East Is West	680	Sunny	517
Chauve Souris	673	Victoria Regina	517
Irene	670	The Vagabond King	511
Boy Meets Girl	669	The New Moon	509
*Junior Miss	658	Shuffle Along	504
Blithe Spirit	657	Chauve-Souris	502
The Women	657	Personal Appearance	501
A Trip to Chinatown	657	Panama Hattie	501
*Sons o' Fun	653	Bird in Hand	500
Rain	648	Sailor, Beware!	500
*Angel Street	643	Room Service	500

DRAMA CRITICS' CIRCLE AWARD

Last season the New York Drama Critics' Circle had some little difficulty agreeing not to agree on any one play as being worthy the Circle's annual award, which goes to the best play written that season by an American and produced in New York. This season six plays were mentioned as being acceptable on the critics' first ballot. It required seven ballots to determine a majority choice in favor of Sidney Kingsley's "The Patriots" as opposed to Thornton Wilder's "The Skin of Our Teeth." Scattering votes were cast naming Maxwell Anderson's "The Eve of St. Mark," Florence Ryerson and Colin Clement's "Harriet," Irving Berlin's and the U. S. Army's "This Is the Army," and Oscar Hammerstein, 2d, and Richard Rodger's "Oklahoma." The Critics' citation named "The Patriots" "for its dignity of material, its thoughtful projection of a great American theme, its vigorous approach to the characters portrayed, and, in spite of certain limitations, its driving final effect on the stage." No choice was made of the best foreign play of the season. Drama Critics' Circle awards have been:

1935-36—Winterset, by Maxwell Anderson
1936-37—High Tor, by Maxwell Anderson
1937-38—Of Mice and Men, by John Steinbeck
1938-39—No decision. ("The Little Foxes" and "Abe Lincoln in Illinois" led voting.)
1939-40—The Time of Your Life, by William Saroyan
1940-41—Watch on the Rhine, by Lillian Hellman
1941-42—No award.
1942-43—The Patriots, by Sidney Kingsley

PULITZER PRIZE WINNERS

"For the original American play performed in New York which shall best represent the educational value and power of the stage in raising the standard of good morals, good taste and good manners."—The Will of Joseph Pulitzer, dated April 16, 1904.

In 1929 the advisory board, which, according to the terms of the will, "shall have the power in its discretion to suspend or to change any subject or subjects . . . if in the judgment of the board such suspension, changes or substitutions shall be conducive to the public good," decided to eliminate from the above paragraph relating to the prize-winning play the words "in raising the standard of good morals, good taste and good manners."

The Pulitzer Committee, which had also failed to select a prize-winning play for the season of 1941-42, settled this season on Thornton Wilder's controversial "The Skin of Our Teeth" by what was reported to be a unanimous vote. Pulitzer awards have been:

1917-18—Why Marry? by Jesse Lynch Williams
1918-19—None
1919-20—Beyond the Horizon, by Eugene O'Neill
1920-21—Miss Lulu Bett, by Zona Gale
1921-22—Anna Christie, by Eugene O'Neill
1922-23—Icebound, by Owen Davis
1923-24—Hell-bent fer Heaven, by Hatcher Hughes
1924-25—They Knew What They Wanted, by Sidney Howard
1925-26—Craig's Wife, by George Kelly
1926-27—In Abraham's Bosom, by Paul Green
1927-28—Strange Interlude, by Eugene O'Neill
1928-29—Street Scene, by Elmer Rice
1929-30—The Green Pastures, by Marc Connelly
1930-31—Alison's House, by Susan Glaspell
1931-32—Of Thee I Sing, by George S. Kaufman, Morrie Ryskind, Ira and George Gershwin
1932-33—Both Your Houses, by Maxwell Anderson
1933-34—Men in White, by Sidney Kingsley
1934-35—The Old Maid, by Zoe Akins
1935-36—Idiot's Delight, by Robert E. Sherwood

1936-37—You Can't Take It with You, by Moss Hart and George S. Kaufman
1937-38—Our Town, by Thornton Wilder
1938-39—Abe Lincoln in Illinois, by Robert E. Sherwood
1939-40—The Time of Your Life, by William Saroyan
1940-41—There Shall Be No Night, by Robert E. Sherwood
1941-42—No award.
1942-43—The Skin of Our Teeth, by Thornton Wilder

THE BEST PLAYS OF 1942-43   495

PREVIOUS VOLUMES OF BEST PLAYS

Plays chosen to represent the theatre seasons from 1899 to 1942 (1899-1909 issue to be published in January) are as follows:

1899-1909

"Barbara Frietchie," by Clyde Fitch. Published by Life Publishing Company, New York.

"The Climbers," by Clyde Fitch. Published by the Macmillan Co., New York.

"If I Were King," by Justin Huntly McCarthy. Published by Samuel French, New York and London.

"The Darling of the Gods," by David Belasco. Published by Little, Brown & Co., Boston, Mass.

"The County Chairman," by George Ade. Published by Samuel French, New York and London.

"Leah Kleschna," by C. M. S. McLellan. Published by Samuel French, New York.

"The Squaw Man," by Edwin Milton Royle.

"The Great Divide," by William Vaughn Moody. Published by Samuel French, New York, London and Canada.

"The Witching Hour," by Augustus Thomas. Published by Samuel French, New York and London.

"The Man from Home," by Booth Tarkington and Harry Leon Wilson. Published by Samuel French, New York, London and Canada.

1909-1919

"The Easiest Way," by Eugene Walter. Published by G. W. Dillingham, New York; Houghton Mifflin Co., Boston.

"Mrs. Bumpstead-Leigh," by Harry James Smith. Published by Samuel French, New York.

"Disraeli," by Louis N. Parker. Published by Dodd, Mead and Co., New York.

"Romance," by Edward Sheldon. Published by the Macmillan Co., New York.

"Seven Keys to Baldpate," by George M. Cohan. Published by Bobbs-Merrill Co., Indianapolis, as a novel by Earl Derr Biggers; as a play by Samuel French, New York.

"On Trial," by Elmer Reizenstein. Published by Samuel French, New York.

"The Unchastened Woman," by Louis Kaufman Anspacher. Published by Harcourt, Brace and Howe, Inc., New York.

"Good Gracious Annabelle," by Clare Kummer. Published by Samuel French, New York.

"Why Marry?" by Jesse Lynch Williams. Published by Charles Scribner's Sons, New York.

"John Ferguson," by St. John Ervine. Published by the Macmillan Co., New York.

1919-1920

"Abraham Lincoln," by John Drinkwater. Published by Houghton Mifflin Co., Boston.

"Clarence," by Booth Tarkington. Published by Samuel French, New York.

"Beyond the Horizon," by Eugene G. O'Neill. Published by Boni & Liveright, Inc., New York.

"Déclassée," by Zoe Akins. Published by Liveright, Inc., New York.

"The Famous Mrs. Fair," by James Forbes. Published by Samuel French, New York.

"The Jest," by Sem Benelli. (American adaptation by Edward Sheldon.)

"Jane Clegg," by St. John Ervine. Published by Henry Holt & Co., New York.

"Mamma's Affair," by Rachel Barton Butler. Published by Samuel French, New York.

"Wedding Bells," by Salisbury Field. Published by Samuel French, New York.

"Adam and Eva," by George Middleton and Guy Bolton. Published by Samuel French, New York.

1920-1921

"Deburau," adapted from the French of Sacha Guitry by H. Granville Barker. Published by G. P. Putnam's Sons, New York.

"The First Year," by Frank Craven. Published by Samuel French, New York.

"Enter Madame," by Gilda Varesi and Dolly Byrne. Published by G. P. Putnam's Sons, New York.

"The Green Goddess," by William Archer. Published by Alfred A. Knopf, New York.

"Liliom," by Ferenc Molnar. Published by Boni & Liveright, New York.

"Mary Rose," by James M. Barrie. Published by Charles Scribner's Sons, New York.

"Nice People," by Rachel Crothers. Published by Charles Scribner's Sons, New York.

"The Bad Man," by Porter Emerson Browne. Published by G. P. Putnam's Sons, New York.

"The Emperor Jones," by Eugene G. O'Neill. Published by Boni & Liveright, New York.

"The Skin Game," by John Galsworthy. Published by Charles Scribner's Sons, New York.

1921-1922

"Anna Christie," by Eugene G. O'Neill. Published by Boni & Liveright, New York.

"A Bill of Divorcement," by Clemence Dane. Published by the Macmillan Company, New York.

"Dulcy," by George S. Kaufman and Marc Connelly. Published by G. P. Putnam's Sons, New York.

"He Who Gets Slapped," adapted from the Russian of Leonid Andreyev by Gregory Zilboorg. Published by Brentano's, New York.

"Six Cylinder Love," by William Anthony McGuire.

"The Hero," by Gilbert Emery.

"The Dover Road," by Alan Aelxander Milne. Published by Samuel French, New York.

"Ambush," by Arthur Richman.

"The Circle," by William Somerset Maugham.

"The Nest," by Paul Geraldy and Grace George.

1922-1923

"Rain," by John Colton and Clemence Randolph. Published by Liveright, Inc., New York.

"Loyalties," by John Galsworthy. Published by Charles Scribner's Sons, New York.

"Icebound," by Owen Davis. Published by Little, Brown & Company, Boston.

"You and I," by Philip Barry. Published by Brentano's, New York.

"The Fool," by Channing Pollock. Published by Brentano's, New York.

"Merton of the Movies," by George Kaufman and Marc Connelly, based on the novel of the same name by Harry Leon Wilson.

"Why Not?" by Jesse Lynch Williams. Published by Walter H. Baker Co., Boston.

"The Old Soak," by Don Marquis. Published by Doubleday, Page & Company, New York.

"R.U.R.," by Karel Capek. Translated by Paul Selver. Published by Doubleday, Page & Company.

"Mary the 3d," by Rachel Crothers. Published by Brentano's, New York.

1923-1924

"The Swan," translated from the Hungarian of Ferenc Molnar by Melville Baker. Published by Boni & Liveright, New York.

"Outward Bound," by Sutton Vane. Published by Boni & Liveright, New York.

"The Show-Off," by George Kelly. Published by Little, Brown & Company, Boston.

"The Changelings," by Lee Wilson Dodd. Published by E. P. Dutton & Company, New York.

"Chicken Feed," by Guy Bolton. Published by Samuel French, New York and London.

"Sun-Up," by Lula Vollmer. Published by Brentano's, New York.

"Beggar on Horseback," by George Kaufman and Marc Connelly. Published by Boni & Liveright, New York.

"Tarnish," by Gilbert Emery. Published by Brentano's, New York.

"The Goose Hangs High," by Lewis Beach. Published by Little, Brown & Company, Boston.

"Hell-bent fer Heaven," by Hatcher Hughes. Published by Harper Bros., New York.

1924-1925

"What Price Glory?" by Laurence Stallings and Maxwell Anderson. Published by Harcourt, Brace & Co., New York.

"They Knew What They Wanted," by Sidney Howard. Published by Doubleday, Page & Company, New York.

"Desire Under the Elms," by Eugene G. O'Neill. Published by Boni & Liveright, New York.

"The Firebrand," by Edwin Justus Mayer. Published by Boni & Liveright, New York.

"Dancing Mothers," by Edgar Selwyn and Edmund Goulding.

"Mrs. Partridge Presents," by Mary Kennedy and Ruth Warren. Published by Samuel French, New York.

"The Fall Guy," by James Gleason and George Abbott. Published by Samuel French, New York.

"The Youngest," by Philip Barry. Published by Samuel French, New York.

"Minick," by Edna Ferber and George S. Kaufman. Published by Doubleday, Page & Company, New York.

"Wild Birds," by Dan Totheroh. Published by Doubleday, Page & Company, New York.

1925-1926

"Craig's Wife," by George Kelly. Published by Little, Brown & Company, Boston.

"The Great God Brown," by Eugene G. O'Neill. Published by Boni & Liveright, New York.

"The Green Hat," by Michael Arlen.

"The Dybbuk," by S. Ansky, Henry G. Alsberg-Winifred Katzin translation. Published by Boni & Liveright, New York.

"The Enemy," by Channing Pollock. Published by Brentano's, New York.

"The Last of Mrs. Cheyney," by Frederick Lonsdale. Published by Samuel French, New York.

"Bride of the Lamb," by William Hurlbut. Published by Boni & Liveright, New York.

"The Wisdom Tooth," by Marc Connelly. Published by George H. Doran & Company, New York.

"The Butter and Egg Man," by George Kaufman. Published by Boni & Liveright, New York.

"Young Woodley," by John Van Druten. Published by Simon and Schuster, New York.

1926-1927

"Broadway," by Philip Dunning and George Abbott. Published by George H. Doran Company, New York.

"Saturday's Children," by Maxwell Anderson. Published by Longmans, Green & Company, New York.

"Chicago," by Maurine Watkins. Published by Alfred A. Knopf, Inc., New York.

"The Constant Wife," by William Somerset Maugham. Published by George H. Doran Company, New York.

"The Play's the Thing," by Ferenc Molnar and P. G. Wodehouse. Published by Brentano's, New York.

"The Road to Rome," by Robert Emmet Sherwood. Published by Charles Scribner's Sons, New York.

"The Silver Cord," by Sidney Howard. Published by Charles Scribner's Sons, New York.

"The Cradle Song," translated from the Spanish of G. Martinez Sierra by John Garrett Underhill. Published by E. P. Dutton & Company, New York.

"Daisy Mayme," by George Kelly. Published by Little, Brown & Company, Boston.

"In Abraham's Bosom," by Paul Green. Published by Robert M. McBride & Company, New York.

1927-1928

"Strange Interlude," by Eugene G. O'Neill. Published by Boni & Liveright, New York.

"The Royal Family," by Edna Ferber and George Kaufman. Published by Doubleday, Doran & Company, New York.

"Burlesque," by George Manker Watters. Published by Doubleday, Doran & Company, New York.

"Coquette," by George Abbott and Ann Bridgers. Published by Longmans, Green & Company, New York, London, Toronto.

"Behold the Bridegroom," by George Kelly. Published by Little, Brown & Company, Boston.

"Porgy," by DuBose Heyward. Published by Doubleday, Doran & Company, New York.

"Paris Bound," by Philip Barry. Published by Samuel French, New York.

"Escape," by John Galsworthy. Published by Charles Scribner's Sons, New York.

"The Racket," by Bartlett Cormack. Published by Samuel French, New York.

"The Plough and the Stars," by Sean O'Casey. Published by the Macmillan Company, New York.

1928-1929

"Street Scene," by Elmer Rice. Published by Samuel French, New York.

"Journey's End," by R. C. Sherriff. Published by Brentano's, New York.

"Wings Over Europe," by Robert Nichols and Maurice Browne. Published by Covici-Friede, New York.

"Holiday," by Philip Barry. Published by Samuel French, New York.

"The Front Page," by Ben Hecht and Charles MacArthur. Published by Covici-Friede, New York.

"Let Us Be Gay," by Rachel Crothers. Published by Samuel French, New York.

"Machinal," by Sophie Treadwell.

"Little Accident," by Floyd Dell and Thomas Mitchell.

"Gypsy," by Maxwell Anderson.

"The Kingdom of God," by G. Martinez Sierra; English version by Helen and Harley Granville-Barker. Published by E. P. Dutton & Company, New York.

1929-1930

"The Green Pastures," by Marc Connelly (adapted from "Ol' Man Adam and His Chillun," by Roark Bradford). Published by Farrar & Rinehart, Inc., New York.

"The Criminal Code," by Martin Flavin. Published by Horace Liveright, New York.

"Berkeley Square," by John Balderston. Published by the Macmillan Company, New York.

"Strictly Dishonorable," by Preston Sturges. Published by Horace Liveright, New York.

"The First Mrs. Fraser," by St. John Ervine. Published by the Macmillan Company, New York.

"The Last Mile," by John Wexley. Published by Samuel French, New York.

"June Moon," by Ring W. Lardner and George S. Kaufman. Published by Charles Scribner's Sons, New York.

"Michael and Mary," by A. A. Milne. Published by Chatto & Windus, London.

"Death Takes a Holiday," by Walter Ferris (adapted from the Italian of Alberto Casella). Published by Samuel French, New York.

"Rebound," by Donald Ogden Stewart. Published by Samuel French, New York.

1930-1931

"Elizabeth the Queen," by Maxwell Anderson. Published by Longmans, Green & Co., New York.

"Tomorrow and Tomorrow," by Philip Barry. Published by Samuel French, New York.

"Once in a Lifetime," by George S. Kaufman and Moss Hart. Published by Farrar and Rinehart, New York.

"Green Grow the Lilacs," by Lynn Riggs. Published by Samuel French, New York and London.

"As Husbands Go," by Rachel Crothers. Published by Samuel French, New York.

"Alison's House," by Susan Glaspell. Published by Samuel French, New York.

"Five-Star Final," by Louis Weitzenkorn. Published by Samuel French, New York.

"Overture," by William Bolitho. Published by Simon & Schuster, New York.

"The Barretts of Wimpole Street," by Rudolf Besier. Published by Little, Brown & Company, Boston.

"Grand Hotel," adapted from the German of Vicki Baum by W. A. Drake.

1931-1932

"Of Thee I Sing," by George S. Kaufman and Morrie Ryskind; music and lyrics by George and Ira Gershwin. Published by Alfred Knopf, New York.

"Mourning Becomes Electra," by Eugene G. O'Neill. Published by Horace Liveright, Inc., New York.

"Reunion in Vienna," by Robert Emmet Sherwood. Published by Charles Scribner's Sons, New York.

"The House of Connelly," by Paul Green. Published by Samuel French, New York.

"The Animal Kingdom," by Philip Barry. Published by Samuel French, New York.

"The Left Bank," by Elmer Rice. Published by Samuel French, New York.

"Another Language," by Rose Franken. Published by Samuel French, New York.

"Brief Moment," by S. N. Behrman. Published by Farrar & Rinehart, New York.

"The Devil Passes," by Benn W. Levy. Published by Martin Secker, London.

"Cynara," by H. M. Harwood and R. F. Gore-Browne. Published by Samuel French, New York.

1932-1933

"Both Your Houses," by Maxwell Anderson. Published by Samuel French, New York.

"Dinner at Eight," by George S. Kaufman and Edna Ferber. Published by Doubleday, Doran & Co., Inc., Garden City, New York.

"When Ladies Meet," by Rachel Crothers. Published by Samuel French, New York.

"Design for Living," by Noel Coward. Published by Doubleday, Doran & Co., Inc., Garden City, New York.

"Biography," by S. N. Behrman. Published by Farrar & Rinehart, Inc., New York.

"Alien Corn," by Sidney Howard. Published by Charles Scribner's Sons, New York.

"The Late Christopher Bean," adapted from the French of René Fauchois by Sidney Howard. Published by Samuel French, New York.

"We, the People," by Elmer Rice. Published by Coward-McCann, Inc., New York.

"Pigeons and People," by George M. Cohan.

"One Sunday Afternoon," by James Hagan. Published by Samuel French, New York.

1933-1934

"Mary of Scotland," by Maxwell Anderson. Published by Doubleday, Doran & Co., Inc., Garden City, N. Y.

"Men in White," by Sidney Kingsley. Published by Covici, Friede, Inc., New York.

"Dodsworth," by Sinclair Lewis and Sidney Howard. Published by Harcourt, Brace & Co., New York.

"Ah, Wilderness," by Eugene O'Neill. Published by Random House, New York.

"They Shall Not Die," by John Wexley. Published by Alfred A. Knopf, New York.

"Her Master's Voice," by Clare Kummer. Published by Samuel French, New York.

"No More Ladies," by A. E. Thomas.

"Wednesday's Child," by Leopold Atlas. Published by Samuel French, New York.

"The Shining Hour," by Keith Winter. Published by Doubleday, Doran & Co., Inc., Garden City, New York.

"The Green Bay Tree," by Mordaunt Shairp. Published by
Baker International Play Bureau, Boston, Mass.

1934-1935

"The Children's Hour," by Lillian Hellman. Published by
Alfred Knopf, New York.

"Valley Forge," by Maxwell Anderson. Published by Anderson
House, Washington, D. C. Distributed by Dodd, Mead & Co.,
New York.

"The Petrified Forest," by Robert Sherwood. Published by
Charles Scribner's Sons, New York.

"The Old Maid," by Zoe Akins. Published by D. Appleton-
Century Co., New York.

"Accent on Youth," by Samson Raphaelson. Published by
Samuel French, New York.

"Merrily We Roll Along," by George S. Kaufman and Moss
Hart. Published by Random House, New York.

"Awake and Sing," by Clifford Odets. Published by Random
House, New York.

"The Farmer Takes a Wife," by Frank B. Elser and Marc
Connelly.

"Lost Horizons," by John Hayden.

"The Distaff Side," by John Van Druten. Published by Alfred
Knopf, New York.

1935-1936

"Winterset," by Maxwell Anderson. Published by Anderson
House, Washington, D. C.

"Idiot's Delight," by Robert Emmet Sherwood. Published by
Charles Scribner's Sons, New York.

"End of Summer," by S. N. Behrman. Published by Random
House, New York.

"First Lady," by Katharine Dayton and George S. Kaufman.
Published by Random House, New York.

"Victoria Regina," by Laurence Housman. Published by
Samuel French, Inc., New York and London.

"Boy Meets Girl," by Bella and Samuel Spewack. Published
by Random House, New York.

"Dead End," by Sidney Kingsley. Published by Random
House, New York.

"Call It a Day," by Dodie Smith. Published by Samuel French, Inc., New York and London.

"Ethan Frome," by Owen Davis and Donald Davis. Published by Charles Scribner's Sons, New York.

"Pride and Prejudice," by Helen Jerome. Published by Doubleday, Doran & Co., Garden City, New York.

1936-1937

"High Tor," by Maxwell Anderson. Published by Anderson House, Washington, D. C.

"You Can't Take It with You," by Moss Hart and George S. Kaufman. Published by Farrar & Rinehart, Inc., New York.

"Johnny Johnson," by Paul Green. Published by Samuel French, Inc., New York.

"Daughters of Atreus," by Robert Turney. Published by Alfred A. Knopf, New York.

"Stage Door," by Edna Ferber and George S. Kaufman. Published by Doubleday, Doran & Co., Garden City, New York.

"The Women," by Clare Boothe. Published by Random House, Inc., New York.

"St. Helena," by R. C. Sherriff and Jeanne de Casalis. Published by Samuel French, Inc., New York and London.

"Yes, My Darling Daughter," by Mark Reed. Published by Samuel French, Inc., New York.

"Excursion," by Victor Wolfson. Published by Random House, New York.

"Tovarich," by Jacques Deval and Robert E. Sherwood. Published by Random House, New York.

1937-1938

"Of Mice and Men," by John Steinbeck. Published by Covici-Friede, New York.

"Our Town," by Thornton Wilder. Published by Coward-McCann, Inc., New York.

"Shadow and Substance," by Paul Vincent Carroll. Published by Random House, Inc., New York.

"On Borrowed Time," by Paul Osborn. Published by Alfred A. Knopf, New York.

"The Star-Wagon," by Maxwell Anderson. Published by Anderson House, Washington, D. C. Distributed by Dodd, Mead & Co., New York.

"Susan and God," by Rachel Crothers. Published by Random House, Inc., New York.

"Prologue to Glory," by E. P. Conkle. Published by Random House, Inc., New York.

"Amphitryon 38," by S. N. Behrman. Published by Random House, Inc., New York.

"Golden Boy," by Clifford Odets. Published by Random House, Inc., New York.

"What a Life," by Clifford Goldsmith. Published by Dramatists' Play Service, Inc., New York.

1938-1939

"Abe Lincoln in Illinois," by Robert E. Sherwood. Published by Charles Scribner's Sons, New York and Charles Scribner's Sons, Ltd., London.

"The Little Foxes," by Lillian Hellman. Published by Random House, Inc., New York.

"Rocket to the Moon," by Clifford Odets. Published by Random House, Inc., New York.

"The American Way," by George S. Kaufman and Moss Hart. Published by Random House, Inc., New York.

"No Time for Comedy," by S. N. Behrman. Published by Random House, Inc., New York.

"The Philadelphia Story," by Philip Barry. Published by Coward-McCann, Inc., New York.

"The White Steed," by Paul Vincent Carroll. Published by Random House, Inc., New York.

"Here Come the Clowns," by Philip Barry. Published by Coward-McCann, Inc., New York.

"Family Portrait," by Lenore Coffee and William Joyce Cowen. Published by Random House, Inc., New York.

"Kiss the Boys Good-bye," by Clare Boothe. Published by Random House, Inc., New York.

1939-1940

"There Shall Be No Night," by Robert E. Sherwood. Published by Charles Scribner's Sons, New York.

"Key Largo," by Maxwell Anderson. Published by Anderson House, Washington, D. C.

"The World We Make," by Sidney Kingsley.

"Life with Father," by Howard Lindsay and Russel Crouse. Published by Alfred A. Knopf, New York.

"The Man Who Came to Dinner," by George S. Kaufman and Moss Hart. Published by Random House, Inc., New York.

"The Male Animal," by James Thurber and Elliott Nugent. Published by Random House, Inc., New York, and MacMillan Co., Canada.

"The Time of Your Life," by William Saroyan. Published by Harcourt, Brace and Company, Inc., New York.

"Skylark," by Samson Raphaelson. Published by Random House, Inc., New York.

"Margin for Error," by Clare Boothe. Published by Random House, Inc., New York.

"Morning's at Seven," by Paul Osborn. Published by Samuel French, New York.

1940-1941

"Native Son," by Paul Green and Richard Wright. Published by Harper & Bros., New York.

"Watch on the Rhine," by Lillian Hellman. Published by Random House, Inc., New York.

"The Corn Is Green," by Emlyn Williams. Published by Random House, Inc., New York.

"Lady in the Dark," by Moss Hart. Published by Random House, Inc., New York.

"Arsenic and Old Lace," by Joseph Kesselring. Published by Random House, Inc., New York.

"My Sister Eileen," by Joseph Fields and Jerome Chodorov. Published by Random House, Inc., New York.

"Flight to the West," by Elmer Rice. Published by Coward, McCann, Inc., New York.

"Claudia," by Rose Franken Maloney. Published by Farrar & Rinehart, Inc., New York and Toronto.

"Mr. and Mrs. North," by Owen Davis. Published by Samuel French, New York.

"George Washington Slept Here," by George S. Kaufman and Moss Hart. Published by Random House, Inc., New York.

1941-1942

"In Time to Come," by Howard Koch. Published by Dramatists' Play Service, Inc., New York.

"The Moon Is Down," by John Steinbeck. Published by The Viking Press, New York.

"Blithe Spirit," by Noel Coward. Published by Doubleday, Doran & Co., Garden City, New York.

"Junior Miss," by Jerome Chodorov and Joseph Fields. Published by Random House, Inc., New York.

"Candle in the Wind," by Maxwell Anderson. Published by Anderson House, Washington, D. C.

"Letters to Lucerne," by Fritz Rotter and Allen Vincent. Published by Samuel French, Inc., New York.

"Jason," by Samson Raphaelson. Published by Random House, Inc., New York.

"Angel Street," by Patrick Hamilton. Published by Constable & Co., Ltd., London, under the title "Gaslight."

"Uncle Harry," by Thomas Job. Published by Samuel French, Inc., New York.

"Hope for a Harvest," by Sophie Treadwell. Published by Samuel French, Inc., New York.

WHERE AND WHEN THEY WERE BORN

(Compiled from the most authentic records available.)

Abba, Marta	Milan, Italy	1907
Abbott, George	Hamburg, N. Y.	1895
Abel, Walter	St. Paul, Minn.	1898
Adams, Maude	Salt Lake City, Utah	1872
Addy, Wesley	Omaha, Neb.	1912
Adler, Luther	New York City	1903
Adler, Stella	New York City	1904
Aherne, Brian	King's Norton, England	1902
Akins, Zoe	Humansville, Mo.	1886
Allgood, Sara	Dublin, Ireland	1883
Ames, Florenz	Rochester, N. Y.	1884
Anders, Glenn	Los Angeles, Cal.	1890
Anderson, Gwen	Holland, Ia.	1921
Anderson, Judith	Australia	1898
Anderson, Mary	Trussville, Ala.	1917
Anderson, Maxwell	Atlantic City, Pa.	1888
Andrews, A. G.	Buffalo, N. Y.	1861
Andrews, Ann	Los Angeles, Cal.	1895
Angel, Heather	Oxford, England	1909
Anglin, Margaret	Ottawa, Canada	1876
Anson, A. E.	London, England	1879
Arden, Eve	San Francisco, Cal.	1912
Arling, Joyce	Memphis, Tenn.	1911
Arliss, George	London, England	1868
Ashcroft, Peggy	Croydon, England	1907
Astaire, Fred	Omaha, Neb.	1899
Atwater, Edith	Chicago, Ill.	1912
Atwell, Roy	Syracuse, N. Y.	1880
Atwill, Lionel	London, England	1885
Bainter, Fay	Los Angeles, Cal.	1892
Baker, Lee	Michigan	1880
Bankhead, Tallulah	Huntsville, Ala.	1902
Banks, Leslie J.	West Derby, England	1890
Barbee, Richard	Lafayette, Ind.	1887
Barrett, Edith	Roxbury, Mass.	1904

Carlisle, Kitty ....New Orleans, La. 1912
Carminati, Tullio ....Zara, Dalmatia 1894
Carnovsky, Morris ....St. Louis, Mo. 1898
Carpenter, Edward Childs .....Philadelphia, Pa. 1871
Carroll, Earl ....Pittsburgh, Pa. 1892
Carroll, Leo G. ....Weedon, England 1892
Carroll, Nancy ....New York City 1906
Catlett, Walter ....San Francisco, Cal. 1889
Caulfield, Joan ....New York City 1924
Chandler, Helen ....Charleston, N. C. 1906
Chaplin, Charles Spencer .....London 1889
Chase, Ilka ....New York 1900
Chatterton, Ruth ....New York 1893
Christians, Mady ....Vienna, Austria 1907
Churchill, Berton ....Toronto, Can. 1876
Claire, Helen ....Union Springs, Ala. 1908
Claire, Ina ....Washington, D. C. 1892
Clark, Bobby ....Springfield, Ohio 1888
Clive, Colin ....St. Malo, France 1900
Coburn, Charles ....Macon, Ga. 1877
Cohan, George M. ....Providence, R. I. 1878
Cohan, Georgette ....Los Angeles, Cal. 1900
Colbert, Claudette ....Paris.................1905
Collier, Constance ....Windsor, England 1882
Collier, William ....New York 1866
Collinge, Patricia ....Dublin, Ireland 1894
Collins, Russell ....New Orleans, La. 1901
Colt, Ethel Barrymore ....Mamaroneck, N. Y. 1911
Colt, John Drew ....New York 1914
Conklin, Peggy ....Dobbs Ferry, N. Y. 1912
Conroy, Frank ....London, England 1885
Conte, Nicholas ....Jersey City, N. J. 1916
Cook, Donald ....Portland, Ore. 1902
Cook, Joe ....Evansville, Ind. 1890
Cooper, Gladys ....Lewisham, England 1888
Cooper, Violet Kemble ....London, England 1890
Corbett, Leonora ....London, England 1908
Cornell, Katharine ....Berlin, Germany 1898
Corthell, Herbert ....Boston, Mass. 1875
Cossart, Ernest ....Cheltenham, England 1876
Coulouris, George ....Manchester, England 1906
Courtleigh, Stephen ....New York City 1912
Coward, Noel ....Teddington, England 1899

Cowl, Jane .... Boston, Mass. 1887
Craig, Helen .... Mexico City 1914
Craven, Frank .... Boston, Mass. 1880
Crews, Laura Hope .... San Francisco, Cal. 1880
Cronyn, Hume .... Canada 1912
Crosman, Henrietta .... Wheeling, W. Va. 1865
Crothers, Rachel .... Bloomington, Ill. 1878
Cummings, Constance .... Seattle, Wash. 1911

Dale, Margaret .... Philadelphia, Pa. 1880
Davis, Donald .... New York 1907
Davis, Owen .... Portland, Me. 1874
Davis, Owen, Jr. .... New York 1910
De Cordoba, Pedro .... New York 1881
Digges, Dudley .... Dublin, Ireland 1880
Dinehart, Allan .... Missoula, Mont. 1889
Dixon, Jean .... Waterbury, Conn. 1905
Dowling, Eddie .... Woonsocket, R. I. 1895
Drake, Alfred .... New York City 1914
Dressler, Eric .... Brooklyn, N. Y. 1900
Dressler, Marie .... Cobourg, Canada 1869
Dudley, Doris .... New York City 1918
Duncan, Augustin .... San Francisco 1873
Duncan, Todd .... Danville, Ky. 1900
Dunn, Emma .... England 1875
Dunning, Philip .... Meriden, Conn. 1890
Dupree, Minnie .... San Francisco, Cal. 1875
Durante, Jimmy .... New York City 1893

Edney, Florence .... London, England 1879
Eldridge, Florence .... Brooklyn, N. Y. 1901
Ellerbe, Harry .... Georgia 1905
Emery, Gilbert .... Naples, New York 1875
Emery, Katherine .... Birmingham, Ala. 1908
Erickson, Leif .... California 1917
Errol, Leon .... Sydney, Australia 1881
Ervine, St. John Greer .... Belfast, Ireland 1883
Evans, Edith .... London, England 1888
Evans, Madge .... New York City 1909
Evans, Maurice .... Dorchester, England 1901

Farley, Morgan .... Mamaroneck, N. Y. 1901
Farmer, Frances .... Seattle, Wash. 1914

Haines, Robert T. ....Muncie, Ind. 1870
Hall, Bettina ....North Easton, Mass. 1906
Hall, Natalie ....North Easton, Mass. 1904
Hall, Thurston ....Boston, Mass. 1882
Halliday, John ....Brooklyn, N. Y. 1880
Halliday, Robert ....Loch Lomond, Scotland ...1893
Hampden, Walter ....Brooklyn, N. Y. 1879
Hannen, Nicholas ....London, England 1881
Hardie, Russell ....Griffin Mills, N. Y. 1906
Hardwicke, Sir Cedric ....Lye, Stourbridge, England.1893
Hargrave, Roy ....New York City 1908
Harrigan, William ....New York 1893
Harris, Sam H. ....New York 1872
Haydon, Julie ....Oak Park, Ill. 1910
Hayes, Helen ....Washington, D. C. 1900
Hector, Louis ....England 1882
Heflin, Van ....Walters, Okla. 1909
Heineman, Eda ....Japan 1891
Heming, Violet ....Leeds, England 1893
Henie, Sonja ....Oslo, Norway 1912
Hepburn, Katharine ....Hartford, Conn. 1907
Hernreid, Paul ....Trieste, Italy 1905
Hobart, Rose ....New York 1906
Hoey, Dennis ....London, England 1893
Holm, Celeste ....New York City 1916
Hopkins, Arthur ....Cleveland, Ohio 1878
Hopkins, Miriam ....Bainbridge, Ga. 1904
Holmes, Taylor ....Newark, N. J. 1872
Homeier, Skippy ....Chicago, Ill. 1930
Howard, Leslie ....London, England 1890
Huber, Paul ....Wilkes-Barre, Pa. 1895
Hull, Henry ....Louisville, Ky. 1893
Humphreys, Cecil ....Cheltenham, England 1880
Hunter, Glenn ....Highland Mills, N. Y. 1896
Huston, Walter ....Toronto 1884
Hutchinson, Josephine ....Seattle, Wash. 1898

Inescort, Frieda ....Hitchin, Scotland 1905
Ingram, Rex ....Dublin, Ireland 1892

Jagger, Dean ....Columbus Grove, Ohio 1904
Jameson, House ....Austin, Texas 1902

NECROLOGY

June 15, 1942—June 13, 1943

Besier, Rudolf, dramatist, 63. First play "The Virgin Goddess" (1906); others "Kips" (with H. G. Wells), "Robin's Father" (with Hugh Walpole), "The Ninth Earl" (with May Edginton), and "The Barretts of Wimpole Street," which Katharine Cornell played for more than 700 performances. Born Java; died London, June 15, 1942.

Charters, Spencer, actor, 68. On stage 36 years; appeared in 475 plays; remembered in "The Tavern" ("What's all the shootin' for?"), "The Bells," "Enoch Arden," "Dr. Jekyll and Mr. Hyde" and "Whoopee." Died Hollywood, January 25, 1943.

Cohan, George M., actor, author, composer, producer, 64. First appeared at Haverstraw, R. I., in "Daniel Boone" (1888); wrote "The Governor's Son," "Little Johnny Jones," "Get Rich Quick Wallingford," "Forty-five Minutes from Broadway," "The Song and Dance Man," etc.; dramatized "Seven Keys to Baldpate," "The Miracle Man," etc.; played notably in "Ah, Wilderness" and "I'd Rather Be Right"; with Sam Harris produced fifty plays; they were lessees of New Gaiety and George M. Cohan Theatres, New York, and Four Cohans' Theatre, Chicago; gained additional fame for war song, "Over There." Born Providence, R. I.; died New York City, November 5, 1942.

Crews, Laura Hope, actress, 62. On stage 58 years; professional debut at four in "Bootle's Baby"; child actress in "Editha's Burglar"; remembered in "Mr. Pim Passes By," "The Silver Cord," "Her Master's Voice," etc.; notable films, "The Man Who Came to Dinner" and "Gone with the Wind." Born San Francisco, Calif.; died New York City, November 13, 1942.

Cruze, James (Bosen), actor, director, 58. Outstanding in silent screen era; directed "Merton of the Movies," "Ruggles of Red Gap," "The Covered Wagon," etc. Born Ogden, Utah; died Hollywood, Calif., August 4, 1942.

Dalton, Charles, actor, 77. First appearance in British Provinces in 1883; last appearance in Maurice Evans' revival of "King

Richard II" New York (1940); first appearance in New York in "The Prodigal Daughter" (1893); supported Helen Hayes in "Mary of Scotland," Katharine Cornell in repertory and Ethel Barrymore in "Mid-Channel." Born England; died Riverbank Road, Conn., June 11, 1942.

Denniston, Reynolds, actor, 62. Served in Boer War; made stage debut in Johannesburg in "Charley's Aunt"; played subsequently in Australia, New Zealand, Hawaii, China, Japan and Malay States; first appeared in New York in "Whispering Wires" (1923). Born Dunedin, New Zealand; died New York City, January 29, 1943.

Dixey, Henry E., actor, 84. Sixty-three years on American stage; first appearance at Howard Atheneum Theatre, Boston, in "Under the Gaslight"; last appearance in "Napi" in Brooklyn (1931); popular star in extensive repertoire including "Adonis," "H.M.S. Pinafore," "Becky Sharpe," etc.; last appearance on Broadway in The Players' revival of "The Beaux Stratagem" (1929). Born Boston, Mass.; died Atlantic City, New Jersey, February 25, 1943.

Ellsler, Effie, actress, 87. Stage favorite of the 1880's and screen character actress more recently; most successful part, Hazel Kirke, in play of that name (1880); was leading lady for Edwin Booth, Lawrence Barrett, John McCullough, etc. Born Cleveland, Ohio; died Los Angeles, California, October 8, 1942.

Erskine, Wallace, actor, 81. First appearance Blackfoot, England (1881); supported Kyrle Bellew, Eleanor Robson and many other stars in America; most recent role Baron Cesarea in "Death Takes a Holiday" (1929). Born England; died Massapequa, L. I., New York, January 6, 1943.

Fiske, Harrison Grey, drama critic, playwright, producer, 81. President and editor of *New York Dramatic Mirror* from 1879 until 1911; wrote "Fontenelle" with his wife, Minnie Maddern Fiske; "Hester Crewe," "The District Attorney" with Charles Klein; was lessee of Manhattan Theatre, New York; fought Theatrical Trust for 10 years. Born Harrison, New York; died New York City, September 3, 1942.

Fokine, Michel, choreographer and maître-de-ballet, 62. Internationally recognized as "father of the modern ballet"; created "The Dying Swan" for Anna Pavlova, "Scheherazade," "Firebird" and "Les Sylphides"; headed Ballet de Monte Carlo (1936), Ballet Russe (1937). Born Leningrad, Russia; died New York City, August 22, 1942.

Gillmore, Frank, actor, 75. First appearance on stage at Maidstone, England, in "Jack and the Beanstalk" (1879); first appearance on New York stage in "The Better Part" (1893); leading man for Mrs. Fiske, Mary Mannering and others; retired in 1916; was one of Equity's Founders and longtime executives; president of Associated Actors and Artistes of America; president emeritus of Actors Equity Association. Born New York City; died New York City, March 29, 1943.

Haines, Robert T., actor, 73. In theatre forty years; first New York success in "The Palace of the King," supporting Viola Allen; played Prince Kara in "The Garden of the Gods" with Blanche Bates (1903); member of Equity Council for 12 years. Born Muncie, Indiana; died New York City, May 6, 1943.

Herne, Katherine Corcoran, actress, 86. Made stage debut in San Francisco in 1877 in "Peg Woffington"; played leading feminine parts in her husband's, James A. Herne's plays, "Margaret Fleming," "Shore Acres," etc.; mother of Julie and Chrystal Herne. Born Abbeyleix, Ireland; died Astoria, New York, February 8, 1943.

Hibbard, Edna, actress, 47. Child actress with Bertha Kalich in "The Kreutzer Sonata" (1907); remembered in "Rock-a-bye Baby," "Ladies of the Evening," "Gentlemen Prefer Blondes," etc. Born California; died New York City, December 26, 1942.

Holmes, Phillips, actor, 33. Appeared with his father, Taylor Holmes, in "The Great Necker"; appeared in many screen plays; left stage to join Royal Canadian Air Force in December, 1941; killed in plane collision. Born Grand Rapids, Michigan; died Ontario, Canada, August 12, 1942.

Jeffreys, Ellis, actress, 74. First appeared in America in "The Notorious Mrs. Ebbsmith" (1895); afterward toured in "She Stoops to Conquer," "The Two Orphans," etc. Born Colombo, Ceylon; died Surrey, England, January 21, 1943.

Latham, Fred G., manager and director, 90. Manager of Drury Lane, Adelphi and other London theatres; manager for Maurice Grau Opera Company at Metropolitan Opera House, New York (1897); manager for Sarah Bernhardt and Coquelin in American coast-to-coast tour. Born England; died New York City, January 31, 1943.

Love, Montagu, actor, 66. Matinee idol of the 1900's; first appearance in America in "The Second in Command" (1913); played in "Grumpy" with Cyril Maude; in films for years.

Born Portsmouth, Hants, England; died Beverly Hills, California, May 17, 1943.

Marshall, Tully, actor, 78. Fifty-seven years on stage and screen; started in San Francisco stock company; subsequently played with Dion Boucicoult, Modjeska, E. H. Sothern, etc. Born Nevada City, California; died Encino, California, March 9, 1943.

Montgomery, Marshall, ventriloquist, 55. Internationally known in vaudeville; appearances abroad included command performances in London and St. Petersburg; last engagement in Billy Rose's "Mrs. Astor's Pet Horse." Born Brooklyn, N. Y.; died Brooklyn, September 30, 1942.

Nemirovitch-Dantchenko, Vladimir Ivanovich, actor, producer, 85. Founded the Moscow Art Theatre with Stanislavsky in 1898; directed the Moscow Art Players in New York in 1925, and toured the United States. Born Tiflis, Russia; died Moscow, Russia, April 25, 1943.

Nielsen, Alice, singer, 66. Light opera star for whom Victor Herbert wrote "The Fortune Teller," "The Singing Girl," etc.; first appeared professionally in San Francisco; was with Bostonians; made grand opera debut in Italy in 1903; sang opposite Caruso at Metropolitan; in 1917 toured United States with Alice Neilsen Opera Co. Born Nashville, Tenn.; died New York City, March 8, 1943.

O'Connell, Hugh, actor, 45. Started in San Francisco with Alcazar Stock Co.; first New York appearance in "Face Value," 1921; remembered in "The Wisdom Tooth," "Once in a Lifetime," "The Milky Way," etc.; member Lambs and Players. Born New York City, died Hollywood, California, January 19, 1943.

Oliver, Edna May, actress, 59. Started as pianist in all-girl orchestra, 1900; first stage success in "Oh, Boy!"; remembered particularly in "Cradle Snatchers" and "Show Boat"; in many films and on radio; descendant of John Quincy Adams. Born Malden, Massachusetts; died Hollywood, California, November 9, 1942.

Overman, Lynne, actor, 55. Started as song and dance man with Ward and Wade Minstrels; in vaudeville; ensign in Navy First World War; Broadway debut in "Fair and Warmer, 1916"; acted in many films; born Maryville, Missouri; died Hollywood, California, February 19, 1943.

Powers, James T., actor, 81. Popular comedian for more than half a century; first professional appearance at Variety

Theatre, Long Branch, N. J., 1878; played in many early Hoyt comedies, "A Bunch of Keys," "A Straight Tip," etc.; with Augustin Daly Musical Co., 1897-1902; created Wun Hi in "The Geisha"; played Bob Acres in revival of "The Rivals," 1931; last appearance in Players' revival of "Seven Keys to Baldpate," 1935. Born New York City; died New York City, February 10, 1943.

Pryor, Arthur, composer and bandmaster, 71. Started as child prodigy; first trombonist with John Philip Sousa many years; head of Pryor's Band for thirty years; 300 compositions included light opera, "Jingaboo," and "Uncle Tom's Cabin." Born St. Joseph, Missouri; died West Long Branch, New Jersey, June 18, 1942.

Robson, May, actress, 78. First appearance in "Hoop of Gold," in Brooklyn, 1884; subsequently played with Empire Theatre Stock; starred in "The Rejuvenation of Aunt Mary" and "Tish"; was in many screen plays, including "Lady for a Day." Born Melbourne, Australia; died Beverly Hills, California, October 20, 1942.

Roeder, Benjamin F., manager, 77. Forty-four years manager for David Belasco; beneficiary and executor of the Belasco estate; wrote "The Old, Old Story," with Walter C. Bellows (1891); member Players and Lambs. Born New York City; died New York City, May 4, 1943.

Rowland, Mabel, actress, 61. Prominent as monologist; founded Metropolitan Players; founded Women's Theatre to aid young Broadway actresses; wrote "Bert Williams, Son of Laughter" and "Life with Laughter." Born Philadelphia, Pennsylvania; died Hollywood, California, February 21, 1943.

Seeley, James L., actor, 76. Many years with Castle Square Players in Boston; first appeared on New York stage in 1903 with James K. Hackett; last appearance in "Flight to the West," 1940. Born Rushville, Ill.; died New York, February 15, 1943.

Sutherland, Anne, actress, 75. On stage sixty years; debut in "H.M.S. Pinafore" as Little Buttercup in Chicago, 1881; with Henry E. Dixey in "Adonis," with Joseph Jefferson in "Rip Van Winkle," with Mrs. Leslie Carter in "Zaza"; conducted Chicago stock company 1916-17; last Broadway role in "Craig's Wife." Born Washington, D. C.; died Brentwood, L. I., June 22, 1942.

Tempest, Dame Marie, 78. Fifty-six years on stage; began as concert singer; first appearance in "Boccacio" in London, 1885; notable successes included "The Red Hussar," "The Fencing Master," "The Geisha" and "San Toy"; many Gilbert and Sullivan operas; toured United States and Canada 1890-91 in light opera; remembered in New York in "Hay Fever," "The Marriage of Kitty," and "Her Husband's Wife"; appeared with Paderewski in "Moonlight Sonata" picture in 1936. Born London, England; died London, October 15, 1942.

Van Brugh, Violet, actress, 75. Came to New York with the Kendals in 1889; first New York appearance in "A Scrap of Paper"; in 1905 appeared by command of King Edward at Windsor Castle as Portia in "The Merchant of Venice"; more recently appeared in "This Way to Paradise" and "Evensong." Born Exeter, England; died London, November 10, 1942.

Wayburn, Ned, director and producer, 68. Dance director for Klaw and Erlanger, Ziegfeld and the Shuberts; started in Chicago as singer and dancer; in vaudeville originated "ragtime" piano playing; composed first ragtime song, "Syncopated Sandy"; maintained dancing school where many distinguished performers were trained. Born Pittsburgh, Pennsylvania; died New York City, September 2, 1942.

Westley, Helen, actress, 63. Organized Washington Square Players; was on Board of Managers of the Theatre Guild; started career in "Captain of the Nonesuch," 1897; featured in many Theatre Guild plays before going to Hollywood for films. Born Brooklyn, New York; died Middlebush, New Jersey, December 12, 1942.

Whiteside, Walker, actor, 73. First appearance in "Hamlet," 1884, in Chicago; first New York appearance in "Hamlet," 1893, with his own company, when he was 24; produced many of the plays in which he appeared; remembered in "The Melting Pot," "The Typhoon," "Mr. Wu," etc.; toured in "The Master of Ballantrae," 1934-35. Born Logansport, Indiana; died Hastings-on-Hudson, New York, August 17, 1942.

Williams, Hattie, actress, 72. Started career in "1492"; played in many Charles Hoyt farces; played leads in "The Girl from Maxim's," "Vivian's Papas," etc.; last appearance in vaudeville sketch "A Slice of Life" by James M. Barrie,

1914-15. Born Boston, Massachusetts; died New York City, August 17, 1942.

Woollcott, Alexander, author, actor, drama critic, commentator, 56. Critic of New York *Times*, 1914; afterward critic of New York *Herald*, New York *Sun* and New York *World;* acted in "Brief Moment," "Wine of Choice" and "The Man Who Came to Dinner"; co-author with George S. Kaufman of "The Channel Road" and "The Dark Tower"; books included "While Rome Burns," "Shouts and Murmurs," "First Reader," etc.; known as the "Town Crier" on radio; editor *Stars and Stripes* during World War I. Born Phalanx, New Jersey; died New York City, January 23, 1943.

Wright, Haidee, actress, 75. Began stage career at ten in "Hoop of Gold," London; continued on stage for sixty-five years; gained wide fame as character actress; played Queen Elizabeth many times. Born London, England; died London, January 29, 1942.

York, Oswald, actor, 75. On stage for fifty-eight years; toured with F. R. Benson Repertory Co. and with E. S. Willard, John Drew and Maude Adams; member of Empire Theatre Stock Co.; in charge of entertaining American troops in France during First World War; married and co-starred with Annie Russell. Born London, England; died New York City, January 25, 1943.

THE DECADES' TOLL

(Persons of Outstanding Prominence in the Theatre
Who Have Died in Recent Years)

	Born	Died
Aborn, Milton	1864	1933
Ames, Winthrop	1871	1937
Anderson, Mary (Navarro)	1860	1940
Baker, George Pierce	1866	1935
Barrymore, John	1882	1942
Belasco, David	1856	1931
Benson, Sir Frank	1859	1939
Bernhardt, Sarah	1845	1923
Campbell, Mrs. Patrick	1865	1940
Cohan, George Michael	1878	1942
Crabtree, Charlotte (Lotta)	1847	1924
De Koven, Reginald	1861	1920
De Reszke, Jean	1850	1925
Drew, John	1853	1927
Drinkwater, John	1883	1937
Du Maurier, Sir Gerald	1873	1934
Duse, Eleanora	1859	1924
Fiske, Minnie Maddern	1865	1932
Frohman, Daniel	1851	1940
Galsworthy, John	1867	1933
Gorky, Maxim	1868	1936
Greet, Sir Philip (Ben)	1858	1936
Herbert, Victor	1859	1924
Patti, Adelina	1843	1919
Pinero, Sir Arthur Wing	1855	1934
Pirandello, Luigi	1867	1936
Rejane, Gabrielle	1857	1920
Rogers, Will	1879	1935
Russell, Annie	1864	1936
Schumann-Heink, Ernestine	1861	1936
Sembrich, Marcella	1859	1935
Shaw, Mary	1860	1929

INDEX OF AUTHORS

531

INDEX OF PLAYS AND CASTS

535

INDEX OF PRODUCERS, DIRECTORS AND DESIGNERS